S0-ABQ-356

SEVENTH EDITION

THE
ENDURING
QUESTIONS

TRADITIONAL AND
CONTEMPORARY
VOICES

JERRY H. GILL

WADSWORTH

THOMSON LEARNING

Australia · Canada · Mexico · Singapore · Spain · United Kingdom · United States

WADSWORTH

THOMSON LEARNING ™

Acquisitions Editor: David Tatom
Marketing Strategist: Adrienne Krysiuk
Project Editor: Jon Davies
Production Manager: Lois West
Manufacturing Manager: Elaine Curda
Permissions Editor: Shirley Webster

Text Designer: Garry Harman
Copy Editor: Sandy Mann
Cover Designer: Garry Harman
Cover Printer: Malloy Lithographing
Compositor: UG / GGS Information Services, Inc.
Printer: Malloy Lithographing

COPYRIGHT © 2002 Thomson Learning, Inc. Thomson LearningTM is a trademark used herein under license.

ALL RIGHTS RESERVED. No part of this work covered by the copyright hereon may be reproduced or used in any form or by any means—graphic, electronic, or mechanical, including but not limited to photocopying, recording, taping, Web distribution, information networks, or information storage and retrieval systems—without the written permission of the publisher.

Printed in the United States of America
1 2 3 4 5 6 7 05 04 03 02 01

For more information about our products, contact us at:
Thomson Learning Academic Resource Center
1-800-423-0563

For permission to use material from this text, contact us by:
Phone: 1-800-730-2214
Fax: 1-800-730-2215
Web: http://www.thomsonrights.com

Library of Congress Catalog Card Number: 2001089592
ISBN: 0-15-506286-7

Asia
Thomson Learning
60 Albert Street, #15-01
Albert Complex
Singapore 189969

Australia
Nelson Thomson Learning
102 Dodds Street
South Melbourne, Victoria 3205
Australia

Canada
Nelson Thomson Learning
1120 Birchmount Road
Toronto, Ontario M1K 5G4
Canada

Europe/Middle East/Africa
Thomson Learning
Berkshire House
168-173 High Holborn
London WC1 V7AA
United Kingdom

Latin America
Thomson Learning
Seneca, 53
Colonia Polanco
11560 Mexico D.F.
Mexico

Spain
Paraninfo Thomson Learning
Calle/Magallanes, 25
28015 Madrid, Spain

For

Kathy, John, Wendy,
and Hannah

good friends from way back

PREFACE

The Enduring Questions, initially edited by Professor Melvin Rader, may well be the oldest introductory philosophy text in existence. It was first published in 1955 and is now in its seventh edition; it, like the questions it raises, has endured the test of time.

It has been my pleasure and honor to be involved in making this important introductory anthology continuously available to teachers and students over the past fifteen years. In the previous edition, a more contemporary essay, representing a minority or "marginal voice," was added to each major part, and I have retained these additions in the present edition.

The major editorial alteration in this seventh edition involves placing an introductory "case study" at the beginning of each major part in order to provide a point of focus for the issues raised by the subsequent readings. These cases are drawn from contemporary people and events embodying many of the philosophical questions taken up in the writings presented in each section of the text. New to this edition, as well, the index has been replaced by a glossary of philosophical terms, and the bibliography has been shortened. Also, selections from Charles Hartshorne and Albert Camus have replaced those of Søren Kierkegaard and William Montague.

I am grateful to David Tatom at Harcourt College Publishers for making it possible to continue the life of this significant anthology, as well as to Drake Bush and Michele Tomiak, who guided the manuscript to completion. In addition, the suggestions of the various readers and reviewers were frequently helpful. As always, I am indebted to my wife and colleague, Mari Sorri, for her insight and encouragement.

J. H. G.
Tucson, AZ
February 2001

CONTENTS

PREFACE *v*

INTRODUCTION THE NATURE OF PHILOSOPHY ... 1

The General Interpretation of Experience 1
The Pursuit of Meaning 2
The Cultivation of Wisdom 3
The Socratic Quest 7
Plato: *Apology* **10**
      Euthyphro **27**

Comment **40**

PART I   THE WAYS OF UNDERSTANDING........ 42

A Case in Point: Can Machines Think? 44

1   **Rationalism 47**
Plato: *Meno* **47**
      René Descartes: *Rules for the Direction of the Mind* **55**

Comment **63**

2   **Empiricism and Its Limits 69**
David Hume: *Knowledge and Causality* **69**
      Immanuel Kant: *The Limits of Knowledge* **84**

Comment **96**

3   Common Sense 101

Thomas Reid: *An Inquiry into the Human Mind* **101**

Comment **118**

4   Intuition and Acquaintance 121

Henri Bergson: *Intuition* **121**

    Bertrand Russell: *Knowledge by Acquaintance and Knowledge by Description* **131**

Comment **139**

5   Pragmatism 142

William James: *What Pragmatism Means* **142**

    John Dewey: *Scientific Philosophy* **149**

Comment **163**

6   Existentialism 167

Albert Camus: *An Absurd Reasoning* **167**

    Gabriel Marcel: *Problems and Mystery* **172**

Comment **180**

7   Perspectivism 185

Sandra Harding: *"Strong Objectivity" and Socially Situated Knowledge* **185**

Comment **202**

PART II   THE NATURE OF REALITY..................... **204**

A Case in Point: Two Persons in One? 206

8   Theism 209

Saint Anselm: *The Ontological Argument* **209**

    Saint Thomas Aquinas: *Five Proofs of God's Existence* **210**

    David Hume: *A Critique of Natural Theology* **213**

Charles Hartshorne: *What Went Wrong in Classical Theism* **222**

Comment **232**

9 Materialism **239**

Titus Lucretius Carus: *On the Nature of the Universe* **239**

Comment **252**

10 Idealism **257**

George Berkeley: *Mind and Its Objects* **257**

Comment **276**

11 Dualism **280**

René Descartes: *Meditations* **280**

Comment **294**

12 Relationalism **296**

Alfred North Whitehead: *Objects and Subjects* **296**

Comment **303**

13 Interactionism **305**

Paulo Freire: *The Political Construction of Reality* **305**

Comment **319**

PART III THE BASIS OF MORALITY...................... **322**

A Case in Point: Euthanasia or Assisted Suicide? **324**

14 The Way of Reason **327**

Aristotle: *Happiness and Virtue* **327**

Comment **344**

15   The Way of Acceptance 347

Marcus Aurelius: *Harmony with Nature* **347**

Comment **356**

16   The Way of Duty 359

Immanuel Kant: *The Categorical Imperative* **359**

Comment **368**

17   The Way of Utility 373

Jeremy Bentham: *The Hedonistic Calculus* **373**
John Stuart Mill: *Utilitariansim* **378**

Comment **391**

18   The Way of Freedom 397

Jean-Paul Sartre: *Existentialism Is a Humanism* **397**

Comment **403**

19   The Way of Experiment 405

John Dewey: *Reconstruction in Moral Conceptions* **405**

Comment **413**

20   The Way of Feminism 419

Annette C. Baier: *What Do Women Want in a Moral Theory?* **419**

Comment **428**

PART IV SOCIAL IDEALS...................................... **430**

A Case in Point: Civil Disobedience or Criminal Activity? 432

21   Aristocracy 435

Plato: *The Ideal Republic* **435**

Comment **459**

22   Peace and Security 464

Thomas Hobbes: *Leviathan* **464**

Comment **472**

23   Social Contract 478

John Locke: *The Basis of Civil Society* **478**

Comment **488**

24   Liberal Democracy 490

John Stuart Mill: *On Liberty* **490**

Comment **509**

25   Communism 512

Karl Marx: *Communism and History* **512**

Comment **526**

26   Colonialism and Nationalism 528

Frantz Fanon: *The Pitfalls of National Consciousness* **528**

Comment **540**

GLOSSARY   *543*

BIBLIOGRAPHY FOR INTRODUCTORY STUDENTS   *546*

THE NATURE OF PHILOSOPHY

THE GENERAL INTERPRETATION OF EXPERIENCE

If the philosopher can be called a "specialist," he or she is a specialist in the general. Socrates (in Plato's *Republic*) defines the philosopher as "the spectator of all time and all existence"; and William James declares that philosophy deals "with the principles of explanation that underlie all things without exception, the element common to gods and men and animals and stones, the first *whence* and the last *whither* of the whole cosmic procession, the conditions of all knowing, and the most general rules of human conduct."[1]

C. D. Broad similarly characterizes philosophy. He distinguishes between *critical* and *speculative* philosophy, both of which deal with what is general. The task of critical philosophy is to analyze and define our most fundamental and general concepts, such as "goodness," "truth," "reality," and "causation." The object of speculative philosophy is "to take over the results of the various sciences, to add to them the results of the religious and ethical experiences of mankind, and then to reflect upon the whole" in an attempt "to reach some general conclusions as to the nature of the Universe, and as to our position and prospects in it."[2]

These characterizations seem to fit the problems that philosophers most often discuss: What is a good life? What is the relation between mind and body? Do we have free will? Is there a God? Is the world fundamentally material or spiritual? Can we know the ultimate nature of reality? These are basic questions involved in a general interpretation of the world. Accordingly, Herbert Spencer defines philosophy as "knowledge of the highest degree of generality."[3]

There are certain difficulties in this view. First, science is sometimes *very* general. Newton's theory of gravitation, for example, characterizes the nearest and the most remote, the least and the greatest of objects—the pin in one's bedroom as well as the most distant galaxy. Similarly, modern atomic physics is

---

[1] *Some Problems of Philosophy* (New York: Longmans, Green, 1911), p. 5.
[2] *Scientific Thought* (New York: Harcourt Brace, 1923), p. 152.
[3] *First Principles* (New York: Burt, 1880), p. 111.

applicable to every material entity in the universe; and the theory of evolution, summarizing the whole history of life from the first germs in the primordial sea to the highest stages of human life, is also exceedingly wide in scope. Second, the synthesis of all the sciences, or the interpretation of the whole of reality, is a pretty big order. A person would need to be a kind of god, or at least a universal genius, to succeed at so prodigious an undertaking. But philosophy is not the peculiar business of the gods or of rare geniuses; it is everyone's business.

THE PURSUIT OF MEANING

Such considerations have led many philosophers to define their field in a more restricted way. One of the most widely accepted definitions is that philosophy is the analysis, or systematic study, of meanings. This definition would in effect limit the field to what C. D. Broad calls critical philosophy.

Those who adopt this interpretation sometimes cite Socrates as an example of a philosopher. In employing his favorite conversational method of giving and receiving questions and answers, he is usually trying to analyze the meaning of some basic concept, such as "knowledge," "justice," "courage," "friendship," or "beauty."

One of the most influential philosophers of modern times, Moritz Schlick, has said,

> … Socrates' philosophy consists of what we may call "The Pursuit of Meaning." He tried to clarify thought by analyzing the meaning of our expressions and the real sense of our propositions. Here then we find a definite contrast between this philosophic method, which has for its object the discovery of meaning, and the method of the sciences, which have for their object the discovery of truth.…
> Science should be defined as the "pursuit of truth" and philosophy as the "pursuit of meaning." Socrates has set the example of the true philosophic method for all times.[4]

This is not an adequate characterization of the method of Socrates or the nature of philosophy. Socrates was engaged not only in the pursuit of meaning but also in the pursuit of truth, and the former was largely instrumental to the latter. His definitions were intended not as arbitrary or merely verbal: They were what philosophers call "real" definitions—that is, they sought to characterize actually existent things. When Socrates asserted that justice or friendship or beauty was this or that, he implied that justice or friendship or beauty really existed and actually possessed the character marked off and fixed in the definition. Consequently, he kept referring to the facts of experience so as to make his definitions truthful. Also, he was interested in fitting together the various insights thus gained into a critical interpretation of human nature, human destiny, and human values.

---

[4] "The Future of Philosophy," in D. J. Bronstein, Y. H. Krikorian, and P. P. Wiener, *Basic Problems of Philosophy* (Englewood Cliffs, NJ: Prentice-Hall, 1947), p. 739.

To define philosophy as the pursuit of meaning is at once too broad and too narrow. It is too broad because scientists as well as philosophers seek to clarify meanings. As C. J. Ducasse has said,

> To mention but a few, such concepts as salt, acid, gas, liquid, solid, water, air, iron, etc. are concepts the exact meaning of which is investigated and discovered not by metaphysicians, logicians, or mathematicians, but by chemists and physicists; and the same is true of such even more basic physical concepts as light, electricity, matter, mass, etc. Moreover, although physicians do give us precise accounts of the meaning of these and numerous other concepts, they do so in their capacity as natural scientists, i.e., on the basis, ultimately, of observations and experiments....[5]

In another sense, Schlick's definition of philosophy is too narrow. If Plato, Aristotle, Aquinas, Descartes, Spinoza, and Kant, for example, are to be considered philosophers—and no one has a better claim—it would appear that their field includes what Broad calls "speculative philosophy." Schlick seeks to dismiss the problems of speculative philosophy as either nonsensical or nonphilosophical. "Some of them will disappear by being shown to be mistakes and misunderstandings of our language," he declares, "and the others will be found to be ordinary scientific questions in disguise."[6] However, it is unlikely that all the problems of speculative philosophy will either vanish when they are stated clearly or will turn out to be nonphilosophical problems, more appropriately treated by science. Moreover, the sharp distinction between the pursuit of meaning and the pursuit of truth is artificial, for the clarification of meaning and the discovery of truth go hand in hand. Broad rightly includes under "critical philosophy" not only the clarification of concepts but also the resolute criticism of our fundamental beliefs.

THE CULTIVATION OF WISDOM

Philosophy, we conclude, involves both the analysis of meanings and the search for generic truths: To complete our definition, we need to distinguish the kinds of meanings and generic truths that are essentially philosophical from the kinds that are scientific.

It will help us to consider the original meaning of *philosophy.* Etymologically, *philosophy* means "the love of wisdom" (from the Greek *philein,* "to love," and *sophia,* "wisdom"). The word has ordinarily been used to designate an activity rather than an emotion—the activity of pursuing wisdom rather than the emotion motivating that pursuit. The essential question that we need to consider is what, exactly, is the wisdom that the philosopher seeks.

Wisdom has been used in two senses. First, it is contrasted with ignorance. The wise person is one who knows and therefore is not ignorant. This meaning,

---

[5] *Philosophy as a Science* (New York: Oskar Piest, 1941), pp. 77–78.
[6] Ibid., p. 745.

however, does not help us to distinguish philosophy from science since the scientist also, of course, is trying to replace ignorance by knowledge. In the second sense, wisdom is contrasted with foolishness. The wise person is one who has good judgment and therefore is not foolish. Fools may have a great deal of knowledge about ordinary matters of fact, but they lack the balance and maturity and ripe insight that make it possible not only to live but also to live well.

If philosophy is the pursuit of wisdom as contrasted with foolishness, it is marked off from ordinary science. The subject matter of science is facts, and science attempts to discover verifiable laws—regularities—among these facts. These laws give a *description* of the facts. It is obvious that the physicist does not talk about wicked atoms or beneficent motions, and even the sociologist, in a purely scientific role, tries to *describe* rather than to *evaluate* the behavior of social groups. If philosophy, on the other hand, seeks wisdom as the opposite of foolishness, it must be a kind of critical activity concerned with appraisals. Matthew Arnold has defined poetry as "the criticism of life," but this definition fits philosophy better than poetry. It is similar to the definition of Ducasse, who maintains that "philosophy is the general theory of criticism,"[7] and the definition of John Dewey, who declares that "philosophy is inherently criticism, having its distinctive position among various modes of criticism in its generality: a criticism of criticisms, as it were."[8]

It is characteristic of criticism that it is yea-saying or nay-saying—a favoring or a disfavoring. The ways of saying *yea* or *nay* are quite various, and they correspond to different pairs of adjectives. In logic, for example, we speak of *valid* or *fallacious;* in epistemology, of *true* or *false;* in metaphysics, of *real* or *unreal;* in theology, of *holy* or *unholy;* in esthetics, of *beautiful* or *ugly;* in ethics, of *right* or *wrong.* In using these adjectives, we are making judgments. The function of philosophy is to provide the intellectual bases of sound judgments about the great issues of life.

Even when philosophy wears the garb of science, it is distinctive. For example, Lucretius was not primarily concerned with the hypotheses of atoms and evolution as scientific descriptions of the nature of things. He was concerned with the right way to think and live in the sort of universe that he regarded as real. Metaphysics should not be interpreted—as it often is—as potential or generalized natural science; rather, it should be regarded as the attempt to achieve a true understanding of humankind and our place in the cosmos so that we can distinguish the deep and permanent from the superficial and temporary, the important from the unimportant. Thus, to distinguish is *to judge,* and metaphysics, like other branches of philosophy, provides a basis for judgment.

Philosophy resembles science not so much in its aim as in its method. Both employ reason and evidence as means to the discovery of truth and the clarification of meaning. Both are forms of inquiry—science being an inquiry into the laws of nature; philosophy, into the norms of criticism. The faith of the

---

[7] *The Philosophy of Art* (New York: Dial, 1929), p. 3.

[8] *Experience and Nature* (Chicago: Open Court, 1925), p. 398.

philosopher, like that of the scientist, is that inquiry is worthwhile. In the *Apology*, Socrates expresses the fundamental conviction of all true philosophers: "The unexamined life," he declares, "is not worth living." Likewise, in the *Meno*, his faith rings out sharp and clear:

> Some things I have said of which I am not altogether confident. But that we shall be better and braver and less helpless if we think that we ought to inquire, than we should have been if we indulged in the idle fancy that there was no knowing and no use in seeking to know what we do not know—that is a theme upon which I am ready to fight, in word and deed, to the utmost of my power.[9]

We can fully appreciate the brave words of Socrates only if we too engage in the quest for wisdom. The proof of the pudding is in the eating—we can best judge the value of philosophy after we have philosophized. Each person must oneself taste of the pudding; no one else can do it. Of course, it is immensely helpful to study the great thinkers, such as Plato, Aristotle, David Hume, and Immanuel Kant, or, nearer to us, William James, George Santayana, and Bertrand Russell. As Descartes declares in the opening chapter of his *Discourse on Method*, "The reading of good books is, as it were, to engage in talk with their authors, the finest minds of past ages, artfully contrived talk in which they give us none but the best and most select of their thoughts."[10] However, like all the very good things of life, wisdom is something that cannot be given and that each must attain for himself.

Here is a definition of philosophy that sums up much that has been said: "Philosophy is an effort to give unity to human arts and sciences by a critical examination of the grounds of our meanings, values, and beliefs."

The foregoing discussion of the analytic and speculative modes of philosophizing serves to distinguish philosophy from two other major areas of human cognitive activity, namely science and religion. Science seeks general truth about the behavior of the natural, animal, and human aspects of reality. Unlike philosophy, it is limited to "factual" truth based on sensory observation and empirical verification. Ideally, scientific hypotheses arise from such observations and are confirmed or discredited by them. On the other hand, religion is concerned about beliefs as they bear on human meaning and destiny. Religion seeks to develop liturgical and ethical practices that will enhance human well-being both now and for eternity. While science aims at theories that *explain* natural events and human behavior, religion constructs theories in order to *guide* human thought and life.

Philosophy, in its analytic mode, may be seen as overlapping with science, while its speculative mode has something in common with religion. In each case, however, philosophy is best understood as a "second-order" activity. That is to say, during and after scientists and theologians engage in their respective endeavors, philosophers engage in theirs: probing and seeking to clarify the meaning,

---

[9] *The Dialogues of Plato*, trans. Benjamin Jowett (London: Oxford University Press, 1924), II, p. 47.

[10] *Discourse on Method*, in *Descartes' Philosophical Writings* (London: Macmillan, 1952), p. 119.

implications, and presuppositions of the various methods employed by scientists and theologians. Indeed, some philosophers suggest that the primary function of philosophy is this process of "conceptual clarification," of exploring and charting the crucial moves made by theoreticians in other disciplines.

Generally speaking, philosophy may be subdivided into five main areas of interest: logic, epistemology, metaphysics, ethics, and social or political philosophy. *Logic* has been defined as the study of the standards of rational thought. As such, it is to be distinguished from psychology, which studies the ways various people actually *do* think, not how they are *supposed* to think. Logic focuses on the relationships within and among various assertions, such as what follows from what (implication), what is presupposed by what (entailment), or whether an argument is rational (valid). Logic itself is usually divided into two parts: deductive (including symbolic logic) and inductive (pertaining to scientific reasoning and probability). Although all of these specific considerations come into play in this volume, the actual principles of logic are not specifically discussed here since the study of logic is a course all its own.

The second main area of philosophy is that of *epistemology*, the study of the basis and nature of knowledge. Once again, it is important to distinguish this branch of philosophy from a parallel field, cognitive psychology. Epistemology is concerned with how knowledge and truth are *defined* and *established*, not with how they are acquired. In Part I of this edition, the main schools of thought in this dimension of philosophy are presented, along with interrelated issues.

A third area of philosophy is usually termed *metaphysics* or *ontology* and may be defined as the study of the nature of reality. Here, too, a cautionary distinction is in order. In popular discourse, the term *metaphysics* has come to designate anything that transcends the normal; whatever is mystical, occult, or supernatural. In philosophy, by contrast, metaphysics refers to theories about what constitutes "the real"—what makes the world what it is and what makes it work the way it does. Part II is comprised of chapters representing major points of view in metaphysical theory, including many relevant issues.

Fourth, there is *ethics*, the area of philosophy dealing with the study of the standards of right conduct. As before, this aspect of philosophy must not be confused with sociology, which studies how people do, in fact, conduct themselves in relation to one another. Ethics explores the various standards for judging the moral worth of human behavior: what constitutes the Good, and what comprises the "good life." At the same time, philosophical ethics is to be distinguished from religious ethics, which represents one type of moral standard. Part III of this book presents several of the more important approaches to the question of the proper criterion by means of which human behavior is to be judged.

A subdivision of ethics, one that has recently become a field of study in its own right, is social or *political philosophy.* Here the central questions and issues have to do with how human beings should organize and govern themselves. This area of philosophy is treated under the heading of "Social Ideals" and makes up Part IV of this text. Although closely related to questions of morality and virtue, the issues discussed in these chapters are broader and more complex. Here one must be careful to distinguish between this area of philosophy and political science, which considers how people actually do organize and govern themselves but does not try to say how they *should* do so.

A further area of philosophy, one that is too large and specialized for inclusion in a text of this sort, is *esthetics*. Here the focus is generally on the "study of the standards of artistic value." Such questions as what makes a work of art beautiful, how esthetic value is related to taste, and even what is art are at the center of philosophical discussions of esthetic meaning.

Finally, a few words about how to "do" philosophy. Although it is very valuable and interesting to study what the great philosophers have thought about "the enduring questions," it should be remembered that philosophy—like business, art, science, and religion—is an *activity* that people actively engage in. Thus, the content of the following chapters is no more important than the process they represent. This means that an introduction to philosophy should challenge students to learn to think philosophically themselves while exposing them to the ideas of other thinkers. To achieve this purpose, readers of the following pages will need to discuss and write both *empathetically* and *assertively*.

Empathetic skills are not highly regarded in our culture, and thus are likely to be more difficult for us to acquire. The term *empathy* is used here to designate the process of placing oneself in another person's position in order to understand and appreciate the person's perspective more fairly and thoroughly. Obviously, this process involves giving the thinker in question—whether a philosopher included in this book, your professor, or a fellow student—the benefit of the doubt at the outset. It involves learning to *listen* to what is actually being said without trying to evaluate it too quickly. This process of empathetic understanding can be even applied to one's own ideas by asking how someone coming from a different perspective might think.

Being assertive means not being passive in relation to what is being read or discussed. Three questions that may help one focus upon this assertive attitude are: (1) What exactly is being said here? (2) What are its ramifications (presuppositions and implications)? and (3) What are its strong points and potential difficulties? It is, of course, important not to confuse being assertive with being aggressive. The goal of philosophy is, after all, increased clarity and understanding, not winning arguments. With these suggestions in mind, and recalling Socrates' confidence about the importance and value of continually asking questions, the reader is in a good position to begin his or her own quest for wisdom. We shall begin with Socrates' own defense of his philosophical activity and then move on to an example of his particular technique.

THE SOCRATIC QUEST

Socrates (470?–399 B.C.)

We have been considering the meaning of philosophy and its relation to the sciences. However, to understand the nature of philosophy, we must have in mind more than a set of definitions and abstract distinctions. *Philosophy,* as we have said, means literally "the love of wisdom," and this is what philosophy at its best has always meant. As Henry David Thoreau put it, to be a philosopher means to love wisdom so as to live according to its dictates.

There is no better way in which to grasp the personal import of philosophy than to study the life and character of Socrates. More than anyone else in the history of thought, he represents the very type and ideal of the philosopher. His portrait, drawn by the genius of Plato, has for more than two thousand years been the standard by which all philosophy and philosophers have been measured. No one has loved wisdom more fervently than Socrates, and no one has lived more truly according to its dictates. In him, philosophy is not merely a way of thinking but a way of living.

Born about 470 B.C., Socrates grew up during the time of Athens' greatest power and achievement—the half century following the victories over the Persians—and he lived through the supreme crisis of Athenian history—the bitter, protracted, and catastrophic war with Sparta. He was a contemporary of many of the greatest figures in the history of culture, among them Sophocles, Herodotus, Phidias, and Pericles. Thus, he knew the city both in the height of its glory and in the depths of its crisis and defeat.

His father was a sculptor or stonemason and his mother a midwife. The family was apparently of good standing and aristocratic connections. Socrates, perhaps in jest, declared that the family pedigree could be traced back to Daedalus, a legendary maker of wooden images. Whatever his background, Socrates moved with ease in the best and most select circles of Athenian society.

It was inevitable that a man of Socrates' bent should display a penchant for philosophy. He is said to have studied under Archelaus, the first native Athenian philosopher, and he was also familiar with the teachings of the Sophists—humanistic philosophers and paid educators who traveled from city to city. However, preferring intellectual leisure to lucrative employment, he was too poor to take formal instruction from the Sophists, whose "wisdom," moreover, he regarded as somewhat hollow. He also studied science, becoming familiar with the doctrines of the Sicilian Empedocles about biological evolution, the theories of the Italian Alcmaeon about the brain as the organ of mental life, the mathematical doctrines of Pythagoras and Zeno, and the theory of Diogenes of Apollonia that everything consists of "air." However, he soon became disillusioned by the flat contradictions of such rival tenets; and when one day he read in the book of Anaxagoras (the first important philosopher to live in Athens) that "mind" is the natural order, the concept struck him with the force of revelation. Reading on, he discovered that Anaxagoras introduced a cosmic mind to explain only the initial impetus given to matter and then employed mechanical principles to explain the general structure of reality. Socrates, in contrast, vowed that he would try really to understand mind and its place in the cosmos. Thereafter, his main endeavor was to search his own mind and the minds of his fellow citizens in an attempt to discover the essence of humankind and of goodness.

In pursuing his "mission," Socrates was trying to explore the human mind and to reach the truth by dint of question and answer, dialogue, and debate. This give-and-take method of investigation by discussion is called "dialectic" or "the Socratic method"—and it is still the essential method of the philosopher. It may be carried on between two or more persons or within the mind of a single inquirer, as one puts questions to oneself and wrestles with one's answers. Usually its objective is to establish a definition, to fix in mind the essential reality of some basic value or property. Each proposed definition is tested by a process of critical examination. Is it internally consistent? Does it fit the facts? Does it agree with what we already know? In formulating and testing the definition, the philosopher continually refers to the particular data of experience; but he or she examines the particulars as instances of a type and defines the type—the "idea," "form," or "universal"—by establishing its significance in the particulars.

The years of Socrates' mission and the last thirty years of his life fell mainly in the period of the war with Sparta, when Athens was fighting for its existence. As we gather from the pages of the great historian Thucydides, it was a period of intense crisis and civil strife. Toward the close of this difficult time, it became apparent that Athens was losing the war, and revolutions were taking place within the city. Socrates, by his independence, his critical spirit, and his refusal to adopt unjust methods, offended both the democratic and aristocratic parties.

In 404 B.C. the city was finally compelled to surrender. After a short and bloody interval of oligarchical dictatorship, the old democratic form of government was restored. However, the political situation remained tense, and the ruling democrats were fearful of counterrevolution. It was Socrates' misfortune that a number of his former close associates had proved themselves traitors or vicious enemies of the democratic cause. Alcibiades, Socrates' young friend, had been a brilliant general of the Athenian army, but when he was accused of religious sacrilege and ordered to stand trial, he deserted to Sparta and became a most formidable enemy of the Athenian state. Similarly, Critias and Charmides, two associates of Socrates, had been leaders of the violent oligarchical dictatorship that was established at the conclusion of the war. Inevitably, Socrates, who had long been known as a vigorous critic of democratic follies, was suspected of subversive activities. Political motives, combined with their intense dislike of Socrates' unconventional teachings, prompted Anytus, a prominent democratic politician, and two lesser associates, Meletus and Lycon, to bring charges against Socrates in 399 B.C., about four years after the war's end. The indictment, as recorded by the later historian Diogenes Laertius, read, "Socrates is guilty of not worshipping the gods whom the State worships, but introducing new and unfamiliar religious practices; and, further, of corrupting the young. The prosecutor demands the death penalty."

The main "offense," not specified in the indictment or at the trial, was that Socrates had fostered the antidemocratic spirit that had inspired the oligarchical revolutions. According to an amnesty that had been officially declared in the year 404–403 B.C., no one could be prosecuted for political offenses committed before that date. Hence the accusations in the formal indictment were, to some extent, trumpery charges, designed to bring Socrates to trial for an offense that, perforce, remained unspecified. Yet the charges were not merely manufactured: There was widespread hostility against Socrates for his critical spirit and his unremitting search for a new rationale and norm for life. In the eyes of conservatives, he *had* blasphemed and corrupted youth. Indeed, he had questioned the very foundation of the social order, and the guardians of the status quo, hurt to the quick, retaliated by seeking to impose the ultimate penalty—death.

Tried before 500 jurors selected by lot, Socrates spoke with such uncompromising independence that he angered the jury and provoked the death penalty. Some of his friends made a last-minute attempt to effect his escape, but he would brook no such disgraceful tactics. After a serene philosophical conversation with a group of intimates in his prison cell, he drank the fatal hemlock.

The following dialogues of Plato are two that scholars generally acknowledge as presenting the most genuine portrait of Socrates and his method of *philosophizing*. In the *Apology* Socrates defends himself and his *calling* against the charges of the state, and in the *Euthyphro* he displays his commitment to the search for truth by relentlessly pressing for the definition of a concept that nearly everyone else takes for granted. It is this commitment, rather than particular answers, that exemplifies the true philosophic spirit.

APOLOGY

Characters

Socrates

Meletus

SCENE: The Court of Justice.

Socrates. I cannot tell what impression my accusers have made upon you, Athenians: for my own part, I know that they nearly made me forget who I was, so plausible were they; and yet they have scarcely uttered one single word of truth. But of all their many falsehoods, the one which astonished me most, was when they said that I was a clever speaker, and that you must be careful not to let me mislead you. I thought that it was most impudent of them not to be ashamed to talk in that way; for as soon as I open my mouth the lie will be exposed, and I shall prove that I am not a clever speaker in any way at all: unless, indeed, by a clever speaker they mean a man who speaks the truth. If that is their meaning, I agree with them that I am a much greater orator than they. My accusers, then I repeat, have said little or nothing that is true; but from me you shall hear the whole truth. Certainly you will not hear an elaborate speech, Athenians, drest up, like theirs, with words and phrases. I will say to you what I have to say, without preparation, and in the words which come first, for I believe that my cause is just; so let none of you expect anything else. Indeed, my friends, it would hardly be seemly for me, at my age, to come before you like a young man with his specious falsehoods. But there is one thing, Athenians, which I do most earnestly beg and entreat of you. Do not be surprised and do not interrupt, if in my defence I speak in the same way that I am accustomed to speak in the market-place, at the tables of the money-changers, where many of you have heard me, and elsewhere. The truth is this. I am more than seventy years old, and this is the first time that I have ever come before a Court of Law; so your

The dialogues of Plato are from the translation by F. J. Church, first published by Macmillan and Company, London, 1880.

manner of speech here is quite strange to me. If I had been really a stranger, you would have forgiven me for speaking in the language and the fashion of my native country: and so now I ask you to grant me what I think I have a right to claim. Never mind the style of my speech—it may be better or it may be worse—give your whole attention to the question, Is what I say just, or is it not? That is what makes a good judge, as speaking the truth makes a good advocate.

I have to defend myself, Athenians, first against the old false charges of my old accusers, and then against the later ones of my present accusers. For many men have been accusing me to you, and for very many years, who have not uttered a word of truth: and I fear them more than I fear Anytus and his companions, formidable as they are. But, my friends, those others are still more formidable; for they got hold of most of you when you were children, and they have been more persistent in accusing me with lies, and in trying to persuade you that there is one Socrates, a wise man, who speculates about the heavens, and who examines into all things that are beneath the earth, and who "makes the worse appear the better reason." These men, Athenians, who can spread abroad this report, are the accusers whom I fear; for their hearers think that persons who pursue such inquiries never believe in the gods. And then they are many, and their attacks have been going on for a long time: and they spoke to you when you were at the age most readily to believe them: for you were all young and many of you were children: and there was no one to answer them when they attacked me. And the most unreasonable thing of all is that commonly I do not even know their names: I cannot tell you who they are, except in the case of the comic poets. But all the rest who have been

trying to prejudice you against me, from motives of spite and jealousy, and sometimes, it may be, from conviction, are the enemies whom it is hardest to meet. For I cannot call any one of them forward in Court, to cross-examine him: I have, as it were, simply to fight with shadows in my defence, and to put questions which there is no one to answer. I ask you, therefore, to believe that, as I say, I have been attacked by two classes of accusers—first by Meletus and his friends, and then by those older ones of whom I have spoken. And, with your leave, I will defend myself first against my old enemies, for you heard their accusations first, and they were much more persistent than my present accusers are.

Well, I must make my defence, Athenians, and try in the short time allowed me to remove the prejudice which you have had against me for a long time. I hope that I may manage to do this, if it be good for you and for me, and that my defence may be successful; but I am quite aware of the nature of my task, and I know that it is a difficult one. Be the issue, however, as God wills, I must obey the law, and make my defence.

Let us begin again, then, and see what is the charge which has given rise to the prejudice against me, which was what Meletus relied on when he drew his indictment. What is the calumny which my enemies have been spreading about me? I must assume that they are formally accusing me, and read their indictment. It would run somewhat in this fashion. "Socrates is an evildoer, who meddles with inquiries into things beneath the earth, and in heaven, and who 'makes the worse appear the better reason,' and who teaches others these same things." That is what they say; and in the Comedy of Aristophanes [The Clouds] you yourselves saw a man called Socrates swinging round in a basket, and saying that he walked the air, and talking a great deal of nonsense about matters of which I understand nothing, either more or less. I do not mean to disparage that kind of knowledge, if there is any man who possesses it. I trust Meletus may never be able to prosecute me for that. But, the truth is, Athenians, I have nothing to do with these matters, and almost all of you are yourselves my witnesses of this. I beg all of you who have ever heard me converse, and they are many, to inform your neighbors and tell them if any of you have ever heard me conversing about such matters, either more or less. That will show you that the other common stories about me are as false as this one.

But, the fact is, that not one of these stories is true; and if you have heard that I undertake to educate men, and exact money from them for so doing, that is not true either; though I think that it would be a fine thing to be able to educate men, as Gorgias of Leontini, and Prodicus of Ceos, and Hippias of Elis do. For each of them, my friends, can go into any city, and persuade the young men to leave the society of their fellow-citizens, with any of whom they might associate for nothing, and to be only too glad to be allowed to pay money for the privilege of associating with themselves. And I believe that there is another wise man from Paros residing in Athens at this moment. I happened to meet Callias, the son of Hipponicus, a man who has spent more money on the Sophists than every one else put together. So I said to him—he has two sons—Callias, if your two sons had been foals or calves, we could have hired a trainer for them who would have made them perfect in the excellence which belongs to their nature. He would have been either a groom or a farmer. But whom do you intend to take to train them, seeing that they are men? Who understands the excellence which belongs to men and to citizens? I suppose that you must have thought of this, because of your sons. Is there such a person, said I, or not? Certainly there is, he replied. Who is he, said I, and where does he come from, and what is his fee? His name is Evenus, Socrates, he replied: he comes from Paros, and his fee is five minae. Then I thought that Evenus was a fortunate person if he really understood this art and could teach so cleverly. If I had possessed knowledge of that kind, I should have given myself airs and prided myself on it. But, Athenians, the truth is that I do not possess it.

Perhaps some of you may reply: But, Socrates, what is this pursuit of yours? Whence come these calumnies against you? You must have been engaged in some pursuit out of the common. All these stories and reports of you would never have gone about, if you had not been in some way different from other men. So tell us what your pursuits are, that we may not give our verdict in the dark. I think that is a fair question, and I will try to explain to you what it is that has raised these calumnies against me, and given me this name. Listen, then: some of you perhaps will think that I am jesting; but I assure you that I will tell you the whole truth. I have gained this name, Athenians, simply by reason of a certain wisdom. But by what kind of wisdom? It is by just that wisdom which is, I believe, possible to men. In that, it may be, I am really wise. But the men of whom I was speaking just now must be wise in a wisdom which is greater than human wisdom, or in some way which I cannot describe, for certainly I know nothing of it myself, and if any man says that I do, he lies and wants to slander me. Do not interrupt me, Athenians, even if you think that I am speaking arrogantly. What I am going to say is not my own: I will tell you who says it, and he is worthy of your credit. I will bring the god of Delphi to be the witness of the fact of my wisdom and of its nature. You remember Chærephon. From youth upwards he was my comrade; and he went into exile with the people,[1] and with the people he returned. And you remember, too, Chærephon's character; how vehement he was in carrying through whatever he took in hand. Once he went to Delphi and ventured to put this question to the oracle—I entreat you again, my friends, not to cry out—he asked if there was any man who was wiser than I: and the priestess answered that there was no man. Chærephon himself is dead, but his brother here will confirm what I say.

Now see why I tell you this. I am going to explain to you the origin of my unpopularity. When I heard of the oracle I began to reflect: What can God mean by this dark saying? I know very well that I am not wise, even in the smallest degree. Then what can he mean by saying that I am the wisest of men? It cannot be that he is speaking falsely, for he is a god and cannot lie. And for a long time I was at a loss to understand his meaning: then, very reluctantly, I turned to seek for it in this manner. I went to a man who was reputed to be wise, thinking that there, if anywhere, I should prove the answer wrong, and meaning to point out to the oracle its mistake, and to say, "You said that I was the wisest of men, but this man is wiser than I am." So I examined the man—I need not tell you his name, he was a politician—but this was the result, Athenians. When I conversed with him I came to see that, though a great many persons, and most of all he himself, thought that he was wise, yet he was not wise. And then I tried to prove to him that he was not wise, though he fancied that he was: and by

so doing I made him, and many of the bystanders, my enemies. So when I went away, I thought to myself, "I am wiser than this man: neither of us probably knows anything that is really good, but he thinks that he has knowledge, when he has not, while I, having no knowledge, do not think that I have. I seem, at any rate, to be a little wiser than he is on this point: I do not think that I know what I do not know." Next I went to another man who was reputed to be still wiser than the last, with exactly the same result. And there again I made him, and many other men, my enemies.

Then I went on to one man after another, seeing that I was making enemies every day, which caused me much unhappiness and anxiety: still I thought that I must set God's command above everything. So I had to go to every man who seemed to possess any knowledge, and search for the meaning of the oracle: and, Athenians, I must tell you the truth; verily, by the dog of Egypt, this was the result of the search which I made at God's bidding. I found that the men, whose reputation for wisdom stood highest, were nearly the most lacking in it; while others, who were looked down on as common people, were much better fitted to learn. Now, I must describe to you the wanderings which I undertook, like a series of Heraclean labors, to make full proof of the oracle. After the politicians, I went to the poets, tragic, dithyrambic, and others, thinking that there I should find myself manifestly more ignorant than they. So I took up the poems on which I thought that they had spent most pains, and asked them what they meant, hoping at the same time to learn something from them. I am ashamed to tell you the truth, my friends, but I must say it. Almost any one of the bystanders could have talked about the works of these poets better than the poets themselves. So I soon found that it is

---

[1] Chærephon was forced into exile during the antidemocratic dictatorship of the Thirty in 404 B.C.

not by wisdom that the poets create their works but by a certain natural power and by inspiration, like soothsayers and prophets, who say many fine things, but who understand nothing of what they say. The poets seemed to me to be in a similar case. And at the same time I perceived that, because of their poetry, they thought that they were the wisest of men in other matters too, which they were not. So I went away again, thinking that I had the same advantage over the poets that I had over the politicians.

Finally, I went to the artisans, for I knew very well that I possessed no knowledge at all, worth speaking of, and I was sure that I should find that they knew many fine things. And in that I was not mistaken. They knew what I did not know, and so far they were wiser than I. But, Athenians, it seemed to me that the skilled artisans made the same mistake as the poets. Each of them believed himself to be extremely wise in matters of the greatest importance, because he was skillful in his own art: and this mistake of theirs threw their real wisdom into the shade. So I asked myself, on behalf of the oracle, whether I would choose to remain as I was, without either wisdom or their ignorance, or to possess both, as they did. And I made answer to myself and to the oracle that it was better for me to remain as I was.

By reason of this examination, Athenians, I have made many enemies of a very fierce and bitter kind, who have spread abroad a great number of calumnies about me, and people say that I am "a wise man." For the bystanders always think that I am wise myself in any matter wherein I convict another man of ignorance. But, my friends, I believe that only God is really wise: and that by this oracle he meant that men's wisdom is worth little or nothing. I do not think that he meant that Socrates was wise. He only made

use of my name, and took me as an example, as though he would say to men, "He among you is the wisest, who, like Socrates, knows that in very truth his wisdom is worth nothing at all." And therefore I still go about testing and examining every man whom I think wise, whether he be a citizen or a stranger, as God has commanded me; and whenever I find that he is not wise, I point out to him on the part of God that he is not wise. And I am so busy in this pursuit that I have never had leisure to take any part worth mentioning in public matters, or to look after my private affairs. I am in very great poverty by reason of my service to God.

And besides this, the young men who follow me about, who are the sons of wealthy persons and have a great deal of spare time, take a natural pleasure in hearing men cross-examined: and they often imitate me among themselves: then they try their hands at cross-examining other people. And, I imagine, they find a great abundance of men who think that they know a great deal, when in fact they know little or nothing. And then the persons who are cross-examined, get angry with me instead of with themselves, and say that Socrates is an abominable fellow who corrupts young men. And when they are asked, "Why, what does he do? what does he teach?" they do not know what to say; but, not to seem at a loss, they repeat the stock charges against all philosophers, and allege that he investigates things in the air and under the earth, and that he teaches people to disbelieve in the gods, and "to make the worse appear the better reason." For, I fancy, they would not like to confess the truth, which is that they are shown up as ignorant pretenders to knowledge that they do not possess. And so they have been filling your ears with their bitter calumnies for a long time, for they are zealous and numerous and bitter against me; and they are well disciplined and plausible in speech. On these grounds Meletus and Anytus and Lycon have attacked me. Meletus is indignant with me on the part of the poets, and Anytus on the part of the artisans and politicians, and Lycon on the part of the orators. And so, as I said at the beginning, I shall be surprised if I am able, in the short time allowed me for my defence, to remove from your minds this prejudice which has grown so strong. What I have told you, Athenians, is the truth: I neither conceal, nor do I suppress anything, small or great. And yet I know that it is just this plainness of speech which makes me enemies. But that is only a proof that my words are true, and that the prejudice against me, and the causes of it, are what I have said. And whether you look for them now or hereafter, you will find that they are so.

What I have said must suffice as my defence against the charges of my first accusers. I will try next to defend myself against that "good patriot" Meletus, as he calls himself, and my later accusers. Let us assume that they are a new set of accusers, and read their indictment, as we did in the case of the others. It runs thus. He says that Socrates is an evildoer who corrupts the youth, and who does not believe in the gods whom the city believes in, but in other new divinities. Such is the charge. Let us examine each point in it separately. Meletus says that I do wrong by corrupting the youth: but I say, Athenians, that he is doing wrong; for he is playing off a solemn jest by bringing men lightly to trial, and pretending to have a great zeal and interest in matters to which he has never given a moment's thought. And now I will try to prove to you that it is so.

Come here, Meletus. Is it not a fact that you think it very important that the younger men should be as excellent as possible?

Meletus. It is.

Socrates. Come then: tell the judges, who is it who improves them? You take so much interest in the matter that of course you know that. You are accusing me, and bringing me to trial, because, as you say, you have discovered that I am the corrupter of the youth. Come now, reveal to the judges who improves them. You see, Meletus, you have nothing to say; you are silent. But don't you think that this is a scandalous thing? Is not your silence a conclusive proof of what I say, that you have never given a moment's thought to the matter? Come, tell us, my good sir, who makes the young men better citizens?

Meletus. The laws.

Socrates. My excellent sir, that is not my question. What man improves the young, who starts with a knowledge of the laws?

Meletus. The judges here, Socrates.

Socrates. What do you mean, Meletus? Can they educate the young and improve them?

Meletus. Certainly …

Socrates. All of them? or only some of them?

Meletus. All of them.

Socrates. By Hera that is good news! There is a great abundance of benefactors. And do the listeners here improve them, or not?

Meletus. They do.

Socrates. And do the senators?

Meletus. Yes.

Socrates. Well then, Meletus; do the members of the Assembly corrupt the younger men? or do they again all improve them?

Meletus. They too improve them.

Socrates. Then all the Athenians, apparently, make the young into fine fellows except me, and I alone corrupt them. Is that your meaning?

Meletus. Most certainly; that is my meaning.

Socrates. You have discovered me to be a most unfortunate man. Now tell me: do you think that the same holds good in the case of horses? Does one man do them harm and every one else improve them? On the contrary, is it not one man only, or a very few—namely, those who are skilled in horses—who can improve them; while the majority of men harm them, if they use them, and have to do with them? Is it not so, Meletus, both with horses and with every other animal? Of course it is, whether you and Anytus say yes or no. And young men would certainly be very fortunate persons if only one man corrupted them, and every one else did them good. The truth is, Meletus, you prove conclusively that you have never thought about the youth in your life. It is quite clear, on your own showing, that you take no interest at all in the matters about which you are prosecuting me.

Now, be so good as to tell us, Meletus, is it better to live among good citizens or bad ones? Answer, my friend: I am not asking you at all a difficult question. Do not bad citizens do harm to their neighbors and good citizens good?

Meletus. Yes.

Socrates. Is there any man who would rather be injured than benefited by his companions? Answer, my good sir: you are obliged by the law to answer. Does any one like to be injured?

Meletus. Certainly not.

Socrates. Well then; are you prosecuting me for corrupting the young, and making them worse men, intentionally or unintentionally?

Meletus. For doing it intentionally.

Socrates. What, Meletus? Do you mean to say that you, who are so much younger than I, are yet so much wiser than I, that you know that bad citizens always do evil, and that good citizens always do good, to those with whom they come in contact, while I am so extraordinarily stupid as not to know that if I make any of my companions a rogue, he will probably injure me in some way, and as to commit this great crime, as you allege, intentionally? You will not make me believe that, nor any one else either, I should think. Either I do not corrupt the young at all; or if I do, I do so unintentionally: so that you are a liar in either case. And if I corrupt them unintentionally, the law does not call upon you to prosecute me for a fault like that, which is an involuntary one: you should take me aside and admonish and instruct me: for of course I shall cease from doing wrong involuntarily, as soon as I know that I have been doing wrong. But you declined to instruct me: you would have nothing to do with me: instead of that, you bring me up before the Court, where the law sends persons, not for instruction, but for punishment.

The truth is, Athenians, as I said, it is quite clear that Meletus has never paid the slightest attention to these matters. However, now tell us, Meletus, how do you say that I corrupt the younger men? Clearly, according to your indictment, by teaching them not to believe in the gods of the city, but in other new divinities instead. You mean that I corrupt young men by that teaching, do you not?

Meletus. Yes: most certainly; I mean that.

Socrates. Then in the name of these gods of whom we are speaking, explain yourself a little more clearly to me and to the judges here. I cannot understand what you mean. Do you mean that I teach young men to believe in some gods, but not in the gods of the city? Do you accuse me of teaching them to believe in strange gods? If that is your meaning, I myself believe in some gods, and my crime is not that of absolute atheism. Or do you mean that I do not believe in the gods at all myself, and that I teach other people not to believe in them either?

Meletus. I mean that you do not believe in the gods in any way whatever.

Socrates. Wonderful, Meletus! Why do you say that? Do you mean that I believe neither the sun nor the moon to be gods, like other men?

Meletus. I swear he does not, judges: he says that the sun is a stone, and the moon earth.

Socrates. My dear Meletus, do you think that you are prosecuting Anaxagoras? You must have a very poor opinion of the judges, and think them very unlettered men, if you imagine that they do not know that the works of Anaxagoras of Clazomeæ are full of these doctrines. And so young men learn these things from me when they can often buy places in the theater[2] for a drachma at most, and laugh Socrates to scorn, were he to pretend that these doctrines, which are very peculiar doctrines, too, were his. But please tell me, do you really think that I do not believe in the gods at all?

----

[2] Socrates here alludes to the references to Anaxagoras by Aristophanes, Euripides, and other Greek dramatists. Anaxagoras' doctrine that the sun is a stone is mentioned in the Orestes of Euripedes.

Meletus. Most certainly I do. You are a complete atheist.

Socrates. No one believes that, Meletus, and I think that you know it to be a lie yourself. It seems to me, Athenians, that Meletus is a very insolent and wanton man, and that he is prosecuting me simply in the insolence and wantonness of youth. He is like a man trying an experiment on me, by asking me a riddle that has no answer. "Will this wise Socrates," he says to himself, "see that I am jesting and contradicting myself? or shall I outwit him and every one else who hears me?" Meletus seems to me to contradict himself in his indictment: it is as if he were to say, "Socrates is a wicked man who does not believe in the gods, but who believes in the gods." But that is mere trifling.

Now, my friends, let us see why I think that this is his meaning. Do you answer me, Meletus: and do you, Athenians, remember the request which I made to you at starting, and do not interrupt me if I talk in my usual way.

Is there any man, Meletus, who believes in the existence of things pertaining to men and not in the existence of men? Make him answer the question, my friends, without these absurd interruptions. Is there any man who believes in the existence of horsemanship and not in the existence of horses? or in flute-playing and not in flute-players? There is not, my excellent sir. If you will not answer, I will tell both you and the judges that. But you must answer my next question. Is there any man who believes in the existence of divine things and not in the existence of divinities?

Meletus. There is not.

Socrates. I am very glad that the judges have managed to extract an answer from you. Well then, you say that I believe in divine beings, whether they be old or new ones, and that I teach others to believe in them; at any rate, according to your statement, I believe in divine beings. That you have sworn in your deposition. But if I believe in divine beings, I suppose it follows necessarily that I believe in divinities. Is it not so? It is. I assume that you grant that, as you do not answer. But do we not believe that divinities are either gods themselves or the children of the gods? Do you admit that?

Meletus. I do.

Socrates. Then you admit that I believe in divinities: now, if these divinities are gods, then, as I say, you are jesting and asking a riddle, and asserting that I do not believe in the gods, and at the same time that I do, since I believe in divinities. But if these divinities are the illegitimate children of the gods, either by the nymphs or by other mothers, as they are said to be, then, I ask, what man could believe in the existence of the children of the gods and not in the existence of the gods? That would be as strange as believing in the existence of the offspring of horses and asses, and not in the existence of horses and asses. You must have indicted me in this manner, Meletus, either to test my skill, or because you could not find any crime that you could accuse me of with truth. But you will never contrive to persuade any man, even of the smallest understanding, that a belief in divine things and things of the gods does not necessarily involve a belief in divinities, and in the gods, and in heroes.

But in truth, Athenians, I do not think that I need say very much to prove that I have not committed the crime for which Meletus is prosecuting me. What I have said is enough to prove that. But, I repeat, it is certainly true, as I have already told you, that I have incurred much unpopularity and made many enemies. And that is what will cause my condemnation, if I am condemned; not Meletus, nor Anytus either, but the prejudice and suspicion of the multitude. They have been the destruction of many good men before me, and I think that they will be so again. There is no fear that I shall be their last victim.

Perhaps some one will say: "Are you not ashamed, Socrates, of following pursuits which are very likely now to cause your death?" I should answer him with justice, and say: My friend, if you think that a man of any worth at all ought to reckon the chances of life and death when he acts, or that he ought to think of anything but whether he is acting rightly or wrongly, and as a good or a bad man would act, you are grievously mistaken. According to you, the demigods who died at Troy would be men of no great worth, and among them the son of Thetis, who thought nothing of danger when the alternative was disgrace. For when his mother, a goddess, addressed him, as he was burning to slay Hector, I suppose in this fashion, "My son, if thou avengest the death of thy comrade Patroclus, and slayest Hector, thou wilt die thyself, for 'fate awaits thee straightway after Hector's death,'" he heard what she said, but he scorned danger and death; he feared much more to live a coward, and not to avenge his friend. "Let me punish the evil-doer and straightway die," he said, "that I may not remain here by the beaked ships, a scorn of men, encumbering the earth." Do you suppose that he thought of danger or of death? For this, Athenians, I believe to be the truth. Wherever a man's post is, whether he has chosen it of his own will, or whether he has been placed at it by his commander, there it is his duty to remain and face the danger, without thinking of death, or of any other thing, except dishonor.

When the generals whom you chose to command me, Athenians, placed me at my post at Potidæ, and at Amphipolis, and at Delium, I remained where they placed me, and ran the risk of death, like other men: and it would be very strange conduct on my part if I were to desert my post now from fear of death or of any other thing, when God has commanded me, as I am persuaded that he has done, to spend my life in searching for wisdom, and in examining myself and others. That would indeed be a very strange thing: and then certainly I might with justice be brought to trial for not believing in the gods: for I should be disobeying the oracle, and fearing death, and thinking myself wise, when I was not wise. For to fear death, my friends, is only to think ourselves wise, without being wise: for it is to think that we know what we do not know. For anything that men can tell, death may be the greatest good that can happen to them: but they fear it as if they knew quite well that it was the greatest of evils. And what is this but that shameful ignorance of thinking that we know what we do not know? In this matter too, my friends, perhaps I am different from the mass of mankind: and if I were to claim to be at all wiser than others, it would be because I do not think that I have any clear knowledge about the other world, when, in fact, I have none. But I do know very well that it is evil and base to do wrong, and to disobey my superior, whether he be man or god. And I will never do what I know to be evil, and shrink in fear from what, for all that I can tell, may be a good. And so, even if you acquit me now, and do not listen to Anytus' argument that, if I am to be acquitted, I ought never to have been brought to trial at all; and that, as it is, you are bound to put me to death, because, as he said, if I escape, all your children will forthwith be utterly corrupted by practicing what Socrates teaches; if you were therefore to say to me, "Socrates, this time we will not listen to Anytus: we will let you go; but on this condition, that you cease from carrying on this search of yours, and from philosophy; if you are found following those pursuits again, you shall die": I say, if you offered to let me go on these terms, I should reply— Athenians, I hold you in the highest regard and love; but I will obey God rather than you: and as long as I have breath and strength I will not cease from philosophy, and from exhorting you, and declaring the truth to every one of you whom I meet, saying, as I am wont: "My excellent friend, you are a citizen of Athens, a city which is very great and very famous for wisdom and power of mind; are you not ashamed of caring so much for the making of money, and for reputation, and for honor? Will you not think or care about wisdom and truth, and the perfection of your soul?" And if he disputes my words, and says that he does care about these things, I shall not forthwith release him and go away: I shall question him and cross-examine him and test him: and if I think that he has not virtue, though he says that he has, I shall reproach him for setting the lower value on the most important things, and a higher value on those that are of less account. This I shall do to every one whom I meet, young or old, citizen or stranger: but more especially to the citizens, for they are more nearly akin to me. For, know well, God has commanded me to do so. And I think that no better piece of fortune has ever befallen you in Athens than my service to God. For I spend my whole life in going about and persuading you all to give your first and chiefest care to the perfection of your souls, and not till you have done that to think of your bodies, or your wealth; and telling you that virtue does not come from wealth, but that wealth, and every other good thing which men have, whether in public, or in private, comes from virtue. If then I corrupt the youth by this teaching, the mischief is great: but if any man says that I teach anything else, he speaks falsely. And therefore, Athenians, I say, either listen to Anytus, or do not listen to him: either acquit me, or do not acquit me: but be sure that I shall not alter my way of life; no, not if I have to die for it many times.

Do not interrupt me, Athenians. Remember the request which I made to you, and listen to my words. I think that it will profit you to hear them. I am going to say something more to you, at which you may be inclined to cry out: but do not do that. Be sure that if you put me to death, who am what I have told you that I am, you will do yourselves more harm than me. Meletus and Anytus can do me no harm: that is impossible: for I am sure that God will not allow a good man to be injured by a bad one. They may indeed kill me, or drive me into exile, or deprive me of my civil rights; and perhaps Meletus and others think those things great evils. But I do not think so: I think that it is a much greater evil to do what he is doing now, and to try to put a man to death unjustly. And now, Athenians, I am not arguing in my own defence at all, as you might expect me to do: I am trying to persuade you not to sin against God, by condemning me, and rejecting his gift to you. For if you put me to death, you will not easily find another man to fill my place. God has sent me to attack the city, as if it were a great and noble horse, to use a quaint simile, which was rather sluggish from its size, and which needed to be aroused by a gadfly: and I think that I am the gadfly that God has sent to the city to attack it; for I never cease from settling upon you, as it were, at every point, and rousing, and exhorting, and reproaching each man of you all day long. You will not easily find any one

else, my friends, to fill my place: and if you take my advice, you will spare my life. You are vexed, as drowsy persons are, when they are awakened, and of course, if you listened to Anytus, you could easily kill me with a single blow, and then sleep on undisturbed for the rest of your lives, unless God were to care for you enough to send another man to arouse you. And you may easily see that it is God who has given me to your city: a mere human impulse would never have led me to neglect all my own interests, or to endure seeing my private affairs neglected now for so many years, while it made me busy myself unceasingly in your interests, and go to each man of you by himself, like a father, or an elder brother, trying to persuade him to care for virtue. There would have been a reason for it, if I had gained any advantage by this conduct, or if I had been paid for my exhortations; but you see yourselves that my accusers, though they accuse me of everything else without blushing, have not had the effrontery to say that I ever either exacted or demanded payment. They could bring no evidence of that. And I think that I have sufficient evidence of the truth of what I say in my poverty.

Perhaps it may seem strange to you that, though I am so busy in going about in private with my counsel, yet I do not venture to come forward in the assembly, and take part in the public councils. You have often heard me speak of my reason for this, and in many places: it is that I have a certain divine sign from God, which is the divinity that Meletus has caricatured in his indictment. I have had it from childhood: it is a kind of voice, which whenever I hear it, always turns me back from something which I was going to do, but never urges me to act. It is this which forbids me to take part in politics. And I think that it does well to forbid me. For, Athenians, it is quite certain that if I had attempted to take part in politics, I should have perished at once and long ago, without doing any good either to you or to myself. And do not be vexed with me for telling the truth. There is no man who will preserve his life for long, either in Athens or elsewhere, if he firmly opposes the wishes of the people, and tries to prevent the commission of much injustice and illegality in the State. He who would really fight for injustice, must do so as a private man, not in public, if he means to preserve his life, even for a short time.

I will prove to you that this is so by very strong evidence, not by mere words, but by what you value highly, actions. Listen then to what has happened to me, that you may know that there is no man who could make me consent to do wrong from the fear of death; but that I would perish at once rather than give way. What I am going to tell you may be a commonplace in the Courts of Law; nevertheless it is true. The only office that I ever held in the State, Athenians, was that of Senator. When you wished to try the ten generals, who did not rescue their men after the battle of Arginusæ, in a body, which was illegal, as you all came to think afterwards, the tribe Antiochis, to which I belong, held the presidency. On that occasion I alone of all the presidents opposed your illegal action, and gave my vote against you. The speakers were ready to suspend me and arrest me; and you were clamoring against me, and crying out to me to submit. But I thought that I ought to face the danger out in the cause of law and justice, rather than join with you in your unjust proposal, from fear of imprisonment or death. That was before the destruction of the democracy. When the oligarchy came, the Thirty sent for me, with four others, to the Council-Chamber, and ordered us to bring over Leon the Salaminian from Salamis, that they might put him to death. They were in the habit of frequently giving similar orders to many others, wishing to implicate as many men as possible in their crimes. But then I again proved, not by mere words, but by my actions, that, if I may use a vulgar expression, I do not care a straw for death; but that I do care very much indeed about not doing anything against the laws of God or man. That government with all its power did not terrify me into doing anything wrong; but when we left the Council-Chamber, the other four went over to Salamis, and brought Leon across to Athens; and I went away home: and if the rule of the Thirty had not been destroyed soon afterwards, I should very likely have been put to death for what I did then. Many of you will be my witnesses in this matter.

Now do you think that I should have remained alive all these years, if I had taken part in public affairs, and had always maintained the cause of justice like an honest man, and had held it a paramount duty, as it is, to do so? Certainly not, Athenians, nor any other man either. But throughout my whole life, both in private, and in public, whenever I have had to take part in public affairs, you will find that I have never yielded a single point in a question of right and wrong to any man; no, not to those whom my enemies falsely assert to have been my pupils.[3] But I was never any man's teacher. I have never withheld myself from any one, young or old, who was anxious to hear me converse while I was about my mission; neither do I converse for payment; and refuse to converse without payment: I am ready to ask questions of rich and poor alike, and if any man wishes to answer me, and then listen to what I have to say, he

---

[3] For example, Critias and Alcibiades.

may. And I cannot justly be charged with causing these men to turn out good or bad citizens: for I never either taught, or professed to teach any of them any knowledge whatever. And if any man asserts that he ever learnt or heard anything from me in private, which every one else did not hear as well as he, be sure that he does not speak the truth.

Why is it, then, that people delight in spending so much time in my company? You have heard why, Athenians. I told you the whole truth when I said that they delight in hearing me examine persons who think that they are wise when they are not wise. It is certainly very amusing to listen to that. And, I say, God has commanded me to examine men in oracles, and in dreams, and in every way in which the divine will was ever declared to man. This is the truth, Athenians, and if it were not the truth, it would be easily refuted. For if it were really the case that I have already corrupted some of the young men, and am now corrupting others, surely some of them, finding as they grew older that I had given them evil counsel in their youth, would have come forward today to accuse me and take their revenge. Or if they were unwilling to do so themselves, surely their kinsmen, their fathers, or brothers, or other relatives, would, if I had done them any harm, have remembered it, and taken their revenge. Certainly I see many of them in Court. Here is Crito, of my own deme and of my own age, the father of Critobulus; here is Lysanias of Sphettus, the father of Æschinus: here is also Antiphon of Cephisus, the father of Epigenes. Then here are others, whose brothers have spent their time in my company; Nicostratus, the son of Theozotides, and brother of Theodotus—and Theodotus is dead, so he at least cannot entreat his brother to be silent: here is Paralus, the son of Demodocus, and the brother of

Theages: here is Adeimantus, the son of Ariston, whose brother is Plato here: and Æantodorus, whose brother is Aristodorus. And I can name many others to you, some of whom Meletus ought to have called as witnesses in the course of his own speech: but if he forgot to call them then, let him call them now—I will stand aside while he does so—and tell us if he has any such evidence. No, on the contrary, my friends, you will find all these men ready to support me, the corrupter, the injurer of their kindred, as Meletus and Anytus call me. Those of them who have been already corrupted might perhaps have some reason for supporting me: but what reason cam their relatives, who are grown up, and who are uncorrupted, have, except the reason of truth and justice, that they know very well that Meletus is a liar, and that I am speaking the truth?

Well, my friends, this, together it may be with other things of the same nature, is pretty much what I have to say in my defence. There may be some one among you who will be vexed when he remembers how, even in a less important trial than this, he prayed and entreated the judges to acquit him with many tears, and brought forward his children and many of his friends and relatives in Court, in order to appeal to your feelings; and then finds that I shall do none of these things, though I am in what he would think the supreme danger. Perhaps he will harden himself against me when he notices this: it may make him angry, and he may give his vote in anger. If it is so with any of you—I do not suppose that it is, but in case it should be so—I think that I should answer him reasonably if I said: "My friend, I have kinsmen too, for, in the words of Homer, 'I am not born of sticks and stones,' but of woman"; and so, Athenians, I have kinsmen, and I have three sons, one of them a lad, and the other two still children. Yet I will not bring any of them forward before you, and implore you to acquit me. And why will I do none of these things? It is not from arrogance, Athenians, nor because I hold you cheap: whether or not I can face death bravely is another question: but for my own credit, and for your credit, and for the credit of our city, I do not think it well, at my age, and with my name, to do anything of that kind. Rightly or wrongly, men have made up their minds that in some way Socrates is different from the mass of mankind. And it will be a shameful thing if those of you who are thought to excel in wisdom, or in bravery, or in any other virtue, are going to act in this fashion. I have often seen men with a reputation behaving in a strange way at their trial, as if they thought it a terrible fate to be killed, and as though they expected to live for ever, if you did not put them to death. Such men seem to me to bring discredit on the city: for any stranger would suppose that the best and most eminent Athenians, who are selected by their fellow-citizens to hold office, and for other honors, are no better than women. Those of you, Athenians, who have any reputation at all, ought not to do these things: and you ought not to allow us to do them: you should show that you will be much more merciless to men who make the city ridiculous by these pitiful pieces of acting, than to men who remain quiet.

But apart from the question of credit, my friends, I do not think that it is right to entreat the judge to acquit us, or to escape condemnation in that way. It is our duty to convince his mind by reason. He does not sit to give away justice to his friends, but to pronounce judgment: and he has sworn not to favor any man whom he would like to favor, but to decide questions according to law. And therefore we ought not to teach you to forswear yourselves; and you ought not to allow yourselves to be taught, for then neither you nor we would be acting righteously. Therefore, Athenians, do not require me to do these things, for I believe them to be neither good nor just nor holy; and, more especially do not ask me to do them today, when Meletus is prosecuting me for impiety. For were I to be successful, and to prevail on you by my prayers to break your oaths, I should be clearly teaching you to believe that there are no gods; and I should be simply accusing myself by my defence of not believing in them. But, Athenians, that is very far from the truth. I do believe in the gods as no one of my accusers believes in them: and to you, and to God I commit my cause to be decided as is best for you and for me.

[He is found guilty by 281 votes to 220.]

I am not vexed at the verdict which you have given, Athenians, for many reasons. I expected that you would find me guilty; and I am not so much surprised at that, as at the numbers of the votes. I, certainly, never thought that the majority against me would have been so narrow. But now it seems that if only thirty votes had changed sides, I should have escaped. So I think that I have escaped Meletus, as it is: and not only have I escaped him; for it is perfectly clear that if Anytus and Lycon had not come forward to accuse me too, he would not have obtained the fifth part of the votes, and would have had to pay a fine of a thousand drachmæ.

So he proposes death as the penalty. Be it so. And what counter-penalty shall I propose to you, Athenians? What I deserve, of course, must I not? What then do I deserve to pay or to suffer for having determined not to spend my life in ease? I neglected the things which most men value, such as wealth, and family interests, and military commands, and popular oratory, and all the political appointments, and clubs, and factions, that there are in Athens; for I thought that I was really too conscientious a man to preserve my life if I engage in these matters. So I did not go where I should have done no good either to you or to myself. I went instead to each one of you by himself, to do him, as I say, the greatest of services, and strove to persuade him not to think of his affairs, until he had thought of himself, and tried to make himself as perfect and wise as possible; nor to think of the affairs of Athens, until he had thought of Athens herself; and in all cases to bestow his thoughts on things in the same manner. Then what do I deserve for such a life? Something good, Athenians, if I am really to propose what I deserve; and something good which it would be suitable to me to receive. Then what is a suitable reward to be given to a poor benefactor, who requires leisure to exhort you? There is no reward, Athenians, so suitable for him as a public maintenance in the Prytaneum. It is a much more suitable reward for him than for any of you who has won a victory at the Olympic games with his horse or his chariots. Such a man only makes you seem happy, but I make you really happy: and he is not in want, and I am. So if I am to propose the penalty which I really deserve, I propose this, a public maintenance in the Prytaneum.

Perhaps you think me stubborn and arrogant in what I am saying now, as in what I said about the entreaties and tears. It is not so, Athenians; it is rather that I am convinced that I never wronged any man intentionally, though I cannot persuade you of that, for we have conversed together only a little time. If there were a law at Athens, as there is elsewhere, not to finish a trial of life and death in a single day, I think that I could have convinced you of it:

but now it is not easy in so short a time to clear myself of the gross calumnies of my enemies. But when I am convinced that I have never wronged any man, I shall certainly not wrong myself, or admit that I deserve to suffer any evil, or propose any evil for myself as a penalty. Why should I? Lest I should suffer the penalty which Meletus proposes, when I say that I do not know whether it is a good or an evil? Shall I choose instead of it something which I know to be an evil, and propose that as a penalty? Shall I propose imprisonment? And why should I pass the rest of my days in prison, the slave of successive officials? Or shall I propose a fine, with imprisonment until it is paid? I have told you why I will not do that. I should have to remain in prison for I have no money to pay a fine with. Shall I then propose exile? Perhaps you would agree to that. Life would indeed be very dear to me, if I were unreasonable enough to expect that strangers would cheerfully tolerate my discussions and reasonings, when you who are my fellow-citizens cannot endure them, and have found them so burdensome and odious to you, that you are seeking now to be released from them. No, indeed, Athenians, that is not likely. A fine life I should lead for an old man, if I were to withdraw from Athens, and pass the rest of my days in wandering from city to city, and continually being expelled. For I know very well that the young men will listen to me, wherever I go, as they do here; and if I drive them away, they will persuade their elders to expel me: and if I do not drive them away, their fathers and kinsmen will expel me for their sakes.

Perhaps some one will say, "Why cannot you withdraw from Athens, Socrates, and hold your peace?" It is the most difficult thing in the world to make you understand why I cannot do that. If I say that I cannot hold my peace, because that would be to disobey God, you will think that I am not in earnest and will not believe me. And if I tell you that no better thing can happen to a man than to converse every day about virtue and the other matters about which you have heard me conversing and examining myself and others, and that an unexamined life is not worth living, then you will believe me still less. But that is the truth, my friends, though it is not easy to convince you of it. And, what is more, I am not accustomed to think that I deserve any punishment. If I had been rich, I would have proposed as large a fine as I could pay: that would have done me no harm. But I am not rich enough to pay a fine, unless you are willing to fix it at a sum within my means. Perhaps I could pay you a mina: so I propose that. Plato here, Athenians, and Crito, and Critobulus, and Apollodorus bid me propose thirty minæ and they will be sureties for me. So I propose thirty minæ. They will be sufficient sureties to you for the money.

[He is condemned to death.]

You have not gained very much time, Athenians, and, as the price of it, you will have an evil name from all who wish to revile the city, and they will cast in your teeth that you put Socrates, a wise man, to death. For they will certainly call me wise, whether I am wise or not, when they want to reproach you. If you would have waited for a little while, your wishes would have been fulfilled in the course of nature; for you see that I am an old man, far advanced in years, and near to death. I am speaking not to all of you, only to those who have voted for my death. And now I am speaking to them still. Perhaps, my friends, you think that I have been defeated because I was wanting in the arguments by which I could have persuaded you to acquit me, if, that is, I had thought it right to do or to say

anything to escape punishment. It is not so. I have been defeated because I was wanting, not in arguments, but in overboldness and effrontery: because I would not plead before you as you would have liked to hear me plead, or appeal to you with weeping and wailing, or say and do many other things, which I maintain are unworthy of me, but which you have been accustomed to from other men. But when I was defending myself, I thought that I ought not to do anything unmanly because of the danger which I ran, and I have not changed my mind now. I would very much rather defend myself as I did, and die, than as you would have had me do, and live. Both in a law suit, and in war, there are some things which neither I nor any other man may do in order to escape from death. In battle a man often sees that he may at least escape from death by throwing down his arms and falling on his knees before the pursuer to beg for his life. And there are many other ways of avoiding death in every danger, if a man will not scruple to say and to do anything. But, my friends, I think that it is a much harder thing to escape from wickedness than from death; for wickedness is swifter than death. And now I, who am old and slow, have been overtaken by the slower pursuer: and my accusers, who are clever and swift, have been overtaken by the swifter pursuer, which is wickedness. And now I shall go hence, sentenced by you to death; and they will go hence, sentenced by truth to receive the penalty of wickedness and evil. And I abide by this award as well as they. Perhaps it was right for these things to be so: and I think that they are fairly measured.

And now I wish to prophesy to you, Athenians who have condemned me. For I am going to die, and that is the time when men have most prophetic power. And I prophesy to you who have sentenced me to death, that a far severer punishment than you have inflicted on me, will surely overtake you as soon as I am dead. You have done this thing, thinking that you will be relieved from having to give an account of your lives. But I say that the result will be very different from that. There will be more men who will call you to account, whom I have held back, and whom you did not see. And they will be harder masters to you than I have been, for they will be younger, and you will be more angry with them. For if you think that you will restrain men from reproaching you for your evil lives by putting them to death, you are very much mistaken. That way of escape is hardly possible, and it is not a good one. It is much better, and much easier, not to silence reproaches, but to make yourselves as perfect as you can. This is my parting prophecy to you who have condemned me.

With you who have acquitted me I should like to converse touching this thing that has come to pass, while the authorities are busy, and before I go to the place where I have to die. So, I pray you, remain with me until I go hence: there is no reason why we should not converse with each other while it is possible. I wish to explain to you, as my friends, the meaning of what has befallen me. A wonderful thing has happened to me, judges—for you I am right in calling judges. The prophetic sign, which I am wont to receive from the divine voice, has been constantly with me all through my life till now, opposing me in quite small matters if I were not going to act rightly. And now you yourselves see what has happened to me; a thing which might be thought, and which is sometimes actually reckoned, the supreme evil. But the sign of God did not withstand me when I was leaving my house in the morning, nor when I was coming up hither to the Court, nor at any point in my speech, when I was going to say anything:

though at other times it has often stopped me in the very act of speaking. But now, in this matter, it has never once withstood me, either in my words or my actions. I will tell you what I believe to be the reason of that. This thing that has come upon me must be a good: and those of us who think that death is an evil must needs be mistaken. I have a clear proof that is so; for my accustomed sign would certainly have opposed me, if I had not been going to fare well.

And if we reflect in another way we shall see that we may well hope that death is a good. For the state of death is one of two things: either the dead man wholly ceases to be, and loses all sensation; or, according to the common belief, it is a change and a migration of the soul unto another place. And if death is the absence of all sensation, and like the sleep of one whose slumbers are unbroken by any dreams, it will be a wonderful gain. For if a man had to select that night in which he slept so soundly that he did not even see any dreams, and had to compare with it all the other nights and days of his life, and then had to say how many days and nights in his life he had spent better and more pleasantly than this night, I think that a private person, nay, even the great King [of Persia] himself, would find them easy to count, compared with the others. If that is the nature of death, I for one count it a gain. For then it appears that eternity is nothing more than a single night. But if death is a journey to another place, and the common belief be true, that there are all who have died, what good could be greater than this, my judges? Would a journey not be worth taking, at the end of which, in the other world, we should be released from the self-styled judges who are here, and should find the true judges, who are said to sit in judgment below, such as Minos, and Rhadamanthus, and Æacus, and Triptolemus, and the other demi-gods who were just in their lives? Or what would you not give to converse with Orpheus and Musæus and Hesiod and Homer? I am willing to die many times, if this be true. And for my own part I should have a wonderful interest in meeting there Palamedes, and Ajax the son of Telamon, and the other men of old who have died through an unjust judgment, and in comparing my experiences with theirs. That I think would be no small pleasure. And, above all, I could spend my time in examining those who are there, as I examine men here, and in finding out which of them is wise, and which of them thinks himself wise, when he is not wise. What would we not give, my judges, to be able to examine the leader of the great expedition against Troy, or Odysseus, or Sisyphus, or countless other men and women whom we could name? It would be an infinite happiness to converse with them, and to live with them, and to examine them. Assuredly there they do not put men to death for doing that. For besides the other ways in which they are happier than we are, they are immortal, at least if the common belief be true.

And you too, judges, must face death with a good courage, and believe this as a truth, that no evil can happen to a good man, either in life, or after death. His fortunes are not neglected by the gods; and what has come to me today has not come by chance. I am persuaded that it was better for me to die now, and to be released from trouble: and that was the reason why the sign never turned me back. And so I am hardly angry with my accusers, or with those who have condemned me to die. Yet it was not with this mind that they accused me and condemned me, but meaning to do me an injury. So far I may find fault with them.

Yet I have one request to make of them. When my sons grow up, visit them with punishment, my friends, and vex them in the same way that I have vexed you, if they seem to you to care for riches, or for any other thing, before virtue: and if they think that they are something, when they are nothing at all, reproach them, as I have reproached you, for not caring for what they should, and for thinking that they are great men when in fact they are worthless. And if you will do this, I myself and my sons will have received our deserts at your hands.

But now the time has come, and we must go hence; I to die, and you to live. Whether life or death is better is known to God, and to God only.

EUTHYPHRO

Characters

Euthyphro

Socrates

Euthyphro. What strange thing has happened, Socrates, that you have left

Reprinted by permission of the publishers from Loeb Classical Library, H. N. Fowler, trans., Plato, *Euthyphro*, Cambridge, MA: Harvard University Press, 1947.

your accustomed haunts in the Lyceum and are now haunting the portico where the king archon sits? For it cannot be that you have an action before the kings, as I have.

Socrates. Our Athenians, Euthyphro, do not call it an action, but an indictment.

Euthyphro. What? Somebody has, it seems, brought an indictment against you; for I don't accuse you of having brought one against anyone else.

Socrates. Certainly not.

Euthyphro. But someone else against you?

Socrates. Quite so.

Euthyphro. Who is he?

Socrates. I don't know the man very well myself, Euthyphro, for he seems to be a young and unknown person. His name, however, is Meletus, I believe. And he is of the deme of Pitthus, if you remember any Pitthian Meletus, with long hair and only a little beard, but with a hooked nose.

Euthyphro. I don't remember him, Socrates. But what sort of an indictment has he brought against you?

Socrates. What sort? No mean one, it seems to me; for the fact that, young as he is, he has apprehended so important a matter reflects no small credit upon him. For he says he knows how the youth are corrupted and who those are who corrupt them. He must be a wise man; who, seeing my lack of wisdom and that I am corrupting his fellows, comes to the State, as a boy runs to his mother, to accuse me. And he seems to me to be the only one of the public men who begins in the right way; for the right way is to take care of the young men first, to make them as good as possible, just as a good husbandman will naturally take care of the young plants first and afterwards of the rest. And so Meletus, perhaps, is first clearing away us who corrupt the young plants, as he says; then after this, when he has turned his attention to the older men, he will bring countless most precious blessings upon the State, at least, that is the natural outcome of the beginning he has made.

Euthyphro. I hope it may be so, Socrates; but I fear the opposite may result. For it seems to me that he begins by injuring the State at its very heart, when he undertakes to harm you. Now tell me, what does he say you do that corrupts the young?

Socrates. Absurd things, my friend, at first hearing. For he says I am a maker of gods; and because I make new gods and do not believe in the old ones, he indicted me for the sake of these old ones, as he says.

Euthyphro. I understand, Socrates; it is because you say the divine monitor keeps coming to you. So he has brought the indictment against you for making innovations in religion, and he is going into court to slander you, knowing that slanders on such subjects are readily accepted by the people. Why, they even laugh at me and say I am crazy when I say anything in the assembly about divine things and fortell the future to them. And yet there is not one of the things I have foretold that is not true; but they are jealous of all such men as you and I are. However, we must not be disturbed, but must come to close quarters with them.

Socrates. My dear Euthyphro, their ridicule is perhaps of no consequence. For the Athenians, I fancy, are not much concerned, if they think a man is clever, provided he does not impart his clever notions to others; but when they think he makes others to be like himself, they are angry with him, either through jealousy, as you say, or for some other reason.

Euthyphro. I don't much desire to test their sentiments toward me in this matter.

Socrates. No, for perhaps they think that you are reserved and unwilling to impart your wisdom. But I fear that because of my love of men they think that I not only pour myself out copiously to anyone and everyone without payment, but that I would even pay something myself, if anyone would listen to me. Now if, as I was saying just now, they were to laugh at me, as you say they do at you, it would not be at all unpleasant to pass the time in the court with jests and laughter; but if they are in earnest, then only soothsayers like you can tell how this will end.

Euthyphro. Well, Socrates, perhaps it won't amount to much, and you will bring your case to a satisfactory ending, as I think I shall mine.

Socrates. What is your case, Euthyphro? Are you defending or prosecuting?

Euthyphro. Prosecuting.

Socrates. Whom?

Euthyphro. Such a man that they think I am insane because I am prosecuting[1] him.

Socrates. Why? Are you prosecuting one who has wings to fly away with?

Euthyphro. No flying for him at his ripe old age.

Socrates. Who is he?

Euthyphro. My father.

Socrates. Your father, my dear man?

Euthyphro. Certainly.

Socrates. But what is the charge, and what is the suit about?

Euthyphro. Murder, Socrates.

Socrates. Heracles! Surely, Euthyphro, most people do not know where the right lies; for I fancy it is not everyone

who can rightly do what you are doing, but only one who is already very far advanced in wisdom.

Euthyphro. Very far, indeed, Socrates, by Zeus.

Socrates. Is the one who was killed by your father a relative? But of course he was; for you would not bring a charge of murder against him on a stranger's account.

Euthyphro. It is ridiculous, Socrates, that you think it matters whether the man who was killed was a stranger or a relative, and do not see that the only thing to consider is whether the action of the slayer was justified or not, and that if it was justified one ought to let him alone, and if not, one ought to proceed against him, even if he share one's hearth and eat at one's table. For the pollution is the same if you associate knowingly with such a man and do not purify yourself and him by proceeding against him. In this case, the man who was killed was a hired workman of mine, and when we were farming at Naxos, he was working there on our land. Now he got drunk, got angry with one of our house slaves, and butchered him. So my father bound him hand and foot, threw him into a ditch, and sent a man here to Athens to ask the religious adviser what he ought to do. In the meantime he paid no attention to the man as he lay there bound, and neglected him, thinking that he was a murderer and it did not matter if he were to die. And that is just what happened to him. For he died of hunger and cold and his bonds before the messenger came back from the adviser. Now my father and the rest of my relatives are angry with me, because for the sake of this murderer I am prosecuting my father for murder. For they say he did not kill him, and if he had killed him never so much, yet since the dead man was a murderer I

---

[1] The Greek word has much the same meaning as the Latin *prosequor* from which the English "prosecute" is derived, "follow," "pursue," and is at the same time the technical term for "prosecute."

ought not to trouble myself about such a fellow, because it is unholy for a son to prosecute his father for murder. Which shows how little they know what the divine law is in regard to holiness and unholiness.

Socrates. But, in the name of Zeus, Euthyphro, do you think your knowledge about divine laws and holiness and unholiness is so exact that, when the facts are as you say, you are not afraid of doing something unholy yourself in prosecuting your father for murder?

Euthyphro. I should be of no use, Socrates, and Euthyphro would be in no way different from other men, if I did not have exact knowledge about all such things.

Socrates. Then the best thing for me, my admirable Euthyphro, is to become your pupil and, before the suit with Meletus comes on, to challenge him and say that I always thought it very important before to know about divine matters and that now, since he says I am doing wrong by acting carelessly and making innovations in matters of religion, I have become your pupil. And "Meletus," I should say, "if you acknowledge that Euthyphro is wise in such matters, then believe that I also hold correct opinions, and do not bring me to trial; and if you do not acknowledge that, then bring a suit against him, my teacher, rather than against me, and charge him with corrupting the old, namely, his father and me, which he does by teaching me and by correcting and punishing his father." And if he does not do as I ask and does not release me from the indictment or bring it against you in my stead, I could say in the court the same things I said in my challenge to him, could I not?

Euthyphro. By Zeus, Socrates, if he should undertake to indict me, I fancy I should find his weak spot, and it would be much more a question about him in court than about me.

Socrates. And I, my dear friend, perceiving this, wish to become your pupil; for I know that neither this fellow Meletus, nor anyone else, seems to notice you at all, but he has seen through me so sharply and so easily that he has indicted me for impiety. Now in the name of Zeus, tell me what you just now asserted that you knew so well. What do you say is the nature of piety and impiety, both in relation to murder and to other things? Is not holiness always the same with itself in every action, and, on the other hand, is not unholiness the opposite of all holiness, always the same with itself and whatever is to be unholy possessing some one characteristic quality?

Euthyphro. Certainly, Socrates.

Socrates. Tell me then, what do you say holiness is, and what unholiness?

Euthyphro. Well then, I say that holiness is doing what I am doing now, prosecuting the wrongdoer who commits murder or steals from the temples or does any such thing, whether he be your father or your mother or anyone else, and not prosecuting him is unholy. And, Socrates, see what a sure proof I offer you—a proof I have already given to others—that this is established and right and that we ought not to let him who acts impiously go unpunished, no matter who he may be. Men believe that Zeus is the best and most just of the gods, and they acknowledge that he put his father in bonds because he wickedly devoured his children, and he in turn had mutilated his father for similar reasons; but they are incensed against me because I proceed against my father when he has done wrong, and so they are inconsistent in what they say about the gods and about me.

Socrates. Is not this, Euthyphro, the reason why I am being prosecuted, because when people tell such stories about the gods I find it hard to accept them? And therefore, probably, people will say I am wrong. Now if you, who know so much about such things, accept these tales, I suppose I too must give way. For what am I to say, who confess frankly that I know nothing about them? But tell me, in the name of Zeus, the god of friendship, do you really believe these things happened?

Euthyphro. Yes, and still more wonderful things than these, Socrates, which most people do not know.

Socrates. And so you believe that there was really war between the gods, and fearful enmities and battles and other things of the sort, such as are told of by the poets and represented in varied designs by the great artists in our sacred places and especially on the robe which is carried up to the Acropolis at the great Panathenaea? for this is covered with such representations. Shall we agree that these things are true, Euthyphro?

Euthyphro. Not only these things, Socrates; but, as I said just now, I will, if you like, tell you many other things about the gods, which I am sure will amaze you when you hear them.

Socrates. I dare say. But you can tell me those things at your leisure some other time. At present try to tell more clearly what I asked you just now. For, my friend, you did not give me sufficient information before, when I asked what holiness was, but you told me that this was holy which you are now doing, prosecuting your father for murder.

Euthyphro. Well, what I said was true, Socrates.

Socrates. Perhaps. But, Euthyphro, you say that many other things are holy, do you not?

Euthyphro. Why, so they are.

Socrates. Now call to mind that this is not what I asked you, to tell me one or two of the many holy acts, but to tell the essential aspect, by which all holy acts are holy; for you said that all unholy acts were unholy and all holy ones holy by one aspect. Or don't you remember?

Euthyphro. I remember.

Socrates. Tell me then what this aspect is, that I may keep my eye fixed upon it and employ it as a model and, if anything you or anyone else does agrees with it, may say that the act is holy, and if not, that it is unholy.

Euthyphro. If you wish me to explain in that way, I will do so.

Socrates. I do wish it.

Euthyphro. Well then, what is dear to the gods is holy, and what is not dear to them is unholy.

Socrates. Excellent, Euthyphro; now you have answered as I asked you to answer. However, whether it is true, I am not yet sure; but you will, of course, show that what you say is true.

Euthyphro. Certainly.

Socrates. Come then, let us examine our words. The thing and the person that are dear to the gods are holy, and the thing and the person that are hateful to the gods are unholy; and the two are not the same, but the holy and the unholy are the exact opposites of each other. Is not this what we have said?

Euthyphro. Yes, just this.

Socrates. And it seems to be correct?

Euthyphro. I think so, Socrates.

Socrates. Well then, have we said this also, that the gods, Euthyphro, quarrel and disagree with each other, and that there is enmity between them?

Euthyphro. Yes, we have said that.

Socrates. But what things is the disagreement about, which causes enmity and anger? Let us look at it in this way. If you and I were to disagree about number, for instance, which of two numbers were the greater, would the disagreement about these matters make us enemies and make us angry with each other, or should we not quickly settle it by resorting to arithmetic?

Euthyphro. Of course we should.

Socrates. Then, too, if we were to disagree about the relative size of things, we should quickly put an end to the disagreement by measuring?

Euthyphro. Yes.

Socrates. And we should, I suppose, come to terms about relative weights by weighing?

Euthyphro. Of course.

Socrates. But about what would a disagreement be, which we could not settle and which would cause us to be enemies and be angry with each other? Perhaps you cannot give an answer offhand; but let me suggest it. Is it not about right and wrong, and noble and disgraceful, and good and bad? Are not these the questions about which you and I and other people become enemies, when we do become enemies, because we differ about them and cannot reach any satisfactory agreement?

Euthyphro. Yes, Socrates, these are the questions about which we should become enemies.

Socrates. And how about the gods, Euthyphro? If they disagree, would they not disagree about these questions?

Euthyphro. Necessarily.

Socrates. Then, my noble Euthyphro, according to what you say, some of the gods too think some things are right or wrong and noble or disgraceful, and good or bad, and others disagree; for they would not quarrel with each other if they did not disagree about these matters. Is that the case?

Euthyphro. You are right.

Socrates. Then the gods in each group love the things which they consider good and right and hate the opposites of these things?

Euthyphro. Certainly.

Socrates. But you say that the same things are considered right by some of them and wrong by others; and it is because they disagree about these things that they quarrel and wage war with each other. Is not this what you said?

Euthyphro. It is.

Socrates. Then, as it seems, the same things are hated and loved by the gods, and the same things would be dear and hateful to the gods.

Euthyphro. So it seems.

Socrates. And then the same things would be both holy and unholy, Euthyphro, according to this statement.

Euthyphro. I suppose so.

Socrates. Then you did not answer my question, my friend. For I did not ask you what is at once holy and unholy; but, judging from your reply, what is dear to the gods is also hateful to the gods. And so, Euthyphro, it would not be surprising if, in punishing your father as you are doing, you were performing an act that is pleasing to Zeus, but hateful to Cronus and Uranus, and pleasing to Hephaestus, but hateful to Hera, and so forth in respect to the other gods, if any disagree with any other about it.

Euthyphro. But I think, Socrates, that none of the gods disagrees with any other about this, or holds that he who kills anyone wrongfully ought not to pay the penalty.

Socrates. Well, Euthyphro, to return to men, did you ever hear anybody arguing that he who had killed anyone wrongfully, or had done anything else whatever wrongfully, ought not to pay the penalty?

Euthyphro. Why, they are always arguing these points, especially in the law courts. For they do very many wrong things; and then there is nothing they will not do or say, in defending themselves, to avoid the penalty.

Socrates. Yes, but do they acknowledge, Euthyphro, that they have done wrong and, although they acknowledge it, nevertheless say that they ought not to pay the penalty?

Euthyphro. Oh, no, they don't do that.

Socrates. Then there is something they do not do and say. For they do not, I fancy, dare to say and argue that, if they have really done wrong, they ought not to pay the penalty; but, I think, they say they have not done wrong; do they not?

Euthyphro. You are right.

Socrates. Then they do not argue this point, that the wrongdoer must not pay the penalty; but perhaps they argue about this, who is a wrongdoer, and what he did, and when.

Euthyphro. That is true.

Socrates. Then is not the same thing true of the gods, if they quarrel about right and wrong, as you say, and some say others have done wrong, and some say they have not? For surely, my friend, no one, either of gods or men, has the face to say that he who does wrong ought not to pay the penalty.

Euthyphro. Yes, you are right about this, Socrates, in the main.

Socrates. But I think, Euthyphro, those who dispute, both men and gods, if the gods do dispute, dispute about each separate act. When they differ with one another about any act, some say it was right and others that it was wrong. Is it not so?

Euthyphro. Certainly.

Socrates. Come now, my dear Euthyphro, inform me, that I may be made wiser, what proof you have that all the gods think that the man lost his life wrongfully, who, when he was a servant, committed a murder, was bound by the master of the man he killed, and died as a result of his bonds before the master who had bound him found out from the advisers what he ought to do with him and that it is right on account of such a man for a son to proceed against his father and accuse him of murder. Come, try to show me clearly about this, that the gods surely believe that this conduct is right; and if you show it to my satisfaction, I will glorify your wisdom as long as I live.

Euthyphro. But perhaps this is no small task, Socrates; though I could show you quite clearly.

Socrates. I understand; it is because you think I am slower to understand than the judges; since it is plain that you will show them that such acts are wrong and that all the gods hate them.

Euthyphro. Quite clearly, Socrates; that is, if they listen to me.

Socrates. They will listen, if they find that you are a good speaker. But this occurred to me while you were talking, and I said to myself: "If Euthyphro should prove to me no matter how clearly that all the gods think such a death is wrongful," what have I learned from Euthyphro about the question, What is holiness and what is unholiness? For this act would, as it seems, be hateful to the gods; but we saw just now that holiness and its opposite are not defined in this way; for we saw that what is hateful to the gods is also dear to them; and so I let you off any discussion of this point, Euthyphro. If you like, all the gods may think it wrong and may hate it. But shall we now emend our definition and say that whatever all the gods hate is unholy and whatever they all love is holy, and what some love and others hate is neither or both? Do you wish this now to be our definition of holiness and unholiness?

Euthyphro. What is to hinder, Socrates?

Socrates. Nothing, so far as I am concerned, Euthyphro, but consider your own position, whether by adopting this definition you will most easily teach me what you promised.

Euthyphro. Well, I should say that what all the gods love is holy and, on the other hand, what they all hate is unholy.

Socrates. Then shall we examine this again, Euthyphro, to see if it is correct, or shall we let it go and accept our own statement, and those of others, agreeing that it is so, if anyone merely says that it is? Or ought we to inquire into the correctness of the statement?

Euthyphro. We ought to inquire. However, I think this is now correct.

Socrates. We shall soon know more about this, my friend. Just consider this question:—Is that which is holy loved by the gods because it is holy, or is it holy because it is loved by the gods?

Euthyphro. I don't know what you mean, Socrates.

Socrates. Then I will try to speak more clearly. We speak of being carried and of carrying, of being led and of leading, of being seen and seeing; and you understand—do you not?—that in all such expressions the two parts differ one from the other in meaning, and how they differ.

Euthyphro. I think I understand.

Socrates. Then, too, we conceive of a thing being loved and of a thing loving, and the two are different?

Euthyphro. Of course.

Socrates. Now tell me, is a thing which is carried a carried thing because one carries it, or for some other reason?

Euthyphro. No, for that reason.

Socrates. And a thing which is led because one leads it, and a thing which is seen is so because one sees it?

Euthyphro. Certainly.

Socrates. Then one does not see it because it is a seen thing, but, on the contrary, it is a seen thing because one sees it; and one does not lead it because it is a led thing, but it is a led thing because one leads it; and one does not carry it because it is a carried thing, but it is a carried thing because one carries it. Is it clear, Euthyphro, what I am trying to say? I am trying to say this, that if anything becomes or undergoes, it does not become because it is in a state of becoming, but it is in a state of becoming because it becomes, and it does not undergo because it is a thing which undergoes, but because it undergoes it is a thing which undergoes; or do you not agree to this?

Euthyphro. I agree.

Socrates. Is not that which is beloved a thing which is either becoming or undergoing something?

Euthyphro. Certainly.

Socrates. And is this case like the former ones: those who love it do not love it because it is a beloved thing, but it is a beloved thing because they love it?

Euthyphro. Obviously.

Socrates. Now what do you say about that which is holy, Euthyphro? It is loved by all the gods, is it not, according to what you said?

Euthyphro. Yes.

Socrates. For this reason, because it is holy, or for some other reason?

Euthyphro. No, for this reason.

Socrates. It is loved because it is holy, not holy because it is loved?

Euthyphro. I think so.

Socrates. But that which is dear to the gods is dear to them and beloved by them because they love it.

Euthyphro. Of course.

Socrates. Then that which is dear to the gods and that which is holy are not identical, but differ one from the other.

Euthyphro. How so, Socrates?

Socrates. Because we are agreed that the holy is loved because it is holy and that it is not holy because it is loved; are we not?

Euthyphro. Yes.

Socrates. But we are agreed that what is dear to the gods is dear to them because they love it, that is, by reason of this love, not that they love it because it is dear.

Euthyphro. Very true.

Socrates. But if that which is dear to the gods and that which is holy were identical, my dear Euthyphro, then if the holy were loved because it is holy, that which is dear to the gods would be loved because it is dear, and if that which is dear to the gods is dear because it is loved, then that which is holy would be holy because it is loved; but now you see that the opposite is the case, showing that the two are entirely different from each other. For the one becomes lovable from the fact that it is loved, whereas the other is loved because it is in itself lovable. And, Euthyphro, it seems that when you were asked what holiness is you were unwilling to make plain its essence, but you mentioned something that has happened to this holiness, namely, that it is loved by the gods. But you did not tell as yet what it really is. So, if you please, do not hide it from me, but begin over again and tell me what holiness is, no matter whether it is loved by the gods or anything else happens to it; for we shall not quarrel about that. But tell me frankly, What is holiness, and what is unholiness?

Euthyphro. But, Socrates, I do not know how to say what I mean. For whatever statement we advance, somehow or other it moves about and won't stay where we put it.

Socrates. Your statements, Euthyphro, are like works of my ancestor Daedalus, and if I were the one who made or advanced them you might laugh at me and say that on account of my relationship to him my works in words run away and won't stay where they are put. But now–well, the statements are yours; so some other jest is demanded; for they won't stay fixed, as you yourself see.

Euthyphro. I think the jest does very well as it is; for I am not the one who makes these statements move about and not stay in the same place, but you are the Daedalus; for they would have stayed, so far as I am concerned.

Socrates. Apparently then, my friend, I am a more clever artist than Daedalus, inasmuch as he made only his own works move, whereas I, as it seems, give motion to the works of others as well as to my own. And the most exquisite thing about my art is that I am clever against my will; for I would rather have my words stay fixed and stable than possess the wisdom of Daedalus and the wealth of Tantalus besides. But enough of this. Since you seem to be indolent, I will aid you myself, so that you may instruct me about holiness. And do not give it up beforehand. Just see whether you do not think that everything that is holy is right.

Euthyphro. I do.

Socrates. But is everything that is right also holy? Or is all which is holy right, and not all which is right holy, but part of it holy and part something else?

Euthyphro. I can't follow you, Socrates.

Socrates. And yet you are as much younger than I as you are wiser; but, as I said, you are indolent on account of your wealth of wisdom. But exert yourself, my friend; for it is not hard to understand what I mean. What I mean is the opposite of what the poet said, who wrote: "Zeus the creator, him who made all things, thou wilt not name; for where fear is, there also is reverence." Now I disagree with the poet. Shall I tell you how?

Euthyphro. By all means.

Socrates. It does not seem to me true that where fear is, there also is reverence; for many who fear diseases and poverty and other such things seem to me to fear, but not to reverence at all these things which they fear. Don't you think so, too?

Euthyphro. Certainly.

Socrates. But I think that where reverence is, there also is fear; for does not everyone who has a feeling of reverence and shame about any act also dread and fear the reputation for wickedness?

Euthyphro. Yes, he does fear.

Socrates. Then it is not correct to say "where fear is, there also is reverence." On the contrary, where reverence is, there also is fear; but reverence is not everywhere where fear is, since, as I think, fear is more comprehensive than reverence; for reverence is a part of fear, just as the odd is a part of number, so that it is not true that where number is, there also is the odd, but that where the odd is, there also is number. Perhaps you follow me now?

Euthyphro. Perfectly.

Socrates. It was something of this sort that I meant before, when I asked whether where the right is, there also is holiness, or where holiness is, there also is the right; but holiness is not everywhere where the right is, for holiness is a part of the right. Do we agree to this, or do you dissent?

Euthyphro. No, I agree; for I think the statement is correct.

Socrates. Now observe the next point. If holiness is a part of the right, we must, apparently, find out what part of the right holiness is. Now if you asked me about one of the things I just mentioned, as, for example, what part of number even was, and what kind of a number it was I should say, "that which is not indivisible by two, but divisible by two"; or don't you agree?

Euthyphro. I agree.

Socrates. Now try in your turn to teach me what part of the right holiness is, that I may tell Meletus not to wrong me any more or bring suits against me for impiety, since I have now been duly instructed by you about what is, and what is not, pious and holy.

Euthyphro. This then is my opinion, Socrates, that the part of the right which has to do with attention to the gods constitutes piety and holiness, and that the remaining part of the right is that which has to do with the service of men.

Socrates. I think you are correct Euthyphro; but there is one little point about which I still want information, for I do not yet understand what you mean by "attention." I don't suppose you mean the same kind of attention to the gods which is paid to other things. We say, for example, that not everyone knows how to attend to horses, but only he who is skilled in horsemanship, do we not?

Euthyphro. Certainly.

Socrates. Then horsemanship is the art of attending to horses?

Euthyphro. Yes.

Socrates. And not everyone knows how to attend to dogs, but only the huntsman?

Euthyphro. That is so.

Socrates. Then the huntsman's art is the art of attending to dogs?

Euthyphro. Yes.

Socrates. And the oxherd's art is that of attending to oxen?

Euthyphro. Certainly.

Socrates. And holiness and piety is the art of attending to the gods? Is that what you mean, Euthyphro?

Euthyphro. Yes.

Socrates. Now does attention always aim to accomplish the same end? I mean something like this: It aims at some good or benefit to the one to whom it is given, as you see that horses, when attended to by the horseman's art are benefited and made better; or don't you think so?

Euthyphro. Yes, I do.

Socrates. And dogs are benefited by the huntsman's art and oxen by the oxherd's and everything else in the same way? Or do you think care and attention are ever meant for the injury of that which is cared for?

Euthyphro. No, by Zeus, I do not.

Socrates. But for its benefit?

Euthyphro. Of course.

Socrates. Then holiness, since it is the art of attending to the gods, is a benefit to the gods, and makes them better? And you would agree that when you do a holy or pious act you are making one of the gods better?

Euthyphro. No, by Zeus, not I.

Socrates. Nor do I, Euthyphro, think that is what you meant. Far from it. But I asked what you meant by "attention to the gods" just because I did not think you meant anything like that.

Euthyphro. You are right, Socrates; that is not what I mean.

Socrates. Well, what kind of attention to the gods is holiness?

Euthyphro. The kind, Socrates, that servants pay to their masters.

Socrates. I understand. It is, you mean, a kind of service to the gods?

Euthyphro. Exactly.

Socrates. Now can you tell me what result the art that serves the physician serves to produce? Is it not health?

Euthyphro. Yes.

Socrates. Well then; what is it which the art that serves shipbuilders serves to produce?

Euthyphro. Evidently, Socrates, a ship.

Socrates. And that which serves housebuilders serves to build a house?

Euthyphro. Yes.

Socrates. Then tell me, my friend; what would the art which serves the gods serve to accomplish? For it is evident that you know, since you say you know more than any other man about matters which have to do with the gods.

Euthyphro. And what I say is true, Socrates.

Socrates. Then, in the name of Zeus, tell me, what is that glorious result which the gods accomplish by using us as servants?

Euthyphro. They accomplish many fine results, Socrates.

Socrates. Yes, and so do generals, my friend; but nevertheless, you could easily tell the chief of them, namely, that they bring about victory in war. Is that not the case?

Euthyphro. Of course.

Socrates. And farmers also, I think, accomplish many fine results; but still the chief result of their work is food from the land?

Euthyphro. Certainly.

Socrates. But how about the many fine results the gods accomplish? What is the chief result of their work?

Euthyphro. I told you a while ago, Socrates, that it is a long task to learn accurately all about these things. However, I say simply that when one knows how to say and do what is gratifying to the gods, in praying and sacrificing, that is holiness, and such things bring salvation to individual families and to states; and the opposite of what is gratifying to the gods is impious, and that overturns and destroys everything.

Socrates. You might, if you wished, Euthyphro, have answered much more briefly the chief part of my question. But it is plain that you do not care to instruct me. For now, when you were close upon it you turned aside; and if you had answered it, I should already have obtained from you all the instruction I need about holiness. But, as things are, the questioner must follow the one questioned wherever he leads. What do you say the holy, or holiness, is? Do you not say that it is a kind of science of sacrificing and praying?

Euthyphro. Yes.

Socrates. And sacrificing is making gifts to the gods and praying is asking from them?

Euthyphro. Exactly, Socrates.

Socrates. Then holiness, according to this definition, would be a science of giving and asking.

Euthyphro. You understand perfectly what I said, Socrates.

Socrates. Yes, my friend, for I am eager for your wisdom, and give my mind to it, so that nothing you say shall fall to the ground. But tell me, what is this service of the gods? Do you say that it consists in asking from them and giving to them?

Euthyphro. Yes.

Socrates. Would not the right way of asking be to ask of them what we need from them?

Euthyphro. What else?

Socrates. And the right way of giving, to present them with what they need from us? For it would not be scientific giving to give anyone what he does not need.

Euthyphro. You are right, Socrates.

Socrates. Then holiness would be an art of barter between gods and men?

Euthyphro. Yes, of barter, if you like to call it so.

Socrates. I don't like to call it so, if it is not true. But tell me, what advantage accrues to the gods from the gifts they get from us? For everybody knows what they give, since we have nothing good which they do not give. But what advantage do they derive from what they get from us? Or have we so much the better of them in our bartering that we get all good things from them and they nothing from us?

Euthyphro. Why you don't suppose, Socrates, that the gods gain any advantage from what they get from us, do you?

Socrates. Well then, what would those gifts of ours to the gods be?

Euthyphro. What else than honour and praise, and, as I said before, gratitude?

Socrates. Then, Euthyphro, holiness is grateful to the gods, but not advantageous or precious to the gods?

Euthyphro. I think it is precious, above all things.

Socrates. Then again, it seems, holiness is that which is precious to the gods.

Euthyphro. Certainly.

Socrates. Then will you be surprised, since you say this, if your words do not remain fixed but walk about, and will you accuse me of being the Daedalus who makes them walk, when you are yourself much more skillful than Daedalus and make them go round in a circle? Or do you not see that our definition has come round to the point from which it started? For you remember, I suppose, that a while ago we found that holiness and what is dear to the gods were not the same, but different from each other, or do you not remember?

Euthyphro. Yes, I remember.

Socrates. Then don't you see that now you say that what is precious to the gods is holy? And is not this what is dear to the gods?

Euthyphro. Certainly.

Socrates. Then either our agreement a while ago was wrong, or if that was right, we are wrong now.

Euthyphro. So it seems.

Socrates. Then we must begin again at the beginning and ask what holiness is. Since I shall not willingly give up until I learn. And do not scorn me, but by all means apply your mind now to the utmost and tell me the truth; for you know, if any one does, and like Proteus, you must be held until you speak. For if you had not clear knowledge of holiness and unholiness, you would surely not have undertaken to prosecute your aged father for murder for the sake of a servant. You would have been afraid to risk the anger of the gods, in case your conduct should be wrong, and would have been ashamed in the sight of men. But now I am sure you think you know what is holy and what is not. So tell me, most excellent

Euthyphro, and do not conceal your thought.

Euthyphro. Some other time, Socrates. Now I am in a hurry and it is time for me to go.

Socrates. Oh my friend, what are you doing? You go away and leave me cast down from the high hope I had that I should learn from you what is holy, and what is not, and should get rid of Meletus' indictment by showing him that I have been made wise by Euthyphro about divine matters and am no longer through ignorance acting carelessly and making innovations in respect to them, and that I shall live a better life henceforth.

COMMENT

In Plato's *Apology,* we do not encounter traditional philosophical questions directly, but several can be felt lurking in the background, especially those having to do with issues of legal processes and social values. Primarily, however, we encounter the person of Socrates himself and his own understanding of life and philosophy.

In this situation, Socrates could have chosen a different course of action. He could have begged and pleaded to be forgiven, promising never to disturb the minds of the Athenians again. Clearly, he felt that such a posture would contradict everything he had spent his recent years teaching and thus compromise his personal integrity. It is probably true that he would have been let off lightly had he taken this course.

The political situation at that time seemed to call for a scapegoat, someone to blame for the city's unfortunate state of affairs; and had Socrates played along, he would have been reprimanded but set free. However, not only did he refuse to follow this course of action, he seems to have decided to take this trial as an opportunity to continue his efforts to teach his fellow citizens a lesson.

Regardless of whether we read his tactics as taking the "high road" of moral integrity or as an effort to embarrass those who were pretending to lead Athenian society, the fact remains that Socrates was absolutely correct in his judgment that down through history his name would be honored while the names of those who were prosecuting him would be forgotten. After all, who ever heard the name "Meletus" before reading the *Apology?*

Although *Euthyphro* presents us with a conversation that took place prior to Socrates' trial as depicted in the *Apology,* the latter serves better as an introduction to his life and personality. In *Euthyphro,* we encounter a typical platonic dialogue between Socrates and one of his acquaintances about familiar yet difficult-to-define concepts. This dialogue is an atypical example in that it seems far more circular and unresolved than many of Plato's dialogues, but it probably represents Socrates and his teaching method rather well.

The paradox encased in this method, on the one hand, is focused on the tension between Socrates' obvious belief that it is possible in the end to get clear about the meaning of crucial concepts like "justice," "truth," and "piety" and, on the other hand, his own, in conjunction with his friends', inability to do so. This paradox lies at the very heart of what is known as the "Socratic Method" of teaching, which seeks to draw truth and knowledge out by means of an insistent exploration of the implications and presuppositions inherent in key ideas and beliefs.

It may prove helpful when reading and discussing these dialogues to pay closer attention to the process involved than to the proposed resultant product—or lack thereof. It should be clear that very often we all employ concepts and terms as if their meanings were perfectly understood when, in fact, they are not. Although we may never be able to achieve "absolute" precision about such notions, and what *that* means is itself worth discussing, we may be able to achieve "significant" precision. And along the way, we may learn a good deal about ourselves and related matters.

PART I

THE WAYS OF UNDERSTANDING

One of the main divisions of philosophy is epistemology, the theory of knowledge. Epistemology asks such fundamental questions as: How much do we know? How do we know? How can we distinguish between appearance and reality? What is the nature of truth and how can we separate it from falsehood? In addition, it asks questions concerning the nature of philosophy: What is its scope and function? Is its method the same as that of science or is it distinctive in method? We shall be dealing with questions such as these in Part I.

After the presentation of "A Case in Point," the plan of our discussion will be as follows: First, we shall examine rationalism, with its emphasis on pure reason, using the philosophy of Plato and Descartes as our examples. Second, we shall take up David Hume's empiricism, with its stress on sensory experience, together with Immanuel Kant's critique of it. Third, we shall consider the commonsense philosophy of Thomas Reid, who was critical of both Hume and Kant. Next, we shall ponder the contribution of direct insight, both the "intuitionism" of Henri Bergson and Bertrand Russell's "knowledge by acquaintance." Then we shall turn to the ideas of the great American philosophers William James and John Dewey as advocates of pragmatism, a movement closely related to the philosophy of Charles Peirce. Next, we shall examine the sharply contrasting movement of "existentialism" as represented by Albert Camus and his twentieth-century counterpart, Gabriel Marcel. Finally, in the concluding chapter of Part I, we shall encounter the challenge raised by Sandra Harding, who questions the very idea of objective knowledge independent of its sociohistorical context.

A CASE IN POINT:

CAN MACHINES THINK?

In February 1996, Garry Kasparov, the world's chess champion, played a six-game match against Deep Blue, the high-powered computer designed by IBM. Deep Blue won the first game, but Kasparov won the second and fifth games, with games three and four ending in a draw. The final game was also won by Kasparov, earning him a decisive victory over the human-made machine. Beneath all the media hoopla about whether machines will ever be superior to humans, and whether Kasparov had successfully defended humanity's "honor," there lay very serious and difficult questions about the nature of knowledge and thought.

These questions were not put to rest by the results of a second match between Kasparov and Deep Blue, which took place several years later. This match was clearly won by the IBM computer. And so now the debate concerning who is "superior" heats up, while the really interesting questions about the nature of thought and knowledge generally go unaddressed. It is the purpose of this section of our text to explore these questions by examining the writings of several philosophers who devoted a good deal of time and effort in answering them.

But first, it may prove helpful to focus on the issues involved by reviewing certain aspects of these famous chess matches and some of the responses that they generated. Deep Blue represents the culmination of some thirty years and millions of dollars of investment on the part of IBM to work toward documenting the claim that machines can, in fact, be designed to perform basic and high-level cognitive functions as well as, if not better than, human beings.

The "skills" that Deep Blue brought to these chess games revolve around its ability to scan upwards of 200 million potential chess moves per second! In short, it operates at a rate that far exceeds that of the human brain, even that of a chess wizard like Kasparov. This ability enables Deep Blue to have far, far more data at its disposal within the established time frame for making each move in a given game. Thus, its moves will always have a more thorough basis in probability than those made by a human player such as Kasparov.

For his part, Kasparov brings to the table a great many years of playing chess against the world's best chess masters, under extremely competitive pressure and circumstances. It should be pointed out that the category of "chess master" is not the same as simply being a very good player of the game. Those given this designation are truly in a class set apart from other chess players, no matter how good they may be. This special gift of genius for chess is often compared with that of mathematical and musical "savants" who accomplish amazing deeds in their fields, which neither they nor those who study these individuals can really explain. It is not often that a player comes along who is recognized as a gifted chess "genius," a person who may not be especially intelligent in other areas but who exhibits an extraordinary, uncanny ability at chess.

In previous decades, many computers have been invented that consistently outplay any outstanding chess champions. However, none of these machines has ever beaten a true chess "master." Until, of course, Deep Blue arrived on the scene.

On the one hand, there are those supporters of the claim that machines in general, and Deep Blue in particular, can be said to "think" or "reason" as well as, if not better than, we humans. Clearly, a great deal depends here on how we go about defining terms like "think," "reason," and "cognition." The chess machine does, in fact, draw conclusions, in the sense that after reviewing hundreds of millions of possibilities in relation to the criteria that it has been programmed with, it selects the move that is the most advantageous for producing a winning result.

On the other hand, however, there are those who insist that all such machines are simply capable of extremely rapid calculation rather than cognition. The range and speed of the "thinking machine," they say, do not enable it to make judgments and imaginatively project possibilities as chess masters must do on a routine basis. Indeed, it is clear that these players, as they consider a given move, make antecedent, yet unconscious, decisions about which possibilities are even worth exploring. It has been pointed out that Deep Blue frequently makes moves that any experienced player would avoid.

This distinction between high-speed calculation and cognitive judgment may be illustrated by the fact that in one of their games, Kasparov made a move early on that would have been recognized immediately by chess players as having no real consequence for the future of the game. Deep Blue, however, treated this move exactly like any other move, searching out all the possibilities without being able to make a judgment about its insignificance. The two processes followed by the machine and the human brain are essentially different.

Clearly, a case such as this is relevant to the sorts of questions with which the philosophers represented in this section of readings wrestle. Rationalists, who define knowledge and truth in terms of the principles of logic and coherence, will approach this case quite differently from empiricists, who define these notions strictly in terms of sensory experience. Moreover, pragmatists, who are primarily interested in the real-life consequences of differing claims to knowledge and truth, might well approach the whole question, including this case, from an altogether different angle, as would those who are classified as existentialists.

Those thinkers who seek to ground cognitive achievement in common sense or intuition may turn out to have something in common with several of the above approaches. In addition, the perspectivism expressed in the final chapter of this section raises issues that could cause one to rethink this whole area of philosophy. It would be fascinating to listen in on a discussion among these thinkers about whether or not machines can be said—or ever will be said—to think. We shall have to construct the contours of such a discussion for ourselves as we engage these thinkers through their writings.

Our focal issue, then, is what do we, or should we, mean by terms like "knowledge," "truth," and "thinking," especially in light of the controversy surrounding the chess matches between Garry Kasparov and Deep Blue. It may be that we will not be able to decide whether machines think until we determine what is meant by the key terms involved. Another way to focus this issue is to ask whether the question is a factual one, which may be settled by empirical investigation, or a conceptual one, which can be resolved only by logical analysis.

RATIONALISM

PLATO (428/7–348/7 B.C.)

As a member of one of the most distinguished families in Athens, Plato was in touch with political and social developments from his early childhood. He grew to manhood during the long, turbulent period of the Peloponnesian War, and his mind must have been deeply disturbed by war and revolution. Athens was finally defeated by Sparta when Plato was twenty-three, and he watched the ensuing oligarchical dictatorship, of which his uncle Charmides and his cousin Critias were leaders, with great hope. This hope soon turned to horror and anger, however, when his old friend Socrates was eventually tried and executed by the restored democratic faction. The shock of this event, occurring when he was just twenty-eight, was the decisive influence on his entire career. He concluded that good government depends on the rare union of power and wisdom, and he resolved to emulate, and as far as possible complete the work of, Socrates. Retiring from Athens to Megara, he began to write his famous dialogues, which lovingly portray his old master.

He is said to have spent the next ten years traveling in Greece, Italy, Egypt, and Asia Minor. For a time he lived at the court of Dionysius I, the tyrant of Syracuse, whose son-in-law, Dion, became Plato's friend and ardent admirer. At the age of forty, he returned to Athens to found the Academy, a school for philosophers, mathematicians, and statesmen. This school was the main center of his interest for the remainder of his long life. In addition to teaching, he continued to write dialogues, which became more technical as he grew older. This quiet, academic life was interrupted in 367 B.C., when he was close to sixty. Dion, his old friend, persuaded him to return to Syracuse as a tutor to Dionysius II, a young man of thirty, who had succeeded to the throne. The venture turned out badly. Dionysius and Dion eventually quarreled, and Plato went back to Athens. Not easily dismayed, he returned to Syracuse six years later in the hope of remedying the situation—and once again met with broken promises and barely escaped with his life. Then he settled down in the Academy to spend the last years of his life teaching and writing. He died at the age of eighty or eighty-one and, according to Cicero, was hard at work at the very end. Generally considered the greatest of the Greek philosophers, he has exercised an immense influence on the thought and literature of the world to this day. The following selection from Plato's dialogue *Meno* begins in the middle of the discussion.

MENO

Socrates. Then begin again and answer: What is virtue, according to you and your friend?

Meno. Well now, my dear Socrates, you are just like what I always heard before I met you: always puzzled yourself and puzzling everybody else. And now you seem to me to be a regular wizard, you dose me with drugs and bewitch me with charms and spells, and drown me in puzzledom. I'll tell you just what you are like, if you will forgive a little jest: your looks and the rest of you are exactly like a flatfish and you sting like this stingray—only go near and touch one of those fish and you go numb, and that is the sort of thing you seem to have done to me. Really and truly, my soul is numb and my mouth is numb, and what to answer you I do not know. Yet I have a thousand times made long speeches about virtue, before many a large audience, and good speeches, too, as I was convinced; but now I have not a word to say at all as to what it is. I must say you are wise not to sail away or travel abroad; for if you did this as a foreigner in a foreign city, you would probably be run in for a wizard.

Socrates. You are a young rogue, Meno, and you almost took me in.

Meno. How, Socrates?

Socrates. I know why you made that comparison of me.

Meno. Why, do you think?

Socrates. That I might make another of you.[1] I know this—that all the famous beauties love being put into comparisons; it pays them, you see, for comparisons of the beautiful are beautiful, I think; but I will not do it with you in return. Well, if this stingray is numb itself as well as making others numb, I am like it; if not, I am not. For I am not clearheaded myself when I make others puzzled, but I am as puzzled as puzzled can be, and thus I make others puzzled too. So now, what virtue is I do not know; but you knew, perhaps, before you touched me, although now you resemble one who does not know. All the same, I wish to investigate, with your help, that we may both try to find out what it is.

Meno. And how will you try to find out something, Socrates, when you have no notion at all what it is? Will you lay out before us a thing you don't know, and then try to find it? Or, if at best you meet it by chance, how will you know this is that which you did not know?

Socrates. I understand what you wish to say, Meno. You look on this as a piece of chop-logic, don't you see, as if a man cannot try to find either what he knows or what he does not know. Of course he would never try to find what he knows, because he knows it, and in that case he needs no trying to find; or what he does not know, because he does not know what he will try to find.

Meno. Then you don't think that is a good argument, Socrates?

Socrates. Not I.

Meno. Can you tell me why?

From *The Great Dialogues of Plato*, by Plato, trans. W. H. D. Rouse, Translation copyright © 1956, renewed 1984 by J. C. G. Rouse. Used by permission of Dutton Signet, a division of Penguin Books USA Inc.

---

[1] A favorite game in society.

Socrates. Oh yes. I have heard wise men and women on the subject of things divine—

Meno. And what did they say?

Socrates. True things and fine things, to my thinking.

Meno. What things, and who were the speakers?

Socrates. The speakers were some priests and priestesses who have paid careful attention to the things of their ministry, so as to be able to give a reasoned explanation of them; also inspired poets have something to say, Pindar and many others. What they say I will tell you; pray consider, if they seem to you to be speaking truth. They say that the soul of man is immortal, and sometimes it comes to an end—which they call death—and sometimes it is born again, but it is never destroyed; therefore we must live our lives as much as we can in holiness: for from whomsoever

> Persephone shall accept payment for ancient wrong,
> She gives up again their souls to the upper sun in the ninth year;
> From these grow lordly kings, and men of power and might,
> And those who are chief in wisdom; these for time to come
> Are known among men for holy heroes.[2]

Then, since the soul is immortal and often born, having seen what is on earth and what is in the house of Hades, and everything, there is nothing it has not learnt; so there is no wonder it can remember about virtue and other things, because it knew about these before. For since all nature is akin, and the soul has learnt everything, there is nothing to hinder a man, remembering one thing only—which men call learning[3] from—himself finding out all else, if he is brave and does not weary in seeking; for seeking and learning is all remembrance. Then we must not be guided by this chop-logic argument; for this would make us idle, and it is pleasant for soft people to hear, but our way makes them active and enquiring. I have faith that this is true, and I wish with your help to try to find out what virtue is.

Meno. Yes, Socrates. But what do you mean by saying that we do not learn, but what we call learning is remembering? Can you teach me how this is?

Socrates. You are a young rogue, as I said a moment ago, Meno, and now you ask me if I can teach you, when I tell you there is no such thing as teaching, only remembering. I see you want to show me up at once as contradicting myself.

Meno. I swear that isn't true, my dear Socrates; I never thought of that, it was just habit. But if you know any way to show me how this can be as you say, show away!

Socrates. That is not easy, but still I want to do my best for your sake. Here, just call up one of your own men from all this crowd of servants, any one you like, and I'll prove my case in him.

Meno. All right. (To a boy) Come here.

Socrates. Is he Greek, can he speak our language?

Meno. Rather! Born in my house.

---

[2] From Pindar. Persephone was Pluto's consort in Hades.

[3] I.e., the one thing needed to remember is how to learn; also remembering is learning. Both statements are covered here.

Socrates. Now, kindly attend and see whether he seems to be learning from me, or remembering.

Meno. All right, I will attend.

Socrates. Now my boy, tell me: Do you know that a four-cornered space is like this? [*Diagram 1*][4]

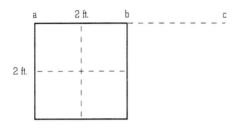

Diagram 1

Boy. I do.

Socrates. Is this a four-cornered space having all these lines[5] equal, all four?

Boy. Surely.

Socrates. And these across the middle, are they not equal too?

Boy. Yes.

Socrates. Such a space might be larger or smaller?

Boy. Oh yes.

Socrates. Then if this side is two feet long and this two, how many feet would the whole be? Or look at it this way: if it were two feet this way, and only one the other, would not the space[6] be once two feet?

---

[4] There are no diagrams in the Greek text; they and the lettering have been added to assist the reader.

[5] I.e., sides.

[6] I.e., area.

Boy. Yes.

Socrates. But as it is two feet this way also, isn't it twice two feet?

Boy. Yes, so it is.

Socrates. So the space is twice two feet?

Boy. Yes.

Socrates. Then how many are twice two feet? Count and tell me.

Boy. Four, Socrates.

Socrates. Well, could there be another such space, twice as big, but of the same shape, with all the lines equal like this one?

Boy. Yes.

Socrates. How many feet will there be in that, then?

Boy. Eight.

Socrates. Very well, now try to tell me how long will be each line of that one. The line of this one is two feet; how long would the line of the double one be?

Boy. The line would be double, Socrates, that is clear.

Socrates. (*aside to* Meno): You see, Meno, that I am not teaching this boy anything: I ask him everything; and now he thinks he knows what the line is from which the eight-[square] foot space is to be made. Don't you agree?

Meno. Yes, I agree.

Socrates. Does he know then?

Meno. Not at all.

Socrates. He *thinks* he knows, from the double size which is wanted?

Meno. Yes.

Socrates. Well, observe him while he remembers bit by bit, as he ought to remember.

Now, boy, answer me. You say the double space is made from the double line. You know what I mean; not long this way and short this way, it must be equal every way like this, but double this—eight [square] feet. Just look and see if you think it will be made from the double line.

Boy. Yes, I do.

Socrates. Then this line [*ac*]⁷ is double this [*ab*], if we add as much [*bc*] to it on this side.

Boy. Of course!

Socrates. Then if we put four like this [*ac*], you say we shall get the eight-foot space.

Boy. Yes.

Socrates. Then let us draw these four equal lines [*ac, cd, de, ea*].⁸ Is that the space which you say will be eight feet?

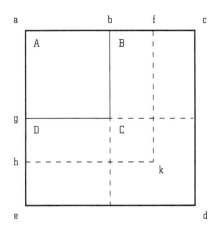

Diagram 2

---

⁷ In Diagram 1.

⁸ In Diagram 2.

Boy. Of course.

Socrates. Can't you see in it these four spaces here [*A, B, C, D*] each of them equal to the one we began with, the four-foot space?

Boy. Yes.

Socrates. Well, how big is the new one? Is it not four times the old one?

Boy. Surely it is!

Socrates. Is four times the old one, double?

Boy. Why no, upon my word!

Socrates. How big, then?

Boy. Four times as big!

Socrates. Then, my boy, from a double line we get a space four times as big, not double.

Boy. That's true.

Socrates. Four times four is sixteen, isn't it?

Boy. Yes.

Socrates. But what line will make an eight-foot space? This line makes one four times as big, sixteen, doesn't it?

Boy..That's what I say.

Socrates. And this four-foot space [*A*] comes from this line [*ab*], half the length of the long one?

Boy. Yes.

Socrates. Good. The eight-foot space will be double this [double A] and half this [*half A, B, C, D*].

Boy. Yes.

Socrates. Then its line must be longer than this [*ab*], and shorter than this [*ac*]. What do you think?

Boy. That's what I think.

Socrates. That's right, just answer what you think. Tell me also: Was not this line [*ab*] two feet, and this [*ac*] four?

Boy. Yes.

Socrates. Then the line of the eight-foot space must be longer than this line of two feet, and shorter than the line of four feet.

Boy. Yes, it must.

Socrates. Try to tell me, then, how long you say it must be.

Boy. Three feet.

Socrates. Three feet, very well: If we take half this bit [*half of bc*] and add it on, that makes three feet [*af*] doesn't it? For here we have two [*ab*], and here one [*bf*], the added bit; and, on the other side, in the same way, here are two [*ag*], here one [*gh*]; and that makes the space you say [*afkh*].

Boy. Yes.

Socrates. Then if the space is three feet this way and three feet that way, the whole space will be three times three feet?

Boy. It looks like it.

Socrates. How much is three times three feet?

Boy. Nine.

Socrates. How many feet was the double to be?

Boy. Eight.

Socrates. So we have not got the eight-foot space from the three-foot line after all.

Boy. No, we haven't.

Socrates. Then how long ought the line to be? Try to tell us exactly, or if you don't want to give it in numbers, show it if you can.

Boy. Indeed, Socrates, on my word I don't know.

Socrates. Now, Meno, do you notice how this boy is getting on in his remembering? At first he did not know what line made the eight-foot space, and he does not know yet; but he thought he knew then, and boldly answered as if he did know, and did not think there was any doubt; now he thinks there is a doubt, and as he does not know, so he does not think he does know.

Meno. Quite true.

Socrates. Then he is better off as regards the matter he did not know?

Meno. Yes, I think so too.

Socrates. So now we have put him into a difficulty, and like the stingray we have made him numb, have we done him any harm?

Meno. I don't think so.

Socrates. At least we have brought him a step onwards, as it seems, to find out how he stands. For now he would go on contentedly seeking, since he does not know; but then he could easily have thought he would be talking well about the double space, even before any number of people again and again, saying how it must have a line of double length.

Meno. It seems so.

Socrates. Then do you think he would have tried to find out or to learn what he thought he knew, not knowing, until he tumbled into a difficulty by thinking he did not know, and longed to know?

Meno. I do not think he would, Socrates.

Socrates. So he gained by being numbed?

Meno. I think so.

Socrates. Just notice now that after this difficulty he will find out by seeking along with me, while I do nothing but ask questions and give no instruction. Look out if you find me teaching and explaining to him, instead of asking for his opinions. Now, boy, answer me. Is not this our four-foot space [A]?[9] Do you understand?

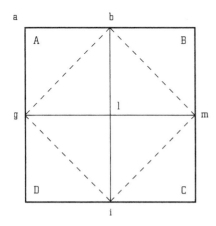

Diagram 3

Boy. I do.

Socrates. Shall we add another equal to it, thus [B]?

Boy. Yes.

Socrates. And a third equal to either of them, thus [C]?

Boy. Yes.

Socrates. Now shall we not also fill in this space in the corner [D]?

Boy. Certainly.

Socrates. Won't these be four equal spaces?

---

[9] In Diagram 3.

Boy. Yes.

Socrates. Very well. How many times the small one is this whole space?

Boy. Four times.

Socrates. But we wanted a double space; don't you remember?

Boy. Oh yes, I remember.

Socrates. Then here is a line running from corner to corner, cutting each of these spaces in two parts [*draws lines bm, mi, ig, gb*].

Boy. Yes.

Socrates. Are not these four lines equal, and don't they contain this space within them [*bmig*]?

Boy. Yes, that is right.

Socrates. Just consider: how big is the space?

Boy. I don't understand.

Socrates. Does not each of these lines cut each of the spaces, four spaces, in half? Is that right?

Boy. Yes.

Socrates. How many spaces as big as that [*blg*] are in this middle space?

Boy. Four.

Socrates. How many in this one [A]?

Boy. Two.

Socrates. How many times two is four?

Boy. Twice.

Socrates. Then how many [square] feet big is this middle space?

Boy. Eight [square] feet.

Socrates. Made from what line?

Boy. This one [*gb*].

Socrates. From the line drawn from corner to corner of the four-foot space?

Boy. Yes.

Socrates. The professors[10] call this a diameter [diagonal]: so if this is a diagonal, the double space would be made from the diagonal, as you say, Meno's boy!

Boy. Certainly, Socrates.

Socrates. Now then, Meno, what do you think? Was there one single opinion which the boy did not give as his own?

Meno. No, they were all his own opinions.

Socrates. Yet he did not know, as we agreed shortly before.

Meno. Quite true, indeed.

Socrates. Were these opinions in him, or not?

Meno. They were.

Socrates. Then in one who does not know, about things he does not know, there are true opinions about the things which he does not know?

Meno. So it appears.

Socrates. And now these opinions have been stirred up in him as in a dream; and if someone will keep asking him these same questions often and in various forms, you can be sure that in the end he will know about them as accurately as anybody.

Meno. It seems so.

Socrates. And no one having taught him, only asked questions, yet he will know, having got the knowledge out of himself?

Meno. Yes.

Socrates. But to get knowledge out of yourself is to remember, isn't it?

Meno. Certainly it is.

Socrates. Well then: This knowledge which he now has—he either got it sometime, or he had it always?

Meno. Yes.

Socrates. Then if he had it always, he was also always one who knew; but if he got it sometime, he could not have got it in this present life. Or has someone taught him geometry? For he will do just these same things in all matters of geometry, and so with all other sciences. Then is there anyone who has taught him everything? You are sure to know that, I suppose, especially since he was born and brought up in your house.

Meno. Well, I indeed know that no one has ever taught him.

Socrates. Has he all these opinions, or not?

Meno. He has, Socrates, it must be so.

Socrates. Then if he did not get them in this life, is it not clear now that he had them and had learnt at some other time?

Meno. So it seems.

---

[10] Sophists, experts in some subject who gave lessons for a fee.

RENÉ DESCARTES (1596–1650)

René Descartes' father was councillor of the Parliament of Brittany and owner of a fair amount of landed property. His mother, apparently consumptive, died during his infancy and left him with enfeebled health. Anxious to surround the delicate boy with every care, his father entrusted Descartes' education to the Jesuits. It was at the newly established Jesuit college at La Flèche that the young Descartes fell in love with geometry.

Leaving school at seventeen, Descartes spent the next four years in Paris studying law. Thereafter for several years, he lived as a traveler and a soldier, serving as a volunteer in three European armies, in the Netherlands, Bavaria, and Hungary. During this period, when he had a good deal of time to reflect, he came to doubt the value of everything he had learned with the single exception of mathematics.

On November 10, 1619, he had the remarkable experience to which he refers at the beginning of Part II of the *Discourse on Method*. He spent this cold November day in a stove-heated room, meditating about the mathematical and scientific ideas that had been tumbling through his mind for several days. Nervously exhausted, he finally fell asleep and had three strange dreams, which he interpreted as pointing to a life of philosophical reflection. As a result of these dreams, which he thought were inspired by God, and the intense intellectual activity that preceded them, he saw himself at the parting of the ways, and he resolved thenceforth to follow the path of philosophy and scientific research.

Although Descartes did not give us a detailed account of "the foundations of a wonderful science" that he discovered at this time, we know he had the conviction that the method of mathematics could be generalized to apply to all the sciences and that thereby certainty could be gained. Moreover, he conceived the method of applying algebraic symbolism to geometry and of using coordinates to describe geometrical figures; in other words, he founded analytical geometry. Finally, he was convinced that science and philosophy should form one whole, subject to a single method.

He vowed that no ties of marriage or society should deter him from a life of intellectual research devoted to the development of these insights. Although he continued to travel and to study "the great book of the world" for the next nine years (1619–1628), he still found time to work on various problems of mathematics and science. Growing tired of his wanderings at last, in 1628 he sold his inherited estates in France and settled in a quiet country house in Holland. With abundant leisure and a few servants to take care of his material needs, he formed the habit of staying in bed until about noon, reading, writing, and meditating. He soon acquired a wide reputation and was visited by, or corresponded with, many notable scientists and philosophers of the age. During this sojourn in Holland, he had what was apparently his only love affair. The daughter who was the product of this alliance died at the age of five, much to her father's sorrow.

In the autumn of 1649, Descartes accepted an invitation from Queen Christina of Sweden to spend a winter at her court. An imperious though learned monarch, Christina thought that she had the right to command his services at any hour she chose. Daily at five in the morning throughout the bitterly cold winter, Descartes was ushered into the presence of the queen, where he discoursed to her about philosophy while he stood shivering on the marble floor. Unused to the biting climate and the rigors of such early rising, he caught pneumonia and died in March 1650, a few days before his fifty-fifth birthday.

RULES FOR THE DIRECTION
OF THE MIND

Rule I

The end of study should be to direct the mind towards the enunciation of sound and correct judgments on all matters that come before it.

Whenever men notice some similarity between two things, they are wont to ascribe to each, even in those respects in which the two differ, what they have found to be true of the other. Thus they erroneously compare the sciences, which entirely consist in the cognitive exercise of the mind, with the arts, which depend upon an exercise and disposition of the body. They see that not all the arts can be acquired by the same man, but that he who restricts himself to one, most readily becomes the best executant, since it is not so easy for the same hand to adapt itself both to agricultural operations and to harp-playing, or to the performance of several such tasks as to one alone. Hence they have held the same to be true of the sci-

ences also, and distinguishing them from one another according to their subject matter, they have imagined that they ought to be studied separately, each in isolation from all the rest. But this is certainly wrong. For since the sciences taken all together are identical with human wisdom, which always remains one and the same, however applied to different subjects, and suffers no more differentiation proceeding from them than the light of the sun experiences from the variety of the things which it illumines, there is no need for minds to be confined at all within limits; for neither does the knowing of one truth have an effect like that of the acquisition of one art and prevent us from finding out another, it rather aids us to do so. . . . Hence we must believe that all the sciences are so interconnected, that it is much easier to study them all together than to isolate one from all the others. . . .

Rule II

Only those objects should engage our attention, to the sure and indubitable knowledge of which our mental powers seem to be adequate.

The following excerpts from the *Rules* are from *The Philosophical Works of Descartes*, translated by Elizabeth S. Haldane and G. R. T. Ross. Copy-right 1911 by the Cambridge University Press. Reprinted by permission.

Science in its entirety is true and evident cognition. He is no more learned who has doubts on many matters than the man who has never thought of them; nay he appears to be less learned if he has formed wrong opinions on any particulars. Hence it were better not to study at all than to occupy one's self with objects of such difficulty, that, owing to our inability to distinguish true from false, we are forced to regard the doubtful as certain; for in those matters any hope of augmenting our knowledge is exceeded by the risk of diminishing it. Thus in accordance with the above maxim we reject all such merely probable knowledge and make it a rule to trust only what is completely known and incapable of being doubted. . . .

But if we adhere closely to this rule we shall find left but few objects of legitimate study. For there is scarce any question occurring in the sciences about which talented men have not disagreed. But whenever two men come to opposite decisions about the same matter one of them at least must certainly be in the wrong, and apparently there is not even one of them in the right; for if the reasoning of the second was sound and clear he would be able so to lay it before the other as finally to succeed in convincing his understanding also. Hence apparently we cannot attain to a perfect knowledge in any such case of probable opinion, for it would be rashness to hope for more than others have attained to. Consequently if we reckon correctly, of the sciences already discovered, Arithmetic and Geometry alone are left, to which the observance of this rule reduces us. . . .

Now let us proceed to explain more carefully our reasons for saying that of all the sciences known as yet, Arithmetic and Geometry alone are free from any taint of falsity or uncertainty. We must note then that there are two ways by which we arrive at the knowledge of facts, viz., by experience and by deduction. We must further observe that while our inferences from experience are frequently fallacious, deduction, or the pure illation of one thing from another, though it may be passed over, if it is not seen through, cannot be erroneous when performed by an understanding that is in the least degree rational. . . . My reason for saying so is that none of the mistakes which men can make (men, I say, not beasts) are due to faulty inference; they are caused merely by the fact that we base inferences upon poorly comprehended experiences, or that propositions are posited which are hasty and groundless.

This furnishes us with an evident explanation of the great superiority in certitude of Arithmetic and Geometry to other sciences. The former alone deal with an object so pure and uncomplicated, that they need make no assumptions at all which experience renders uncertain, but wholly consist in the rational deduction of consequences. They are on that account much the easiest and clearest of all, and possess an object such as we require, for in them it is scarce humanly possible for anyone to err except by inadvertence. And yet we should not be surprised to find that plenty of people of their own accord prefer to apply their intelligence to other studies. The reason for this is that every person permits himself the liberty of making guesses in the matter of an obscure subject with more confidence than in one which is clear, and that it is much easier to have some vague notion about any subject, no matter what, than to arrive at the real truth about a single question however simple that may be.

But one conclusion now emerges out of these considerations, viz., not, indeed, that Arithmetic and Geometry are the sole sciences to be studied, but only that in our search for the direct road towards truth we should busy ourselves with no object about which we cannot attain a certitude equal to that of the demonstrations of Arithmetic and Geometry.

Rule III

In the subjects we propose to investigate, our inquiries should be directed, not to what others have thought, nor to what we ourselves conjecture, but to what we can clearly and perspicuously behold and with certainty deduce; for knowledge is not won in any other way.

To study the writings of the ancients is right, because it is a great boon for us to be able to make use of the labours of so many men; and we should do so, both in order to discover what they have correctly made out in previous ages, and also that we may inform ourselves as to what in the various sciences is still left for investigation. But yet there is a great danger lest in a too absorbed study of these works we should become infected with their errors, guard against them as we may. For it is the way of writers, whenever they have allowed themselves rashly and credulously to take up a position in any controverted matter, to try with the subtlest of arguments to compel us to go along with them. But when, on the contrary, they have happily come upon something certain and evident, in

displaying it they never fail to surround it with ambiguities, fearing, it would seem, lest the simplicity of their explanation should make us respect their discovery less, or because they grudge us an open vision of the truth.

Further, supposing now that all were wholly open and candid, and never thrust upon us doubtful opinions as true, but expounded every matter in good faith, yet since scarce anything has been asserted by any one man the contrary of which has not been alleged by another, we should be eternally uncertain which of the two to believe. It would be no use to total up the testimonies in favour of each, meaning to follow that opinion which was supported by the greater number of authors; for it is a question of difficulty that is in dispute, it is more likely that the truth would have been discovered by few than by many. But even though all these men agreed among themselves, what they teach us would not suffice for us. For we shall not, e.g., all turn out to be mathematicians though we know by heart all the proofs that others have elaborated, unless we have an intellectual talent that fits us to resolve difficulties of any kind. Neither, though we have mastered all the arguments of Plato and Aristotle, if yet we have not the capacity for passing a solid judgment on these matters, shall we become Philosophers; we should have acquired the knowledge not of a science, but of history.

I lay down the rule also, that we must wholly refrain from ever mixing up conjectures with our pronouncements on the truth of things. This warning is of no little importance. There is no stronger reason for our finding nothing in the current Philosophy which is so evident and certain as not to be capable of being controverted, than the fact that the learned, not content with the recognition of what is clear and certain, in the first instance hazard the assertion of obscure and ill-comprehended theories, at which they have arrived merely by probable conjecture. Then afterwards they gradually attach complete credence to them, and mingling them promiscuously with what is true and evident, they finish by being unable to deduce any conclusion which does not appear to depend upon some proposition of the doubtful sort, and hence is not uncertain.

But lest we in turn should slip into the same error, we shall here take note of all those mental operations by which we are able, wholly without fear of illusion, to arrive at the knowledge of things. Now I admit only two, viz., intuition and deduction.

By *intuition* I understand, not the fluctuating testimony of the senses, nor the misleading judgment that proceeds from the blundering constructions of imagination, but the conception which an unclouded and attentive mind gives us so readily and distinctly that we are wholly freed from doubt about that which we understand. Or, what comes to the same thing, *intuition* is the undoubting conception of an unclouded and attentive mind, and springs from the light of reason alone; it is more certain than deduction itself, in that it is simpler, though deduction, as we have noted above, cannot by us be erroneously conducted. Thus each individual can mentally have intuition of the fact that he exists, and that he thinks; that the triangle is bounded by three lines only, the sphere by a single superficies, and so on. Facts of such a kind are far more numerous than many people think, dis-

daining as they do . . . to direct their attention upon such simple matters. . . .

This evidence and certitude, however, which belongs to intuition, is required not only in the enunciation of propositions, but also in discursive reasoning of whatever sort. For example consider this consequence: 2 and 2 amount to the same as 3 and 1. Now we need to see intuitively not only that 2 and 2 make 4, and likewise 3 and 1 make 4, but further that the third of the above statements is a necessary conclusion from these two.

Hence now we are in a position to raise the question as to why we have, besides intuition, given this supplementary method of knowing, viz., knowing by *deduction*, by which we understand all necessary inference from other facts that are known with certainty. This, however, we could not avoid, because many things are known with certainty, though not by themselves evident, but only deduced from true and known principles by the continuous and uninterrupted action of a mind that has a clear vision of each step in the process. It is in a similar way that we know that the last link in a long chain is connected with the first, even though we do not take in by means of one and the same act of vision all the intermediate links on which that connection depends, but only remember that we have taken them successively under review and that each single one is united to its neighbour, from the first even to the last. Hence we distinguish this mental intuition from deduction by the fact that into the conception of the latter there enters a certain movement or succession, into that of the former there does not. Further deduction does not require an immediately presented evidence such as intuition possesses;

its certitude is rather conferred upon it in some way by memory. The upshot of the matter is that it is possible to say that those propositions indeed which are immediately deduced from first principles are known now by intuition, now by deduction, i.e., in a way that differs according to our point of view. But the first principles themselves are given by intuition alone, while, on the contrary, the remote conclusions are furnished only by deduction.

These two methods are the most certain routes to knowledge, and the mind should admit no others. All the rest should be rejected as suspect of error and dangerous. . . .

Rule IV

There is need of a method for finding out the truth.

So blind is the curiosity by which mortals are possessed, that they often conduct their minds along unexplored routes, having no reason to hope for success, but merely being willing to risk the experiment of finding whether the truth they seek lies there. As well might a man burning with an unintelligent desire to find treasure, continuously roam the streets, seeking to find something that a passerby might have chanced to drop. This is the way in which most Chemists, many Geometricians, and Philosophers not a few prosecute their studies. I do not deny that sometimes in these wanderings they are lucky enough to find something true. But I do not allow that this argues greater industry on their part, but only better luck. But, however that may be, it were far better never to think of investigating truth at all, than to do so without a method. For it is very certain that unregulated inquiries and confused reflections of this kind only confound the natural light and blind our mental powers. Those who so become accustomed to walk in darkness weaken their eyesight so much that afterwards they cannot bear the light of day. This is confirmed by experience; for how often do we not see that those who have never taken to letters, give a sounder and clearer decision about obvious matters than those who have spent all their time in the schools? Moreover by a method I mean certain and simple rules, such that, if a man observe them accurately, he shall never assume what is false as true, and will never spend his mental efforts to no purpose, but will always gradually increase his knowledge and so arrive at a true understanding of all that does not surpass his powers. . . .

Rule V

Method consists entirely in the order and disposition of the objects towards which our mental vision must be directed if we would find out any truth. We shall comply with it exactly if we reduce involved and obscure propositions step by step to those that are simpler, and then starting with the intui- tive apprehension of all those that are absolutely simple, attempt to ascend to the knowledge of all others by precisely similar steps.

In this alone lies the sum of all human endeavour, and he who would approach the investigation of truth must hold to this rule as closely as he who enters the labyrinth must follow the thread which guided Theseus. But many people either do not reflect on the precept at all, or ignore it altogether, or presume not to need it. Consequently they often investigate the most difficult questions with so little regard to order, that, to my mind, they act like a man who should attempt to leap with one bound from the base to the summit of a house, either making no account of the ladders provided for his ascent or not noticing them. It is thus that all Astrologers behave, who, though in ignorance of the nature of the heavens, and even without having made proper observations of the movements of the heavenly bodies, expect to be able to indicate their effects. This is also what many do who study Mechanics apart from Physics, and readily set about devising new instruments for producing motion. Along with them go also those Philosophers who, neglecting experience imagine that truth will spring from their brain like Pallas from the head of Zeus.

Now it is obvious that all such people violate the present rule. But since the order here required is often so obscure and intricate that not everyone can make it out, they can scarcely avoid error unless they diligently observe what is laid down in the following proposition.

Rule VI

In order to separate out what is quite simple from what is complex, and to arrange these matters methodically, we ought, in the case of every series in which we have deduced certain facts the one from the other, to notice which fact is simple, and to mark the interval, greater, less or equal, which separates all the others form this.

Although this proposition seems to teach nothing very new, it contains, nevertheless, the chief secret of method, and none in the whole of this treatise is of greater utility. For it tells us that all facts can be arranged in certain series, not indeed in the sense of being referred to some ontological genus such as the categories employed by Philosophers in their classification, but in so far as certain truths can be known from others; and thus, whenever a difficulty occurs we are able at once to perceive whether it will be profitable to examine certain others first, and which, and in what order.

Further, in order to do that correctly, we must note first that for the purpose of our procedure, which does not regard things as isolated realities, but compares them with one another in order to discover the dependence in knowledge of one upon the other, all things can be said to be either absolute or relative.

I call that absolute which contains within itself the pure and simple essence of which we are in quest. Thus the term will be applicable to whatever is considered as being independent, or a cause, or simple, universal, one, equal, like, straight, and so forth; and the absolute I call the simplest and the easiest of all, so that we can make use of it in the solution of questions.

But the relative is that which, while participating in the same nature, or at least sharing in it to some degree which enables us to relate it to the absolute and to deduce it from that by a chain of operations, involves in addition something else in its concept which I call relativity. Examples of this are found in whatever is said to be dependent, or an effect, composite, particular, many, unequal, unlike, oblique, etc. These relatives are the further removed from the absolute, in proportion as they contain more elements of relativity subordinate the one to the other. We state in this rule that these should all be distinguished and their correlative connection and natural order so observed, that we may be able by traversing all the intermediate steps to proceed from the most remote to that which is in the highest degree absolute. . . .

Finally we must note that our inquiry ought not to start with the investigation of difficult matters. Rather, before setting out to attack any definite problem, it behooves us first, without making any selection, to assemble those truths that are obvious as they present themselves to us, and afterwards, proceeding step by step, to inquire whether any others can be deduced from these, and again any others from these conclusions and so on, in order. This done, we should attentively think over the truths we have discovered and mark with diligence the reasons why we have been able to detect some more easily than others, and which these are. Thus, when we come to attack some definite problem we shall be able to judge what previous questions it were best to settle first. For example, if it comes into my thought that the number 6 is twice 3, I may then ask what is twice 6, viz., 12; again, perhaps I seek for the double of this, viz., 24, and again of this, viz., 48. Thus I may deduce that there is the same proportion between 3 and 6, as between 6 and 12, and likewise 12 and 24, and so on, and hence that the numbers 3, 6, 12, 24, 48, etc., are in continued proportion. But though these facts are all so clear as to seem almost childish, I am now able by attentive reflection to understand what is the form involved by all questions that can be propounded about the proportions or relations of things, and the order in which they should be investigated; and this discovery embraces the sum of the entire science of Pure Mathematics.

Rule VII

If we wish our science to be complete, those matters which promote the end we have in view must one and all be scrutinized by a movement of thought which is continuous and nowhere interrupted; they must also be included in an enumeration which is both adequate and methodical.

It is necessary to obey the injunctions of this rule if we hope to gain admission among the certain truths for those which, we have declared above, are not immediate deductions from primary and self-evident principles. For this deduction frequently involves such a long series of transitions from ground to consequent that when we come to the conclusion we have difficulty in recalling the whole of the route by which we have arrived at it. This is why I say that there must be a continuous movement of thought to make good this weakness of the memory. Thus, e.g., if I have first found out by separate mental operations what the relation is between the magnitudes A and B, then what between B and C, between C and D, and finally between D and E, that does not entail my seeing what the relation is between A and E, nor can the truths previously learnt give me a precise knowledge of it unless I recall them all. To remedy this I would run them over from time to time, keeping the imagination moving continuously in such a way that while it is intuitively perceiving each fact it simultaneously passes on to the next; and this I would do until I had learned to pass from the first to the last so quickly, that no stage in the process was left to the care of the memory, but I seemed to have the whole in intuition before me at the same time. This method will both relieve the memory, diminish the sluggishness of our thinking, and definitely enlarge our mental capacity.

But we must add that this movement should nowhere be interrupted. Often people who attempt to deduce a conclusion too quickly and from remote principles do not trace the whole chain of intermediate conclusions with sufficient accuracy to prevent them from passing over many steps without due consideration. But it is certain that wherever the smallest link is left out the chain is broken and the whole of the certainty of the conclusion falls to the ground. . . .

Rule VIII

If in the matters to be examined we come to a step in the series of which our understanding is not sufficiently well able to have an intuitive cognition, we must stop short there. We must make no attempt to examine what follows; thus we shall spare ourselves superfluous labour.

. . . If a man proposes to himself the problem of examining all the truths for the knowledge of which human reason suffices—and I think that this is a task which should be undertaken once at least in his life by every person who seriously endeavors to attain equilibrium of thought—he will, by the rules given above, certainly discover that nothing can be known prior to the understanding, since the knowledge of all things else depends upon this and not conversely. Then, when he has clearly grasped all those things which follow proximately on the knowledge of the naked understanding, he will enumerate among other things whatever instruments of thought we have other than the understanding; and these are only two, viz., imagination and sense. He will therefore devote all his energies to the distinguishing and examining of these three modes of cognition, and seeing that in the strict sense truth and falsity can be a matter of the understanding alone, though often it derives its origin from the other two faculties, he will attend carefully to every source of deception in order that he may be on his guard. He will also enumerate exactly all the ways leading to truth which lie open to us, in order that he may follow the right way. They are not so many that they cannot all be easily discovered and embraced in an adequate enumeration. And though this will seem marvellous and incredible to the inexpert, as soon as in each matter he has distinguished those cognitions which only fill and embellish the memory, from those which cause one to be deemed really more instructed, which it will be easy for him to do, he will feel assured that any absence of further knowledge is not due to lack of intelligence or of skill, and that nothing at all can be known by anyone else which he is not capable of knowing, provided only that he gives to it his utmost mental application.

COMMENT

Plato's Meno

Classical rationalism differs from its modern version in many respects, as a comparison of these readings from Plato and Descartes clearly reveals. Nonetheless, both versions argue that knowledge is the result of rational analysis alone and is achieved completely independently of sensory experience. In addition, both

Plato and Descartes take geometric reasoning as the paradigm of cognitive activity since it is strictly a function of intellectual processes and leaves no margin for error.

Plato's *Meno* begins, as most of his works do, with a good deal of verbal byplay, followed by the admission of both Socrates and his interlocutor that they do not know how to define the key concept in question, in this case "virtue." We pick up the conversation at the point where a fresh and more serious start is made. Meno expresses their problem in the form of a paradoxical dilemma: Knowledge of any truth would seem to be impossible since *either* one already knows it and thus cannot learn it, *or* one does not know it and thus would not recognize it when confronted with it.

After rehearsing a common belief of the day concerning the immortality of the soul, including the mind, Socrates suggests the possibility that all human knowledge is merely a remembering or recollecting of that which was known by the soul in its previous existence. If this is the case, all that is necessary to prove it is to draw some seemingly fresh knowledge out of an uneducated young person without relying in any way on sensory input. This Socrates proceeds to do with the help of Meno's slave boy. Simply by means of pure logic, aided by a diagram, he leads the slave, step by step, to a "discovery" of the truth of what has come to be called the "Pythagorean Theorem."

The results of such analysis, according to the rationalist approach to knowledge, clearly establish the conceptual rather than the perceptual basis of all truth. Thus, even the knowledge of such abstract notions as "virtue" can be obtained through the rational, albeit arduous, analysis of their implicit and essential meanings. By beginning with simple, undefined yet unquestionable concepts and axioms, and then moving by the laws of logic to conclusions entailed by them, anyone with sufficient intellectual ability will be able to arrive at knowledge.

The heart of the rationalist claim is that apart from the activity of the mind, which enables a person to grasp the connection or similarity between various experiential objects or qualities, our sensory encounters would remain mere "exposures," with no pattern or coherence. It is the mind, what Plato called "the eye of the soul," that enables one to see what things have in common and what follows from what and why. Other animals have sensory exposure to trees, sounds, and fears, for instance, but only humans *understand* the concept of a "tree," the meaning of sounds, and how to alleviate fears—or so claims the rationalist.

The critics of rationalism, however, question whether Socrates actually drew the knowledge of geometry out of the slave's mind. The use of the diagram is itself a *perceptual* device, and throughout their conversation, Socrates is said to be relying on the boy's sensory experience with other aspects of life. At best, this is another version of the famous "chicken or egg" controversy: How is it possible to prove or know anything until you already know something else? Every idea seems to be dependent on another idea; both mental activity and sensory experience would seem to be necessary for knowledge to exist.

Another, more modern criticism of the rationalist approach to knowledge focuses on the nature of mathematical reasoning. Many thinkers suggest that the reason Socrates is able to help the boy pull the rabbit out of the logical hat is that it was already in the hat, rather than in the boy's mind, at the outset. That is, the very concepts with which Socrates began, such as "four-cornered space," "equal," "larger or smaller," "twice two," and so on, are defined and used in such a way as to necessitate certain conclusions. In other words, many modern thinkers believe that mathematical "knowledge" is empty of any factual information about the world, that it is strictly a matter of setting up certain definitions and axioms and then squeezing them to see what is entailed by them, because the information was built into them at the beginning. Such knowledge can only be *a priori*, or independent of experience, because it is "analytic" in the sense that its meaning and truth are, strictly speaking, obtainable only by analyzing the original terms used at the outset. Such knowledge is absolutely certain, but the price for certainty is, according to these critics, emptiness.

Descartes' Method

The question of method became a matter of keen and widespread interest with the great flowering of science in the seventeenth and eighteenth centuries. The discoveries by such great scientists as Kepler, Galileo, Newton, Gilbert, and Harvey and the rapid development of mathematics and natural science forced people to reflect on the nature of scientific knowledge and the means to its attainment.

The principal cleavage among the philosophers was between the *rationalists* and the *empiricists*. The rationalists, among them Descartes, Spinoza, and Leibniz, relied chiefly on reason as the source of genuine knowledge, taking the methods of mathematics, especially geometry, as their model. The empiricists, among them Locke, Berkeley, and Hume, depended mainly on experience, regarding the methods of hypothesis, observation, and experiment as the principal foundations of knowledge. Actually, the differences between the two groups were not so sharp as they are often represented. Both groups recognized the necessity of a combination of experience and reason, but they veered toward opposite sides in their emphasis.

Of primary significance in considering Descartes' philosophy as an example of rationalism is his intense desire for certainty: "I always had an excessive desire to learn to distinguish the true from the false, in order to see clearly in my actions and to walk with confidence in the life."[1] He believed that the key to certainty, the way in which to dispel his innumerable doubts, lay in a sound and logical method of reasoning. The proper employment of reason, he believed, would make vast provinces accessible to human knowledge.

---

[1] *Discourse on Method*, in *The Philosophical Works of Descartes*, trans. Elizabeth S. Haldane and G. R. T. Ross (Cambridge: Cambridge University Press, 1931), I, p. 87.

Descartes asserted that all certain knowledge is based on two mental opera-tions: *intuition*—which he also called "the natural light of reason"—and *deduction*. His definitions of these terms are contained in his *Rules for the Direction of the Mind*:

> By *intuition* I understand, not the fluctuating testimony of the senses, nor the misleading judgment that proceeds from the blundering constructions of imagination, but the conception which an unclouded and attentive mind gives us so readily and distinctly that we are wholly freed from doubt about that which we understand. Or, what comes to the same thing, *intuition* is the undoubting conception of an unclouded and attentive mind, and springs from the light of reason alone. . . .
>
> By *deduction* ... we understand all necessary inference from other facts that are known with certainty. ... Many things are known with certainty, though not by themselves evident, but only deduced from true and known principles by the continuous and uninterrupted action of a mind that has a clear vision of each step in the process. It is in a similar way that we know that the last link in a long chain is connected with the first, even though we do not take in by means of one and the same act of vision all the intermediate links on which that connection depends, but only remember that we have taken them successively under review and that each single one is united to its neighbour, from the first even to the last.[2]

In formulating these definitions, Descartes was thinking specifically of the method of mathematics, particularly geometry. The certainty of rigorous mathe-matical reasoning, he believed, consists in starting with meanings and insights so clear and distinct that they cannot be doubted, and then accepting nothing as true unless it follows no less evidently from these foundations. An intuited truth is such that reason has only to understand its meaning fully to see that it *must* be true. Examples of intuitions are the insights that five is more than four, that a trian-gle is bounded by only three lines, and that things equal to the same thing are equal to each other. Given such manifest and self-evident premises, our conclu-sion will be certain provided that it is *necessarily* implied by what precedes and that nothing is admitted in the steps of reasoning that does not thus necessarily follow. Thus, in a chain of reasoning symbolized by letters, if p implies q, and q implies r, and r implies s, then s is certain provided that p is certain and that each subsequent step leading to s is also certain. Descartes believed that thinkers have succeeded in the past and will succeed in the future to the extent that they have rigorously employed, or will employ, intuition and deduction.

With this conception of reasoning in mind, he summed up his method in four rules, which are stated in Part II of the *Discourse*:

1. *The rule of certainty.* This rule is (1) to accept nothing as true that we do not unquestionably recognize to be such and (2) to carefully avoid all precipitation and prejudice so as to reach judgments so clear and distinct that they cannot be doubted. Only what we *know* to be true is to be admitted into the sphere of belief:

---

[2] *Rules for the Direction of the Mind,* in ibid., pp. 7–8.

Thus, Descartes aimed not at mere probability but at absolute certainty. This rule compelled him to reject all beliefs that are at all dubious.

He recognized two causes as chiefly responsible for error: precipitate judgment, due to insufficient care, and prejudiced judgment, due to habit or emotional bias. Many beliefs are tenaciously held not because they are seen with clearness and distinctness to be true but because, in our haste or bias, we feel a very strong inclination to believe them. "I term that clear," he declared, "which is present and apparent to an attentive mind. . . . But the distinct is that which is so precise and different from all other objects that it contains within itself nothing but what is clear."[3] A judgment is worthy of belief only if all the ideas in it and the judgment as a whole are thus clear and distinct.

2. *The rule of division.* We should analyze each of the difficulties involved in our problem into its smallest and simplest parts. If we then attack each of the subordinate parts separately, we shall find it easier to understand and deal with the simple than the complex. When we have thus discovered elements so simple, so clear, and so distinct that the mind cannot break them down into still simpler parts, we can know these elements by a direct awareness exempt from illusion and error; and after this analysis, reason can more surely reconstruct the complex objects of thought.

3. *The rule of order.* We should carry on our reflections in due order, starting with the simplest ideas and proceeding, step by step, to the more and more complex. Descartes had in mind a deductive chain of reasoning in which each stage follows necessarily from the preceding stage, reason always being careful to follow the one and only order. Every step in this process must command certainty since it is guaranteed by intuition, that "undoubting conception of an unclouded and attentive mind."

4. *The rule of enumeration and review.* In a long chain of reasoning, we are apt to make a slip—to think that we grasp something clearly and distinctly, when in fact we do not, or to remember incorrectly some earlier stage in the reasoning. Whenever the smallest link is thus impaired, the chain of reasoning is broken, and all certainty is lost. Hence, it is necessary to recount and review the steps again and again to be absolutely sure that there has been no trick of memory or mistake in reasoning. Certainty is attained only when every link is so firmly grasped, and every connection has been so often reviewed, that the mind finally gathers together the links into an indissoluble, self-evident whole, which it views, as it were, all at the same time. Intuition then can grasp this whole as certain, just as it has grasped the initial premises and each successive step as certain.

Systematic Doubt

The success of the Cartesian method depends on having a sure foundation on which to build and thereafter on successfully applying the first rule to admit nothing that is uncertain. Therefore, Descartes resolved to doubt everything that he

---

[3] *The Principles of Philosophy,* in ibid., I, p. 237.

could possibly doubt, provisionally retaining only those ordinary maxims of conduct that are necessary in order to live decently. To doubt in this methodical way is not to consider something false or improbable but to recognize that it is not *absolutely* certain. The function of systematic doubt is to find a solid foundation for science and philosophy and thus to dispel skepticism.

The kind of indubitable foundation for which Descartes was searching is not any formal principle of logic or mathematics, such as the principle that one and the same proposition cannot be both true and false. Such a principle, although a necessary foundation of reasoning, tells us nothing about *what exists* and hence cannot provide the necessary basis for a philosophy or science of *reality*. The kind of premise that he sought, therefore, must be such that its truth cannot be doubted, it must be self-evident and not deduced from something else, and it must refer to something actually existing.

In resolutely admitting nothing except what is certain, Descartes was forced to doubt almost everything that he had ever believed: sensory experience, memory, expectation, the existence of other people, his body, the external physical world, and even simple mathematical truths such as two plus two equals four. His argument is so lucid that the reader should have no difficulty in understanding it.

It would seem that nothing at all is left to believe; but something remains even when doubt has done its worst. "I suppose myself to be deceived," Descartes exclaimed; "doubtless, then, I exist, since I am deceived. My very act of doubting proves something that I cannot doubt, I think, therefore I am."

Here is the first principle—the absolute the indubitable certainty—for which Descartes was searching, and here also is the main point of departure of modern epistemology: The certainty of self-consciousness had been proclaimed earlier by St. Augustine (354–430) and St. Thomas Aquinas (1225?–1274). But Descartes gave the idea wide currency, backing it up with systematic doubt, and without admitting the element of faith essential to Augustine and Aquinas. No one before him had so deliberately adopted doubt as a method of procedure or employed it so boldly and sweepingly.

It is instructive at this point to consider the case study presented at the beginning of this section from the rationalist perspective. What would Plato and Descartes say about the sort of knowledge exhibited by a chess-playing computer? What sort of "self-evident" truths or axioms might this computer be operating with? How are deduction and systematic doubt involved? What would it mean to ask whether the notions of "truth" and "reason" are relevant to the computer's calculations?

2

EMPIRICISM AND ITS LIMITS

▄▄▄▄▄▄▄▄▄▄▄▄▄▄▄▄▄▄

DAVID HUME (1711–1776)

Born in Edinburgh, David Hume was the youngest son of a gentleman landowner. His father died when he was an infant, and he was reared by his mother, who, somewhat critical of his bookish tendencies, is said to have remarked that "oor Davie's a fine good-natured crater but uncommon wake-minded." Hume's studies at the University of Edinburgh instilled in him a love of literature and philosophy, which kept him from settling down to a legal or business career. He decided to devote his life to scholarly pursuits, and at the age of twenty-three crossed the Channel to live in France, studying at La Flèche, where Descartes had gone to school.

There he completed, before he reached the age of twenty-five, his greatest philosophical work, the *Treatise of Human Nature*. In his brief autobiography, he remarked that the book "fell dead-born from the press." Although this remark is an exaggeration, it suggests Hume's great disappointment that his ideas did not find a wider public. His *An Enquiry Concerning Human Understanding* (1748) and *An Enquiry Concerning the Principles of Morals* (1751), which restated principal parts of the *Treatise*, were somewhat more popular, but his literary reputation was based mainly on his *Political Discourses* (1752) and his *History of England*, published in 1755 and following years. He also wrote *Dialogues Concerning Natural Religion*, which he regarded as a bit too shocking to publish during his own lifetime.

Although the income from his books gradually increased and he remained a frugal bachelor, he had to find other means of livelihood. Early in his career, he applied first to the University of Edinburgh and then to the University of Glasgow for a teaching position, but both universities rejected him because of the heterodoxy of his views. For a short time, he was tutor to a lunatic, the Marquis of Annandale, and then later became secretary to General St. Clair. Thereafter he secured a six-year post as keeper of Advocates' Library in Edinburgh, and from 1763 to 1765 served as secretary to the British Embassy in Paris. His French acquaintances included the most famous intellectuals of the period—D'Alembert, Diderot, Holbach, and Rousseau. After his sojourn in France, he spent two years in London (1767–1769) as undersecretary of state for Scotland. In Great Britain as in France, he was a friend of distinguished wits, such as Burke, Gibbon, and Adam Smith. Having received a moderate pension, he finally retired to Edinburgh, where he lived quietly with his sister until his death in 1776.

In a self-obituary, he describes himself as follows: "I was a man of mild disposition, of command of temper, of an open, social and cheerful humor, capable of attachment but little susceptible of enmity, and of great moderation in all my passions. Even my love of literary fame, my ruling passion, never soured my temper, notwithstanding my frequent disappointments." This characterization appears to be entirely accurate. Hume was a canny Scot, with a kindly, humorous, equable disposition.

KNOWLEDGE AND CAUSALITY

1. [Impressions and Ideas]

Everyone will readily allow, that there is a considerable difference between the perceptions of the mind, when a man feels the pain of excessive heat, or the pleasure of moderate warmth, and when he afterwards recalls to his memory this sensation, or anticipates it by his imagination. These faculties may mimic or copy the perceptions of the senses; but they never can entirely reach the force and vivacity of the original sentiment. The utmost we say of them, even when they operate with greatest vigor, is, that they represent their object in so lively a manner, that we could *almost* say we feel or see it: But, except the mind be disordered by disease or madness, they never can arrive at such a pitch of vivacity, as to render these perceptions altogether undistinguishable. All the colors of poetry, however splendid, can never paint natural objects in such a manner as to make the description be taken for a real landskip. The most lively thought is still inferior to the dullest sensation.

We may observe a like distinction to run through all the other perceptions of the mind. A man in a fit of anger, is actuated in a very different manner from one who only thinks of that emotion. If you tell me, that any person is in love, I easily understand your meaning, and form a just conception of his situation; but never can mistake the conception for the real disorders and agitations of the passion. When we reflect on our past sentiments and affections, our thought is a faithful mirror, and copies its objects truly; but the colors which it employs are faint and dull, in comparison of those in which our original perceptions were clothed. It requires no nice discernment or metaphysical head to mark the distinction between them.

Here therefore we may divide all the perceptions of the mind into two classes or species, which are distinguished by their different degrees of force and vivacity. The less forcible and lively are commonly denominated *Thoughts* or *Ideas*. The other species want a name in our language, and in most others; I suppose, because it was not requisite for any, but philosophical purposes, to rank them under a general term or appellation. Let us, therefore, use a little freedom, and call them *Impressions;* employing that word in a sense somewhat different from the usual. By the term *impression*, then, I mean all our more lively perceptions, when we hear, or see, or feel, or love, or hate, or desire, or will.

Section I combines excerpts from the *Treatise* and the *Enquiry;* sections 2, 4, 5, 6, and 8 are from the *Enquiry;* sections 3 and 7 are from the *Treatise*. The *Treatise* was published in 1739; the *Enquiry* in 1748.

And impressions are distinguished from ideas, which are the less lively perceptions, of which we are conscious, when we reflect on any of those sensations or movements above mentioned. . . .

Impressions may be divided into two kinds, those of *sensation,* and those of *reflection.* The first kind arises in the soul originally, from unknown causes. The second is derived, in a great measure, from our ideas, and that in the following order. An impression first strikes upon the senses, and makes us perceive heat or cold, thirst or hunger, pleasure or pain, of some kind or other. Of this impression there is a copy taken by the mind, which remains after the impression ceases; and this we call an idea. This idea of pleasure or pain, when it returns upon the soul, produces the new impressions of desire and aversion, hope and fear, which may properly be called impressions of reflection, because derived from it. These again are copied by the memory and imagination, and become ideas: which perhaps, in their turn, give rise to other impressions and ideas; so that the impressions of reflection, are not only antecedent to their correspondent ideas, but posterior to those of sensation, and derived from them. . . .

We find, by experience, that when any impression has been present with the mind, it again makes its appearance there as an idea; and this it may do after two different ways: either when, in its new appearance, it retains a considerable degree of its first vivacity, and is somewhat intermediate betwixt an impression and an idea; or when it entirely loses that vivacity, and is a perfect idea. The faculty by which we repeat our impressions in the first manner, is called the *memory,* and the other the *imagination.* It is evident, at first sight, that the ideas of the memory are much more lively and strong than those of the imagination, and that the former faculty paints its objects in more distinct colors than any which are employed by the latter. When we remember any past event, the idea of it flows in upon the mind in a forcible manner; whereas, in the imagi-

nation, the perception is faint and languid, and cannot, without difficulty, be preserved by the mind steady and uniform for any considerable time. Here, then, is a sensible difference betwixt one species of ideas and another.

There is another difference betwixt these two kinds of ideas, which is no less evident, namely, that though neither the ideas of the memory nor imagination, neither the lively nor faint ideas, can make their appearance in the mind, unless their correspondent impressions have gone before to prepare the way for them, yet the imagination is not restrained to the same order and form with the original impressions; while the memory is in a manner tied down in that respect, without any power of variation.

Nothing, at first view, may seem more unbounded than the thought of man, which not only escapes all human power and authority, but is not even restrained within the limits of nature and reality. To form monsters, and join incongruous shapes and appearances, costs the imagination no more trouble than to conceive the most natural and familiar objects. And while the body is confined to one planet, along which it creeps with pain and difficulty; the thought can in an instant transport us into the most distant regions of the universe; or even beyond the universe, into the unbounded chaos, where nature is supposed to lie in total confusion. What never was seen, or heard of, may yet be conceived; nor is anything beyond the power of thought; except what implies an absolute contradiction.

But though our thought seems to possess this unbounded liberty, we shall find, upon a nearer examination, that it is really confined within very narrow limits, and that all this creative power of the mind amounts to no more than the faculty of compounding, transposing, augmenting, or diminishing the materials afforded us by the senses and experience. When we think of a golden mountain, we only join two consistent ideas, *gold,* and *mountain,* with which we were formerly acquainted. A virtuous horse we can conceive; because, from our own feeling, we can conceive virtue; and this we may unite to the figure and shape of a horse, which is an animal familiar to us. In short, all the materials of thinking are derived either: from our outward or inward sentiment: the mixture and composition of these belongs alone to the mind and will. Or, to express myself in philosophical language, all our ideas or more feeble perceptions are copies of our impressions or more lively ones. . . .

Here, therefore, is a proposition, which not only seems, in itself, simple and intelligible; but, if a proper use were made of it, might render every dispute equally intelligible, and banish all that jargon, which has so long taken possession of metaphysical reasonings, and drawn disgrace upon them. All ideas, especially abstract ones, are naturally faint and obscure: the mind has but a slender hold of them: they are apt to be confounded with other resembling ideas; and when we have often employed any term, though without a distinct meaning, we are apt to imagine it has a determinate idea annexed to it. On the contrary, all impressions, that is, all sensations, either outward or inward, are strong and vivid: the limits between them are more exactly determined: nor is it easy to fall into any error or mistake with regard to them. When we entertain, therefore, any suspicion that a philosophical term is employed without any meaning or idea (as is but too frequent), we need but enquire, *from what impression is that supposed idea derived?* And if it be impossible to assign any, this will serve to confirm our suspicion. By bringing ideas into so clear a light we may reasonably hope to remove all dispute, which may arise, concerning their nature and reality.

2. [The Forms of Reasoning]

All the objects of human reason or enquiry may naturally be divided into two kinds, to wit, *Relations of Ideas*, and *Matters of Fact*.

Of the first kind are the sciences of Geometry, Algebra, and Arithmetic; and in short, every affirmation which is either intuitively or demonstratively certain. *That the square of the hypothenuse is equal to the square of the two sides,* is a proposition which expresses a relation between these figures. *That three times five is equal to the half of thirty,* expresses a relation between these numbers. Propositions of this kind are discoverable by the mere operation of thought, without dependence on what is anywhere existent in the universe. Though there never were a circle or triangle in nature, the truths demonstrated by Euclid would for ever retain their certainty and evidence.

Matters of fact, which are the second objects of human reason, are not ascertained in the same manner; nor is our evidence of their truth, however great, of a like nature with the foregoing. The contrary of every matter of fact is still possible; because it can never imply a contradiction, and is conceived by the mind with the same facility and distinctness, as if ever so comformable to reality. *That the sun will not rise tomorrow* is no less intelligible a proposition, and implies no more contradiction than the affirmation, *that it will rise.* We should in vain, therefore, attempt to demonstrate its falsehood. Were it demonstratively false, it would imply a contradiction, and could never be distinctly conceived by the mind.

It may, therefore, be a subject worthy of curiosity, to enquire what is the nature of that evidence which assures us of any real existence and matter of fact, beyond the present testimony of our senses, or the records of our memory. This part of philosophy, it is observable, has been little cultivated, either by the ancients or moderns; and therefore our doubts and errors, in the prosecution of so important an enquiry, may be the more excusable; while we march through such difficult paths without any guide or direction. They may even prove useful, by exciting curiosity, and destroying that implicit faith and security, which is the bane of all reasoning and free enquiry. The discovery of defects in the common philosophy, if any such there be, will not, I presume, be a discouragement, but rather an incitement, as is usual, to attempt something more full and satisfactory than has yet been proposed to the public.

All reasonings concerning matter of fact seem to be founded on the relation of *Cause and Effect.* By means of that relation alone we can go beyond the evidence of our memory and senses. If you were to ask a man, why he believes any matter of fact, which is absent; for instance, that his friend is in the country, or in France; he would give you a reason; and this reason would be some other fact; as a letter received from him or the knowledge of his former resolutions and promises. A man finding a watch or any other machine in a desert island, would conclude that there had once been men in that island. All our reasonings concerning fact are of the same nature. And here it is constantly supposed that there is a connection between the present fact and that which is inferred from it. Were there nothing to bind them together, the inference would be entirely precarious. The hearing of an articulate voice and rational discourse in the dark assures us of the presence of some person: Why? because these are the effects of the human make and fabric, and closely connected with it. If we anatomize all the other reasonings of this nature, we shall find that they are founded on the relation of cause and effect, and that this relation is either near or remote, direct or collateral. Heat and light are collateral effects of fire, and the one effect may justly be inferred from the other.

If we would satisfy ourselves, therefore, concerning the nature of that evidence, which assures us of matters of fact, we must enquire how we arrive at the knowledge of cause and effect.

I shall venture to affirm, as a general proposition, which admits of no exception, that the knowledge of this relation is not, in any instance, attained by reasonings *a pri-*

ori; but arises entirely from experience, when we find that any particular objects are constantly conjoined with each other. Let an object be presented to a man of ever so strong natural reason and abilities; if that object be entirely new to him, he will not be able, by the most accurate examination of its sensible qualities, to discover any of its causes or effects. Adam, though his rational faculties be supposed, at the very first, entirely perfect, could not have inferred from the fluidity and transparency of water that it would suffocate him, or from the light and warmth of fire that it would consume him. No object ever discovers, by the qualities which appear to the senses, either the causes which produced it, or the effects which will arise from it; nor can our reason, unassisted by experience, ever draw any inference concerning real existence and matter of fact.

This proposition, *that causes and effects are discoverable, not by reason but by experience,* will readily be admitted with regard to such objects, as we remember to have once been altogether unknown to us; since we must be conscious of the utter inability, which we then lay under, of foretelling what would arise from them. Present two smooth pieces of marble to a man who has no tincture of natural philosophy; he will never discover that they will adhere together in such a manner as to require great force to separate them in a direct line, while they make so small a resistance to a lateral pressure. Such events, as bear little analogy to the common course of nature, are also readily confessed to be known only by experience; nor does any man imagine that the explosion of gunpowder, or the attraction of a loadstone, could ever be discovered by arguments *a priori.* In like manner, when an effect is supposed to depend upon an intricate machinery or secret structure of parts, we make no difficulty in attributing all our knowledge of it to experience. Who will assert that he can give the ultimate reason why milk or bread is proper nourishment for a man, not for a lion or a tiger? . . .

3. [The Idea of Causation]

We must consider the idea of *causation,* and see from what origin it is derived. It is impossible to reason justly, without understanding perfectly the idea concerning which we reason; and it is impossible perfectly to understand any idea, without tracing it up to its origin, and examining that primary impression, from which it arises. The examination of the impression bestows a clearness on the idea; and the examination of the idea bestows a like clearness on all our reasoning.

Let us therefore cast our eye on any two objects, which we call cause and effect, and turn them on all sides, in order to find that impression, which produces an idea of such prodigious consequence. At first sight I perceive, that I must not search for it in any of the particular *qualities* of the objects; since, whichever of these qualities I pitch on, I find some object that is not possessed of it, and yet falls under the denomination of cause or effect. And indeed there is nothing existent, either externally or internally, which is not to be considered either as a cause or an effect; though it is plain there is no one quality which universally belongs to all beings, and gives them a title to that denomination.

The idea then of causation must be derived from some *relation* among objects; and that relation we must now endeavor to discover. I find in the first place, that whatever objects are considered as causes or effects, are *contiguous;* and that nothing can operate in a time or place, which is ever so little removed from those of its existence. Though distant objects may sometimes seem productive of each other, they are commonly found upon examination to be linked by a chain of causes, which are contiguous among themselves, and to the distant objects; and when in any particular instance we cannot discover this connection, we still presume it to exist. We may therefore consider the relation of *contiguity* as essential to that of causation. ...

The second relation I shall observe as essential to causes and effects, is ... that of *priority* of time in the cause before the effect. ...

[A third] relation betwixt cause and effect ... is their *constant conjunction.* Contiguity and succession are not sufficient to make us pronounce any two objects to be cause and effect, unless we perceive that these two relations are preserved in several instances. ... Thus we remember to have seen that species of object we call *flame,* and to have felt that species of sensation we call *heat.* We likewise call to mind their constant conjunction in all past instances. Without any farther ceremony, we call the one *cause* and the other *effect,* and infer the existence of the one from that of the other. ...

There is [also] a *necessary connection* to be taken into consideration; and that relation is of much greater importance. ...

What is our idea of necessity, when we say that two objects are necessarily connected to-gether? Upon this head I repeat, what I have often had occasion to observe, that as we have no idea that is not derived from an impression, we must find some impression that gives rise to this idea of necessity, if we assert we have really such an idea. In order to do this, I consider in what objects necessity is commonly supposed to lie; and, finding that it is always ascribed to causes and effects, I turn my eye to two objects supposed to be placed in that relation, and examine them in all the situations of which they are susceptible. I immediately perceive that they are contiguous in time and place, and that the object we call cause *precedes* the other we call effect. In no one instance can I go any further, nor is it possible for me to discover any third relation betwixt these objects. I therefore enlarge my view to comprehend several instances, where I find like objects always existing in like relations of contiguity and succession. At first sight this seems to serve but little to my purpose. The reflection on several instances only repeats the same objects; and therefore can never give rise to a new idea. But upon further enquiry I find, that the repetition is not in every particular the same, but produces a new impression, and by that means the idea which I at present examine. For after a frequent repetition I find, that upon the appearance of one of the objects, the mind is *determined* by custom to consider its usual attendant, and to consider it in a stronger light upon account of its relation to the first object. It is this impression, then, or *determination*, which affords me the idea of necessity. ...

Suppose two objects to be presented to us, of which the one is the cause and the other the effect; it is plain that, from the simple consideration of one, or both these objects, we never shall perceive the tie by which they are united, or be able certainly to pronounce, that there is a connection betwixt them. It is not, therefore, from any one instance, that we arrive at the idea of cause and effect, of a necessary connection of power, of force, of energy, and of efficacy. Did we never see any but particular conjunctions of objects, entirely different from each other, we should never be able to form any such ideas [as cause and effect].

But, again, suppose we observe several instances in which the same objects are always conjoined together, we immediately conceive a connection betwixt them, and begin to draw an inference from one to another. This multiplicity of resembling instances, therefore, constitutes the very essence of power or connection, and is the source from which the idea of it arises. ...

Though the several resembling instances, which give rise to the idea of power, have no influence on each other, and can never produce any new quality *in the object*, which can be the model of that idea, yet the *observation* of this resemblance produces a new impression *in the mind*, which is its real model. For after we have observed the resemblance in a sufficient number of instances, we immediately feel a determination of the mind to pass from one object to its usual attendant, and

to conceive it in a stronger light upon account of that relation. This determination is the only effect of the resemblance; and, therefore, must be the same with power or efficacy, whose idea is derived from the resemblance. The several instances of resembling conjunctions lead us into the notion of power and necessity. These instances are in themselves totally distinct from each other, and have no union but in the mind, which observes them, and collects their ideas. Necessity, then, is the effect of this observation, and is nothing but an internal impression of the mind, or a determination to carry our thoughts from one object to another. Without considering it in this view, we can never arrive at the most distant notion of it, or be able to attribute it either to external or internal objects, to spirit or body, to causes or effects. ...

The idea of necessity arises from some impression. There is no impression conveyed by our senses, which can give rise to that idea. It must, therefore, be derived from some internal impression, or impression of reflection. There is no internal impression which has any relation to the present business, but that propensity, which custom produces, to pass from an object to the idea of its usual attendant. This, therefore, is the essence of necessity. Upon the whole, necessity is something that exists in the mind, not in objects; nor is it possible for us ever to form the most distant idea of it, considered as a quality in bodies. Either we have no idea of necessity, or necessity is nothing but that determination of the thought to pass from causes to effects, and from effects to causes, according to their experienced union.

Thus, as the necessity, which makes two times two equal to four, or three angles of a triangle equal to two right ones, lies only in the act of the understanding, by which we consider and compare these ideas; in like manner, the necessity of power, which unites causes and effects, lies in the determination of the mind to pass from the one to the other. The efficacy or energy of causes is neither placed in the causes themselves, nor in the Deity, nor in the concurrence of these two principles; but belongs entirely to the soul, which considers the union of two or more objects in all past instances. It is here that the real power of causes is placed, along with their connection and necessity. ...

4. [Of Liberty and Necessity]

I have frequently considered, what could possibly be the reason why all mankind, though they have ever, without hesitation, acknowledged the doctrine of necessity in their whole practice and reasoning, have yet discovered such a reluctance to acknowledge it in words, and have rather shown a propensity, in all ages, to profess the contrary opinion. The matter, I think, may be accounted for after the following manner if we examine the operations of body, and the production of effects from their causes, we shall find that all our faculties can never carry us farther in our knowledge of this relation than barely to observe that particular objects are *constantly conjoined* together, and that the mind is carried, by a *customary transition*, from the appearance of one to the belief of the other. But though this conclusion concerning human ignorance be the result of the strictest scrutiny of this subject, men still entertain a strong propensity to believe that they penetrate farther into the powers of nature, and perceive something like a necessary connexion between the cause and the effect. When again they turn their reflections towards the operations of their own minds, and feel no such connexion of the motive and the action; they are thence apt to suppose, that there is a difference between the effects which result from material force, and those which arise from thought and intelligence. But being once convinced that we know nothing farther of causation of any kind than merely the *constant conjunction* of objects, and the consequent *inference* of the mind from one to another, and finding that these two circumstances are universally allowed to have

place in voluntary actions; we may be more easily led to own the same necessity common to all causes. ...

It would seem, indeed, that men begin at the wrong end of this question concerning liberty and necessity, when they enter upon it by examining the faculties of the soul, the influence of the understanding, and the operations of the will. Let them first discuss a more simple question, namely, the operations of body and of brute unintelligent matter; and try whether they can there form any idea of causation and necessity, except that of a constant conjunction of objects, and subsequent inference of the mind from one to another. If these circumstances form, in reality, the whole of that necessity, which we conceive in matter, and if these circumstances be also universally acknowledged to take place in the operations of the mind, the dispute is at an end; at least, must be owned to be thenceforth merely verbal. But as long as we will rashly suppose, that we have some farther idea of necessity and causation in the operations of external objects; at the same time, that we can find nothing farther in the voluntary actions of the mind; there is no possibility of bringing the question to any determinate issue, while we proceed upon so erroneous a supposition. The only method of undeceiving us is to mount up higher; to examine the narrow extent of science when applied to material causes; and to convince ourselves that all we know of them is the constant conjunction and inference above mentioned. We may, perhaps, find that it is with difficulty we are induced to fix such narrow limits to human understanding: But we can afterwards find no difficulty when we come to apply this doctrine to the actions of the will. For as it is evident that these have a regular conjunction with motives and circumstances and characters, and as we always draw inferences from one to the other, we must be obliged to acknowledge in words that necessity, which we have already avowed, in every deliberation of our lives, and in every step of our conduct and behaviour. ...

But to proceed in this reconciling project with regard to the question of liberty and necessity; the most contentious question of metaphysics, the most contentious science; it will not require many words to prove, that all mankind have ever agreed in the doctrine of liberty as well as in that of necessity, and that the whole dispute, in this respect also, has been hitherto merely verbal. For what is meant by liberty, when applied to voluntary actions? We cannot surely mean that actions have so little connexion with motives, inclinations, and circumstances, that one does not follow with a certain degree of uniformity from the other, and that one affords no inference by which we can conclude the existence of the other. For these are plain and acknowledged matters of fact. By liberty, then, we can only mean *a power of acting or not acting, according to the determinations of the will;* that is, if we choose to remain at rest, we may; if we choose to move, we also may. Now this hypothetical liberty is universally allowed to belong to every one who is not a prisoner and in chains. Here, then, is no subject of dispute.

Whatever definition we may give of liberty, we should be careful to observe two requisite circumstances; *first,* that it be consistent with plain matter of fact; *secondly,* that it be consistent with itself. If we observe these circumstances, and render our definition intelligible, I am persuaded that all mankind will be found of one opinion with regard to it.

It is universally allowed that nothing exists without a cause of its existence, and that chance, when strictly examined, is a mere negative word, and means not any real power which has anywhere a being in nature. But it is pretended that some causes are necessary, some not necessary. Here then is the advantage of definitions. Let any one *define* a cause, without comprehending, as a part of the definition, a necessary connexion with its effect; and let him show distinctly the origin of the idea, expressed by the definition; and I shall readily give up the whole controversy. But if the foregoing explication of the matter be received, this must be absolutely impracticable. Had not objects a regular conjunction with each other, we should never have entertained any notion of cause and effect; and this regular conjunction produces that inference of the understanding, which is the only connexion, that we can have any comprehension of. Whoever attempts a definition of cause, exclusive of these circumstances, will be obliged either to employ unintelligible terms or such as are synonymous to the term which he endeavours to define. And if the definition above mentioned be admitted; liberty, when opposed to necessity, not, to constraint, is the same thing with chance; which is universally allowed to have no existence.

5. [Will the Future Resemble the Past?]

It must certainly be allowed, that nature has kept us at a great distance from all her secrets, and has afforded us only the knowledge of a few superficial qualities of objects; while she conceals from us those powers and principles on which the influence of those objects entirely depends. Our senses inform us of the color, weight, and consistence of bread; but neither sense nor reason can ever inform us of those qualities which fit it for the nourishment and support of a human body. Sight or feeling conveys an idea of the actual motion of bodies; but as to that wonderful force or power, which would carry on a moving body for ever in a continued change of place, and which bodies never lose but by communicating it to others; of this we cannot form the most distant conception. But notwithstanding this ignorance of natural powers and principles, we always presume, when we see like sensible qualities, that they have like secret powers, and expect that effects, similar to those which we have experienced, will follow from them. If a body of like color and consistence with that bread, which we have formerly eat, be presented to us, we make no scruple of repeating the experiment, and foresee, with certainty, like nourishment and support. Now this is a process of the mind or thought, of which I would willingly know the foundation. It is allowed on all hands that there is no known connexion between the sensible qualities and the secret powers; and consequently, that the mind is not led to form such a conclusion concerning their constant and regular conjunction, by anything which it knows of their nature. As to past *Experience,* it can be allowed to give *direct* and *certain* information of those precise objects only, and that precise period of time, which fell, under its cognizance: but why this experience should be extended to future times, and to other objects, which for aught we know, may be only in appearance similar; this is the main question on which I would insist. The bread, which I formerly eat, nourished me; that is, a body of such sensible qualities was, at that time, endued with such secret powers: but does it follow, that other bread must also nourish me at another time, and that like sensible qualities must always be attended with like secret powers? The consequence seems nowise necessary. At least, it must be acknowledged that there is here a consequence drawn by the mind; that there is a certain step taken; a process of thought, and an inference, which wants to be explained. These two propositions are far from being the same, *I have found that such an object has always been attended with such an effect, and I foresee, that other objects, which are, in appearance, similar, will be attended with similar effects.* I shall allow, if you please, that the one proposition may justly be inferred from the other: I know, in fact, that it always is inferred. But if you insist that the inference is made by a chain of reasoning, I desire you to produce that reasoning. . . .

All reasonings may be divided into two kinds, namely, demonstrative reasoning, or that concerning relations of ideas, and moral reasoning, or that concerning matter of fact and existence. That there are no demonstrative arguments in the case seems evident; since it implies no contradiction that the cause of nature may change, and that an object, seemingly like those which we have experienced, may be attended with different or contrary effects. May I not clearly and distinctly conceive that a body, falling from the clouds, and which, in all other respects, resembles snow, has yet the taste of salt or feeling of fire? Is there any more intelligible proposition than to affirm, that all the trees will flourish in December and January, and decay in May and June? Now whatever is intelligible, and can be distinctly conceived, implies no contradiction, and can never be proved false by any demonstrative argument or abstract reasoning *a priori.*

If we be, therefore, engaged by arguments to put trust in past experience, and make it the standard of our future judgment, these arguments must be probable only, or such as regard matter of fact and real existence, according to the division above mentioned. But that there is no argument of this kind, must appear, if our explication of that species of reasoning be admitted as solid and satisfactory. We have said that all arguments concerning existence are founded on the relation of cause, and effect; that our knowledge of that relation is derived entirely from experience; and that all our experimental conclusions proceed upon the supposition that the future will be conformable to the past. To endeavour, therefore, the proof of this last supposition by probable arguments, or arguments regarding existence, must be evidently going in a circle, and taking that for granted, which is the very point in question. . . .

Should it be said that, from a number of uniform experiments, we *infer* a connexion between the sensible qualities and the secret powers; this, I must confess, seems the same difficulty, couched in different terms. The question still recurs, on what process of argument this *inference* is founded? Where is the medium, the interposing ideas, which join propositions so very wide of each other? It is confessed that the color, consistence, and other sensible qualities of bread appear not, of themselves, to have any connexion with the secret powers of nourishment and support. For otherwise we could infer these secret powers from the first appearance of these sensible qualities, without the aid of experience; contrary to the sentiment of all, philosophers; and contrary to plain matter of fact. Here, then, is our natural state of ignorance with regard to the powers and influence of all objects. How is this remedied by experience? It only shows us a number of uniform effects, resulting from certain objects, and teaches us that those particular objects, at that particular time, were endowed with such powers and forces. When a new object, endowed with similar sensible qualities, is produced, we expect similar powers and forces, and look for a like effect. From a body of like color and consistence with bread we expect like nourishment and support. But this surely is a step or progress of the mind, which wants to be explained. When a man says, *I have found in all past instances, such sensible qualities conjoined with such secret powers*: And when he says, *Similar sensible qualities will always be conjoined with similar secret powers,* he is not guilty of a tautology, nor are these propositions in any respect the same. You say that the one proposition is an inference from the other. But you must confess that the inference is not intuitive; neither is it demonstrative: Of what nature is it, then? To say it is experimental is begging the question. For all inferences from experience suppose, as their foundation, that the future will resemble the past, and that similar powers will be conjoined with similar sensible qualities. If there be any suspicion that the course of nature may change, and that the past may be no rule for the future, all experience becomes useless, and can give rise to no inference or conclusion. It is impossible, therefore, that any arguments from experience can prove this resemblance of the past to the future; since all these arguments are founded on the supposition of that resemblance. Let the course of things be allowed hitherto ever so regular; that alone, without some new argument or inference, proves not that, for the future, it will continue so. In vain, do you pretend to have learned the nature of bodies from your past experience. Their secret nature, and consequently all their effects and influence, may change, without any change in their sensible qualities. This happens sometimes, and with regards to some objects: Why may it not happen always, and with regard to all objects? What logic, what process of argument secures you against this supposition? My practice, you say, refutes my doubts. But you mistake the purport, of my question. As an agent, I am quite satisfied in the point; but as a philosopher, who has some share of curiosity, I will not say scepticism, I want to learn the foundation of this inference. No reading, no enquiry has yet been able to remove my difficulty, or give me satisfaction in a matter of such importance. Can I do better than propose the difficulty to the public, even though, perhaps, I have small hopes of obtaining a solution? We shall at least, by this means, be sensible of our ignorance, if we do not augment our knowledge.

6. [Can We Know External Objects?]

It seems evident, that men are carried, by a natural instinct or prepossession, to repose faith in their senses; and that, without any reasoning, or even almost before the use of reason, we always suppose an external universe, which depends not on our perception, but would exist, though we and every sensible creature were absent or annihilated. Even the animal creation are governed by a like opinion, and preserve this belief of external objects, in all their thoughts, designs, and actions.

It seems also evident, that, when men follow this blind and powerful instinct of nature, they always suppose the very images, presented by the senses, to be the external objects, and never entertain any suspicion, that the one are nothing but representations of the other. This very table, which we see white, and which we feel hard, is believed to exist, independent of our perception, and to be something external to our mind, which perceives it. Our presence bestows not being on it: our absence does not annihilate it. It preserves its existence uniform and entire, independent of the situation of intelligent beings, who perceive or contemplate it.

But this universal and primary opinion of all men is soon destroyed by the slightest philosophy, which teaches us, that nothing can ever be present to the mind but an image or perception, and that the senses are only the inlets, through which these images are conveyed, without being able to produce any immediate intercourse between the mind and the object. The table, which we see, seems to diminish, as we remove farther from it: but the real table, which exists independent of us, suffers no alteration: it was, therefore, nothing but its image, which was present to the mind. These are the obvious dictates of reason; and no man, who reflects, ever doubted, that the existences, which we consider, when we say, *this house* and *that tree,* are nothing but perceptions in the mind, and fleeting copies or representations of other existences, which remain uniform and independent.

So far, then, we are necessitated by reasoning to contradict or depart from the primary instincts of nature, and to embrace a new system with regard to the evidence of our senses. But here philosophy finds herself extremely embarrassed, when she would justify this new system, and obviate the cavils and objections of the sceptics. She can no longer plead the infallible and irresistible instinct of nature: for that led us to a quite different system, which is acknowledged fallible and even erroneous. And to justify this pretended philosophical system, by a chain of clear and convincing argument, or even any appearance of argu-

ment, exceeds the power of all human capacity.

By what argument can it be proved, that the perceptions of the mind must be caused by external objects, entirely different from them, though resembling them (if that be possible) and could not arise either from the energy of the mind itself, or from the suggestion of some invisible and unknown spirit, or from some other cause still more unknown to us? It is acknowledged, that, in fact, many of these perceptions arise not from anything external, as in dreams, madness, and other diseases. And nothing can be more inexplicable than the manner, in which body should so operate upon mind as ever to convey an image of itself to a substance, supposed of so different, and even contrary a nature.

It is a question of fact, whether the perceptions of the senses be produced by external objects, resembling them: how shall this question be determined? By experience surely; as all other questions of a like nature. But here experience is, and must be entirely silent. The mind has never anything present to it but the perceptions, and cannot possibly reach any experience of their connection with objects. The supposition of such a connexion is, therefore, without any foundation in reasoning.

To have recourse to the veracity of the Supreme Being, in order to prove the veracity of our senses, is surely making a very unexpected circuit. If his veracity were at all concerned in this matter, our senses would be entirely infallible; because it is not possible that he can ever deceive. Not to mention, that, if the external world be once called in question, we shall be at a loss to find arguments, by which we may prove the existence of that Being or any of his attributes.

This is a topic, therefore, in which the profounder and more philosophical sceptics will always triumph, when they endeavour to introduce an universal doubt into all subjects of human knowledge and enquiry.

Do you follow the instincts and propensities of nature may they say, in assenting to the veracity of sense? But these lead you to believe that the very perception or sensible image is the external object. Do you disclaim this principle, in order to embrace a more rational opinion, that the perceptions are only representations of something external? You here depart from your natural propensities and more obvious sentiments; and yet are not able to satisfy your reason, which can never find any convincing argument from experience to prove, that the perceptions are connected with any external objects. . . .

It is universally allowed by modern enquirers, that all the sensible qualities of objects, such as hard, soft, hot, cold, white, black, etc. are merely secondary, and exist not in the objects themselves, but are perceptions of the mind, without any external archetype or model, which they represent. If this be allowed, with regard to secondary qualities, it must also follow, with regard to the supposed primary qualities of extension and solidity; nor can the latter be any more entitled to that denomination than the former. The idea of extension is entirely acquired from the senses of sight and feeling; and if all the qualities, perceived by the senses, be in the mind, not in the object, the same conclusion must reach the idea of extension, which is wholly dependent on the sensible ideas or the ideas of secondary qualities. . . .

Thus the first philosophical objection to the evidence of sense or to the opinion of external existence consists in this, that such an opinion, if rested on natural instinct, is contrary to reason, and if referred to reason, is contrary to natural instinct, and at the same time carries no rational evidence with it, to convince an impartial enquirer. The second objection goes farther, and represents this opinion as contrary to reason: at least, if it be a principle of reason, that all sensible qualities are in the mind, not in the object. Bereave matter of all its intelligible qualities, both primary and secondary, you in a manner annihilate it, and leave only a certain unknown, inexplicable *something*, as the cause of our perceptions; a notion so imperfect, that no sceptic will think it worth while to contend against it.

7. [The Idea of Self]

There are some philosophers, who imagine we are every moment intimately conscious of what we call our *self;* that we feel its existence and its continuance in existence; and are certain, beyond the evidence of a demonstration, both of its perfect identity and simplicity. The strongest sensation, the most violent passion, say they, instead of distracting us from this view, only fix it the more intensely, and make us consider their influence on *self* either by their pain or pleasure. To attempt a further proof of this were to weaken its evidence; since no proof can be derived from any fact of which we are so intimately conscious; nor is there any thing of which we can be certain, if we doubt of this.

Unluckily all these positive assertions are contrary to that very experience which is pleaded for them; nor have we any idea of *self,* after the manner it is here explained. For, from what impression could this idea be derived? This question it is impossible to answer without a manifest contradiction and absurdity; and yet it is a question which must necessarily be answered, if we would have the idea of self pass for clear and intelligible. It must be some one impression that gives rise to every real idea. But self or person is not any one impression, but that to which our several impressions, and ideas are supposed to have a reference. If any impression gives rise to the idea of self, that impression must continue invariably the same, through the whole course of our lives; since self is supposed to exist after that manner. But there is no impression constant and invariable. Pain and pleasure, grief and joy, passions and sensations succeed each other, and never all exist at the same time. It cannot therefore be from any of these impressions, or from any other, that the idea of self is derived; and consequently there is no such idea.

But further, what must become of all our particular perceptions upon this hypothesis? All these are different, and distinguishable, and separable from each other, and may be separately considered, and may exist separately, and have no need of any thing to support their existence. After what manner therefore do they belong to self, and how are they connected with it? For my part, when I enter most intimately into what I call *myself,* I always stumble on some particular perception or other, of heat or cold, light or shade, love or hatred, pain or pleasure. I never can catch *myself* at any time without a perception, and never can observe any thing but the perception. When my perceptions are removed for any time, as by sound sleep, so long am I insensible of *myself,* and may truly be said not to exist. And were all my perceptions removed by death, and could I neither think, nor feel, nor see, nor love, nor hate, after the dissolution of my body, I should be entirely annihilated, nor do I conceive what is further requisite to make me a perfect nonentity. If any one, upon serious and unprejudiced reflection, thinks he has a different notion of *himself,* I must confess I can reason no longer with him. All I can allow him is, that he may be in the right as well as I, and that we are essentially different in this particular. He may; perhaps, perceive something simple and continued, which he calls *himself:* though I am certain there is no such principle in me.

But setting aside some metaphysicians of this kind, I may venture to affirm of the rest of mankind, that they are nothing but a bundle or collection of different perceptions, which succeed each other with an inconceivable rapidity, and are in a perpetual flux and movement. Our eyes cannot turn in their sockets without varying our perceptions. Our thought is still more variable than our sight; and all our other senses and faculties contribute to this change; nor is there any single power of the soul, which remains unalterably the same, perhaps for one moment. The mind is a kind of theater, where several perceptions successively make their appearance; pass, repass, glide away, and mingle in an infinite variety of postures and situations. There is properly no *simplicity* in it at one time, nor identity in different, whatever natural propension we may have to imagine that simplicity and identity. The comparison of the theater must not mislead us. They are the successive perceptions only, that constitute the mind; nor have we the most distant notion of the place where these scenes are represented, or of the materials of which it is composed.

8. [On the Proper Limits of Enquiry]

The *imagination* of man is naturally sublime, delighted with whatever is remote and extraordinary, and running, without control, into the most distant parts of space and time in order to avoid the objects, which custom has rendered too familiar to it. A correct *Judgment* observes a contrary method, and avoiding all distant and high enquiries, confines itself to common life and to such subjects as fall under daily practice and experience; leaving the more sublime topics to the embellishment of poets and orators, or to the arts of priests and politicians. . . . Those who have a propensity to philosophy, will still continue their researches; because they reflect, that, besides the immediate pleasure, attending such an occupation, philosophical decisions are nothing but the reflections of common life, methodized and corrected. But they will never be tempted to go beyond common life so long as they consider the imperfection of those faculties which they employ, their narrow reach, and their inaccurate operations. While we cannot give a satisfactory reason, why we believe, after a thousand experiments, that a stone will fall, or fire burn; can we ever satisfy ourselves concerning any determination, which we may form, with regard to the origin of worlds, and the situation of nature, from, and to eternity?

This narrow limitation; indeed, of our enquiries, is, in every respect, so reasonable that it suffices to make the slightest examination into the natural powers of the human mind and to compare them with their objects, in order to recommend it to us. We shall then find what are the proper subjects of science and enquiry.

It seems to me, that the only objects of the abstract science or of demonstration are quantity and number, and that all attempts to extend this more perfect species of knowledge beyond these bounds are mere sophistry and illusion. As the component parts of quantity and number are entirely similar, their relations become intricate and involved; and nothing can be more curious, as well as useful, than to trace, by a variety of mediums, their equality or inequality, through their different appearances. But as all other ideas are clearly distinct and different from each other, we can never advance farther, by our utmost scrutiny, than to observe this diversity, and, by an obvious reflection, pronounce one thing not to be another. Or if there be any difficulty in these decisions, it proceeds entirely from the undeterminate meaning of words, which is corrected by juster definitions. That the *square of the hypothenuse is equal to the squares of the other two sides*, cannot be known, let the terms be ever so exactly defined, without a train of reasoning and enquiry. But to convince us of this proposition, *that where there is no property, there can be no injustice*, it is only necessary to define the terms, and explain injustice, to be a violation of property. This proposition is, indeed, nothing but a more imperfect definition It is the same case with all those pretended syllogistical reasonings, which may be found in every other branch of learning, except the sci-

ences of quantity and number; and these may safely, I think, be pronounced the only proper objects of knowledge and demonstration.

All other enquiries of men regard only matter of fact and existence; and these are evidently incapable of demonstration. Whatever *is* may *not be*. No negation of a fact can involve a contradiction. The nonexistence of any being, without exception, is as clear and distinct an idea as its existence. The proposition, which affirms it not to be, however false, is no less conceivable and intelligible, than that which affirms it to be. The case is different with the sciences, properly so called. Every proposition, which is not true, is there confused and unintelligible. That the cube root of 64 is equal to the half of 10, is a false proposition, and can never be distinctly conceived. But that Caesar, or the angel Gabriel, or any being never existed, may be a false proposition, but still is perfectly conceivable, and implies no contradiction.

The existence, therefore, of any being can only be proved by arguments from its cause or its effect; and these arguments are founded entirely on experience. If we reason *a priori*, anything may appear able to produce anything. The falling of a pebble may, for aught we know, extinguish the sun; or the wish of a man control the planets in their orbits. It is only experience, which teaches us the nature and bounds of cause and effect, and enables us to infer the existence of one object from that of another. . . .

When we run over libraries, persuaded of these principles, what havoc must we make? If we take in our hand any volume; of divinity or school metaphysics, for instance; let us ask, *Does it contain any abstract reasoning concerning quantity or number? No. Does it contain any experimental reasoning concerning matter of fact and existence?* No. Commit it then to the flames: for it can contain nothing but sophistry and illusion.

IMMANUEL KANT (1724–1804)

The fourth child of a humble saddle maker, Immanuel Kant was born in Königsberg, East Prussia. His parents belonged to the Pietists, a revivalist sect within the Lutheran Church, and their family life was characterized by simple religious devotion. Kant detested the mechanical discipline and narrow range of ideas of the Pietist school to which he was sent. At sixteen, he enrolled in the University of Königsberg, supporting himself mainly by tutoring well-to-do students. There his intellectual interests turned to physics and astronomy. After six years at the university, Kant became a private tutor in several homes in East Prussia, a profession that he followed for some nine years. Returning to the university in 1755, he obtained a higher degree and a subordinate post on the faculty. For the next fifteen years he lived in academic poverty, until in 1770 he was finally appointed a full professor. In his lectures, he enthralled his student audiences with his knowledge, eloquence, and wit. The popular form of his teaching was in marked contrast to the difficult and technical style of his writing.

He never married, and the clocklike regularity of his bachelor ways became proverbial. His servant awakened him at 4:45 every morning; he spent the next hour drinking tea, smoking his pipe, and planning the day's work; from 6:00 to 7:00 he prepared his lectures; from 7:00 to 9:00 or 10:00 he taught; then he wrote until 11:30; at 12:00 he ate a hearty dinner; in the afternoon, rain or shine, he took a regular walk; after that, he read or wrote until, at 10:00, he went to bed. The rigidity of his routine did not prevent him from enjoying the society of women and enlivening many social gatherings with his dry wit. He had many friends in the town, and until he was old, he always dined with friends. His gallantry never deserted him; even when he was so old and feeble that he lost his footing and fell in the street, he courteously presented one of the two unknown women who helped him to his feet with the rose that he happened to be carrying.

Although he never traveled far from Königsberg, he was fond of travel books and sympathetic with intellectual and political emancipation the world over. "Have the courage to use your own intelligence!" he advised. He applauded the American and French revolutions, but not the Reign of Terror. "It was a time in Königsberg," wrote one of his colleagues, "when anyone who judged the Revolution even mildly, let alone favorably, was put on a black list as a Jacobin. Kant did not allow himself by that fact to be deterred from speaking up for the Revolution even at the table of noblemen."

Except for a remarkable astronomical treatise (1755), in which he anticipated Laplace's nebular hypothesis, all of his more important works were published late in his life, after he was awakened by Hume from his "dogmatic slumber." In an amazing decade, from 1780 to 1790, there appeared a series of epoch-making books: *The Critique of Pure Reason* (1781), *The Prolegomena to All Future Metaphysics* (1783), *The Foundations of the Metaphysic of Morals* (1785),

The Critique of Practical Reason (1788), and *The Critique of Judgment* (1790). He subsequently published works on politics and religion, but his main task was done. After 1796, his health gradually declined, and he died in 1804, aged nearly eighty.

THE LIMITS OF KNOWLEDGE

1. [Kant's Indebtedness to Hume]

Since the essays of Locke and Leibniz were written, or better, since the beginning of metaphysics, as history records it, no event has been more decisive for this science than the attack of David Hume. He shed no light but he did strike a spark from which a light might be kindled in receptive tinder, if its glow were carefully tended.

Hume began with one important metaphysical idea. It was the supposed connection of cause and effect. He challenged the claim that this connection was conceived in the mind itself. He wanted to know how anyone could think anything so constituted that its mere existence necessarily called for the existence of something else; for this is what the notion of cause means. He proved conclusively that it is quite impossible to conceive the connection of cause and effect abstractly, solely by means of thought, because it involves the idea of necessity. We do not see that if one thing exists, another has to exist in consequence, and we do not know how an abstract idea of this relation could occur to anyone.

Hume concluded that the idea of cause constitutes a delusion which seems to be a human brain child but is just the

bastard of imagination sired by experience. Thus, certain perceptions are joined together as the law of association provides. Then habit, which is a psychological necessity, is passed off as objective and as being discovered through insight. He then inferred that we cannot conceive a causal connection between events, even in general; for if we did, our ideas would be fictional and knowledge, which is supposed to be abstract and necessary, would be nothing but common experience under a false label. This, plainly, means that there is not and cannot be such a thing as metaphysics.

However hasty and mistaken Hume's conclusion may be, it was at least based on investigation. This made it worthwhile for the bright people of the day to co-operate in finding a happier solution to the problem as he explained it. The outcome might well have been a complete reform of the science, but the unhappy genius of metaphysicians caused him not to be understood.

I frankly confess that many years ago it was the memory of David Hume that first interrupted my dogmatic slumber and gave new direction to my studies in the field of speculative philosophy.

I tired first to see if Hume's objection could be put in a general form. I soon found that the idea of a connection between cause and effect was by no means the only idea we conceive abstractly of relations between things. Metaphysics consists first and last of such ideas. I tried to count them and when I had succeeded as I wished, taking first one and then another, I went on to explain them. I was now certain that they are not derived from experience,

Excerpts from *An Immanuel Kant Reader,* trans. and ed. Raymond Bernard Blakney. Copyright © 1960 by Raymond Bernard Blakney, renewed 1988. Reprinted by permission of HarperCollins Publishers Inc. The first section is from *The Prolegomena to All Future Metaphysics,* and the final section is from *The Critique of Judgment.* All else is from *The Critique of Pure Reason.*

as Hume has asserted, but that they spring from the mind alone. These explanations had seemed impossible to my smart predecessor and had not even occurred to anyone else, although everyone used such ideas without asking what the security behind them might be. This, I say, was the most difficult work ever undertaken on behalf of metaphysics. The worst of it was that no help at all could be had from metaphysics itself because the very possibility of metaphysics depends on this kind of explanation.

Having now succeeded in the solution of Hume's problem, not only in special cases but with a view to the whole reasoning function of mind, I could proceed safely, if slowly, to survey the field of pure reasoning, its boundaries as well as its contents, and I could do this working from general principles. This is exactly what metaphysics needs to build a system which is securely planned.

2. [A New Way of Thinking]

In metaphysics, thought is continually coming to a dead end, even when laws which common experience supports are under examination, purely as laws. Times without number it is necessary to go back to the fork because the road does not take us where we want to go. As for unanimity among the practitioners of metaphysics, there is so little of it that the discipline seems more like an arena, a ring constructed for those who like to exercise their skills in mock combat. At any rate, no contestant has yet succeeded in getting and holding a spot of his own. It appears, then, that to date, the procedure in metaphysics has just been to grope and worse than that, to grope among ideas.

How can it be explained that in this field, scientific certainty has not yet been found? Can it be impossible? If it is, why has nature visited our minds with a restless drive for certainty, as if this were the most important business of all? Not only that but there would be little reason ever to trust the

powers of thought, if they fail in one of the most important projects of human curiosity, proffering illusions and giving at last betrayal. Perhaps it is only that up to now we have failed to read the road signs correctly. If we renew the search, may we hope to have better luck than has been the lot of those who preceded us?

It seems to me that the examples of mathematics and physics, having become what they are by sudden revolution, are remarkable enough to warrant attention to the essential element of their change, the change that proved so beneficial. It may be worth our while also to make the experiment of imitating them, to the degree the analogy between these two rational disciplines and metaphysics permits.

Hitherto it has been assumed that knowledge must conform to the things known; but on this basis all attempts to find out about the world of things by abstract thought, and thus to permit an extension of human knowledge, have come to nothing. Let us then experiment to see whether or not we do better with the problems of metaphysics if we assume that things to be known must conform in advance to our knowing process. This would appear to lead to what we want, namely, knowledge that tells us something about an object of thought before it becomes a part of our experience.

If my perception of an object has to conform to the object, I do not see how there could be any abstract knowledge of it; but if the objects of my perceptions conform to the laws by which I know them, it is easy to conceive of abstract knowledge, for all experience is a kind of knowledge involving the mind, the laws of which I must suppose were a part of me before I ever saw anything. Those laws get expressed in abstract terms but all my experience must agree with them.

This experiment succeeds as well as could be desired. It promises scientific certainty for the part of metaphysics that deals in abstract ideas, the corresponding objects of which may be checked off in experience.

It involves a new way of thinking which enables us to explain perfectly how abstract knowledge, knowledge prior to experience, is possible. It also furnishes satisfactory proofs of the laws which form the mental framework of the natural world. Both of these achievements had been impossible heretofore.

3. [Empirical and *A Priori* Knowledge]

There is no doubt that knowledge begins with experience. How else could mental powers be awakened to action, if not by the objects that excite our senses, in part arousing images and in part stimulating the mental activity by which the images are compared? Images must then be combined or separated and the raw material of sense impressions worked over into the knowledge of things called experience. In the order of time, life begins with experience; there is no knowledge before that.

But if knowledge begins with experience, it does not follow that all of it is derived from experience. It may well be that whatever knowledge we do get from experience is already a combination of impressions and mental activity, the sense impressions being merely the occasion. It may be that the mental additive cannot be distinguished from the basic stuff until long practice makes one alert to it and skilled to pick it out.

This then is a question that needs close study and for which no offhand answer will do: Is there knowledge apart from both experience and sense impressions? This kind of knowledge is called abstract and prior (*a priori*) in contrast to knowledge derived from experience, which is empirical (*a posteriori*).

The word *"a priori"* is not yet definite enough to indicate the full meaning of the question at hand. It is often said of knowledge derived from experience that it is abstract because it does not come immediately from experience, but from some general rule borrowed from experience. Of a man who undermines the foundations of his house, we might say that he might have known *a priori*, that is, abstractly and beforehand, that the house would fall. He need not have waited for the actual experience of seeing it go down. He could not, however, have known about the house falling, from abstract principles only. He needs first to learn that bodies are heavy and that they fall when supports are removed; this would have to be learned from experience.

In what follows, by *abstract* knowledge we do not mean knowledge independent of this or that experience but knowledge *utterly independent of all experience*. In contrast, there is empirical, or *a posteriori* knowledge which we get only through experience. Abstract knowledge is called *pure* when it contains no trace of experience. So, for example, the proposition, "Every change has its cause," is abstract, but not *pure* because *change* is an idea drawn only from experience.

We need now a criterion by which to distinguish pure from empirical knowledge. Experience teaches one that an object is what it is, but not that it could not be otherwise. So, first, if a proposition cannot be conceived without thinking it *necessary,* it is *abstract*. Secondly, a judgment based on experience is never truly or strictly universal but only relatively so. But if a judgment is strictly *universal* and there is no possible exception to this, then it is not derived from experience and is valid, absolutely *abstract, pure*.

We need also to distinguish between two kinds of judgments, or statements: *analytic,* in which the predicate merely analyzes the subject; and *synthetic,* or *amplifying* in which the predicate adds something to the subject. If A is the subject of a statement and B is the predicate, there are two choices. If B is contained in A, the statement is analytic; if B is not contained in A but is related to it otherwise, the statement is synthetic, or amplifying.

For example, if I say, "All bodies are extended," this is an analytic statement of judgment. I need not go beyond the very idea of "body" to find the idea of "extension." On the other hand when I say, "All bodies are heavy," the predicate is quite different from what I think in the idea of "body" as such, and the addition of this kind of predicate to the subject makes the statement synthetic. Statements of experience always amplify the subject.

In abstract, amplifying judgments, no help can be had from experience. If I go beyond idea A and find idea B related to it, on what could such an amplification be based? Take, for example, the proposition: Everything that happens has a cause. In the idea of "something that happens" I can think of a time before the event and from it derive analytic judgments. But the idea of "cause" is something else; it does not fall within the idea of "something that happens." How then can I say something about this subject that is entirely unrelated to it? How do I know that cause belongs necessarily to that "something that happens," even when that something does not contain any notion of it? What is the unknown X on which one depends when he discovers a predicate B, foreign to A, which is, nevertheless, connected with it?

The unknown X cannot be experience because the principle just discussed adds a second conception (cause) to the first (existence), not only with wider generalization than experience can proffer but with an assertion of necessity. It is therefore wholly abstract and unrelated to experience. The whole aim of our speculative, abstract knowledge depends on synthetic, or amplifying propositions of this kind. Analytic judgments are of the highest importance and necessary, but only to clarify conception. This, in turn, is required for the secure and broader amplification by which something really new may be added to the matter of knowledge.

Examples from science. Mathematical judgments always amplify. One might think at first that $7+5 = 12$ is a straight analytic proposition. On closer inspection, it appears that the sum $7+5$ contains nothing

more than the combination of these two numbers. There is nothing to indicate what number embraces both. Arithmetical propositions always amplify.

Nor are geometric propositions analytic. That a straight line is the shortest distance between two points is an amplifying conception. Straightness has nothing to do with quantity, but only with quality. The idea of shortness is thus additive, and intuition is necessary at this point. Without it, amplification would be impossible.

The science of physics also contains principles which are abstract and amplifying. For example, there is the proposition that in all the changes of the physical world, the total quantity of matter remains unchanged. But in the idea of matter, I do not imagine its permanency. I think only of its presence in the space it fills. So I really have to go beyond the idea of matter itself and attribute something to it abstractly, something I never thought it involved. The proposition is thus not analytic but synthetic, or amplifying and yet it is abstractly conceived.

There must be amplifying and abstract knowledge in metaphysics too, even if metaphysics is regarded only as a pseudo science, necessary to human nature. It is not the duty of metaphysicians merely to dissect subjects and so, analytically, to illustrate abstract ideas. It is their duty to extend abstract knowledge and for this purpose they use principles which add to their ideas matter not originally contained in them. By means of abstract, amplifying judgments they may even go where experience cannot follow, as, for example, in the statement that "the world must have a beginning," and the like. So, metaphysics, at least by aim, consists of pure, amplifying propositions.

The characteristic problem then of pure reason is: How are abstract, amplifying judgments possible? That metaphysics has so far remained in the state of vacillating uncertainty and contradiction, is due to the fact that this problem was not recognized sooner, nor, perhaps, was the difference between analytic and amplifying judgment made clear.

4. [The Matter and Form of Intuition]

Of the varied processes by which things become known, there is one from which all thought stems. It is awareness (intuition), and it alone is direct, or immediate. Ultimately all food for thought comes from the outside world through our awareness of it, but among humans this occurs only when mind is involved.

The property of mind by which external things are recognized may be called sensitivity. Objects appear to mind because of its sensitivity, and this is the only way awareness can occur. In functioning mind, then, awareness gives rise to thoughts and finally to concepts. Directly or indirectly, all thought goes back to awareness and so to sensitivity, because there is no other way to know external things. Sensation is the effect an object has on the sen-sitive mind. If awareness comes through sensation, it is said to be empirical;, and the object so revealed, whatever it may be, is called "phenomenon," or simply "thing."

By matter, I mean the substance of a thing, to which sensations are traceable; by form, I refer to my awareness that the substance of something is arranged in a given order.

It is clear that sensations are not put in form by other sensations. The matter of which things are composed may be known through sensation but their form is provided by the mind, and form is therefore separate from sensation.

I call awareness (intuition) which does not participate in sensation, pure (that is, belonging only to mind). The pure form which sense impressions take on, the form or order in which the many elements of things are arranged by the mind, must be in mind beforehand. The pure form of sensitivity may be called pure awareness.

If, from your awareness of a body, you subtract the contribution of thought processes such as substance, forces, divisi-bility, etc., and then take away all that pertains to sensation, such as impenetrability, color, etc., there will still remain extension and form. These belong to pure awareness and exist only in mind, as forms for sense impressions, even if there were present no external objects or sensations from them.

5. [The Pure Forms of Intuition—Space and Time]

There is a sense or sensitivity of mind, by which we reach out to things and see them located in external space. Within this space their form, size, and relative positions are or can be fixed.

There is an internal sense by which the mind is aware of itself or its internal states. This sense does not present the soul as an object to be observed. It is, however, a fixed function without which an awareness of internal states of mind would be impossible. Its operations pertain to the relationships of time. Time cannot appear as an external matter any more than space can appear to be something within.

What then are space and time? Are they real entities? Or if not are they the delimitations of things or relations between things which exist whether anyone observes them or not? Or are they delimitations and relations which are inherent in one's awareness of the world and thus in the subjective character of the mind? If so, then without these properties of mind, predicates like space and time would never appear anywhere.

To understand this matter more clearly, let us first consider space.

(1.) Space is not an idea derived from experience of the external world. If my sensations are to be referred to things outside me, i.e., to things located at some point of space other than where I am, or if I am to be able to refer my sensations to differing objects located at several points, the idea of space must be present in advance. My conception of space therefore cannot be the product of experience or borrowed from the relations of things to each other.

On the contrary, it is only by means of the idea of space that external experience becomes possible at all.

(2.) Space is the visualization which is necessary to the mind, and the basis of all external perceptions. One might imagine space with no objects to fill it, but it is impossible to imagine that there should be no space. Space is therefore a condition of the possibility of phenomena and not a form required by them. It is subjective, a visualization which precedes all external experience.

(3.) The demonstrable certainty of geometric propositions depends on the necessity of this mental visualization of space. If space were a conception gained empirically or borrowed from general external experience, the first principles of mathematical definition would be merely perceptions. They would be subject to all the accidents of perception and there would be no necessity that there should be only one straight line between two points. A theorem would be something to be learned in each case by experience. Whatever is derived from experience possesses only relative generality, based on reasoning from observations. We should accordingly be able to say only that so far as anyone can see, there is no space having more than three dimensions.

(4.) Space is not a discursive or general idea of the relations between things. It is pure awareness or mental visualization. First of all, only one space is imaginable, and if many spaces are mentioned, they are all parts of the one space. They are not to be considered as leading up to the one all-embracing space, or the component parts from which an aggregate of space is formed.

Space is essentially one. The general idea of a multiplicity of spaces is the result of imposing limitations on space. Hence, it follows that the foundation of all ideas of space is a mental awareness, and it is thus not derived from experience. So geometrical principles, such as "The sum of two sides of a triangle is greater than the third,"

may never be derived from the general conception of sides and triangles but from an awareness of visualization which is purely mental and which is derived thence with demonstrable certainty.

(5.) Space is visualized as an infinite quantity. The general idea of space, which is to be found in a foot as well as a yard, would furnish no information about the quantity of the space involved if there were not infinity in the reach of awareness. Without this, no conception of relations in space could ever contain the principle of infinity.

Space is not in any sense a property of things or the relation between them. It is nothing but the form the appearances of things take to man's outer senses. It is the mental basis of sensitivity and makes possible one's awareness of the external world.

One may speak of space, extension, etc., only from the human point of view. Apart from one's awareness of the outer world, the idea of space means nothing at all. The space predicate is attributed to things only as they are sensed.

The rule that "things are juxtaposed in space" is valid within the limitation that "things" are taken only as objects of awareness. Add one condition and say that "things as they appear externally are juxtaposed in space," and the rule is universally valid.

This exposition therefore teaches the *reality* (objective validity) of space. Space is as real as anything else in the world. At the same time, it teaches the *ideality* of space, when things are viewed as only the mind can view them, as they are by themselves, apart from the activity of human sense. We also assert the reality of space as verifiable fact in human experience of the external world.

The *formal* idea of phenomena in space is a critical reminder that there is nothing of which one is aware that is a thing-itself (that is, something apart from man's perception of it). Space is not the form of things-themselves. The phenomena of which we are aware tell us nothing about things as they are apart from us, and in experience nobody ever asks about them as such.

[Kant's treatment of time parallels that of space and need not be quoted. Time, like space, is a form of perception, not a thing perceived. Just as phenomena are spread out in space, above or below, near or far, to the right or the left, so likewise are they ordered in time, before, after, or simultaneous with other events. Anything experienced as spatial is thought of as belonging to the outer world, but temporal order applies to one's psychological acts of apprehension. Hence time is "the form of inner sense, that is, of our awareness of ourselves and our own inner states." But both space and time are necessary forms of human perception, and cannot be ascribed to objects in themselves apart from experience.]

6. [How the Categories of the Understanding Unify and Organize Our Experience]

Among the many strands from which the complicated web of human knowledge is woven there are some which are destined from the start to be used abstractly and to continue independent of experience. The claims made for these ideas generally require special demonstration (deduction). Their legitimacy is not established by a deduction based on experience, even though we do want to know how these ideas can refer to objects within one's experience, and yet be derived apart from it. The explanation of the way abstract and prior ideas refer to objects is to be called *formal deduction*. This is distinguished from *empirical deduction*, which shows how an idea is derived by reflection from experience. *Empirical deduction* applies not to the legitimacy of the use of the ideas but to the facts from which they arise.

Without doubt an investigation of the functioning of man's power to know, beginning with single perceptions and climbing to general ideas, is useful. We have to thank the celebrated John Locke for opening up this avenue. The deduction of pure ideas is not, however, to be achieved along these lines; it is to be worked out in another direction. Their future use, independent of experience, requires for them a very particular birth certificate, in which descent from experience is denied. Locke's attempted

psychological derivation is not deduction at all, because it depends on matters of fact. It is rather an explanation of the possession of pure knowledge. It is clear, therefore, that only a formal deduction of pure ideas is usable and that empirical deductions will not do.

Our entire investigation of the formal deduction of pure ideas should be based on this principle: Pure ideas are the abstract and prior conditions of experience. They supply the objective ground of experience and are, accordingly, necessary. To know how they occur, the abstract and prior conditions necessary to experience must be discovered and kept separate from knowledge derived from experience. The categories are pure ideas which express the formal and objective conditions of experience with sufficient generality and which contain the pure thought involved in every experience. It is really a sufficient deduction of the categories and a justification of their objective validity to prove that no object is conceivable without them.

The famous John Locke, lacking these considerations and having come across pure ideas in the course of experience, proceeded to derive them from experience itself. Then, inconsistently, he went far beyond the bounds of experience in studies of knowledge. David Hume saw that to do this, ideas from pure origins are needed. He could not explain, however, how it was that ideas, disconnected in one's mind, came together in some object of thought. It never occurred to him that mind itself might be the author of the experience of its object.

So he, too, was led to derive pure ideas from experience, or habit, i.e., from a subjective necessity begotten of frequent associations of experiences. This finally came to be accepted as objective, but falsely so. Subsequently Hume explained, and quite consistently this time, that with ideas so derived and with their attendant principles, it is not possible to get beyond personal experience. The deduction of pure ideas from experience, as practiced by

Locke and Hume, cannot be reconciled with the abstract and prior knowledge encountered in pure mathematics and natural science. It is therefore refuted by the facts.

The first of these men left the door wide open to fantasy. It is hard to keep reasoning within due bounds once it has had unlimited prestige. The second gave in entirely to skepticism because he believed he had found in the knowing process an illusion which generally passed as reasonable. We now turn to study whether or not reasoning can be steered between these two cliffs, its limits indicated, and still keep its proper field of function open.

If every perception or idea were isolated from every other, there could be no knowledge as we know it, because knowledge consists of perceptions and ideas conjoined and compared to each other. Since the senses cover a whole field of awareness, they need a synopsis corresponding to the organization that makes knowledge possible when mind spontaneously comprehends sense data. Spontaneity is the beginning of a threefold organization which is necessary to every kind of knowledge. It consists of (1) *comprehension,* in which awareness is made into perception by ideas; (2) imagination in the *recollection* of the various elements necessary to knowledge; (3) *recognition* of the resultant ideas. Thus we have three inner sources of knowledge which make understanding and its empirical product, experience, possible.

However ideas or images arise, whether from the influence of external things or inner causes, or abstractly, or empirically as phenomena, they belong to man's inner sense because they are simply modifications of mind. All knowledge is, accordingly, subject to the formal condition of inner sense, namely, time. Everything is arranged, connected, and related by time. This general remark is fundamental to all subsequent discussion.

Generally speaking, awareness means being aware of many things at once, and this could not be imagined if time were not marked in the mind by a succession of impressions. In any given instant each impression is an absolute unity by itself; so, in order to get unity in awareness (as the idea of space requires), it is first necessary to let the various elements of awareness run in succession through the mind and then pull them together. This is the act which I call the organization of apprehension, or understanding. It is applied directly to awareness, which actually is multiple and so requires organization if it is to be unified or comprehended by means of a single idea.

The synthesis, or organization of understanding must be carried out abstractly and in advance, since ideas which are not empirical are involved. The ideas of space and time would be impossible without it; the many elements of sense data must be organized before they appear. This is how the pure organization of understanding is accomplished.

Again, it is apparent that if I draw an imaginary line, or consider the time lapse from one noon to the next, or even think of a certain number, I must begin by getting a general idea of the aggregates or sets of perceptions involved. If I were to lose from thought the antecedent part of either of them, say the first part of the line, the first hours of the day, or the digits preceding my number, and if I were unable to reproduce the lost parts as I went on, then no general idea of either of these sets would be possible to me. Neither could I, in that case, have the foregoing thoughts of even the first and purest ideas of space and time.

The organization of understanding is inseparably connected with recollection. Since the former is the formal basis of all knowledge, both empirical and pure, the organization of recollection by imagination belongs to the formal activity of mind and is here to be called *formal imagination.*

Again, if I were not aware that what I now think is the same as what I was thinking a moment ago, recollection of a lost step in a series of perceptions would be useless. Each perception in its place would be new, and not part of the action that made the series. A series of experiences could never be complete because it would lack the unity which only consciousness can give it. When I count, if I forget how the series of numbers now in my thought has been added up, one by one, I can never understand how the final sum is produced. The sum is a concept which depends on my consciousness of the organized unity of the number series.

The very word "idea" could have been the occasion of these remarks; consciousness gathers up the items in a series or a field, one by one, then recollection pulls them all together in a single idea. The consciousness involved may be so weak that it is felt, not in the act or process of production but only in the final idea. Nevertheless, even though it is not very clear, consciousness must always be there. Without it, ideas and all knowledge of objects would be impossible. . . .

If it is desired to follow up the inward connections among perceptions to their point of convergence, where they are unified as experience requires, we must begin with pure self-consciousness. Awareness amounts to nothing until it merges into consciousness, directly or indirectly. If this did not happen there would be no knowledge. Among all the perceptions of a given moment, we are conscious, abstractly and in advance, of our own identity. This is how any perception becomes possible, and it is a firm principle which may be called the formal principle of unity in one's perception of a field of sense data.

This unity, however, presupposes or involves an organization which is as necessary to knowledge and as prior and abstract as the unity itself. Unification depends on pure imagination to organize a field of perceptions into knowledge. Such an organization is said to be formal if, ignoring differences of awareness, it effects only the necessary unification of the field. The unity involved is also formal when it refers only to the original unity of self and thus becomes prior and necessary. Formal and organizing imagination is thus the pure

form of knowledge by means of which—both abstractly and in advance—objects of experience become known.

Understanding is the self at work in imagination, unifying and organizing experience; pure understanding is the self at work when imagination effects a formal organization. Understanding, therefore, involves pure, abstract forms for knowledge, which carry the unity the imagination uses to organize the data or experience into phenomena. These forms are the categories; that is, they are the mind's pure conceptions, or ideas. This then is how man learns from experience: Mind focuses on objects of sense by its own necessity, via awareness and by means of an organizing imagination; then phenomena, the data of experience, conform to mind; by means of the categories, pure mind constitutes a formal and organizing principle of experience, and this shows how, necessarily, phenomena are related to mind. . . .

Imagination, therefore, is man's prior and necessary capacity to organize things, and this makes us call it *productive imagination*. If imagination effects only necessary unity in the organization of phenomena, it can be called formal. The foregoing may appear strange, but it must be clear by now that the affinity, the association of phenomena and their recollection according to law, which is to say the whole of human experience, is made possible by formal imagination. Without this, ideas of objects could never foregather in a single experience.

It is permanent and unchanging "I" (pure apperception) that correlates perceptions when we become conscious of them. All consciousness belongs to one all-embracing pure apperception, "I," as sense awareness, belongs to one pure inner awareness, namely, time. So that this "I" may function mentally, imagination is added and the organization effected by imagination, though of itself prior and necessary, is carried out in the senses. Phenomena are connected in a field of impressions only as they appear in awareness: for example, a triangle. When the field is once related to the "I," ideas of it fit into the mind, and imagination relates them to sense awareness.

Pure imagination is therefore a fundamental operation of the soul, and abstractly, in advance, all knowledge depends on it. It connects all that one is aware of with the unitary "I." It brings the two extremes of sense and mind together. Without it, the senses might report phenomena but not empirical knowledge, and so experience would be impossible. Real experience comes of apprehension, association, and recognition of phenomena and contains the ultimate and highest ideas, the ideas that formally unify experience and validate empirical knowledge objectively. These ideas constitute the basis on which a field of sense data is recognized. If they concern only the form of experience, they are, accordingly, categories. The whole formal unity of recognition by means of imagination depends on the categories, and in turn the whole empirical use of the categories (in recognition, recollection, association, and apprehension), even down to phenomena, depends on imagination. These four elements of knowing make it possible for a phenomenon to belong to our consciousness and so to ourselves.

It is we who bring order and regularity to phenomena and call the result "nature." These properties would not be discovered in nature if our own minds had not first put them there; for unity in nature means a prior, necessary, and certain connection of phenomena. How indeed could organized unity in nature be conceived in advance, if the original source of knowledge, the inner core of our minds, did not first contain it? What would there be to see if this mental condition of ours were not objectively valid, valid because it is the condition by which objects become part of experience?

7. [Phenomena and Noumena]

We have now explored the land of pure reasoning and carefully surveyed every part of it. We have measured its extent and put everything in its right place. It is an island, by nature enclosed within unchangeable limits. It is the land of truth (enchanting name!) surrounded by a wide and stormy ocean, the native home of illusion, where cloud banks and icebergs falsely prophesy new lands and incessantly deceive adventurous seafarers with empty hopes, engaging them in romantic pursuits which they can neither abandon nor fulfill. Before we venture on this sea, we ought to glance at the map of the island and consider whether or not to be satisfied with it, lest there be no other territory on which to settle. We should know what title we have to it, by which we may be secure against opposing claims.

We have seen that the produce of mind is not borrowed from experience but is for use only in experience. The mind's principles may be either abstract and constitutive, like mathematical principles, or merely regulative, like dynamic principles. In either case they contain nothing but the pure schema of possible experience. Unity comes into experience from the organizing unity of mind, which the mind confers on self-consciousness via imagination; and phenomena, as the data of possible experience, must fit into that unity abstractly and in advance. These rules of mind not only are true but also are the source of all truth, the reason for the agreement of our knowledge with objects. They contain the basis on which experience is possible, that is, experience viewed as the sum of one's knowledge of objects. We are not, however, satisfied with an exposition merely of what is true; we want also to know what mankind otherwise wants to know. This long, critical inquiry would hardly seem worthwhile if at the end of it, we have learned only what would have gone on anyway in everyday mental operations.

Even if our minds do work satisfactorily without such an inquiry as this, the inquiry has one advantage. The mind that is in us is unable to determine for itself the limits of its own uses. That is why the deep inquiry we have set up is required. If we cannot decide whether certain questions lie within our mental horizon, we must be prepared for getting lost among the delusions that result from overstepping our limitations.

If we can know certainly whether the mind can use its principles only within experience and never purely formally, this knowledge will have important consequences. The formal use of an idea is its application to things in general and to entities for which we have no sense data; the empirical use of an idea is its application to phenomena, or to objects of possible experience. It is evident that only the latter application is practicable. For example, consider the ideas of mathematics, first, as pure awareness: space has three dimensions; there can be but one straight line between two points; etc. Although these principles are generated abstractly in the mind, they would mean nothing if their meaning could not be demonstrated in phenomena. It is therefore required that a pure idea be made sensible, that is, that one should or can be aware of an object corresponding to it. Otherwise, the idea, we say, would make no sense, i.e., it would be meaningless.

The mathematician meets this need by the construction of a figure which is, to the senses, a phenomenon, even though abstractly produced. In the same science, the idea of size finds its meaning and support in number, whether by fingers, or abacus beads, or in strokes and points on the printed page. The idea is always abstractly conceived, as are the amplifying principles and formulas derived from them; but finally, their use and their relation to their indicated objects appear only in experience, even though they contain the formal conditions of the possibility of that experience.

That this is the case with all the categories and, the principles spun out of them, appears as follows. We cannot really define the categories, or make the possibility of their objects intelligible, without descending at once to the conditions of sense and the forms of phenomena, to which, as their

only objects, the categories must be limited. If this condition is removed, all meaning, all relation to an object disappears, and no example will make the meaning of such an idea comprehensible. ...

If *noumenon* means something which is not an object of sense and so is abstracted from awareness, this is the negative sense of the term. If, however, it means an object of nonsensible awareness, we presuppose a special kind of awareness, which is purely mental, not part of our equipment, and of which we cannot imagine even the possibility. That would be *noumenon* in the positive sense of the word. ...

The division of objects into phenomena and noumena, and the world into a world of the senses and a world of mind, is not admissible in the positive sense, even though the division of ideas as sensible and mental is legitimate. For we cannot conceive a mind which knows objects, not discursively or through categories, but by a nonsensible awareness. What mind acquires through the idea of noumenon is a negative extension. It is not then limited by sense but rather, it limits sense by applying the term "noumena" to things-themselves, which are not phenomena. It also limits itself, since noumena are not to be known by means of categories. They can be thought of only as unknown somethings.

8. [God, Freedom, and Immortality]

God, freedom, and the immortality of the soul are the problems to the solution of which all the labors of metaphysics are directed. It used to be believed that the doctrine of freedom was necessary only as a negative condition of practical philosophy, and that the ideas of God and the soul belonged to theoretical philosophy; they had to be demonstrated separately. Religion was achieved subsequently by adding morality to these ideas.

It soon appears, however, that such an attempt must miscarry. It is absolutely impossible to conceive an original Being whose characteristics make him experienceable, and therefore knowable, if one starts with only simple, abstract, ontological ideas. Neither would an idea based on the experience of physical appropriateness in nature adequately demonstrate morality or acquaintance with God. Just as little would knowledge of the soul, acquired from experience in this life, provide an idea of the soul's spiritual, immortal nature, adequate to morality. Neither theology nor spiritualism can be established by empirical data. They deal with matters that transcend human knowledge. Ideas of God and the immortal soul can be defined only by predicates drawn from supersensible sources, predicates whose reality is demonstrated by experience. This is the only way a supersensible Being can be known.

The freedom of man under moral law conjoined with the final end which freedom prescribes by means of the moral law compose the only predicate of this kind. This combination of ideas contains the conditions necessary to the possibility of both God and man. An inference can then be made to the actuality and the nature of God and the soul, both of which would otherwise be entirely hidden from us.

Theoretical proofs of God and immortality fail because natural ideas tell us nothing about supersensible matters. Proofs via morality and freedom do succeed because there is causality in these ideas and their roots are supersensible. The causal law of freedom here establishes its own actuality by the way men behave. It also provides means of knowing other supersensible objects, such as the final moral end and its practicability. The conception of freedom's causality is, of course, based on practical considerations, but that happens to be all religion needs.

It is remarkable that of the three pure, rational ideas—God, freedom, and immortality—whose objects are supersensible, freedom alone proves its objective reality in the world of nature by what it can effect there. Freedom, therefore, makes possible the connection of the other two ideas with nature and of all three with religion. We may thus conceive the supersensible realm within man and around him, so that it becomes practical knowledge. Speculative philosophy, which offers only a negative idea even of freedom itself, can never accomplish anything like this. The idea of freedom, fundamental to unconditioned practical law, reaches beyond the limits within which natural, theoretical ideas remain hopelessly restricted.

COMMENT

Impressions and Ideas

The supreme advocate of the skeptical spirit is David Hume. He is a member of the sequence of classic British empiricists, which includes such great figures as Bacon, Hobbes, Locke, Berkeley, and Mill. More consistent in his empiricism than his predecessors, Hume pushed the skeptical implications of this approach to its logical extreme. Many philosophers have tried to refute his arguments, but his influence continues to be immense.

A thorough empiricist, Hume traced all knowledge back to some original basis in experience. The stream of experience, he pointed out, is made up of *perceptions,* a term he employed to designate any mental content whatever. He divided perceptions into *impressions;* the original sensations or feelings, and *ideas,* the images, copies, or representations of these originals. It is important to note that Hume, unlike Locke and Berkeley, reserved the word *idea* for mental copies, or representations of original data.

Hume's practice of tracing ideas back to their original impressions becomes a *logical test* of the soundness of concepts. If a concept, such as that of substance, cannot be traced back to some reliable basis in impressions, it immediately becomes suspect. A fertile source of confusion in our thinking is the tendency to impute to outer things the qualities that belong to internal impressions. Thus an internal feeling of necessity may be falsely imputed to some outer chain of events. The human mind, if it does not carefully analyze the sources of its ideas, is prone to fall into such errors. Hume's philosophy consists largely in exposing these pitfalls in our thinking.

Criticism of the Idea of Causation

The most famous example of this critical method is Hume's analysis of the idea of causation. He began by pointing out that this idea is extremely crucial in our thinking. "The only connection or relation of objects," he declared, "which can lead us beyond the immediate impressions of our memory and senses, is that of cause and effect; and that because it is the only one on which we can found a just inference from one object to another."[1] We infer external objects only because we suppose them to be the causes of the immediate data of experience. The idea of causation is thus the basis of empirical science and the ultimate ground for belief in an external world. For Hume, scientific knowledge as a whole stands or falls according to whether causation can be validated as a principle of reasoning.

Upon analysis, the idea of causation breaks up into four notions: (1) *succession*, (2) *contiguity*, (3) *constant conjunction*, and (4) *necessary connection*. Hume maintained that the first three notions can be defended—we can verify them by recalling the original sensory impressions from which they are derived. However, *necessity* cannot thus be verified—try as we may, we cannot trace it back to any sensory impressions. It turns out, therefore, to be a confused and illegitimate notion. An analysis of the details of his argument will not be given since this exercise in analysis is excellent practice for students.

Skeptical Implications

Hume was quick to draw the consequences from his theory of causation. One implication is that our commonsense idea that the future will resemble the past is merely an assumption, an expectation begotten by habit, not a rational conviction. Since we never discover an objective necessity binding effect to cause, we have no reason to assume that this cause-and-effect relation must continue to hold. The sun has risen many times, but this does not mean that it will rise tomorrow. There is no "law" that the sun must rise: There is only inexplicable repetition.

One of the most significant applications of Hume's analysis of causation is his attack on the arguments for an external world. Both Locke and Berkeley, whose arguments Hume had primarily in mind, inferred the existence of an external world on the basis of a theory of causation. They reasoned that the regular

---

[1] *An Enquiry Concerning Human Understanding*, ed. L. A. Selby-Bigge (Oxford: Clarendon Press, 1902), p. 89.

character of experience, which is largely determined for us independently of our wills, must have some external cause. Locke found the cause in material substances and primary qualities; Berkeley, in God and the ideas that God imprints on our minds. Now Hume, in attack, went to the nerve of the argument and maintained that we are not justified in employing the idea of cause in this way.

> The only conclusion we can draw from the existence of one thing to that of another is by means of the relation of cause and effect, which shows that there is a connection betwixt them, and that the existence of one is dependent on that of the other. ... But as no beings are ever present to the mind but perceptions, it follows that we may observe a conjunction or a relation of cause and effect between different perceptions, but can never observe it between perceptions and objects. 'Tis impossible, therefore, that from the existence of any of the qualities of the former, we can ever form any conclusion concerning the existence of the latter. ...[2]

What emerges from this devastating criticism? If we are resolved thus to stay within the closed circle of experience, we can either accept our perceptions as the ultimate character of existence or say that there may be something more—*some* kind of external world—but that we cannot know what something more is. There is little basis here for positive belief.

A final twist to Hume's skepticism is his denial of a substantial self. Just as Berkeley rejected Locke's doctrine of material substance, so Hume for similar reasons rejected Berkeley's doctrine of a mental substance. He denied that we ever have an *impression* of a self, and in the absence of any such impression, he saw no way of proving that a self exists. All the content of experience is fleeting, evanescent, whereas the self is supposed to be identical through succeeding states. Impressions, being variable and evanescent, are incapable of revealing a permanent self; and to *infer* an unexperienced self as the necessary cause of our mental states is to project illegitimately the relation of cause and effect, which is through experiential, beyond the circle of experience.

Hume thus reduced reality, as far as it can be verified, to a stream of "perceptions" neither caused nor sustained by any mental or material substance. Existence is made up of mental facts, perceptions, with no selves, to which the perceptions belong and no material world in which they reside.

How Kant Differed from Hume

Kant was struck, as Hume himself had been struck, by the largely negative results of Hume's inquiry. "I am ... affrighted and confounded with the forlorn solitude in which I am placed by my philosophy," Hume confessed, "and fancy myself some strange uncouth monster, utterly abandoned and disconsolate." The effect of Hume's skepticism on Kant was different—not to fill his mind with fright and confusion, but to awaken him from his "dogmatic slumber." Hume convinced Kant

---

[2] *A Treatise of Human Nature*, ed. L. A. Selby-Bigge (Oxford: Clarendon Press, 1896), p. 212.

that traditional metaphysics was bankrupt and that a new start was necessary. However, Kant was also convinced that there must be something fundamentally wrong with an empiricism that led to such devastating conclusions. He was not content to fall back on "natural instinct" but sought some kind of rationale for his trust in science and his moral and religious convictions. The task that he set himself, in the words of one of his contemporaries, was "to limit Hume's scepticism on the one hand, and the old dogmatism on the other, and to refute and destroy materialism, fatalism, atheism, as well as sentimentalism and superstition."

In *The Critique of Pure Reason*, Kant undertook to prove that all genuine scientific knowledge, whether in mathematics or in the natural sciences, is universally valid, but that speculative metaphysics, which seeks to go beyond experience to determine the ultimate and absolute nature of things, cannot be established on any sound and dependable basis. Science is reliable because it deals with *phenomena*—things as they *appear* in human experiences—but metaphysics is unreliable because it tries to interpret *noumena*— things as they are in themselves, apart from experience. The world of ultimate reality, in contrast to the world of appearance, can never be known to reason. The noumenal realities must be interpreted, if at all by moral conviction and religious faith—not by science or pure theoretical philosophy.

The phenomena, Kant insisted, exhibit spatial and temporal forms of rational connections, such as cause and effect. In grasping these forms and connections, consciousness is an awareness of meanings—not passive contemplation but active judgment, not mere perception but synthetic interpretation. We can never know things as they are apart from these synthetic modes of apprehension and judgment, which are the necessary conditions of all human experience. To interpret *ultimate* reality as either finite or infinite, one or many, mechanistic or teleological, mental or material, is to attempt to probe the supersensible nature of existence—and this human reason can never do. However, if the positive claims of transcendent metaphysics are thus overthrown, so are its negative claims. The metaphysician is as powerless to *disprove* the existence of God as to prove His existence, or to *disprove* an idealistic account of reality as to prove it. When the overweening claims of "pure reason" are thus refuted, our "practical reason" is no longer inhibited by atheism, materialism, or mechanistic determinism.

To sum up Kant's answer to Hume's skepticism, Kant tries to make secure the foundations of natural science by demonstrating that the order and regularity necessary to science—the sensory forms of space and time and the intelligible order of substance, causation, and the other "categories"—inhere necessarily in phenomena because they are contributed by the mind in the very act of knowing (knowledge being a joint product of mind and things-in-themselves). To Hume's reduction of the mind to a succession of awarenesses, Kant opposes the mind's awareness of succession, which he says is unaccountable without more synthesis and continuity than Hume recognized. Although he agrees with Hume that the doctrines of speculative metaphysics cannot be demonstrated, he tries to justify the ideas of God, freedom, and immortality on moral grounds.

Here, again, it should prove useful to ask how Hume and Kant would differ from the rationalists, as well as from each other, over the kind of knowledge involved in the case study introduced at the outset of this part. Is there a difference between how Gary Kasparov and Deep Blue do their "thinking"? Can the computer be said to rely on sensory perception? What sort of inferential reasoning is operative in the game of chess? How does the question of causation enter into our understanding of such reasoning?

3

COMMON SENSE

THOMAS REID (1710–1796)

Thomas Reid was born and raised in Scotland to a family with a strong religious heritage. His father was a Presbyterian minister and Reid himself became a minister as well. During his youth, he was a librarian while studying mathematics and physics. After serving as a pastor for fifteen years, during which time he studied philosophy on his own, he was appointed to a professorship at King's College in Aberdeen. Reid began as a follower of Bishop (of Cloyne) Berkeley's philosophy, but like Immanuel Kant, was jolted by his reading of David Hume's *Treatise of Human Nature*. In 1764 Reid succeeded Adam Smith as professor of moral philosophy at the University of Glasgow and published his own *Inquiry* in which he attacks both rationalism and empiricism in the name of common sense. During the last years of his life, he published several important essays. After having been nearly eclipsed by the philosophies of Descartes, Hume, and Kant, as well as their twentieth-century followers, Reid's thought has recently undergone something of a revival.

AN INQUIRY INTO THE HUMAN MIND

... Upon the whole, it appears that our philosophers have imposed upon themselves and upon us, in pretending to deduce from sensation the first origin of our notions of external existences, of space, motion, and extension, and all the primary qualities of body that is, the qualities whereof we have the most clear and distinct conception. These qualities do not at all tally with any system of the human faculties that hath been advanced. They have no resemblance to any sensation, or to any operation of our minds; and, therefore, they cannot be ideas either of sensation or of reflection. The very conception of them is irreconcilable to the principles of all our philosophic systems of the understanding. The belief of them is no less so.

Section VII: Of the Existence of a Material World

It is beyond our power to say when, or in what order, we came by our notions of these qualities. When we trace the operations of our minds as far back as memory

Reprinted by permission of the publishers from *Thomas Reid's Inquiry and Essays*, ed. Ronald Beanblossom and Keith Lehrer, (Indianapolis: Hackett Publishing Company, 1983).

and reflection can carry us, we find them already in possession of our imagination and belief, and quite familiar to the mind: but how they came first into its acquaintance, or what has given them so strong a hold of our belief, and what regard they deserve, are, no doubt, very important questions in the philosophy of human nature.

Shall we, with the Bishop of Cloyne, serve them with a *quo warranto*, and have them tried at the bar of philosophy, upon the statute of the ideal system? Indeed, in this trial they seem to have come off very pitifully; for, although they had very able counsel, learned in the law—viz., Des Cartes, Malebranche, and Locke, who said everything they could for their clients—the Bishop of Cloyne, believing them to be aiders and abetters of heresy and schism, prosecuted them with great vigour, fully answered all that had been pleaded in their defense, and silenced their ablest advocates, who seem, for half a century past, to decline the argument, and to trust to the favour of the jury rather than to the strength of their pleadings.

Thus, the wisdom of *philosophy* is set in opposition to the *common sense* of mankind. The first pretends to demonstrate, *a priori*, that there can be no such thing as a material world; that sun, moon, stars, and earth, vegetable and animal bodies, are, and can be nothing else, but sensations in the mind, or images of those sensations in the memory and imagination; that, like pain and joy, they can have no existence when they are not thought of. The last can conceive no otherwise of this opinion, than as a kind of metaphysical lunacy, and concludes that too much learning is apt to make men mad; and that the man who seriously entertains this belief, though in other respects he may be a very good man, as a man may be who believes that he is made of glass; yet, surely he bath a soft place in his understanding, and hath been hurt by much thinking.

This opposition betwixt philosophy and common sense, is apt to have a very unhappy influence upon the philosopher himself. He sees human nature in an odd, unamiable, and mortifying light. He considers himself, and the rest of his species, as born under a necessity of believing ten thousand absurdities and contradictions, and endowed with such a pittance of reason as is just sufficient to make this unhappy discovery: and this is all the fruit of his profound speculations. Such notions of human nature tend to slacken every nerve of the soul, to put every noble purpose and sentiment out of countenance, and spread a melancholy gloom over the whole face of things.

If this is wisdom, let me be deluded with the vulgar. I find something within me that recoils against it, and inspires more reverent sentiments of the human kind, and of the universal administration. Common Sense and Reason have both one author; that Almighty Author in all whose other works we observe a consistency, uniformity, and beauty which charm and delight the understanding: there must, therefore, be some order and consistency in the human faculties, as well as in other parts of his workmanship. A man that thinks reverently of his own kind, and esteems true wisdom and philosophy, will not be fond, nay, will be very suspicious, of such strange and paradoxical opinions. If they are false, they disgrace philosophy; and, if they are true, they degrade the human species, and make us justly ashamed of our frame.

To what purpose is it for philosophy to decide against common sense in this or any other matter? The belief of a material world is older, and of more authority, than any principles of philosophy. It declines the tribunal of reason, and laughs at all the artillery of the logician. It retains its sovereign authority in spite of all the edicts of philosophy, and reason itself must stoop to its orders. Even those philosophers who have disowned the authority of our notions of an external material world, confess that they find themselves under a necessity of submitting to their power.

Methinks, therefore, it were better to make a virtue of necessity; and, since we cannot get rid of the vulgar notion and belief of an external world, to reconcile our reason to it as well as we can; for, if Reason should stomach and fret ever so much at this yoke, she cannot throw it off; if she will not be the servant of Common Sense, she must be her slave.

In order, therefore, to reconcile Reason to Common Sense in this matter, I beg leave to offer to the consideration of philosophers these two observations. First, that, in all this debate about the existence of a material world, it hath been taken for granted on both sides, that this same material world, if any such there be, must be the express image of our sensations; that we can have no conception of any material thing which is not like some sensation in our minds; and particularly that the sensations of touch are images of extension, hardness, figure, and motion. Every argument brought again: the existence of a material world, either by the Bishop of Cloyne, or by the author of the "Treatise of Human Nature," supposeth this. If this is true, their arguments are conclusive and unanswerable; but, on the other hand, if it is not true, there is no shadow of argument left. Have those philosophers, then, given any solid proof of this hypothesis, upon which the whole weight of so strange a system rests? No. They have not so much as attempted to do it. But, because ancient and modern philosophers have agreed in this opinion, they have taken it for granted. But let us, as becomes philosophers, lay aside authority; we need not, surely, consult Aristotle or Locke, to know whether pain be like the point of a sword. I have as clear a conception of extension, hardness, and motion, as I have of the point of a sword; and, with some pains and practice, I can form as clear a notion of the other sensations of touch as I have of pain. When I do so, and compare them together, it appears to me clear as daylight, that the former are not of kin to the latter, nor resemble them in any one feature. They are as unlike, yea as certainly and manifestly unlike, as pain is to the point of a sword. It

may be true, that those sensations first introduced the material world to our acquaintance; it may be true that it seldom or never appears without their company; but, for all that, they are as unlike as the passion of anger is to those features of the countenance which attend it.

So that, in the sentence those philosophers have passed against the material world, there is an *error personae*. Their proof touches not matter, or any of its qualities; but strikes directly against an idol of their own imagination, a material world made of ideas and sensations, which never had, nor can have an existence.

Secondly, the very existence of our conceptions of extension, figure, and motion, since they are neither ideas of sensation nor reflection, overturns the whole ideal system, by which the material world hath been tried and condemned; so that there hath been likewise in this sentence an *error juris*.

It is a very fine and a just observation of Locke, that, as no human art can create a single particle of matter, and the whole extent of our power over the material world consists in compounding, combining, and disjoining the matter made to our hands; so, in the world of thought, the materials are all made by nature, and can only be variously combined and disjoined by us. So that it is impossible for reason or prejudice, true or false philosophy, to produce one simple notion or conception, which is not the work of nature, and the result of our constitution. The conception of extension, motion, and the other attributes of matter, cannot be the effect of error or prejudice; it must be the work of nature. And the power or faculty by which we acquire those conceptions, must be something different from any power of the human mind that bath been explained, since it is neither sensation nor reflection.

This I would, therefore, humbly propose, as an *experimentum crucis*, by which the ideal system must stand or fall; and it brings the matter to a short issue: Extension, figure, motion, may any one, or all of them, be taken for the subject of this experiment. Either they are ideas of sensation, or they are not. If any one of them can be shewn to be an idea of sensation, or to have the least resemblance to any sensation, I lay my hand upon my mouth, and give up all pretence to reconcile reason to common sense in this matter, and must suffer the ideal scepticism to triumph. But if, on the other hand, they are not ideas of sensation, nor like to any sensation, then the ideal system is a rope of Sand, and all the laboured arguments of the sceptical philosophy against a material world, and against the existence of every thing but impressions and ideas, proceed upon a false hypothesis. ...

Bishop Berkeley hath proved, beyond the possibility of reply, that we cannot by reasoning infer the existence of matter from our sensations: and the author of the "Treatise of Human Nature" hath proved no less clearly, that we cannot by reasoning infer the existence of our own or other minds from our sensations. But are we to admit nothing but what can be proved by reasoning? Then we must be sceptics indeed, and believe nothing at all. The author of the "Treatise of Human Nature" appears to me to be but a half-sceptic. He hath not followed his principles so far as they lead him; but, after having, with unparalleled intrepidity and success, combated vulgar prejudices, when he had but one blow to strike, his courage fails him, he fairly lays down his arms, and yields himself a captive to the most common of all vulgar prejudice—I mean the belief of the existence of his own impressions and ideas.

I beg, therefore, to have the honour of making an addition to the sceptical system, without which I conceive it cannot hang together. I affirm, that the belief of the existence of impressions and ideas, is as little supported by reason, as that of the existence of minds and bodies. No man ever did or could offer any reason for this belief. Des Cartes took it for granted, that he thought, and had sensations and ideas; so have all his followers done. Even the hero of scepticism hath yielded this point, I

crave leave to say, weakly and imprudently. I say so, because I am persuaded that there is no principle of his philosophy that obliged him to make this concession. And what is there in impressions and ideas so formidable, that this all-conquering philosophy, after triumphing over every other existence, should pay homage to them? Besides, the concession is dangerous: for belief is of such a nature, that, if you leave any root, it will spread; and you may more easily pull it up altogether, than say, Hitherto shalt thou go and no further: the existence of impressions and ideas I give up to thee; but see thou pretend to nothing more. A thorough and consistent sceptic will never, therefore, yield this point; and while he holds it, you can never oblige him to yield anything else.

To such a sceptic I have nothing to say; but of the semisceptics, I should beg to know, why they believe the existence of their impressions and ideas. The true reason I take to be, because they cannot help it; and the same reason will lead them to believe many other things.

All reasoning must be from first principles; and for first principles no other reason can be given but this, that, by the constitution of our nature, we are under a necessity of assenting to them. Such principles are parts of our constitution, no less than the power of thinking: reason can neither make nor destroy them; nor can it do anything without them: it is like a telescope, which may help a man to see farther, who hath eyes; but, without eyes, a telescope shews nothing at all. A mathematician cannot prove the truth of his axioms, nor can he prove anything, unless he takes them for granted. We cannot prove the existence of our minds, nor even of our thoughts and sensations. A historian, or a witness, can prove nothing, unless it is taken for granted that the memory and senses may be trusted. A natural philosopher can prove nothing, unless it is taken for granted that the course of nature is steady and uniform.

How or when I got such first principles, upon which I build all my reasoning, I know not; for I had them before I can remember: but I am sure they are parts of my constitution, and that I cannot throw them off. That our thoughts and sensations must have a subject, which we call *ourself* is not therefore an opinion got by reasoning, but a natural principle. That our sensations of touch indicate something external, extended, figured, hard or soft, is not a deduction of reason, but a natural principle. The belief of it, and the very conception of it, are equally parts of our constitution. If we are deceived in it, we are deceived by Him that made us, and there is no remedy.

I do not mean to affirm, that the sensations of touch do, from the very first, suggest the same notions of body and its qualities which they do when we are grown up. Perhaps Nature is frugal in this, as in her other operations. The passion of love, with all its concomitant sentiments and desires, is naturally suggested by the perception of beauty in the other sex; yet the same perception does not suggest the tender passion till a certain period of life. A blow given to an infant, raises grief and lamentation; but when he grows up, it as naturally stirs resentment, and prompts him to resistance. Perhaps a child in the womb, or for some short period of its existence, is merely a sentient being; the faculties by which it perceives an external world, by which it reflects on its own thoughts, and existence, and relation to other things, as well as its reasoning and moral faculties, unfold themselves by degrees so that it is inspired with the various principles of common sense, as with the passions of love and resentment, when it has occasion for them.

Section VIII: Of the Systems of Philosophers Concerning the Senses

All the systems of philosophers about our senses and their objects have split upon this rock, of not distinguishing properly sensations which can have no existence but when they are felt, from the things suggested by them. Aristotle—with as distinguishing a head as ever applied to philosophical disquisitions—confounds these two; and makes every sensation to be the form, without the matter, of the thing perceived by it. As the impression of a seal upon wax has the form of the seal but nothing of the matter of it, so he conceived our sensations to be impressions upon the mind, which bear the image, likeness, or form of the external thing perceived, without the matter of it. Colour, sound, and smell, as well as extension, figure, and hardness, are, according to him, various forms of matter: our sensations are the same forms imprinted on the mind, and perceived in its own intellect. It is evident from this, that Aristotle made no distinction between primary and secondary qualities of bodies, although that distinction was made by Democritus, Epicurus, and others of the ancients.

Des Cartes, Malebranche, and Locke, revived the distinction between primary and secondary qualities; but they made the secondary qualities mere sensations, and the primary ones resemblances of our sensations. . . .

Bishop Berkeley gave new light to this subject, by shewing that the qualities of an inanimate thing, such as matter is conceived to be, cannot resemble any sensation; that it is impossible to conceive anything like the sensations of our minds, but the sensations of other minds. Every one that attends properly to his sensations must assent to this; yet it had escaped all the philosophers that came before Berkeley. . . .

But let us observe what use the Bishop makes of this important discovery. Why, he concludes, that we can have no conception of an inanimate substance, such as matter is conceived to be, or of any of its qualities; and that there is the strongest ground to believe that there is no existence in nature but minds, sensations, and ideas: if there is any other kind of existence, it must be what we neither have nor can have any conception of. But how does this follow? Why, thus: We can have no conception of anything but what resembles some sensation or idea in our minds; but the sensations and ideas in our minds can resemble nothing but the sensations and ideas in other minds; therefore, the conclusion is evident. This argument, we see, leans upon two propositions. The last of them the ingenious author hath, indeed, made evident to all that understand his reasoning, and can attend to their own sensations: but the first proposition he never attempts to prove; it is taken from the doctrine of ideas, which hath been so universally received by philosophers, that it was thought to need no proof.

We may here again observe, that this acute writer argues from a hypothesis against fact, and against the common sense of mankind. That we can have no conception of anything, unless there is some impression, sensation, or idea, in our minds which resembles it, is indeed an opinion which hath been very generally received among philosophers; but it is neither self-evident, nor hath it been clearly proved; and therefore it hath been more reasonable to call in question this doctrine of philosophers, than to discard the material world, and by that means expose philosophy to the ridicule of all men who will not offer up common sense as a sacrifice to metaphysics.

We ought, however, to do this justice both to the Bishop of Cloyne and to the author of the "Treatise of Human Nature," to acknowledge, that their conclusions are justly drawn from the doctrine of ideas, which has been so universally received. On the other hand, from the character of Bishop Berkeley, and of his predecessors, Des Cartes, Locke, and Malebranche, we may venture to say, that, if they had seen all the consequences of this doctrine, as clearly as the author before mentioned did, they would have suspected it vehemently, and examined it more carefully than they appear to have done.

The theory of ideas, like the Trojan horse, had a specious appearance both of innocence and beauty; but if those philosophers had known that it carried in its belly death and destruction to all science and common sense, they would not have broken down their walls to give it admittance.

That we have clear and distinct conceptions of extension, figure, motion, and other attributes of body, which are neither sensations, nor like any sensation, is a fact of which we may be as certain as that we have sensations. And that all mankind have a fixed belief of an external material world—a belief which is neither got by reasoning nor education, and a belief which we cannot shake off, even when we seem to have strong arguments against it and no shadow of argument for it—is likewise a fact, for which we have all the evidence that the nature of the thing admits. These facts are phenomena of human nature, from which we may justly argue against any hypothesis, however generally received. But to argue from a hypothesis against facts, is contrary to the rules of true philosophy. . . .

Section XX: Of Perception in General

Sensation, and the perception of external objects by the senses, though very different in their nature, have commonly been considered as one and the same thing. The purposes of common life do not make it necessary to distinguish them, and the received opinions of philosophers tend rather to confound them. But, without attending carefully to this distinction, it is impossible to have any just conception of the operations of our senses. The most simple operations of the mind, admit not of a logical definition: all we can do is to describe them, so as to lead those who are conscious of them in themselves, to attend to them, and reflect upon them; and it is often very difficult to describe them so as to answer this intention.

The same mode of expression is used to denote sensation and perception: and, therefore, we are apt to look upon them as things of the same nature. Thus, *I feel a pain; I see a tree:* the first denoteth a sensation, the last a perception. The grammatical analysis of both expressions is the same: for both consist of an active verb and an object. But, if we attend to the things signified by these expressions, we shall find that, in the first, the distinction between the act and the object is not real but grammatical: in the second, the distinction is not only grammatical but real.

The form of the expression, *I feel pain*, might seem to imply that the feeling is something distinct from the pain felt; yet, in reality, there is no distinction. As *thinking a thought* is an expression which could signify no more than *thinking*, so *feeling a pain* signifies no more than *being pained*. What we have said of pain is applicable to every other mere sensation. It is difficult to give instances, very few of our sensations having names; and, where they have, the name being common to the sensation, and to something else which is associated with it. But, when we attend to the sensation by itself, and separate it from other things which are conjoined with it in the imagination, it appears to be something which can have no existence but in a sentient mind, no distinction from the act of the mind by which it is felt.

Perception, as we here understand it, hath always an object distinct from the act by which it is perceived; an object which may exist whether it be perceived or not. I perceive a tree that grows before my window; there is here an object which is perceived, and an act of the mind by which it is perceived; and these two are not only distinguishable, but they are extremely unlike in their natures. The object is made up of a trunk, branches, and leaves; but the act of the mind by which it is perceived hath neither trunk, branches, nor leaves. I am conscious of this act of my mind, and I can reflect upon it; but it is too simple to admit of an analysis, and I cannot find proper words to describe it. I find nothing that resembles it so much as the remembrance of the tree, or the imagination of it. Yet both these differ essentially from perception; they differ likewise one from another. It is in

vain that a philosopher assures me, that the imagination of the tree, the remembrance of it, and the perception of it, are all one, and differ only in degree of vivacity. I know the contrary; for I am as well acquainted with all the three as I am with the apartments of my own house. I know this also, that the perception of an object implies both a conception of its form, and a belief of its present existence. I know, moreover, that this belief is not the effect of argumentation and reasoning; it is the immediate effect of my constitution.

I am aware that this belief which I have in perception stands exposed to the strongest batteries of scepticism. But they make no great impression upon it. The sceptic asks me, Why do you believe the existence of the external object which you perceive? This belief, sir, is none of my manufacture; it came from the mint of Nature; it bears her image and superscription; and, if it is not right, the fault is not mine: I even took it upon trust, and without suspicion. Reason, says the sceptic, is the only judge of truth, and you ought to throw off every opinion and every belief that is not grounded on reason. Why, sir, should I believe the faculty of reason more than that of perception?—they came both out of the same shop and were made by the same artist; and if he puts one piece of false ware into my hands, what should hinder him from putting another?

Perhaps the sceptic will agree to distrust reason, rather than give any credit to perception. For, says he, since, by your own concession, the object which you perceive, and that act of your mind by which you perceive it, are quite different things, the one may exist without the other; and, as the object may exist without being perceived, so the perception may exist without an object. There is nothing so shameful in a philosopher as to be deceived and deluded; and, therefore, you ought to resolve firmly to withhold assent, and to throw off this belief of external objects, which may be all delusion. For my part, I will never attempt to throw it off; and, although the sober part of mankind will not be very anxious to know my reasons, yet, if they can be of use to any sceptic, they are these:—

First, because it is not in my power: why, then, should I make a vain attempt? It would be agreeable to fly to the moon, and to make a visit to Jupiter and Saturn; but, when I know that Nature has bound me down by the law of gravitation to this planet which I inhabit, I rest contented, and quietly suffer myself to be carried along in its orbit. My belief is carried along by perception, as irresistibly as my body by the earth. And the greatest sceptic will find himself to be in the same condition. He may struggle hard to disbelieve the informations of his senses, as a man does to swim against a torrent; but, ah! it is in vain. It is in vain that he strains every nerve, and wrestles with nature, and with every object that strikes upon his senses. For, after all, when his strength is spent in the fruitless attempt, he will be carried down the torrent with the common herd of believers.

Secondly, I think it would not be prudent to throw off this belief, if it were in my power. If Nature intended to deceive me, and impose upon me by false appearances, and I, by my great cunning and profound logic, have discovered the imposture, prudence would dictate to me, in this case, even to put up [with] this indignity done me, as quietly as I could, and not to call her an impostor to her face, lest she should be even with me in another way. For what do I gain by resenting this injury? You ought at least not to believe what she says. This indeed seems reasonable, if she intends to impose upon me. But what is the consequence? I resolve not to believe my senses. I break my nose against a post that comes in my way; I step into a dirty kennel; and, after twenty such wise rational actions, I am taken up and clapped into a madhouse. Now, I confess I would rather make one of the credulous fools whom Nature imposes upon, than of those wise and rational philosophers who resolve to withhold assent at all this expense. If a man pretends

to be a sceptic with regard to the informations of sense, and yet prudently keeps out of harm's way as other men do, he must excuse my suspicion, that be either acts the hypocrite, or imposes upon himself. For, if the scale of his belief were so evenly poised as to lean no more to one side than to the contrary, it is impossible that his actions could be directed by any rules of common prudence.

Thirdly, although the two reasons already mentioned are perhaps two more than enough, I shall offer a third. I gave implicit belief to the informations of Nature by my senses, for a considerable part of my life, before I had learned so much logic as to be able to start a doubt concerning them. And now, when I reflect upon what is past, I do not find that I have been imposed upon by this belief. I find that without it I must have perished by a thousand accidents. I find that without it I should have been no wiser now than when I was born. I should not even have been able to acquire that logic which suggests these sceptical doubts with regard to my senses. Therefore, I consider this instinctive belief as one of the best gifts of Nature. I thank the Author of my being, who bestowed it upon me before the eyes of my reason were opened, and still bestows it upon me, to be my guide where reason leaves me in the dark. And now I yield to the direction of my senses, not from instinct only, but from confidence and trust in a faithful and beneficent Monitor, grounded upon the experience of his paternal care and goodness.

In all this I deal with the Author of my being, no otherwise than I thought it reasonable to deal with my parents and tutors, I believed by instinct whatever they told me, long before I had the idea of a lie, or thought of the possibility of their deceiving me. Afterwards, upon reflection, I found they had acted like fair and honest people, who wished me well. I found that, if I had not believed what they told me, before I could give a reason of my belief, I had to this day been little better than a changeling. And although this natural credulity hath sometimes occasioned my being imposed upon by deceivers, yet it hath been of infinite advantage to me upon the whole; therefore, I consider it as another good gift of Nature. And I continue to give that credit, from reflection, to those of whose integrity and veracity I have had experience, which before I gave from instinct.

There is a much greater similitude than is commonly imagined, between the testimony of nature given by our senses, and the testimony of men given by language. The credit we give to both is at first the effect of instinct only. When we grow up, and begin to reason about them, the credit given to human testimony is restrained and weakened, by the experience we have of deceit. But the credit given to the testimony of our senses, is established and confirmed by the uniformity and constancy of the laws of nature.

Our perceptions are of two kinds: some are natural and original; others acquired, and the fruit of experience. When I perceive that this is the taste of cyder, that of brandy; that this is the smell of an apple, that of an orange; that this is the noise of thunder, that the ringing of bells; this the sound of a coach passing, that the voice of such a friend; these perceptions, and others of the same kind, are not original—they are acquired. But the perception which I have, by touch, of the hardness and softness of bodies, of their extension, figure, and motion, is not acquired—it is original.

In all our senses, the acquired perceptions are many more than the original, especially in sight. By this sense we perceive originally the visible figure and colour of bodies only, and their visible place; but we learn to perceive by the eye, almost everything which we can perceive by touch. The original perceptions of this sense serve only as signs to introduce the acquired.

The signs by which objects are presented to us in perception, are the language of Nature to man: and as, in many respects, it hath great affinity with the language of man to man, so particularly in this, that both are partly natural and original, partly acquired by custom. Our original or natural perceptions are analogous to the natural language of man to man, of which we took notice in the fourth chapter; and our acquired perceptions are analogous to artificial language, which, in our mother tongue, is got very much in the same manner with our acquired perceptions—as we shall afterwards more fully explain. . . .

Perception ought not only to be distinguished from sensation, but likewise from that knowledge of the objects of sense which is got by reasoning. There is no reasoning in perception, as hath been observed. The belief which is implied in it, is the effect of instinct. But there are many things, with regard to sensible objects, which we can infer from what we perceive; and such conclusions of reason ought to be distinguished from what is merely perceived. When I look at the moon, I perceive her to be sometimes circular, sometimes horned, and sometimes gibbous. This is simple perception, and is the same in the philosopher and in the clown: but from these various appearances of her enlightened part, I infer that she is really of a spherical figure. This conclusion is not obtained by simple perception, but by reasoning. Simple perception has the same relation to the conclusions of reason drawn from our perceptions, as the axioms in mathematics have to the propositions. I cannot demonstrate that two quantities which are equal to the same quantity, are equal to each other; neither can I demonstrate that the tree which I perceive, exists. But, by the constitution of my nature, my belief is irresistibly carried along by my apprehension of the axiom; and, by the constitution of my nature, my belief is no less irresistibly carried along by my perception of the tree. All reasoning is from principles. The first principles of mathematical reasoning are mathematical axioms and definitions; and the first principles of all our reasoning about existences, are our perceptions. The first principles of every kind of reasoning are given us by Nature, and are of equal authority with the faculty of reason itself, which is also the gift of Nature. The conclusions of reason are all built upon first principles, and can have no other foundation. Most justly, therefore, do such principles disdain to be tried by reason and laugh at all the artillery of the logician, when it is directed against them.

When a long train of reasoning is necessary in demonstrating a mathematical proposition, it is easily distinguished from an axiom; and they seem to be things of a very different nature. But there are some propositions which lie so near to axioms, that it is difficult to say whether they ought to be held as axioms, or demonstrated as propositions. The same thing holds with regard to perception, and the conclusions drawn from it. Some of these conclusions follow our perceptions so easily, and are so immediately connected with them, that it is difficult to fix the limit which divides the one from the other. . . .

Section: XXIV: Of the Analogy between Perception and the Credit We Give to Human Testimony

The objects of human knowledge are innumerable; but the channels by which it is conveyed to the mind are few. Among these, the perception of external things by our senses, and the informations which we receive upon human testimony, are not the least considerable; and so remarkable is the analogy between these two, and the analogy between the principles of the mind which are subservient to the one and those which are subservient to the other, that, without further apology, we shall consider them together.

In the testimony of Nature given by the senses, as well as in human testimony given by language, things are signified to us by signs: and in one as well as the other, the mind, either by original principles or by custom, passes from the sign to the conception and belief of the things signified.

We have distinguished our perceptions into original and acquired; and language, into natural and artificial. Between acquired perception and artificial language, there is a great analogy; but still a greater between original perception and natural language.

The signs in original perception are sensations, of which Nature hath given us a great variety, suited to the variety of the things signified by them. Nature hath established a real connection between the signs and the things signified; and Nature hath also taught us the interpretation of the signs; so that, previous to experience, the sign suggests the thing signified, and creates the belief of it.

The signs in natural language are features of the face, gestures of the body, and modulations of the voice; the variety of which is suited to the variety of the things signified by them. Nature hath established a real connection between these signs, and the thoughts and dispositions of the mind which are signified by them; and Nature hath taught us the interpretation of these signs; so that, previous to experience, the signs suggest the thing signified, and create the belief of it.

A man in company, without doing good or evil, without uttering an articulate sound, may behave himself gracefully, civilly, politely; or, on the contrary, meanly, rudely, and impertinently. We see the dispositions of his mind by their natural signs in his countenance and behaviour, in the same manner as we perceive the figure and other qualities of bodies by the sensations which nature hath connected with them.

The signs in the natural language of the human countenance and behavior, as well as the signs in our original perceptions, have the same signification in all climates and in all nations; and the skill of interpreting them is not acquired, but innate.

In acquired perception the signs are either sensations, or things which we perceive by means of sensations. The connection between the sign and the thing signified, is established by nature; and we discover this connection by experience; but not without the aid of our original perceptions, or of those which we have already acquired. After this connection is discovered, the sign, in like manner as in original perception, always suggests the things signified, and creates the belief of it.

In artificial language, the signs are articulate sounds, whose connection with the things signified by them, is established by the will of men; and, in learning our mother tongue, we discover this connection by experience; but not without the aid of natural language, or of what we had before attained of artificial language. And, after this connection is discovered, the sign, as in natural language, always suggests the thing signified, and creates the belief of it.

Our original perceptions are few, compared with the acquired; but, without the former, we could not possibly attain the latter. In like manner, natural language is scanty, compared with artificial; but, without the former, we could not possibly attain the latter.

Our original perceptions, as well as the natural language of human features and gestures, must be resolved into particular principles of the human constitution. Thus, it is by one particular principle of our constitution that certain features express anger; and, by another particular principle, that certain features express benevolence. It is, in like manner, by one particular principle of our constitution that a certain sensation signifies hardness in the body which I handle; and it is by another particular principle that a certain sensation signifies motion in that body.

But our acquired perceptions, and the information we receive by means of artificial language, must be resolved into general principles of the human constitution. When a painter perceives that this picture is the work of Raphael, that the work of Titian; a jeweller, that this is a true diamond, that a counterfeit; a sailor, that this is a ship of five hundred ton, that of four hundred; these different acquired perceptions are produced by the same general principles of the human mind, which have a different operation in the same person according as they are variously applied, and in different persons according to the diversity of their education and manner of life. In like manner, when certain articulate sounds convey to my mind the knowledge of the battle of Pharsalia, and others, the knowledge of the battle of Poltowa—when a Frenchman and an Englishman receive the same information by different articulate sounds—the Signs used in these different cases, produce the knowledge and belief of the things signified, by means of the same general principles of the human constitution.

Now, if we compare the general principles of our constitution, which fit us for receiving information from our fellow-creatures by language, with the general principles which fit us for acquiring the perception of things by our senses, we shall find them to be very similar in their nature and manner of operation.

When we begin to learn our mother tongue, we perceive, by the help of natural language, that they who speak to us use certain sounds to express certain things. We imitate the same sounds when we would express the same things; and find that we are understood.

But here a difficulty occurs which merits our attention, because the solution of it leads to some original principles of the human mind, which are of great importance, and of very extensive influence. We know by experience that men have used such words to express such things; but all experience is of the past, and can, of itself, give no notion or belief of what is future. How come we, then, to believe, and to rely upon it with assurance, that men, who have it in their power to do otherwise, will continue to use the same words when they think the same things? Whence comes this knowledge and belief—this foresight, we ought rather to call it—of the future and voluntary actions of our fellow-creatures? Have they promised that they will never impose upon us by equivocation or falsehood? No, they have not. And, if they had, this would not solve the difficulty; for such promise must be expressed by words or by other signs; and, before we can rely upon it, we must be assured that they put the usual meaning upon the signs which express that promise. No man of common sense ever thought of taking a man's own word for his honesty; and it is evident that we take his veracity for granted when we lay any stress upon his word or promise. I might add, that this reliance upon the declarations and testimony of men is found in children long before they know what a promise is.

There is, therefore, in the human mind an early anticipation, neither derived from experience, nor from reason, nor from any compact or promise, that our fellow-creatures will use the same signs in language, when they have the same sentiments.

This is, in reality, a kind of prescience of human actions; and it seems to me to be an original principle of the human constitution, without which we should be incapable of language, and consequently incapable of instruction.

The wise and beneficent Author of Nature, who intended that we should be social creatures, and that we should receive the greatest and most important part of our knowledge by the information of others, hath, for these purposes, implanted in our natures two principles that tally with each other.

The first of these principles is, a propensity to speak truth, and to use the signs of language so as to convey our real sentiments. This principle has a powerful operation, even in the greatest liars; for where they lie once, they speak truth a hundred times. Truth is always uppermost, and is the natural issue of the mind: It requires no art or training, no inducement or temptation, but only that we yield to a natural impulse. Lying, on the contrary, is doing violence to our nature; and is never practised, even by the worst men, without some temptation. Speaking truth is like using our natural food; which we would do from appetite, although it answered no end; but lying is like taking physic, which is nauseous to the taste, and which no man takes but for some end which he cannot otherwise attain.

If it should be objected, That men may be influenced by moral or political considerations to speak truth, and, therefore, that their doing so is no proof of such an original principle as we have mentioned—I answer, First, That moral or political considerations can have no influence until we arrive at years of understanding and reflection; and it is certain, from experience, that children keep to truth invariably, before they are capable of being influenced by such considerations. Secondly, When we are influenced by moral or political considerations, we must be conscious of that influence, and capable of perceiving it upon reflection. Now, when I reflect upon my actions most attentively, I am not conscious that, in speaking truth, I am influenced on ordinary occasions by any motive, moral or political. I find that truth is always at the door of my lips, and goes forth spontaneously, if not held back. It requires neither good nor bad intention to bring it forth, but only that I be artless and undesigning. There may indeed be temptations to falsehood, which would be too strong for the natural principle of veracity, unaided by principles of honour or virtue; but where there is no such temptation, we speak truth by instinct—and this instinct is the principle I have been explaining.

By this instinct, a real connection is formed between our words and our thoughts, and thereby the former become fit to be signs of the latter, which they could not otherwise be. And although this connection is broken in every instance of lying and equivocation, yet these instances being comparatively few, the authority of human testimony is only weakened by them but not destroyed.

Another original principle implanted in us by the Supreme Being, is a disposition to confide in the veracity of others, and to believe what they tell us. This is the counterpart to the former; and, as that may be called *the principle of veracity*, we shall, for want of a more proper name, call this *the principle of credulity*. It is unlimited in children, until they meet with instances of deceit and falsehood; and it retains a very considerable degree of strength through life.

If Nature had left the mind of the speaker in *aequilibrio,* without any inclination to the side of truth more than to that of falsehood, children would lie as often as they speak truth, until reason was so far ripened as to suggest the imprudence of lying, or conscience, as to suggest its immorality. And if Nature had left the mind of the hearer *in aequilibrio*, without any inclination to the side of belief more than to that of disbelief, we should take no man's word until we had positive evidence that he spoke truth. His testimony would, in this case, have no more authority than his dreams; which may be true or false, but no man is disposed to believe them, on this account, that they were dreamed. It is evident that, in the matter of testimony, the balance of human judgment is by nature inclined to the side of belief; and turns to that side of itself, when there is nothing put into the opposite scale. If it was not so, no proposition that is uttered in discourse would be believed, until it was examined and tried by reason; and most men would be unable to find reasons for believing the thousandth part of what is told them. Such distrust and incredulity would deprive us of the greatest benefits of society, and place us in a worse condition than that of savages.

Children, on this supposition, would be ab-solutely incredulous, and, therefore, absolutely incapable of instruction: those who had little knowledge of human life, and of the manners and characters of men, would be in the next degree incredulous: and the most credulous men would be those of greatest experience, and of the deepest penetration: because, in many cases, they would be able to find good reasons for believing testimony, which the weak and the ignorant could not discover.

In a word, if credulity were the effect of reasoning and experience, it must grow up and gather strength, in the same proportion as reason and experience do. But, if it is the gift of Nature, it will be strongest in childhood, and limited and restrained by experience; and the most superficial view of human life shews, that the last is really the case, and not the first.

It is the intention of Nature, that we should be carried in arms before we are able to walk upon our legs; and it is likewise the intention of Nature, that our belief should be guided by the authority and reason of others, before it can be guided by our own reason. The weakness of the infant, and the natural affection of the mother, plainly indicate the former; and the natural credulity of youth, and authority of age, as plainly indicate the latter. The infant, by proper nursing, and care, acquires strength to walk without support. Reason hath likewise her infancy, when she must be carried in arms: then she leans entirely upon authority, by natural instinct, as if she was conscious of her own weakness; and, without this support, she becomes vertiginous. When brought to maturity by proper culture, she begins to feel her own strength, and leans less upon the reason of others; she learns to suspect testimony in some cases, and to disbelieve it in others; and sets bounds to that authority to which she was at first entirely subject. But still, to the end of life, she finds a necessity of borrowing light from testimony, where she has none within herself, and of leaning, in some degree, upon the reason of others, where she is conscious of her own imbecility.

And as, in many instances, Reason, even in her maturity, borrows aid from testimony, so in others she mutually gives aid to it, and strengthens its authority. For, as we find good reason to reject testimony in some cases, so in others we find good reason to rely upon it with perfect security, in our most important concerns. The character, the number, and the disinterestedness of witnesses, the impossibility of collusion, and the incredibility of their concurring in their testimony without collusion, may give an irresistible strength to testimony, compared to which its native and intrinsic authority is very inconsiderable.

Having now considered the general principles of the human mind which fit us for receiving information from our fellow-creatures, by the means of language, let us next consider the general principles which fit us for receiving the information of Nature by our acquired perceptions.

It is undeniable, and indeed is acknowledged by all, that when we have found two things to have been constantly conjoined in the course of nature, the appearance of one of them is immediately followed by the conception and belief of the other. The former becomes a natural sign of the latter; and the knowledge of their constant conjunction in time past, whether got by experience or otherwise, is sufficient to make us rely with assurance upon the continuance of that conjunction.

This process of the human mind is so familiar that we never think of inquiring into the principles upon which it is founded. We are apt to conceive it as a self-evident truth, that what is to come must be similar to what is past. Thus, if a certain degree of cold freezes water today, and has been known to do so in all time past, we have no doubt but the same degree of cold will freeze water tomorrow, or a year hence. That this is a truth which all men believe as soon as they understand it, I readily admit; but the question is, Whence does its evidence arise? Not from comparing the ideas, surely. For, when I compare the idea of cold with that of water hardened into a transparent solid body, I can perceive no connection between them: no man can shew the one to be the necessary effect of the other; no man can give a shadow of reason why Nature hath conjoined them. But do we not learn their conjunction from experience? True; experience informs us that they have been conjoined in time *past*; but no man ever had any experience of what is *future*: and this is the very question to be resolved. How we come to believe that the *future* will be like the *past*? Hath the Author of nature promised this? Or were we admitted to his council, when he established the pres-ent laws of nature, and

determined the time of their continuance. No, surely. Indeed, if we believe that there is a wise and good Author of nature, we may see a good reason why he should continue the same laws of nature, and the same connections of things, for a long time: because, if he did otherwise, we could learn nothing from what is past, and all our experience would be of no use to us. But, though this consideration, when we come to the use of reason, may confirm our belief of the continuance of the present course of nature, it is certain that it did not give rise to this belief; for children and idiots have this belief as soon as they know that fire will burn them. It must, therefore, be the effect of instinct, not of reason.

The wise Author of our nature intended, that a great and necessary part of our knowledge should be derived from experience, before we are capable of reasoning and he hath provided means perfectly adequate to this intention. For, First, He governs nature by fixed laws, so that we find innumerable connections of things which continue from age to age. Without this stability of the course of nature, there could be no experience; or, it would be a false guide, and lead us into error and mischief. If there were not a principle of veracity in the human mind, men's words would not be signs of their thoughts: and if there were no regularity in the course of nature, no one thing could be a natural sign of another. Secondly, He hath implanted in human minds an original principle by which we believe and expect the continuance of the course of nature, and the continuance of those connections which we have observed in time past. It is by this general principle of our nature, that, when two things have been found connected in time past, the appearance of the one produces the belief of the other.

I think the ingenious author of the "Treatise of Human Nature" first observed, That our belief of the continuance of the laws of nature cannot be founded either upon knowledge or probability: but, far from conceiving it to be an original principle of the mind, he endeavours to account for it from his favourite hypothesis, That belief is nothing but a certain degree of vivacity in the idea of the thing believed. I made a remark upon this curious hypothesis in the second chapter, and shall now make another.

The belief which we have in perception, is a belief of the present existence of the object; that which we have in memory, is a belief of its past existence; the belief of which we are now speaking is a belief of its future existence; and in imagination there is no belief at all. Now, I would gladly know of this author, how one degree of vivacity fixes the existence of the object to the present moment; another carries it back to time past; a third, taking a contrary direction, carries it into futurity; and a fourth carries it out of existence altogether. Suppose, for instance, that I see the sun rising out of the sea: I remember to have seen him rise yesterday; I believe he will rise tomorrow near the same place; I can likewise imagine him rising in that place, without any belief at all. Now, according to this sceptical hypothesis, this perception, this memory, this foreknowledge, and this imagination, are all the same idea, diversified only by different degrees of vivacity. The perception of the sun rising is the most lively idea; the memory of his rising yesterday is the same idea a little more faint; the belief of his rising tomorrow is the same idea yet fainter; and the imagination of his rising is still the same idea, but faintest of all. One is apt to think, that this idea might gradually pass through all possible degrees of vivacity without stirring out of its place. But, if we think so, we deceive ourselves; for no sooner does it begin to grow languid than it moves backward into time past. Supposing this to be granted. we expect, at least, that, as it moves backward by the decay of its vivacity, the more that vivacity decays it will go back the farther, until it remove quite out of sight. But here we are deceived again; for there is a certain period of this declining vivacity, when, as if it had met an elastic obstacle in its motion backward, it suddenly rebounds from the past to the future, without taking the present in its way. And now, having got into the regions of futurity, we are apt to think that it has room enough to spend all its remaining vigour: but still we are deceived; for, by another sprightly bound, it mounts up into the airy region of imagination. So that ideas, in the gradual declension of their vivacity, seem to imitate the inflection of verbs in grammar. They begin with the present, and proceed in order to the preterite, the future and the indefinite. This article of the sceptical creed is indeed so full of mystery, on whatever side we view it, that they who hold that creed are very injuriously charged with incredulity; for, to me, it appears to require as much faith as that of St. Athanasius.

However, we agree with the author of the "Treatise of Human Nature," in this, That our belief of the continuance of nature's laws is not derived from reason. It is an instinctive prescience of the operations of nature, very like to that prescience of human actions which makes us rely upon the testimony of our fellow-creatures; and as, without the latter, we should he incapable of receiving information from men by language, so, without the former, we should be incapable of receiving the information of nature by means of experience.

All our knowledge of nature beyond our original perceptions, is got by experience, and consists in the interpretation of natural signs. The constancy of nature's laws connects the sign with the thing signified; and, by the natural principle just now explained, we rely upon the continuance of the connections which experience hath discovered; and thus the appearance of the sign is followed by the belief of the thing signified. Upon this principle of our constitution, not only acquired perception, but all inductive reasoning, and all our reasoning from analogy, is grounded; and, therefore, for want of another name, we shall beg leave to call it *the inductive principle*. It is from the force of this principle that we immediately assent to that axiom upon which all our knowledge of nature is built.

That effects of the same kind must have the same cause; for *effects* and *causes*, in the operations of nature, mean nothing but signs and the things signified by them. We perceive no proper causality or efficiency in any natural cause; but only a connection established by the course of nature between it and what is called its effect. Antecedently to all reasoning, we have, by our constitution, an anticipation that there is a fixed and steady course of nature: and we have an eager desire to discover this course of nature. We attend to every conjunction of things which presents itself, and expect the continuance of that conjunction. And, when such a conjunction has been often ob-served, we conceive the things to be naturally connected, and the appearance of one, without any reasoning or reflection, carries along with it the belief of the other.

If any reader should imagine that the inductive principle may be resolved into what philosophers usually call the *association of ideas*, let him observe, that, by this principle, natural signs are not associated with the idea only, but with the belief of the things signified. Now, this can with no propriety be called an association of ideas, unless ideas and belief be one and the same thing. A child has found the prick of a pin conjoined with pain; hence he believes, and knows, that these things are naturally connected; he knows that the one will always follow the other. If any man will call this only an association of ideas, I dispute not about words, but I think he speaks very improperly. For, if we express it in plain English, it is a prescience that things which he hath found conjoined in time past, will be conjoined in time to come. And this prescience is not the effect of reasoning, but of an original principle of human nature, which I have called the *inductive principle*.

This principle, like that of credulity, is unlimited in infancy, and gradually restrained and regulated as we grow up. It leads us often into mistakes; but is of infinite advantage upon the whole. By it, the child once burnt shuns the fire; by it, he likewise runs away from the surgeon by whom he was inoculated. It is better that he should do the last, than he should not do the first.

But the mistakes we are led into by these two natural principles, are of a different kind. Men sometimes lead us into mistakes, when we perfectly understand their language, by speaking lies. But Nature never misleads us in this way: her language is always true; and it is only by misinterpreting it that we fall into error. There must be many accidental conjunctions of things, as well as natural connections; and the former are apt to be mistaken for the latter. Thus, in the instance above mentioned, the child connected the pain of inoculation with the surgeon; whereas it was really connected with the incision only. Philosophers, and men of science, are not exempted from such mistakes; indeed, all false reasoning in philosophy is owing to them; it is drawn from experience and analogy, as well as just reasoning, otherwise it could have no verisimilitude; but the one is an unskillful and rash, the other a just and legitimate interpretation of natural signs. If a child, or a man of common understanding, were put to interpret a book of science, written in his mother-tongue, how many blunders and mistakes would he be apt to fall into? Yet he knows as much of this language as is necessary for his manner of life.

The language of Nature is the universal study; and the students are of different classes. Brutes, idiots, and children employ themselves in this study, and owe to it all their acquired perception. Men of common understanding make a greater progress, and learn, by a small degree of reflection, many things of which children are ignorant. ...

From the time that children begin to use their hands, Nature directs them to handle everything over and over, to look at it while they handle it, and to put it in various positions, and at various distances from the eye. We are apt to excuse this as a childish diversion, because they must be doing something, and have not reason to entertain themselves in a more manly way. But, if we think more justly, we shall find, that they are engaged in the most serious and important study; and, if they had all the reason of a philosopher, they could not be more properly employed. For it is this childish employment that enables them to make the proper use of their eyes. They are thereby every day acquiring habits of perception, which are of greater importance than anything we can teach them. The original perceptions which Nature gave them are few, and insufficient for the purposes of life; and, therefore, she made them capable of acquiring many more perceptions by habit. And, to complete her work, she hath given them an unwearied assiduity in applying to the exercises by which those perceptions are acquired. ...

We have shewn, on the contrary, that every operation of the senses, in its very nature, implies judgment or belief, as well as simple apprehension. Thus, when I feel the pain of the gout in my toe, I have not only a notion of pain, but a belief of its existence, and a belief of some disorder in my toe which occasions it; and this belief is not produced by comparing ideas, and perceiving their agreements and disagreements; it is included in the very nature of the sensation. When I perceive a tree before me, my faculty of seeing gives me not only a notion or simple apprehension of the tree, but a belief of its existence, and of its figure, distance, and magnitude; and this judgment or belief is not got by comparing ideas, it is included in the very nature of the perception. We have taken notice of several original principles of belief in the course of this inquiry; and when other faculties of the mind are examined, we shall find more, which have not occurred in the examination of the five senses.

Such original and natural judgments are, therefore, a part of that furniture which Nature hath given to the human understanding. They are the inspiration of the Almighty, no less than our notions or simple apprehensions. They serve to direct us in the common affairs of life, where our reasoning faculty would leave us in the dark.

They are a part of our constitution; and all the discoveries of our reason are grounded upon them. They make up what is called the *common sense of mankind;* and, what is manifestly contrary to any of those first principles, is what we call *absurd.* The strength of them is *good sense,* which is often found in those who are not acute in reasoning. A remarkable deviation from them, arising from a disorder in the constitution, is what we call *lunacy;* as when a man believes that he is made of glass. When a man suffers himself to be reasoned out of the principles of common sense, by metaphysical arguments, we may call this *metaphysical lunacy;* which differs from other species of the distemper in this, that it is not continued, but intermittent: it is apt to seize the patient in solitary and speculative moments; but, when he enters into society, Common Sense recovers her authority. A clear explication and enumeration of the principles of common sense, is one of the chief *desiderata* in logic. We have only considered such of them as occurred in the examination of the five senses.

The last observation that I shall make upon the new system is, that, although it professes to set out in the way of reflection, and not of analogy, it hath retained some of the old analogical notions concerning the operations of the mind; particularly, that things which do not now exist in the mind itself, can only be perceived, remembered or imagined, by means of ideas or images of them in the mind, which are the immediate objects of perception, remembrance, and imagination. This doctrine appears evidently to be borrowed from the old system; which taught that external things make impressions upon the mind, like the impressions of a seal upon wax; that it is by means of those impressions that we perceive, remember, or imagine them; and that those impressions must resemble the things from which they are taken. When we form our notions of the operations of the mind by analogy, this way of conceiving them seems to be very natural, and offers itself to our thoughts; for, as everything which is felt must make some impression upon the body, we are apt to think that everything which is understood must make some impression upon the mind.

From such analogical reasoning, this opinion of the existence of ideas or images of things in the mind, seems to have taken its rise, and to have been so universally received among philosophers. It was observed already, that Berkeley, in one instance, apostatizes from this principle of the new system, by affirming that we have no ideas of spirits, and that we can think of them immediately, without ideas. But I know not whether in this he has had any followers. There is some difference, likewise, among modern philosophers with regard to the ideas or images by which we perceive, remember, or imagine sensible things. For, though all agree in the existence of such images they differ about their place; some placing them in a particular part of the brain, where the soul is thought to have her residence, and others placing them in the mind itself. Des Cartes held the first of these opinions; to which Newton seems likewise to have inclined.... But Locke seems to place the ideas of sensible things in the mind; and that Berkeley, and the author of the "Treatise of Human Nature," were of the same opinion, is evident. The last makes a very curious application of this doctrine, by endeavouring to prove from it, that the mind either is no substance, or that it is an extended and divisible substance; because the ideas of extension cannot be in a subject which is indivisible and unextended.

I confess I think his reasoning in this, as in most cases, is clear and strong. For whether the idea of extension be only another name for extension itself, as Berkeley and this author assert; or whether the idea of extension be an image and resemblance of extension, as Locke conceived; I appeal to any man of common sense, whether extension, or any image of extension, can be in an unextended and indivisible subject. But while I agree with him in his reasoning, I would make a different application of it. He takes it for granted, that there are ideas of extension in the mind; and thence infers, that, if it is at all a substance, it must be an extended and divisible substance. On the contrary, I take it for granted, upon the testimony of common sense, that my mind is a substance—that is, a permanent subject of thought; and my reason convinces me that it is an unextended and indivisible substance; and hence I infer that there cannot be in it anything that resembles extension. If this reasoning had occurred to Berkeley, it would probably have led him to acknowledge that we may think and reason concerning bodies, without having ideas of them in the mind, as well as concerning spirits.

I intended to have examined more particularly and fully this doctrine of the existence of ideas or images of things in the mind; and likewise another doctrine, which is founded upon it—to wit, That judgment or belief is nothing but a perception of the agreement or disagreement of our ideas; but, having already shewn, through the course of this inquiry, that the operations of the mind which we have examined, give no countenance to either of these doctrines, and in many things contradict them, I have thought it proper to drop this part of my design. It may be executed with more advantage, if it is at all necessary, after inquiring into some other powers of the human understanding.

COMMENT

Reid's complaint against the dominant philosophies of his time—rationalism and empiricism—in the name of common sense must not be misunderstood as a criticism of philosophy itself. He well knew that to claim that philosophy is useless or harmful is *itself* a philosophical point of view, which in turn needs examination and evaluation. Rather, Reid argues that the basis or starting point for all thought, including philosophy, must be the commonsense beliefs we have all acquired as part of our enculturation as human beings. Thus, for Reid, to question the existence of material objects, or the "external world," is technically impossible since the questioner is *simultaneously* taking the material world for granted. Consider Descartes seated in a chair, writing with a pen on paper, which is resting on a table, asking whether or not such objects are real!

Reid's answer to skepticism does not involve arriving at different conclusions by inferring from similar observational premises. Rather, he insists that we must begin our reasonings from certain "first principles," the truth of which can neither be established by deductive nor by inductive inference. These first principles must simply be "taken for granted." Otherwise no living, let alone reasoning, can take place. The first principles of common sense, according to Reid, are given by God to enable us to live in the world. Nature and our senses are bound together by a kind of "language" that can only be questioned at the cost of self-contradiction or fantasy.

The sort of thing Reid has in mind here is, as he says, the predisposition to believe that other people speak the truth. A moment's reflection will make it clear that without this "assumption," language would be impossible. Lying and pretending are parasitic on truth telling; otherwise we could never get started in language, let alone survive as families and societies. Another propensity, one that speaks directly to causation—the central difficulty encountered by Hume and Kant—is that of induction. According to Reid, our anticipation that the future will be like the past is preinferential, or "instinctive"; it can neither be given a rational justification nor be in need of one. All reasoning, even Hume's critique of inductive inference, is based on and makes use of the inferential process. After all, Hume himself gives a "causal explanation" of the psychological basis of the inferential process.

There are two highly influential philosophers in the twentieth century who take up a position quite similar to that of Reid. One is Ludwig Wittgenstein,[1] who in his later philosophy sought to undermine the "foundationalist" posture of nearly all modern thought; to wit, that some things must simply be accepted as "bedrock" or taken as "certain" in order for any language and thought to be possible. The other is Michael Polanyi,[2] whose notion of "tacit knowledge," whereby we accredit our cognitive powers as reliable (even when raising skeptical questions) suggests that we always "know more than we can say." Space will not permit a further discussion of these two thinkers here, but the interested reader is encouraged to consult their major works for the view sometimes called "reliablism."

There are, to be sure, certain difficulties that arise in connection with Reid's appeal to common sense as the basis and ultimate test for knowledge. Cultural anthropology has taught us to ask whether what is taken for granted in one culture is necessarily taken as such in others. Also, there is something somewhat

---

[1] See *Philosophical Investigations* (New York: Macmillan, 1953).
[2] See *Personal Knowledge* (Chicago: University of Chicago Press, 1958).

"rationalistic" about Reid's position, something that smacks of Descartes' "self-evident axioms" or innate ideas. On the surface, at least, it would seem that some sort of justification for these "first principles" must be given. Reid, of course, could reply, with Wittgenstein, that justifications "must come to an end, otherwise they would not be justifications." However, not all philosophers agree with this antifoundationalist posture and at the very least more work needs to be done to clarify the nature of any supposed "truths" that are claimed to be beyond scrutiny.

Finally, it can be asked whether Reid's approach is all that different from that of Kant. Kant, too, argues that our belief in causation, among other first principles, is the result of the very structure of the human mind. Thus both he and Reid assert that to believe in and practice inductive inference is part of what it means to have a mind in the first place and that there is nothing "irrational" about such beliefs and practice. In fact, it would be irrational not to so believe and act. It would be worthwhile to ask what differences there are between Reid's view and that of Kant. It would also be valuable to construct the reply to them that Hume might have given had he been able or so inclined. The reader is encouraged to follow up on these suggestions, both in private and in class discussion, as they will serve as an excellent bridge to the next chapters in this epistemological unit.

Once more, the reader may profit from exploring the initial case study about the sort of cognition displayed by the chess-playing computer. Would Reid say that Deep Blue could engage in the use of "common sense"? How would Reid distinguish between Kasparov and Deep Blue as "thinkers"? How are causal inferences and mistakes to be explained by Reid in the thinking of these two chess players?

4

INTUITION AND ACQUAINTANCE

HENRI BERGSON (1859-1941)

Henri Bergson was born in Paris of an English mother and a Polish father. From his father, an accomplished musician, he may have inherited the artistic temperament that is reflected throughout his work. Although interested in literature and science, he devoted himself to philosophy, which he taught in various lycées and, from 1900 to 1921, at the Collège de France.

In 1888 he published his first major work, *Time and Free Will*, but it was not until 1908, with the appearance of his *Creative Evolution*, that he suddenly became the most popular figure in the philosophic world. The audience gathered in the lecture hall an hour in advance to secure seats, and people from many countries flocked to his lectures. Among his honors were election to the Council of the Legion of Honor, the French Academy, and the Academy of Sciences, and the award of the Nobel Prize in literature.

After World War I, he devoted himself to the cause of peace, presiding over the International Commission for Intellectual Cooperation of the League of Nations. When the French Vichy government introduced anti-Semitic measures under the Nazi occupation during World War II, it proposed to exempt Bergson despite his Jewish extraction. As a protest against the infamy of the regime, he refused exemption and renounced his various honors. Finally, at the age of eighty-one, he rose from his sickbed and waited in line to register as a Jew. He died a few days later.

INTUITION

A comparison of the definitions of metaphysics and the various concepts of the absolute leads to the discovery that philoso-

From *An Introduction to Metaphysics*, trans. T. E. Hulme, New York: G.P. Putnam's Sons, 1912. Copyright © 1912 by Bergson.

phers, in spite of their apparent divergencies, agree in distinguishing two profoundly different ways of knowing a thing. The first implies that we move round the object; the second that we enter into it. The first depends on the point of view at which we are placed and on the symbols by which we express ourselves. The second neither depends on a point of view nor relies on any symbol. The first kind of knowledge may be said to stop at the *relative*; the second, in those cases where it is possible, to attain the *absolute*.

Consider, for example, the movement of an object in space. My perception of the motion will vary with the point of view, moving or stationary, from which I observe it. My expression of it will vary with the systems of axes, or the points or reference to which I relate it; that is, with the symbols by which I translate it. For this double reason I call such motion *relative*: in the one case, as in the other, I am placed outside the object itself. But when I speak of an *absolute* movement, I am attributing to the moving object an interior and, so to speak, states of mind; I also imply that I am in sympathy with those states, and that I insert myself in them by an effort of imagination. Then, according as the object is moving or stationary, according as it adopts one movement or another, what I experience will vary. And what I experience will depend neither on the point of view I may take up in regard to the object, since I am inside the object itself, nor on the symbols by which I may translate the motion, since I have rejected all translations in order to possess the original. In short, I shall no longer grasp the movement from without, remaining where I am, but from where it is, from within, as it is in itself. I shall possess an absolute.

Consider, again, a character whose adventures are related to me in a novel. The author may multiply the traits of his hero's character, may make him speak and act as much as he pleases, but all this can never be equivalent to the simple and indivisible feeling which I should experience if I were able for an instant to identify myself with the person of the hero himself. Out of that indivisible feeling; as from a spring, all the words, gestures, and actions of the man would appear to me to flow naturally. They would no longer be accidents which, added to the idea I had already formed of the character, continually enriched that idea, with-

out ever completing it. The character would be given to me all at once, in its entirety, and the thousand incidents which manifest it, instead of adding themselves to the idea and so enriching it, would seem to me, on the contrary, to detach themselves from it, without, however, exhausting it or impoverishing its essence. All the things I am told about the man provide me with so many points of view from which I can observe him. All the traits which describe him, and which can make him known to me only by so many comparisons with persons or things I know already, are signs by which he is expressed more or less symbolically. Symbols and points of view, therefore, place me outside him; they give me only what he has in common with others, and not what belongs to him and to him alone. But that which is properly himself, that which constitutes his essence, cannot be perceived from without, being internal by definition, nor be expressed by symbols, being incommensurable with everything else. Description, history, and analysis leave me here in the relative. Coincidence with the person himself would alone give me the absolute.

It is in this sense, and in this sense only, that *absolute* is synonymous with *perfection*. Were all the photographs of a town, taken from all possible points of view, to go on indefinitely completing one another, they would never be equivalent to the solid town in which we walk about. Were all the translations of a poem into all possible languages to add together their various shades of meaning and, correcting each other by a kind of mutual retouching, to give a more and more faithful image of the poem they translate, they would yet never succeed in rendering the inner meaning of the original. A representation taken from a certain point of view, a translation made with certain symbols, will always remain imperfect in comparison with the object of which a view has been taken, or which the symbols seek to express. But the absolute, which is the object and not its representation, the original and not its translation, is perfect, by being perfectly what it is.

It is doubtless for this reason that the *absolute* has often been identified with the *infinite*. Suppose that I wished to communicate to some one who did not know Greek the extraordinarily simple impression that a passage in Homer makes upon me; I should first give a translation of the lines, I should then comment on my translation, and then develop the commentary; in this way, by piling up explanation on explanation, I might approach nearer and nearer to what I wanted to express; but I should never quite reach it. When you raise your arm, you accomplish a movement of which you have, from within, a simple perception; but for me, watching it from the outside, your arm passes through one point, then through another, and between these two there will be still other points; so that, if I began to count, the operation would go on forever. Viewed from the inside, then, an absolute is a simple thing; but looked at from the outside, that is to say, relatively to other things, it becomes, in relation to these signs which express it, the gold coin for which we never seem able to finish giving small change. Now, that which lends itself at the same time both to an indivisible apprehension and to an inexhaustible enumeration is, by the very definition of the word, an infinite.

It follows from this that an absolute could only be given in an *intuition*, whilst everything else falls within the province of *analysis*. By intuition is meant the kind of *intellectual sympathy* by which one places oneself within an object in order to coincide with what is unique in it and consequently inexpressible. Analysis, on the contrary, is the operation which reduces the object to elements already known, that is, to elements common both to it and other objects. To analyze, therefore, is to express a thing as a function of something other than itself. All analysis is thus a translation, a development into symbols, a representation taken from successive points of view from which we note as many resemblances as possible between the new object which we are studying and others

which we believe we know already. In its eternally unsatisfied desire to embrace the object around which it is compelled to turn, analysis multiplies without end the number of its points of view in order to complete its always incomplete representation, and ceaselessly varies its symbols that it may perfect the always imperfect translation. It goes on, therefore, to infinity. But intuition, if intuition is possible, is a simple act.

Now it is easy to see that the ordinary function of positive science is analysis. Positive science works, then, above all, with symbols. Even the most concrete of the natural sciences, those concerned with life, confine themselves to the visible form of living beings, their organs and anatomical elements. They make comparisons between these forms, they reduce the more complex to the more simple; in short, they study the workings of life in what is, so to speak, only its visual symbol. If there exists any means of possessing a reality absolutely instead of knowing it relatively, of placing oneself within it instead of looking at it from outside points of view, of having the intuition instead of making the analysis: in short, of seizing it without any expression, translation, or symbolic representation—metaphysics is that means. *Metaphysics, then, is the science which claims to dispense with symbols.*

There is one reality, at least, which we all seize from within, by intuition and not by simple analysis. It is our own personality in its flowing through time—our self which endures. We may sympathize intellectually with nothing else, but we certainly sympathize with our own selves.

When I direct my attention inward to contemplate my own self (supposed for the moment to be inactive), I perceive at first, as a crust solidified on the surface, all the perceptions which come to it from the material world. These perceptions are clear, distinct, juxtaposed or juxtaposable one with another; they tend to group themselves into objects. Next, I notice the memories which more or less adhere to these perceptions and which serve to interpret them. These memories have been detached, as it were, from the depth of my personality, drawn to the surface by the perceptions which resemble them; they rest on the surface of my mind without being absolutely myself. Lastly, I feel the stir of tendencies and motor habits—a crowd of virtual actions, more or less firmly bound to these perceptions and memories. All these clearly defined elements appear more distinct from me, the more distinct they are from each other. Radiating, as they do, from within outwards, they form, collectively, the surface of a sphere which tends to grow larger and lose itself in the exterior world. But if I draw myself in from the periphery towards the center; if I search in the depth of my being that which is most uniformly, most constantly, and most enduringly myself, I find an altogether different thing.

There is, beneath these sharply cut crystals and this frozen surface a continuous flux which is not comparable to any flux I have ever seen. There is a succession of states, each of which announces that which follows and contains that which precedes it. They can, properly speaking, only be said to form multiple states when I have already passed them and turn back to observe their track. Whilst I was experiencing them they were so solidly organized, so profoundly animated with a common life, that I could not have said where any one of them finished or where another commenced. In reality no one of them begins or ends, but all extend into each other.

This inner life may be compared to the unrolling of a coil, for there is no living being who does not feel himself coming gradually to the end of his rôle; and to live is to grow old. But it may just as well be compared to a continual rolling up, like that of a thread on a ball, for our past follows us, it swells incessantly with the present that it picks up on its way; and consciousness means memory.

But actually it is neither an unrolling nor a rolling up, for these two similes evoke the idea of lines and surfaces whose parts are homogeneous and superposable on one another. Now, there are no two identical moments in the life of the same conscious being. Take the simplest sensation, suppose it constant, absorb in it the entire personality: the consciousness which will accompany this sensation cannot remain identical with itself for two consecutive moments, because the second moment always contains, over and above the first, the memory that the first has bequeathed to it. A consciousness which could experience two identical moments would be a consciousness without memory. It would die and be born again continually. In what other way could one represent unconsciousness?

It would be better, then, to use as a comparison the myriad-tinted spectrum, with its insensible gradations leading from one shade to another. A current of feeling which passed along the spectrum, assuming in turn the tint of each of its shades, would experience a series of gradual changes, each of which would announce the one to follow and would sum up those which preceded it. Yet even here the successive shades of the spectrum always remain external one to another. They are juxtaposed; they occupy space. But pure duration, on the contrary, excludes all idea of juxtaposition, reciprocal externality, and extension.

Let us, then, rather, imagine an infinitely small elastic body, contracted, if it were possible, to a mathematical point. Let this be drawn out gradually in such a manner that from the point comes a constantly lengthening line. Let us fix our attention not on the line as a line, but on the action by which it is traced. Let us bear in mind that this action, in spite of its duration, is indivisible if accomplished without stopping, that if a stopping-point is inserted, we have two actions instead of one, that each of these separate actions is then the indivisible operation of which we speak, and that it is not the moving action itself which is divisible, but, rather, the stationary line it leaves behind it as its track in space. Finally, let us free ourselves from the space which underlies the movement in order to consider only the movement itself, the act of tension or extension; in short, pure mobility. We shall have this time a more faithful image of the development of our self in duration.

However, even this image is incomplete, and, indeed, every comparison will be insufficient, because the unrolling of our duration resembles in some of its aspects the unity of an advancing movement and in others the multiplicity of expanding states; and, clearly, no metaphor can express one of these two aspects without sacrificing the other. If I use the comparison of the spectrum with its thousand shades, I have before me a thing already made, whilst duration is continually in the making. If I think of an elastic which is being stretched, or of a spring which is extended or relaxed, I forget the richness of color, characteristic of duration that is lived, to see only the simple movement by which consciousness passes from one shade to another. The inner life is all this at once: variety of qualities, continuity of progress, and unity of direction. It cannot be represented by images.

But it is even less possible to represent it by *concepts*, that is by abstract general, or simple ideas. It is true that no image can reproduce exactly the original feeling I have of the flow of my own conscious life. But it is not even necessary that I should attempt to render it. If a man is incapable of getting for himself the intuition of the constitutive duration of his own being, nothing will ever give it to him, concepts no more than images. Here the single aim of the philosopher should be to promote a certain effort, which in most men is usually fettered by habits of mind more useful to life. Now the image has at least this advantage, that it keeps us in the concrete. No image can replace the intuition of duration, but many diverse images, borrowed from very different orders of things, may, by the convergence of their action, direct consciousness to the precise point where there is a certain

intuition to be seized. By choosing images as dissimilar as possible, we shall prevent any one of them from usurping the place of the intuition it is intended to call up, since it would then be driven away at once by its rivals. By providing that, in spite of their differences of aspect, they all require from the mind the same kind of attention, and in some sort the same degree of tension, we shall gradually accustom consciousness to a particular and clearly-defined disposition—that precisely which it must adopt in order to appear to itself as it really is, without any veil. But, then, consciousness must at least consent to make the effort. For it will have been shown nothing: It will simply have been placed in the attitude it must take up in order to make the desired effort, and so come by itself to the intuition. Concepts on the contrary—especially if they are simple—have the disadvantage of being in reality symbols substituted for the object they symbolize, and demand no effort on our part. Examined closely, each of them, it would be seen, retains only that part of the object, which is common to it and to others, and expresses, still more than the image does, a *comparison* between the object and others which resemble it. But as the comparison has made manifest a resemblance, as the resemblance is a property of the object, and as a property has every appearance of being *a part* of the object which possesses it, we easily persuade ourselves that by setting concept beside concept we are reconstructing the whole of the object with its parts, thus obtaining, so to speak, its intellectual equivalent. In this way we believe that we can form a faithful representation of duration by setting in line the concepts of unity, multiplicity, continuity, finite or infinite divisibility, etc. There precisely is the illusion. There also is the danger. Just in so far as abstract ideas can render service to analysis, that is, to the scientific study of the object in its relations to other objects, so far are they incapable of replacing intuition, that is, the metaphysical investigation of what is essential and unique in the object. For on the one hand these concepts, laid side by side, never actually give us more than an artificial reconstruction of the object, of which they can only symbolize certain general, and, in a way, impersonal aspects; it is therefore useless to believe that with them we can seize a reality of which they present to us the shadow alone. And, on the other hand, besides the illusion there is also a very serious danger. For the concept generalizes at the same time as it abstracts. The concept can only symbolize a particular property by making it common to an infinity of things. It therefore always more or less deforms the property by the extension it gives to it. Replaced in the metaphysical object to which it belongs, a property coincides with the object, or at least moulds itself on it, and adopts the same outline. Extracted from the metaphysical object, and presented in a concept, it grows indefinitely larger, and goes beyond the object itself, since henceforth it has to contain it, along with a number of other objects. Thus the different concepts that we form of the properties of a thing inscribe round it so many circles, each much too large and none of them fitting it exactly. And yet, in the thing itself the properties coincided with the thing, and coincided consequently with one another. So that if we are bent on reconstructing the object with concepts, some artifice must be sought whereby this coincidence of the object and its properties can be brought about. For example, we may choose one of the concepts and try, starting from it, to get round to the others. But we shall then soon discover that according as we start from one concept or another, the meeting and combination of the concepts will take place in an altogether different way. According as we start, for example, from unity or from multiplicity, we shall have to conceive differently the multiple unity of duration. Everything will depend on the weight we attribute to this or that concept, and this weight will always be arbitrary, since the concept extracted from the object has no weight, being only the shadow of a body. In this way, as many different *systems* will spring up as there are external points of view from which the reality can be examined, or larger circles in which it can be enclosed. Simple concepts have, then, not only the inconvenience of dividing the concrete unity of the object into so many symbolical expressions; they also divide philosophy into distinct schools, each of which takes its seat, chooses its counters, and carries on with the others a game that will never end. Either metaphysics is only this play of ideas, or else, if it is a serious occupation of the mind, if it is a science and not simply an exercise, it must transcend concepts in order to reach intuition. Certainly, concepts are necessary to it, for all the other sciences work as a rule with concepts, and metaphysics cannot dispense with the other sciences. But it is only truly itself when it goes beyond the concept, or at least when it frees itself from rigid and ready-made concepts in order to create a kind very different from those which we habitually use; I mean supple, mobile, and almost fluid representations, always ready to mould themselves on the fleeting forms of intuition. We shall return later to this important point. Let it suffice us for the moment to have shown that our duration can be presented to us directly in an intuition, that it can be suggested to us indirectly by images, but that it can never—if we confine the word *concept* to its proper meaning—be enclosed in a conceptual representation. . . .

Thinking usually consists in passing from concepts to things, and not from things to concepts. To know a reality, in the usual sense of the word "know," is to take ready-made concepts, to portion them out and to mix them together until a practical equivalent of the reality is obtained. But it must be remembered that the normal work of the intellect is far from being disinterested. We do not aim generally at knowledge for the sake of knowledge, but in order to take sides, to draw profit—in short, to satisfy an interest. We inquire up to what point the object we seek to know is *this or that*, to what known class it belongs, and what kind of action, bearing, or attitude it should suggest to us. These different possible actions and attitudes are so many *conceptual directions* of our thought, determined once for all; it remains only to follow them: in that precisely consists the application of concepts to things. To try to fit a concept on an object is simply to ask what we can do with the object, and what it can do for us. To label an object with a certain concept is to mark in precise terms the kind of action or attitude the object should suggest to us. All knowledge, properly so called, is then oriented in a certain direction, or taken from a certain point of view. It is true that our interest is often complex. This is why it happens that our knowledge of the same object may face several successive directions and may be taken from various points of view. It is this which constitutes, in the usual meaning of the terms, a "broad" and "comprehensive" knowledge of the object; the object is then brought not under one single concept, but under several in which it is supposed to "participate." How does it participate in all these concepts at the same time? This is a question which does not concern our practical action and about which we need not trouble. It is, therefore, natural and legitimate in daily life to proceed by the juxtaposition and portioning out of concepts; no philosophical difficulty will arise from this procedure, since by a tacit agreement we shall abstain from philosophizing. But to carry this *modus operandi* into philosophy, to pass here also from concepts to the thing, to use in order to obtain a disinterested knowledge of an object (that this time we desire to grasp as it is in itself) a manner of knowing inspired by a determinate interest, consisting by definition in an externally-taken view of the object, is to go against the end that we have chosen, to condemn philosophy to an eternal skirmishing between the schools and to install contradiction in the very heart of the object and of the method. Either there is no philosophy possible, and all knowledge of things is a practical knowledge aimed at the profit to be drawn from

them, or else philosophy consists in placing oneself within the object itself by an effort of intuition.

. . . Analysis operates always on the immobile, whilst intuition places itself in mobility, or, what comes to the same thing, in duration. There lies the very distinct line of demarcation between intuition and analysis. The real, the experienced, and the concrete are recognized by the fact that they are variability itself, the element by the fact that it is invariable. And the element is invariable by definition, being a diagram, a simplified reconstruction, often a mere symbol, in any case a motionless view of the moving reality.

But the error consists in believing that we can reconstruct the real with these diagrams. As we have already said and may as well repeat here—from intuition one can pass to analysis, but not from analysis to intuition.

Out of variability we can make as many variations, qualities and modifications as we please, since these are so many static views, taken by analysis, of the mobility given to intuition. But these modifications, put end to end, will produce nothing which resembles variability, since they are not parts of it, but elements, which is quite a different thing.

Consider, for example, the variability which is nearest to homogeneity, that of movement in space. Along the whole of this movement we can imagine possible stoppages; these are what we call the positions of the moving body, or the points by which it passes. But with these positions, even with an infinite number of them, we shall never make movement. They are not parts of the movement, they are so many snapshots of it; they are, one might say, only supposed stopping-places. The moving body is never really in any of the points; the most we can say is that it passes through them. But passage, which is movement, has nothing in common with stoppage, which is immobility. A movement cannot be superposed on an immobility, or it would then coincide with it, which would be a contradiction. The points are not in the movement, as parts, nor even *beneath* it, as positions occupied by the moving body. They are simply projected by us under the movement, as so many places where a moving body, which by hypothesis does not stop, would be it if were to stop. They are not, therefore, properly speaking, positions, but "suppositions," aspects, or points of view of the mind. But how could we construct a thing with points of view?

Nevertheless, this is what we try to do whenever we reason about movement, and also about time, for which movement serves as a means of representation. As a result of an illusion deeply rooted in our mind, and because we cannot prevent ourselves from considering analysis as the equivalent of intuition, we begin by distinguishing along the whole extent of the movement, a certain number of possible stoppages or points, which we make, whether they like it or no, parts of the movement. Faced with our impotence to reconstruct the movement with these points, we insert other points, believing that we can in this way get nearer to the essential mobility in the movement. Then, as this mobility still escapes us, we substitute for a fixed and finite number of points an "indefinitely increasing" number—thus vainly trying to counterfeit, by the movement of a thought that goes on indefinitely adding points to points, the real and undivided motion of the moving body. Finally, we say that movement is composed of points, but that it comprises, in addition, the obscure and mysterious passage from one position to the next. As if the obscurity was not due entirely to the fact that we have supposed immobility to be clearer than mobility and rest anterior to movement! As if the mystery did not follow entirely from our attempting to pass from stoppages to movement by way of addition, which is impossible, when it is so easy to pass, by simple diminution, from movement to the slackening of movement, and so to immobility! It is movement that we must accustom ourselves to look upon as simplest and clearest, immobility being only the extreme limit of the slowing down of movement, a limit reached only, perhaps, in thought and never realized in nature. What we have done is to seek for the meaning of the poem in the form of the letters of which it is composed; we have believed that by considering an increasing number of letters we would grasp at last the ever-escaping meaning, and in desperation, seeing that it was useless to seek for a part of the sense in each of the letters, we have supposed that it was between each letter and the next that this long-sought fragment of the mysterious sense was lodged! But the letters, it must be pointed out once again, are not parts of the thing, but elements of the symbol. Again, the positions of the moving body are not parts of the movement; they are points of the space which is supposed to underlie the movement. This empty and immobile space which is merely conceived, never perceived, has the value of a symbol only. How could you ever manufacture reality by manipulating symbols?

But the symbol in this case responds to the most inveterate habits of our thought. We place ourselves as a rule in immobility, in which we find a point of support for practical purposes, and with this immobility we try to reconstruct motion. We only obtain in this way a clumsy imitation, a counterfeit of real movement, but this imitation is much more useful in life than the intuition of the thing itself would be. Now our mind has an irresistible tendency to consider that idea clearest which is most often useful to it. That is why immobility seems to it clearer than mobility, and rest anterior to movement.

The difficulties to which the problem of movement has given rise from the earliest antiquity have originated in this way. They result always from the fact that we insist on passing from space to movement, from the trajectory to the flight, from immobile positions to mobility, and on passing from one to the other by way of addition. But it is movement which is anterior to immobility, and the relation between positions and a displacement is not that of parts to a whole, but that of the diversity of possible points of view to the real indivisibility of the object.

Many other problems are born of the same illusion. What stationary points are to the movement of a moving body, concepts of different qualities are to the qualitative change of an object. The various concepts into which a change can be analyzed are therefore so many stable views of the instability of the real. And to think of an object—in the usual meaning of the word "think"—is to take one or more of these immobile views of its mobility. It consists, in short, in asking from time to time where the object is, in order that we may know what to do with it. Nothing could be more legitimate, moreover, than this method of procedure, so long as we are concerned only with a practical knowledge of reality. Knowledge, in so far as it is directed to practical matters, has only to enumerate the principal possible attitudes of the thing towards us, as well as our best possible attitude towards it. Therein lies the ordinary function of ready-made concepts, those stations with which we mark out the path of becoming. But to seek to penetrate with them into the inmost nature of things, is to apply to the mobility of the real a method created in order to give stationary points of observation on it. It is to forget that, if metaphysics is possible, it can only be a laborious, and even painful, effort to remount the natural slope of the work of thought, in order to place oneself directly, by a kind of intellectual expansion, within the thing studied: in short, a passage from reality to concepts and no longer from concepts to reality. Is it astonishing that, like children trying to catch smoke by closing their hands, philosophers so often see the object they would grasp fly before them? It is in this way that many of the quarrels between the schools are perpetuated, each of them reproaching the others with having allowed the real to slip away.

... The inherent difficulties of metaphysics, the antinomies which it gives rise to, and the contradictions into which it falls, the division into antagonistic schools, and the irreducible opposition between systems are largely the result of our applying, to the disinterested knowledge of the real, processes which we generally employ for practical ends. They arise from the fact that we place ourselves in the immobile in order to lie in wait for the moving thing as it passes, instead of replacing ourselves in the moving thing itself, in order to traverse with it the immobile positions. They arise from our professing to reconstruct reality—which is tendency and consequently mobility—with percepts and concepts whose function it is to make it stationary. With stoppages, however numerous they may be, we shall never make mobility; whereas, if mobility is given, we can, by means of diminution, obtain from it by thought as many stoppages as we desire. In other words, *it is clear that fixed concepts may be extracted by our thought from mobile reality; but there are no means of reconstructing the mobility of the real with fixed concepts.* Dogmatism, however, in so far as it has been a builder of systems, has always attempted this reconstruction.

In this it was bound to fail. It is on this impotence and on this impotence only that the sceptical, idealist, critical doctrines really dwell: in fact, all doctrines that deny to our intelligence the power of attaining the absolute. But because we fail to reconstruct the living reality with stiff and ready-made concepts, it does not allow that we cannot grasp it in some other way. *The demonstrations which have been given of the relativity of our knowledge are therefore tainted with an original vice; they imply, like the dogmatism they attack, that all knowledge must necessarily start from concepts with fixed outlines, in order to clasp with them the reality which flows.*

But the truth is that our intelligence can follow the opposite method. It can place itself within the mobile reality, and adopt its ceaselessly changing direction; in short, can grasp it by means of that *intellectual sympathy* which we call intuition. This is extremely difficult. The mind has to do violence to itself, has to reverse the direction of the operation by which it habitually thinks, has perpetually to revise, or rather to recast, all its categories. But in this way it will attain to fluid concepts, capable of following reality in all its sinuosities and of adopting the very movement of the inward life of things. Only thus will a progressive philosophy be built up, freed from the disputes which arise between the various schools, and able to solve its problems naturally, because it will be released from the artificial expression in terms of which such problems arc posited. *To philosophize, therefore, is to invert the habitual direction of the work of thought.*

This inversion has never been practised in a methodical manner; but a profoundly considered history of human thought would show that we owe to it all that is greatest in the sciences, as well as all that is permanent in metaphysics. The most powerful of the methods of investigation at the disposal of the human mind, the infinitesimal calculus, originated from this very inversion. Modern mathematics is precisely an effort to substitute the *being made* for the *ready made*, to follow the generation of magnitudes, to grasp motion no longer from without and in its displayed result, but from within and in its tendency to change; in short, to adopt the mobile continuity of the outlines of things. It is true that it is confined to the outline, being only the science of magnitudes. It is true also that it has only been able to achieve its marvelous applications by the invention of certain symbols, and that if the intuition of which we have just spoken lies at the origin of invention, it is the symbol alone which is concerned in the application. But metaphysics, which aims at no application, can and usually must abstain from converting intuition into symbols. Liberated from the obligation of working for practically useful results, it will indefinitely enlarge the domain of its investigations. What it may lose in comparison with science in utility and exactitude, it will regain in range and extension. Though mathematics is only the science of magni-

tudes, though mathematical processes are applicable only to quantities, it must not be forgotten that quantity is always quality in a nascent state; it is, we might say, the limiting case of equality. It is natural, then, that metaphysics should adopt the generative idea of our mathematics in order to extend it to all qualities; that is, to reality in general. It will not, by doing this, in any way be moving towards universal mathematics, that chimera of modern philosophy. On the contrary, the farther it goes, the more untranslatable into symbols will be the objects it encounters. But it will at least have begun by getting into contact with the continuity and mobility of the real, just where this contact can be most marvelously utilized. It will have contemplated itself, much shrunken, no doubt, but for thai reason very luminous. It will have seen with greater clearness what the mathematical processes borrow from concrete reality, and it will continue in the direction of concrete reality, and not in that of mathematical processes. Having then discounted beforehand what is too modest, and at the same time too ambitious, in the following formula, we may say that *the object of metaphysics is to perform* qualitative *differentiations and integrations.*

The reason why this object has been lost sight of, and why science itself has been mistaken in the origin of the processes it employs, is that intuition, once attained, must find a mode of expression and of application which conforms to the habits of our thought, and one which furnishes us, in the shape of well-defined concepts, with the solid points of support which we so greatly need. In that lies the condition of what we call exactitude and precision, and also the condition of the unlimited extension of a general method to particular cases. Now this extension and this work of logical improvement can be continued for centuries, whilst the act which creates the method lasts but for a moment. That is why we so often take the logical equipment of science for science itself, forgetting the metaphysical intuition from which all the rest has sprung.

From the overlooking of this intuition proceeds all that has been said by philosophers and by men of science themselves about the "relativity" of scientific knowledge. *What is relative is the symbolic knowledge by pre-existing concepts, which proceeds from the fixed to the moving, and not the intuitive knowledge which installs itself in that which is moving and adopts the very life of things.* This intuition attains the absolute.

Science and metaphysics therefore come together in intuition. A truly intuitive philosophy would realize the much-desired union of science and metaphysics. While it would make of metaphysics a positive science—that is, a progressive and indefinitely perfectible one—it would at the same time lead the positive sciences, properly so-called, to become conscious of their true scope, often far greater than they imagine. It would put more science into metaphysics, and more metaphysics into science. It would result in restoring the continuity between the intuitions which the various sciences have obtained here and there in the course of their history, and which they have obtained only by strokes of genius.

BERTRAND RUSSELL (1872–1970)

The second son of Viscount Amberly and grandson of Lord John Russell, a famous liberal prime minister, Bertrand Russell was born on May 18, 1872, in the lovely valley of the Wye (described in Wordsworth's *Tintern Abbey*). His mother died when he was two years old and his father when he was three, so the boy was brought up in the home of his grandfather. Until he went to Cambridge University, at the age of eighteen, he lived a solitary life, supervised by German and Swiss governesses and English tutors and seeing little of other children. However, Cambridge opened to him "a new world of infinite delight." Here he found mathematics and philosophy extremely exciting and formed warm friendships with a number of brilliant young men, including the philosophers McTaggart McTaggart, G. E. Moore, and Alfred North Whitehead.

After leaving Cambridge in 1894, Russell spent time abroad, at first as attaché at the British Embassy in Paris. He married at the end of a year's service in the embassy—he was then twenty-two—and went to Germany to study economics and politics. His wife, the sister of Logan Pearsall Smith, well-known essayist and a Philadelphia Quaker, persuaded him to spend three months in America in 1896. After these travels, the young couple settled down in a workman's cottage in Sussex, where Russell, with enough income to support his family without other remuneration, devoted himself intensively to philosophy and mathematics.

The next two decades were the most intellectually productive in his long career. During this period, he wrote a series of important books, including *A Critical Exposition of the Philosophy of Leibniz* (1900), The *Principles of Mathematics*, (1903), *Principia Mathematica* (with Whitehead, 1910–1913), and *Our Knowledge of the External World* (1914). These books, especially *Principia Mathematica*, which was the result of twelve years of intense labor, firmly established Russell's reputation as one of the great figures in modern thought.

Always interested in politics, Russell was profoundly disturbed by the outbreak of World War I and was quite unsatisfied with the melodramatic pronouncements of the belligerent governments. His bold defense of conscientious objectors and his antiwar publications brought him fines and imprisonment, as well as loss of his position as fellow at Trinity College, Cambridge. He emerged from the war a changed man, aware of great social perils and pathological evil in human nature that he had never suspected. He subsequently devoted a large part of his time and energy to writing about political, educational, and moral affairs.

In 1921, after seventeen years of married life, his first marriage was dissolved, and he then wed Dora Winifred Black, who bore him a daughter and son, and from whom he was later divorced. Upon the death of his elder brother in 1931, he succeeded to the family earldom; and in 1934 he remarried, thus making Helen Patricia Spence, a young and beautiful woman, the Countess Russell. In 1950 he received the Nobel Prize for literature, the same honor that Bergson had been awarded. Despite his advanced age, he continued to live a busy and adventurous life, writing prolifically and espousing the cause of peace, until his death in 1970.

KNOWLEDGE BY ACQUAINTANCE AND KNOWLEDGE BY DESCRIPTION

It is often said, as though it were a self-evident truism, that we cannot know that anything exists which we do not know. It is inferred that whatever can in any way be relevant to our experience must be at least capable of being known by us; whence it follows that if matter were essentially something with which we could not become acquainted, matter would be something which we could not know to exist, and which could have for us no importance whatever. It is generally also implied, for reasons which remain obscure, that what can have no importance for us cannot be real, and that therefore matter, if it is not composed of minds or of mental ideas, is impossible and a mere chimaera.

To go into this argument fully at our present stage would be impossible, since it raises points requiring a considerable preliminary discussion; but certain reasons for rejecting the argument may be noticed at

once. To begin at the end: there is no reason why what cannot have any *practical* importance for us should not be real. It is true that, if *theoretical* importance is included, everything real is of *some* importance to us, since, as persons desirous of knowing the truth about the universe, we have some interest in everything that the universe contains. But if this sort of interest is included, it is not the case that matter has no importance for us, provided it exists, even if we cannot know that it exists. We can, obviously, suspect that it may exist, and wonder whether is does; hence it is connected with our desire for knowledge, and has the importance of either satisfying or thwarting this desire.

Again, it is by no means a truism, and is in fact false, that we cannot know that anything exists which we do not know. The word 'know' is here used in two different senses. (1) In its first use it is applicable to the sort of knowledge which is opposed to error, the sense in which what we know is *true*, the sense which applies to our beliefs and convictions, i.e. to what are called *judgements*. In this sense of the word we

From *The Problems of Philosophy*, (London, New York, and Toronto: Oxford University Press, 1912). Reprinted by permission.

know that something is the case. This sort of knowledge may be described as knowledge of *truths*. (2) In the second use of the word 'know' above, the word applies to our knowledge of *things*, which we may call *acquaintance*. This is the sense in which we know sense-data. (The distinction involved is roughly that between *savoir* and *connaître* in French, or between *wissen* and *kennen* in German.)

Thus the statement which seemed like a truism becomes, when restated, the following: 'We can never truly judge that something with which we are not acquainted exists.' This is by no means a truism, but on the contrary a palpable falsehood. I have not the honour to be acquainted with the Emperor of China, but I truly judge that he exists. It may be said, of course, that I judge this because of other people's acquaintance with him. This, however, would be an irrelevant retort, since, if the principle were true, I could not know that any one else is acquainted with him. But further: there is no reason why I should not know of the existence of something with which *nobody* is acquainted. This point is important, and demands elucidation.

If I am acquainted with a thing which exists, my acquaintance gives me the knowledge that it exists. But it is not true that, conversely, whenever I can know that a thing of a certain sort exists, I or some-one else must be acquainted with the thing. What happens, in cases where I have true judgement without acquaintance, is that the thing is known to me by *description*, and that, in virtue of some general principle, the existence of a thing answering to this description can be inferred from the existence of something with which I am acquainted. In order to understand this point fully, it will be well first to deal with the difference between knowledge by acquaintance and knowledge by description, and then to consider what knowledge of general principles, if any, has the same kind of certainty as our knowledge of the existence of our own experiences.

... We saw that there are two sorts of knowledge: knowledge of things, and knowledge of truths. ... We shall be concerned exclusively with knowledge of things, of which in turn we shall have to distinguish two kinds. Knowledge of things, when it is of the kind we call knowledge by *acquaintance*, is essentially simpler than any knowledge of truths, and logically independent of knowledge of truths, though it would be rash to assume that human beings ever, in fact, have acquaintance with things without at the same time knowing some truth about them. Knowledge of things by *description*, on the contrary, always involves, as we shall find in the course of the present chapter, some knowledge of truths as its source and ground. But first of all we must make clear what we mean by 'acquaintance' and what we mean by 'description.'

We shall say that we have *acquaintance* with anything of which we are directly aware, without the intermediary of any process of inference or any knowledge of truths. Thus in the presence of my table I am acquainted with the sense-data that make up the appearance of my table—its colour, shape, hardness, smoothness, etc.; all these are things of which I am immediately conscious when I am seeing and touching my table. The particular shade of colour that I am seeing may have many things said about it—I may say that it is brown, that it is rather dark, and so on. But such statements, though they make me know truths *about* the colour, do not make me know the colour itself any better than I did before: so far as concerns knowledge of the colour itself, as opposed to knowledge of truths about it, I know the colour perfectly and completely when I see it, and no further knowledge of it itself is even theoretically possible. Thus the sense-data which make up the appearance of my table are things with which I have acquaintance, things immediately known to me just as they are.

My knowledge of the table as a physical object, on the contrary, is not direct knowledge. Such as it is, it is obtained through acquaintance with the sense-data that make up the appearance of the table. We have seen that it is possible, without absurdity, to doubt whether there is a table at all, whereas it is not possible to doubt the sense-data. My knowledge of the table is of the kind which we shall call 'knowledge by description.' The table is 'the physical object which causes such-and-such sense-data." This *describes* the table by means of the sense-data. In order to know anything at all about the table, we must know truths connecting it with things with which we have acquaintance: we must know that 'such-and-such sense-data are caused by a physical object.' There is no state of mind in which we are directly aware of the table; all our knowledge of the table is really knowledge of *truths*, and the actual thing which is the table is not, strictly speaking, known to us at all. We know a description, and we know that there is just one object to which this description applies, though the object itself is not directly known to us. In such a case, we say that our knowledge of the object is knowledge by description.

All our knowledge, both knowledge of things and knowledge of truths, rests upon acquaintance as its foundation. It is therefore important to consider what kinds of things there are with which we have acquaintance.

Sense-data, as we have already seen, are among the things with which we are acquainted; in fact, they supply the most obvious and striking example of knowledge by acquaintance. But if they were the sole example, our knowledge would be very much more restricted than it is. We should only know what is now present to our senses: we could not know anything about the past—not even that there was a past— nor could we know any truths about our sense-data, for all knowledge of truths, as we shall show, demands acquaintance with things which are of an essentially different character from sense-data, the things which

are sometimes called 'abstract ideas,' but which we shall call 'universals.' We have therefore to consider acquaintance with other things besides sense-data if we are to obtain any tolerably adequate analysis of our knowledge.

The first extension beyond sense-data to be considered is acquaintance by *memory*. It is obvious that we often remember what we have seen or heard or had otherwise present to our senses, and that in such cases we are still immediately aware of what we remember, in spite of the fact that it appears as past and not as present. This immediate knowledge by memory is the source of all our knowledge concerning the past: without it, there could be no knowledge of the past by inference, since we should never know that there was anything past to be inferred.

The next extension to he considered is acquaintance by *introspection*. We are not only aware of being aware of things, but we are often aware of being aware of them. When I see the sun, I am often aware of my seeing the sun; thus 'my seeing the sun' is an object with which I have acquaintance. When I desire food, I may be aware of my desire for food; thus 'my desiring food' is an object with which I am acquainted. Similarly we may be aware of our feeling pleasure or pain, and generally of the events which happen in our minds. This kind of acquaintance, which may be called self-consciousness, is the source of all our knowledge of mental things. It is obvious that it is only what goes on in our own minds that can be thus known immediately. What goes on in the minds of others is known to us through our perception of their bodies, that is, through the sense-data in us which are associated with their bodies. But for our acquaintance with the contents of our own minds, we should be unable to imagine the minds of others, and therefore we could never arrive at the knowledge that they have minds. It seems natural to suppose that self-consciousness is one of the things that distinguish men from animals:

animals, we may suppose, though they have acquaintance with sense-data, never become aware of this acquaintance. I do not mean that they *doubt* whether they exist, but that they have never become conscious of the fact that they have sensations and feelings, nor therefore of the fact that they, the subjects of their sensations and feelings, exist.

We have spoken of acquaintance with the contents of our minds as *self*-consciousness, but it is not, of course consciousness of our *self*: it is consciousness of particular thoughts and feelings. The question whether we are also acquainted with our bare selves, as opposed to particular thoughts and feelings, is a very difficult one, upon which it would be rash to speak positively. When we try to look into ourselves we always seem to come upon some particular thought or feeling, and not upon the 'I' which has the thought or feeling. Nevertheless there are some reasons for thinking that we are acquainted with 'I,' though the acquaintance is hard to disentangle from other things. To make clear what sort of reason there is, let us consider for a moment what our acquaintance with particular thoughts really involves.

When I am acquainted with 'my seeing the sun,' it seems plain that I am acquainted with two different things in relation to each other. On the one hand there is the sense-datum which represents the sun to me, on the other hand there is that which sees this sense-datum. All acquaintance, such as my acquaintance with the sense-datum which represents the sun, seems obviously a relation between the person acquainted and the object with which the person is acquainted. When a case of acquaintance is one with which I can be acquainted (as I am acquainted with my acquaintance with the sense-datum representing the sun), it is plain that the person acquainted is myself. Thus, when I am acquainted with my seeing the sun, the whole fact with which I am acquainted is 'Self-acquainted-with-sense-datum.'

Further, we know the truth 'I am acquainted with this sense-datum.' It is hard to see how we could know this truth, or even understand what is meant by it, unless we were acquainted with something which we call 'I.' It does not seem necessary to suppose that we are acquainted with a more or less permanent person, the same to-day as yesterday, but it does seem as though we must be acquainted with that thing, whatever its nature, which sees the sun and has acquaintance with sense-data. Thus, in some sense it would seem we must be acquainted with Selves as opposed to our particular experiences. But the question is difficult, and complicated arguments can be adduced on either side. Hence, although acquaintance with ourselves seems *probably* to occur, it is not wise to assert that it undoubtedly does occur.

We may therefore sum up as follows what has been said concerning acquaintance with things that exist. We have acquaintance in sensation with the data of the outer senses, and in introspection with the data of what may be called the inner sense—thoughts, feelings, desires, etc.; we have acquaintance in memory with things which have been data either of the outer senses or of the inner sense. Further, it is probable, though not certain, that we have acquaintance with Self, as that which is aware of things or has desires towards things.

In addition to our acquaintance with particular existing things, we also have acquaintance with what we shall call *universals*, that is to say, general ideas, such as *whiteness, diversity, brotherhood*, and so on. Every complete sentence must contain at least one word which stands for a universal, since all verbs have a meaning which is universal.... For the pres-ent, it is only necessary to guard against the supposition that whatever we can be acquainted with must be something particular and existent. Awareness of universals is called *conceiving*, and a universal of which we are aware is called a *concept*.

It will be seen that among the objects with which we are acquainted are not included physical objects (as opposed to sense-data), nor other people's minds. These things are known to us by what I call 'knowledge by description,' which we must now consider.

By a 'description' I mean any phrase of the form 'a so-and-so' or 'the so-and-so.' A phrase of the form 'a so-and-so' I shall call an 'ambiguous' description; a phrase of the form 'the so-and-so' (in the singular) I shall call a 'definite' description. Thus 'a man' is an ambiguous description, and 'the man with the iron mask' is a definite description. There are various problems connected with ambiguous descriptions, but I pass them by, since they do not directly concern the matter we are discussing, which is the nature of our knowledge concerning objects in cases where we know that there is an object answering to a definite description, though we are not *acquainted* with any such object. This is a matter which is concerned exclusively with *definite* descriptions. I shall therefore, in the sequel, speak simply of 'descriptions' when I mean 'definite descriptions.' Thus a description will mean any phrase of the form 'the so-and-so' in the singular.

We shall say that an object is 'known by description' when we know that it is 'the so-and-so,' i.e. when we know that there is one object, and no more, having a certain property; and it will generally be implied that we do not have knowledge of the same object by acquaintance. We know that the man with the iron mask existed, and many propositions are known about him; but we do not know who he was. We know that the candidate who gets the most votes will be elected, and in this case we are very likely also acquainted (in the only sense in which one can be acquainted with someone else) with the man who is, in fact, the candidate who will get most votes; but we do not know which of the candidates he is, i.e. we do not know any proposition of the form 'A is the candidate who will get most votes'

where A is one of the candidates by name. We shall say that we have 'merely descriptive knowledge' of the so-and-so when, although we know that the so-and-so exists, and although we may possibly be acquainted with the object which is, in fact, the so-and-so, yet we do not know any proposition '*a* is the so-and-so,' where *a* is something with which we are acquainted.

When we say 'the so-and-so exists,' we mean that there is just one object which is the so-and-so. The proposition '*a is* the so-and-so' means that *a* has the property so-and-so, and nothing else has. 'Mr. A. is the Unionist candidate for this constituency' means 'Mr. A. is the Unionist candidate for this constituency, and no one else is.' 'The Unionist candidate for this constituency exists' means 'some one is a Unionist candidate for this constituency, and no one else is.' Thus, when we are acquainted with an object which is the so-and-so, we know that the so-and-so exists; but we may know that the so-and-so exists when we are not acquainted with any object which we know to be the so-and-so, and even when we are not acquainted with any object which, in fact, is the so-and-so.

Common words, even proper names, are usually really descriptions. That is to say, the thought in the mind of a person using a proper name correctly can generally only be expressed explicitly if we replace the proper name by a description. Moreover, the description required to express the thought will vary for different people, or for the same person at different times. The only thing constant (so long as the name is rightly used) is the object to which the name applies. But so long as this remains constant, the particular description involved usually makes no difference to the truth or falsehood of the proposition in which the name appears.

Let us take some illustrations. Suppose some statement made about Bismarck. Assuming that there is such a thing as direct acquaintance with oneself, Bismarck himself might have used his name directly to designate the particular person with whom he was acquainted. In this case, if he made a judgement about himself, he himself might be constituent of the judgement. Here the proper name has the direct use which it always wishes to have, as simply standing for a certain object, and not for a description of the object. But if a person who knew Bismarck made a judgement about him, the case is different. What this person was acquainted with were certain sense-data which he connected (rightly, we will suppose) with Bismarck's body. His body, as a physical object, and still more his mind, were only known as the body and the mind connected with these sense-data. That is, they were known by description. It is, of course, very much a matter of chance which characteristics of a man's appearance will come into a friend's mind when he thinks of him; thus the description actually in the friend's mind is accidental. The essential point is that he knows that the various descriptions all apply to the same entity, in spite of not being acquainted with the entity in question.

When we, who did not know Bismarck, make a judgement about him, the description in our minds will probably be some more or less vague mass of historical knowledge—far more, in most cases, than is required to identify him. But for the sake of illustration, let us assume that we think of him as 'the first Chancellor of the German Empire.' Here all the words are abstract except 'German.' The word 'German' will, again, have different meanings for different people. To some it will recall travels in Germany, to some the look of Germany on the map, and so on. But if we are to obtain a description which we know to be applicable, we shall be compelled, at some point, to bring in a reference to a particular with which we are acquainted. Such reference is involved in any mention of past, present, and future (as opposed to definite dates), or of here and there, or of what others have told us. Thus it would seem that, in some way or other, a description known to be applicable to a particular must involve some reference to a particular with which we are acquainted, if our knowledge about the thing described is not to be merely what follows *logically* from the description. For example, 'the most longlived of men' is a description involving only universals, which must apply to some man, but we can make no judgements concerning this man which involve knowledge about him beyond what the description gives. If, however, we say, 'The first Chancellor of the German Empire was an astute diplomatist,' we can only be assured of the truth of our judgement in virtue of something with which we are acquainted—usually a testimony heard or read. Apart from the information we convey to others, apart from the fact about the actual Bismarck, which gives importance to our judgement, the thought we really have contains the one or more particulars involved, and otherwise consists wholly of concepts.

All names of places—London, England, Europe, the Earth, the Solar System—similarly involve, when used, descriptions which start from some one or more particulars with which we are acquainted. I suspect that even the Universe, as considered by metaphysics, involves such a connexion with particulars. In logic, on the contrary, where we are concerned not merely with what does exist, but with whatever might or could exist or be, no reference to actual particulars is involved.

It would seem that, when we make a statement about something only known by description, we often *intend* to make our statement, not in the form involving the description, but about the actual thing described. That is to say, when we say anything about Bismarck, we should like, if we could, to make the judgement which Bismarck alone can make, namely, the judgement of which he himself is a constituent. In this we are necessarily defeated, since the actual Bismarck is unknown to us. But we know that there is an object B, called Bismarck, and that B was an astute diplomatist.

We can thus *describe* the proposition we should like to affirm, namely, 'B was an astute diplomatist,' where B is the object which was Bismarck. If we are describing Bismarck as 'the first Chancellor of the German Empire,' the proposition we should like to affirm may be described as 'the proposition asserting, concerning the actual object which was the first Chancellor of the German Empire, that this object was an astute diplomatist,' that enables us to communicate in spite of the varying descriptions we employ is that we know there is a true proposition concerning the actual Bismarck, and that however we may vary the description (so long as the description is correct) the proposition described is still the same. This proposition, which is described and is known to be true, is what interests us; but we are not acquainted with the proposition itself, and do not know it, though we know it is true.

It will be seen that there are various stages in the removal from acquaintance with particulars: there is Bismarck to people who knew him; Bismarck to those who only know of him through history; the man with the iron mask; the longest-lived of men. These are progressively further removed from acquaintance with particulars; the first comes as near to acquaintance as is possible in regard to another person; in the second, we shall still be said to know 'who Bismarck was'; in the third, we do not know who was the man with the iron mask, though we can know many propositions about him which are not logically deducible from the fact that he wore an iron mask; in the fourth, finally, we know nothing beyond what is logically deducible from the definition of the man. There is a similar hierarchy in the region of universals. Many universals, like many particulars, are only known to us by description. But here, as in the case of particulars, knowledge concerning what is known by description is ultimately reducible to knowledge concerning what is known by acquaintance.

The fundamental principle in the analysis of propositions containing descriptions is this: *Every proposition which we can understand must be composed wholly of constituents with which we are acquainted.*

We shall not at this stage attempt to answer all the objections which may be urged against this fundamental principle. For the present, we shall merely point out that in some way or other, it must be possible to meet these objections, for it is scarcely conceivable that we can make a judgement or entertain a supposition without knowing what it is that we are judging or supposing about. We must attach *some* meaning to the words we use, if we are to speak significantly and not utter mere noise; and the meaning we attach to words must be something with which we are acquainted. Thus when, for example, we make a statement about Julius Caesar, it is plain that Julius Caesar himself is not before our minds, since we are not acquainted with him. We have in mind some *description* of Julius Caesar: 'the man who was assassinated on the Ides of March,' 'the founder of the Roman Empire,' or, perhaps, merely 'the man whose name was *Julius Caesar*.' (In this last description, *Julius Caesar* is a noise or shape with which we are acquainted.) Thus our statement does not mean quite what it seems to mean, but means something involving, instead of Julius Caesar, some description of him which is composed wholly of particulars and universals with which we are acquainted.

The chief importance of knowledge by description is that it enables us to pass beyond the limits of our private experience. In spite of the fact that we can only know truths which are wholly composed of terms which we have experienced in acquaintance, we can yet have knowledge by description of things which we have never experienced. In view of the very narrow range of our immediate experience, this result is vital, and until it is understood much of our knowledge must remain mysterious and therefore doubtful.

COMMENT

The word *intuition* is derived from the Latin *intuere*—"to look at." The looking or directness of the insight, is its fundamental mark. In intuitive knowledge, as John Locke wrote, "the mind … perceives the truth as the eye doth the light, only by being directed towards it." [1] Intuition can be defined as the direct apprehension that a proposition is true, or that something is the case.

Both Descartes and Bergson regard intuition as basic to philosophic method, but each differs in his conception of intuitive insight. For Descartes, it is the immediate grasp of truths, for example, that six is more than five. As the source of axiomatic truths, it provides the premises from which deduction draws forth, by a process of logical inference, the conclusions that necessarily follow. For Bergson, in contrast, intuition is the direct apprehension by a knowing subject of oneself, of one's mental states, or of anything with which one is immediately acquainted. It is more akin to sympathetic imagination than to abstract reasoning, and valued more for its own sake than as a foundation for deductive inference. It is an imaginative realization of the real rather than the fictitious.

The Bergsonian type of intuition is vividly illustrated by a number of passages in letters of John Keats. Consider, for example, his characterization of a poet's grasp of things:

> As to the poetical Character itself … it is not itself—it has no self—it is everything and nothing—It has no character—it enjoys light and shade; it lives in gusto, be it foul or fair, high or low, rich or poor, mean or elevated—It has as much delight in conceiving an Iago as an Imogen. What shocks the virtuous philosopher, delights the camelion Poet. It does not harm from its relish of the dark side of things any more than from its taste for the bright one; because they both end in speculation. A Poet is the most unpoetical of anything in existence; because he has no Identity—he is continually in for[ming?]—and filling some other Body—The Sun, the Moon, the Sea and Men and Women who are creatures of impulse are poetical and have about them an unchangeable attribute—the poet has none; no identity—he is certainly the most unpoetical of all God's Creatures. … It is a wretched thing to confess; but is a very fact that not one word I ever utter can be taken for granted as an opinion growing out of my identical nature—how can it, when I have no nature? When I am in a room with People if I ever am free from speculating on creations of my own brain, then not myself goes home to myself but the identity of every one in the room begins to press upon me [so] that I am in a very little time an[ni]hilated—not only among Men; it would be the same in a Nursery of children.

Keats was aware in his keen, intuitive way not only of human beings but also of animals and even inanimate things. "I go among the Fields," he wrote, "and catch a glimpse of a Stoat or a fieldmouse peeping out of the withered grass—the creature hath a purpose and its eyes are bright with it." In another letter he remarked, "… If a Sparrow come before my window I take part in its existence and

---

[1] *An Essay Concerning Human Understanding,* Book IV, Chap. 2.

pick about the Gravel." Keats claimed that he could imaginatively project himself into a moving billiard ball, and conceive, as though its qualities were his own, the "roundness, smoothness and volubility and the rapidity of its motion."

According to Bergson, all humans have the ability to intuit but only a genius exhibits it to a high degree. "Between nature and ourselves," he declares, "nay, between ourselves and our own consciousness a veil is interposed: a veil that is dense and opaque for the common herd—thin, almost transparent, for the artist and the poet." The ordinary man moves about amid "generalities and symbols," but the intuitive person, whether called an artist or not, brushes aside "the utilitarian symbols, the conventional and socially accepted generalities, in short everything that veils reality from us, in order to bring us face to face with reality itself."[2] In its innermost character, this reality is *duration*—the ceaseless, undivided flow of time, not clock time, with its mathematical abstractness, but *living* time, in its qualitative richness, fullness, and density.

Bergson distinguishes between *intellect*, the analytical faculty whose function is to facilitate action by dissecting and classifying, and *intuition*, the synthetic faculty whose function is to grasp the wholeness and concrete individuality of things. On the basis of these distinctions, he rejects the claims of mechanistic and materialistic philosophy and espouses a theory of free will and creative evolution. There is an irreducible life force, or *élan vital*, moving not toward any fixed or final goal but thrusting upward toward new and higher forms of existence. The downward movement of usable matter governed by the law of entropy is counter to this vital impetus.

There is much in this metaphysics and methodology with which Russell disagrees. Superficially, at least, he and Bergson could scarcely be farther apart. "I prefer sharp outlines and definite separations,"[3] he has remarked, deploring the opposite tendency of Bergson. Whereas the latter leans toward art and mysticism, Russell clings tenaciously to logic, mathematics, and science. "He seems very early to have felt, with justice," G. J. Warnock writes, "that by contrast with his own work and that of a few others in logic and the philosophy of mathematics, the writings of most contemporary philosophers were exceedingly loose, amateurish, and obscure. He was fond of saying that philosophy ought to be, as it had never yet been, 'scientific'—not only not less rigorous and exact, but more so, than mathematics and the physical sciences."[4] Judged by this standard, Bergson's "irrationalism" seemed to Russell deplorable.

During the very long period in which Russell had been writing, he had continued to develop, modify, and change his ideas. The views we are here considering are those expressed in *The Problems of Philosophy* (1912)—an early work. It is here that he develops, in the excerpt reprinted in this book, the distinction between "knowledge by acquaintance" and "knowledge by description," the latter being ultimately based on the former. However, it is unnecessary to summarize an

---

[2] *Laughter* (London: Macmillan, 1921), pp. 151, 157.
[3] *Portraits from Memory* (London: Allen & Unwin, 1956), p. 38.
[4] *English Philosophy Since 1900* (New York: Oxford University Press, 1966), p. 21.

argument that is so lucid. To refute those who would exaggerate the opposition between Bergson and Russell, it is sufficient to point out the similarity of "intuition" and "acquaintance." On the basis of this link, the two men stand together in contrast to such rationalists as Descartes, Spinoza, and Leibniz.

Finally, how would Bergson and Russell deal with the question of whether or not Deep Blue, the chess-playing computer, is actually thinking? Would they agree that some sort of intuitive knowledge is involved, or would they disagree? How do rationalism, with its emphasis on self-evident truths, and intuitionism, with its focus on direct knowledge, differ with respect to the above questions? Would Bergson acknowledge any intuition or "internal" activity on the part of the computer? Does he need to? What about Russell?

5

PRAGMATISM

Born in New York City in 1842, William James grew up in a family remarkable for its high spirits, intelligence, and congeniality. His father, Henry James, Sr., a man of intense religious and philosophical disposition, used his considerable inherited fortune to surround his five children with an atmosphere of culture. The family traveled a great deal, and William, like his sister and three brothers, was educated in various schools in the United States, England, France, Germany, and Switzerland. Thus he acquired the cosmopolitanism and *savoir faire* that distinguished him throughout his life. Uncertain of the choice of a career, he dabbled in painting, then studied chemistry, physiology, and medicine at Harvard. Still unable to reach a decision, he accompanied Louis Agassiz, the great naturalist, on a field trip up the Amazon and spent the next two years studying in Europe, mainly Germany. During this period and the subsequent three years spent in America, he suffered from a profound mental depression, at times even considering suicide.

Although he completed the work for his doctor's degree at the Harvard Medical School in 1869, it was not until 1872, when he was appointed to the post of instructor in physiology at Harvard, that he found regular employment. This appointment, which he called "a perfect God-send to me," contributed to a happier outlook. The last traces of his morbid mental state had apparently disappeared by 1878, when he married Alice Gibbens.

By this time, aged thirty-six, he was an established teacher of physiology and psychology at Harvard. In 1880, he became assistant professor of philosophy and before long, professor. During his tenure, the Department of Philosophy attained a high point of distinction, including among its faculty Josiah Royce, Hugo Münsterberg, and George Santayana. James' own importance as an original thinker was established with the publication, in 1890, of his masterwork, *Principles of Psychology*, the product of eleven years of labor. Although he finally won great acclaim as a philosopher, he never succeeded in writing a philosophical work as substantial and comprehensive as this great treatise in psychology.

Among his favorite recreations was mountain climbing. In June 1899, while climbing alone in the Adirondacks, he lost his way and overstrained his heart in a desperate thirteen-hour scramble. The result was an irreparable lesion, which forced him to curtail his intellectual activities. Finally, in 1910, his heart trouble became very serious, and he died in his New Hampshire home in August of that year.

Witty, kindly, urbane, but restless and neurasthenic, James was a remarkably complex and attractive character—"a being," to quote his sister, "who would bring life and charm to a treadmill." This charm he communicated in his writing, which often lends a rollicking sprightliness to the most abstruse subjects. Despite his artistic flair, he had the scientist's keen sense of fact and the moralist's high seriousness. However, his seriousness was never stuffy—he was always opposed to the snobs, the dogmatists, the pedants, and the goody-goodies that would fence in the human spirit.

WHAT·PRAGMATISM MEANS

Some years ago, being with a camping party in the mountains, I returned from a solitary ramble to find every one engaged in a ferocious metaphysical dispute. The *corpus* of the dispute was a squirrel—a live squirrel supposed to be clinging to one side of a tree-trunk; while over against the tree's opposite side a human being was imagined to stand. This human witness tries to get sight of the squirrel by moving rapidly round the tree, but no matter how fast he goes, the squirrel moves as fast in the opposite direction, and always keeps the tree between himself and the man, so that never a glimpse of him is caught. The resultant metaphysical problem now is this: *Does the man go round the squirrel or not?* He goes round the tree, sure enough, and the squirrel is on the tree; but does he go round the squirrel? In the unlimited leisure of the wilderness, discussion had been worn threadbare. Every one had taken sides, and was obstinate; and the numbers on both sides were even. Each side, when I appeared, therefore appealed to me to make it a majority. Mindful of the scholastic adage that whenever you meet a contradiction you must make a distinction, I immediately sought and found one, as follows: "Which party is right," I said, "depends on what you *practically mean* by 'going round'

the squirrel. If you mean passing from the north of him to the east, then to the south, then to the west, and then to the north of him again, obviously the man does go round him, for he occupies these successive positions. But if on the contrary you mean being first in front of him, then on the right of him, then behind him, then on his left, and finally in front again, it is quite as obvious that the man fails to go round him, for by the compensating movements the squirrel makes, he keeps his belly turned towards the man all the time, and his back turned away. Make the distinction, and there is no occasion for any further dispute. You are both right and both wrong according as you conceive the verb 'to go round' in one practical fashion or the other."

Although one or two of the hotter disputants called my speech a shuffling evasion, saying they wanted no quibbling or scholastic hair-splitting, but meant just plain honest English "round," the majority seemed to think that the distinction had assuaged the dispute.

I tell this trivial anecdote because it is a peculiarly simple example of what I wish now to speak of as the pragmatic method. The *pragmatic method* is primarily a method of settling metaphysical disputes that otherwise might be interminable. Is the world one or many?—fated or free?—material or spiritual?—here are notions either of which may or may not hold good of the world; and disputes over such notions are unending. The pragmatic method in such

From *Pragmatism: A New Name for Some Old Ways of Thinking.* Lectures II and VI (New York: Longmans, Green, 1907). Reprinted by permission.

cases is to try to interpret each notion by tracing its respective practical consequences. What difference would it practically make to any one if this notion rather than that notion were true? If no practical difference whatever can be traced, then the alternatives mean practically the same thing, and all dispute is idle. Whenever a dispute is serious, we ought to be able to show some practical difference that must follow from one side or the other's being right.

A glance at the history of the idea will show you still better what pragmatism means. The term is derived from the same Greek word πράγμα, meaning action, from which our words "practice" and "practical" come. It was first introduced into philosophy by Mr. Charles Peirce in 1878. In an article entitled "How to Make Our Ideas Clear," in the *Popular Science Monthly* for January of that year Mr. Peirce, after pointing out that our beliefs are really rules for action, said that, to develop a thought's meaning, we need only determine what conduct it is fitted to produce: that conduct is for us its sole significance. And the tangible fact at the root of all our thought-distinctions, however subtle, is that there is no one of them so fine as to consist in anything but a possible difference of practice. To attain perfect clearness in our thoughts of an object, then, we need only consider what conceivable effects of a practical kind the object may involve—what sensations we are to expect from it, and what reactions we must prepare. Our conception of these effects, whether immediate or remote, is then for us the whole of our conception of the object, so far as that conception has positive significance at all.

This is the principle of Peirce, the principle of pragmatism. It lay entirely unnoticed by any one for twenty years, until I, in an address before Professor Howison's Philosophical Union at the University of California, brought it forward again and made a special application of it to religion. By that date (1898) the time seemed ripe for its reception. The word "pragmatism" spread, and at present it fairly spots the pages of the philosophic journals. On all hands we find the "pragmatic movement" spoken of, sometimes with respect, sometimes with contumely, seldom with clear understanding. It is evident that the term applies itself conveniently to a number of tendencies that hitherto have lacked a collective name, and that it has "come to stay."

To take in the importance of Peirce's principle, one must get accustomed to applying it to concrete cases. I found a few years ago that Ostwald, the illustrious Leipzig chemist, had been making perfectly distinct use of the principle of pragmatism in his lectures on the philosophy of science, though he had not called it by that name.

"All realities influence our practice," he wrote me, "and that influence is their meaning for us. I am accustomed to put questions to my classes in this way: In what respects would the world be different if this alternative or that were true? If I can find nothing that would become different, then the alternative has no sense."

That is, the rival views mean practically the same thing, and meaning, other than practical, there is for us none. Ostwald in a published lecture gives this example of what he means. Chemists have long wrangled over the inner constitution of certain bodies called "tautomerous." Their properties seemed equally consistent with the notion that an instable hydrogen atom oscillates inside of them, or that they are instable mixtures of two bodies. Controversy raged, but never was decided. "It would never have begun," says Ostwald, "if the combatants had asked themselves what particular experimental fact could have been made different by one or the other view being correct. For it would then have appeared that no difference of fact could possibly ensue; and the quarrel was as unreal as if, theorizing in primitive times about the raising of dough by yeast, one party should have invoked a 'brownie,' while another insisted on an 'elf' as the true cause of the phenomenon."[1]

It is astonishing to see how many philosophical disputes collapse into insignificance the moment you subject them to this simple test of tracing a concrete consequence. There can *be* no difference anywhere that doesn't *make* a difference elsewhere—no difference in abstract truth that doesn't express itself in a difference in concrete fact and in conduct consequent upon that fact, imposed on somebody, somehow, somewhere, and somewhen. The whole function of philosophy ought to find out what definite difference it will make to you and me, at definite instants of our life, if this world-formula or that world-formula be the true one.

There is absolutely nothing new in the pragmatic method. Socrates was an adept at it. Aristotle used it methodically. Locke, Berkeley, and Hume made momentous contributions to truth by its means. Shadworth Hodgson keeps insisting that realities are only what they are "known as." But these forerunners of pragmatism used it in fragments: they were preluders only. Not until in our time has it generalized itself, become conscious of a universal mission, pretended to a conquering destiny. I believe in that destiny, and I hope I may end by inspiring you with my belief.

Pragmatism represents a perfectly familiar attitude in philosophy, the empiricist attitude, but it represents it, as it seems to me, both in a more radical and in a less objectionable form than it has ever yet

---

[1] "Theorie und Praxis." *Zeitschrift des Oesterreichischan Ingenieur-u Architecten Vereines*; 1905, Nr. 4 u. 6. I find a still more radical pragmatism than Ostwald's in an address by Professor W. S. Franklin: "I think that the sickliest notion of physics, even if a student gets it, is that it is 'the science of masses, molecules, and the ether.' And I think that the healthiest notion, even if a student does not wholly get it, is that physics is the science of the ways of taking hold of bodies and pushing them!" (*Science, January 2, 1903.*)

assumed. A pragmatist turns his back resolutely and once for all upon a lot of inveterate habits dear to professional philosophers. He turns away from abstraction and insufficiency, from verbal solutions, from bad *a priori* reasons, from fixed principles, closed systems, and pretended absolutes and origins. He turns towards concreteness and adequacy, towards fact, towards action and towards power. That means the empiricist temper regnant and the rationalist temper sincerely given up. It means the open air and possibilities of nature, as against dogma, artificiality, and the pretence of finality in truth.

At the same time it does not stand for any special results. It is a method only. But the general triumph of that method would mean an enormous change in ... the "temperament" of philosophy. Teachers of the ultrarationalistic type would be frozen out, much as the courtier type is frozen out in republics, as the ultramontane type of priest is frozen out in protestant lands. Science and metaphysics would come much nearer together, would in fact work absolutely hand in hand.

Metaphysics has usually followed a very primitive kind of quest. You know how men have always hankered after unlawful magic, and you know what a great part in magic *words* have always played. If you have his name, or the formula of incantation that binds him, you can control the spirit, genie, afrite, or whatever the power may be. Solomon knew the names of all the spirits, and having their names, he held them subject to his will. So the universe has always appeared to the natural mind as a kind of enigma, of which the key must be sought in the shape of some illuminating or power-bringing word or name. That word names the universe's *principle*, and to possess it is after a fashion to possess the universe itself. "God," 'Matter," "Reason", "the Absolute," "Energy," are so many solving names. You can rest when you have them. You are at the end of your metaphysical quest.

But if you follow the pragmatic method, you cannot look on any such word as closing your quest. You must bring out of each word its practical cash-value, set it at work within the stream of your experience. It appears less as a solution, then, than as a program for more work, and more particularly as an indication of the ways in which existing realities may be *changed*.

Theories thus become instruments, not answers to enigmas, in which we can rest. We don't lie back upon them, we move forward, and, on occasion, make nature over again by their aid. Pragmatism unstiffens all our theories, limbers them up and sets each one at work. Being nothing essentially new, it harmonizes with many ancient philosophic tendencies. It agrees with nominalism, for instance, in always appealing to particulars; with utilitarianism in emphasizing practical aspects; with positivism in its disdain for verbal solutions, useless questions and metaphysical abstractions.

All these, you see, are *anti-intellectualist* tendencies. Against rationalism as a pretension and a method pragmatism is fully armed and militant. But, at the outset, at least, it stands for no particular results. It has no dogmas, and no doctrines save its method. As the young Italian pragmatist Papini has well said, it lies in the midst of our theories, like a corridor in a hotel. Innumerable chambers open out of it. In one you may find a man writing an atheistic volume; in the next some one on his knees praying for faith and strength; in a third a chemist investigating a body's properties. In a fourth a system of idealistic metaphysics is excogitated; in a fifth the impossibility of metaphysics is being shown. But they all own the corridor, and all must pass through it if they want a practicable way of getting into or out of their respective rooms.

No particular results then, so far, but only an attitude of orientation, is what the pragmatic method means. *The attitude of looking away from first things, principles, "categories," supposed necessities; and of looking towards last things, fruits, consequences, facts.*

So much for the pragmatic method!... Meanwhile the word pragmatism has come to be used in a still wider sense, as meaning also a certain *theory of truth.* ...

Truth, as any dictionary will tell you, is a property of certain of our ideas. It means their "agreement," as falsity means their "disagreement," with "reality." Pragmatists and intellectualists both accept this definition as a matter of course. They begin to quarrel only after the question is raised as to what may precisely be meant by the term "agreement," and what by the term "reality," when reality is taken as something for our ideas to agree with.

In answering these questions the pragmatists are more analytic and painstaking, the intellectualists more offhand and irreflective. The popular notion is that a true idea must copy its reality. Like other popular views, this one follows the analogy of the most usual experience. Our true ideas of sensible things do indeed copy them. Shut your eyes and think of yonder clock on the wall, and you get just such a true picture or copy of its dial. But your idea of its "works" (unless you are a clockmaker) is much less of a copy, yet it passes muster, for it in no way clashes with the reality. Even though it should shrink to the mere word "works," that word still serves you truly; and when you speak of the "timekeeping function" of the clock, or of its spring's "elasticity," it is hard to see exactly what your ideas can copy.

You perceive that there is a problem here. Where our ideas cannot copy definitely their object, what does agreement with that object mean? Some idealists seem to say that they are true whenever they are what God means that we ought to think about that subject. Others hold the copy-view all through, and speak as if our ideas possessed truth just in proportion as they approach to being copies of the Absolute's eternal way of thinking.

These views, you see, invite pragmatistic discussion. But the great assumption of the intellectualists is that truth means essentially an inert static relation. When you've got your true idea of anything, there's an end of the matter. You're in possession; you *know;* you have fulfilled your thinking destiny. You are where you ought to be mentally; you have obeyed your categorical imperative; and nothing more need follow on that climax of your rational destiny. Epistemologically you are in stable equilibrium.

Pragmatism, on the other hand, asks its usual question. "Grant an idea or belief to be true," it says, "what concrete difference will its being true make in any one's actual life? How will the truth be realized? What experiences will be different from those which would obtain if the belief were false? What, in short, is the truth's cash-value in experiential terms?"

The moment pragmatism asks this question, it sees the answer: *True ideas are those that we can assimilate, validate, corroborate and verify. False ideas are those that we cannot.* That is the practical difference it makes to us to have true ideas; that, therefore, is the meaning of truth, for it is all that truth is known as.

This thesis is what I have to defend. The truth of an idea is not a stagnant property inherent in it. Truth *happens* to an idea. It *becomes* true, is made true by events. Its verity is in fact an event, a process: the process namely of its verifying itself, its veri-*fication.* Its validity is the process of its valid-*ation.*

But what do the words verification and validation themselves pragmatically mean? They again signify certain practical consequences of the verified and validated idea. It is hard to find any one phrase that characterizes these consequences better than the ordinary agreement-formula—just such consequences being what we have in mind whenever we say that our ideas "agree" with reality. They lead us, namely, through the acts and other ideas which they instigate, into or up to, or towards, other parts of experience with which we feel all the while—such feeling being among our potentialities—that the original ideas remain in agreement.

The connections and transitions come to us from point to point as being progressive, harmonious, satisfactory. This function of agreeable leading is what we mean by an idea's verification.

To "agree" in the widest sense with a reality *can only mean to be guided either straight up to it or into its surroundings, or to be put into such working touch with it as to handle either it or something connected with it better than if we disagreed.* Better either intellectually or practically! And often agreement will only mean the negative fact that nothing contradictory from the quarter of that reality comes to interfere with the way in which our ideas guide us elsewhere. To copy a reality is, indeed, one very important way of agreeing with it, but it is far from being essential. The essential thing is the process of being guided. Any idea that helps us to deal, whether practically or intellectually, with either the reality or its belongings, that doesn't entangle our progress in frustrations, that *fits,* in fact, and adapts our life to the reality's whole setting, will agree sufficiently to meet the requirement. It will hold true of that reality.

Thus, *names* are just as "true" or "false" as definite mental pictures are. They set up similar verification-processes, and lead to fully equivalent practical results. ...

The overwhelming majority of our true ideas admit of no direct or face-to-face verification—those of past history, for example, as of Cain and Abel. The stream of time can be remounted only verbally, or verified indirectly by the present prolongations or effects of what the past harbored. Yet if they agree with these verbalities and effects, we can know that our ideas of the past are true. *As true as past time itself was*, so true was Julius Caesar, so true were antediluvian monsters, all in their proper dates and settings. That past time itself was, is guaranteed by its coherence with everything that's present. True as the present is, the past *was* also.

Agreement thus turns out to be essentially an affair of leading—leading that is useful because it is into quarters that contain objects that are important. True ideas lead us into useful verbal and conceptual quarters as well as directly up to useful sensible termini. They lead to consistency, stability and flowing human intercourse. They lead away from eccentricity and isolation, from foiled and barren thinking. The untrammeled flowing of the leading-process, its general freedom from clash and contradiction, passes for its indirect verification; but all roads lead to Rome, and in the end and eventually, all true processes must lead to the face of directly verifying sensible experiences *somewhere*, which somebody's ideas have copied.

Such is the large loose way in which the pragmatist interprets the word agreement. He treats it altogether practically. He lets it cover any process of conduction from a present idea to a future terminus, provided only it run prosperously. It is only thus that "scientific" ideas, flying as they do beyond common sense, can be said to agree with their realities. It is, as I have already said, *as if* reality were made of ether, atoms or electrons, but we mustn't think so literally. The term "energy" doesn't even pretend to stand for anything "objective." It is only a way of measuring the surface of phenomena so as to string their changes on a simple formula.

Yet in the choice of these man-made formulas we cannot be capricious with impunity any more than we can be capricious on the common-sense practical level. We must find a theory that will *work*; and that means something extremely difficult; for our theory must mediate between all previous truths and certain new experiences. It must derange common sense and previous belief as little as possible, and it must lead to some sensible terminus or other that can be verified exactly. To "work" means both these things; and the squeeze is so tight that there is little loose play for any hypothesis. Our theories are wedged and controlled as nothing else is. Yet sometimes alternative theoretic formulas are equally compatible with all the truths we know, and then we choose between them for subjective reasons. We choose the kind of theory to which

we are already partial; we follow "elegance" or "economy." Clerk-Maxwell somewhere says it would be "poor scientific taste" to choose the more complicated of two equally well-evidenced conceptions; and you will all agree with him. Truth in science is what gives us the maximum possible sum of satisfactions, taste included, but consistency both with previous truth and with novel fact is always the most imperious claimant. . . .

Our account of truth is an account of truths in the plural, of processes of leading, realized *in rebus* [in things], and having only this quality in common, that they *pay*. They pay by guiding us into or towards some part of a system that dips at numerous points into sense-percepts, which we may copy mentally or not, but with which at any rate we are now in the kind of commerce vaguely designated as verification. Truth for us is simply a collective name for verification-processes, just as health, wealth, strength, etc., are names for other processes connected with life, and also pursued because it pays to pursue them. Truth is *made*, just as health, wealth and strength are made, in the course of experience. . . .

"*The true*," to put it *very briefly*, *is only the expedient in the way of our thinking, just as "the right" is only the expedient in the way of our behaving.* Expedient in almost any fashion; and expedient in the long run and on the whole of course; for what meets expediently all the experience in sight won't necessarily meet all further experiences equally satisfactorily. Experience, as we know, has ways of *boiling over*, and making us correct our present formulas.

The "absolutely" true, meaning what no further experience will ever alter, is that ideal vanishing-point towards which we imagine that all our temporary truths will some day converge. It runs on all fours with the perfectly wise man, and with the absolutely complete experience; and, if these ideals are ever realized, they will all be realized together. Meanwhile we have to live today by what truth we can get today, and be ready tomorrow to call it falsehood. Ptolemaic astronomy, Euclidean space, Aristotelian logic, Scholastic metaphysics, were expedient for centuries, but human experience has boiled over those limits, and we now call these things only relatively true, or true within those borders to experience. "Absolutely" they are false: for we know that those limits were causal, and might have been transcended by past theorists just as they are by present thinkers. ...

The trail of the human serpent is thus over everything. Truth independent; truth that we *find* merely; truth no longer malleable to human need; truth incorrigible, in a word; such truth exists indeed superabundantly—or is supposed to exist by rationalistically minded thinkers; but then it means

only the dead heart of the living tree, and its being there means only that truth also has its paleontology, and its "prescription," and may grow stiff with years of veteran service and petrified in men's regard by sheer antiquity. But how plastic even the oldest truths nevertheless really are has been vividly shown in our day by the transformation of logical and mathematical ideas, a transformation which seems even to be invading physics. The ancient formulas are reinterpreted as special expressions of much wider principles, principles that our ancestors never got a glimpse of in their present shape and formulation. ...

Such then would be the scope of pragmatism—first, a method; and second, a genetic theory of what is meant by truth.

JOHN DEWEY (1859–1952)

John Dewey was born in the beautiful New England town of Burlington, Vermont. "All my forefathers," he has said, "earned an honest living as farmers, wheelwrights, coopers. I was absolutely the first one in seven generations to fall from grace."[1] However, his father, a grocer, loved to recite from Shakespeare and Milton, and his parents gave their four sons the advantages of a college education and of a liberal moral and religious outlook. Dewey took his undergraduate degree at the University of Vermont and his doctorate degree in philosophy at Johns Hopkins in 1884.

He taught at the University of Michigan from 1884 to 1894 (except for one year at the University of Minnesota) and then, for an additional ten-year period, at the University of Chicago. During these years, he gradually shifted from Hegelian idealism to his own version of pragmatism, or as he preferred to call it, "instrumentalism." His ideas had begun to cause some controversy even before he went to Chicago, but this was mild compared with the storm that broke out when he began to apply his pragmatic ideals as director of the "Laboratory School" for children at the University of Chicago. Aided by his wife, for seven and a half years Dewey conducted a bold educational experiment based on the concepts of "learning by doing" and "education for democracy." Whereas traditional education had sought to instill obedience and receptivity, he sought to cultivate activity, initiative, diversity, and voluntary cooperation; and in so doing,

[1] Edwin E. Slosson, *Six Major Prophets* (Boston: Little, Brown, 1917), p. 268. (From a letter of Dewey to Slosson.)

he wrought a veritable revolution in educational theory and practice. The volume in which he explained what he was trying to do, *School and Society*, was first published in 1899 and has since been translated into a dozen European and Oriental languages and reprinted many times.

Having achieved fame both as an educator and as a philosopher, Dewey in 1904 was called to Columbia University, where he remained until his retirement in 1929. With prodigious energy, he poured forth an immense volume of publications and engaged in many educational, political, and civic activities. In 1919 he lectured at the Imperial University of Japan in Tokyo, and during the next two years at the National Universities at Peking and at Nanking, where he made a profound impression on Chinese students and intellectuals. For briefer periods, he visited Turkey in 1924, Mexico in 1926, and Soviet Russia in 1928. Later he served as a member of the international Commission of Inquiry into the charges made against Leon Trotsky at the famous Moscow trial of Trotsky's alleged confederates. This commission, which met in Mexico City, finally issued a report *Not Guilty* (1937), which became the object of heated political controversy.

During the later years of his life, Dewey's interests continued to broaden, as indicated by the wide range of his writings—on education, religion, art, politics, ethics, logic, epistemology, and metaphysics. His many social and intellectual activities, however, did not prevent him from rearing a large family and forming many warm personal friendships. When he died at the age of ninety-two, he had had a more comprehensive and profound impact on the modern world than any other American philosopher.

His personality was not as vivid as James', and his literary style is not as readable. Modest, unobtrusive, somewhat halting in speech, and ultrademocratic in manner, Dewey the human being has sometimes seemed to be quite different from Dewey the bold and independent thinker. This contrast has led many people to misinterpret and vulgarize his ideas and to underestimate his native radicalism. But if, as has been claimed, Dewey is more representative of democratic America than any other thinker, it is an intellectually adventurous and daring America that he represents.

SCIENTIFIC PHILOSOPHY

The Copernican Revolution

Kant claimed that he had effected a Copernican revolution in philosophy by treating the world and our knowledge of it from the

Reprinted by permission of the Putnam Publishing Group from *The Quest for Certainty* by John Dewey. © Copyright 1929 by John Dewey. Renewed © 1957 by Frederick A. Dewey.

standpoint of the knowing subject. To most critics, the endeavor to make the known world turn on the constitution of the knowing mind, seems like a return to an ultra-Ptolemaic system. But Copernicus, as Kant understood him, effected a straightening out of astronomical phenomena by interpreting their perceived subject, instead of treating them as inherent in the things perceived. The revolution of the sun about the earth as it offers itself to sense-perception was regarded as due to the conditions of human observation and not to the movements of the sun itself. Disregarding the consequences of the changed point of view, Kant settled upon this one feature as characteristic of the method of Copernicus. He thought he could generalize this feature of Copernican method, and thus clear up a multitude of philosophical difficulties by attributing the facts in question to the constitution of the human subject in knowing.

That the consequence was Ptolemaic rather than Copernican is not to be wondered at. In fact, the alleged revolution of Kant consisted in making explicit what was implicit in the classic tradition. In words, the latter had asserted that knowledge is determined by the objective constitution of the universe. But it did so only after it had first assumed that the universe is itself constituted after the pattern of reason. Philosophers first constructed a rational system of nature and then borrowed from it the features by which to characterize their knowledge of it. Kant, in effect, called attention to the borrowing; he insisted that credit for the borrowed material be assigned to human reason instead of to divine. His "revolution" was a shift from a theological to a human authorship; beyond that point, it was an explicit acknowledgement of what philosophers in the classic line of descent had been doing unconsciously before him. For the basic assumption of this tradition was the inherent correspondence subsisting between *intellectus* and the structure of Nature—the principle so definitely stated by Spinoza. By the time of Kant difficulties in this rationalistic premise had become evident. He thought to maintain the underlying idea and remedy the perplexities it entailed by placing the locus of intellect in man as a knowing subject. The irritation which this performance arouses in some minds is due rather to this transfer than to any doubt about the valid function of reason in the constitution of nature.

Kant refers incidentally to the experimental method of Galileo as an illustration of the way in which thought actually takes the lead, so that an object is known because of conformity to a prior conception—because of its conformity to the specifications of the latter. The reference makes clear by contrast the genuine reversal contained in the experimental way of knowing. It is true that experimentation proceeds on the basis of a directive idea. But the difference between the office of the idea in determining a known object and the office assigned to it in Kant's theory is as great as between the Copernican and the Ptolemaic systems. For an idea in experiment is tentative, conditional, not fixed and rigorously determinative. It controls an action to be performed, but the consequences of the operation determine the worth of the directive idea; the directive does not fix the nature of the object.

Moreover, in experiment everything takes place aboveboard, in the open. Every step is overt and capable of being observed. There is a specified antecedent state of things; a specified operation using means, both physical and symbolic, which are externally exhibited and reported. The entire process by which the conclusion is reached that such and such a judgment of an object is valid is overt. It can be repeated step by step by any one. Thus every one can judge for himself whether or not the conclusion reached as to the object justifies assertion of knowledge, or whether there are gaps and deflections. Moreover, the whole process goes on where other existential processes go on, in time. There is a temporal sequence as definitely as in any art, as in, say, the making of cotton cloth from ginning of raw material, through carding and spinning to the operation of the loom. A public and manifest series of definite operations, all capable of public notice and report, distinguishes scientific knowing from the knowing carried on by inner "mental" processes accessible only to introspection, or inferred by dialectic from assumed premises.

There is accordingly opposition rather than agreement between the Kantian determination of objects by thought and the determination by thought that takes place in experimentation. There is nothing hypothetical or conditional about Kant's forms of perception and conception. They work uniformly and triumphantly; they need no differential testing by consequences. The reason Kant postulates them is to secure universality and necessity instead of the hypothetical and the probable. Nor is there anything overt, observable and temporal or historical in the Kantian machinery. Its work is done behind the scenes. Only the result is observed, and only an elaborate process of dialectic inference enables Kant to assert the existence of his apparatus of forms and categories. These are as inaccessible to observation as were the occult forms and essences whose rejection was a prerequisite of development of modern science.

These remarks are not directed particularly against Kant. For, as has been already said, he edited a new version of old conceptions about mind and its activities in knowing, rather than evolved a brand new theory. But since he happens to be the author of the phrase "Copernican revolution," his philosophy forms a convenient point of departure for consideration of a genuine reversal of traditional ideas about the mind, reason, conceptions, and mental processes. Phases of this revolution have concerned us in the previous lectures. We have seen how the opposition between knowing and doing, theory and practice, has been abandoned in the actual enterprise of scientific inquiry, how knowing goes forward by means of doing. We have seen how the cognitive quest for absolute certainty by purely mental means has been surrendered in behalf of, search for a security, having a high degree of probability, by means of preliminary active regulation of conditions. We have considered some of the definite steps by which security has come to attach to regulation of change rather than absolute certainty to the unchangeable. We have noted how in sequence of this transformation the stan-

dard of judgment has been transferred from antecedents to consequents from inert dependence upon the past to intentional construction of a future.

If such changes do not constitute, in the depth and scope of their significance, a reversal comparable to a Copernican revolution, I am at a loss to know where such a change can be found or what it would be like. The old center was mind knowing by means of an equipment of powers complete within itself, and merely exercised upon an antecedent external material equally complete in itself. The new center is indefinite interactions taking place within a course of nature which is not fixed and complete, but which is capable of direction to new and different results through the mediation of intentional operations. Neither self nor world, neither soul nor nature (in the sense of something isolated and finished in its isolation) is the center, any more than either earth or sun is the absolute center of a single universal and necessary frame of reference. There is a moving whole of interacting parts; a center emerges wherever there is effort to change them in a particular direction.

The reversal has many phases, and these are interconnected. It cannot be said that one is more important than another. But one change stands out with an extraordinary distinctness. Mind is no longer a spectator beholding the world from without and finding its highest satisfaction in the joy of self-sufficing contemplation. The mind is within the world as a part of the latter's own on-going process. It is marked off as mind by the fact that wherever it is found, changes take place in a *directed* way, so that a movement in a definite one-way sense—from the doubtful and confused to the clear, resolved and settled—takes place. From knowing as an outside beholding to knowing as in active participant in the drama of an on-moving world is the historical transition whose record we have been following.

As far as philosophy is concerned, the first direct and immediate effect of this shift from knowing which makes a difference to the knower but none in the world, to knowing which is a directed change within the world, is the complete abandonment of what we may term the intellectualist fallacy. By this is meant something which may also be termed the ubiquity of knowledge as a measure of reality. Of the older philosophies, framed before experimental knowing had made any significant progress, it may be said that they made a definite separation between the world in which man thinks and knows and the world in which he lives and acts. In his needs and in the acts that spring from them, man *was* a part of the world, a sharer in its fortunes, sometimes willingly, sometimes perforce; he was exposed to its vicissitudes and at the mercy of its irregular and unforeseeable changes. By acting in and upon the world he made his earthly way, sometimes failing, sometimes achieving. He was acted upon by it, sometimes carried forward to unexpected glories and sometimes overwhelmed by its disfavor.

Being unable to cope with the world in which he lived, he sought some way to come to terms with the universe as a whole. Religion was, in its origin, an expression of this endeavor. After a time, a few persons with leisure and endowed by fortune with immunity from the rougher impacts of the world, discovered the delights of thought and inquiry. They reached the conclusion that through rational thought they could rise above the natural world in which, with their body, and those mental processes that were connected with the body, they lived. In striving with the inclemencies of nature, suffering its buffetings, wresting sustenance from its resources, they were parts of Nature. But in knowledge, true knowledge which is rational, occupied with objects that are universal and immutable, they escaped from the world of vicissitude and uncertainty. They were elevated above the realm in which needs are felt and laborious effort imperative. In rising above this world of sense and time, they came into rational communion with the divine which was

untroubled and perfect mind. They became true participants in the realm of ultimate reality. Through knowledge, they were without the world of chance and change, and within the world of perfect and unchanging Being.

How far this glorification by philosophers and scientific investigators of a life of knowing, apart from and above a life of doing, might have impressed the popular mind without adventitious aid there is no saying. But external aid came. Theologians of the Christian Church adopted this view in a form adapted to their religious purposes. The perfect and ultimate reality was God; to know Him was eternal bliss. The world in which man lived and acted was a world of trials and troubles to test and prepare him for a higher destiny. Through thousands of ways, including histories arid rites, with symbols that engaged the emotions and imagination, the essentials of the doctrine of classic philosophy filtered its way into the popular mind.

It would be a one-sided view which held that this story gives the entire account of the elevation of knowing and its object above practical action and its objects. A contributing cause was found in the harshness, cruelties and tragic frustrations of the world of action. Were it not for its brutalities and failures, the motive for seeking refuge in a higher realm of knowledge would have been lacking. It was easy and, as we say, "natural" to associate these evils with the fact that the world in which we act is a realm of change. The generic fact of change was made absolute and the source of all the troubles and defects of the world in which we directly live. At the very best, good and excellence are insecure in a world of change; good can be securely at home only in a realm of fixed unchanging substance. When the source of evil was once asserted to reside in the inherent deficiencies of a realm of change, responsibility was removed from human ignorance, incapacity arid insusceptibility. It remained only to change our own attitude and disposition, to turn the soul from perishable things toward perfect Being. In this idea religion stated in one language precisely what the great philosophic tradition stated in another.

Nor is this the whole of the story. There was, strangely enough, a definitely practical ground for the elevation of knowledge above doing and making. Whenever knowledge is actually obtained, a measure of security through ability to control ensues. There is a natural inclination to treat value as a measure of reality. Since knowledge is the mode of experience that puts in our hands the key to controlling our other dealings with experienced objects, it has a central position. There is no *practical* point gained in asserting that a thing is what it is *experienced* to be apart from knowledge. If a man has typhoid fever, he has it; he does not have to search for or pry into it. But to *know* it, he does have to search:—to *thought*, to intellect, the fever is what it is known to be. For when it is known, the various phenomena of *having* it, the direct experiences, fall into order; we have at least that kind of control called understanding, and with this comes the possibility of a more active control. The very fact that other experiences speak, so to say, for themselves makes it unnecessary to ask *what* they are. When the nature of an existence is in doubt and we have to seek for it, the idea of reality is consciously present. Hence the thought of existence becomes exclusively associated with knowing. Other ways of experiencing things exist so obviously that we do not *think* of existence in connection with them.

At all events, whatever the explanation, the idea that cognition is the measure of the reality found in other modes of experience is the most widely distributed premise of philosophies. The equation of the real and the known comes to explicit statement in idealistic theories. If we remind ourselves of the landscape with trees and grasses waving in the wind and waves dancing in sunlight, we recall how scientific thought of these things strips off the qualities significant in perception and

direct enjoyment, leaving only certain physical constants stated in mathematical formulæ. What is more natural, then, than to call upon mind to reclothe by some contributory act of thought or consciousness the grim skeleton offered by science? Then if only it can be shown that mathematical relations are themselves a logical construction of thought, the knowing mind is enstated as the constitutive author of the whole scheme. Realistic theories have protested against doctrines that make the knowing mind the source of the thing known. But they have held to a doctrine of a partial equation of the real and the known; only they have read the equation from the side of the object instead of the subject. Knowledge must be the grasp or vision of the real as it "is in itself," while emotions and affections deal with it as it is affected with an alien element supplied by the feeling and desiring subject. The postulate of the unique and exclusive relation among experienced things of knowledge and the real is shared by epistemological idealist and realist.

The meaning of a Copernican reversal is that we do not have to go to knowledge to obtain an exclusive hold on reality. The world as we experience it is a real world. But it is not in its primary phases a world that is known, a world that is understood, and is intellectually coherent and secure. Knowing consists of operations that give experienced objects a form in which the relations, upon which the onward course of events depends, are securely experienced. It marks a transitional redirection and rearrangement of the real. It is intermediate and instrumental; it comes between a relatively casual and accidental experience of existence and one relatively settled and defined. The knower is within the world of existence; his knowing, as experimental, marks an interaction of one existence with other existences. There is, however, a most important difference between it and other existential interactions. The difference is not between something going on within nature as a part of itself and something else taking place outside it, but is that between a regulated course of changes and an uncontrolled one. In knowledge, causes become means and effects become consequences, and thereby things have meanings. The known object is an antecedent object as that is intentionally rearranged and redisposed, an eventual object whose value is tested by the reconstruction it effects. It emerges, as it were, from the fire of experimental thought as a refined metal issues from operations performed on crude material. It is the same object but the same object with a difference, as a man who has been through conditions which try the temper of his being comes out the same man and a different man.

Knowledge then does not encompass the world as a whole. But the fact that it is not coextensive with experienced existence is no defect nor failure on its part. It is an expression of the fact that knowledge attends strictly to its own business:—transformation of disturbed and unsettled situations into those more controlled and more significant. Not all existence asks to be known, and it certainly does not ask leave from thought to exist. But some existences as they are experienced do ask thought to direct them in their course so that they may be ordered and fair and be such as to commend themselves to admiration, approval and appreciation. Knowledge affords the sole means by which this redirection can be effected. As the latter is brought about, parts of the experienced world have more luminous and organized meaning and their significance is rendered more secure against the gnawing tooth of time. The problem of knowledge is the problem of discovery of methods for carrying on this enterprise of redirection. It is a problem never ended, always in process; one problematic situation is resolved and another takes its place. The constant gain is not in approximation to universal solution but in betterment of methods and enrichment of objects experienced.

Man as a natural creature acts as masses and molecules act; he lives as animals live, eating, fighting, fearing, reproduc-

ing. As he lives, some of his actions yield understanding and things take on meaning, for they become signs of one another; means of expectation and of recall, preparations for what is to come and celebrations of what has gone. Activities take on ideal quality. Attraction and repulsion become love of the admirable and hate of the harsh and ugly, and they seek to find and make a world in which they may be securely at home. Hopes and fears, desires and aversions, are as truly responses to things as are knowing and thinking. Our affections, when they are enlightened by understanding, are organs by which we enter into the meaning of the natural world as genuinely as by knowing, and with greater fullness and intimacy. This deeper and richer intercourse with things can be effected only by thought and its resultant knowledge; the arts in which the potential meanings of nature are realized demand an intermediate and transitional phase of detachment and abstraction. The colder and less intimate transactions of knowing involve temporary disregard of the qualities and values to which our affections and enjoyments are attached. But knowledge is an indispensable medium of our hopes and fears, of loves and hates, if desires and preferences are to be steady, ordered, charged with meaning, secure.

The glorification of knowledge as the exclusive avenue of access to what is real is not going to give way soon nor all at once. But it can hardly endure indefinitely. The more widespread become the habits of intelligent thought, the fewer enemies they meet from those vested interests and social institutions whose power depends upon immunity from inspection by intelligence, in short, the more matter of course they become, the less need will there seem to be for giving knowledge an exclusive and monopolistic position. It will be prized for its fruits rather than for the properties assigned to it when it was a new and precarious enterprise. The common fact that we prize in proportion to rarity has a good deal to do with the exclusive esteem in which knowledge has been held. There is so much unintelligent appetite and impulse, so much routine action, so much that is dictated by the arbitrary power of other persons, so much, in short, that is not informed and enlightened by knowledge, that it is not surprising that action and knowledge should have been isolated in thought from one another, and knowledge treated as if it alone had dealings with real existence. I do not know when knowledge will become naturalized in the life of society. But when it is fully acclimatized, its instrumental, as distinct from its monopolistic, role in approach to things of nature and society will be taken for granted without need for such arguments as I have been engaging in. Meantime, the development of the experimental method stands as a prophecy of the possibility of the accomplishment of this Copernican Revolution.

Whenever anyone speaks about the relation of knowledge (especially if the word science be used) to our moral, artistic and religious interests, there are two dangers to which he is exposed. There exists on one hand efforts to use scientific knowledge to substantiate moral and religious beliefs, either with respect to some specific form in which they are current or in some vague way that is felt to he edifying and comforting. On the other hand, philosophers derogate the importance and necessity of knowledge in order to make room for an undisputed sway of some set of moral and religious tenets. It may be that preconceptions will lead some to interpret what has been said in one or other of these senses. If so, it is well to state that not a word has been said in depreciation of science; what has been criticized is a philosophy and habit of mind on the ground of which science is prized for false reasons. Nor does this negative statement cover the whole ground. Knowledge is instrumental. But the purport of our whole discussion has been in. praise of tools, instrumentalities, means, putting them on a level equal in value to ends and consequences, since without them the latter are merely acciden-

tal, sporadic and unstable. To call known objects, in their capacity of being objects of knowledge, means is to appreciate them, not to depreciate them.

Affections, desires, purposes, choices are going to endure as long as man is man; therefore as long as man is man, there are going to be ideas, judgments, beliefs about values. Nothing could be sillier than to attempt to justify their existence at large; they are going to exist anyway. What is inevitable needs no proof for its existence. But these expressions of our nature need *direction*, and direction is possible only through knowledge. When they are informed by knowledge, they themselves constitute, in their directed activity, intelligence in operation. Thus as far as concerns particular value-beliefs, particular moral and religious ideas and creeds, the import of what has been said is that they need to be tested and revised by the best knowledge at command. The moral of the discussion is anything but a reservation for them of a position in which they are exempt from the impact, however disintegrative it may be, of new knowledge.

The relation between objects as known and objects with respect to value is that between the actual and the possible. "The actual" consists of given conditions; "the possible" denotes ends or consequences not now existing but which the actual may through its use bring into existence. The possible in respect to any given actual situation is thus an ideal for that situation; from the standpoint of operational definition—of thinking in terms of action—the ideal and the possible are equivalent ideas. Idea and ideal have. more in common than certain letters of the alphabet. Everywhere an idea, in its intellectual content, is a projection of what something existing may come to be. One may report a quality already sensed in a proposition, as when standing before the fire I remark upon how hot it is. When seeing something at a distance, I judge without sensible contact that it must be hot; "hot" expresses a consequence which I infer would be experienced if I were to approach close enough; it designates a possibility of what is actually there in experience. The instance is a trivial one, but it sets forth what happens in every case where any predicate, whether quality or relation, expresses an *idea* rather than a sensibly perceived characteristic. The difference is not between one mental state called a sensation and another called an image. It is between what is experienced as being already there and what marks a possibility of being experienced. If we agree to leave out the eulogistic savor of "ideal" and define it in contrast with the actual, the possibility denoted by an idea is the ideal phase of the existent.

The problem of the connection or lack of connection of the actual and the ideal has always been the central problem of philosophy in its metaphysical aspect, just as the relation between existence and idea has been the central theme of philosophy on the side of the theory of knowledge. Both issues come together in the problem of the relation of the actual and the possible. Both problems are derived from the necessities of action if that is to be intelligently regulated. Assertion of an idea or of an ideal, if it is genuine, is a claim that it is possible to modify what exists so that it will take on a form possessed of specifiable traits. This statement as it relates to an idea, to the cognitive aspect, takes us back to what has been said about ideas as designations of operations and their consequences. Its bearing upon the "ideal" concerns us at this point.

In this basic problem of the relation of the actual and ideal, classic philosophies have always attempted to prove that the ideal is already and eternally a property of the real. The quest for absolute cognitive certainty has come to a head in the quest for an ideal which is one with the ultimately real. Men have not been able to trust either the world or themselves to realize the values and qualities which are the possibilities of nature. The sense of incompetency and the sloth born of desire for irresponsibility have combined to create an overwhelming longing for the ideal and rational as an antecedent possession of actuality, and consequently something upon which we can fall back on for emotional support in times of trouble.

The assumption of the antecedent inherent identity of actual and ideal has generated problems which have not been solved. It is the source of the problem of evil; of evil not merely in the moral sense, but in that of the existence of defect and aberration, of uncertainty and error, of all deviation from the perfect. If the universe is in itself ideal, why is there so much in our experience of it which is so thoroughly unideal? Attempts to answer this question have always been compelled to introduce lapse from perfect Being:—some kind of fall to which is due the distinction between noumena and phenomena, things as they really are and as they seem to be. There are many versions of this doctrine. The simplest, though not the one which has most commended itself to many philosophers, is the idea of the "fall of man," a fall which, in the words of Cardinal Newman, has implicated all creation in an aboriginal catastrophe. I am not concerned to discuss them and their respective weaknesses and strengths. It is enough to note that the philosophies which go by the name of Idealism are attempts to prove by one method or another, cosmological, ontological or epistemological, that the Real and the Ideal are one, while at the same time they introduce qualifying additions to explain why after all they are not one.

There are three ways of idealizing the world. There is idealization through purely intellectual and logical processes, in which reasoning alone attempts to prove that the world has characters that satisfy our highest aspirations. There are again, moments of intense emotional appreciation when, through a happy conjunction of the state of the self and of the surrounding world, the beauty and harmony of existence is disclosed in experiences which are the immediate consummation of all for which we long. Then there is an idealization through actions that are directed by thought, such as are manifested in the works of fine art and in all human relations perfected by loving care. The first path has been taken by many philosophies. The second while it lasts is the most engaging. It sets the measure of our ideas of possibilities that are to be realized by intelligent endeavor. But its objects depend upon fortune and are insecure. The third method represents the way of deliberate quest for security of the values that are enjoyed by grace in our happy moments.

That in fortunate moments objects of complete and approved enjoyment are had is evidence that nature is capable of giving birth to objects that stay with us as ideal. Nature thus supplies potential material for embodiment of ideals. Nature, if I may use the locution, is idealizable. It lends itself to operations by which it is perfected. The process is not a passive one. Rather nature gives, not always freely but in response to search, means and material by which the values we judge to have supreme quality may be embodied in existence. It depends upon the choice of man whether he employs what nature provides and for what ends he uses it.

Idealism of this type is not content with dialectical proofs that the perfect is already and immutably in Being, either as a property of some higher power or as an essence. The emotional satisfactions and encouragements thus supplied are not an adequate substitute for an ideal which is projected in order to be a guide of our doings. While the happy moment brings us objects to admire, approve and revere, the security and extent in which the beautiful, the true and the revered qualify the world, depend upon the way in which our own affections and desires for that kind or world engage activities. Things loved, admired and revered, things that spiritualistic philosophies have seized upon as the defining characters of ultimate Being, are genuine elements of nature. But without the aid and support of deliberate action based on understanding of conditions, they are transitory and unstable, as well as narrow and confined in the number of those who enjoy them.

Religious faiths have come under the influence of philosophies that have tried to demonstrate the fixed union of the actual and ideal in ultimate Being. Their interest in persuading to a life of loyalty to what is esteemed good, has been bound up with a certain creed regarding historical origins. Religion has also been involved in the metaphysics of substance, and has thrown in its lot with acceptance of certain cosmogonies. It has found itself fighting a battle and a losing one with science, as if religion were a rival theory about the structure of the natural world. It has committed itself to assertions about astronomical, geological, biological subject-matter; about questions of anthropology, literary criticism, and history. With the advances of science in these fields it has in consequence found itself involved in a series of conflicts, compromises, adjustments and retreats.

The religious attitude as a sense of the possibilities of existence and as devotion to the cause of these possibilities, as distinct from acceptance of what is given at the time, gradually extricates itself from these unnecessary intellectual commitments. But religious devotees rarely stop to notice that what lies at the basis of recurrent conflicts with scientific findings is not this or that special dogma so much as it is alliance with philosophical schemes which hold that the reality and power of whatever is excellent and worthy of supreme devotion, depends upon proof of its antecedent existence, so that the ideal of perfection loses its claim over us unless it can be demonstrated to exist in the sense in which the sun and stars exist.

Were it not because of this underlying as-sumption, there could be no conflict between science and religion. The currency of attempts to reconcile scientific conclusions with special doctrines of religion may unfortunately suggest, when such a statement is made, the idea of some infallible recipe for conciliation. But nothing is further from its meaning. It signifies that a religious attitude would surrender once for all commitment to beliefs about matters of fact, whether physical, social or metaphysical. It would leave such matters to inquirers in other fields. Nor would it substitute in their place fixed beliefs about values save the one value of the worth of discovering the possibilities of the actual and striving to realize them. Whatever is discovered about actual existence would modify the content of human beliefs about ends, purposes and goods. But it would and could not touch the fact that we are capable of directing our affection and loyalty to the possibilities resident in the actualities discovered. An idealism of action that is devoted to creation of a future, instead of to staking itself upon propositions about the past, is invincible. The claims of the beautiful to be admired and cherished do not depend upon ability to demonstrate statements about the past history of art. The demand of righteousness for reverence does not depend upon ability to prove the existence of an antecedent Being who is righteous.

It is not possible to set forth with any accuracy or completeness just what form religion would take if it were wedded to an idealism of this sort, or just what would happen if it broke away from that quest for certitude in the face of peril and human weakness which has determined its historic and institutional career. But some features of the spirit of the change which would follow may be indicated. Not the least important change would be a shift from the defensive and apologetic position which is practically compulsory as long as religious faith is bound up with defense of doctrines regarding history and physical nature; for this entanglement subjects it to constant danger of conflict with science. The energy which is thus diverted into defense of positions that have in time to be surrendered would be released for positive activity in behalf of the security of the underlying possibilities of actual life. More important still would be liberation from attachment to dogmas framed in conditions very unlike

those in which we live, and the substitution of a disposition to turn to constructive account the results of knowledge.

It is not possible to estimate the amelioration that would result if the stimulus and support given to practical action by science were no longer limited to industry and commerce and merely "secular" affairs. As long as the practical import of the advance of science is confined to these activities, the dualism between the values which religion professes and the urgent concerns of daily livelihood will persist. The gulf between them will continually grow wider, and the widening will not, judging from past history, be at the expense of the territory occupied by mundane and secular affairs. On the contrary, ideal interests will be compelled to retreat more and more to a confined ground.

The philosophy which holds that the realm of essence subsists as an independent realm of Being also emphasizes that this is a realm of possbilities; it offers this realm as the true object of religious devotion. But, by definition, such possibilities are abstract and remote. They have no concern nor traffic with natural and social objects that are concretely experienced. It is not possible to avoid the impression that the idea of such a realm is simply the hypostatizing in a wholesale way of the fact that actual existence has its own possibilities. But in any case devotion to such remote and unattached possibilities simply perpetuates the other-worldliness of religious tradition, although its other-world is not one supposed to exist. Thought of it is a refuge, not a resource. It becomes effective in relation to the conduct of life only when separation of essence from existence is cancelled; when essences are taken to be possibilities to be embodied through action in concrete objects of secure experience. Nothing is gained by reaching the latter through a circuitous course.

Religious faith which attaches itself to the possibilities of nature and associated living would, with its devotion to the ideal, manifest piety toward the actual. It would not be querulous with respect to the defects and hardships of the latter. Respect and esteem would be given to that which is the means of realization of possibilities, and to that in which the ideal is embodied if it ever finds embodiment. Aspiration and endeavor are not ends in themselves; value is not in them in isolation but in them as means to that reorganization of the existent in which approved meanings are attained. Nature and society include within themselves projection of ideal possibilities and contain the operations by which they are actualized. Nature may not be worshiped as divine even in the sense of the intellectual love of Spinoza. But nature, including humanity, with all its defects and imperfections, may evoke heartfelt piety as the source of ideals, of possibilities, of aspiration in their behalf, and as the eventual abode of all attained goods and excellencies.

I have no intention of entering into the field of the psychology of religion, that is to say, the personal attitudes involved in religious experience. But I suppose that no one can deny that the sense of dependence, insisted upon, for example, by Schleiermacher, comes close to the heart of the matter. This sense has taken many different forms in connection with different states of culture. It has shown itself in abject fears, in practice of extreme cruelties designed to propitiate the powers upon which we depend, and in militantly fanatical intolerance on the part of those who felt that they had special access to the ultimate source of power and a peculiar authorization to act in its behalf. It has shown itself in noble humilities and unquenchable ardors. History shows there is no one channel in which the sense of dependence is predestined to express itself.

But of the religious attitude which is allied to acceptance of the ideally good as the to-be-realized possibilities of existence, one statement may be made with confidence. At the best, all our endeavors look to the future and never attain certainty. The lesson of probability holds for all forms of

activity as truly as for the experimental operations of science, and even more poignantly and tragically. The control and regulation of which so much has been said never signifies certainty of outcome, although the greater need of security it may afford will not be known until we try the experimental policy in all walks of life. The unknown surrounds us in other forms of practical activity even more than in knowing, for they reach further into the future, in more significant and less controllable ways. A sense of dependence is quickened by that Copernican revolution which looks to security amid change instead of to certainty in attachment to the fixed.

It would, moreover, alter its dominant quality. One of the deepest of moral traditions is that which identifies the source of moral evil, as distinct from retrievable error, with pride, and which identifies pride with isolation. This attitude of pride assumes many forms. It is found among those who profess the most complete dependence, often preëminently among them. The pride of the zealously devout is the most dangerous form of pride. There is a divisive pride of the learned, as well as of family, wealth and power. The pride of those who feel themselves learned in the express and explicit will of God is the most exclusive. Those who have this pride, one that generates an exclusive institutionalism and then feeds and sustains itself through its connection with an institution claiming spiritual monopoly, feel themselves to be special organs of the divine, and in its name claim authority over others.

The historic isolation of the church from other social institutions is the result of this pride. The isolation, like all denials of interaction and interdependence, confines to special channels the power of those who profess special connection with the ideal and spiritual. In condemning other modes of human association to an inferior position and rôle, it breeds irresponsibility in the latter. This result is perhaps the most serious of the many products of that dualism between nature and spirit in which isolation of the actual and the possible eventuates. The sense of dependence that is bred by recognition that the intent and effort of man are never final but are subject to the uncertainties of an indeterminate future, would render dependence universal and shared by all. It would terminate the most corroding form of spiritual pride and isolation, that which divides man from man at the foundation of life's activities. A sense of common participation in the inevitable uncertainties of existence would be coeval with a sense of common effort and shared destiny. Men will never love their enemies until they cease to have enmities. The antagonism between the actual and the ideal, the spiritual and the natural, is the source of the deepest and most injurious of all enmities.

What has been said might seem to ignore the strength of those traditions in which are enshrined the emotions and imaginations of so many human beings, as well as the force of the established institutions by which these traditions are carried. I am, however, engaged only in pointing out the possibility of a change. This task does not require us to ignore the practical difficulties in the way of realizing it. There is one aspect of these difficulties which is pertinent at this point. It is appropriate to inquire as to the bearing of them upon the future office of philosophy. A philosophy committed to rational demonstration of the fixed and antecedent certainty of the ideal, with a sharp demarcation of knowledge and higher activity from all forms of practical activity, is a philosophy which perpetuates the obstacles in the way of realization of the possibility that has been pointed out. It is easy both to minimize the practical effect of philosophic theories and to exaggerate it. Directly, it is not very great. But as an intellectual formulation and justification of habits and attitudes already obtaining among men its influence is immense. The *vis inertiae* of habit is tremendous, and when it is reinforced by a philosophy which also is embodied in institutions, it is so great as to be a factor in sustaining the pre-sent confusion and conflict of authorities and allegiances.

A final word about philosophy is then in place. Like religion it has come into conflict with the natural sciences, or at least its path has diverged increasingly from theirs since the seventeenth century. The chief cause of the split is that philosophy has assumed for its function a knowledge of reality. This fact makes it a rival instead of a complement to the sciences. It has forced philosophy into claiming a kind of knowledge which is more ultimate than theirs. In consequence it has, at least in its more systematic forms, felt obliged to revise the conclusions of science to prove that they do not mean what they say; or that, in any case they apply to a world of appearances instead of to the superior reality to which philosophy directs itself. Idealistic philosophies have attempted to prove from an examination of the conditions of knowledge that mind is the only reality. What does it matter, they have said in effect, if physical knowledge recognizes only matter, since matter itself is mental? Idealisms in proving that the ideal is once for all the real has absolved itself from the office, more useful if humbler, of attempting that interpretation of the actual by means of which values could be made more extensive and more secure.

General ideas, hypotheses, are necessary in science itself. They serve an indispensable purpose. They open new points of view; they liberate us from the bondage of habit which is always closing in on us, restricting our vision both of what is and of what the actual may become. They direct operations that reveal new truths and new possibilities. They enable us to escape from the pressure of immediate circumstance and provincial boundaries. Knowledge falters when imagination clips its wings or fears to use them. Every great advance in science has issued from a new audacity of imagination. What are now working conceptions, employed as a matter of course because they have withstood the tests of experiment and have emerged triumphant, were once speculative hypotheses.

There is no limit set to the scope and depth of hypotheses. There are those of short and technical range and there are those as wide as experience. Philosophy has always claimed universality for itself. It will make its claim good when it connects this universality with the formation of directive hypotheses instead of with a sweeping pretension to knowledge of universal Being. That hypotheses are fruitful when they are suggested by actual need, are bulwarked by knowledge already attained, and are tested by the consequences of the operations they evoke goes without saying. Otherwise imagination is dissipated into fantasies and rises vaporously into the clouds.

The need for large and generous ideas in the direction of life was never more urgent than in the confusion of tongues, beliefs and purposes that characterizes present life. Knowledge of actual structure and processes of existence has reached a point where a philosophy which has the will to use knowledge has guidance and support. A philosophy which abandoned its guardianship of fixed realities, values and ideals, would find a new career for itself. The meaning of science in terms of science, in terms of knowledge of the actual, may well be left to science itself. Its meaning in terms of the great human uses to which it may be put, its meaning in the service of possibilities of secure value, offers a field for exploration which cries out from very emptiness. To abandon the search for absolute and immutable reality and value may seem like a sacrifice. But this renunciation is the condition of entering upon a vocation of greater vitality. The search for values to be secured and shared by all, because buttressed in the foundations of social life, is a quest in which philosophy would have no rivals but coadjutors in men of good will.

Philosophy under such conditions finds itself in no opposition to science. It is a liaison officer between the conclusions of science and the modes of social and personal action through which attainable possibilities are projected and striven for. No more than a religion devoted to inspiration and cultivation of the sense of ideal possibilities in the actual would it find itself checked by any possible discovery of science. Each new discovery would afford a new opportunity. Such a philosophy would have a wide field of criticism before it. But its critical mind would be directed against the domination exercised by prejudice, narrow interest, routine custom and the authority which issues from institutions apart from the human ends they serve. This negative office would be but the obverse of the creative work of the imagination in pointing to the new possibilities which knowledge of the actual discloses and the projecting methods for their realization in the homely everyday experience of mankind.

Philosophy has often entertained the ideal of a complete integration of knowledge. But knowledge by its nature is analytic and discriminating. It attains large syntheses, sweeping generalizations. But these open up new problems for consideration, new fields for inquiry; they are transitions to more detailed and varied knowledge. Diversification of discoveries and the opening up of new points of view and new methods are inherent in the progress of knowledge. This fact defeats the idea of any complete synthesis of knowledge upon an intellectual basis. The sheer increase of specialized knowledge will never work the miracle of producing an intellectual whole. Nevertheless, the need for integration of specialized results of science remains, and philosophy should contribute to the satisfaction of the need.

The need, however, is practical and human rather than intrinsic to science itself; the latter is content as long as it can move to new problems and discoveries. The need for direction of action in large social fields is the source of a genuine demand for unification of scientific conclusions. They are organized when their bearing on the conduct of life is disclosed. It is at this point that the extraordinary and multifarious results of scientific inquiry are unorganized, scattered, chaotic. The astronomer, biologist, chemist, may attain systematic wholes, at least for a time, within his own field. But when we come to the bearing of special conclusions upon the conduct of social life, we are, outside of technical fields, at a loss. The force of tradition and dogmatic authority is due, more than to anything else, to precisely this defect. Man has never had such a varied body of knowledge in his possession before, and probably never before has he been so uncertain and so perplexed as to what his knowledge means, what it points to in action and in consequences.

Were there any consensus as to the significance of what is known upon beliefs about things of ideal and general value, our life would be marked by integrity instead of by distraction and by conflict of competing aims and standards. Needs of practical action in large and liberal social fields would give unification to our special knowledge; and the latter would give solidity and confidence to the judgment of values that control conduct. Attainment of this consensus would mean that modern life had reached maturity in discovering the meaning of its own intellectual movement. It would find within its own interests and activities the authoritative guidance for its own affairs which it now vainly seeks in oscillation between outworn traditions and reliance upon casual impulse.

The situation defines the vital office of present philosophy. It has to search out and disclose the obstructions; to criticize the habits of mind which stand in the way; to focus reflection upon needs congruous to present life; to interpret the conclusions of science with respect to their consequences for our beliefs about purposes and values in all phases of life. The development of a system of thought capable of giving this service is a difficult undertaking; it can proceed only slowly and through coöperative effort. In these pages I have tried to indicate in outline the nature of the task to be accomplished and to suggest some of the resources at hand for its realization.

COMMENT

The Origin and Development of Pragmatism

The word *pragmatism* was introduced into modern philosophy by Charles Peirce to designate the "method of ascertaining the meaning of hard words and abstract conceptions," which he had advocated in "How to Make Our Ideas Clear" (1878). Even before he wrote this essay, Peirce had expressed the basic principle of his pragmatism in a review (1871) of Fraser's edition of George Berkeley's Works, in which he offered the following "rule for avoiding the deceits of language": "Do things fulfill the same function practically? Then let them be signified by the same word. Do they not? Then let them be distinguished." In neither of these early statements did Peirce use the word *pragmatism*. But in 1898, at the University of California, William James delivered a lecture entitled "Philosophical Conceptions and Practical Results," in which he hailed Peirce not only as the founder of pragmatism but also as the originator of the term. It appears that Peirce used the word orally for some time before he first committed it to print in 1902, when he contributed an article on the subject to Baldwin's *Philosophical Dictionary*.

The terms *pragmatic* and *pragmatism* were suggested to Peirce by his study of Immanuel Kant. In *The Metaphysic of Morals*, Kant distinguished between *pragmatic* and *practical*. The former term, deriving from the Greek *pragma* ("things done"), applies to the rules of art or technique based on experience; the latter term applies to moral rules, which Kant regarded as *a priori*. Hence Peirce, wishing to emphasize an experimental and non-*a priori* type of reasoning, chose the word *pragmatic* to designate his way of clarifying meanings.

The pragmatic movement first sprang to life in the early 1870s in the Metaphysical Club, a philosophical discussion group founded by Peirce, which included among its members William James and Oliver Wendell Holmes, Jr. Two of the brilliant young members of the club, Chauncey Wright and Nicholas St. John Green, emphasized the practical bearing and function of ideas. They thus suggested to Peirce the criterion of clarity, which he expressed in "How to Make Our Ideas Clear." However, this essay lay unnoticed for twenty years, until James, in his address of 1898, pointed to Peirce as the founder of an important new philosophical movement.

As Peirce initially used the term, *pragmatism* referred to a maxim for the clarification of ideas and hypotheses, not for their verification; it was a theory of meaning, not of truth. Later he also used the term to designate the rule that only hypotheses that are *clear* should be admitted in scientific or philosophical inquiry. As interpreted and amplified by James, pragmatism became a theory of truth and so changed into something alien to Peirce's way of thinking. "The modern movement known as pragmatism," Ralph Barton Perry has remarked, "is largely the result of James' misunderstanding of Peirce."[1]

While James was developing his own versions of pragmatism, John Dewey was working along similar lines at the University of Michigan and later at the University of Chicago. As early as 1886, he and James began to exchange letters, and in 1903, in the preface to *Studies in Logical Theory*, Dewey acknowledged "a preeminent obligation" to James. In certain ways, however, Dewey shows a closer affinity to Peirce—for example, in his close study of the experimental methods of natural science, in his rejection of James' criterion of emotional satisfaction as a test of truth, in his emphasis on the *social* bearing of ideas, and in his opposition to all "intuitionist" theories of knowledge.

However much he differed in some respects from James, Dewey fully agreed with the forward-looking and empirical temper of James' pragmatism—"the attitude of looking away from first things, principles, 'categories,' supposed necessities; and of looking toward last things, fruits, consequences, facts." He also agreed that thinking is essentially instrumental to the attainment of human purposes, although the purposes of the scientist are to be distinguished from the purposes of the practical man of affairs. Like James, moreover, he vehemently rejected a dualism of experience and nature. The stuff of the world is natural events such as we directly experience. His interpretation of inquiry, however, was more akin to Peirce's experimentalism than to James' ethical pragmatism. The result is a constellation of ideas that can be described as "experimental naturalism." Perhaps the

---

[1] *The Thought and Character of William James*, Briefer Version (Cambridge, MA: Harvard University Press, 1935), p. 281

best brief expression of this naturalistic philosophy is to be found in Dewey's essay "The Copernican Revolution."

In this essay, Dewey argues that the Copernican revolution in science necessitates a comparable revolution in philosophy. The philosopher, using a method like that of the naturalist, should forswear "inquiry after absolute origins and absolute finalities in order to explore specific values and the specific conditions that generate them." First and final causes, as allegedly lying behind and beyond nature, are beyond the reach of science, and the philosopher should turn away from such illusory objects. For him as for the scientist, things should be understood in terms of their origins and functions, and inquiry should be empirical in method and practical in motivation.

Conceiving philosophical and scientific method in this way, Dewey regards fruitful inquiry as essentially active and prospective rather than passive and retrospective:

> Intelligence develops within the sphere of action for the sake of possibilities not yet given.... Intelligence *as* intelligence is inherently forward-looking.... A pragmatic intelligence is a creative intelligence, not a routine mechanic.... Intelligence is ... instrumental *through* action to the determination of the qualities of future experience.[2]

Accordingly, Dewey proposes to determine meanings and test beliefs by examining the *consequences* that flow from them. What can the idea or belief promise for the future? How can it help us in resolving our perplexities? What predictions are implied by the hypothesis and how can they be verified?

Such questions apply even to propositions about the past, and even these propositions must be verified in terms of future consequences: "The past event has left effects, consequences, that are present and that will continue in the future. Our belief about it, if genuine, must also modify action in *some* way and so have objective effects. If these two sets of effects interlock harmoniously, then the judgment is true."[3] For example, the assassination of Lincoln *had* consequences, such as records of the event. One's belief about it *has* consequences, such as expectations that the records will be so and so. If the two sets of consequences harmoniously coincide so that my expectations are fulfilled, the statement is true.

Dewey regarded this emphasis on consequences as the essential characteristic of pragmatism. "The term 'pragmatic,'" he declared, "means only the rule of referring all thinking, all reflective considerations, to *consequences* for final meaning and test."[4] This insistence on consequent rather than antecedent phenomena is, as we have noted, like the pragmatism of James except that it does not define truth in terms of emotional satisfactions and the play of desires, as James did in his more extreme statements.

---

[2] *Creative Intelligence* (New York: Henry Holt, 1917), p. 65.

[3] *The Influence of Darwin on Philosophy and Other Essays* (New York: Henry Holt, 1910), p. 160.

[4] *Essays in Experimental Logic* (Chicago: University of Chicago Press, 1916), p. 330.

There were other important contributors to pragmatism, such as George Herbert Mead (1863–1931) in America and F. C. S. Schiller (1864–1937) in England; but Peirce, James, and Dewey are the towering figures.

We would be making a mistake to conclude that pragmatism is only a false and outmoded way of thinking. It contains many insights that are both important and salutary. Perhaps its value can be suggested by the following description by John Jay Chapman of a social gathering at the home of a friend, Mrs. Henry Whitman, in Boston:

> I remember a curious Bostonian cockfight at her studio, where Professor Royce and Judge Oliver Wendell Holmes were pitted against each other to talk about the Infinite. Royce won, of course … by involving the subject in such adamantine cobwebs of voluminous rolling speculation that no one could regain his senses thereafter. He not only cut the ground from under everyone's feet; but he pulled down the sun and moon, and raised up the ocean, and everyone was shipwrecked and took to small planks and cups of tea.[5]

Holmes, the friend of James and Peirce, was a pragmatist, whereas Royce was of the old-fashioned school of metaphysics. Holmes lost the argument, but he had a greater humility, a keener sense of reality, and a firmer hold on the perennially human point of view than Royce did. If homely realism and practical concern for humanity's lot have tended to supersede the daring flights of metaphysicians, the pragmatists, such as James, Dewey, and Holmes, are in large measure responsible. This change one may count as either a loss or a gain.

How, then, would pragmatists treat the question of whether or not computers like Deep Blue are capable of knowledge? Is there any pragmatic difference between the activities in which the computer and Gary Kasparov are engaged? Does thinking necessarily involve some sort of behavioral outcome for the pragmatist, and if so, does the computer offer any? What are the "consequences" of Kasparov's and Deep Blue's activities?

---

[5] *Memories and Milestones* (New York: Moffatt, Yard, 1915), p.106. Cited by Max H. Fisch, *Classic American Philosophers* (New York: Appleton-Crofts, 1951), p. 7.

6

EXISTENTIALISM

Albert Camus was born in Mondovi, Algeria. He spent the early years of his life working at various part-time jobs and attending the University of Algiers, where he earned a degree in philosophy. He spent a number of years as a journalist, while directing a theatrical company in Paris. During the Nazi occupation of France in World War II, Camus participated in the resistance movement as editor of *Combat,* an important underground newspaper. He was good friends with, and often disagreed with, his fellow philosophers Jean-Paul Sartre and Maurice Merleau-Ponty. Camus died in a tragic automobile crash in 1960 at the age of forty-seven, after having been awarded the Nobel Prize for Literature in 1957.

Camus wrote a number of plays and philosophical essays, which have been collected in the books *The Rebel* and *The Myth of Sisyphus.* His chief claim to fame, however, centers on his three main novels, *The Stranger, The Plague,* and *The Fall,* which form something of a trilogy dealing with existentialist themes of alienation, suffering and responsibility, and guilt. The main theme of Camus' work is the solitude and seriousness of the human condition together with the necessity of absolute honesty and authenticity in everyday life. He likened the human situation to that of Sisyphus, in ancient Greek mythology, who was condemned for an eternity to roll a huge boulder up a hill only to have it roll back down again. Camus claimed that we can create meaning in our own lives only by embracing the absurdity of our meaningless existence.

In the following selection from his essay "An Absurd Reasoning," Camus brings this point of view to bear on what philosophers call epistemological problems—problems of truth, knowledge, and reasoning. He begins this essay by stating: "There is but one truly serious philosophical problem, and that is suicide." After all, he reasons, before one can go on to deal with other problems, one must choose, if only by default, whether to go on at all.

Camus sought to relate his perspective to the traditional concerns of philosophers about human knowledge and the search for truth by stressing the truly individual character of the cognitive process, especially as it intermingles with the dimensions of feeling and value. His existentialist perspective focuses on the limited, if not absurd, nature of all human efforts to achieve absolute or final understanding of any question, let alone those that pertain to the meaning of life and the cosmos.

At the deepest level, Camus believed that it is absolutely important that a person not "cop out" along the way in this existentialist pilgrimage by making a blind leap of faith to some religious or other absolutist point of view in order to escape the responsibility and hard work inherent in striving for authenticity. He concludes his essay with these words: "But it is bad to stop, hard to be satisfied with a single way of seeing, to go without contradiction, perhaps the most subtle of all spiritual forces. The preceding merely defines a way of thinking. But the point is to live."

AN ABSURD REASONING

The mind's first step is to distinguish what is true from what is false. However, as soon as thought reflects on itself, what it first discovers is a contradiction. Useless to strive to be convincing in this case. Over the centuries no one has furnished a clearer and more elegant demonstration of the business than Aristotle: "The often ridiculed consequence of these opinions is that they destroy themselves. For by asserting that all is true we assert the truth of the contrary assertion and consequently the falsity of our own thesis (for the contrary assertion does not admit that it can be true). And if one says that all is false, that assertion is itself false. If we declare that solely the assertion opposed to ours is false or else that solely ours is not false, we are nevertheless forced to admit an infinite number of true or false judgments. For the one who expresses a true assertion proclaims simultaneously that it is true, and so on *ad infinitum*."

This vicious circle is but the first of a series in which the mind that studies itself gets lost in a giddy whirling. The very simplicity of these paradoxes makes them irreducible. Whatever may be the plays on words and the acrobatics of logic, to understand is, above all, to unify. The mind's deepest desire, even in its most elaborate operations, parallels man's unconscious

feeling in the face of his universe: it is an insistence upon familiarity, an appetite for clarity. Understanding the world for a man is reducing it to the human, stamping it with his seal. The cat's universe is not the universe of the anthill. The truism "All thought is anthropomorphic" has no other meaning. Likewise, the mind that aims to understand reality can consider itself satisfied only by reducing it to terms of thought. If man realized that the universe like him can love and suffer, he would be reconciled. If thought discovered in the shimmering mirrors of phenomena eternal relations capable of summing them up and summing themselves up in a single principle, then would be seen an intellectual joy of which the myth of the blessed would be but a ridiculous imitation. That nostalgia for unity, that appetite for the absolute illustrates the essential impulse of the human drama. But the fact of that nostalgia's existence does not imply that it is to be immediately satisfied. For if, bridging the gulf that separates desire from conquest, we assert with Parmenides the reality of the One (whatever it may be), we fall into the ridiculous contradiction of a mind that asserts total unity and proves by its very assertion its own difference and the diversity it claimed to resolve. This other vicious circle is enough to stifle our hopes.

These are again truisms. I shall again repeat that they are not interesting in themselves but in the consequences that can be deduced from them. I know another truism:

From *The Myth of Sisyphus* by Albert Camus. Translated by Justin O'Brien. Vintage Books, Random House, 1955.

it tells me that man is mortal. One can nevertheless count the minds that have deduced the extreme conclusions from it. It is essential to consider as a constant point of reference in this essay the regular hiatus between what we fancy we know and what we really know, practical assent and simulated ignorance which allows us to live with ideas which, if we truly put them to the test, ought to upset our whole life. Faced with this inextricable contradiction of the mind, we shall fully grasp the divorce separating us from our own creations. So long as the mind keeps silent in the motionless world of its hopes, everything is reflected and arranged in the unity of its nostalgia. But with its first move this world cracks and tumbles: an infinite number of shimmering fragments is offered to the understanding. We must despair of ever reconstructing the familiar, calm surface which would give us peace of heart. After so many centuries of inquiries, so many abdications among thinkers, we are well aware that this is true for all our knowledge. With the exception of professional rationalists, today people despair of true knowledge. If the only significant history of human thought were to be written, it would have to be the history of its successive regrets and its impotences.

Of whom and of what indeed can I say: "I know that!" This heart within me I can feel, and I judge that it exists. This world I can touch, and I likewise judge that it exists. There ends all my knowledge, and the rest is construction. For if I try to seize this self of which I feel sure, if I try to define and to summarize it, it is nothing but water slipping through my fingers. I can sketch one by one all the aspects it is able to assume, all those likewise that have been attributed to it, this upbringing, this origin, this ardor or these silences, this nobility or this vileness. But aspects cannot be added up. This very heart which is mine will forever remain indefinable to me. Between the certainty I have of my existence and the content I try to give to that assurance, the gap will never be filled. Forever I shall be a stranger to myself. In psychology as in logic, there are truths but no truth. Socrates' "Know thyself" has as much value as the "Be virtuous" of our confessionals. They reveal a nostalgia at the same time as an ignorance. They are sterile exercises on great subjects. They are legitimate only in precisely so far as they are approximate.

And here are trees and I know their gnarled surface, water and I feel its taste. These scents of grass and stars at night, certain evenings when the heart relaxes—how shall I negate this world whose power and strength I feel? Yet all the knowledge on earth will give me nothing to assure me that this world is mine. You describe it to me and you teach me to classify it. You enumerate its laws and in my thirst for knowledge I admit that they are true. You take apart its mechanism and my hope increases. At the final stage you teach me that this wondrous and multicolored universe can be reduced to the atom and that the atom itself can be reduced to the electron. All this is good and I wait for you to continue. But you tell me of an invisible planetary system in which electrons gravitate around a nucleus. You explain this world to me with an image. I realize then that you have been reduced to poetry: I shall never know. Have I the time to become indignant? You have already changed theories. So that science that was to teach me everything ends up in a hypothesis, that lucidity founders in metaphor, that uncertainty is resolved in a work of art. What need had I of so many efforts? The soft lines of these hills and the hand of evening on this troubled heart teach me much more. I have returned to my beginning. I realize that if through science I can seize phenomena and enumerate them, I cannot, for all that, apprehend the world. Were I to trace its entire relief with my finger, I should not know any more. And you give me the choice between a description that is sure but that teaches me nothing and hypotheses that claim to teach me but that are not sure. A stranger to myself and to the world, armed solely with a thought that negates itself as soon as it asserts, what is this condition in which I can have peace only by refusing to know and to live, in which the appetite for conquest bumps into walls that defy its assaults? To will is to stir up paradoxes. Everything is ordered in such a way as to bring into being that poisoned peace produced by thoughtlessness, lack of heart, or fatal renunciations.

Hence the intelligence, too, tells me in its way that this world is absurd. Its contrary, blind reason, may well claim that all is clear; I was waiting for proof and longing for it to be right. But despite so many pretentious centuries and over the heads of so many eloquent and persuasive men, I know that is false. On this plane, at least, there is no happiness if I cannot know. That universal reason, practical or ethical, that determinism, those categories that explain everything are enough to make a decent man laugh. They have nothing to do with the mind. They negate its profound truth, which is to be enchained. In this unintelligible and limited universe, man's fate henceforth assumes its meaning. A horde of irrationals has sprung up and surrounds him until his ultimate end. In his recovered and now studied lucidity, the feeling of the absurd becomes clear and definite. I said that the world is absurd, but I was too hasty. This world in itself is not reasonable, that is all that can he said. But what is absurd is the confrontation of this irrational and the wild longing for clarity whose call echoes in the human heart. The absurd depends as much on man as on the world. For the moment it is all that links them together. It binds them one to the other as only hatred can weld two creatures together. This is all I can discern clearly in this measureless universe where my adventure takes place. Let us pause here. If I hold to be true that absurdity that determines my relationship with life, if I become thoroughly imbued with that sentiment that seizes me in face of the world's scenes, with that lucidity imposed on me by the pursuit of a science, I must sacrifice everything to these certainties and I must see them squarely to be able to maintain them. Above all, I must adapt my behavior to them and pursue them in all their consequences. I am speaking here of decency. But I want to know beforehand if thought can live in those deserts.

I already know that thought has at least entered those deserts. There it found its bread. There it realized that it had previously been feeding on phantoms. It justified some of the most urgent themes of human reflection.

From the moment absurdity is recognized, it becomes a passion, the most harrowing of all. But whether or not one can live with one's passions, whether or not one can accept their law, which is to burn the heart they simultaneously exalt—that is the whole question. It is not, however, the one we shall ask just yet. It stands at the center of this experience. There will be time to come back to it. Let us recognize rather those themes and those impulses born of the desert. It will suffice to enumerate them. They, too, are known to all today. There have always been men to defend the rights of the irrational. The tradition of what may be called humiliated thought has never ceased to exist. The criticism of rationalism has been made so often that it seems unnecessary to begin again. Yet our epoch is marked by the rebirth of those paradoxical systems that strive to trip up the reason as if truly it had always forged ahead. But that is not so much a proof of the efficacy of the reason as of the intensity of its hopes. On the plane of history, such a constancy of two attitudes illustrates the essential passion of man torn between his urge toward unity and the clear vision he may have of the walls enclosing him. . . .

How can one fail to feel the basic relationship of these minds! How can one fail to see that they take their stand around a privileged and bitter moment in which hope has no further place? I want everything to be explained to me or nothing. And the reason is impotent when it hears this cry from the heart. The mind aroused by this insistence seeks and finds nothing but contradictions and nonsense. What I fail to

understand is nonsense. The world is peopled with such irrationals. The world itself,
whose single meaning I do not understand,
is but a vast irrational. If one could only say
just once: "This is clear," all would be
saved. But these men vie with one another
in proclaiming that nothing is clear, all is
chaos, that all man has is his lucidity and
his definite knowledge of the walls surrounding him.

All these experiences agree and confirm one another. The mind, when it
reaches its limits, must make a judgment
and choose its conclusions. This is where
suicide and the reply stand. But I wish to
reverse the order of the inquiry and start out
from the intelligent adventure and come
back to daily acts. The experiences called
to mind here were born in the desert that
we must not leave behind. At least it is
essential to know how far they went. At this
point of his effort man stands face to face
with the irrational. He feels within him
his longing for happiness and for reason.
The absurd is born of this confrontation
between the human need and the unreasonable silence of the world. This must not
be forgotten. This must be clung to because
the whole consequence of a life can
depend on it. The irrational, the human
nostalgia, and the absurd that is born of
their encounter—these are the three characters in the drama that must necessarily
end with all the logic of which an existence
is capable. . . .

My reasoning wants to be faithful to
the evidence that aroused it. That evidence
is the absurd. It is that divorce between the
mind that desires and the world that disap-
points, my nostalgia for unity, this frag-
mented universe and the contradiction that
binds them together. Kierkegaard sup-
presses my nostalgia and Husserl gathers
together that universe. That is not what I
was expecting. It was a matter of living and
thinking with those dislocations, of knowing whether one had to accept or refuse.
There can be no question of masking the
evidence, of suppressing the absurd by
denying one of the terms of its equation. It

is essential to know whether one can live
with it or whether, on the other hand, logic
commands one to die of it. I am not interested in philosophical suicide, but rather in
plain suicide. I merely wish to purge it of its
emotional content and know its logic and
its integrity. Any other position implies for
the absurd mind deceit and the mind's
retreat before what the mind itself has
brought to light. Husserl claims to obey the
desire to escape "the inveterate habit of living and thinking in certain well-known and
convenient conditions of existence," but
the final leap restores in him the eternal
and its comfort. The leap does not represent an extreme danger as Kierkegaard
would like it to do. The danger, on the contrary, lies in the subtle instant that precedes
the leap. Being able to remain on that dizzy-
ing crest—that is integrity and the rest is
subterfuge. I know also that never has helplessness inspired such striking harmonies as
those of Kierkegaard. But if helplessness
has its place in the indifferent landscapes of
history, it has none in a reasoning whose
exigence is now known.

Absurd Freedom

Now the main thing is done, I hold certain
facts from which I cannot separate. What I
know, what is certain, what I cannot deny,
what I cannot reject—this is what counts. I
can negate everything of that part of me
that lives on vague nostalgias, except this
desire for unity, this longing to solve, this
need for clarity and cohesion. I can refute
everything in this world surrounding me
that offends or enraptures me, except this
chaos, this sovereign chance and this
divine equivalence which springs from
anarchy. I don't know whether this world
has a meaning that transcends it. But I
know that I do not know that meaning and
that it is impossible for me just now to
know it. What can a meaning outside my
condition mean to me? I can understand
only in human terms. What I touch, what
resists me—that is what I understand. And
these two certainties—my appetite for the

absolute and for unity and the impossibility of reducing this world to a rational and reasonable principle—I also know that I cannot reconcile them. What other truth can I ad-mit without lying, without bringing in a hope I lack and which means nothing within the limits of my condition?

If I were a tree among trees, a cat among animals, this life would have a meaning, or rather this problem would not arise, for I should belong to this world. I should *be* this world to which I am now opposed by my whole consciousness and my whole insistence upon familiarity. This ridiculous reason is what sets me in opposition to all creation. I cannot cross it out with a stroke of the pen. What I believe to be true I must therefore preserve. What seems to me so obvious, even against me, I must support. And what constitutes the basis of that conflict, of that break between the world and my mind, but the awareness of it? If therefore I want to preserve it, I can through a constant awareness, ever revived, ever alert. This is what, for the moment, I must remember. At this moment the absurd, so obvious and yet so hard to win, returns to a man's life and finds its home there. At this moment, too, the mind can leave the arid, dried-up path of lucid effort. That path now emerges in daily life. It encounters the world of the anonymous impersonal pronoun "one," but henceforth man enters in with his revolt and his lucidity. He has forgotten how to hope. This hell of the present is his Kingdom at last. All problems recover their sharp edge. Abstract evidence retreats before the poetry of forms and colors. Spiritual conflicts become embodied and return to the abject and

magnificent shelter of man's heart. None of them is settled. But all are transfigured. Is one going to die, escape by the leap, rebuild a mansion of ideas and forms to one's own scale? Is one, on the contrary, going to take up the heart-rending and marvelous wager of the absurd? Let's make a final effort in this regard and draw all our conclusions. The body, affection, creation, action, human nobility will then resume their places in this mad world. At last man will again find there the wine of the absurd and the bread of indifference on which he feeds his greatness.

Let us insist again on the method: it is a matter of persisting. At a certain point on his path the absurd man is tempted. History is not lacking in either religions or prophets, even without gods. He is asked to leap. All he can reply is that he doesn't fully understand, that it is not obvious. Indeed, he does not want to do anything but what he fully understands. He is assured that this is the sin of pride, but he does not understand the notion of sin; that perhaps hell is in store, but he has not enough imagination to visualize that strange future; that he is losing immortal life, but that seems to him an idle consideration. An attempt is made to get him to admit his guilt. He feels innocent. To tell the truth, that is all he feels—his irreparable innocence. This is what allows him everything. Hence, what he demands of himself is to live *solely* with what he knows, to accommodate himself to what is, and to bring in nothing that is not certain. He is told that nothing is. But this at least is a certainty. And it is with this that he is concerned: he wants to find out if it is possible to live *without appeal*.

GABRIEL MARCEL (1889–1973)

Gabriel Marcel was born and raised in France and is generally regarded as a twentieth-century exponent of "religious existentialism." He began his life as a highly cultured, liberal idealist, but he was shocked into seeking a more "realistic" philosophy by the horrors he saw while working for the Red Cross during World War

I. Marcel converted to Catholicism in 1929 but seems never to have considered himself a religious philosopher. In fact, although his thought bears strong resemblance to that of Søren Kierkegaard, Martin Heidegger, and Martin Buber, Marcel is known to have raised frequently the question of whether or not he was an existentialist thinker.

Nonetheless, like other existentialists, Marcel exhibited a strong interest in the arts. He wrote plays and experimented with music. In all his work he sought to avoid the empty theoretic abstractions often associated with traditional philosophy. Instead he strove to develop an approach that would provide a concrete analysis of thought, faith, and being as they are actually experienced by human beings, while at the same time preserving their mysterious quality.

Marcel's main philosophical works include *Creative Fidelity* (1940), *The Philosophy of Existence* (1949), *The Mystery of Being* (1950), and *Man Against Humanity* (1952). His plays include *The Lantern* (1958), *A Man of God* (1958), *Ariadne* (1965), and *The Funeral Pyre* (1965).

PROBLEMS AND MYSTERY

On the Ontological Mystery

The title of this essay is likely to annoy the philosopher as much as to startle the layman, since philosophers are inclined to leave mystery either to the theologians or else to the vulgarisers, whether of mysticism or of occultism, such as Maeterlinck. Moreover, the term *ontological,* which has only the vaguest meaning for the layman, has become discredited in the eyes of Idealist philosophers; while the term *mystery* is reserved by those thinkers who are imbued with the ideas of Scholasticism for the revealed mysteries of religion.

Thus my terminology is clearly open to criticism from all sides. But I can find no other which is adequate to the body of ideas which I intend to put forward and on which my whole outlook is based. Readers of my *Journal Métaphysique* will see that they represent the term of the whole spiritual and philosophical evolution which I have described in that book.

Rather than to begin with abstract definitions and dialectical arguments which may be discouraging at the outset, I should like to start with a sort of global and intuitive characterization of the man in whom the sense of the ontological—the sense of being—is lacking, or, to speak more correctly, of the man who has lost the awareness of this sense. Generally speaking, modern man is in this condition; if ontological demands worry him at all, it is only dully, as an obscure impulse. Indeed I wonder if a psychoanalytical method, deeper and more discerning than any that has been evolved until now, would not reveal the morbid effects of the repression of this sense and of the ignoring of this need.

The characteristic feature of our age seems to me to be what might be called the misplacement of the idea of function, taking function in its current sense which includes both the vital and the social functions.

The individual tends to appear both to himself and to others as an agglomeration

From *The Philosophy of Existentialism* by Gabriel Marcel, trans. Manya Harari. Copyright © 1956 by Citadel Press. Published by arrangement with Carol Publishing Group.

of functions. As a result of deep historical causes, which can as yet be understood only in part, he has been led to see himself more and more as a mere assemblage of functions, the hierarchical interrelation of which seems to him questionable or at least subject to conflicting interpretations.

To take the vital functions first. It is hardly necessary to point out the role which historical materialism on the one hand, and Freudian doctrines on the other, have played in restricting the concept of man.

Then there are the social functions—those of the consumer, the producer, the citizen, etc.

Between these two there is, in theory, room for the psychological functions as well; but it is easy to see how these will tend to be interpreted in relation either to the social or the vital functions, so that their independence will be threatened and their specific character put in doubt. In this sense, Comte, served by his total incomprehension of psychical reality, displayed an almost prophetic instinct when he excluded psychology from his classification of sciences.

So far we are still dealing only with abstractions, but nothing is easier than to find concrete illustrations in this field.

Travelling on the Underground, I often wonder with a kind of dread what can he the inward reality of the life of this or that man employed on the railway—the man who opens the doors, for instance, or the one who punches the tickets. Surely everything both within him and outside him conspires to identify this man with his functions—meaning not only with his functions as worker, as trade union member or as voter, but with his vital functions as well. The rather horrible expression "time table" perfectly describes his life. So many hours for each function. Sleep too is a function which must be discharged so that the other functions may be exercised in their turn. The same with pleasure, with relaxation; it is logical that the weekly allowance of recreation should be determined by an expert on hygiene; recreation is a psycho-organic function which must not be neglected any more than, for instance, the function of sex. We need go no further; this sketch is sufficient to suggest the emergence of a kind of vital schedule; the details will vary with the country, the climate, the profession, etc., but what matters is that there is a schedule.

It is true that certain disorderly elements—sickness, accidents of every sort—will break in on the smooth working of the system. It is therefore natural that the individual should be overhauled at regular intervals like a watch (this is often done in America). The hospital plays the part of the inspection bench or the repair shop. And it is from this same standpoint of function that such essential problems as birth control will be examined.

As for death, it becomes, objectively and functionally, the scrapping of what has ceased to be of use and must be written off as total loss.

I need hardly insist on the stifling impression of sadness produced by this functionalised world. It is sufficient to recall the dreary image of the retired official, or those urban Sundays when the passers-by look like people who have retired from life. In such a world, there is something mocking and sinister even in the tolerance awarded to the man who has retired from his work.

But besides the sadness felt by the onlooker, there is the dull, intolerable unease of the actor himself who is reduced to living as though he were in fact submerged by his functions. This uneasiness is enough to show that there is in all this some appalling mistake, some ghastly misinterpretation, implanted in defenceless minds by an increasingly inhuman social order and an equally inhuman philosophy (for if the philosophy has prepared the way for the order, the order has also shaped the philosophy).

I have written on another occasion that, provided it is taken in its metaphysical and not its physical sense, the distinction between the *full* and the *empty* seems to me more fundamental than that between the *one* and the *many*. This is particularly applicable to the case in point. Life in a world centered on function is liable to despair because in reality this world is *empty,* it rings hollow; and if it resists this temptation it is only to the extent that there come into play from within it and in its favour certain hidden forces which are beyond its power to conceive or to recognise.

It should be noted that this world is, on the one hand, riddled with problems and, on the other, determined to allow no room for mystery. I shall come back to this distinction between problem and mystery which I believe to be fundamental. For the moment I shall only point out that to eliminate or to try to eliminate mystery is (in this functionalist world) to bring into play in the face of events which break in on the course of existence—such as birth, love and death—that psychological and pseudoscientific category of the "purely natural" which deserves a study to itself. In reality, this is nothing more than the remains of a degraded rationalism from whose standpoint cause explains effect and accounts for it exhaustively. There exists in such a world, nevertheless, an infinity of problems, since the causes are not known to us in detail and thus leave room for unlimited research. And in addition to these theoretical puzzles there are innumerable technical problems, bound up with the difficulty of knowing how the various functions, once they have been inventoried and labelled, can be made to work together without doing one another harm. These theoretical and technical questions are interdependent, for the theoretical problems arise out of the different techniques while the technical problems cannot be solved without a measure of preestablished theoretical knowledge.

In such a world the ontological need, the need of being, is exhausted in exact proportion to the breaking up of personality on the one hand and, on the other, to the triumph of the category of the "purely nat-

ural" and the consequent atrophy of the faculty of *wonder.*

But to come at last to the ontological need itself; can we not approach it directly and attempt to define it? In reality this can only be done to a limited extent. For reasons which I shall develop later, I suspect that the characteristic of this need is that it can never be wholly clear to itself.

To try to describe it without distorting it we shall have to say something like this:

Being is—or should be—necessary. It is impossible that everything should be reduced to a play of successive appearances which are inconsistent with each other ("inconsistent" is essential), or, in the words of Shakespeare, to "a tale told by an idiot." I aspire to participate in this being, in this reality—and perhaps this aspiration is already a degree of participation, however rudimentary.

Such a need, it may be noted, is to be found at the heart of the most inveterate pessimism. Pessimism has no meaning unless it signifies: it would surely be well if there were being, but there is no being, and I, who observe this fact, am therefore nothing.

As for defining the word "being," let us admit that it is extremely difficult. I would merely suggest this method of approach: being is what withstands—or what would withstand—an exhaustive analysis bearing on the data of experience and aiming to reduce them step by step to elements increasingly devoid of intrinsic or significant value. (An analysis of this kind is attempted in the theoretical works of Freud.)

When the pessimist Besme says in *La Ville* that *nothing is,* he means precisely this, that there is no experience that withstands this analytical test. And it is always towards death regarded as the manifestation, the proof of this ultimate nothingness that the kind of inverted apologetic which arises out of absolute pessimism will inevitably gravitate.

A philosophy which refuses to endorse the ontological need is, nevertheless, possible; indeed, generally speaking, contemporary thought tends towards this abstention. But at this point a distinction must be made between two different attitudes which are sometimes confused: one which consists in a systematic reserve (it is that of agnosticism in all its forms), and the other, bolder and more coherent, which regards the ontological need as the expression of an outworn body of dogma liquidated once and for all by the Idealist critique.

The former appears to me to be purely negative: it is merely the expression of an intellectual policy of "not raising the question."

The latter, on the contrary, claims to be based on a positive theory of thought. This is not the place for a detailed critical study of this philosophy. I shall only note that it seems to me to tend towards an unconscious relativism, or else towards a monism which ignores the personal in all its form, ignores the tragic and denies the transcendent, seeking to reduce it to its caricatural expressions which distort its essential character. I shall also point out that, just because the philosophy continually stresses the activity of verification, it ends by ignoring *presence*—that inward realisation of presence through love which infinitely transcends all possible verification because it exists in an immediacy beyond all conceivable mediation. This will be clearer to some extent from what follows.

Thus I believe for my part that the ontological need cannot be silenced by an arbitrary dictatorial act which mutilates the life of the spirit at its roots. It remains true, nevertheless, that such an act is possible, and the conditions of our life are such that we can well believe that we are carrying it out; this must never be forgotten.

These preliminary reflections on the ontological need are sufficient to bring out its indeterminate character and to reveal a fundamental paradox. To formulate this need is to raise a host of questions: Is there such a thing as being? What is it? etc. Yet immediately an abyss opens under my feet: I who ask these questions about being, how can I be sure that I exist?

Yet surely I, who formulate this *problem*, should be able to remain *outside* it— *before* or *beyond* it? Clearly this is not so. The more I consider it the more I find that this problem tends inevitably to invade the proscenium from which it is excluded in theory: it is only by means of a fiction that Idealism in its traditional form seeks to maintain on the margin of being the consciousness which asserts it or denies it.

So I am inevitably forced to ask: Who am I—I who question being? How am I qualified to begin this investigation? If I do not exist, how can I succeed in it? And if I do exist, how can I be sure of this fact?

Contrary to the opinion which suggests itself at this point, I believe that on this plane the *cogito* cannot help us at all. Whatever Descartes may have thought of it himself, the only certainty with which it provides us concerns only the epistemological subject as organ of objective cognition. As I have written elsewhere, the *cogito* merely guards the threshold of objective validity, and that is strictly all; this is proved by the indeterminate character of the *I*. The *I am* is, to my mind, a global statement which it is impossible to break down into its component parts.

There remains a possible objection; it might be said: Either the being designated in the question "What am I?" concerns the subject of cognition, and in this case we are on the plane of the *cogito;* or else that which you call the ontological need is merely the extreme point (or perhaps only the fallacious transposition) of a need which is, in reality, vital and with which the metaphysician is not concerned.

But is it not a mistake arbitrarily to divide the question, *Who am I?* from the ontological "problem" taken as a whole? The truth is that neither of the two can be dealt with separately, but that when they are taken together, they cancel one another out *as problems*.

It should be added that the Cartesian position is inseparable from a form of dualism which I, for my part, would unhesitatingly reject. To raise the ontological problem is to raise the question of being as a whole and of oneself seen as a totality.

But should we not ask ourselves if we must not reject this dissociation between the intellectual and the vital, with its resultant over- or under-estimation of the one or the other? Doubtless it is legitimate to establish certain distinctions within the unity of the being who thinks and who endeavours to *think himself;* but it is only beyond such distinctions that the ontological problem can arise and it must relate to that being seen in his all-comprehensive unity.

To sum up our reflections at this point, we find that we are dealing with an urge towards an affirmation—yet an affirmation which it seems impossible to make, since it is not until it has been made that I can regard myself as qualified to make it.

It should be noted that this difficulty never arises at a time when I am actually faced with a problem to be solved. In such a case I work on the data, but everything leads me to believe that I need not take into account the I who is at work—it is a factor which is presupposed and nothing more.

Here, on the contrary, which I would call the ontological status of the investigator assumes a decisive importance. Yet so long as I am concerned with thought itself I seem to follow an endless regression. But by the very fact of recognising it as endless I transcend it in a certain way: I see that this process takes place within an affirmation of being—an affirmation which I *am* rather than an affirmation which I *utter:* by uttering it I break, I divide it, I am on the point of betraying it.

It might be said, by way of an approximation, that my inquiry into being presupposes an affirmation in regard to which I am, in a sense, passive, *and of which I am the stage rather than the subject.* But this is only at the extreme limit of thought, a limit which I cannot reach without falling into contradiction. I am therefore led to assume or to recognise a form of participation which has the reality of a subject; this participation cannot be, by definition, an *object* of thought; it cannot serve as a solu-

tion—it appears beyond the realm of problems: it is meta-problematical.

Conversely, it will be seen that, if the meta-problematical can be asserted at all, it must be conceived as transcending the opposition between the subject who asserts the existence of being, on the one hand, and being *as asserted by that subject,* on the other, and as underlying it in a given sense. To postulate the meta-problematical is to postulate the primacy of being over knowledge (not of being as *asserted,* but of being as *asserting itself;* it is to recognise that knowledge is, as it were, environed by being, that it is interior to it in a certain sense—a sense perhaps analogous to that which Paul Claudel tried to define in his *Art Poètique.* From this standpoint, contrary to what epistemology seeks vainly to establish, there exists well and truly a mystery of cognition; knowledge is contingent on a participation in being for which no epistemology can account because it continually presupposes it.

At this point we can begin to define the distinction between mystery and problem. A mystery is a problem which encroaches upon its own data, invading them, as it were, and thereby transcending itself as a simple problem. A set of examples will help us to grasp the content of this definition.

It is evident that there exists a mystery of the union of the body and the soul. The indivisible unity always inadequately expressed by such phrases as *I have a body, I make use of my body, I feel my body,* etc., can be neither analysed nor reconstituted out of precedent elements. It is not only data, I would say that it is the basis of data, in the sense of being my own presence to myself, a presence of which the act of self-consciousness is, in the last analysis, only an inadequate symbol.

It will be seen at once that there is no hope of establishing an exact frontier between problem and mystery. For in reflecting on a mystery we tend inevitably to degrade it to the level of a problem. This is particularly clear in the case of the problem of evil.

In reflecting upon evil, I tend, almost inevitably, to regard it as a disorder which I view from outside and of which I seek to discover the causes or the secret aims. Why is it that the "mechanism" functions so defectively? Or is the defect merely apparent and due to a real defect of my vision? In this case the defect is in myself, yet it remains objective in relation to my thought, which discovers it and observes it. But evil which is only stated or observed is no longer evil which is suffered: in fact, it ceases to be evil. In reality, I can only grasp it as evil in the measure in which it *touches* me—that is to say, in the measure in which I am *involved*, as one is involved in a lawsuit. Being "involved" is the fundamental fact; I cannot leave it out of account except by an unjustifiable fiction, for in doing so, I proceed as though I were God, and a God who is an onlooker at that.

This brings out how the distinction between what is in me and what is only *before me* can break down. This distinction falls under the blow of a certain kind of thought: thought at one remove.

But it is, of course, in love that the obliteration of this frontier can best be seen. It might perhaps even be shown that the domain of the meta-problematical coincides with that of love, and that love is the only starting point for the understanding of such mysteries as that of a body and soul, which, in some manner, is its expression.

Actually, it is inevitable that, in being brought to bear on love, thought which has not thought itself—unreflected reflection—should tend to dissolve its meta-problematical character and interpret it in terms of abstract concepts, such as the will to live, the will to power, the *libido*, etc. On the other hand, since the domain of the problematical is that of the objectively valid, it will be extremely difficult—if not impossible—to refute these interpretations without changing to a new ground: a ground on which, to tell the truth, they lose their meaning. Yet I have the assurance, the certainty—and it envelops me like a protective cloak—that for as much as I really love I

must not be concerned with these attempts at devaluation.

It will be asked: What is the criterion of true love? It must be answered that there is no criteriology except in the order of the objective and the problematical; but we can already see at a distance the eminent ontological value to be assigned to fidelity.

Let us take another illustration, more immediate and more particular, which may shed some light on the distinction between problem and mystery.

Say that I have made an encounter which has left a deep and lasting trace on all my life. It may happen to anyone to experience the deep spiritual significance of such a meeting—yet this is something which philosophers have commonly ignored or disdained, doubtless because it effects only the particular person as person—it cannot be universalised, it does not concern rational being in general.

It is clear that such a meeting raises, if you will, a problem; but it is equally clear that the solution of this problem will always fall short of the only question that matters. Suppose that I am told, for instance: "The reason you have met this person in this place is that you both like the same kind of scenery, or that you both need the same kind of treatment for your health"—the explanation means nothing. Crowds of people who apparently share my tastes were in the Engadine or in Florence at the time I was there; and there are always numbers of patients suffering from the same disease as myself at the health resort I frequent. But neither this supposed identity of tastes nor this common affliction has brought us together in any real sense; it has nothing to do with that intimate and unique affinity with which we are dealing. At the same time, it would be transgression of this valid reasoning to treat this affinity as if it were itself the cause and to say: "It is precisely this which has determined our meeting."

Hence I am in the presence of a mystery. That is to say, of a reality rooted in what is beyond the domain of the problematical properly so called. Shall we avoid the difficulty by saying that it was after all nothing but a coincidence, a lucky chance? But the whole of me immediately protests against this empty formula, this vain negation of what I apprehend with the deepest of my being. Once again we are brought back to our first definition of a mystery as a problem which encroaches upon its own data: I who inquire into the meaning and the possibility of this meeting, I cannot place myself outside it or before it; I am engaged in this encounter, I depend upon it, I am inside it in a certain sense, it envelops me and it comprehends me—even if it is not comprehended by me. Thus it is only by a kind of betrayal or denial that I can say: "After all, it might not have happened, I would still have been what I was, and what I am today." Nor must it be said: I have been changed by it as by an outward cause. No, it has developed me from within, it has acted in me as an inward principle.

But this is very difficult to grasp without distortion. I shall be inevitably tempted to react against this sense of the inwardness of the encounter, tempted by my probity itself, by what from a certain standpoint I must judge to be the best—or at least the safest—of myself.

There is a danger that these explanations may strengthen in the minds of my readers a preliminary objection which must be stated at once.

It will be said: The meta-problematical of which you speak is after all a content of thought; how then should we not ask ourselves what is its mode of existence? What assures us of its existence at all? Is it not itself problematical in the highest degree?

My answer is categorical: To think, or, rather, to assert, the meta-problematical is to assert it as indubitably real, as a thing of which I cannot doubt without falling into contradiction. We are in a sphere where it is no longer possible to dissociate the idea itself from the certainty or the degree of certainty which pertains to it. Because this idea is certainty, it is the assurance of itself; it is, in this sense, something other and some-

thing more than an idea. As for the term *content of thought* which figured in the objection, it is deceptive in the highest degree. For content is, when all is said and done, derived from experience; whereas it is only by a way of liberation and detachment from experience that we can possibly rise to the level of the meta-problematical and of mystery. This liberation must be *real;* this detachment must be *real;* they must not be an abstraction, that is to say a fiction recognised as such.

And this at last brings us to recollection, for it is in recollection and in this alone that this detachment is accomplished. I am convinced, for my part, that no ontology—that is to say, no apprehension of ontological mystery in whatever degree—is possible except to a being who is capable of recollecting himself, and of thus proving that he is not a living creature pure and simple, a creature, that is to say, which is at the mercy of its life and without a hold upon it.

It should be noted that recollection, which has received little enough attention from pure philosophers, is very difficult to define—if only because it transcends the dualism of being and action or, more correctly, because it reconciles in itself these two aspects of the antimony. The word means what it says—the act whereby I re-collect myself as a unity; but this hold, this grasp upon myself, is also relaxation and abandon. *Abandon to...relaxation in the presence of...*—yet there is no noun for these prepositions to govern. The way stops at the threshold.

Here, as in every other sphere, problems will be raised, and it is the psychologist who will raise them. All that must be noted is that the psychologist is no more in a position to shed light on the metaphysical bearing of recollection than on the noetic value of knowledge.

It is within recollection that I take up my position—or, rather, I become capable of taking up my position—in regard to my life; I withdraw from it in a certain way, but not as the pure subject of cognition; *in this withdrawal I carry with me that which I am and which perhaps life is not.* This brings out the gap between my being and my life. I am not my life; and if I can judge my life—a fact I cannot deny without falling into a radical scepticism which is nothing other than despair—is only on condition that I encounter myself within recollection beyond all possible judgment and, I would add, beyond all representation. Recollection is doubtless what is least spectacular in the soul; it does not consist in looking at something, it is an inward hold, an inward reflection, and it might be asked in passing whether it should not be seen as the ontological basis of memory—that principle of effective and non-representational unity on which the possibility of remembrance rests. The double meaning of "recollection" in English is revealing.

It may be asked: is not recollection identical with that dialectical moment of the turning to oneself *(retour sur soi)* or else with the *fuer sich sein* which is the central theme of German Idealism?

I do not think so. To withdraw into oneself is not to be for oneself nor to mirror oneself in the intelligible unity of subject and object. On the contrary. I would say that here we come up against the paradox of that actual mystery whereby the I into which I withdraw ceases, for as much, to belong to itself. "You are not your own"— this great saying of St. Paul assumes in this connection its full concrete and ontological significance; it is the nearest approach to the reality for which we are groping. It will be asked: is not this reality an object of intuition? Is not that which you term "recollec-tion" the same as what others have termed "intuition"?

But this again seems to me to call for the utmost prudence. If intuition can be mentioned in this context at all, it is not an intuition which is, or can be, given as such.

The more an intuition is central and basic in the being whom it illuminates, the less it is capable of turning back and apprehending itself.

Moreover, if we reflect on what an intuitive knowledge of being could possibly be, we see that it could never figure in a collection, a procession of simple experiences or *Erlebnisse,* which all have this characteristic that they can be at times absorbed and at others isolated and, as it were, uncovered. Hence, any effort to remember such an intuition, to represent it to oneself, is inevitably fruitless. From this point of view, to be told of an intuitive knowledge of being is like being invited to play on a soundless piano. Such an intuition cannot be brought out into the light of day, for the simple reason that we do not possess it.

We are here at the most difficult point of our whole discussion. Rather than to speak of intuition in this context, we should say that we are dealing with an assurance which underlies the entire development of thought, even of discursive thought; it can therefore be approached only by a second reflection—a reflection whereby I ask myself how and from what starting point I was able to proceed in my initial reflection, which itself postulated the ontological, but without knowing it. This second reflection is recollection in the measure in which recollection can be self-conscious.

COMMENT

Camus and Existentialism

The twentieth century witnessed crises of unparalleled scope and intensity: two world wars, a very severe economic depression, revolutionary movements of tremendous magnitude and fury, the threat of nuclear holocaust. Philosophers have reacted with different degrees of intensity to these world-shaking events.

Apart from the Marxists, the existentialists have been the philosophers most responsive. Existentialism, in fact, is a philosophy of crisis—its popularity can be explained largely in these terms. Although Jean-Paul Sartre and Albert Camus in France, Martin Heidegger and Karl Jaspers in Germany, and the other existentialist philosophers have been able to agree on almost nothing else, they are alike in reflecting a time out of joint, when people have been hungry for meaning, for identity, for some roots in existence, for some structure of purpose in human experience, for some protection against anxieties and frustrations.

Though it has certain historical predecessors, existentialism is, strictly speaking, a twentieth-century phenomenon. Nietzsche, Pascal, Dostoyevsky, and Kierkegaard all share in the existentialist heritage, but it has only been in our time that the emphases which these thinkers have in common have exerted a profound influence in the philosophical and religious worlds. The two thinkers represented in this section reflect the themes of earlier existentialist thinkers, but in a way that is particularly appropriate to our century.

It can be said that Camus and other existentialist thinkers share a common concern for the priority of human values. It is this concern that gives rise to the affinity between existentialism and religious questions. Whereas philosophy has often concerned itself with other questions—such as those of a scientific and logical nature—existentialist thinkers are agreed that the first job of philosophy is to come to grips with the value structure of human existence. Clearly, this concern is of primary importance to religious thinkers as well. Although there are "atheistic" existentialists as well as theistic ones, even these find it necessary to define themselves and their positions in relation to the traditional religious posture.

It is on the basis of their concern with the values of human existence that Camus and the writers in question have been grouped together, for good or for ill, under the heading "existentialist." The questions of the nature of human existence, the proper mode of existence, and the basis of responsibility are all central to these thinkers. In all of these questions, emphasis is placed upon the ultimacy of personal integrity and individuality. Moreover, there is a strong concern to develop a stance toward life that takes full cognizance of the stark realities of human existence, such as anxiety, absurdity, and death. Thus, there is a constant protest against what might be called the naive optimism of all forms of Idealism, religious and nonreligious. Clearly, Camus shares such concerns.

The other side of this positive concern for human, existential values is a negative appraisal of the importance of empirical or scientific reason. While some existentialists have actually taken what must be labeled an "irrationalist" approach, most have been content to mark out the limitations of what might be termed "critical reason" with respect to questions of ethics and religion. By and large, existentialist writers maintain a strict dichotomy between the factual and the valuational dimensions of human existence. Thus, critical reason, which is appropriate to factual considerations, is thought to be essentially irrelevant to valuational considerations. It is claimed that critical reason, with its stress upon objectivity, alienates the knower from the known and systematically avoids all questions of decision and commitment as hopelessly "subjective." Thus, as Camus argues, all of the truly important considerations of human existence are set aside. For these reasons it is thought useless and harmful to subject valuational issues to the structures of critical reason.

Among those existentialists who address themselves to a philosophical consideration of religion, nearly all are agreed that the foregoing remarks apply with equal force to religious questions. Religion is seen as a subdivision within the valuational domain, and thus outside of the scope of critical reason. Here again it is to be noted that this is not an irrationalist claim, since it is maintained both that critical reason has other, more appropriate concerns and that there are other means available for coming to an understanding of the valuational and religious aspects of existence. This is Marcel's posture.

This emphasis, as well as that placed on human values, brings existentialism into direct relationship with religion. On the one hand, there is a concrete effort made by nearly all those writing from within this perspective to analyze the nature of existence in general, or as it is usually put, to understand "Being itself." This effort is often confined to a focus on the "existentials" of human experience, such as anxiety, fear, absurdity, and death, by way of carving out a meaningful place to stand in daily life. This is Camus' posture. On the other hand, there is often an interest among existentialist thinkers in constructing a rather full-blown metaphysical position in order to interrelate the various aspects of experience in a stable and coherent worldview. This interest is in harmony with the Idealist tradition extending from Plato down through Hegel. Thus, it is that the concepts of God, nature, the self, immortality, and the like play a role in both religion and existentialist philosophy.

The connection between this concern for ontology and previously mentioned negative appraisal of critical reason is to be found by zeroing in on the method by means of which existentialist ontology is to be developed. While these thinkers are against the application of critical reason in the valuational and religious realms, some are in favor of the application of what is often termed "speculative reason." Most often philosophy is identified with that enterprise which seeks to draw all the data of human experience and knowledge together by way of making generalizations about the nature of reality as a whole. Sometimes this methodology is equated with some form of intuition or introspection. In the latter case, existentialism is transformed into what is known today as "Phenomenology." Perhaps the most important characteristic of speculative reason, as contrasted with critical reason, is its attempt to "get inside of" reality, rather than to objectively describe it. The methods of doing this are as varied as the thinkers who advocate this approach. Camus preferred to approach these issues through novels and brief essays rather than by engaging in abstract analysis.

Marcel and Self-Knowledge

Gabriel Marcel begins by pointing out the inherent circularity involved in René Descartes' efforts to establish his own existence. No matter which way we come at this issue, we seem to find it necessary in some sense to assume what we are seeking to prove. Surely the act of proving something to be the case must be performed by an agent who would presumably be a self. Thus, when a self engages in proving its own existence, the argument becomes confused. To put it another way, the first "I" in Descartes' famous *Cogito,* "I think, therefore I am," already makes use of and thus presupposes the conclusion.

This difficulty leads Marcel to distinguish between a "problem" and a "mystery." Problems can be separated from the person who is seeking to solve them, whereas mysteries cannot be objectified in this way since "they encroach on their own data." Marcel clearly thinks that the question of self-knowledge is more of a mystery than a problem. In other contexts, he includes our knowledge of other persons and God in this category as well. In a sense, such questions are so "close" to us, so involve our basic commitments and values, that we are inextricably connected with what is being examined and are as much a part of the problem as of the solution.

If this is the case, it is hardly surprising that according to Marcel, whenever we try to apply to a mystery our analytic or strictly intellectual capacities—which are designed for and appropriate to the solving of problems—we turn it into a problem and thereby miss its essence. In other words, Marcel contends, along with Kierkegaard, that not all knowledge is the result of objectifying cognitive activity. Questions that bear on the meaning of human existence, the ultimate nature of reality, the meaning of love, and so on can only be treated "inwardly" because they are mysteries rather than problems.

This inward reflection is termed *recollection* by Marcel. He does not use this term in the sense that Plato used it, as a remembrance of knowledge acquired in a previous existence. Rather, he seems to mean a form of reflective self-consciousness, a kind of self-transcendence in which one is both the knower and the known. Our knowledge of mysteries is, then, *reciprocal* in character: We both know ourselves and are the ones who do the knowing. Although this argument sounds very similar to Bergsonian intuition, Marcel is careful to distinguish his notion of recollection from that of Henri Bergson. What is known with respect to mysteries is not a "datum" in the sense that Bergson or even Bertrand Russell would speak of it. Rather, it is more like the "assurance which underlies the entire development of thought," the confidence with which we participate in the various dimensions of human existence.

Perhaps the most troubling question regarding this way of thinking about knowledge pertains to verification. The same problems that arose with Camus' notion of "subjectivity" would seem to plague Marcel's concept of "inwardness." If the knowledge supposedly appropriate to mystery cannot be articulated and tested in the manner appropriate to problems, how can we establish that it is knowledge? Is not one person's inward "knowledge" the same as another's inward "error"? How are conflicting claims to such knowledge adjudicated?

This is one significant difference between Camus' view and that of Marcel. Whereas the former stresses the individual character of truth, the latter appeals to the common cognitive experience of all humans. Marcel claims that the sort of knowledge he is speaking of, this interaction between the knower and the known, is shared by everyone at various levels of life and in various contexts. We all know ourselves, each other, the world around us, and even the divine presence, in a way that, although not reducible to observation and inferential reasoning, is nonetheless absolutely certain. Indeed, he would say that we must draw on our knowledge of such mysteries even to explore and examine them, as well as to engage in the whole problem-solving procedure itself. Needless to say, not everyone agrees with Marcel's approach. As the British philosopher John Wisdom once said, "In philosophy someone always objects."

It is, to be sure, difficult to know how the existentialist approach to knowledge would relate to the case study presented at the beginning of this section. Would Camus and Marcel take the same approach, or would they differ, and if so, why? Indeed, is this whole question "absurd," or is it an example of a "problem" or of a "mystery"? What would Camus and Marcel say to the claim that Deep Blue's victories over Kasparov prove that humans are not superior to machines because neither involve self-consciousness?

7

PERSPECTIVISM

SANDRA HARDING (1935–   )

For a number of years, Sandra Harding, professor of philosophy at the University of Delaware, has been a leading advocate of critiquing traditional scientific methods from a feminist point of view. In addition to pointing out the generally overlooked social bases for our scientific knowledge, she seeks to focus attention on the feminist perspective in our knowledge of nature and human social life. Harding also attempts to offset the built-in bias of white-male dominance by bringing into the discussion of human knowledge the "marginalized" voices of culturally disenfranchised minorities.

In the following essay, taken from her book *Whose Science? Whose Knowledge?*, Harding wrestles with the notion of "objectivity," a concept crucial to the traditional philosophical understanding of knowledge. She argues that far from undermining the objectivity of scientific research, the inclusion of the sociohistorical factors comprising the context within which knowledge is obtained actually ensures and enhances the deeper meaning of objectivity.

Harding's works include: *The Science Question in Feminism; Discovering Reality: Feminist Perspectives on Epistemology, Metaphysics, Methodology, and Philosophy of Science* (with Merrill Hintikka); *Feminism and Methodology: Social Science Issues*; and *Sex and Scientific Inquiry* (with Jean F. O'Barr).

"STRONG OBJECTIVITY" AND SOCIALLY SITUATED KNOWLEDGE

In the preceding chapter I argued that a feminist standpoint theory can direct the production of less partial and less distorted beliefs. This kind of scientific process will not merely acknowledge the social-situatedness—the historicity—of the very best beliefs any culture has arrived at or could in principle "discover" but will use this fact as a resource for generating those beliefs.[1] Nevertheless, it still might be thought that

Reprinted from Sandra Harding, *Whose Science? Whose Knowledge? Thinking from Women's Lives*, pp. 138–163. Copyright © 1991 by Cornell University. Used by permission of Cornell University Press.

[1] See Donna Haraway, "Situated Knowledges: *The Science Question in Feminism* and the Privilege of Partial Perspective," *Feminist Studies* 14:3 (1988).

this association of objectivity with socially situated knowledge is an impossible combination. Has feminist standpoint theory really abandoned objectivity and embraced relativism? Or, alternatively, has it remained too firmly entrenched in a destructive objectivism that increasingly is criticized from many quarters?

The Declining Status of "Objectivism"

Scientists and science theorists working in many different disciplinary and policy projects have objected to the conventional notion of a value-free, impartial, dispassionate objectivity that is supposed to guide scientific research and without which, according to conventional thought, one cannot separate justified belief from mere opinion, or real knowledge from mere claims to knowledge. From the perspective of this conventional notion of objectivity—sometimes referred to as "objectivism"—it has appeared that if one gives up this concept, the only alternative is not just a cultural relativism (the sociological assertion that what is thought to be a reasonable claim in one society or subculture is not thought to be so in another) but, worse, a judgmental or epistemological relativism that denies the possibility of any reasonable standards for adjudicating between competing claims. Some fear that to give up the possibility of one universally and eternally valid standard of judgment is perhaps even to be left with no way to argue rationally against the possibility that *each person's* judgment about the regularities of nature and their underlying causal tendencies must be regarded as equally valid. The reduction of the critic's position to such an absurdity provides a powerful incentive to question no further the conventional idea that objectivity requires value-neutrality. From the perspective of objectivism, judgmental relativism appears to be the only alternative.

Insistence on this division of epistemological stances between those that firmly support value-free objectivity and those that support judgmental relativism—a dichotomy that unfortunately has gained the consent of many critics of objectivism as well as its defenders—has succeeded in making value-free objectivity look much more attractive to natural and social scientists than it should. It also makes judgmental relativism appear far more progressive than it is. Some critics of the conventional notion of objectivity have openly welcomed judgmental relativism.[2] Others have been willing to tolerate it as the cost they think they must pay for admitting the practical ineffectualness, the proliferation of confusing conceptual contradictions, and the political regressiveness that follow from trying to achieve an objectivity that has been defined in terms of value-neutrality. But even if embracing judgmental relativism could make sense in anthropology and other social sciences, it appears absurd as an epistemological stance in physics or biology. What would it mean to assert that no reasonable standards can or could in principle be found for adjudicating between one culture's claim that the earth is flat and another culture's claim that the earth is round?

The literature on these topics from the 1970s and 1980s alone is huge and located in many disciplines. Prior to the 1960s the issue was primarily one of ethical and cultural absolutism versus relativism. It was the concern primarily of philosophers and anthropologists and was considered relevant only to the social sciences, not the natural sciences. But since then, the recognition has emerged that cognitive, scientific, and epistemic absolutism are both implicated in ethical and cultural issues and are also independently problematic. One incentive to the expansion was Thomas Kuhn's account of how the natural sciences have developed in response to

---

[2] See, e.g., David Bloor, *Knowledge and Social Imagery* (London: Routledge & Kegan Paul, 1977); and many of the papers in *Knowledge and Reflexivity*, ed. Steve Woolgar (Beverly Hills, Calif.: Sage, 1988).

what scientists have found "interesting," together with the subsequent post-Kuhnian philosophy and social studies of the natural sciences.[3]

Another has been the widely recognized failure of the social sciences to ground themselves in methods and theoretical commitments that can share in the scientificity of the natural sciences. Paradoxically, the more "scientific" social research becomes, the less objective it becomes.[4]

Further incentives have been such political tendencies as the U.S. civil rights movement, the rise of the women's movement, the decentering of the West and criticisms of Eurocentrism in international circles, and the increasing prominence within U.S. political and intellectual life of the voices of women and of African Americans and other people of Third World descent. From these perspectives, it appears increasingly arrogant for defenders of the West's intellectual traditions to continue to dismiss the scientific and epistemological stances of Others as caused mainly by biological inferiority, ignorance, underdevelopment, primitiveness, and the like. On the other hand, although diversity, pluralism, relativism, and difference have their valuable political and intellectual uses, embracing them resolves the political—scientific—epistemological conflict to almost no one's satisfaction.

I make no attempt here to summarize the arguments of these numerous and diverse writings.[5] My concern is more narrowly focused: to state as clearly as possible how issues of objectivity and relativism appear from the perspective of a feminist standpoint theory.

Feminist critics of science and the standpoint theorists especially have been interpreted as supporting either an excessive commitment to value-free objectivity or, alternatively, the abandonment of objectivity in favor of relativism. Because there are clear commitments within feminism to tell less partial and distorted stories about women, men, nature, and social relations, some critics have assumed that feminism must be committed to value-neutral objectivity. Like other feminists, however, the standpoint theorists have also criticized conventional sciences for their arrogance in assuming that they could tell one true story about a world that is out there, ready-made for their reporting, without listening to women's accounts or being aware that accounts of nature and social relations have been constructed within men's control of gender relations. Moreover, feminist thought and politics as a

---

[3] Thomas Kuhn, *The Structure of Scientific Revolutions* (Chicago: University of Chicago Press, 1962).

[4] This is an important theme in Richard Bernstein, *Beyond Objectivism and Relativism* (Philadelphia: University of Pennsylvania Press, 1983). Similar doubts about the ability of legal notions of objectivity to advance justice appear in many of the essays in "Women in Legal Education: Pedagogy, Law, Theory, and Practice," *Journal of Legal Education* 38 (1988), special issue, ed. Carrie Menkel-Meadow, Martha Minow, and David Vernon.

[5] Discussions on one or more of these focuses can be found in Martin Hollis and Steven Lukes, eds., *Rationality and Relativism* (Cambridge, Mass: Harvard University Press, 1982); Michael Krausz and Jack Meiland, eds., *Relativism: Cognitive and Moral* (Notre Dame, Ind.: University of Notre Dame Press, 1982); Richard Bernstein, *Beyond Objectivism;* and S. P. Mohanty, "Us and Them: On the Philosophical Bases of Political Criticism," *Yale Journal of Criticism* 2:2 (1989). A good brief bibliographic essay on the recent philosophy of science within and against which the particular discussion of this chapter is located is Steve Fuller, "The Philosophy of Science since Kuhn: Readings on the Revolution That Has Yet to Come," *Choice,* December 1989. For more extended studies that are not incompatible with my arguments here, see Steve Fuller, *Social Epistemology* (Bloomington: Indiana University Press, 1988); and Joseph Rouse, *Knowledge and Power: Toward a Political Philosophy of Science* (Ithaca: Cornell University Press, 1987).

whole are continually revising the ways they bring women's voices and the perspectives from women's lives to knowledge-seeking, and they are full of conflicts between the claims made by different groups of feminists. How could feminists in good conscience do anything but abandon any agenda to legitimate one over another of these perspectives? Many feminists in literature, the arts, and the humanities are even more resistant than those in the natural and social sciences to claims that feminist images or rep-resentations of the world hold any special epistemo-logical or scientific status. Such policing of thought is exactly what they have objected to in criticizing the authority of their disciplinary canons on the grounds that such authority has had the effect of stifling the voices of marginalized groups. In ignoring these views, feminist epistemologists who are concerned with natural or social science agendas appear to sup-port an epistemological divide between the sciences and humanities, a divide that feminism has elsewhere criticized.

The arguments of this book move away from the fruitless and depressing choice between value-neutral objectivity and judgmental relativism. The last chapter stressed the greater objectivity that can be and has been claimed to result from grounding research in women's lives. This chapter draws on some assumptions underlying the analyses of earlier chap-ters in order to argue that the conventional notion of objectivity against which feminist criticisms have been raised should be regarded as excessively weak. A fem-inist standpoint epistemology requires strengthened standards of objectivity. The standpoint episte-molo-gies call for recognition of a historical or sociological or cultural relativism—but not for a judgmental or epistemological relativism. They call for the acknowledgment that all human beliefs—including our best scientific beliefs—are socially situated, but they also require a critical evaluation to determine which social situations tend to generate the most objective knowledge

claims. They require, as judgmental relativism does not, a scientific account of the relationships between historically located belief and maximally objective belief. So they demand what I shall call *strong objectivity* in contrast to the weak objectivity of objectivism and its mirror-linked twin, judgmental relativism. This may appear to be circular reason-ing—to call for scientifically examining the social location of scientific claims—but if so, it is at least not viciously circular.[6]

This chapter also considers two possible objections to the argument presented, one that may arise from scientists and philosophers of science, and another that may arise among feminist themselves.

Objectivism's Weak Conception of Objectivity

The term "objectivism" is useful for the purposes of my argument because its echoes of "scientism" draw attention to ways in which the research prescriptions called for by a value-free objectivity only mimic the

---

[6] Additional writings informing this chapter include esp. Haraway, "Situated Knowledges"; Donna Haraway, *Primate Visions: Gender, Race, and Nature in the World of Modern Science* (New York: Routledge, 1989); Jane Flax, *Thinking Fragments: Psychoanalysis, Feminism, and Postmodernism in the Contemporary West* (Berkeley: University of California Press, 1990); and the writings of standpoint theorists themselves, esp. Nancy Hartsock, "The Feminist Standpoint: Developing the Ground for a Specifically Feminist Historical Materialism," in *Discovering Reality: Feminist Perspectives on Epistemology, Metaphysics, Methodology, and Philosophy of Science*, ed. Sandra Harding and Merrill Hintikka (Dordrecht: Reidel, 1983); Dorothy Smith, *The Everyday World as Problematic: A Feminist Sociology* (Boston: Northeastern University Press, 1987); Hilary Rose, "Hand, Brain, and Heart: A Feminist Epistemology for the Natural Sciences," *Signs* 9:1 (1983); Patricia Hill Collins, "Learning from the Outsider Within: The Sociological Significance of Black Feminist Thought," *Social Problems* 33 (1986)—though each of these theorists would no doubt disagree with various aspects of my argument.

purported style of the most successful scientific practices without managing to produce their effects. Objectivism results only in semiscience when it turns away from the task of critically identifying all those broad, historical social desires, interests, and values that have shaped the agendas, contents, and results of the sciences much as they shape the rest of human affairs. Objectivism encourages only a partial and distorted explanation of why the great moments in the history of the natural and social sciences have occurred.

Let me be more precise in identifying the weaknesses of this notion. It has been conceptualized both too narrowly, and too broadly to be able to accomplish the goals that its defenders claim it is intended to satisfy. Taken at face value it is ineffectively conceptualized, but this is what makes the sciences that adopt weak standards of objectivity so effective socially: objectivist justifications of science are useful to dominant groups that, consciously or not, do not really intend to "play fair" anyway. Its internally contradictory character gives it a kind of flexibility and adaptability that would be unavailable to a coherently characterized notion.

Consider, first, how objectivism operational-izes too narrowly the notion of maximizing objectivity. The conception of value-free, impartial, dispassionate research is supposed to direct the identification of all social values and their elimination from the results of research, yet it has been operationalized to identify and eliminate only those social values and interests that differ among the researchers and critics who are regarded by the scientific community as competent to make such judgments. If the community of "qualified" researchers and critics systematically excludes, for example, all African Americans and women of all races, and if the larger culture is stratified by race and gender and lacks powerful critiques of this stratifica-tion, it is not plausible to imagine that racist and sexist interests and values would be identified within a community of scientists composed

entirely of people who benefit—intentionally or not—from institutional racism and sexism.

This kind of blindness is advanced by the conventional belief that the truly scientific part of knowledge-seeking—the part controlled by methods of research—is only in the context of justification. The context of discovery, where problems are identified as appropriate for scientific investigation, hypotheses are formulated, key concepts are defined—this part of the scientific process is thought to be unexaminable within science by rational methods. Thus "real sci-ence" is restricted to those processes controllable by methodological rules. The methods of science—or, rather, of the special sciences—are restricted to pro-cedures for the testing of already formulated hypothe-ses. Untouched by these careful methods are those values and interests entrenched in the very statement of what problem is to be researched and in the con-cepts favored in the hypotheses that are to be tested. Recent histories of science are full of cases in which broad social assumptions stood little chance of identification or elimination through the very best research procedures of the day.[7] Thus objectivism operationalizes the notion of objectivity in much too narrow a way to

---

[7] This is the theme of many feminist, left, and antiracist analyses of biology and social sciences. See, e.g., Anne Fausto-Sterling, *Myths of Gender: Biological Theories about Women and Men* (New York: Basic Books, 1985); Stephen Jay Gould, *The Mismeasure of Man* (New York: Norton, 1981); Robert V. Guthrie, *Even the Rat Was White: A Historical View of Psychology* (New York: Harper & Row, 1976); Haraway, *Primate Visions*; Sandra Harding, ed., *Feminism and Methodology: Social Science Issues* (Bloomington: Indiana University Press, 1987); Joyce Ladner, ed., *The Death of White Sociology* (New York: Random House, 1973); Hilary Rose and Steven Rose, eds., *Ideology of/in the Natural Sciences* (Cambridge, Mass.: Schenkman, 1979); Londa Schiebinger, *The Mind Has No Sex: Women in the Origins of Modern Science* (Cambridge, Mass.: Harvard University Press, 1989).

permit the achievement of the value-free research that is supposed to be its outcome.

But objectivism also conceptualizes the desired value-neutrality of objectivity too broadly. Objectivists claim that objectivity requires the elimination of *all* social values and interests from the research process and the results of research. It is clear, however, that not all social values and interests have the same bad effects upon the results of research. Some have systematically generated less partial and distorted beliefs than others—or than purportedly value-free research—as earlier chapters have argued.

Nor is this so outlandish an understanding of the history of science as objectivists frequently intimate. Setting the scene for his study of nineteenth-century biological determinism, Stephen Jay Gould says:

> I do not intend to contrast evil determinists who stray from the path of scientific objectivity with enlightened antideterminists who approach data with an open mind and therefore see truth. Rather, I criticize the myth that science itself is an objective enterprise, done properly only when scientists can shuck the constraints of their culture and view the world as it really is.... . Science, since people must do it, is a socially embedded activity. It progresses by hunch, vision, and intuition. Much of its change through time does not record a closer approach to absolute truth, but the alteration of cultural contexts that influence it so strongly.[8]

Other historians agree with Gould.[9] Modern science has again and again been reconstructed by a set of interests and values—distinctively Western, bourgeois, and patriarchal—which were originally formulated by a new social group that intentionally used the new sciences in their struggles against the Catholic Church and feudal state. These interests and values had both positive and negative consequences for the development of the sciences. Political and social interests are not "add-ons" to an otherwise transcendental science that is inherently indifferent to human society; scientific beliefs, practices, institutions, histories, and problematics are constituted in and through contemporary political and social projects, and always have been. It would be far more startling to discover a kind of human knowledge-seeking whose products could—alone among all human products—defy historical "gravity" and fly off the earth, escaping entirely their historical location. Such a cultural phenomenon would be cause for scientific alarm; it would appear to defy principles of "material" causality upon which the possibility of scientific activity itself is based.[10]

Of course, people in different societies arrive at many of the same empirical claims. Farmers, toolmakers, and child tenders in every culture must arrive at similar "facts" about nature and social relations if their work is to succeed. Many of the observations collected by medieval European astronomers are preserved in the data used by astronomers today. But what "facts" these data refer to, what further research they point to, what theoretical statements they support and how such theories are to be applied, what such data signify in terms of human social relations and relations to nature—all these parts of the sciences can differ wildly, as the contrast between medieval and contemporary astronomy illustrates.

There are yet deeper ways in which political values permeate modern science.

---

[8] Gould, *Mismeasure of Man*, 21–22.

[9] E.g., William Leiss, *The Domination of Nature* (Boston: Beacon Press, 1972); Carolyn Merchant, *The Death of Nature: Women, Ecology, and the Scientific Revolution* (New York: Harper & Row, 1980); Wolfgang Van`den Daele, "The Social Construction of Science," in *The Social Production of Scientific Knowledge*, ed. Everett Mendelsohn, Peter Weingart, and Richard Whitley (Dordrecht: Reidel, 1977).

[10] Rouse, *Knowledge and Power*, provides a good analysis of the implications for science of Foucauldian notions of politics and power.

For even relatively conservative tendencies in the post-Kuhnian philosophies of science, the sciences' power to manipulate the world is considered the mark of their success. The "new empiricism" contrasts in this respect with conventional empiricism. As Joseph Rouse puts the point:

If we take the new empiricism seriously, it forces us to reappraise the relation between power and knowledge in a more radical way. The central issue is no longer how scientific claims can be distorted or suppressed by polemic, propaganda, or ideology. Rather, we must look at what was earlier described as the achievement of power through the application of knowledge. But the new empiricism also challenges the adequacy of this description in terms of "application." The received view distinguishes the achievement of knowledge from its subsequent application, from which this kind of power is supposed to derive. New empiricist accounts of science make this distinction less tenable by shifting the locus of knowledge from accurate representation to successful manipulation and control of events. Power is no longer external to knowledge or opposed to it: power itself becomes the mark of knowledge.[11]

The best as well as the worst of the history of the natural sciences has been shaped by—or, more accurately, constructed through and within—political desires, interests, and values. Consequently, there appear to be no grounds left from which to defend the claim that the objectivity of research is advanced by the elimination of all political values and interests from the research process. Instead, the sciences need to legitimate *within scientific research*, as part of practicing science, critical examination of historical values and interests that may be so shared within the scientific community, so invested in by the very constitution of this or that field of study, that they will not show up as a cultural bias between experimenters or between research communities. What objectivism cannot conceptualize is the need for critical examination of the "intentionality of nature"—meaning not that nature is no different from humans (in having intentions, desires, interests, and values or in constructing its own meaningful "way of life," and so on) but that nature as-the-object-of-human-knowledge never comes to us "naked"; it comes only as already constituted in social thought.[12] Nature-as-object-of-study simulates in this respect an intentional being. This idea helps counter the intuitively seductive idea that scientific claims are and should be an epiphenomenon of nature. It is the development of strategies to generate just such critical examination that the notion of strong objectivity calls for.

Not everyone will welcome such a project; even those who share these criticisms of objectivism may think the call for strong objectivity too idealistic, too utopian, not realistic enough. But is it more unrealistic than trying to explain the regularities of nature and their underlying causal tendencies scientifically but refusing to examine all their causes? And even if the ideal of identifying *all* the causes of human beliefs is rarely if ever achievable, why not hold it as a desirable standard? Anti-litter laws improve social life even if they are not always obeyed.[13]

---

[11] Rouse, *Knowledge and Power*, 19. Among the "new empiricist" works that Rouse has in mind are Larry Laudan, *Progress and Its Problems: Toward a Theory of Scientific Growth* (Berkeley: University of California Press, 1977); Mary Hesse, *Revolutions and Reconstructions in the Philosophy of Science* (Bloomington: University of Indiana Press, 1980); Nancy Cartwright, *How the Laws of Physics Lie* (Oxford: Oxford University Press, 1983).

[12] See Haraway, *Primate Visions*, esp. chap. 10 for analysis of differences between the Anglo-American, Japanese, and Indian constructions of "nature" which shape the objects of study in primatology.

[13] Fuller uses the anti-litter law example in another context in *Social Epistemology*.

Weak objectivity, then, is a contradictory notion, and its contradictory character is largely responsible for its usefulness and its widespread appeal to dominant groups. It offers hope that scientists and science institutions, themselves admittedly historically located, can produce claims that will be regarded as objectively valid without their having to examine critically their own historical commitments, from which—intentionally or not—they actively construct their scientific research. It permits scientists and science institutions to be unconcerned with the origins or consequences of their problematics and practices, or with the social values and interests that these problematics and practices support. It offers the possibility of enacting what Francis Bacon promised: "The course I propose for the discovery of sciences is such as leaves but little to the acuteness and strength of wits, but places all wits and understandings nearly on a level." His "way of discovering sciences goes far to level men's wits, and leaves but little to individual excellence; because it performs everything by surest rules and demonstrations."[14]

For those powerful forces in society that want to appropriate science and knowledge for their own purposes, it is extremely valuable to be able to support the idea that ignoring the constitution of science within political desires, values, and interests will somehow increase the reliability of accounts of nature and social life. The ideal of the disinterested rational scientist advances the self-interest of both social elites and, ironically, scientists who seek status and power. Reporting on various field studies of scientific work, Steve Fuller points out that Machiavellian judgments

simulate those of the fabled "rational" scientist, since in order for the Machiavellian to maximize his advantage he must be ready to switch research programs when

he detects a change in the balance of credibility—which is, after all, what philosophers of science would typically have the rational scientist do. To put the point more strikingly, it would seem that as the scientist's motivation approximates total *self-interestedness* (such that he is always able to distance his own interests from those of any social group which supports what may turn out to be a research program with diminishing credibility), his behavior approxi-mates total *disinterestedness*. And so we can imagine the ultimate Machiavellian scientist pursuing a line of research frowned upon by most groups in the society—perhaps determining the racial component in intelligence is an example—simply because he knows of its potential for influencing the course of future research and hence for enhancing his credibility as a scientist.[15]

The history of science shows that research directed by maximally liberatory social interests and values tends to be better equipped to identify partial claims and distorting assumptions even though the credibility of the scientists who do it may not be enhanced during the short run. After all, antiliberatory interests and values are invested in the natural inferiority of just the groups of humans who, if given real equal access (not just the formally equal access that is liberalism's goal) to public voice, would most strongly contest claims about their purported natural inferiority. Antiliberatory interests and values silence and destroy the most likely sources of evidence against their own claims. That is what makes them rational for elites.

Strong Objectivity: A Competency Concept

At this point what I mean by a concept of strong objectivity should be clear. In an important sense, our cultures have agendas

---

[14] Quoted in Van den Daele, "Social Construction of Science," 34.

[15] Fuller, *Social Epistemology*, 267.

and make assumptions that we as individuals cannot easily detect. Theoretically unmediated experience, that aspect of a group's or an individual's experience in which cultural influences cannot be detected, functions as part of the evidence for scientific claims. Cultural agendas and assumptions are part of the background assumptions and auxiliary hypotheses that philosophers have identified. If the goal is to make available for critical scrutiny *all* the evidence marshaled for or against a scientific hypothesis, then this evidence too requires critical examination *within* scientific research processes. In other words, we can think of strong objectivity as extending the notion of scientific research to include systematic examination of such powerful background beliefs. It must do so in order to be competent at maximizing objectivity.

The strong objectivity that standpoint theory requires is like the "strong programme" in the sociology of knowledge in that it directs us to provide symmetrical accounts of both "good" and "bad" belief formation and legitimation.[16] We must be able to identify the social causes of good beliefs, not just of the bad ones to which the conventional "sociology of error" and objectivism restrict causal accounts. However, in contrast to the "strong programme," standpoint theory requires causal analyses not just of the micro processes in the laboratory but also of the macro tendencies in the social order, which shape scientific practices. Moreover, a concern with macro tendencies permits a more robust notion of reflexivity than is currently available in the sociology of knowledge or the philosophy of science. In trying to identify the social causes of good beliefs, we will be led also to examine critically the kinds of bad beliefs that shape our own thought and behaviors, not just the thought behavior of others.

To summarize the argument of the last chapter, in a society structured by gender hierarchy, "starting thought from women's lives" increases the objectivity of the results of research by bringing scientific observation and the perception of the need for explanation to bear on assumptions and practices that appear natural or unremarkable from the perspective of the lives of men in the dominant groups. Thinking from the perspective of women's lives makes strange what had appeared familiar, which is the beginning of any scientific inquiry.[17]

Why is this gender difference a scientific resource? It leads us to ask questions about nature and social relations from the perspective of devalued and neglected lives. Doing so begins research in the perspective from the lives of "strangers" who have been excluded from the culture's ways of socializing the "natives," who are at home in its institutions and who are full-fledged citizens. It starts research in the perspective from the lives of the systematically oppressed, exploited, and dominated, those who have fewer interests in ignorance about how the social order actually works. It begins research in the perspective from the lives of people on the "other side" of gender battles, offering a view different from the "winner's stories" about nature and social life which men's interpretations of men's lives tend to produce. It starts thought in everyday life, for which women are assigned primary responsibility and in which appear consequences of dominant group activities—consequences that are invisible from the perspective of those activities. It starts thought in the lives of those people to whom is assigned the work of mediating many of the culture's ideological dualisms—especially the gap between nature and culture. It starts research in the

---

[16] I use "good" and "bad" here to stand for "true" and "false," "better confirmed" and "less well confirmed," "plausible" and "implausible," and so on.

[17] As emphasized in Chapters 5 and 7, starting thought from women's lives is something that both men and women must learn to do. Women's telling their experiences is not the same thing as thinking from the perspective of women's lives.

lives not just of strangers or outsiders but of "outsiders within," from which the relationship between outside and inside, margin and center, can more easily be detected. It starts thought in the perspective from the life of the Other, allowing the Other to gaze back "shamelessly" at the self who had reserved for himself the right to gaze "anonymously" at whomsoever he chooses. It starts thought in the lives of people who are unlikely to permit the denial of the interpretive core of all knowledge claims. It starts thought in the perspective from lives that at this moment in history are especially revealing of broad social contradictions. And no doubt there are additional ways in which thinking from the perspective of women's lives is especially revealing of regularities in nature and social relations and their underlying causal tendencies.

As analyzed further in Part III, it is important to remember that in a certain sense there are no "women" or "men" in the world—there is no "gender"—but only women, men, and gender constructed through particular historical struggles over just which races, classes, sexualities, cultures, religious groups, and so forth, will have access to resources and power. Moreover, standpoint theories of knowledge, whether or not they are articulated as such, have been advanced by thinkers concerned not only with gender and class hierarchy (recollect that standpoint theory originated in class analyses) but also with other "Others."[18] To make sense of any

actual woman's life or the gender relations in any culture, analyses must begin in real, historic women's lives, and these will be women of particular races, classes, cultures, and sexualities. The historical particularity of women's lives is a problem for narcissistic or arrogant accounts that attempt, consciously or not, to conduct a cultural monologue. But it is a resource for those who think that our understandings and explanations are improved by what we could call an intellectual participatory democracy.

The notion of strong objectivity welds together the strengths of weak objectivity and those of the "weak subjectivity" that is its correlate, but excludes the features that make them only weak. To enact or operationalize the directive of strong objectivity is to value the Other's perspective and to pass over in thought into the social condition that creates it—not in order to stay there, to "go native" or merge the self with the Other, but in order to look back at the self in all its cultural particularity from a more distant, critical, objectifying location. One can think of the subjectivism that objectivism conceptualizes as its sole alternative as only a "premodern" alternative to objectivism; it provides only a premodern solution to the problem we have here and now at the moment of postmodern criticisms of modernity's objectivism. Strong objectivity rejects attempts to resuscitate those organic, occult, "participating consciousness" relationships between self and Other which are characteristic of the premodern world.[19] Strong objectivity requires that we investigate the relation between subject and object rather than deny the existence of, or seek unilateral control over, this relation.

[18] See, e.g., Samir Amin, *Eurocentrism* (New York: *Monthly Review Press*, 1989); Bettina Aptheker, *Tapestries of Life: Women's Work, Women's Consciousness, and the Meaning of Daily Life* (Amherst: University of Massachusetts Press, 1989); Collins, "Learning from the Outsider Within"; Walter Rodney, *How Europe Underdeveloped Africa* (Washington, D.C.: Howard University Press, 1982); Edward Said, *Orientalism* (New York: Pantheon Books, 1978); Edward Said, Foreword to *Selected Subaltern Studies*, ed. Ranajit Guha and Gayatri Chakravorty Spivak (New York: Oxford University Press, 1988), viii.

[19] See Morris Berman, *The Reenchantment of the World* (Ithaca: Cornell University Press, 1981), for an analysis of the world that modernity lost, and lost for good. Some feminists have tried to dismantle modernist projects with premodernist tools.

Historical Relativism versus Judgmental Relativism

It is not that historical relativism is in itself a bad thing. A respect for historical (or sociological or cultural) relativism is always useful in starting one's thinking. Different social groups tend to have different patterns of practice and belief and different standards for judging them; these practices, beliefs, and standards can be explained by different historical interests, values, and agendas. Appreciation of these empirical regularities are especially important at this moment of unusually deep and extensive social change, when even preconceived schemes used in liberatory projects are likely to exclude less-well-positioned voices and to distort emerging ways of thinking that do not fit easily into older schemes. Listening carefully to different voices and attending thoughtfully to others' values and interests can enlarge our vision and begin to correct for inevitable enthnocentrisms. (The dominant values, interests, and voices are not among these "different" ones; they are the powerful tide against which "difference" must swim.)

To acknowledge this historical or sociological fact, as I have already argued, does not commit one to the further epistemological claim that there are therefore no rational or scientific grounds for making judgments between various patterns of belief and their originating social practices, values, and consequences. Many thinkers have pointed out that judgmental relativism is internally related to objectivism. For example, science historian Donna Haraway argues that judgmental relativism is the other side of the very same coin from "the God trick." required by what I have called weak objectivity. To insist that no judgments at all of cognitive adequacy can legitimately be made amounts to the same thing as to insist that knowledge can be produced only from "no place at all": that is, by someone who can be every place at once.[20]

Critical preoccupation with judgmental relativism is the logical complement to the judgmental absolutism characteristic of Eurocentrism. Economist Samir Amin criticizes the preoccupation with relativism in some Western intellectual circles as a kind of inverted "Eurocentrism":

> The view that any person has the right—and even the power—to judge others is replaced by attention to the relativity of those judgments. Without a doubt, such judgments can be erroneous, superficial, hasty, or relative. No case is ever definitely closed; debate always continues. But that is precisely the point. It is necessary to pursue debate and not to avoid it on the grounds that the views that one forms about others are and always will be false: that the French will never understand the Chinese (and vice versa), that men will never understand women, etc; or, in other words, that there is no human species, but only "people." Instead, the claim is made that only Europeans can truly understand Europe, Chinese China, Christians Christianity, and Moslems Islam; the Eurocentrism of one group is completed by the inverted Eurocentrism of others.[21]

Historically, relativism appears as a problematic intellectual possibility only for dominating groups at the point where the hegemony of their views is being challenged. Though the recognition that other cultures do, in fact, hold different beliefs, values, and standards of judgment is as old as human history, judgmental relativism emerged as an urgent intellectual issue only in nineteenth-century Europe, with the belated recognition that the apparently

---

[20] Haraway, "Situated Knowledges" makes these points and uses the phrase "the God trick."

[21] Amin, *Eurocentrism,* 146–47. Amin further makes clear that it takes more than mere debate– i.e., only intellectual work–to come to understand the lives or point of view of "people" who are on trajectories that oppose one's own in political struggles. The following paragraph draws on "Introduction: Is There a Feminist Method?" in *Feminism and Methodology,* p. 10

bizarre beliefs and behaviors of Others had a rationality and logic of their own. Judgmental relativism is not a problem originating in or justifiable in terms of the lives of marginalized groups. It did not arise in misogynous thought about women; it does not arise from the contrast feminism makes between women's lives and men's. Women do not have the problem of how to accommodate intellectually both the sexist claim that women are inferior in some way or another and the feminist claim that they are not. Here relativism arises as a problem only from the perspective of men's lives. Some men want to appear to acknowledge and accept feminist arguments without actually giving up any of their conventional androcentric beliefs and the practices that seem to follow so reasonably from such beliefs. "It's all relative, my dear," is a convenient way to try to accomplish these two goals.

We feminists in higher education may have appeared to invite charges of relativism in our language about disseminating the results of feminist research and scholarship beyond women's studies programs into the entire curriculum and canon. We speak of "mainstreaming" and "integrating" the research, scholarship, and curriculum of Other programs and of encouraging "inclusiveness" in scholarship and the curriculum. We enroll our women's studies courses in campuswide projects to promote "cultural diversity" and "multiculturalism," and we accept students into such courses on these terms. Do these projects conflict with the standpoint logic? Yes and no. They conflict because the notions involved are perfectly coherent with the maintenance of elitist knowledge production and systems. Let me make the point in terms of my racial identity as white. "They (those people of color at the margins of the social order) are to be integrated with us (whites at the center), leaving us unchanged and the rightful heirs of the center of the culture. They are to give up their agendas and interests that conflict with ours in order to insert their contributions

into the research, scholarship, or curriculum that has been structured to accommodate our agendas and interests." This is just as arrogant a posture as the older cultural absolutism. From the perspective of racial minorities, integration has never worked as a solution to ethnic or race relations in the United States. Why is there reason to think it will work any better for the marginalized projects in intellectual circles?

Should we therefore give up attempts at an "inclusive curriculum" and "cultural diversity" because of their possible complicity with sexism, racism, Eurocentrism, heterosexism, and class oppression? Of course the answer must be no. It is true that this kind of language appears to betray the compelling insights of the standpoint epistemology and to leave feminist programs in the compromised position of supporting the continued centering of white, Western, patriarchal visions. But many feminist projects—including women's studies programs themselves—are forced to occupy whatever niches they can find within institutional structures that are fundamentally opposed to them or, at least, "prefeminist." An implicit acceptance of pluralism, if not judgmental relativism—at least at the institutional level—appears to be the only condition under which women's voices and feminist voices, male and female, can be heard at all.

After all, isn't feminism just one "equal voice" among many competing for everyone's attention? The nineteenth-century "natives" whose beliefs and behaviors Europeans found bizarre were not in any real sense competing for an equal voice within European thought and politics. They were safely off in Africa, the Orient and other faraway places. The chances were low that aborigines would arrive in Paris, London, and Berlin to study and report back to their own cultures the bizarre beliefs and behaviors that constituted the "tribal life" of European anthropologists and *their* culture. More important, there was no risk at all that they could have used such knowledge to assist in imposing their rule on Europeans in Europe. Women's voices, while certainly far from silent, were far more effectively contained and muted than is possible today. As a value, a moral prescription, relativism was a safe stance for Europeans to choose; the reciprocity of respect it appeared to support had little chance of having to be enacted. Today, women and feminists are not safely off and out of sight at all. They are present, speaking, within the very social order that still treats women's beliefs and behaviors as bizarre. Moreover, their speech competes for attention and status as most plausible not only with that of misogynists but also with the speech of other Others: African Americans, other peoples of color, gay rights activists, pacifists, ecologists, members of new formations of the left, and so on. Isn't feminism forced to embrace relativism by its condition of being just one among many countercultural voices?

This description of the terrain in which feminists struggle to advance their claims, however, assumes that people must either choose only one among these countercultures as providing an absolute standard for sorting knowledge claims, or else regard all of them as competing and assign them equal cognitive status. Actually, it is a different scenario that the countercultures can envision and even occasionally already enact: the fundamental tendencies of each must permeate each of the others in order for each movement to succeed. Feminism should center the concerns of each of these movements, and each of them must move feminist concerns to its center.

To summarize, then, a strong notion of objec-tivity requires a commitment to acknowledge the his-torical character of every belief or set of beliefs—commitment to cultural, sociological historical relativism. But it also requires that judgmental or epistemological relativism be rejected. Weak objectivity is located in a conceptual interdependency that includes (weak) subjectivity and judgmental relativism. One cannot simply give up weak objectivity without making adjustments throughout the rest of this epistemological system.

Responding to Objections

Two possible objections to the recommendation of a stronger standard for objectivity must be considered here. First, some scientists and philosophers of sci-ence may protest that I am attempting to specify standards of objectivity for all the sciences. What could it mean to attempt to specify *general* standards for increasing the objectivity of research? Shouldn't the task of determining what counts as adequate research be settled within each science by its own practitioners? Why should practicing scientists revise their research practices because of what is thought by a philosopher or anyone else who is not an expert in a particular science?

But the issue of this chapter is an epistemological issue—a metascientific one—rather than an issue within any single science. It is more like a directive to operationalize theoretical concepts than like a directive to operationalize in a certain way some particular theoretical notion within physics or biology. The recommended combination of strong objectivity with the acknowledgement of historical relativism would, if adopted, create a culturewide shift in the kind of epistemology regarded as desirable. Certainly, strategies for enacting commitments to strong objectivity and the acknowledgment of historical relativism would have to be developed within each particular research program; plenty of examples already exist in biology and the social sciences. My position is that the natural sciences are backward in this respect; they are not immune from the reasonableness of these directives, as conventionalists have assumed.

The notion of strong objectivity developed here represents insights that have been emerging from thinkers in a number of disciplines for some decades—

not just "wishful thinking" based on no empirical sciences at all. Criticisms of the dominant thought of the West from both inside and outside the West argue that its partiality and distortions are the consequence in large part of starting that thought only from the lives of the dominant groups in the West. Less partiality and less distortion result when thought starts from peasant life, not just aristocratic life; from slaves' lives, not just slaveowners' lives; from the lives of factory workers, not just those of their bosses and managers; from the lives of people who work for wages and have also been assigned responsibility for husband and child care, not just those of persons who are expected to have little such responsibility. This directive leaves open to be determined within each discipline or research area what a researcher must do to start thought from women's lives or the lives of people in other marginalized groups, and it will be easier—though still difficult—to provide reasonable responses to such a request in history or sociology than in physics or chemistry. But the difficulty of providing an analysis in physics or chemistry does not signify that the question is an absurd one for knowledge-seeking in general, or that there are no reasonable answers for those sciences too.

The second objection may come from femi-nists themselves. Many would say that the notion of objectivity is so hopelessly tainted by its historical complicity in justifying the service of science to the dominant groups that trying to make it function effectively and progressively in alternative agendas only confuses the matter. If feminists want to breathe new life into such a bedraggled notion as objectivity, why not at least invent an alternative term that does not call up the offenses associated with the idea of value neutrality, that is not intimately tied to a faulty theory of representation, to a faulty psychic construction of the ideal agent of knowledge, and to regressive political tendencies.

Let us reorganize some points made earlier in order to get the full force of this objection. The goal of producing results of research that are value-free is part of the notion of the ideal mind as a mir-ror that can reflect a world that is "out there," ready-made (see Chapter 4). In this view, value-free objectivity can locate an Archimedean perspective from which the events and processes of the natural world appear in their proper places. Only false beliefs have social causes—human values and inter-ests that blind us to the real regularities and under-lying causal tendencies in the world, generating biased results of research. True beliefs have only natural causes: those regularities and underlying causal tendencies that are *there*, plus the power of the eyes to see them and of the mind to reason about them. This theory of representation is a historically situated one: it is characteristic only of certain groups in the modern West. Can the notion of objectivity really be separated from this implausi-ble theory of representation?

Value-free objectivity requires also a faulty theory of the ideal agent—the subject—of science, knowledge, and history. It requires a notion of the self as a fortress that must be defended against polluting influences from its social surroundings. The self whose mind would perfectly reflect the world must create and constantly police the borders of a gulf, a no-man's-land, between himself as the subject and the object of his research, knowledge, or action. Feminists have been among the most pointed critics of this self-versus-Other construct,[22] referring to it as "abstract masculinity."[23] Moreover,

---

[22] See, e.g., Nancy Chodorow, *The Reproduction of Mothering* (Berkeley: University of California Press, 1978); Dorothy Dinnerstein, *The Mermaid and the Minotaur: Sexual Arrangements and Human Malaise* (New York: Harper & Row, 1976); Carol Gilligan, *In a Different Voice: Psychological Theory and Women's Development* (Cambridge, Mass.: Harvard University Press, 1982); Evelyn Fox Keller, *Reflections on Gender and Science* (New Haven, Conn.: Yale University Press, 1984).

[23] Hartsock, "The Feminist Standpoint."

its implication in Western constructions of the racial Other against which the "white" West would define its admirable projects is also obvious.[24] Can the notion of objectivity be useful in efforts to oppose such sexism and racism?

Equally important, the notion of value-free objectivity is morally and politically regressive for reasons additional to those already mentioned. It justifies the construction of science institutions and individual scientists as "fast guns for hire." It has been used to legitimate and hold up as the highest ideal institutions and individuals that are, insofar as they are scientific, to be studiously unconcerned with the origins or consequences of their activities or with the values and interests that these activities advance. This nonaccidental, determined, energetic lack of concern is supported by science education that excludes training in critical thought and that treats all expressions of social and political concern—the concerns of the torturer and the concerns of the tortured—as being on the same low level of scientific "rationality." Scandalous examples of the institutional impotence of the sciences as sciences to speak to the moral and political issues that shape their problematics, consequences, values, and interests have been identified for decades (see Chapter 4). The construction of a border between scientific method and violations of human and, increasingly, animal rights must be conducted "outside" that method, by government statements about what constitutes acceptable methods of research on human and animal subjects, what constitutes consent to experimentation, the subsequent formation of "ethics committees," and so on. Can the notion of objectivity be extracted from the morals and politics of "objective science" as a "fast gun for hire"?

These are formidable objections. Nevertheless, the argument of this book is that the notion of objectivity not only can but should be separated from its shameful and damaging history. Research is socially situated, and it can be more objectively conducted without aiming for or claiming to be value-free. The requirements for achieving strong objectivity permit one to abandon notions of perfect, mirrorlike representations of the world, the self as a defended fortress, and the "truly scientific" as disinterested with regard to morals and politics, yet still apply rational standards to sorting less from more partial and distorted belief. Indeed, my argument is that these standards are more rational and more effective at producing maximally objective results than the ones associated with what I have called weak objectivity.

As I have been arguing, objectivity is one of a complex of inextricably linked notions. Science and rationality are two other terms in this network. But it is not necessary to accept the idea that there is only one correct or reasonable way to think about these terms, let alone that the correct way is the one used by dominant groups in the modern West. Not all reason is white, masculinist, modern, heterosexual, Western rea-son. Not all modes of rigorous empirical knowledge-seeking are what the dominant groups think of as science—to understate the point. The procedures institutionalized in conventional science for distinguishing between how we want the world to be and how it is are not the only or best ways to go about maximizing objectivity. It is important to work and think outside the dominant modes, as the minority movements have done. But it is important, also, to bring the insights developed there into the heart of conventional institutions, to disrupt the dominant practices from within by appropriating notions such as objectivity, reason, and science in ways that stand a chance of compelling

---

[24] See, e.g., Sander Gilman, *Difference and Pathology: Stereotypes of Sexuality, Race, and Madness* (Ithaca: Cornell University Press, 1985); V. Y. Mudimbe, *The Invention of Africa: Gnosis, Philosophy, and the Order of Knowledge* (Bloomington: Indiana University Press, 1988); Said, *Orientalism*, and Foreword to Guha and Spivak, *Subaltern Studies.*

reasoned assent while simultaneously shifting and displacing the meanings and referents of the discussion in ways that improve it. It is by thinking and acting as "outsiders within" that feminists and others can transform science and its social relations for those who remain only insiders or outsiders.

One cannot afford to "just say no" to objectivity. I think there are three additional good reasons to retain the notion of objectivity for future knowledge-seeking projects but to work at separating it from its damaging historical associations with value-neutrality.

First, it has a valuable political history. There have to be standards for distinguishing between how I want the world to be and how, in empirical fact, it is. Otherwise, might makes right in knowledge-seeking just as it tends to do in morals and politics. The notion of objectivity is useful because its meaning and history support such standards, Today, as in the past, there are powerful interests ranged against attempts to find out the regularities and underlying causal tendencies in the natural and social worlds. Some groups do not want exposed to public scrutiny the effect on the environment of agribusiness or of pesticide use in domestic gardening. Some do not want discussed the consequences for Third World peasants, for the black underclass in the United States, and especially for women in both groups of the insistence on economic production that generates profit for elites in the West. The notion of achieving greater objectivity has been useful in the past and can be today in struggles over holding people and institutions responsible for the fit between their behavior and the claims they make.

Second, objectivity also can claim a glorious intellectual history. The argument of this chapter has emphasized its service to elites, but it also has been invoked to justify unpopular criticisms of partisan but entrenched beliefs. Standpoint theory can rightfully claim that history as its legacy.

Finally, the appeal to objectivity is an issue not only between feminist and prefeminist sciences but within each feminist and other emancipatory movement. There are many feminisms, some of which result in claims that distort the racial, class, sexuality, and gender relationships in society. Which ones generate less and which more partial and distorted accounts of nature and social life? The notion of objectivity is useful in providing a way to think about the gap we want between how any individual or group wants the world to be and how in fact it is.

The notion of objectivity—like such ideas as science and rationality, democracy and feminism—contains progressive as well as regressive tendencies. In each case, it is important to develop the progressive and to block the regressive ones.

Reflexivity Revisited

The notion of "strong objectivity" conceptualizes the value of putting the subject or agent of knowledge in the same critical; causal plane as the object of her or his inquiry. It permits us to see the scientific as well as the moral and political advantages of this way of trying to achieve a reciprocal relationship between the agent and object of knowledge. The contrast developed here between weak and strong notions of objectivity permits the parallel construction of weak versus strong notions of reflexivity.

Reflexivity has tended to be seen as a problem in the social sciences—and only there. Observation cannot be as separated from its social consequences as the directives of "weak objectivity," originating in the natural sciences, have assumed. In social inquiry, observation changes the field observed. Having recognized his complicity in the lives of his objects of study, the researcher is then supposed to devise various strategies to try to democratize the situation, to inform the "natives" of their options, to make them participants in the account of their activities, and so forth.[25]

Less commonly, reflexivity has been seen as a problem because if the researcher is under the obligation to identify the social causes of the "best" as well as the "worst" beliefs and behaviors of those he studies, then he must also analyze his own beliefs and behaviors in conducting his research project—which have been shaped by the same kinds of social relations that he is interested to identify as causes of the beliefs and behaviors of others. (Here, reflexivity can begin to be conceptualized as a "problem" for the natural sciences, too.) Sociologists of knowledge in the recent "strong programme" school and related tendencies, who emphasize the importance of identifying the social causes of "best belief," have been aware of this problem from the very beginning but have devised no plausible way of resolving it—primarily because their conception of the social causes of belief in the natural sciences (the subject matter of their analyses) is artificially restricted to the micro processes of the laboratory and research community,

explicitly excluding race, gender, and class relations. This restricted notion of what constitutes appropriate subject matter for analyses of the social relations of the sciences is carried into their understanding of their own work. It generates ethnographies of their own and the natural science communities which are complicitous with positivist tendencies in insisting on the isolation of research communities from the larger social, economic, and political currents in their societies. (These accounts are also flawed by their positivist conceptions of the object of natural science study).[26]

These "weak" notions of reflexivity are disabled by their lack of any mechanism for identifying the cultural values and interests of the researchers, which form part of the evidence for the results of research in both the natural and social sciences. Anthropologists, sociologists, and the like, who work within social communities, frequently appear to desire such a mechanism or standard; but the methodological assumptions of their disciplines, which direct them to embrace either weak objectivity or judgmental relativism, have not permitted them to develop one. That is, individuals express "heartfelt desire" not to harm the subjects they observe, to become aware of their own cultural biases, and so on, but such reflexive goals remain at the level of desire rather than competent enactment. In short, such weak reflexivity has no possible operationalization, or no competency standard, for success.

A notion of strong reflexivity would require that the objects of inquiry be conceptualized as gazing back in all their cultural particularity and that the researcher, through theory and methods, stand behind them, gazing back at his own socially situated research

---

[25] A fine account of the travails of such a project reports Robert Blauner and David Weliman's dawning recognition that nothing they did could eliminate the colonial relationship between themselves and their black informants in the community surrounding Berkeley; see their "Toward the Decolonization of Social Research," in Ladner, *The Death of White Sociology*. Economist Vernon Dixon argues that from the perspective of an African or African American world view, the idea that observation would not change the thing observed appears ridiculous; see his "World Views and Research Methodology," in *African Philosophy: Assumptions and Paradigms for Research on Black Persons*, ed. L. M. King, Vernon Dixon, and W. W. Nobles (Los Angeles: Fanon Center, Charles R. Drew Postgraduate Medical School, 1976), and my discussion of the congruence between African and feminine world views in *The Science Question in Feminism* (Ithaca: Cornell University Press, 1986), chap. 7.

[26] See, e.g., Bloor, *Knowledge and Social Imagery*; and Steve Woolgar's nevertheless interesting paper, "Reflexivity Is the Ethnographer of the Text," as well as other (somewhat bizarre) discussions of reflexivity in Woolgar, *Knowledge and Reflexivity*.

project in all its cultural particularity and its relationships to other projects of his culture—many of which (policy development in intentional relations, for example, or industrial expansion) can be seen only from locations far away from the scientist's actual daily work. "Strong reflexivity" requires the development of oppositional theory from the perspective of the lives of those Others ("nature" as already socially constructed, as well as other peoples),

since intuitive experience, for reasons discussed earlier, is frequently not a reliable guide to the regularities of nature and social life and their underlying causal tendencies.

Standpoint theory opens the way to stronger standards of both objectivity and reflexivity. These standards require that research projects use their historical location as a resource for obtaining greater objectivity.

COMMENT

Into the traditional philosophical debate over the nature and basis of knowledge steps a contemporary thinker, Sandra Harding. Building on the growing awareness of the crucial role that individual and practical perspectives play in the acquisition and validation of knowledge, an awareness clearly nascent in both pragmatism and existentialism, Harding tackles the ever-threatening problem of relativism. Following up on the insights and impetus provided by Thomas Kuhn's pivotal work, *The Structure of Scientific Revolutions*, she seeks to move beyond the objectivity/subjectivity dichotomy by redefining the former as necessarily *including*, rather than excluding, the standpoint or perspective of those involved in the acquisition of knowledge, especially women. Harding labels her fresh point of view "strong objectivity," since by incorporating the so-called "subjective" aspects of knowing experience one obtains *more* grounding for one's knowledge claim instead of less. By ignoring such factors, one weakens both the breadth and depth of the resultant understanding being sought.

Harding strives to disengage the rejection of "objectivism" and the affirmation of historical or cultural relativism, on the one hand, from their traditional entanglement with the concept of epistemological or "judgmental" relativism on the other hand. In a word, she argues that a commitment to "strong objectivity," which incorporates sociohistorical factors and perspectives, does not *entail* the acceptance of some form of total relativism. In this way, Harding attempts to avoid the pitfalls of both traditional epistemological absolutism and its subjectivist counterpart. Continued dialogue seems to be the dynamic that she hopes will carry knowledge seekers beyond this familiar impasse.

This bilateral dialogue between observers and those being observed, especially in the acquisition of knowledge concerning social reality, would focus on the idea that Harding terms "reflexivity." As she says, "A notion of strong reflexivity would require that the objects of inquiry be conceptualized as gazing back in all their cultural particularity and that the researcher, through theory and methods, stand behind them, gazing back at his own socially situated research project in all its cultural particularity ..." This acknowledgment, and even affirmation, of the sociohistorical dimensions of *all* efforts to obtain knowledge, according to

Harding, renders the epistemological quest even more "objective" than did the traditional denial of these dimensions.

It is both interesting and instructive to consider what the likes of Plato, Descartes, Hume, Kant, Reid, Bergson, James, Camus, and Marcel would have to say about Harding's proposal. Nearly every thinker up through Kant maintained that unless knowledge was defined at the outset as transcending sociohistorical factors, it could never rise above mere "opinion." Thus they would reject Harding's perspectivism as incapable of providing any real knowledge at all. The deep issue here would seem to be whether knowledge must be understood as something that never changes, or whether it can be viewed as continually in the process of evolving. The traditional Western answer is a clear "Yes" in favor of the first option.

Beginning with Thomas Reid and carrying on down through the existentialists, however, there is a growing concern to incorporate the perspective of the knower, as well as that of the known, into our understanding of human knowledge. The difficulties arise, to be sure, when it comes to deciding on how to identify and weigh such factors within any particular cognitive context.

When different perspectives seem to yield conflicting understandings of a particular situation, how is this cognitive dissonance to be resolved? The dialogical posture recommended by Harding seems to be a good point of departure in an effort to reach such resolutions, but it remains difficult to know how to go on from there. Specifically, the question of criteria for evaluating knowledge claims, which are themselves, at least largely, a function of cultural perspectives, continues to invite the charge of skepticism, namely that because of such difficulties as these, knowledge is ultimately impossible.

In her defense, Harding, and some others we have studied in these chapters, might well argue that skepticism only arises in connection with these issues when one assumes at the outset that knowledge must be conceived of as a static rather than dynamic reality. If one thinks of knowing as a relational process wherein each cognitive exploration and claim is itself part of what constitutes what is to be known, then error is not so much something to be eliminated as it is something with which we must continually cope. Knowing, then, would be more like maintaining one's balance than it would be like answering a question on a television quiz show or devising a formula that describes the motion of the solar system.

Can the reader discern how Harding would come at the questions raised by the case study presented at the beginning of Part One? In what sense is the kind or kinds of thinking engaged in by Gary Kasparov and Deep Blue when playing chess to be understood as "socially situated" knowledge? Are there different sorts of "reasons" being expressed by Kasparov and Deep Blue, and if so, what factors have contributed to their respective formations? Does a computer have any sociopolitical context or "background" for its calculations?

PART II

The Nature of Reality

In Part I we have been concerned mainly with epistemology, the theory of knowledge—especially with the meaning of truth and the methods of its attainment. In Part II we shall be concerned primarily with metaphysics, the theory of reality. It is impossible, however, to separate sharply epistemology and metaphysics. For example, in Part I, we studied the philosophy of René Descartes, which is as important for metaphysics as for epistemology; and in Part II we shall examine the philosophies of Berkeley and Hume, which have contributed as greatly to epistemology as to metaphysics. The difference between Part I and Part II, therefore, is not an absolute difference in subject matter but a relative difference in emphasis.

We shall consider the question "What is the fundamental nature of humanity and the surrounding universe?" This question directs attention to "the metaphysics of the microcosm"—of the "I," or self, as a small part of the whole scheme of things—and to "the metaphysics of the macrocosm"—of the great, all-enveloping system of reality. We shall not attempt to separate these two inquiries, and indeed, any sharp separation would be artificial. However, each of the theories that we shall consider will throw light on the nature of the human being and the nature of the total environment. We shall discuss six answers, not all mutually exclusive:

1. *The answer of the theist.* The view of the theist may be combined with teleology, dualism, idealism, or vitalism, but it is incompatible with a complete materialism or an absolute skepticism. It conceives of human beings and animals as the creatures of God and of nature as God's handiwork.

2. *The answer of the materialist.* As opposed to the teleologist, the materialist tries to explain the present and the future in terms of past or antecedent causes, and these causes are conceived to be material, such as the movement of physical atoms.

3. *The answer of the idealist.* Like the materialist, the idealist denies ultimate dualism, but unlike the materialist; the idealist regards mind rather than matter as the basic stuff.

4. *The answer of the dualist.* The dualist recognizes two distinct and irreducible kinds of being—mind and matter—and regards a human being as a combination of the two. Although Descartes defined the essence of the mind as thought and the essence of the body as extension, he maintained that the two substances, the physical and mental, interact within the pineal gland of the human brain.

5. *The answer of the relationalist.* A relationalist believes that the interaction and interconnectedness among all of the particular things constituting reality are more fundamental than the particulars themselves. Events and relationships are thought to be the essential qualities of reality.

6. *The answer of the interactionist.* The interactionist may be said to build upon the ideas of the relationalists by applying them to the level of interaction between human sociopolitical activity and the world in which we live. It is claimed that the reality we experience and know is actually constructed in and through this interaction.

But first, let us consider yet another "Case in Point."

A CASE IN POINT:

TWO PERSONS IN ONE?

The simple facts are these: On March 7, 1990, twins were born to Patty and Mike Hensel. However, not only were their new daughters joined together, but they were and remain joined together at the shoulders, having two heads but only one body. Abigail and Brittany Hensel came into the world, and have continued to live in it, as two persons sharing a single, common body. They have separate brains and distinct personalities, as well as separate hearts, stomachs, and spinal cords. Yet they share a blood stream and all organs below the waist.

Although it is impossible to physically separate Abby and Britty from each other without one of them dying, they have grown up as two relatively normal children who attend school, ride a bike, swim, and like different kinds of food, music, and books. They even have arguments with each other and can become physically sick as individuals. While the twins were well known within the confines of their small, Midwestern community, their parents kept them from receiving any national attention until 1996. And even though they have now been seen widely in the national media, their parents continue to refuse to allow them to be studied scientifically.

Perhaps the most amazing thing about Abby and Britty is their ability to coordinate one body even though they have two separate brains and thus minds. While they may well have different likes and opinions, it has been relatively easy for them to learn to tie their common shoelaces, for instance, even though each controls only one hand and one leg. The same dexterity characterizes nearly all their other physical activity as well. They really are two persons in one.

There are, to be sure, many interesting and practical questions, to say nothing of the medical questions, that can be asked about the life or lives of these two youngsters. It is not our purpose, however, to probe into the personal details surrounding the twins, their parents, and their futures, as intriguing as they may be. How they will develop as adults, what sort of lives they will lead, whether or not they will have children, and the like, are not our concern in these pages. Rather, we must turn our attention to the philosophical issues raised by this phenomenon of two persons in one body.

One dimension of this phenomenon pertains to the sorts of questions explored in the previous section, namely those having to do with the nature of knowledge. Clearly, there are serious concerns raised by the case of these two girls for our understanding of the relation between perception, thought, and motor knowledge. It would prove fascinating to compare and contrast just how rationalists, empiricists, and other epistemological thinkers would analyze and explain the cognitive functions and patterns in these two knowers.

Another important dimension of philosophy that these twins trigger is the ethical one. In the third part of this text, we shall be taking up questions of morality and its basis, and it would be enlightening to employ this case as a way of focusing on the issues of responsibility, duty, happiness, and the good life. When, for instance, these girls behave in a certain manner or commit a particular act, just which is to be held responsible? What are the specific obligations, if any, these two persons have toward each other that may not confront other siblings?

Our concern in this instance, however, is with what are called the metaphysical or ontological aspects of the case presented by the situation of these two persons in one body. As has been pointed out, this division of philosophy treats questions having to do with what is real and what is not with what there is and how many kinds of reality there might be. This is a quite different use of the concept of metaphysics from that which has gained popular usage among those who are interested in psychic phenomena, reincarnation, and the like. In fact, the term "metaphysics" originally designated the writings of Aristotle that were placed immediately after those in which he dealt with the physical universe.

One important traditional facet of philosophical metaphysics is that relating to the question of religion and/or God. According to the standard interpretation of Christian theology, for instance, the concept of a person is identical with that of a soul. Moreover, it is frequently, if not usually, maintained that in death the soul is separated from the body in order to enter into eternity. Thus, it would appear that Abby and Britty present no particular difficulty for this view of the religious question. The fact that they share a common body is only an incidental feature of their earthly existence. Clearly, according to this interpretation, they have or are two distinct souls.

There are those who would point out, however, that this view of Christian theology is erroneous. For, not only does the New Testament clearly say that Christ was resurrected bodily, but also that believers will be resurrected in a similar manner. Moreover, the Apostle's Creed, which states the main beliefs of the early Church, contains the phrase "I believe in the resurrection of the body." This interpretation would certainly imply that the body is an integral dimension of each individual's personhood, and thus in turn, raises interesting questions for the religious aspects of the twins' existence.

An additional feature of religious philosophy pertains to what is generally called "the problem of evil," wherein it is asked why suffering exists if there is a God who is both all powerful and all loving. The following could be asked in the case of Abby and Britty: Why have they been saddled with this sort of burden above and beyond the difficulties facing others? It might be said that they and their parents have been given the opportunity to learn and grow through this experience, but there are those who would object to a God who would put people in difficult and even dangerous situations in order to "teach them a lesson."

All of the above questions bear on a further metaphysical issue, namely that of personal identity. Just what are the criteria for determining when an entity, in this case a person, is the identical entity it was a year, a day, or even a second ago? Furthermore, just where does Abby end and Britty begin? Frequently, personal identity is said to consist in the conjunction of consciousness and memory, on the one hand, and bodily similarity, on the other. But in this, the two persons have or are a common body, while at the same time they have different consciousnesses and memories. Are they two people or one? Do they both get to vote? Do they have one driver's license? If they have different husbands, are they both mothers of their individual children? How do we answer such questions?

Finally, underlying nearly all of the foregoing issues is the question of the relation between mind and body, ideas and material reality, in these two young people. Materialist thinkers maintain that reality is nothing but complex forms of matter that continually rearrange themselves, while their rivals, idealist thinkers, affirm just the opposite. It should be clear that neither of these terms is being used in the more popular sense of whether one is primarily concerned with the rewards of this world or some other. It would seem that it is difficult if not impossible not only to separate the minds of Abby and Britty from their shared body, but to separate each from the other.

Thus, metaphysical dualists conclude that both mind and matter are real, even though both Plato and Descartes, for instance, saw the material world as inferior to and/or in some way dependent on the ideal or mental world. Nevertheless, dualists are usually hard pressed to explain just how it is that these two forms of reality, having been defined as quite distinct from each other, nonetheless manage to interact. In the case of our twins, this is a special difficulty because they bring two minds to this basic interaction.

In recent decades, a number of thinkers have developed approaches to these questions that center on the concepts of metaphysical and social processes in order to handle the mind/body problem. They tend to see the two—mind and body—as involved in a bipolar, symbiotic dynamic that is fundamentally more real than either of its mental or physical poles. It is possible that this approach might cast some light on the reality comprising the Hensel twins. For, clearly, their minds and body are engaged in an extremely interactive dynamic, both with each other and with those persons by whom they are surrounded.

8

THEISM

SAINT ANSELM (1033?–1109)

Although Italian by birth, Saint Anselm ended his career as archbishop of Canterbury. He is famous not only for his philosophical works but also for his interpretation of Christian theology. As abbot of a monastery in Normandy and as archbishop in England, he was a zealous defender of the Church against the expansion of secular power.

THE ONTOLOGICAL ARGUMENT

...I do not seek to understand that I may believe, but I believe in order to understand. For this also I believe—that unless I believed, I should not understand.

And so, Lord, do thou, who dost give understanding to faith, give me, so far as thou knowest it to be profitable, to understand that thou art as we believe; and that thou art that which we believe. And, indeed, we believe that thou art a being than which nothing greater can be conceived. Or is there no such nature, since the fool hath said in his heart, there is no God? (Psalms xiv. I). But, at any rate, this very fool, when he hears of this being of which I speak—a being than which nothing greater can be conceived—understands what he hears, and what he understands is in his understanding; although he does not understand it to exist.

For, it is one thing for an object to be in the understanding, and another to understand that the object exists. When a painter first conceives of what he will afterwards perform, he has it in his understanding, but he does not yet understand it to be, because he has not yet performed it. But after he has made the painting, he both has it in his understanding, and he understands that it exists, because he has made it.

Hence, even the fool is convinced that something exists in the understanding, at least, than which nothing greater can be conceived. For, when he hears of this, he understands it. And whatever is understood, exists in the understanding. And assuredly that, than which nothing greater can be conceived, cannot exist in the understanding alone. For, suppose it exists in the understanding alone: then it can be conceived to exist in reality; which is greater.

Therefore, if that, than which nothing greater can be conceived, exists in the understanding alone, the very being, than which nothing greater can be conceived, is one, than which a greater can be conceived. But obviously this is impossible.

Translated by Sidney Norton Deane, Open Court Publishing Co., 1903. Reprinted by permission.

Hence, there is no doubt that there exists a being, than which nothing greater can be conceived, and it exists both in the understanding and in reality.

And it assuredly exists so truly, that it cannot be conceived not to exist. For, it is possible to conceive of a being which cannot be conceived not to exist; and this is greater than one which can be conceived not to exist. Hence, if that, than which nothing greater can be conceived, can be conceived not to exist, it is not that, than which nothing greater can be conceived. But this is an irreconcilable contradiction. There is, then, so truly a being than which nothing greater can be conceived to exist, that it cannot even be conceived not to exist; and this being thou art, O Lord, our God.

So truly, therefore, dost thou exist, O Lord, my God, that thou canst not be conceived not to exist; and rightly. For, if a mind could conceive of a being better than thee, the creature would rise above the Creator; and this is most absurd. And, indeed, whatever else there is, except thee alone, can be conceived not to exist. To thee alone, therefore, it belongs to exist more truly than all other beings, and hence in a higher degree than all others. For, whatever else exists does not exist so truly, and hence in a less degree it belongs to it to exist. Why, then, has the fool said in his heart, there is no God, since it is so evident, to a rational mind, that thou dost exist in the highest degree of all? Why, except that he is dull and a fool?

SAINT THOMAS AQUINAS (1225–1274)

Saint Thomas Aquinas, the son of Count Landolfo of Aquino, was born at the ancestral castle near Naples. At the age of five, he was sent to the Benedictine monastery of Monte Cassino to be educated. When ten years old, he entered the University of Naples, where he remained for six years. He then joined the Dominican Order, very much against the will of his parents and so much to the disgust of his brothers that they kidnapped and imprisoned him in the family stronghold for two years. At last he escaped and continued his education at Paris and Cologne. In 1256 he became a master of theology, and thereafter taught at the University of Paris and elsewhere. During his career, he succeeded in constructing the greatest of all systems of Catholic philosophy. He died at the age of forty-nine. Three years after his death, he was censured by the bishop of Paris for his alleged heterodoxy, but in 1323 he was canonized by Pope John XXII.

FIVE PROOFS OF GOD'S EXISTENCE

1. [The Argument from Change]

[In his first argument, St. Thomas argues from the fact of change to an Unmoved Mover; in his second argument, from the fact of causation to an Uncaused

From St. Thomas Aquinas, *Philosophical Texts*, trans. Thomas Gilby (London, New York, Toronto: Oxford University Press, 1951). Reprinted by permission.

Cause; in his third argument, from the fact of non-necessary being to a Necessary Being. In each case the reasoning is an inference from something dependent (change, causation, or contingent being) to something independent and self-sufficient—namely, God. Motion, movement, and change, as employed in the first argument, are synonymous. Note that the argument is not restricted to change of place (motion as we ordinarily use the term), but refers to all change whatsoever.]

The first and most open way is presented by change or motion. It is evident to our senses and certain that in the whole some things are in motion.

Whatever is in motion is set in motion by another. For nothing is in motion unless it be potential to that to which it is in motion; whereas a thing sets in motion inasmuch as it is actual, because to set in motion is naught else than to bring a thing from potentiality to actuality, and from potentiality a subject cannot be brought except by a being that is actual; actually hot makes potentially hot become actually hot, as when fire changes and alters wood. Now for the same thing to be simultaneously and identically actual and potential is not possible, though it is possible under different respects; what is actually hot cannot simultaneously be potentially hot, though it may be potentially cold. It is impossible, therefore, for a thing both to exert and to suffer motion in the same respect and according to the same motion.

If that which sets in motion is itself in motion then it also must be set in motion by another, andthat in its turn by another again. But here we can-not proceed to infinity, otherwise there would beno first mover, and consequently no other mover, seeing that subsequent movers do not initiate motion unless they be moved by a former mover, as stick by hand.

Therefore we are bound to arrive at the first mover set in motion by no other, and this everyone understands to be God.

Summa Theologica, Ia. ii. 3

Having indicated that the attempt to prove God's existence is not hopeless from the outset, we proceed now to fix on the arguments of philosophers and theologians alike, beginning with Aristotle who sets off from the concept of change. His argument takes two directions, of which the first is as follows.

Everything in a process of change is set in motion by another. Our senses tell us that things are in motion, the sun for instance. Therefore they are set in motion by another. Now this setter-in-motion is either itself in motion or it is not. If not, then we have our conclusion, namely the necessity of inferring a motionless mover which we term God. But if it is itself in motion then it must be set in motion by another. Either we have an infinite series or we arrive at a changeless mover. But we cannot go back infinitely. Therefore we must infer a first changeless mover.

There are two propositions to be proved; first, that everything in motion is set in motion by another; second, that an infinite series of things setting and set in motion is impossible.

Summa Contra Gentiles, 1, 13

2. [The Argument from Efficient Causality]

The second approach starts from the nature of efficient causality. Among phenomena we discover an order of efficient causes. But we never come across, nor ever shall, anything that is an efficient cause of itself; such a thing would be prior to itself, which is impossible. It is also impossible to go on to infinity with efficient causes, for in an ordered series the first is the cause of the intermediate and the intermediate is the cause of the last. Whether or not the intermediate causes be one or many is irrelevant. Take away the cause and the effect also goes. Therefore if there were not a first among efficient causes—which would be the case in an infinite series—there would be no intermediate causes nor an ultimate effect. This plainly is not the case. A first cause, generally termed God, must therefore be inferred.

Summa Theologica, Ia. ii. 3

An infinite series of efficient causes in essential subordination is impossible. Causes essentially required for the production of a determinate effect cannot consequently be infinitely multiplied, as if a block could be shifted by a crowbar, which in turn is levered by a hand, and so on to infinity.

But an infinite series of causes in accidental subordination is not reputed impossible, so long as all the causes thus multiplied are grouped as one cause and their multiplication is incidental to the causality at work. For instance a blacksmith may work with many hammers because one after another breaks in his hand, but that one particular hammer is used after another particular one is incidental. Similarly that in begetting a child a man was himself begotten by another man; for he is father as man, not as son. In a genealogy of efficient causes all men have the same status of particular generator. Hence, for such a line to stretch back to infinity is not unthinkable.

Summa Theologica, Ia. xlvi. 2, and 7

3. [The Argument from Contingent Being]

We observe in our environment how things are born and die away; they may or may not exist; to be or not to be—they are open to either alternative. All things cannot be so contingent, for what is able not to be may be reckoned as once a non-being, and were everything like that once there would have been nothing at all. Now were this true, nothing would ever have begun, for what is does not begin to be except because of something which is, and so there would be nothing even now. This is clearly hollow. Therefore all things cannot be might-not-have-beens; among them must be a being whose existence is necessary.

Summa Theologica, Ia. ii. 3

Everything that is a possible-to-be has a cause, since its essence as such is equally uncommitted to the alternatives of existing and not existing. If it be credited with existence, then this must be from some cause. Causality, however, is not an infinite process. Therefore a necessary being is the conclusion. The principle of its necessity is either from outside or not. If not, then the being is inwardly necessary. If necessity comes from without, we must still propose a first being necessary of itself, since we

cannot have an endless series of derivatively necessary beings.

Summa Contra Gentiles, I, 15

4. [The Argument from Degrees of Excellence]

The fourth argument is taken from the degrees of reality we discover in things. Some are truer and better and nobler than others, so also with other perfections. But more or less are attributed to different things in proportion as they variously approach something which is the maximum. Hence, there is something truest, and best, and noblest, and in consequence the superlative being, for the greatest truths are the greatest beings. Now the maximum in any order is the cause of all the other realities of that order. Therefore there is a real cause of being and goodness and all perfections whatsoever in everything; and this we term God.

Summa Theologica, Ia. ii. 3

The argument can be gathered from words let fall by Aristotle in the *Metaphysics*. He says that the truest things are also the most real; and again, that there is a superlative truth. One piece of architecture is more sham than another, one more genuine; throughout a comparison is implied with what is true without qualification and most of all. We can go farther and conclude that there is something most real, and this we call God.

Summa Contra Gentiles, I, 13

5. [The Argument from Purpose or Design]

Contrary and discordant elements ... cannot always, or nearly always, work harmoniously together unless they be directed by something providing each and all with their tendencies to a definite end. Now in the universe we see things of diverse natures conspiring together in one scheme, not rarely or haphazardly, but approximately always or for the most part. There must be something, therefore, whose providence directs the universe.

Summa Contra Gentiles, I, 13

We observe that things without consciousness, such as physical bodies, operate with a purpose, as appears from their co-operating invariably, or almost so, in the same way in order to obtain the best result. Clearly then they reach this end by intention and not by chance. Things lacking knowledge move towards an end only when directed by someone who knows and understands, as an arrow by an archer. There is consequently an intelligent being who directs all natural things to their ends; and this being we call God.

Summa Theologica, Ia. ii. 3

When diverse things are coordinated the scheme depends on their directed unification, as the order of battle of a whole army hangs on the plan of the commander-in-chief. The arrangement of diverse things cannot be dictated by their own private and divergent natures; of themselves they are diverse and exhibit no tendency to make a pattern. It follows that the order of many among themselves is either a matter of chance or it must be resolved into one first planner who has a purpose in mind. What comes about always; or in the great majority of cases, is not the result of accident. Therefore the whole of this world has but one planner or governor.

Summa Contra Gentiles, I, 42

DAVID HUME (1711–1776)

For a biographical note, see pages 69–70.

A CRITIQUE OF NATURAL THEOLOGY

1. [The Argument for a First Cause]

The argument, replied Demea, which I would insist on is the common one. Whatever exists must have a cause or reason of its existence, it being absolutely impossible for anything to produce itself or be the cause of its own existence. In mounting up, therefore, from effects to causes, we must either go on in tracing an infinite succession, without any ultimate cause at all, or must at last have recourse to some ultimate cause that is *necessarily* existent. Now that the first supposition is absurd may be thus

---

From *Dialogues Concerning Natural Religion*. Published in London, 1779. Critical edition by Norman Kemp Smith, Oxford: Oxford University Press, 1935. Reprinted by permission.

proved. In the infinite chain or succession of causes and effects, each single effect is determined to exist by the power and efficacy of that cause which immediately preceded; but the whole eternal chain or succession, taken together, is not determined or caused by anything, and yet it is evident that it requires a cause or reason, as much as any particular object which begins to exist in time. The question is still reasonable why this particular succession of causes existed from eternity, and not any other succession or no succession at all. If there be no necessarily existent being, any supposition which can be formed is equally possible; nor is there any more absurdity in *nothing's* having existed from eternity than there is in that succession of causes which constitutes the universe. What was it, then, which determined something to exist rather than *nothing,* and bestowed being on a particular possibility, exclusive of the rest? *External causes,* there are supposed to be none. *Chance* is a word without a meaning. Was it *nothing?* But that can never produce anything. We must, therefore, have recourse to a necessarily existent Being who carries the reason of his existence in himself, and who cannot be supposed not to exist, without an express contradiction. There is, consequently, such a Being—that is, there is a Deity.

I shall not leave it to Philo, said Cleanthes, though I know that the starting of objections is his chief delight, to point out the weakness of this metaphysical reasoning. It seems to me so obviously ill-grounded, and at the same time of so little consequence to the cause of true piety and religion, that I shall myself venture to show the fallacy of it.

I shall begin with observing that there is an evident absurdity in pretending to demonstrate a matter of fact, or to prove it by any arguments *a priori.* Nothing is demonstrable unless the contrary implies a contradiction. Nothing that is distinctly conceivable implies a contradiction. Whatever we conceive as existent, we can also conceive as non-existent. There is no being, therefore, whose non-existence implies a contradiction. Consequently there is no being whose existence is demonstrable. I propose this argument as entirely decisive, and am willing to rest the whole controversy upon it.

It is pretended that the Deity is a necessarily existent being; and this necessity of his existence is attempted to be explained by asserting that, if we knew his whole essence or nature, we should perceive it to be as impossible for him not to exist, as for twice two not to be four. But it is evident that this can never happen, while our faculties remain the same as at present. It will still be possible for us, at any time, to conceive the non-existence of what we formerly conceived to exist; nor can the mind ever lie under a necessity of supposing any object to remain always in being, in the same manner as we lie under a necessity of always conceiving twice two to be four. The words, therefore, *necessary existence* have no meaning or, which is the same thing, none that is consistent.

But further, why may not the material universe be the necessarily existent Being, according to this pretended explication of necessity? We dare not affirm that we know all the qualities of matter; and, for aught we can determine, it may contain some qualities which, were they known, would make its non-existence appear as great a contradiction as that twice two is five. I find only one argument employed to prove that the material world is not the necessarily existent Being; and this argument is derived from the contingency both of the matter and the form of the world. "Any particle of matter," it is said, "may be *conceived* to be annihilated, and any form may be *conceived* to be altered. Such an annihilation or alteration, therefore, is not impossible." But it seems a great partiality not to perceive that the same argument extends equally to the Deity, so far as we have any conception of him, and that the mind can at least imagine him to be non-existent or his attributes to be altered. It must be some unknown, inconceivable qualities which can make his non-existence appear impossible or his attributes unalterable; and no reason can be assigned why these qualities may not belong to matter. As they are altogether unknown and inconceivable, they can never be proved incompatible with it.

Add to this that in tracing an eternal succession of objects it seems absurd to inquire for a general cause or first author. How can anything that exists from eternity have a cause, since that relation implies a priority in time and a beginning of existence?

In such a chain, too, or succession of objects, each part is caused by that which preceded it, and causes that which succeeds it. Where then is the difficulty? But the *whole,* you say, wants a cause. I answer that the uniting of these parts into a whole, like the uniting of several distinct countries into one kingdom, or several distinct members into one body, is performed merely by an arbitrary act of the mind, and has no influence on the nature of things. Did I show you the particular causes of each individual in a collection of twenty particles of matter, I should think it very unreasonable should you afterwards ask me what was the cause of the whole twenty. This is sufficiently explained in explaining the cause of the parts.

Though the reasonings which you have urged, Cleanthes, may well excuse me, said Philo, from starting any further difficulties, yet I cannot forbear insisting still upon another topic. It is observed by arithmeticians that the products of 9 compose always either 9 or some lesser product of 9 if you add together all the characters of which any of the former products is composed. Thus, of 18, 27, 36, which are products of 9, you make 9 by adding 1 to 8, 2 to 7, 3 to 6. Thus 369 is a product also of 9; and if you add 3, 6, and 9, you make 18, a lesser product of 9. To a superficial observer so wonderful a regularity may be admired as the effect either of chance or design; but a skilful algebraist immediately concludes it to be the work of necessity, and demonstrates that it must for ever result from the nature of these numbers. Is is not probable, I ask, that the whole economy of the universe is conducted by a like necessity, though no human algebra can furnish a key which solves the difficulty? And instead of admiring the order of natural beings, may it not happen that, could we penetrate into the intimate nature of bodies, we should clearly see why it was absolutely impossible they could ever admit of any other disposition? So dangerous is it to introduce this idea of necessity into the present question! and so naturally does it afford an inference directly opposite to the religious hypothesis!

2. [The Argument from Design]

Not to lose any time in circumlocutions, said Cleanthes ... I shall briefly explain how I conceive this matter. Look round the world, contemplate the whole and every part of it: you will find it to be nothing but one great machine, subdivided into an infinite number of lesser machines, which again admit of subdivisions to a degree beyond what human senses and faculties can trace and explain. All these various machines, and even their most minute parts, are adjusted to each other with an accuracy which ravishes into admiration all men who have ever contemplated them. The curious adapting of means to ends, throughout all nature, resembles exactly, though it much exceeds, the productions of human contrivance—of human design, thought, wisdom, and intelligence. Since therefore the effects resemble each other, we are led to infer, by all the rules of analogy, that the causes also resemble, and that the Author of nature is somewhat similar to the mind of man, though possessed of much larger faculties, proportioned to the grandeur of the work which he has executed. By this argument *a posteriori,* and by this argument alone, do we prove at once the existence of a Deity and his similarity to human mind and intelligence.

I shall be free, Cleanthes, said Demea, as to tell you that from the beginning I could not approve of your conclusion concerning the similarity of the Deity to men, still less can I approve of the mediums by which you endeavor to establish it. What! No demonstration of the Being of God! No abstract arguments! No proofs *a priori!* Are these which have hitherto been so much insisted on by philosophers all fallacy, all sophism? Can we reach no farther in this subject than experience and probability? I will not say that this is betraying the cause of a Deity; but surely, by this affected candor, you give advantages to atheists which they never could obtain by the mere dint of argument and reasoning.

What I chiefly scruple in this subject, said Philo, is not so much that all religious arguments are by Cleanthes reduced to experience, as that they appear not to be even the most certain and irrefragable of that inferior kind. That a stone will fall, that fire will burn, that the earth has solidity, we have observed a thousand and a thousand times; and when any new instance of this nature is presented, we draw without hesitation the accustomed inference. The exact similarity of the cases gives us a perfect assurance of a similar event, and a stronger evidence is never desired nor sought after. But wherever you depart, in the least, from the similarity of the cases, you diminish proportionably the evidence, and may at last bring it to a very weak *analogy,* which is confessedly liable to error and uncertainty. After having experienced the circulation of the blood in human creatures, we make no doubt that it takes place in Titius and Maevius; but from its circulation in frogs and fishes it is only a presumption, though a strong one, from analogy that it takes place in men and other animals. The analogical reasoning is much weaker when we infer the circulation of the sap in vegetables from our experience that the blood circulates in animals; and those who hastily followed that imperfect analogy are found, by more accurate experiments, to have been mistaken.

If we see a house, Cleanthes, we conclude, with the greatest certainty, that it had an architect or builder because this is precisely that species of effect which we have experienced to proceed from that species of cause. But surely you will not affirm that the universe bears such a resemblance to a house that we can with the same certainty infer a similar cause, or that the analogy is here entire and perfect. The dissimilitude is so striking that the utmost you can here pretend to is a guess, a conjecture, a presumption concerning a similar cause; and how that pretension will be received in the world, I leave you to consider. . . .

That all inferences, Cleanthes, concerning fact are founded on experience, and that all experimental reasonings are founded on the supposition that similar causes prove similar effects, and similar effects similar causes, I shall not at present much dispute with you. But observe, I entreat you, with what extreme caution all just reasoners proceed in the transferring of

experiments to similar cases. Unless the cases be exactly similar, they repose no perfect confidence in applying their past observation to any particular phenomenon. Every alteration of circumstances occasions a doubt concerning the event; and it requires new experiments to prove certainly that the new circumstances are of no moment or importance. A change in bulk, situation, arrangement, age, disposition of the air, or surrounding bodies—any of these particulars may be attended with the most unexpected consequences. And unless the objects be quite familiar to us, it is the highest temerity to expect with assurance, after any of these changes, an event similar to that which before fell under our observation. The slow and deliberate steps of philosophers here, if anywhere, are distinguished from the precipitate march of the vulgar, who, hurried on by the smallest similitude, are incapable of all discernment or consideration.

But can you think, Cleanthes, that your usual phlegm and philosophy have been preserved in so wide a step as you have taken when you compared to the universe houses, ships, furniture, machines, and, from their similarity in some circumstances, inferred a similarity in their causes? Thought, design, intelligence, such as we discover in men and other animals, is no more than one of the springs and principles of the universe, as well as heat or cold, attraction or repulsion, and a hundred others which fall under daily observation. It is an active cause by which some particular parts of nature, we find, produce alterations on other parts. But can a conclusion, with any propriety, be transferred from parts to the whole? Does not the great disproportion bar all comparison and inference? From observing the growth of a hair, can we learn anything concerning the generation of a man? Would the manner of a leaf's blowing, even though perfectly known, afford us any instruction concerning the vegetation of a tree?

But allowing that we were to take the *operations* of one part of nature upon another for the foundation of our judgment concerning the *origin* of the whole (which never can be admitted), yet why select so minute, so weak, so bounded a principle as the reason and design of animals is found to be upon this planet? What peculiar privilege has this little agitation of the brain which we call *thought*, that we must thus make it the model of the whole universe? Our partiality in our own favor does indeed present it on all occasions, but sound philosophy ought carefully to guard against so natural an illusion.

So far from admitting, continued Philo, that the operations of a part can afford us any just conclusion concerning the origin of the whole, I will not allow any one part to form a rule for another part if the latter be very remote from the former. Is there any reasonable ground to conclude that the inhabitants of other planets possess thought, intelligence, reason, or anything similar to these faculties in men? When nature has so extremely diversified her manner of operation in this small globe, can we imagine that she incessantly copies herself throughout so immense a universe? And if thought, as we may well suppose, be confined merely to this narrow corner and has even there so limited a sphere of action, with what propriety can we assign it for the original cause of all things? The narrow views of a peasant who makes his domestic economy the rule for the government of kingdoms is in comparison a pardonable sophism.

But were we ever so much assured that a thought and reason resembling the human were to be found throughout the whole universe, and were its activity elsewhere vastly greater and more commanding than it appears in this globe, yet I cannot see why the operations of a world constituted, arranged, adjusted, can with any propriety be extended to a world which is in its embryo state, and is advancing towards that constitution and arrangement. By observation we know somewhat of the economy, action, and nourishment of a finished animal, but we must transfer with great caution that observation to the growth of a foetus in the womb, and still more to the formation of an animalcule in the loins of its male parent. Nature, we find, even from our limited experience, possesses an infinite number of springs and principles which incessantly discover themselves on every change of her position and situation. And what new and unknown principles would actuate her in so new and unknown a situation as that of the formation of a universe, we cannot, without the utmost temerity, pretend to determine.

A very small part of this great system, during a very short time, is very imperfectly discovered to us; and do we thence pronounce decisively concerning the origin of the whole?

Admirable conclusion! Stone, wood, brick, iron, brass, have not, at this time, in this minute globe of earth, an order or arrangement without human art and contrivance; therefore, the universe could not originally attain its order and arrangement without something similar to human art. But is a part of nature a rule for another part very wide of the former? Is it a rule for the whole? Is a very small part a rule for the universe? Is nature in one situation a certain rule for nature in another situation vastly different from the former?

And can you blame me, Cleanthes, if I here imitate the prudent reserve of Simonides, who, according to the noted story, being asked by Hiero, *What God was?* desired a day to think of it, and then two days more; and after that manner continually prolonged the term, without ever bringing in his definition or description? Could you even blame me if I had answered, at first, *that I did not know,* and was sensible that this subject lay vastly beyond the reach of my faculties? You might cry out sceptic and rallier, as much as you pleased; but, having found in so many other subjects much more familiar the imperfections and even contradictions of human reason, I never should expect any success from its feeble conjectures in a subject so sublime and so remote from the sphere of our observation. When two *species* of objects have always been observed to be conjoined together, I can *infer*, by custom, the existence of one whenever I *see*–the existence of the other; and this I call an argument from experience. But how this argument can have place where the objects, as in the present case, are single, individual, without parallel or specific resemblance, may be difficult to explain. And will any man tell me with a serious countenance that an orderly universe must arise from some thought and art like the human because we have experience of it? To ascertain this reasoning it were requisite that we had experience of the origin of worlds; and it is not sufficient, surely, that we have seen ships and cities arise from human art and contrivance. …

… I shall endeavor to show you, a little more distinctly, the inconveniences of that anthropomorphism which you have embraced, and shall prove that there is no ground to suppose a plan of the world to be formed in the Divine mind, consisting of distinct ideas, differently arranged, in the same manner as an architect forms in his head the plan of a house which he intends to execute.

It is not easy, I own, to see what is gained by this supposition, whether we judge of the matter by *reason* or by *experience*. We are still obliged to mount higher in order to find the cause of this cause which you had assigned as satisfactory and conclusive.

If *reason* (I mean abstract reason derived from inquiries *a priori*) be not alike mute with regard to all questions concerning cause and effect, this sentence at least it will venture to pronounce: that a mental world or universe of ideas requires a cause as much as does a material world or universe of objects, and, if similar in its arrangement, must require a similar cause. For what is there in this subject which should occasion a different conclusion or inference? In an abstract view, they are entirely alike; and no difficulty attends the one supposition which is not common to both of them.

Again, when we will needs force *experience* to pronounce some sentence, even on these subjects which lie beyond her sphere, neither can she perceive any material difference in this particular between these two kinds of worlds, but finds them to be governed by similar principles, and to depend upon an equal variety of causes in their operations. We have specimens in miniature of both of them. Our own mind resembles the one; a vegetable or animal body the other. Let experience, therefore, judge from these samples. Nothing seems more delicate, with regard to its causes, than thought; and as these causes never operate in two persons after the same manner, so we never find two persons who think exactly alike. Nor indeed does the same person think exactly alike at any two different periods of time. A difference of age, of the disposition of his body, of weather, of food, of company, of books, of passions—any of these particulars, or others more minute, are sufficient to alter the curious machinery of thought and communicate to it very different movements and operations. As far as we can judge, vegetables and animal bodies are not more delicate in their motions, nor depend upon a greater variety or more curious adjustment of springs and principles.

How, therefore, shall we satisfy ourselves concerning the cause of that Being whom you suppose the Author of nature, or, according to your system of anthropomorphism, the ideal world into which you trace the material? Have we not the same reason to trace that ideal world into another ideal world or new intelligent principle? But if we stop and go no farther, why go so far? Why not stop at the material world? How can we satisfy ourselves without going on *in infinitum?* And, after all, what satisfaction is there in that infinite progression? Let us remember the story of the Indian philosopher and his elephant. It was never more applicable than to the present subject. If the material world rests upon a similar ideal world, this ideal world must rest upon some other, and so on without end. It were better therefore, never to look beyond the present material world. By supposing it to contain the principle of its order within itself, we really assert it to be God; and the sooner we arrive at that Divine Being, so much the better. When you go one step beyond the mundane system, you only excite an inquisitive humor which it is impossible ever to satisfy.

To say that the different ideas which compose the reason of the Supreme Being fall into order of themselves and by their own nature is really to talk without any precise meaning. If it has a meaning, I would fain know why it is not as good sense to say that the parts of the material world fall into order of themselves and by their own nature. Can the one opinion be intelligible, while the other is not so?

We have, indeed, experience of ideas which fall into order of themselves and without any *known*–cause. But, I am sure, we have a much larger experience of matter which does the same, as in all instances of generation and vegetation where the accurate analysis of the cause exceeds all human comprehension. We have also experience of particular systems of thought and of matter which have no order; of the first in madness, of the second in corruption. Why, then, should we think that order is more essential to one than the other? And if it requires a cause in both, what do we gain by your system, in tracing the universe of objects into a similar universe of ideas? The first step which we make leads us on for ever. It were, therefore, wise in us to limit all our inquiries to the present world, without looking farther. No satisfaction can ever be attained by these speculations which so far exceed the narrow bounds of human understanding. . . .

But to show you still more inconveniences, continued Philo, in your anthropomorphism, please to take a new survey of your principles. *Likeeffects prove like causes*. This is the experimental argument; and this, you say too, is the sole theological argument. . . .

Now, Cleanthes, said Philo, with an air of alacrity and triumph, mark the consequences. *First,* by this method of reasoning you renounce all claim to infinity in any of the attributes of the Deity. For, as the cause ought only to be proportioned to the effect, and the effect, so far as it falls under our cognizance, is not infinite, what pretensions have we, upon your suppositions, to ascribe that attribute to the Divine Being? You will still insist that, by removing him so much from all similarity to human creatures, we give in to the most arbitrary hypothesis, and at the same time weaken all proofs of his existence.

Secondly, you have no reason, on your theory, for ascribing perfection to the Deity, even in his finite capacity, or for supposing him free from every error, mistake, or incoherence, in his undertakings. There are many inexplicable difficulties in the works of nature which, if we allow a perfect author to be proved *a priori,* are easily solved, and become only seeming difficulties from the narrow capacity of man, who cannot trace infinite relations. But according to your method of reasoning, these difficulties become all real, and, perhaps, will be insisted on as new instances of likeness to human art and contrivance. At least, you must acknowledge that it is impossible for us to tell, from our limited views, whether this system contains any great faults or deserves any considerable praise if compared to other possible and even real systems. Could a peasant, if the *Aeneid* were read to him, pronounce that poem to be absolutely faultless, or even assign to its proper rank among the productions of human wit, he who had never seen any other production?

But were this world ever so perfect a production, it must still remain uncertain whether all the excellences of the work can justly be ascribed to the workman. If we survey a ship, what an exalted idea must we form of the ingenuity of the carpenter who framed so complicated, useful, and beautiful a machine? And what surprise must we feel when we find him a stupid mechanic who imitated others, and copied an art which, through a long succession of ages, after multiplied trials, mistakes, corrections, deliberations, and controversies, had been gradually improving? Many worlds might have been botched and bungled, throughout an eternity, ere this system was struck out; much labor lost, many fruitless trials made, and a slow but continued improvement carried on during infinite ages in the art of world-making.In such subjects, who can determine where the truth, nay, who can conjecture where the probability lies, amidst a great number of hypotheses which may be proposed and a still greater which may be imagined?

And what shadow of an argument, continued Philo, can you produce from your hypothesis to prove the unity of the Deity? A great number of men join in building a house or ship, in rearing a city, in framing a commonwealth; why may not several deities combine in contriving and framing a world? This is only so much greater similarity to human affairs. By sharing the work among several, we may so much further limit the attributes of each, and get rid of that extensive power and knowledge which must be supposed in one deity, and which, according to you, can only serve to weaken the proof of his existence. And if such foolish, such vicious creatures as man can yet often unite in framing and executing one plan, how much more those deities or demons, whom we may suppose several degrees more perfect!

It must be a slight fabric, indeed, said Demea, which can be erected on so tottering a foundation. While we are uncertain whether there is one deity or many, whether the deity or deities, to whom we owe our existence, be perfect or imperfect, subordinate or supreme, dead or alive, what trust or confidence can we repose in them? What devotion or worship address to them? What veneration or obedience pay them? To all the purposes of life the theory of religion becomes altogether useless; and even with regard to speculative consequences its uncertainty, according to you,

must render it totally precarious and unsatisfactory.

To render it still more unsatisfactory, said Philo, there occurs to me another hypothesis which must acquire an air of probability from the method of reasoning so much insisted on by Cleanthes. That like effects arise from like causes—this principle he supposes the foundation of all religion. But there is another principle of the same kind, no less certain and derived from the same source of experience, that, where several known circumstances are observed to be similar, the unknown will also be found similar. Thus, if we see the limbs of a human body, we conclude that it is also attended with a human head, though hid from us. Thus, if we see, through a chink in a wall, a small part of the sun, we conclude that were the wall removed we should see the whole body. In short, this method of reasoning is so obvious and familiar that no scruple can ever be made with regard to its solidity.

Now, if we survey the universe, so far as it falls under our knowledge, it bears a great resemblance to an animal or organized body, and seems actuated with a like principle of life and motion. A continual circulation of matter in it produces no disorder; a continual waste in every part is incessantly repaired; the closest sympathy is perceived throughout the entire system; and each part or member, in performing its proper offices, operates both to its own preservation and to that of the whole. The world, therefore, I infer, is an animal; and the Deity is the *soul* of the world, actuating it, and actuated by it.

You have too much learning, Cleanthes, to be at all surprised at this opinion which, you know, was maintained by almost all the theists of antiquity, and chiefly prevails in their discourses and reasonings. For though, sometimes, the ancient philosophers reason from final causes, as if they thought the world the workmanship of God, yet it appears rather their favorite notion to consider it as his body whose organization renders it subservient to him.

And it must be confessed that, as the universe resembles more a human body than it does the works of human art and contrivance, if our limited analogy could ever, with any propriety, be extended to the whole of nature, the inference seems juster in favor of the ancient than the modern theory.

There are many other advantages, too, in the former theory which recommended it to the ancient theologians. Nothing more repugnant to all their notions, because nothing more repugnant to common experience, than mind without body, a mere spiritual substance which fell not under their senses nor comprehension, and of which they had not observed one single instance throughout all nature. Mind and body they knew because they felt both; an order, arrangement, organization, or internal machinery, in both they likewise knew, after the same manner; and it could not but seem reasonable to transfer this experience to the universe, and to suppose the divine mind and body to be also coeval and to have, both of them, order and arrangement naturally inherent in them and inseparable from them.

Here, therefore, is a new species of anthropomorphism, Cleanthes, on which you may deliberate, and a theory which seems not liable to any considerable difficulties. You are too much superior, surely, to systematical prejudices to find any more difficulty in supposing an animal body to be, originally, of itself or from unknown causes, possessed of order and organization, than in supposing a similar order to belong to mind. But the vulgar prejudice that body and mind ought always to accompany each other ought not, one should think, to be entirely neglected; since it is founded on vulgar experience, the only guide which you profess to follow in all these theological inquiries. And if you assert that our limited experience is an unequal standard by which to judge of the unlimited extent of nature, you entirely abandon your own hypothesis, and must thenceforward adopt our mysticism, as you

call it, and admit of the absolute incomprehensibility of the Divine Nature.

This theory, I own, replied Cleanthes, has never before occurred to me, though a pretty natural one; and I cannot readily, upon so short an examination and reflection, deliver any opinion with regard to it. You are very scrupulous, indeed, said Philo; were I to examine any system of yours, I should not have acted with half that caution and reserve, in stating objections and difficulties to it. However, if anything occur to you, you will oblige us by proposing it.

Why then, replied Cleanthes, it seems to me that, though the world does, in many circumstances, resemble an animal body, yet is the analogy also defective in many circumstances the most material: no organs of sense; no seat of thought or reason; no one precise origin of motion and action. In short, it seems to bear a stronger resemblance to a vegetable than to an animal, and your inference would be so far inconclusive in favor of the soul of the world. . . .

But here, continued Philo, in examining the ancient system of the soul of the world there strikes me, all on a sudden, a new idea which, if just, must go near to subvert all your reasoning, and destroy even your first inferences on which you repose such confidence. If the universe bears a greater likeness to animal bodies and to vegetables than to the works of human art, it is more probable that its cause resembles the cause of the former than that of the latter, and its origin ought rather to be ascribed to generation or vegetation than to reason or design. Your conclusion, even according to your own principles, is therefore lame and defective. . . .

All religious systems, it is confessed, are subject to great and insuperable difficulties. Each disputant triumphs in his turn, while he carries on an offensive war, and exposes the absurdities, barbarities, and pernicious tenets of his antagonist. But all of them, on the whole, prepare a complete triumph for the *sceptic,* who tells them that no system ought ever to be embraced with regard to such subjects: for this plain reason that no absurdity ought ever to be assented to with regard to any subject. A total suspense of judgment is here our only reasonable resource. And if every attack, as is commonly observed, and no defense among theologians is successful, how complete must be *his* victory who remains always, with all mankind, on the offensive, and has himself no fixed station or abiding city which he is ever, on any occasion, obliged to defend?

CHARLES HARTSHORNE (1897–2000)

Charles Hartshorne lived in three centuries, the nineteenth, the twentieth, and the twenty-first. His father was an Episcopal minister descended from a long line of Quakers, but he himself chose to serve in World War I. He then studied at Harvard University under Alfred North Whitehead and became a proponent of Whitehead's "process philosophy." Whitehead's perspective on the nature of reality will be presented a bit later in this part.

In addition to a long teaching career at such schools as the University of Chicago and the University of Texas, Hartshorne also established himself as a world authority on birds and the evolution of their various songs. In fact, one of his many books is entitled *Born to Sing.* Among his many publications are such books as *Creativity in American Philosophy, The Ontological Argument, Insights and Oversights of the Great Thinkers,* and *Omnipotence and Other Theological Mistakes.* The following selection is from *Omnipotence and Other Theological Mistakes.*

Perhaps the strongest objection ever raised against the theistic view of reality is focused on the so-called problem of evil. If God is both all-powerful and all-loving, how can human suffering be explained? Rather than engage in many theological conceptual maneuvers in an effort to save the traditional definition of God, Hartshorne follows Whitehead's "process perspective" and simply proclaims that God is not to be understood as omnipotent. Moreover, he contends that God is as much influenced by human behavior as humans are by God; these two realities are engaged in a symbiotic, interactive relationship.

WHAT WENT WRONG IN CLASSICAL THEISM

Two Meanings of "God Is Perfect and Unchanging"

The word 'perfect' literally means "completely made" or "finished." But God is conceived as the maker or creator of all; so

From *Omnipotence and Other Theological Mistakes,* SUNY Press. Albany, N.Y., 1984.

what could have made God (whether or not the making was properly completed)? 'Perfect' seems a poor word to describe the divine reality.

To describe something as "not perfect" seems a criticism, it implies fault finding; worship excludes criticism and fault finding. God is to be "loved with all one's mind, heart, and soul." Such love seems to rule out the possibility of criticism. Suppose we accept this. Do we then have to admit that God cannot change? Clearly yes, insofar as change is for the worse and capacity for it objectionable, a *fault* or *weakness*. God then cannot change for the worse. The view I wish to defend admits this. But does every conceivable kind of change show a fault or weakness? Is there not change for the better? We praise people when they change in this fashion. All healthy growth is such change. We are delighted in growth in infants and children.Is there nothing to learn from this about how toconceive God?

It is easy to reply that, whereas the human offspring starts as a mere fertilized single cell and before that as an unfertilized one, God is surely not to be so conceived. However, no analogy between something human and the worshipful God is to be taken in simple-minded literalness. There still may be an analogy between growth as a wholly good form of change and the divine life. For it is arguable that even an infinite richness may be open to increase. The great logician Bertrand Russell expressed this opinion to me, although Russell was an atheist and had no interest in supporting my, or any, theology.

The traditional objection, already mentioned, to divine change was that if a being were already perfect, meaning that nothing better was possible, then change for the better must be impossible for the being. The unnoticed assumption here has been (for two thousand and more years) that it makes sense to think of a value so great or marvelous that it could in no sense whatever be excelled or surpassed. How do we know that this even makes sense? In my viewit does not and is either a contradiction or mere nonsense.

Bishop Anselm sought to define God's perfection as "that than which nothing greater (or better) can be conceived." In other words, the divine worth is *in all respects* strictly unsurpassable, incapable of growth as well as of rivalry by another. The words are smoothly uttered; but do they convey a clear and consistent idea? Consider the phrase 'greatest possible number.' It, too, can be smoothly uttered, but does it say anything? It might be used to define infinity; but I am not aware of any mathematician who has thought this a good definition. There are in standard mathematics many infinities unequal to one another, but no highest infinity. "Infinite" was a favorite word among classical theists; but they cannot be said to have explored with due care its possible meanings. In any case "not finite" is a negation, and the significance of the negative depends on that of the positive which is negated. If being finite is in every sense a defect, something objectionable, then did not God in creating a world of finite things act objectionably? This seems to me to follow.

Do or do not finite things contribute something to the greatness of God? If so, then each such contribution is itself finite. Does this not mean that somehow finitude has a valid application to the divine life? Consider that, according to the tradition, God could have refrained from creating our world. Then whatever, if anything, this world contributes to the divine life would have been lacking. Moreover, if God could have created some other world instead of this one, God must actually lack what the other world would have contributed. If you reply that the world contributes nothing to the greatness of God, then I ask, What are we all doing, and why talk about "serving God," who, you say, gains nothing whatever from our existence?

The simple conclusion from the foregoing, and still other lines of reasoning, is that the traditional idea of divine perfection or infinity is hopelessly unclear or ambiguous and that persisting in that tradition is bound to cause increasing skepticism, confusion, and human suffering. It has long bred, and must evermore breed, atheism as a natural reaction.

It is only fair to the founders of our .religious tradition to remember that their Greek philosophical teachers who inclined to think of deity as wholly unchanging also greatly exaggerated the lack of novelty in many nondivine things. The heavenly bodies were unborn and undying, and changed only by moving in circles; species were fixed forever; the Greek atomists or materialists thought that atoms changed only by altering their positions. Heraclitus, it is true, hinted at a far more basic role for change, and Plato partly followed him. Plato's World Soul, best interpreted as an aspect of God, was not purely eternal, but in its temporal dimension "a moving image of eternity." However, Aristotle, in his view of divinity at least, was more of an eternalist even than Plato, and medieval thought was influenced by Aristotle, also by Philo Judaeus and Plotinus, who likewise stressed the eternalistic side of Plato. Today science and philosophy recognize none of the absolute wordly fixities the Greeks assumed—not the stars, not the species, not the atoms. It more and more appears that creative becoming is no secondary, deficient form of reality compared to being, but is, as Bergson says, "reality itself." Mere being is only an abstraction. Then is there no permanence, does "everything change"? On the contrary (see later, under topic 5), past actualities are permanent. My childhood experiences will be changelessly there in reality, just as they occurred. Change is not finally analyzable as destruction, but only as creation of novelty. The old endures, the new is added.

There are two senses in which freedom from faults, defects, or objectional features, and perfection in *that* sense, may be applied theologically. The divine, to be worthy of worship, must excel any conceivable being other than itself: it must be unsurpassable *by another,* exalted beyond all possible rivals. Hence all may worship God as in principle forever superior to any other being. This exaltation beyond possible rivals applies to both of the two senses of perfection that I have in mind. There are two kinds (or norms) of excellence, which differ as follows. With one kind it makes sense to talk of an absolute excellence, unsurpassable not only by another being

but also by the being itself. This is what the tradition had in mind; and there was in it an important truth. The neglected other truth, however, is that an absolute best, unsurpassable not only by others but by the being itself, is conceivable only in certain *abstract* aspects of value or greatness, not in fully concrete value or greatness. And God, I hold, is no mere abstraction.

The abstract aspects of value capable of an absolute maximum are goodness and wisdom, or what ought to be meant by the infallibility, righteousness, or holiness of God (one attribute variously expressed). We should conceive the divine knowledge of the world and divine decision-making about it as forever incapable of rivalry and in its infallible rightness incapable of growth. God is not first more or less wicked or foolish (or, like the lower animals, amoral, unaware of ethical principles) and then righteous and wise, but is always beyond criticism in these abstract respects, always wholly wise and good in relating to the world. It is not in such attributes that God can grow. This is so because goodness and rightness are abstract, in a sense in which some values are not.

Put a man in prison. He is not thereby necessarily forced to entertain wrong beliefs, lose virtue, or make wrong decisions. What he is forced to lose is the aesthetic richness and variety of his impressions. He cannot in the same degree continue to enjoy the beauty of the world. Similarly, a person suffering as Job did is not a happy person, but is not necessarily less virtuous than before. We can go further: ethical goodness and infallibility in knowledge have an upper or absolute limit. Whatever the world may be, God can know without error or ignorance what that world is and can respond to it, taking fully into account the actual and potential values which it involves, and thus be wholly righteous. But if the world first lacks and then acquires new harmonies, new forms of aesthetic richness, then the beauty of the world as divinely known increases. God would be defective in aesthetic capacity were the divine enjoyment not to increase in such a case. Aesthetic value is the most concrete form of value. Everything can contribute to and increase it. *An absolute maximum of beauty is a meaningless idea.* Leibniz tried to define it. Who dares to say that he succeeded? Beauty is unity in variety of experiences. Absolute unity in absolute variety has no clear meaning. Either God lacks any aesthetic sense and then we surpass God in that respect, or there is no upper limit to the divine enjoyment of the beauty of the world.

Plato viewed God as the divine artist, Charles Peirce and A. N. Whitehead termed God the poet of the world. Is the artist not to enjoy the divine work of art, the poet not to enjoy the divine poem? The Hindus attributed bliss to the supreme reality, and many Western theologians have spoken of the divine happiness, but a careful inquiry into the possibility of an absolute upper limit of happiness has not commonly been undertaken. Plato did write about "absolute beauty" but failed to give even a slightly convincing reason for thinking that the phrase has a coherent meaning.

It is not a defect of a Mozart symphony that it lacks the precise form of beauty which a Bach composition has. Aesthetic limitations are not mere defects. The most concrete form of value has no upper limit; there can always be additional values. God can enjoy all the beauty of the actual world and its predecessors, but creativity is inexhaustible and no actual creation can render further creation superfluous. Absolute beauty is a will-o-the-wisp, the search for which has misled multitudes. This is the very rationale of becoming, the reason why mere static being is not enough. Any actual being is less than there could be. There could be more, let there be more. To suppose that this has no application to God is to throw away such clues to value as we have, turn out the light, and use mere words to try to illuminate the darkness that is left.

Two Meanings of "All-Powerful"

The idea of omnipotence in the sense to be criticized came about as follows: to be God, that is, worthy of worship, God must in power excel all others (and be open to criticism by none). The highest conceivable form of power must be the divine power. So far so good. Next question: what is the highest conceivable form of power? This question was scarcely put seriously at all, the answer was felt to be so obvious: it must be the power to determine every detail of what happens in the world. Not, notice, to significantly influence the happenings; no, rather to strictly determine, decide, their every detail. Hence it is that people still today ask, when catastrophe strikes, Why did God do this to me? What mysterious divine reason could there be? Why me? I charge theologians with responsibility for this improper and really absurd question.

Without telling themselves so, the founders of the theological tradition were accepting and applying to deity the *tyrant* ideal of power. "I decide and determine everything, you (and your friends and enemies) merely do what I determine you (and them) to do. Your decision is simply mine for you. You only think you decide: in reality the decision is mine."

Since the theologians were bright people we must not oversimplify. They half-realized they were in trouble. Like many a politician, they indulged in double-talk to hide their mistake even from themselves. They knew they had to define sin as freely deciding to do evil or the lesser good, and as disobeying the will of God. How could one disobey an omnipotent will? There were two devices. One was to say that God does not decide to bring about a sinful act; rather, God decides not to prevent it. God "permits" sin to take place. Taking advantage of this decision, the sinner does his deed. Yet stop! Remember that God is supposed to decide *exactly* what happens in the world. If someone murders me, God has decided there shall be precisely that murderous action. So it turns out that "permits" has here a meaning it ordinarily does not have. Ordinarily, when X gives Y permission to do such and such, there are at least details in the actual doing that are not specified by X (and could not be specified, since human language can give only outlines, not full details, of concrete occurrences). But omnipotence is defined as power to absolutely determine what happens. I have Thomas Aquinas especially in mind here. God gives a creature permission to perform act A, where A is no mere outline but is the act itself in its full concreteness. So nothing at all is left for the creature to decide? What then is left of creaturely freedom?

The most famous of all the scholastics finds the answer, and this is the second of the two devices referred to above. God decides that the creature shall perform act A, but the divine decision is that nevertheless the act shall be performed "freely." Don't laugh, the saintly theologian is serious. Serious, but engaging in double-talk. It is determined exactly what the creature will do, but determined that he or she will do it freely. As the gangsters sometimes say, after specifying what is to be done, "You are going to like it"—in other words, to do it with a will. If this is not the despot's ideal of power, what is?

What, let us ask again, is the highest conceivable form of power? Is it the despot's, magnified to infinity, and by hook or crook somehow reconciled with "benevolence," also magnified to infinity? This seems to have been the (partly unconscious) decision of theologians. Is there no better way? Of course there is.

After all, the New Testament analogy—found also in Greek religions—for deity is the parental role, except that in those days of unchallenged male chauvinism it had to be the father role. What is the ideal parental role? Is it that every detail is to be decided by the parent? The question answers itself. The ideal is that the child shall more and more decide its own behavior as its intelligence grows. Wise parents

do not try to determine everything, even for the infant, much less for the half-matured or fully matured offspring. Those who do not understand this, and their victims, are among the ones who write agonized letters to Ann Landers. In trying to conceive God, are we to forget everything we know about values? To read some philosophers or theologians it almost seems so.

If the parent does not decide everything, there will be some risk of conflict and frustration in the result. The children are not infallibly wise and good. And indeed, as we shall argue later, even divine wisdom cannot completely foresee (or timelessly know) what others will decide. Life simply is a process of decision making, which means that risk is inherent in life itself. Not even God could make it otherwise. *A world without risks is not conceivable*. At best it would be a totally dead world, with neither good nor evil.

Is it the highest ideal of power to rule over puppets who are permitted to think they make decisions but who are really made by another to do exactly what they do? For twenty centuries we have had theologians who seem to say yes to this question.

Some theologians have said that, while God *could* determine everything, yet out of appreciation for the value of having free creatures, God chooses to create human beings to whom a certain freedom is granted. When things go badly, it is because these special creatures make ill use of the freedom granted them. As a solution of the problem of evil, this is perhaps better than the nothing that theorists of religion have mostly given us. But it is not good enough. Many ills cannot plausibly be attributed to *human* freedom. Diseases no doubt are made worse and more frequent by people's not taking care of themselves, not exercising due care in handling food, and so forth. But surely they are not caused only by such misdoings. Human freedom does not cause all the suffering that animals undergo, partly from hunger, partly from wounds inflicted by sexual rivals or predators, also from diseases, parasites, and other causes not controlled by human beings.

There is only one solution of the problem of evil "worth writing home about." It uses the idea of freedom, but generalizes it. Why suppose that only people make decisions? People are much more conscious of the process of decision making than the other animals need be supposed to be; but when it comes to that, how conscious is an infant in determining its activities? If chimpanzees have no freedom, how much freedom has an infant, which by every test that seems applicable is much less intelligent than an adult chimpanzee? (One would never guess this fact from what "pro-lifers" say about a fetus being without qualification a person, so loose is their criterion for personality.)

There are many lines of reasoning that support the conclusion to which theology has been tending for about a century now, which is that our having at least some freedom is not an absolute exception to an otherwise total lack of freedom in nature, but a special, intensified, magnified form of a *general principle* pervasive of reality, down to the very atoms and still farther. Current physics does not contradict this, as many physicists admit. When will the general culture at least begin to see the theological bearings of this fact?

In philosophy of religion there is news, but newspapers know nothing of this. Nay more, periodicals of general interest know nothing of it. We have a population that inclines, in the majority, to be religious, but that shies away from any attempt at rational discussion of religious issues. This is an example of leveling down, rather than leveling up, democracy. People keep implying philosophical doctrines (why has God done this to me?) which philosophy of religion has largely outgrown, as also have the theologies which make some effort to be literate in philosophy and science.

Those who stand deep in the classical tradition are likely to object to the new theology that it fails to acknowledge "the sovereignty of God." To them we may reply,

"Are we to worship the Heavenly Father of Jesus (or the Holy Merciful One of the Psalmist or Isaiah), *or* to worship a heavenly king, that is, a cosmic despot?" These are incompatible ideals; candid thinkers should choose and not pretend to be faithful to both. As Whitehead said, "They gave unto God the properties that belonged unto Caesar." Our diminished awe of kings and emperors makes it easier for us than for our ancestors to look elsewhere for our model of the divine nature. "Divine sovereignty" sounds to some of us like a confession, an admission that it is sheer power, not unstinted love that one most admires.

From childhood I learned to worship divine love. God's power simply is the appeal of unsurpassable love. Again Whitehead put it well: "God's power is the worship he inspires." It is not that we hear Zeus's fearful thunderbolt, see the lightning, and fall down at the sight of such power. No, we feel the divine beauty and majesty, and cannot but respond accordingly. Even the other animals feel it; what they cannot, and we can, do is to think it. Whitehead again: God leads the world by the "majesty" of the divine vision of each creature and its place in the world. God "shares with each actual entity its actual (past) world." "God is the fellow sufferer who understands."

Whitehead read in Plato and Aristotle the wonderfully enlightened doctrine that it is the divine beauty that moves the world. And what is the divine beauty, beyond all other beauties? A thousand voices, alas not quite audible in ancient Greece, have said it; but we still scarcely believe, much less understand, these voices: the beauty beyond all others is the beauty of love, that with which life has a meaning, without which it does not. The Greeks, however, had an argument, a subtly fallacious one, for denying that love is the ultimate principle. Love implies, they saw, that one fails to have in oneself all possible value and hence looks to another for additional value. Overlooked was the question-begging assumption that it even makes sense to "have in oneself all possible value," as though value is something that *could* be exhaustively actualized in one being all by itself. Were that possible, of course its possessor would not need another to love but would exist in solitary glory, incapable of enhancement in any way. And thus the one clue we have to life's meaning is cast away in favor of a merely verbal ideal of the exhaustive realization of possible good. ...

The new idea is that causal order is not absolute but statistical. It admits an element of chance or randomness in nature. Many of the leading physicists of recent times are quite explicit about this. But they were preceded in principle by some great Greek philosophers, some French philosophers of modern times, and the three most distinguished of purely American philosophers, Charles Peirce, William James and John Dewey. All events are "caused," if that means that they had necessary conditions in the past, conditions without which they could not have happened, however, what is technically termed "suffcient condition," that which fully determines what happens, requires qualification. Where there is little freedom, as an inanimate nature, there are often conditions sufficient to determine approximately what happens, and for most purposes this is all we need to consider. Where there is much freedom, as in the behavior of higher, including human, animals, there are still necessary conditions in the past, but sufficient past conditions only for a considerable range of possibilities within which each decision maker finally determines what precisely and concretely happens at the moment in the agent's own mind, that is, what decision is made. Even God, as the French Catholic philosopher Lequier said more than a century ago, waits to see what the individual decides. "Thou hast created me creator of myself." Many decades later Whitehead, also a believer in God, independently put the point with the phrase "the self-created creature"; and the atheist Sartre in France wrote of human consciousness as its own cause, *causa sui.*

Determinists claim that what makes us free is that our "character" as already formed, plus each new situation, determines our decisions. So then the child was determined by the character already formed in its infant past and by the surrounding world, and this character by the preceding fetus and world, and that by the fertilized egg? What kind of freedom is that? By what magic do people miss the fact they are misusing words? Skinner is right; once accept determinism and all talk of freedom is double-talk. The word 'voluntary' (liking it) is good enough for the determinist's freedom; why not stick to it, without trying to borrow the prestige of the glorious word 'freedom'? One's past character is *now* a mere fact, part of the settled world, almost like someone else's past character. One may be capable of creating a partly new and better character by using the genuine freedom, some of which one has already long had but perhaps has too little or too ill made use of.

Our rejection of omnipotence will be attacked by the charge, "So you dare to limit the power of God?" Not so, I impose no such limit if this means, as it seems to imply, that God's power fails to measure up to some genuine ideal. All I have said is that omnipotence as usually conceived is a false or indeed absurd ideal, which in truth *limits* God, denies to him any world worth talking about: a world of living, that is to say, significantly decision-making, agents. It is the *tradition* which did indeed terribly limit divine power, the power to foster creativity even in the least of the creatures.

No worse falsehood was ever perpetrated than the traditional concept of omnipotence. It is a piece of unconscious blasphemy, condemning God to a dead world, probably not distinguishable from no world at all.

The root of evil, suffering, misfortune, wickedness, is the same as the root of all good, joy, happiness, and that is freedom, decision making. If, by a combination of good management and good luck, X and Y harmonize in their decisions, the AB they bring about may be good and happy; if not, not. To attribute all good to good luck, or all to good management, is equally erroneous. Life is not and cannot be other than a mixture of the two. God's good management is the explanation of there being a cosmic order that limits the scope of freedom and hence of chance—limits, but does not reduce to zero. With too much freedom, with nothing like laws of nature (which, some of us believe, are divinely decided and sustained), there could be only meaningless chaos; with too little, there could be only such good as there may be in atoms and molecules by themselves, apart from all higher forms. With no creaturely freedom at all, there could not even be that, but at most God alone, making divine decisions—about what? It is the existence of many decision makers that produces everything, whether good or ill. It is the existence of God that makes it possible for the innumerable decisions to add up to a coherent and basically good world where opportunities justify the risks. Without freedom, no risks—and no opportunities.

Nothing essential in the foregoing is my sheer invention. I am summing up and making somewhat more explicit what a number of great writers have been trying to communicate for several centuries, or at least and especially during the last one hundred and fifty years. ...

I feel that I ought to inform the reader, if he or she is not a philosopher, that today many philosophers defend the doctrine called "compatibilism," holding that determinism is compatible with human freedom. The reason they can do so is that they think of deciding merely as a psychological process of considering various ways of acting with the motives or reasons favoring or disfavoring the ways, and, without any sense of being constrained by anyone, adopting one of the ways. They do not seriously ask what objective significance the process has in the cosmos, what it does to the causal structure of the world. Moreover they are rather vague as to what the causal structure might really be.

Karl Popper says that when a physicist speaks of determinism he has a fairly precise idea of what he is talking about, but when a psychologist or philosopher talks about it "all precision vanishes." Peirce made similar charges. The causal structure of the world was in physics taken to be such that from the state of the whole universe (or an isolated system in it) in two successive moments all earlier and all later states follow exactly, given the natural laws really obtaining. Only ignorance of the previous successions of states and the laws would then explain our uncertainty about future states. But this is all talk about fairyland. We could not conceivably *not* be in partial ignorance, at least about previous states, if not also about the laws. Maxwell saw this over a century ago and remarked that since only God could possibly have the knowledge in question, and it is not the business of physics to discuss theological questions, determinism was not a proper doctrine of physics.

Maxwell probably did not know—few did in his time—that there are theologies which deny even to God knowledge of laws implying determinism, not because of divine limitations but because such laws describe no coherently conceivable world. They leave no room for genuine individuality, that is, for truly individual actions; and without individuals there are also no crowds or aggregates. To be is to act; to be individual is to act individually, that is, as not fully determined by another individual or set of individuals, past or eternal, according to strict law. From the universal to the fully individual there can be no deduction, no necessity. Laws are universals. If they have any role in reality it can only be to limit individual actions without fully determining them. They do forbid individuals to act in certain ways. This is true of many legal laws and moral principles. The principle of kindness does not tell us what in particular to do, but forbids whole classes of unkind actions. The "motives" that psychological determinism says determine actions are always more or less universal. We want to be "helpful" to someone we like, but no abstract idea like "helpful" can be as particular as what we actually do. Always finer decisions are left open by motives, ideals, or laws.

The idea of God fully determining, without constraining, our decisions can appeal to certain analogies. There is the hypnotic analogy. I take an actual case. The hypnotist says, "You will (later on) open the window." It is a cold day, the room is not in the least overwarm. You do open the window, giving some ingenious reasons for this. Has the hypnotist preprogrammed a particular piece of decision making? Not really. He has limited the options, at least as a matter of probabilities. (There is no proof that opening the window was *certain* to happen; there might have been a slight probability of its not happening.) But there are countless particular, subtly differing ways of opening a window. And those ingenious reasons for an odd action were not preprogrammed at all, so far as the data can prove. They were the real decisions, along with the exact timing, exact motions of the arm, and the like.

Again we can put pressure on people, or exert charm or more or less subtle suggestions, to get people to do what we want them, or think they ought, to do. But the actions themselves are always more particular than the wanting, or the idea of moral obligation.

There is no analogy that unambiguously supports determinism. It is a leap in the dark. No matter how brilliant a hypnotist, no matter how charming or subtly suggestive, God may be, the creature's concrete, fully definite decision has to be made by it, not by God. Whitehead's terminology is the most exact in history, by a good margin, to express the point. The creature must "prehend" God's "initial subjective aim" proposed to it. The proposed aim is in terms of universals called by Whitehead "eternal objects"—my own view does not eternalize universals to the extent Whitehead does—but the final subjective aim, which is the creature's fully particular decision, cannot follow or be uniquely specified by the initial subjective aim,

which is really an outline, not an exact qualitative duplicate of the final aim.

Peirce, Bergson, and Whitehead realize, as many do not, that the ultimate freedom is not in "behavior" but in experience, just *how* that particular experience prehends its past, including in that past God's decision, already made, for the particular occasion. No matter what motives the past, including me as past, and other actualities offer me-now, I-now must still decide the precise concrete way in which I respond to this offering, just what relative prominence this or that factor receives in my experience of it. "The many become one and are increased by one." My past is a many of events or experiences, including my previous experiences; what is called my character as already formed is simply an aspect of the past history of experiences constituting a sequence of the type that used to be called one's stream of consciousness, the members of this stream having special prehensive relations to previous members and to that complicated society of societies of subhuman actualities making up what is called one's body. (More of this in Chapter 2.)

When determinists talk about freedom as action determined by one's own character, they are blurring together several factors which need distinguishing (illustrating Popper's lack of precision in nonphysicists). If the character in question is your or my *pres-ent* quality as experiencer, that and the present experience are simply two aspects of one actuality. Self-determination in that sense does not imply determinism; but, on the contrary, it means that my character as definite before the decision does not determine but only influences (via present prehension) the pres-ent character, decision, or experience. . . .

The remaining theoretical option is that God, being supremely free, decides for creatures that are less than supremely, but still somewhat, free. Thus no unqualified determinism. By this sacrifice (what really is lost by it?) we gain—I am tempted to say—*everything*. A "world" now means an ordered, but not absolutely ordered, system of decision makers, whose decisions will have some chance aspects, with their mixtures of risks and opportunities. A world, any world, will be exciting, since in it agents really decide things every moment that previously (or from any purely eternal standpoint) were not decided. In any world, at every moment, even God encounters novelties, so that 'becoming' (in total abstraction from which no being can be anything but an empty cipher) applies even to God. In such a world there will be conflicts and frustrations. There is no longer the classical problem of evil. The question now is only, Is there not too much freedom, too great risk of evil, to be justified by the opportunities also open to the freedom? Thus the question becomes one of degree, and then the ancient defence, we are not wise like God and probably not in a position to second-guess divine decisions, becomes at least far stronger than it could be under the old idea of all-determining power (dealing only with the powerless). And at least we are no longer living in fairyland. We can recognize our world as a specimen of what has been abstractly described.

An interesting special case of the omnipotence problem is Abraham Lincoln's thought about it during the Civil War. "The will of God prevails," he said, and derived from this, though with some hesitation, that the war would last exactly as long as God willed it to last, since God, by "working in quiet" on the minds of men, could determine it to end at any time. It is not clear just how far Lincoln went toward absolute theological determinism. Perhaps he thought that God made definite decisions only about fairly large-scale matters like the ending of a war. He suggested that a long war might mean God's will that the monstrous crime of slavery should be adequately punished. Yet "God's purposes are not our purposes." Lincoln also speaks about "the attributes we attribute to God," presumably referring especially to power and goodness. Like many theologians he

seems somewhat more willing to confess our possible ignorance of God's goodness than of his power. Or is he about equally modest in both respects? Surely, unless we are to worship power more than goodness, it is at least as important that we should have a meaning applicable to God for 'goodness' as for 'power'; and what does "God is good" mean if the kind of purpose it implies is hopelessly opaque to us?

What use could Lincoln really be making of his view that God would determine the exact length of the war? How would it illuminate his own actions? Consider, too, that at the end of the war some Northerners would be much concerned to see to it that the South suffered as its rebellion made it "deserve" to suffer. If a long war occurred in order, in the divine judgment, to adequately punish the South (or the South and the North), this would not tell Northerners anything about what to do to prolong or shorten the war. For, only after the end came could one know what God willed in the matter. And if, after the end, one concluded that God had evidently willed the South's suffering to end, this would really be illogical, since other ways to make the South suffer than in war would be quite possible. So Lincoln's forgiveness of the South might be against the will of God? Ah, but wait and see! The will of God prevails. Then was the assassination divinely willed so that the punishment of the South could continue? Where do we stop in this second-guessing of God?

The only livable doctrine of divine power is that it influences all that happens but determines nothing in its concrete particularity. "Knowing" afterwards exactly what God has willed to happen is useless. We can, I believe, know the *general principle* of God's purpose. It is the beauty of the world (or the harmonious happiness of the creatures), a beauty of which every creature enjoys its own glimpses and to which it makes its unique contributions, but each created stage of which only God enjoys adequately, everlastingly, and as a whole, once it has been created.

Lincoln was a noble soul, supremely great, and he made no bad use of the theology he knew. But he could perhaps have gained something from a better theology. Still more could many souls, less wise and strong, gain what they sorely lack if they were spared useless riddles about divine power and could focus on the inspiration of seeing life as, even in its least moments, permanent contributions to the stores of beauty available selectively and partially to future moments and inclusively and fully to God. Also of believing in God as ideally powerful—in whatever sense this is compatible with having free creatures whose satisfactions and dissatisfactions are divinely participated in—God, who can hurt no one without vicariously suffering Him-Her-self, and can gratify no one without vicariously enjoying this gratification. So God's purpose is the welfare of the creatures as the means, finally, to increase the divine happiness, whose value is no absolute maximum but an ever-enriched infinity.

As a final verbal clarification, I remark that if by 'all-powerful' we mean that God has the highest conceivable form of power and that this power extends to all things—not as, with us, being confined to a tiny corner of the cosmos—and if this is what the word 'omnipotent' can be understood to mean, then yes, God is omnipotent. But the word has been so fearfully misdefined, and has so catastrophically misled so many thinkers, that I incline to say that the word itself had better be dropped. God has power uniquely excellent in quality and scope, in no respect inferior to any coherently conceivable power. In power, as in all properties, God is exalted beyond legitimate criticism or fault finding. In this power I believe. But it is not power to have totally unfree or "absolutely controlled" creatures. For that is nonsense. . . .

COMMENT

The Meaning of Theism

For the theist, the key to reality lies in God and divine design. This belief does not exclude several positions that we have already examined, since a theist can be a teleologist, a dualist, or an idealist; but cannot be a complete materialist or an absolute skeptic.

God has been defined as "a being who is personal, supreme, and good." This definition is in accord with what most people mean when they use the word "God." They think of God as personal—that is, as conscious mind or spirit. Of course, God's mind is conceived as much larger or greater than any human mind, but still somewhat like mind or spirit as we know it. God is also thought of as supreme—if not omnipotent, at least immensely great and powerful—so powerful, indeed, as to profoundly affect the whole world. Finally, a personal and supreme being would not be called God if it were not also good—perhaps not perfect, but at least good in a measure that far surpasses our poor human capacities.

If it be granted that the concept of God should be so defined, the question arises whether the belief in God is mature and defensible—whether it is consistent with the life of reason, which Socrates declared is alone worth living. Is faith in God, as Sigmund Freud maintained, a mere illusory compensation for fear, repression, and catastrophe? Or is it an inalienable possession of spiritual life, as rational as it is emotionally satisfying? Can this faith withstand the criticism of philosophy? What *reasons* are there for believing in the existence of God, and how valid are these reasons?

The main arguments *pro* and *con* are contained in this chapter. The ontological proof ("ontological" means "pertaining to the nature of being") as stated by St. Anselm is an *a priori* argument. From his definition of God as "that being than which no greater can be conceived," he reasons that we cannot, without contradiction, assert that God does not exist. St. Thomas rejected this form of proof, his five arguments all being *a posteriori*. They start with some fact given in experience—change, causality, nonnecessary being, degrees of excellence, or design—and they proceed to reason from this fact to the conclusion that God exists. The arguments of both St. Anselm and St. Thomas are intended to prove the existence of a perfect and omnipotent God. The argument of Hartshorne resembles the fifth proof of St. Thomas but concludes that God must be limited in power.

Hume's *Dialogues Concerning Natural Religion* are conversations (sometimes long speeches) between three characters: Demea, a partisan of "the argument for a first cause," Cleanthes, a defender of "the argument from design," and Philo, who is skeptical of both arguments. Demea's argument resembles the first three proofs of St. Thomas, but Demea also falls back upon St. Anselm's contention that the nonexistence of God would be a logical contradiction. Cleanthes' argument is like the fifth proof of St. Thomas.

The arguments themselves will not be restated because the reader, perhaps with help from an instructor, should be able to understand them, but something can be said about the criticisms that have been brought to bear against these arguments.

Criticism of the Ontological Argument

The ontological argument has had a checkered history. It was immediately criticized by an aged monk, Gaunilo, and was rejected by the greatest medieval philosopher, St. Thomas Aquinas. Then it was revived by Descartes, restated by Spinoza and Leibniz, and sharply criticized by Locke, Hume, and Kant. Relatively few philosophers in more recent times have accepted it.

The import of the argument is clarified by Gaunilo's objection and Anselm's reply. As interpreted by Gaunilo, the argument can be restated as follows: God is thought of as perfect; existence is necessary to perfection; therefore, God exists. This argument, said Gaunilo, is fallacious because by the same kind of reasoning I could "prove" the existence of a perfect island, to wit: If the island did not exist it would lack one of the elements of perfection, namely, real existence, and hence it would not be a perfect island. However, the conclusion that a perfect island must exist is obviously absurd, and hence this type of argument is fallacious.

Anselm promptly replied to this attempted *reductio ad absurdum* by pointing out that a "perfect island" is perfect only in a weak and limited sense. By its very nature, an island is finite, and hence can be "perfect" only in a relative or inaccurate manner of speaking—it cannot be *infinitely* perfect. God, and not the hypothetical island, is that being than which no greater can be conceived—a being perfect in the sense of being incomparably greatest. Such absolute and infinite perfection applies to God and to God alone, and only such perfection requires existence.

Another objection was advanced by St. Thomas Aquinas. Going to the root of the argument, he questioned whether we really have in mind the concept of an utterly infinite or perfect being. He pointed out that we finite human beings have only an inadequate and indirect knowledge of God. Because of the infirmity of our understanding, we cannot discern God as divine in itself, but only by the effects that God produces. If we could know God's essence absolutely, we would surely see that God's essence involves existence. However, since we know God only relatively, God's existence is not self-evident to us. We cannot leap from our imperfect idea of God to the conclusion that an absolutely perfect being exists.

Perhaps the most profound criticism of the ontological argument was advanced by Immanuel Kant, whose objection turns on the meaning of the word "exists." Suppose we say that God exists. Are we making the same sort of statement as when we say that God is omnipotent? Kant would say no. The first statement asserts nothing about the *characteristics* of God; it merely tells us that God, whatever that is, exists, just as a rabbit, a cabbage, a stone, or a planet exists. This statement can be denied in only one way—namely, by denying that God exists. The second statement, that God is omnipotent, does tell us something about the character of God, and this statement, unlike the first, can be denied in two ways—either by denying that there is a God or by denying that God is omnipotent.

Since the question of a thing's existence is thus *additional* to the question of its characteristics, we can grasp its characteristics without knowing whether it exists. Take the following illustration. As you sit at your desk, you may wonder whether there is a dollar bill in your pocket. Before reaching into your pocket to find out, you have in mind what the dollar bill would be like. The characteristics of the dollar bill that you are thinking about are the same whether or not there really is a dollar bill in your pocket. Hence, you can grasp the characteristics of a dollar bill without knowing that it exists. Can we likewise grasp God's characteristics without knowing whether God exists? Yes, declares Kant. It is logically possible to think of an infinite and perfect Being without knowing that there is such a Being. However, suppose we *mean* by God a necessarily existent God. It would still not follow that there really is such a Being. It would merely follow that *if* there is a God, then God is a necessarily existent Being—because that is what we mean. At best, Anselm's argument shows only that the thought of God implies the *thought* of God's existence. The thought of perfection implies the thought of existence, and real perfection implies real existence. However, the *thought* of perfection does imply *real* existence. This is the tenor of Kant's criticism.

The evaluation of the original argument and these criticisms shall be left to the reader. Regardless of the criticisms, Anselm's distinction between "essence" and "existence" has had a very stimulating influence on later philosophical thought. Existentialism, which we examined in Chapter 6, is based in large measure on this distinction. The ontological proof, moreover, still fascinates both students and philosophers. Two very able American philosophers, Norman Malcolm and Charles Hartshorne, have reformulated and defended the argument.

Criticism of the Cosmological Proof

The term "cosmological proof" has been used in a blanket way to cover arguments like the first three of St. Thomas. These arguments are alike in maintaining that the insufficiency of nature requires the self-sufficiency of God to explain it. *Change* ("motion" in the sense of actualization of potentialities) cannot explain itself but requires an Unchanged Changer ("Unmoved Mover"—a fully actualized being) for its explanation. *Causation* (in the sense of bringing something into existence) cannot explain itself but requires an Uncaused Cause. *Contingent being* cannot explain itself but requires a Necessary Being for its explanation. Because these proofs are parallel, they can be grouped together. It is the third that we shall take as the most instructive and consider in some detail.

Fundamental to the third argument is the contention that we cannot explain one dependent event merely by another or yet another dependent event, even if we push back the regress indefinitely. St. Thomas is prepared to admit, apart from Revelation, that contingent events may be causally linked to one another in a never-ending regress. What he denies is that we can have a *sufficient* explanation in terms of such an infinite regress of *dependent* causes.

So long as we merely have a series of causes, however infinitely extended, we are explaining one dependent event by another dependent event by still another dependent event, and so on. This is unsatisfactory for two reasons. First, each event is dependent upon its antecedents, and hence no event is more than *conditionally* necessary. If everything is dependent upon something else, the whole process hangs on nothing. An explanation that thus never gives us an *ultimate* necessity is incomplete and hence is not a full and satisfactory explanation. Secondly, even if there is an infinite regress of causes, we can always ask why this chain occurs rather than some other chain. Or even if we consider the sum total of nature, we can ask why we have *this* totality rather than some quite different totality. The only *sufficient* explanation is that natural events, and even the whole of nature, must ultimately depend upon a necessary Being. Such a Being cannot have had an external cause, because it is an infinite and eternal Being—namely, God—whose essence is to exist. The argument arrives at the same conclusion as the ontological proof but via a different route.

This argument can be criticized in a number of ways. First, we can ask what is meant by saying that God is a necessary Being. The word "necessity" applies to *propositions* whose denial would be contradictory. "Two plus two equals four" is a necessary proposition, since it would be contradictory to deny it. However, does "necessity" apply to *things* as well as to propositions? The character Cleanthes, in Hume's dialogue, answers: "Nothing is demonstrable unless the contrary implies a contradiction. Nothing that is distinctly conceivable implies a contradiction. Whatever we conceive as existent, we can also conceive as nonexistent. There is no being, therefore, whose nonexistence implies a contradiction." If necessity thus applies to logically necessitated propositions and not to things, nothing, not even God, is a necessary Being.

If, in some mysterious way, a Being can be necessary, why might not the natural universe be this necessarily existent Being? If you reply that every natural event is seen to be nonnecessary (in the sense that its absence involves no contradiction), it does not follow that the whole of nature is nonnecessary. A whole need not have the character of its parts. It does not follow from the fact that every note in a musical composition is short that the whole composition is short. Similarly, it does not follow from the fact that every natural thing or event is nonnecessary that the whole of nature is nonnecessary. If we are to insist upon a necessity that we do not understand, this necessity would seem as applicable to nature as to supernature.

However, should we demand such an ultimate necessity? Why not simply suppose that the causal series of linked events stretches back infinitely and that there is no other explanation? If each part is determined by its antecedents, is not the whole sufficiently determined? It would seem to be absurd to demand an external cause for an infinite regress without beginning, since the causal relation implies priority in time and hence a beginning of existence. Our whole experience of causal connections, moreover, lies *within* nature, and we have no sufficient basis for projecting this relation *outside* of nature. Can we assume that what is true of particular things in the world—namely, that *they* are caused—is true of the universe in its totality? Must the universe have a cause outside its own nature? Or must it have any cause at all? To a consistent empiricist, such as Hume, the extension of the concept of causation beyond the field of all actual or possible experience offers special difficulties. On the other hand, if we understand the "necessity" of a necessary Being as logical rather than causal, we are faced by the difficulty already mentioned—that the necessity here involved is mysterious and seems applicable to the whole of nature no less than to supernature.

Despite these objections of Hume, most Catholic and some non-Catholic philosophers believe that the argument retains its cogency. It seems to them that the evident self-insufficiency of natural events requires an ultimate self-sufficient foundation. Nature as a composite whole, moreover, seems *not* self-sufficient, because any composite *could* be composed in a different way. Why should there be this total natural constellation rather than some other? Does not the existence of such dependent and conditioned being require existence of independent and unconditioned Being? Only an infinite, eternal, completely actualized, and noncomposite Being—a pure spirit—could be thus independent and unconditioned, the guarantor of its own existence and all else besides. We may have to fall back upon other arguments to establish some of the attributes of God, but the cosmological argument at least proves that nature is dependent upon supernature, and this conclusion carries us a long way—or so the believer in the cosmological argument would continue to maintain.

Criticism of the Teleological Argument

The teleological argument, or argument from design, is very ancient but still popular. It was first expressly formulated by Plato, in the *Laws,* and has been restated by innumerable philosophers, among them St. Augustine, St. Thomas (in his fifth proof), Locke, and Rousseau. It was especially popular in the seventeenth and eighteenth centuries, when the astronomy and physics of Isaac Newton were interpreted as the disclosure of a wonderful natural order requiring God as its source.

The criticisms of Hume, as set forth by the character Philo in the *Dialogues Concerning Natural Religion,* constitute a powerful attack upon the design argument. Are these criticisms conclusive? Evidently Hume did not think so. The criticisms are not presented as his but are put in the mouth of Philo, one of the three characters in the *Dialogues*. Hume abstains from indicating his own sympathies except at the very end of the book, where he suggests that "the opinions" of Cleanthes, the proponent of the design argument, are nearer to the truth than those of Philo. In a letter to a friend, George Elliot (dated March 10, 1751), Hume refers to Cleanthes as the "hero" of the dialogues, and asks for any suggestions that will strengthen that side of the dispute. Even Philo, in a final passage not quoted here, is made to remark that the apparent design in nature proves that its cause bears an analogy, though somewhat remote, to the human mind. Probably Hume felt that Philo's criticisms were weighty but by no means decisive.

One thing to note about most of these criticisms is that they do not tend to prove the *absence* of a designing agency or agencies. They indicate limitations rather than fatal defects in the design argument. They show that the finite order and goodness of nature are an insufficient basis for inferring an infinite, perfect, unitary, external, and conscious designer. Kant later pointed out an additional limitation—that the design argument can prove only a kind of architect, but it cannot prove a creator who makes the world out of nothing. Just as a watchmaker uses materials already in existence to make a watch, so the designer of a natural order may use preexisting materials to compose his design. However, these considerations are consistent with some kind of teleological explanation of the goodness and higher levels of order to be found in nature. It is true that Philo's final point, that the natural order may be the result of mere natural selection, is opposed to a teleological hypothesis, but the further course of the dialogue suggests that neither Cleanthes nor Philo regarded natural selection as sufficient, in itself, to explain the whole order of nature. It is also noteworthy that John Stuart Mill and William James could not bring themselves to the view that the Darwinian hypothesis of natural selection was alone sufficient to explain the higher levels of evolution. They preferred to believe in a finite God, struggling against evil but not wholly able to eliminate it. Moreover, this finite God need not be thought of as an external, transcendent Deity but can be construed as the total society of natural forces that are pushing on toward the good. Admittedly, this concept alters the usual meaning of "God," but some modern philosophers nevertheless prefer it.

As can be seen from reading Hartshorne's essay on the shortcomings of the traditional definition of God, there are approaches to the relationship between creation and evolution that do not see the two processes as opposed. Indeed, Pierre Teilhard de Chardin, along with Hartshorne, became quite well known for identifying the two, for seeing the latter as the means through which the former takes place. In fact, it can be argued that evolution actually serves as evidence for the existence of a higher, creative power at work in the universe because it contradicts the Second Law of Thermodynamics.

This law of physics states that the universe is becoming ever more diffused and random in nature and thus will eventually run out of energy. Evolution, on the other hand, seems to entail increasingly complex life forms, which in turn serve to concentrate energy. It would seem, according to this line of reasoning, that creative energy is being infused into the evolving universe from some outside source. Thus, there need be no conflict between evolutionary and creation theory.

Also, Hartshorne not only approaches the problem of evil by rethinking the traditional definition of God and affirming the role of human free will in the overall scheme of things, but he also suggests that there may be just as much difficulty explaining the presence of goodness in the universe as there is in explaining the reality of suffering. Moreover, he says, our conceptual and linguistic efforts to describe God can only be based on the highest and most praiseworhty characteristics we encounter in the world. Surely, sheer despotic power is not such a characteristic. Rather, only a God who loves, who is faithful, and who suffers with humanity is worthy of worship.

Before moving on to additional metaphysical perspectives, it may prove useful to consider how the theistic perspective would approach the case study set out at the beginning of this section. How does the very existence of Abby and Britty Hensel, as two persons in one body, relate to the question of the existence and nature of God? Does it count as evidence for or against God's existence and control over the universe? Is there a difference between how traditional theists, like Anselm and Aquinas, would approach this case and the way Hartshorne would do so? Are Abby and Britty examples of the "problem of evil"?

9

MATERIALISM

TITUS LUCRETIUS CARUS (96?–55? B.C.)

We know nothing certain about the life of Lucretius. St. Jerome, a hostile critic, declared that he had fits of madness, composed his poem during intervals of sanity, and killed himself in his forty-fourth year. This report, as George Santayana has remarked, must be taken with a large grain of salt. From Lucretius' book, we discover that he revered Epicurus, detested religious superstition, and delighted in the bounty of nature.

ON THE NATURE OF THE UNIVERSE

1. [Prayer to the Creative Force of Nature (Personified as Venus) to Inspire the Poet, to Bless His Patron Memmius, and to Bring Peace to the World.]

Mother of Aeneas and his race, delight of men and gods, life-giving Venus, it is your doing that under the wheeling constellations of the sky all nature teems with life, both the sea that buoys up our ships and the earth that yields our food. Through you all living creatures are conceived and come forth to look upon the sunlight. Before you the winds flee, and at your coming the clouds forsake the sky. For you the inventive earth flings up sweet flowers. For you the ocean levels laugh, the sky is calmed and glows with diffused radiance. When first the day puts on the aspect of spring, when in all its force the fertilizing breath of Zephyr is unleashed, then, great goddess, the birds of air give the first intimation of your entry; for yours is the power that has pierced them to the heart. Next the cattle run wild frisk through the lush pastures and swim the swift-flowing streams. Spell-bound by your charm, they follow your lead with fierce desire. So throughout seas and uplands, rushing torrents, verdurous meadows and the leafy shelters of the birds, into the breasts of one and all you instil alluring love, so that with passionate longing they reproduce their several breeds.

Since you alone are the guiding power of the universe and without you nothing emerges into the shining sunlit world to grow in joy and loveliness, yours is the partnership I seek in striving to compose these lines *On the Nature of the Universe* for my noble Memmius. For him, great goddess, you have willed outstanding excellence in every field and everlasting

From *On the Nature of the Universe* by Lucretius, trans. R. E. Latham, Harmondsworth, England: Penguin Classics, 1951. Copyright © 1951 by Ronald Latham. Reproduced by permission of Penguin Books Ltd.

fame. For his sake, therefore, endow my verse with everlasting charm.

Meanwhile, grant that this brutal business of war by sea and land may everywhere be lulled to rest. For you alone have power to bestow on mortals the blessing of quiet peace. In your bosom Mars himself, supreme commander in this brutal business, flings himself down at times, laid low by the irremediable wound of love. Gazing upward, his neck a prostrate column, he fixes hungry eyes on you, great goddess, and gluts them with love. As he lies outstretched, his breath hangs upon your lips. Stoop, then, goddess most glorious, and enfold him at rest in your hallowed bosom and whisper with those lips sweet words of prayer, beseeching for the people of Rome untroubled peace. In this evil hour of my country's history, I cannot pursue my task with a mind at ease, as an illustrious scion of the house of Memmius cannot at such a crisis withhold his service from the common well.

2. [Exhortation to Memmius to Listen to an Exhortation of "True Reason."]

For what is to follow, my Memmius, lay aside your cares and lend undistracted ears and an attentive mind to true reason. Do not scornfully reject, before you have understood them, the gifts I have marshalled for you with zealous devotion. I will set out to discourse to you on the ultimate realities of heaven and the gods. I will reveal those *atoms* from which nature creates all things and increases and feeds them and into which, when they perish, nature again resolves them. To these in my discourse I commonly give such names as the 'raw material,' or 'generative bodies' or 'seeds' of things. Or I may call them 'primary particles,' because they come first and everything else is composed of them.

3. [Praise of Epicurus for Delivering Mankind from Superstition.]

When human life lay groveling in all men's sight, crushed to the earth under the dead weight of superstition whose grim features loured menacingly upon mortals from the four quarters of the sky, a man of Greece was first to raise mortal eyes in defiance, first to stand erect and brave the challenge. Fables of the gods did not crush him, nor the lightning flash and the growling menace of the sky. Rather, they quickened his manhood, so that he, first of all men, longed to smash the constraining locks of nature's doors. The vital vigour of his mind prevailed. He ventured far out beyond the flaming ramparts of the world and voyaged in mind throughout infinity. Returning victorious, he proclaimed to us what can be and what cannot: how a limit is fixed to the power of everything and an immovable frontier post. Therefore superstition in its turn lies crushed beneath his feet, and we by his triumph are lifted level with the skies.

4. [Superstition, Its Cause and Cure.]

One thing that worries is the fear that you may fancy yourself embarking on an impious course, setting your feet on the path of sin. Far from it. More often it is this very superstition that is the mother of sinful and impious deeds. Remember how at Aulis the altar of the Virgin Goddess was foully stained with the blood of Iphigeneia by the leaders of the Greeks, the patterns of chivalry. The headband was bound about her virgin tresses and hung down evenly over both her cheeks. Suddenly she caught sight of her father standing sadly in front of the altar, the attendants beside him hiding the knife and her people bursting into tears when they saw her. Struck dumb with terror, she sank on her knees to the ground. Poor girl, at such a moment it did not help her that she had been first to give the name of father to a king. Raised by the hands of men, she was led trembling to the altar. Not for her the sacrament of marriage and the loud chant of Hymen. It was her fate in the very hour of marriage to fall a sinless victim to a sinful rite, slaughtered to her greater grief by a father's hand, so that a fleet might sail under happy auspices. Such are the heights of wickedness to which men are driven by superstition.

You yourself, if you surrender your judgement at any time to the blood-curdling declamations of the prophets, will want to desert our ranks. Only think what phantoms they can conjure up to overturn the tenor of your life and wreck your happiness with fear. And not without cause. For, if men saw that a term was set to their troubles, they would find strength in some way to withstand the hocus-pocus and intimidations of the prophets. As it is, they have no power of resistance, because they are haunted by the fear of eternal punishment after death. They know nothing of the nature of the spirit. Is it born, or is it implanted in us at birth? Does it perish with us, dissolved by death, or does it visit the murky depths and dreary sloughs of Hades? Or is it transplanted by divine power into other creatures, as described in the poems of our own Ennius, who first gathered on the delectable slopes of Helicon an evergreen garland destined to win renown among the nations of Italy? Ennius indeed in his immortal verses proclaims that there is also a Hell, which is peopled not by our actual spirits or bodies but only by shadowy images, ghastly pale. It is from this realm that he pictures the ghost of Homer, of unfading memory, as appearing to him, shedding salt tears and revealing the nature of the universe.

I must therefore give an account of celestial phenomena, explaining the movements of sun and moon and also the forces that determine events on earth. Next, and no less important, we must look with keen insight into the make-up of spirit and mind: we must consider those alarming phantasms that strike upon our minds when they are awake but disordered by sickness, or when they are buried in slumber, so that we seem to see and hear before us men whose dead bones lie in the embraces of earth.

I am well aware that it is not easy to elucidate in Latin verse the obscure discoveries of the Greeks. The poverty of our language and the novelty of the theme compel me often to coin new words for the purpose. But your merit and the joy I hope to derive from our delightful friendship encourage me to face any task however hard. This it is that leads me to stay awake through the quiet of the night, studying how by choice of words and the poet's art I can display before your mind a clear light by which you can gaze into the heart of hidden things.

5. [Nothing Is Ever Created Out of Nothing.]

This dread and darkness of the mind cannot be dispelled by the sunbeams, the shining shafts of day, but only by an understanding of the outward form and inner workings of nature. In tackling this theme, our starting-point will be this principle: *Nothing can ever be created by divine power out of nothing*. The reason why all mortals are so gripped by fear is that they see all sorts of things happening on the earth and in the sky with no discernible cause, and these they attribute to the will of a god. Accordingly, when we have seen that nothing can be created out of nothing, we shall then have a clearer picture of the path ahead, the problem of how things are created and occasioned without the aid of the gods.

First then, if things were made out of nothing, any species could spring from any source and nothing would require seed. Men could arise from the sea and scaly fish from the earth, and birds could be hatched out of the sky. Cattle and other domestic animals and every kind of wild beast, multiplying indiscriminately, would occupy cultivated and waste lands alike. The same fruits would not grow constantly on the same trees, but they would keep changing: any tree might bear any fruit. If each species were not composed of its own generative bodies, why should each be born always of the same kind of mother? Actually, since each is formed out of specific seeds, it is born and emerges into the sunlit world only from a place where there exists the right material, the right kind of atoms. This is why everything cannot be born of everything, but a specific power of generation inheres in specific objects.

Again, why do we see roses appear in spring, grain in summer's heat, grapes under the spell of autumn? Surely, because it is only after specific seeds have drifted together at their own proper time that every created thing stands revealed, when the season is favourable and the life-giving earth can safely deliver delicate growths into the sunlit world. If they were made out of nothing, they would spring up suddenly after varying lapses of time and at abnormal seasons, since there would of course be no primary bodies which could be prevented by the harshness of the season from entering into generative unions. Similarly, in order that things might grow, there would be no need of any lapse of time for the accumulation of seed. Tiny tots would turn suddenly into grown men, and trees would shoot up spontaneously out of the earth. But it is obvious that none of these things happens, since everything grows gradually, as is natural, from a specific seed and retains its specific character. It is a fair inference that each is increased and nourished by its own raw material.

Here is a further point. Without seasonable showers the earth cannot send up gladdening growths. Lacking food, animals cannot reproduce their kind or sustain life. This points to the conclusion that many elements are common to many things, as letters are to words, rather than to the theory that anything can come into existence without atoms.

Or again, why has not nature been able to produce men on such a scale that they could ford the ocean on foot or demolish high mountains with their hands or prolong their lives over many generations? Surely, because each thing requires for its birth a particular material which determines what can be produced. It must therefore be admitted that nothing can be made out of nothing, because everything must be generated from a seed before it can emerge into the unresisting air.

Lastly, we see that tilled plots are superior to untilled, and their fruits are improved by cultivation. This is because the earth contains certain atoms which we rouse to productivity by turning the fruitful clods with the ploughshare and stirring up the soil. But for these, you would see great improvements arising spontaneously without any aid from our labours.

6. [Nothing Is Ever Annihilated.]

The second great principle is this: *nature resolves everything into its component atoms and never reduces anything to nothing*. If anything were perishable in all its parts, anything might perish all of a sudden and vanish from sight. There would be no need of any force to separate its parts and loosen their links. In actual fact, since everything is composed of indestructible seeds, nature obviously does not allow anything to perish till it has encountered a force that shatters it with a blow or creeps into chinks and unknits it.

If the things that are banished from the scene by age are annihilated through the exhaustion of their material, from what source does Venus bring back the several races of animals into the light of life? And, when they are brought back, where does the inventive earth find for each the special food required for its sustenance and growth? From what fount is the sea replenished by its native springs and the streams that flow into it from afar? Whence does the ether draw nutriment for the stars? For everything consisting of a mortal body must have been exhausted by the long day of time, the illimitable past. If throughout this bygone eternity there have persisted bodies from which the universe has been perpetually renewed, they must certainly be possessed of immortality. Therefore things cannot be reduced to nothing.

Again, all objects would regularly be destroyed by the same force and the same cause, were it not that they are sustained by imperishable matter more or less tightly fastened together. Why, a mere touch would be enough to bring about destruction supposing there were no imperishable bodies whose union could be dissolved only by the appropriate force. Actually, because the fastenings of the atoms are of various kinds while their matter is imperishable, compound objects remain intact until one of them encounters a force that proves strong enough to break up its particular constitution. Therefore nothing returns to nothing, but everything is resolved into its constituent bodies.

Lastly, showers perish when father ether has flung them down into the lap of mother earth. But the crops spring up fresh and gay; the branches on the trees burst into leaf; the trees themselves grow and are weighed down with fruit. Hence in turn man and brute draw nourishment. Hence we see flourishing cities blest with children and every leafy thicket loud with new broods of songsters. Hence in lush pastures cattle wearied by their bulk fling down their bodies, and the white milky juice oozes from their swollen udders. Hence a new generation frolic friskily on wobbly legs through the fresh grass, their young minds tipsy with undiluted milk. Visible objects therefore do not perish utterly, since nature repairs one thing from another and allows nothing to be born without the aid of another's death.

7. [Matter Exists in the Form of Invisible Particles (Atoms).]

Well, Memmius, I have taught you that things cannot be created out of nothing nor, once born be summoned back to nothing. Perhaps, however, you are becoming mistrustful of my words, because these atoms of mine are not visible to the eye. Consider, therefore, this further evidence of *bodies whose existence you must acknowledge though they cannot be seen*. First, wind, when its force is roused, whips up waves, founders tall ships and scatters cloudrack. Sometimes scouring plains with hurricane force it strews them with huge trees and batters mountain peaks with blasts that hew down forests. Such is wind in its fury, when it whoops aloud with a mad menace in its shouting. Without question, therefore, there must be invisible particles of wind which sweep sea and land and the clouds in the sky, swooping upon them and whirling them along in a headlong hurricane. In the way they flow and the havoc they spread they are no different from a torrential flood of water when it rushes down in a sudden spate from the mountain heights, swollen by heavy rains, and heaps together wreckage from the forest and entire trees. Soft though it is by nature, the sudden shock of oncoming water is more than even stout bridges can withstand, so furious is the force with which the turgid, storm-flushed torrent surges against their piers. With a mighty roar it lays them low, rolling huge rocks under its waves and brushing aside every obstacle from its course. Such, therefore, must be the movement of blasts of wind also. When they have come surging along some course like a rushing river, they push obstacles before them and buffet them with repeated blows; and sometimes, eddying round and round, they snatch them up and carry them along in a swiftly circling vortex. Here then is proof upon proof that winds have invisible bodies, since in their actions and behaviour they are found to rival great rivers, whose bodies are plain to see.

Then again, we smell the various scents of things though we never see them approaching our nostrils. Similarly, heat and cold cannot be detected by our eyes, and we do not see sounds. Yet all these must be composed of bodies, since they are able to impinge upon our senses. For nothing can touch or be touched except body.

Again, clothes hung out on a surf-beaten shore grow moist. Spread in the sun they grow dry. But we do not see how the moisture has soaked into them, nor again how it has been dispelled by the heat. If follows that the moisture is split up into minute parts which the eye cannot possibly see.

Again, in the course of many annual revolutions of the sun a ring is worn thin next to the finger with continual rubbing. Dripping water hollows a stone. A curved ploughshare, iron though it is, dwindles imperceptibly in the furrow. We see the cobble-stones of the highway worn by the feet of many wayfarers. The bronze statues by the city gates show their right hands worn thin by the touch of travellers who have greeted them in passing. We see that all these are being diminished, since they are worn away. But to perceive what particles drop off at any particular time is a power grudged to us by our ungenerous sense of sight.

To sum up, whatever is added to things gradually by nature and the passage of days, causing a cumulative increase, eludes the most attentive scrutiny of our eyes. Conversely, you cannot see what objects lose by the wastage of age—sheer sea-cliffs, for instance, exposed to prolonged erosion by the mordant brine—or at what time the loss occurs. It follows that nature works through the agency of invisible bodies.

8. [Besides Matter, the Universe Contains Empty Space (Vacuity).]

On the other hand, things are not hemmed in by the pressure of solid bodies in a tight mass. This is because *there is vacuity in things*. A grasp of this fact will be helpful to you in many respects and will save you from much bewildered doubting and questioning about the universe and from mistrust of my teaching. Well then, by vacuity I mean intangible and empty space. If it did not exist, things could not move at all. For the distinctive action of matter, which is counteraction and obstruction, would be in force always and everywhere. Nothing could proceed, because nothing would give it a starting point by receding. As it is, we see with our own eyes at sea and on land and high up in the sky that all sorts of

things in all sorts of ways are on the move. If there were no empty space, these things would be denied the power of restless movement—or rather, they could not possibly have come into existence, embedded as they would have been in motionless matter.

Besides, there are clear indications that things that pass for solid are in fact porous. Even in rocks a trickle of water seeps through into caves, and copious drops ooze from every surface. Food percolates to every part of an animal's body. Trees grow and bring forth their fruit in season, because their food is distributed throughout their length from the tips of the roots through the trunk and along every branch. Noises pass through walls and fly into closed buildings. Freezing cold penetrates to the bones. If there were no vacancies through which the various bodies could make their way, none of these phenomena would be possible.

Again, why do we find some things outweigh others of equal volume? If there is as much matter in a ball of wool as in one of lead, it is natural that it should weigh as heavily, since it is the function of matter to press everything downwards, while it is the function of space on the other hand to remain weightless. Accordingly, when one thing is not less bulky than another but obviously lighter, it plainly declares that there is more vacuum in it, while the heavier object proclaims that there is more matter in it and much less empty space. We have therefore reached the goal of our diligent inquiry: there is in things an admixture of what we call vacuity.

In case you should be misled on this question by the idle imagining of certain theorists, I must anticipate their argument. They maintain that water yields and opens a penetrable path to scaly bodies of fish that push against it, because they leave spaces behind them into which the yielding water can flow together. In the same way, they suppose, other things can move by mutually changing places, although every place remains filled. This theory has been adopted utterly without warrant. For how can the fish advance till the water has given way? And how can the water retire when the fish cannot move? There are thus only two alternatives: either all bodies are devoid of movement, or you must admit that things contain an admixture of vacuity whereby each is enabled to make the first move.

Lastly, if two bodies suddenly spring apart from contact on a broad surface, all the intervening space must be void until it is occupied by air. However quickly the air rushes in all round, the entire space cannot be filled instantaneously. The air must occupy one spot after another until it has taken possession of the whole space. If anyone supposes that this consequence of such springing apart is made possible by the condensation of air, he is mistaken. For condensation implies that something that was full becomes empty, or *vice versā*. And I contend that air could not condense so as to produce this effect; or at any rate, if there were no vacuum, it could not thus shrink into itself and draw its parts together.

However many pleas you may advance to prolong the argument, you must end by admitting that there is vacuity in things. There are many other proofs I could add to the pile in order to strengthen conviction; but for an acute intelligence these small clues should suffice to enable you to discover the rest for yourself. As hounds that range the hills often smell out the lairs of wild beasts screened in thickets, when once they have got on to the right trail, so in such questions one thing will lead on to another, till you can succeed by yourself in tracking down the truth to its lurking-places and dragging it forth.

If you grow weary and relax from the chase, there is one thing, Memmius, that I can safely promise you: my honeyed tongue will pour from the treasury of my breast such generous draughts, drawn from inexhaustible springs, that I am afraid slow-plodding age may creep through my limbs and unbolt the bars of my life before the full flood of my arguments on any single point has flowed in verse through your ears.

9. [The Universe Consists of Matter (With Its Properties and Accidents) and of Vacuity and Nothing Else.]

To pick up the thread of my discourse, all nature as it is in itself consists of two things—bodies and the vacant space in which the bodies are situated and through which they move in different directions. The existence of bodies is vouched for by the agreement of the senses. If a belief resting directly on this foundation is not valid, there will be no standard to which we can refer any doubt on obscure questions for rational confirmation. If there were no place and space, which we call vacuity, these bodies could not be situated anywhere or move in any direction whatever. This I have just demonstrated. It remains to show that *nothing exists that is distinct both from body and from vacuity* and could be ranked with the others as a third substance. For whatever is must also be something. If it offers resistance to touch, however light and slight, it will increase the mass of body by such amount, great or small, as it may amount to, and will rank with it. If, on the other hand, it is intangible, so that it offers no resistance whatever to anything passing through it, then it will be that empty space which we call vacuity. Besides, whatever it may be in itself, either it will act in some way, or react to other things acting upon it, or else it will be such that things can be and happen in it. But without body nothing can act or react; and nothing can afford a place except emptiness and vacancy. Therefore, besides matter and vacuity, we cannot include in the number of things any third substance that can either affect our senses at any time or be grasped by the reasoning of our minds.

You will find that anything that can be named is either a property or an accident of these two. A *property* is something that cannot be detached or separated from a thing without destroying it, as weight is a property of rocks, heat of fire, fluidity of water, tangibility of all bodies, intangibility of vacuum. On the other hand, servitude and liberty, poverty and riches, war and peace, and all other things whose advent or departure leaves the essence of a thing intact, all these it is our practice to call by their appropriate name, *accidents.*

Similarly, time by itself does not exist; but from things themselves there results a sense of what has already taken place, what is now going on and what is to ensue. It must not be claimed that anyone can sense time by itself apart from the movement of things or their restful immobility.

Again, when men say it is a fact that Helen was ravished or the Trojans were conquered, do not let anyone drive you to the admission that any such event is independently of any object, on the ground that the generations of men of whom these events were accidents have been swept away by the irrevocable lapse of time. For we could put it that whatever has taken place is an accident of a particular tract of earth or of the space it occupied. If there had been no matter and no space or place in which things could happen, no spark of love kindled by the beauty of Tyndareus' daughter would ever have stolen into the breast of Phrygian Paris to light that dazzling blaze of pitiless war; no Wooden Horse, unmarked by the sons of Troy, would have set the towers of Ilium aflame through the midnight issue of Greeks from its womb. So you may see that events cannot be said to *be* by themselves like matter or in the same sense as space. Rather, you should describe them as accidents of matter, or of the place in which things happen.

10. [The Atoms Are Indestructible.]

Material objects are of two kinds, atoms and compounds of atoms. The atoms themselves cannot be swamped by any force, for they are preserved indefinitely by their absolute solidity. Admittedly, it is hard to believe that anything can exist that is absolutely solid. The lightning stroke from the sky penetrates closed buildings, as do shouts and other noises. Iron glows molten in the fire, and hot rocks are cracked by untempered scorching. Hard gold is softened and melted by heat; and bronze, ice-like, is liquefied by flame. Both heat and piercing cold seep through silver, since we feel both alike when a cooling shower of water is poured into a goblet that we hold ceremonially in our hands. All these facts point to the conclusion that nothing is really solid. But sound reasoning and nature itself drive us to the opposite conclusion. Pay attention, therefore, while I demonstrate in a few lines that there exist certain bodies that are absolutely solid and indestructible, namely those atoms which according to our teaching are the seeds or prime units of things from which the whole universe is built up.

In the first place, we have found that nature is twofold, consisting of two totally different things, matter and the space in which things happen. Hence each of these must exist by itself without admixture of the other. For, where there is empty space (what we call vacuity), there matter is not; where matter exists, there cannot be a vacuum. Therefore the prime units of matter are solid and free from vacuity.

Again, since composite things contain some vacuum, the surrounding matter must be solid. For you cannot reasonably maintain that anything can hide vacuity and hold it within its body unless you allow that the container itself is solid. And what contains the vacuum in things can only be an accumulation of matter. Hence matter, which possesses absolute solidity, can be everlasting when other things are decomposed.

Again, if there were no empty space, everything would be one solid mass; if there were not material objects with the property of filling the space they occupy, all existing space would be utterly void. It is clear, then, that there is an alternation of matter and vacuity, mutually distinct, since the whole is neither completely full nor completely empty. There are therefore solid bodies, causing the distinction between empty space and full. And these, as I have just shown, can be neither decomposed by blows from without nor invaded and unknit from within nor destroyed by any other form of assault. For it seems that a thing without vacuum can be neither knocked to bits nor snapped nor chopped in two by cutting; nor can it let in moisture or seeping cold or piercing fire, the universal agents of destruction. The more vacuum a thing contains within it, the more readily it yields to these assailants. Hence, if the units of matter are solid and without vacuity, as I have shown, they must be everlasting.

Yet again, if the matter in things had not been everlasting, everything by now would have gone back to nothing, and the things we see would be the product of rebirth out of nothing. But, since I have already shown that nothing can be created out of nothing nor any existing thing be summoned back to nothing, the atoms must be made of imperishable stuff into which everything can be resolved in the end, so that there may be a stock of matter for building the world anew. The atoms, therefore, are absolutely solid and unalloyed. In no other way could they have survived throughout infinite time to keep the world in being.

Furthermore, if nature had set no limit to the breaking of things, the particles of matter in the course of ages would have been ground so small that nothing could be generated from them so as to attain in the fullness of time to the summit of its growth. For we see that anything can be more speedily disintegrated than put together again. Hence, what the long day of time, the bygone eternity, has already shaken and loosened to fragments could never in the residue of time be reconstructed. As it is, there is evidently a limit set to breaking, since we see that everything is renewed and each according to its kind has a fixed period in which to grow to its prime.

Here is a further argument. Granted that the particles of matter are absolutely solid, we can still explain the composition and behaviour of soft things—air, water,

earth, fire—by their intermixture with empty space. On the other hand, supposing the atoms to be soft, we cannot account for the origin of hard flint and iron. For there would be no foundation for nature to build on. Therefore there must be bodies strong in their unalloyed solidity by whose closer clustering things can be knit together and display unyielding toughness.

If we suppose that there is no limit set to the breaking of matter, we must still admit that material objects consist of particles which throughout eternity have resisted the forces of destruction. To say that these are breakable does not square with the fact that they have survived throughout eternity under a perpetual bombardment of innumerable blows.

Again, there is laid down for each thing a specific limit to its growth and its tenure of life, and the laws of nature ordain what each can do and what it cannot. No species is ever changed, but each remains so much itself that every kind of bird displays on its body its own specific markings. This is a further proof that their bodies are composed of changeless matter. For, if the atoms could yield in any way to change, there would be no certainty as to what could arise and what could not, at what point the power of everything was limited by an immovable frontier-post; nor could successive generations so regularly repeat the nature, behaviour, habits and movements of their parents.

To proceed with our argument, there is an ultimate point in visible objects which represents the smallest thing that can be seen. So also there must be an ultimate point in objects that lie below the limit of perception by our senses. This point is without parts and is the smallest thing that can exist. It never has been and never will be able to exist by itself, but only as one primary part of something else. It is with a mass of such parts, solidly jammed together in order, that matter is filled up. Since they cannot exist by themselves, they must needs stick together in a mass from which they cannot by any means be pried loose. The atoms therefore are absolutely solid and unalloyed, consisting of a mass of least parts tightly packed together. They are not compounds formed by the coalescence of their parts, but bodies of absolute and everlasting solidity. To these nature allows no loss or diminution, but guards them as seeds for things. If there are no such least parts, even the smallest bodies will consist of an infinite number of parts, since they can always be halved and their halves halved again without limit. On this showing, what difference will there be between the whole universe and the very least of things? None at all. For, however endlessly infinite the universe may be, yet the smallest things will equally consist of an infinite number of parts. Since true reason cries out against this and denies that the mind can believe it, you must needs give in and admit that there are least parts which themselves are partless. Granted that these parts exist, you must needs admit that the atoms they compose are also solid and everlasting. But, if all things were compelled by all-creating nature to be broken up into these least parts, nature would lack the power to rebuild anything out of them. For partless objects cannot have the essential properties of generative matter—those varieties of attachment, weight, impetus, impact and movement on which everything depends. …

11. [Occasionally They Swerve Slightly from the Vertical.]

…There is another fact that I want you to grasp. *When the atoms are travelling straight down through empty space by their own weight, at quite indeterminate times and places they swerve ever so little from their course,* just so much that you can call it a change of direction. If it were not for this swerve, everything would fall downwards like rain-drops through the abyss of space. No collision would take place and no impact of atom on atom would be created. Thus nature would never have created anything.

If anyone supposes that heavier atoms on a straight course through empty space could outstrip lighter ones and fall on them from above, thus causing impacts that might give, rise to generative motions, he is going far astray from the path of truth. The reason why objects falling through water or thin air vary in speed according to their weight is simply that the matter composing water or air cannot obstruct all objects equally, but is forced to give way more speedily to heavier ones. But empty space can offer no resistance to any object in any quarter at any time, so as not to yield free passage as its own nature demands. Therefore, through undisturbed vacuum all bodies must travel at equal speed though impelled by unequal weights. The heavier will never be able to fall on the lighter from above or generate of themselves impacts leading to that variety of motions out of which nature can produce things. We are thus forced back to the conclusion that the atoms swerve a little—but only a very little, or we shall be caught imagining slantwise movements, and the facts will prove us wrong. For we see plainly and palpably that weights, when they come tumbling down, have no power of their own to move aslant, so far as meets the eye. But who can possibly perceive that they do not diverge in the very least from a vertical course?

Again, if all movement is always interconnected, the new arising from the old in a determinate order—if the atoms never swerve so as to originate some new movement that will snap the bonds of fate, the everlasting sequence of cause and effect—what is the source of the free will possessed by living things throughout the earth? What, I repeat, is the source of that will-power snatched from the fates, whereby we follow the path along which we are severally led by pleasure, swerving from our course at no set time or place but at the bidding of our own hearts? There is no doubt that on these occasions the will of the individual originates the movements that trickle through his limbs. Observe, when the starting barriers are flung back, how the racehorses in the eagerness of their strength cannot break away as suddenly as their hearts desire. For the whole supply of matter must first be mobilized throughout every member of the body: only then, when it is mustered in a continuous array, can it respond to the prompting of the heart. So you may see that the beginning of movement is generated by the heart; starting from the voluntary action of the mind, it is then transmitted throughout the body and the limbs. Quite different is our experience when we are shoved along by a blow inflicted with compulsive force by someone else. In that case it is obvious that all the matter of our body is set going and pushed along involuntarily, till a check is imposed through the limbs by the will. Do you see the difference? Although many men are driven by an external force and often constrained involuntarily to advance or to rush headlong, yet there is within the human breast something that can fight against this force and resist it. At its command the supply of matter is forced to take a new course through our limbs and joints or is checked in its course and brought once more to a halt. So also in the atoms you must recognize the same possibility: besides weight and impact there must be a third cause of movement, the source of this inborn power of ours, since we see that nothing can come out of nothing. For the weight of an atom prevents its movements from being completely determined by the impact of other atoms. But the fact that the mind itself has no internal necessity to determine its every act and compel it to suffer in helpless passivity—this is due to the slight swerve of the atoms at no determinate time or place. ...

14. [And of Sentience.]

At this stage you must admit that whatever is seen to be sentient is nevertheless composed of atoms that are insentient. The phenomena open to our observation do not contradict this conclusion or conflict with it.

Rather, they lead us by the hand and compel us to believe that the animate is born, as I maintain, of the insentient.

As a particular instance, we can point to living worms, emerging from foul dung when the earth is soaked and rotted by intemperate showers. Besides, we see every sort of substance transformed in the same way. Rivers, foliage and lush pastures are transformed into cattle; the substance of cattle is transformed into our bodies; and often enough our bodies go to build up the strength of predatory beasts or the bodies of the lords of the air. So nature transforms all foods into living bodies and generates from them all the senses of animate creatures, just as it makes dry wood blossom out in flame and transfigures it wholly into fire. So now do you see that it makes a great difference in what order the various atoms are arranged and with what others they are combined so as to impart and take over motions?

What is it, then, that jogs the mind itself and moves and compels it to express certain sentiments, so that you do not believe that the sentient is generated by the insentient? Obviously it is the fact that a mixture of water and wood and earth cannot of itself bring about vital sensibility. There is one relevant point you should bear in mind: I am not maintaining that sensations are generated automatically from all the elements out of which sentient things are created. Everything depends on the size and shape of the sense-producing atoms and on their appropriate motions, arrangements and positions. None of these is found in wood or clods. And yet these substances, when they are fairly well rotted by showers, give birth to little worms, because the particles of matter are jolted out of their old arrangements by a new factor and combined in such a way that animate objects must result.

Again, those who would have it that sensation can be produced only by sensitive bodies, which originate in their turn from others similarly sentient—these theorists are making the foundations of our senses perishable, because they are making them soft. For sensitivity is always associated with flesh, sinews, veins—all things that we see to be soft and composed of perishable stuff.

Let us suppose, for argument's sake, that particles of these substances could endure everlastingly. The sensation with which they are credited must be either that of a part or else similar to that of an animate being as a whole. But it is impossible for parts by themselves to experience sensation: all the sensations felt in our limbs are felt by us as a whole; a hand or any other member severed from the whole body is quite powerless to retain sensation on its own. There remains the alternative that such particles have senses like those of an animate being as a whole. They must then feel precisely what we feel, so as to share in all our vital sensations. How then can they pass for elements and escape the path of death, since they are animate beings, and animate and mortal are one and the same thing? Even supposing they could escape death, yet they will make nothing by their combination and conjunction but a mob or horde of living things, just as men and cattle and wild beasts obviously could not combine so as to give birth to a single thing. If we suppose that they shed their own sentience from their bodies and acquire another one, what is the point of giving them the one that is taken away? Besides, as we saw before, from the fact that we perceive eggs turning into live fledgelings and worms swarming out when the earth has been rotted by intemperate showers, we may infer that sense can be generated from the insentient.

Suppose someone asserts that sense can indeed emerge from the insentient, but only by some transformation or some creative process comparable to birth. He will be adequately answered by a clear demonstration that birth and transformation occur only as the result of union or combination. Admittedly sensation cannot arise in any body until an animate creature has been born. This of course is because the requisite matter is dispersed through air and streams and earth and the products of earth: it has not come together in the appropriate manner, so as to set in mutual operation those vitalizing motions that kindle the all-watchful senses which keep watch over every animate creature.

When any animate creature is suddenly assailed by a more powerful blow than its nature can withstand, all the senses of body and mind are promptly thrown into confusion. For the juxtapositions of the atoms are unknit, and the vitalizing motions are inwardly obstructed, until the matter, jarred and jolted throughout every limb, loosens the vital knots of the spirit from the body and expels the spirit in scattered particles through every pore. What other effect can we attribute to the infliction of a blow than this of shaking and shattering everything to bits? Besides, it often happens, when the blow is less violently inflicted, that such vitalizing motions as survive emerge victorious; they assuage the immense upheavals resulting from the shock, recall every particle to its own proper courses, break up the lethal motion when it is all but master of the body and rekindle the well-nigh extinguished senses. How else could living creatures on the very threshold of death rally their consciousness and return to life rather than make good their departure by a route on which they have already travelled most of the way?

Again, pain occurs when particles of matter have been unsettled by some force within the living flesh of the limbs and stagger in their inmost stations. When they slip back into place, that is blissful pleasure. It follows that the atoms cannot be afflicted by any pain or experience any pleasure in themselves, since they are not composed of any primal particles, by some reversal of whose movements they might suffer anguish or reap some fruition of vitalizing bliss. They cannot therefore be endowed with any power of sensation.

Again, if we are to account for the power of sensation possessed by animate creatures in general by attributing sentience to their atoms, what of those atoms that specifically compose the human race? Presumably they are not merely sentient, but also shake their sides with uproarious guffaws and besprinkle their cheeks with dewy teardrops and even discourse profoundly and at length about the composition of the universe and proceed to ask of what elements they are themselves composed. If they are to be likened to entire mortals, they must certainly consist of other elemental particles, and these again of others. There is no point at which you may call a halt, but I will follow you there with your argument that whatever speaks or laughs or thinks is composed of particles that do the same. Let us acknowledge that this is stark madness and lunacy: one can laugh without being composed of laughing particles, can think and proffer learned arguments though sprung from seeds neither thoughtful nor eloquent. Why then cannot the things that we see gifted with sensation be compounded of seeds that are wholly senseless?

Lastly, we are all sprung from heavenly seed. All alike have the same father, from whom all-nourishing mother earth receives the showering drops of moisture. Thus fertilized, she gives birth to smiling crops and lusty trees, to mankind and all the breeds of beasts. She it is that yields the food on which they all feed their bodies, lead their joyous lives and renew their race. So she has well earned the name of mother. In like manner this matter returns: what came from earth goes back into the earth; what was sent down from the ethereal vault is readmitted to the precincts of heaven. Death does not put an end to things by annihilating the component particles but by breaking up their conjunction. Then it links them in new combinations, making everything change in shape and colour and give up in an instant its acquired gift of sensation. So you may realize what a difference it makes in what combinations and positions the same elements occur, and what motions they mutually pass on and take over. You will thus avoid

the mistake of conceiving as permanent properties of the atoms the qualities that are seen floating on the surface of things, coming into being from time to time and as suddenly perishing. Obviously it makes a great difference in these verses of mine in what context and order the letters are arranged. If not all, at least the greater part is alike. But differences in their position distinguish word from word. Just so with actual objects: when there is a change in the combination, motion, order, position or shapes of the component matter, there must be a corresponding change in the object composed. . . .

15. [Mind and Spirit Were Born and Will Die.]

A tree cannot exist high in air, or clouds in the depths of the sea, as fish cannot live in the fields, or blood flow in wood or sap in stones. There is a determined and allotted place for the growth and presence of everything. So mind cannot arise alone without body or apart from sinews and blood. If it could do this, then surely it could much more readily function in head or shoulders or the tips of the heels and be born in any other part, so long as it was held in the same container, that is to say in the same man. Since, however, even in the human body we see a determined and allotted place set aside for the growth and presence of spirit and mind, we have even stronger grounds for denying that they could survive or come to birth outside the body altogether. You must admit, therefore, that when the body has perished there is an end also of the spirit diffused through it. It is surely crazy to couple a mortal object with an eternal and suppose that they can work in harmony and mutually interact. What can be imagined more incongruous, what more repugnant and discordant, than that a mortal object and one that is immortal and everlasting should unite to form a compound and jointly weather the storms that rage about them?

Again, there can be only three kinds of everlasting objects. The first, owing to the absolute solidity of their substance, can repel blows and let nothing penetrate them so as to unknit their close texture from within. Such are the atoms of matter, whose nature I have already demonstrated. The second kind can last for ever because it is immune from blows. Such is empty space, which remains untouched and unaffected by any impact. Last is that which has no available place surrounding it into which its matter can disperse and disintegrate. It is for this reason that the sum total of the universe is everlasting, having no space outside it into which the matter can escape and no matter that can enter and disintegrate it by the force of impact.

Equally vain is the suggestion that the spirit is immortal because it is shielded by life-preserving powers; or because it is unassailed by forces hostile to its survival; or because such forces, if they threaten, are somehow arrested before we are conscious of the threat. Apart from the spirit's participation in the ailments of the body, it has maladies enough of its own. The prospect of the future torments it with fear and wearies it with worry, and past misdeeds leave the sting of remorse. Lastly, it may fall a prey to the mind's own specific afflictions, madness and amnesia, and plunge into the black waters of oblivion.

From all this it follows that *death is nothing to us* and no concern of ours, since our tenure of the mind is mortal. In days of old, we felt no disquiet when the hosts of Carthage poured in to battle on every side—when the whole earth, dizzied by the convulsive shock of war, reeled sickeningly under the high ethereal vault, and between realm and realm the empire of mankind by land and sea trembled in the balance. So, when we shall be no more—when the union of body and spirit that engenders us has been disrupted—to us, who shall then be nothing, nothing by any hazard will happen any more at all. Nothing will have power to stir our senses, not though earth be fused with sea and sea with sky. ...

COMMENT

Ancient and Modern Materialism

Although Lucretius wrote his poem more than two thousand years ago, his vision of a materialistic universe remains as fresh and vivid as ever. This may seem strange to a reader familiar with the history of ideas. Have not science and the naturalistic philosophy based on it undergone an immense revolution since the time of Lucretius? Even the more modern materialism of Thomas Hobbes and Julien La Mettrie appears quaint and archaic in the light of recent science and philosophy. We can no longer conceive of matter in the form of tiny indivisible particles, like the motes of dust that we see dancing about in a shaft of sunlight. The atomic theory has been transplanted from metaphysical speculation to experimental research, and the resulting discoveries have radically transformed it.

Few people would not question the existence of atoms, but the atoms are no longer conceived as inert, eternal, and indivisible particles moving in a featureless void. Instead of being inert, they are made up of electrical charges, which behave like waves. Instead of being eternal, they emit radiations and are subject to splittings and fusions. Instead of being indivisible, they can be analyzed into electrons, protons, neutrons, mesons, positrons, and so on. Instead of moving in a void, they are enmeshed in electromagnetic fields within curved space-time.

These modern concepts of radiation, fission, quanta, waves, fields, and relativity are a far cry from Lucretius.

Yet the naturalistic temper of his philosophy as distinguished from the arcane details of his science remains as up to date as ever. Nothing in modern physics contradicts his vision of all things arising from and returning to a material base. The view of the world that some philosophers prefer to call naturalism rather than materialism remains as plausible as ever. This is the view that the universe as revealed in the physical sciences is primary and fundamental in the nature of things.

Can Materialism Explain Perceptual Appearances?

Extreme materialism tries to explain every process in terms of matter and motion quantitatively described. "Primary qualities," which are abstract and measurable, are conceived to be more ultimate or objective, whereas "secondary qualities," which are concrete and unmeasurable, are regarded as more derivative or subjective. This distinction was first clearly stated by Democritus: "There are two kinds of knowledge: real knowledge and obscure knowledge. To obscure knowledge belong all things of sight, sound, odor, taste, and touch; real knowledge is distinct from this.... Sweet and bitter, heat and cold, and color, are only opinions; there is nothing true but atoms and the void."[1] For Democritus, the only objective properties of things are size, shape, weight, and motion. All other qualities, such as sound, color, odor, taste, and touch, are sensations in us caused by the motions and arrangements of the atoms.

This theory was revived by Galileo and was reformulated by Hobbes, Locke, Newton, and other influential modern thinkers. It has figured very prominently in modern theories of perception. Warmth, for example, is explained as the reaction of our sense organs and nervous systems to molecular motions; sound, as our reaction to air waves; color, as our reaction to electromagnetic vibrations. Thus the "secondary qualities"—colors, sound, odors, and so on—exist, as such, only for our minds. In the absence of our mental reactions, the universe is a pretty dull and abstract affair—a collection of soundless, colorless, and odorless particles, in various arrangements, drifting through space and time.

Lucretius, departing from the views of Democritus, had a different theory. He agreed that the atoms individually are without any of the secondary qualities but maintained that these qualities spring into existence when the atoms are combined in certain ways. "The first-bodies," he tells us, are not only "bereft ... of color, they are also sundered altogether from warmth and cold, and fiery heat, and are carried along barren of sound and devoid of taste, nor do they give off any scent of their own from their body." However, these qualities *are* properties of compounds, formed by combinations of atoms. The compounds, being new and different entities, have color, sound, odor, taste, and heat, none of which can

---

[1] *The Way of Philosophy*, trans. Philip Wheelwright (New York: Odyssey Press, 1954), p. 162.

belong to the atoms as individual particles. When we perceive these secondary qualities we are grasping real objective properties, for the complex body perceived by our senses is as real as the atoms.

Whatever interpretation is adopted, whether that of Democritus, Lucretius, or a modern materialist, is subject to all the difficulties discussed by Bertrand Russell in Chapter 4. The qualities of perception belong to appearances ("sense–data"), which depend at least in part on the reactions of the sentient organism. To profess to know what is behind the sensory appearances is to leap into conjecture. Russell indicates just how conjectural this leap is.

Even if we accept the conclusions drawn from modern physical science, the electrons, protons, neutrons, mesons, positrons, and other abstract entities, with their fields of force and curved space-time environment, are very unlike human perceptions. To what extent are the appearances verifiable? To what extent are the *inferences* from these appearances also verifiable? To what extent are the appearances merely reactions in us? To what extent are they like "things" in the real external world? These are questions that should not be answered without reviewing the difficulties pointed out by Russell.

Can Materialism Explain Life?

Can a materialist account for the differences between animate and inanimate things?

Extreme materialists will not admit any such fundamental cleavage. Plant and animal activity, they will maintain, is reducible simply to physical and chemical forces exactly like those found in inorganic bodies. Living things are composed exclusively of substances that may also be found in nonliving things, and there are no teleological or vitalistic forces that explain life. In opposition to this point of view, "vitalists" such as Henri Bergson maintain that life is distinct and fundamentally different from nonlife.

Vitalism is not as plausible as it was earlier in this century. We are now aware of intermediate forms such as viruses that cannot be easily classified as either organic or inorganic. There are chemical substances that grow and multiply—they behave in some ways as if they were alive and in other ways as if they were not. Even machines display marks of behavior that were hitherto regarded as characteristic of living things only. It has become increasingly difficult to differentiate between the behavior of living and lifeless things.

More plausible than a sharp and everlasting dualism of the inorganic and the organic is the doctrine of emergence. This is the theory that life and mind evolve out of the nonliving and the nonmental. Lucretius can be called a believer in emergence. He pointed out that men can speak and laugh and think, whereas it would be absurd to attribute these capacities to atoms. A human organism, made up of innumerable atoms, has vital characteristics, which the atoms taken singly do not possess. Just as the meaning of a sentence results from the combinations of meaningless letters, so life and mind result from the meetings and configurations of lifeless and mindless atoms. Applied to evolution, this theory means the recognition of diverse levels of complexity and organization, each with its emergent qualities, and the interpretation of these levels as successive stages in an evolutionary process. We associate this type of theory with such modern philosophers as Samuel Alexander (1859–1938), but it was maintained by Lucretius two thousand years ago.

Its implications are, in the wide sense of the word, "materialistic." Mind, it declares, arises out of matter and is a function of complex material bodies. "Out of dust man arises and to dust will he return." Vital processes, including thought, cannot survive the dissolution of the body any more than a football game can continue after the disbanding of the opposing teams.

The type of materialism called *epiphenomenalism* admits that there are mental processes but regards them as mere ineffectual by-products of physical processes. The only causal relations are between physical events and other physical events, or between physical antecedents and mental consequents. Our thoughts and feelings are caused by molecular changes in the brain or other physical processes and have no causal efficacy of their own. The mind has as little to do with the movement of the body as the shadow cast by a locomotive has to do with the racing of the locomotive.

Lucretius is not consistent enough to be called an epiphenomenalist, but for the most part he clings to a materialistic interpretation of the *causes* of mental events. He maintains, for example, that all knowledge is derived from sensations caused by the impact on the mind-atoms of surface-films emanating from external physical objects. However, he departs from epiphenomenalism with its extreme mechanistic implications in his theory of "swerving" atoms and concomitant free will.

Consideration of these alternative theories—vitalism, emergence, and epiphenomenalism—will provide ample ground for discussion.

Can Materialism Explain Mind?

Can a materialist account for mental characteristics?

The most extreme kind of materialism, exemplified by some radical mechanists and behaviorists, is the virtual denial that we have minds at all. Since we are all aware that there are mental processes, such as reasoning, willing, feeling, perceiving, remembering, and imagining, we need not argue the point.

More sensible than the denial that human beings experience mental processes is the contention that machines can, in a sense "think." Since World War II there has been an amazing development of "electronic brains" or "thinking machines." They can perform lightning computations of the most complex kind—they can play chess, prove theorems, translate from one language to another, and guide rockets through interplanetary space. These astounding performances have reinforced the contention that the human mind is just a very complicated mechanism. In his article "Computing Machines and Intelligence," A. M. Turing argues that technicians will eventually be able to create machines with artificial intelligence so sophisticated that it cannot, under certain conditions (for example, "the imitation game"), be distinguished from human intelligence. Turing contends that we should then concede that machines can think.

An opponent would object that we cannot determine whether a machine can think by the mere observation of outputs, however cleverly they might simulate human behavior. It is not simply *what* the machine does but *how* it does it that must be considered. If by thought one means *conscious* deliberations and initiatives, the machine does not think.

Every conscious human being is aware of his or her own mental life—the sensations, feelings of pleasure and pain, hopes and dreams and fancies, loves and hates, plans and purposes. No machine has such an "inner life" or any self-conscious awareness. As Wladyslaw Sluckin, who is both a psychologist and an engineer, has written:

> Machines do not form their purposes in the manner of human beings, the purposes of machines are decided for them by their inventors or operators. It would be absurd to praise or blame a machine for results of its operations other than in a metaphorical way. Machines have no ethical sentiments and no effective attitudes. In no situation are machines expected to pass moral judgement. The question as to whether machines could possibly exhibit purpose in this sense of the word is nonsensical because it does not appear in any way feasible to describe robot behavior in terms which ascribe to it morality.[2]

---

[2] *Minds and Machines*, rev. ed. (Baltimore: Penguin Books, 1960), p. 213.

10

IDEALISM

GEORGE BERKELEY (1685–1753)

George Berkeley was born in Kilkenny County, Ireland. His parents, having a comfortable income, gave him a good education at Kilkenny School and Trinity College, Dublin. While scarcely more than a boy, he began to fill notebooks with original philosophical reflections. His first major publication, *An Essay Toward a New Theory of Vision,* appeared when he was twenty-four, and *Principles of Human Knowledge,* which set forth his whole idealistic philosophy, was published only a year later. Finding that his ideas were ridiculed, if not neglected, he reformulated his argument in *Three Dialogues Between Hylas and Philonous,* which appeared in 1713. Thus, by the time he was twenty-eight, he had published his three major works, remarkable both for the felicity of their style and for the daring and profundity of their thought.

During this period of his greatest literary activity, Berkeley was a fellow and tutor at Trinity College, but he spent the next years after publishing his *Dialogues* in London, France, and Italy. In London he became a friend of Alexander Pope, Richard Steele, Joseph Addison, and Jonathan Swift. Subsequently he traveled in Europe as secretary and chaplain to an earl and tutor to a bishop's son. While in Sicily, he lost the manuscript of the second part of *The Principles of Human Knowledge* and never had the heart to rewrite it.

Returning to Ireland, he was appointed lecturer in Greek and theology at Trinity College and eventually an ecclesiastical dean (1724). Shortly thereafter, to his immense surprise, he inherited three thousand pounds from Hester Van Homrigh (Swift's former friend "Vanessa"), a lady whom he had met once and then only casually.

At about the same time, he conceived the project of founding a college in the Bermudas for training missionaries to the Indians and clergy for the American colonists. By his eloquence and personal charm, he was able to obtain a considerable sum to finance his project from private donors and the promise of twenty thousand pounds from the House of Commons. With a new wife, he set sail for America in 1728. However, Robert Walpole, the prime minister, refused to fulfill the promise of Parliament, and Berkeley remained for three years at Newport, Rhode Island, his hopes gradually diminishing. Finally, in 1731, despairing of further aid and saddened by the death of an infant daughter, he sailed with his wife and tiny son back to England.

His later life was spent as bishop of Cloyne and head of a growing family. He divided his time between ecclesiastical duties, philosophical studies, agitation for social reform, and family affairs. His main publication in these years was *Siris* (1744), a rather odd work in which he extolled the medicinal virtues of tar-water and expounded an idealistic interpretation of the universe. In the final year of his life, Berkeley and his family moved to Oxford, where, "suddenly and without the least previous notice or pain," he died in 1753.

MIND AND ITS OBJECTS

The First Dialogue

Philonous. Good morning, Hylas: I did not expect to find you abroad so early.

Hylas. It is indeed something unusual; but my thoughts were so taken up with a subject I was discoursing of last night, that finding I could not sleep, I resolved to rise and take a turn in the garden.

Philonous. It happened well, to let you see what innocent and agreeable pleasures you lose every morning. Can there be a pleasanter time of the day, or a more delightful season of the year? That purple sky, those wild but sweet notes of birds, the fragrant bloom upon the trees and flowers, the gentle influence of the rising sun, these and a thousand nameless beauties of nature inspire the soul with secret transports; its faculties too being at this time fresh and lively, are fit for these meditations, which the solitude of a garden and tranquillity of the morning naturally dispose us to. But I am afraid I interrupt your thoughts: for you seemed very intent on something.

Hylas. It is true, I was, and shall be obliged to you if you will permit me to go in the same vein; not that I would by any

means deprive myself of your company, for my thoughts always flow more easily in conversation with a friend, than when I am alone: but my request is, that you would suffer me to impart my reflections to you.

Philonous. With all my heart, it is what I should have requested myself if you had not prevented me.

Hylas. I was considering the odd fate of those men who have in all ages, through an affectation of being distinguished from the vulgar, or some unaccountable turn of thought, pretended either to believe nothing at all, or to believe the most extravagant things in the world. This however might be borne, if their paradoxes and scepticism did not draw after them some consequences of general disadvantage to mankind. But the mischief lieth here; that when men of less leisure see them who are supposed to have spent their whole time in the pursuits of knowledge professing an entire ignorance of all things, or advancing such notions as are repugnant to plain and commonly received principles, they will be tempted to entertain suspicions concerning the most important truths, which they had hitherto held sacred and unquestionable.

Philonous. I entirely agree with you, as to the ill tendency of the affected doubts

London, 1713. Second unchanged edition, 1725. Third edition, 1734. The present text is that of A. Campbell Fraser, *The Works of George Berkeley,* (Oxford: Clarendon Press, 1871). (With omissions.)

of some philosophers, and fantastical conceits of others. . . .

Hylas. I am glad to find there was nothing in the accounts I heard of you.

Philonous. Pray, what were those?

Hylas. You were represented in last night's conversation, as one who maintained the most extravagant opinion that ever entered into the mind of man, to wit, that there is no such thing as *material substance* in the world.

Philonous. That there is no such thing as what Philosophers call *material substance,* I am seriously persuaded: but, if I were made to see anything absurd or sceptical in this, I should then have the same reason to renounce this that I imagine I have now to reject the contrary opinion.

Hylas. What! can anything be more fantastical, more repugnant to common sense, or a more manifest piece of Scepticism, than to believe there is no such thing as *matter?*

Philonous. Softly, good *Hylas.* What if it should prove, that you, who hold there is, are, by virtue of that opinion, a greater sceptic, and maintain more paradoxes and repugnances to common sense, than I who believe no such thing?

Hylas. You may as soon persuade me, the part is greater than the whole, as that, in order to avoid absurdity and Scepticism, I should ever be obliged to give up my opinion in this point.

Philonous. Well then, are you content to admit that opinion for true, which, upon examination, shall appear most agreeable to common sense, and remote from Scepticism?

Hylas. With all my heart. Since you are for raising disputes about the plainest

things in nature, I am content for once to hear what you have to say. . . .

Philonous. Shall we therefore examine which of us it is that denies the reality of sensible things, or professes the greatest ignorance of them; since, if I take you rightly, he is to be esteemed the greatest sceptic?

Hylas. That is what I desire.

Philonous. What mean you by Sensible Things?

Hylas. Those things which are perceived by the senses. Can you imagine that I mean anything else?

Philonous. Pardon me, *Hylas,* if I am desirous clearly to apprehend your notions, since this may much shorten our inquiry. Suffer me then to ask you this further question. Are those things only perceived by the senses which are perceived immediately? Or, may those things properly be said to be *sensible* which are perceived mediately, or not without the intervention of others?

Hylas. I do not sufficiently understand you.

Philonous. In reading a book, what I immediately perceive are the letters, but mediately, or by means of these, are suggested to my mind the notions of God, virtue, truth, &c. Now, that the letters are truly sensible things, or perceived by sense, there is no doubt: but I would know whether you take the things suggested by them to be so too.

Hylas. No, certainly; it were absurd to think *God or virtue* sensible things, though they may be signified and suggested to the mind by sensible marks, with which they have an arbitrary connection.

Philonous. It seems then, that by *sensible* things you mean those only which can be perceived *immediately* by sense?

Hylas. Right.

Philonous. Doth it not follow from this, that though I see one part of the sky red, and another blue, and that my reason doth thence evidently conclude there must be some cause of that diversity of colors, yet that cause cannot be said to be a sensible thing, or perceived by the sense of seeing?

Hylas. It doth.

Philonous. In like manner, though I hear variety of sounds, yet I cannot be said to hear the causes of those sounds?

Hylas. You cannot.

Philonous. And when by my touch I perceive a thing to be hot and heavy, I cannot say, with any truth or propriety, that I feel the cause of its heat or weight?

Hylas. To prevent any more questions of this kind, I tell you once for all, that by *sensible things* I mean those only which are perceived by sense, and that in truth the senses perceive nothing which they do not perceive immediately: for they make no inferences. The deducing therefore of causes or occasions from effects and appearances, which alone are perceived by sense, entirely relates to reason.

Philonous. This point then is agreed between us—that *sensible things are those only which are immediately perceived by sense.* You will further inform me, whether we immediately perceive by sight anything beside light, and colors, and figures; or by hearing, anything but sounds; by the palate, anything beside tastes; by the smell, beside odors; or by the touch, more than tangible qualities.

Hylas. We do not.

Philonous. It seems, therefore, that if you take away all sensible qualities, there remains nothing sensible?

Hylas. I grant it.

Philonous. Sensible things therefore are nothing else but so many sensible qualities, or combinations of sensible qualities?

Hylas. Nothing else.

Philonous. Heat is then a sensible thing?

Hylas. Certainly.

Philonous. Doth the reality of sensible things consist in being perceived? or, is it something distinct from their being perceived, and that bears no relation to the mind?

Hylas. To *exist* is one thing, and to be *perceived* is another.

Philonous. I speak with regard to sensible things only: and of these I ask, whether by their real existence you mean a subsistence exterior to the mind, and distinct from their being perceived?

Hylas. I mean a real absolute being, distinct from, and without any relation to their being perceived.

Philonous. Heat therefore, if it be allowed a real being, must exist without the mind?

Hylas. It must.

Philonous. Tell me, *Hylas,* is this real existence equally compatible to all degrees of heat, which we perceive; or is there any reason why we should attribute it to some, and deny it to others? and if there be, pray let me know that reason.

Hylas. Whatever degree of heat we perceive by sense, we may be sure the same exists in the object that occasions it.

Philonous. What! the greatest as well as the least?

Hylas. I tell you, the reason is plainly the same in respect of both: they are both perceived by sense; nay, the greater degree of heat is more sensibly perceived; and consequently, if there is any difference, we are more certain of its real existence than we can be of the reality of a lesser degree.

Philonous. But is not the most vehement and intense degree of heat a very great pain?

Hylas. No one can deny it.

Philonous. And is any unperceiving thing capable of pain or pleasure?

Hylas. No certainly.

Philonous. Is your material substance a senseless being, or a being endowed with sense and perception?

Hylas. It is senseless without doubt.

Philonous. It cannot therefore be the subject of pain?

Hylas. By no means.

Philonous. Nor consequently of the greatest heat perceived by sense, since you acknowledge this to be no small pain?

Hylas. I grant it.

Philonous. What shall we say then of your external object; is it a material Substance, or no?

Hylas. It is a material substance with the sensible qualities inhering in it.

Philonous. How then can a great heat exist in it, since you own it cannot in a material substance? I desire you would clear this point.

Hylas. Hold, *Philonous*, I fear I was out in yielding intense heat to be a pain. It should seem rather, that pain is something distinct from heat, and the consequence or effect of it.

Philonous. Upon putting your hand near the fire, do you perceive one simple uniform sensation, or two distinct sensations?

Hylas. But one simple sensation.

Philonous. Is not the heat immediately perceived?

Hylas. It is.

Philonous. And the pain?

Hylas. True.

Philonous. Seeing therefore they are both immediately perceived at the same time, and the fire affects you only with one simple, or uncompounded idea, it follows that this simple idea is both the intense heat immediately perceived, and the pain; and, consequently, that the intense heat immediately perceived, is nothing distinct from a particular sort of pain.

Hylas. It seems so.

Philonous. Again, try in your thoughts, *Hylas,* if you can conceive a vehement sensation to be without pain or pleasure.

Hylas. I cannot.

Philonous. Or can you frame to yourself an idea of sensible pain or pleasure, in general, abstracted from every particular idea of heat, cold, tastes, smells? etc.

Hylas. I do not find that I can.

Philonous. Doth it not therefore follow, that sensible pain is nothing distinct from those sensations or ideas—in an intense degree?

Hylas. It is undeniable; and, to speak the truth, I begin to suspect a very great heat cannot exist but in a mind perceiving it.

Philonous. What! are you then in that *sceptical* state of suspense, between affirming and denying?

Hylas. I think I may be positive in the point. A very violent and painful heat cannot exist without the mind.

Philonous. It hath not therefore, according to you, any real being?

Hylas. I own it.

Philonous. Is it therefore certain, that there is no body in nature really hot?

Hylas. I have not denied there is any real heat in bodies. I only say, there is no such thing as an intense real heat.

Philonous. But, did you not say before that all degrees of heat were equally real; or, if there was any difference, that the greater were more undoubtedly real than the lesser?

Hylas. True: but it was because I did not then consider the ground there is for distinguishing between them, which I now plainly see. And it is this:— because intense heat is nothing else but a particular kind of painful sensation; and pain cannot exist but in a perceiving being; it follows that no intense heat can really exist in an unperceiving corporeal substance. But this is no reason why we should deny heat in an inferior degree to exist in such a substance.

Philonous. But how shall we be able to discern those degrees of heat which exist only in the mind from those which exist without it?

Hylas. That is no difficult matter. You know the least pain cannot exist unperceived; whatever, therefore, degree of heat is a pain exists only in the mind. But, as for all other degrees of heat, nothing obliges us to think the same of them.

Philonous. I think you granted before that no unperceiving being was capable of pleasure, any more than of pain.

Hylas. I did.

Philonous. And is not warmth, or a more gentle degree of heat than what causes uneasiness, a pleasure?

Hylas. What then?

Philonous. Consequently, it cannot exist without the mind in an unperceiving substance, or body.

Hylas. So it seems.

Philonous. Since, therefore, as well those degrees of heat that are not painful, as those that are, can exist only in a thinking substance; may we not conclude that external bodies are absolutely incapable of any degree of heat whatsoever?

Hylas. On second thoughts, I do not think it so evident that warmth is a pleasure, as that a great degree of heat is a pain.

Philonous. I do not pretend that warmth is as great a pleasure as heat is a pain. But, if you grant it to be even a small pleasure, it serves to make good my conclusion.

Hylas. I could rather call it an *indolence*. It seems to be nothing more than a privation of both pain and pleasure. And that such a quality or state as this may agree to an unthinking substance, I hope you will not deny.

Philonous. If you are resolved to maintain that warmth, or a gentle degree of heat, is no pleasure, I know not how to convince you otherwise, than by appealing to your own sense. But what think you of cold?

Hylas. The same that I do of heat. An intense degree of cold is a pain; for to feel a very great cold, is to perceive a great uneasiness: it cannot therefore exist without the mind; but a lesser degree of cold may, as well as a lesser degree of heat.

Philonous. Those bodies, therefore, upon whose application to our own, we perceive a moderate degree of heat, must be concluded to have a moderate degree of heat or warmth in them; and those, upon whose application we feel a like degree of cold, must be thought to have cold in them.

Hylas. They must.

Philonous. Can any doctrine be true that necessarily leads a man into an absurdity?

Hylas. Without doubt it cannot.

Philonous. Is it not an absurdity to think that the same thing should be at the same time both cold and warm?

Hylas. It is.

Philonous. Suppose now one of your hands hot, and the other cold, and that they are both at once put into the same vessel of water, in an intermediate state; will not the water seem cold to one hand, and warm to the other?

Hylas. It will.

Philonous. Ought we not therefore, by our principles, to conclude it is really both cold and warm at the same time, that is, according to your own concession to believe an absurdity?

Hylas. I confess it seems so.

Philonous. Consequently, the principles themselves are false, since you have granted that no true principle leads to an absurdity.

Hylas. But, after all, can anything be more absurd than to say, *there is no heat in the fire?*

Philonous. To make the point still clearer; tell me whether, in two cases exactly alike, we ought not to make the same judgment?

Hylas. We ought.

Philonous. When a pin pricks your finger, doth it not rend and divide the fibers of your flesh?

Hylas. It doth.

Philonous. And when a coal burns your finger, doth it any more?

Hylas. It doth not.

Philonous. Since, therefore, you neither judge the sensation itself occasioned by the pin, nor anything like it to be in the pin; you should not, conformably to what you have now granted, judge the sensation occasioned by the fire, or anything like it, to be in the fire.

Hylas. Well, since it must be so, I am content to yield this point, and acknowledge that heat and cold are only sensations existing in our minds. But there still remain qualities enough to secure the reality of external things.

Philonous. But what will you say, *Hylas,* if it shall appear that the case is the same with regard to all other sensible qualities, and that they can no more be supposed to exist without the mind, than heat and cold?

Hylas. Then indeed you will have done something to the purpose; but that is what I despair of seeing proved.

Philonous. Let us examine them in order. What think you of _tastes_—do they exist without the mind, or no?

Hylas. Can any man in his senses doubt whether sugar is sweet, or wormwood bitter?

Philonous. Inform me, *Hylas.* Is a sweet taste a particular kind of pleasure or pleasant sensation, or is it not?

Hylas. It is.

Philonous. And is not bitterness some kind of uneasiness or pain?

Hylas. I grant it.

Philonous. If therefore sugar and wormwood are unthinking corporeal substances existing without the mind, how can sweetness and bitterness, that is, pleasure and pain, agree to them?

Hylas. Hold *Philonous,* I now see what it was deluded me all this time. You asked whether heat and cold, sweetness and bitterness, were not particular sorts of pleasure and pain; to which I answered simply, that they were. Whereas I should have thus distinguished:—those qualities, as perceived by us, are pleasures or pains; but not as existing in the external objects. We must not therefore conclude absolutely, that there is no heat in the fire, or sweetness in the sugar, but only that heat or sweetness, as perceived by us, are not in the fire or sugar. What say you to this?

Philonous. I say it is nothing to the purpose. Our discourse proceeded altogether concerning sensible things, which you define to be, *the things we only immediately perceive by our senses.* Whatever other qualities, therefore, you speak of, as distinct from these, I know nothing of them, neither do they at all belong to the point in dispute. You may, indeed, pretend to have discovered certain qualities which you do not perceive, and assert those insensible qualities exist in fire and sugar. But what use can be made of this to your present purpose, I am at a loss to conceive. Tell me then once more, do you acknowledge that heat and cold, sweetness and bitterness

(meaning those qualities which are perceived by the senses), do not exist without the mind? . . .

Hylas. I frankly own, *Philonous,* that it is in vain to stand out any longer. Colors, sounds, tastes, in a word all those termed *secondary qualities,* have certainly no existence without the mind. But, by this acknowledgment I must not be supposed to derogate anything from the reality of Matter or external objects; seeing it is no more than several philosophers maintain, who nevertheless are the farthest imaginable from denying Matter. For the clearer understanding of this, you must know sensible qualities are by philosophers divided into *primary* and *secondary.* The former are Extension, Figure, Solidity, Gravity, Motion, and Rest. And these they hold exist really in bodies. The latter are those above enumerated; or, briefly, all sensible qualities beside the Primary, which they assert are only so many sensations or ideas existing nowhere but in the mind. But all this, I doubt not, you are apprised of. For my part, I have been a long time sensible there was such an opinion current among philosophers, but was never thoroughly convinced of its truth until now.

Philonous. You are still then of opinion that *extension* and *figures* are inherent in external unthinking substances?

Hylas. I am.

Philonous. But what if the same arguments which are brought against Secondary Qualities will hold good against these also?

Hylas. Why then I shall be obliged to think, they too exist only in the mind.

Philonous. Is it your opinion the very figure and extension which you perceive by sense exist in the outward object or material substance?

Hylas. It is.

Philonous. Have all other animals as good grounds to think the same of the figure and extension which they see and feel?

Hylas. Without doubt, if they have any thought at all.

Philonous. Answer me, *Hylas*. Think you the senses were bestowed upon all animals for their preservation and well-being in life? or were they given to men alone for this end?

Hylas. I make no question but they have the same use in all other animals.

Philonous. If so, is it not necessary they should be enabled by them to perceive their own limbs, and those bodies which are capable of harming them?

Hylas. Certainly.

Philonous. A mite therefore must be supposed to see his own foot, and things equal or even less than it, as bodies of some considerable dimension; though at the same time they appear to you scarce discernible, or at best as so many visible points?

Hylas. I cannot deny it.

Philonous. And to creatures less than the mite they will seem yet larger?

Hylas. They will.

Philonous. Insomuch that what you can hardly discern will to another extremely minute animal appear as some huge mountain?

Hylas. All this I grant.

Philonous. Can one and the same thing be at the same time in itself of different dimensions?

Hylas. That were absurd to imagine.

Philonous. But, from what you have laid down it follows that both the extension by you perceived, and that perceived by the mite itself, as likewise all those perceived by lesser animals, are each of them the true extension of the mite's foot; that is to say, by your own principles you are led into an absurdity.

Hylas. There seems to be some difficulty in the point.

Philonous. Again, have you not acknowledged that no real inherent property of any object can be changed without some change in the thing itself?

Hylas. I have.

Philonous. But, as we approach to or recede from an object, the visible extension varies, being at one distance ten or a hundred times greater than at another. Doth it not therefore follow from hence likewise that it is not really inherent in the object?

Hylas. I own I am at a loss what to think.

Philonous. Your judgement will soon be determined, if you will venture to think as freely concerning this quality as you have done concerning the rest. Was it not admitted as a good argument, that neither heat nor cold was in the water, because it seemed warm to one hand and cold to the other?

Hylas. It was.

Philonous. Is it not the very same reasoning to conclude there is no extension or figure in an object, because to one eye it shall seem little, smooth, and round, when at the same time it appears to the other, great, uneven, and angular?

Hylas. The very same. But does this latter fact ever happen?

Philonous. You may at any time make the experiment, by looking with one eye bare, and with the other through a microscope.

Hylas. I know not how to maintain it, and yet I am loath to give up *extension*, I see so many odd consequences following upon such a concession.

Philonous. Odd, say you? After the concessions already made, I hope you will stick at nothing for its oddness. But, on the other hand, should it not seem very odd, if the general reasoning which includes all other sensible qualities did not also include extension? If it be allowed that no idea nor anything like an idea can exist in an unperceiving substance, then surely it follows that no figure or mode of extension, which we can either perceive or imagine, or have any idea of, can be really inherent in Matter; not to mention the peculiar difficulty there must be in conceiving a material substance, prior to and distinct from extension, to be the *substratum* of extension. Be the sensible quality what it will—figure, or sound, or color; it seems alike impossible it should subsist in that which doth not perceive it.

Hylas. I give up the point for the present, reserving still a right to retract my opinion, in case I shall hereafter discover any false step in my progress to it.

Philonous. That is a right you cannot be denied. Figures and extensions being dispatched, we proceed next to *motion*. *Can* a real motion in any external body be at the same time both very swift and very slow?

Hylas. It cannot.

Philonous. Is not the motion of a body swift in a reciprocal proportion to the time it takes up in describing any given space? Thus a body that describes a mile in an hour moves three times faster than it would in case it described only a mile in three hours.

Hylas. I agree with you.

Philonous. And is not time measured by the succession of ideas in our minds?

Hylas. It is.

Philonous. And is it not possible ideas should succeed one another twice as fast in your mind as they do in mine, or in that of some spirit of another kind?

Hylas. I own it.

Philonous. Consequently, the same body may to another seem to perform its motion over any space in half the time that it doth to you. And the same reasoning will hold as to any other proportion: that is to say, according to your principles (since the motions perceived are both really in the object) it is possible one and the same body shall be really moved the same way at once, both very swift and very slow. How is this consistent either with common sense, or with what you just now granted?

Hylas. I have nothing to say to it.

Philonous. Then as for *solidity;* either you do not mean any sensible quality by that word, and so it is beside our inquiry: or if you do, it must be either hardness or resistance. But both the one and the other are plainly relative to our senses: it being evident that what seems hard to one animal may appear soft to another, who hath greater force and firmness of limbs. Nor is it less plain that the resistance I feel is not in the body.

Hylas. I own the very sensation of resistance, which is all you immediately perceive, is not in the *body*, but the cause of that sensation is.

Philonous. But the causes of our sensations are not things immediately perceived, and therefore not sensible. This point I thought had been already determined.

Hylas. I own it was; but you will pardon me if I seem a little embarrassed: I know not how to quit my old notions.

Philonous. To help you out, do but consider that if *extension* be once acknowledged to have no existence without the mind, the same must necessarily be granted of motion, solidity, and gravity—since they all evidently suppose extension. It is therefore superfluous to inquire particularly concerning each of them. In denying extension, you have denied them all to have any real existence.…

Hylas. It is just come into my head, *Philonous*, that I have somewhere heard of a distinction between absolute and sensible extension. Now, though it be acknowledged that *great* and *small*, consisting merely in the relation which other extended beings have to the parts of our own bodies do not really inhere in the Substances themselves; yet nothing obliges us to hold the same with regard to *absolute extension,* which is something abstracted from *great* and *small,* from this or that particular magnitude or figure. So likewise as to motion; *swift* and *slow* are altogether relative to the succession of ideas in our own minds. But, it doth not follow, because those modifications of motion exist not without the mind, that therefore absolute motion abstracted from them doth not.

Philonous. Pray what is it that distinguishes one motion, or one part of extension, from another? Is it not something sensible, as some degree of swiftness or slowness, some certain magnitude or figure peculiar to each?

Hylas. I think so.

Philonous. These qualities, therefore, stripped of all sensible properties, are without all specific and numerical differences, as the schools call them.

Hylas. They are.

Philonous. That is to say, they are extension in general, and motion in general.

Hylas. Let it be so.

Philonous. But it is a universally received maxim that *Everything which exists is particular.* How then can motion in general, or extension in general, exist in any corporeal Substance?

Hylas. I will take time to solve your difficulty.

Philonous. But I think the point may be speedily decided. Without doubt you can tell whether you are able to frame this or that idea. Now I am content to put our dispute on this issue. If you can frame in your thoughts a distinct abstract idea of motion or extension; divested of all those sensible modes, as swift and slow, great and small, round and square, and the like, which are acknowledged to exist only in the mind, I will then yield the point you contend for. But, if you cannot, it will be unreasonable on your side to insist any longer upon what you have no notion of.

Hylas. To confess ingenuously, I cannot.

Philonous. Can you even separate the ideas of extension and motion from the ideas of all those qualities which they who make the distinction term *secondary?*

Hylas. What! is it not an easy matter to consider extension and motion by themselves, abstracted from all other sensible qualities? Pray how do the mathematicians treat of them?

Philonous. I acknowledge, *Hylas,* it is not difficult to form general propositions and reasonings about those qualities, without mentioning any other; and, in this sense, to consider or treat of them abstractedly. But, how doth it follow that, because I can pronounce the word *motion* by itself, I can form the idea of it in my mind exclusive of body? Or, because theorems may be made of extension and figures, without any mention of *great* or *small*, or any other sensible mode or quality, that therefore it is possible such an abstract idea of extension, without any particular size or figure, or sensible quality, should be distinctly formed, and apprehended by the mind? Mathematicians treat of quantity, without regarding what other sensible qualities it is attended with, as being altogether indifferent to their demonstrations. But when laying aside the words, they contemplate the bare ideas, I believe you will find, they are not the pure abstracted ideas of extension.

Hylas. But what say you to *pure intellect?* May not abstracted ideas be framed by that faculty?

Philonous. Since I cannot frame abstract ideas at all, it is plain I cannot frame them by the help of *pure intellect;* whatsoever faculty you understand by those words. Besides, not to inquire into the nature of pure intellect and its spiritual objects, as *virtue, reason, God,* or the like, thus much seems manifest, that sensible things are only to be perceived by sense, or represented by the imagination. Figures, therefore, and extension, being originally perceived by sense, do not belong to pure intellect: but, for your further satisfaction, try if you can frame the idea of any figure, abstracted from all particularities of size, or even from other sensible qualities.

Hylas. Let me think a little.... I do not find that I can.

Philonous. And can you think it possible that should really exist in nature which

implies a repugnancy in its conception?

Hylas. By no means.

Philonous. Since therefore it is impossible even for the mind to disunite the ideas of extension and motion from all other sensible qualities, doth it not follow, that where the one exist there necessarily the other exist likewise?

Hylas. It should seem so.

Philonous. Consequently, the very same arguments which you admitted as conclusive against the Secondary Qualities are, without any further application of force, against the Primary too. Besides, if you will trust your senses, is it not plain all sensible qualities coexist, or to them appear as being in the same place? Do they ever represent a motion, or figure, as being divested of all other visible and tangible qualities?

Hylas. You need say no more on this head. I am free to own, if there be no secret error to oversight in our proceedings hitherto, that all sensible qualities are alike to be denied existence without the mind. But, my fear is that I have been too liberal in my former concessions, or overlooked some fallacy or other. In short, I did not take time to think.

Philonous. For that matter, *Hylas,* you may take what time you please in reviewing the progress of our inquiry. You are at liberty to recover any slips you might have made, or offer whatever you have omitted which makes for your first opinion.

Hylas. One great oversight I take to be this—that I did not sufficiently distinguish the *object* from the *sensation.* Now, though this latter may not exist without the mind, yet it will not thence follow that the former cannot.

Philonous. What object do you mean? The object of the senses?

Hylas. The same.

Philonous. It is then immediately perceived?

Hylas. Right.

Philonous. Make me to understand the difference between what is immediately perceived, and a sensation.

Hylas. The sensation I take to be an act of the mind perceiving; besides which, there is something perceived; and this I call the *object*. For example, there is red and yellow on that tulip. But then the act of perceiving those colors, is in me only, and not in the tulip.

Philonous. What tulip do you speak of? Is it that which you see?

Hylas. The same.

Philonous. And what do you see beside color, figure, and extension?

Hylas. Nothing.

Philonous. What you would say then is that the red and yellow are coexistent with the extension, is it not?

Hylas. That is not all; I would say they have a real existence without the mind, in some unthinking substance.

Philonous. That the colors are really in the tulip which I see is manifest. Neither can it be denied that this tulip may exist independent of your mind or mine; but, that any immediate object of the senses—that is, any idea, or combination of ideas—should exist in an unthinking substance, or exterior to all minds, is in itself an evident contradiction. Nor can I imagine how this follows from what you said just now, to wit, that the red and yellow were on the tulip *you saw,* since you do not pretend to *see* that unthinking substance. . . .

Hylas. Pray what think you of this? It is just come into my head that the ground of all our mistake lies in your treating of each quality by itself. Now, I grant that each quality cannot singly subsist without the mind. Color cannot without extension, neither can figure without some other sensible quality. But, as the several qualities united or blended together form entire sensible things, nothing hinders why such things may not be supposed to exist without the mind.

Philonous. Either, *Hylas,* you are jesting, or have a very bad memory. Though indeed we went through all the qualities by name one after another, yet my arguments, or rather your concessions, nowhere tended to prove that the Secondary Qualities did not subsist each alone by itself; but, that they were not *at all* without the mind. Indeed, in treating of figure and motion we concluded they could not exist without the mind, because it was impossible even in thought to separate them from all secondary qualities, so as to conceive them existing by themselves. But then this was not the only argument made use of upon that occasion. But (to pass by all that hath been hitherto said, and reckon it for nothing, if you will have it so) I am content to put the whole upon this issue. If you can conceive it possible for any mixture or combination of qualities, or any sensible object whatever, to exist without the mind, then I will grant it actually to be so.

Hylas. If it comes to that the point will soon be decided. What more easy than to conceive a tree or house existing by itself, independent of, and unperceived by, any mind whatsover? I do at this present time conceive them existing after that manner.

Philonous. How say you, *Hylas*, can you see a thing which is at the same time unseen?

Hylas. No, that were a contradiction.

Philonous. Is it not as great a contradiction to talk of *conceiving* a thing which is *unconceived?*

Hylas. It is.

Philonous. The tree or house therefore which you think of is conceived by you?

Hylas. How should it be otherwise?

Philonous. And what is conceived is surely in the mind?

Hylas. Without question, that which is conceived is in the mind.

Philonous. How then came you to say, you conceived a house or tree existing independent and out of all minds whatsoever?

Hylas. That was I own an oversight; but stay, let me consider what led me into it.—It is a pleasant mistake enough. As I was thinking of a tree in a solitary place where no one was present to see it, methought that was to conceive a tree as existing unperceived or unthought of—not considering that I myself conceived it all the while. But now I plainly see that all I can do is to frame ideas in my own mind. I may indeed conceive in my own thoughts the idea of a tree, or a house, or a mountain, but that is all. And this is far from proving that I can conceive them existing *out of the minds of all Spirits*.

Philonous. You acknowledge then that you cannot possibly conceive how any one corporeal sensible thing should exist otherwise than in a mind? ...

Hylas. To speak the truth, *Philonous*, I think there are two kinds of objects:— the one perceived immediately, which are likewise called *ideas;* the other are real things or external objects, perceived by the mediation of ideas, which are their images and representations. Now, I own ideas do not exist without the mind; but the latter sort of objects do. I am sorry I did not think of this distinction sooner; it would probably have cut short your discourse.

Philonous. Are those external objects perceived by sense, or by some other faculty?

Hylas. They are perceived by sense.

Philonous. How! is there anything perceived by sense which is not immediately perceived?

Hylas. Yes, *Philonous*, in some sort there is. For example, when I look on a picture or statue of Julius Caesar, I may be said after a manner to perceive him (though not immediately) by my senses.

Philonous. It seems then you will have our ideas, which alone are immediately perceived, to be pictures of external things: and that these also are perceived by sense, inasmuch as they have a conformity or resemblance to our ideas?

Hylas. That is my meaning.

Philonous. And, in the same way that Julius Caesar, in himself invisible, is nevertheless perceived by sight; real things, in themselves imperceptible, are perceived by sense.

Hylas. In the very same.

Philonous. Tell me, *Hylas*, when you behold the picture of Julius Caesar, do you see with your eyes any more than some colors and figures, with a certain symmetry and composition of the whole?

Hylas. Nothing else.

Philonous. And would not a man who had never known anything of Julius Caesar see as much?

Hylas. He would.

Philonous. Consequently he hath his sight, and the use of it, in as perfect a degree as you?

Hylas. I agree with you.

Philonous. Whence comes it then that your thoughts are directed to the Roman emperor, and his are not? This cannot proceed from the sensations or ideas of sense by you then perceived; since you acknowledge you have no advantage over him in that respect. It should seem therefore to proceed from reason and memory: should it not?

Hylas. It should.

Philonous. Consequently, it will not follow from that instance that anything is perceived by sense which is not immediately perceived. Though I grant we may, in one acceptation, be said to perceive sensible things mediately by sense—that is, when, from a frequently perceived connection, the immediate perception of ideas by one sense suggest to the mind others, perhaps belonging to another sense, which are wont to be connected with them. For instance, when I hear a coach drive along the streets, immediately I perceive only the sound; but, from the experience I have had that such a sound is connected with a coach, I am said to hear the coach. It is nevertheless evident that, in truth and strictness, nothing can be *heard* but *sound;* and the coach is not then properly perceived by sense, but suggested from experience. So likewise when we are said to see a red-hot bar of iron; the solidity and heat of the iron are not the objects of sight, but suggested to the imagination by the color and figure which are properly perceived by that sense. In short, those things alone are actually and strictly perceived by any sense, which would have been perceived in case that same sense had then been first conferred on us. As for other things, it is plain they are only suggested to the mind by experience, grounded on former perceptions. But, to return to your comparison of Caesar's picture, it is plain, if you keep to that, you must hold the real things or archetypes of our ideas are not perceived by sense, but by some internal faculty of the soul, as reason or memory. I would therefore fain know what arguments you can draw from reason for the existence of what you call *real things* or *material objects,* or, whether you remember to have seen them formerly as they are in themselves; or, if you have heard or read of any one that did.

Hylas. I see, *Philonous,* you are disposed to raillery; but that will never convince me.

Philonous. My aim is only to learn from you the way to come at the knowledge of *material beings.* Whatever we perceive is perceived immediately or mediately: by sense; or by reason and reflection. But, as you have excluded sense, pray show me what reason you have to believe their existence; or what *medium* you can possibly make use of to prove it, either to mine or your own understanding.

Hylas. To deal ingenuously, *Philonous,* now I consider the point, I do not find I can give you any good reason for it. But, thus much seems pretty plain, that it is at least possible such things may really exist. And, as long as there is no absurdity in supposing them, I am resolved to believe as I did, till you bring good reasons to the contrary.

Philonous. What! is it come to this, that you only believe the existence of material objects, and that your belief is founded barely on the possibility of its being true? Then you will have me bring reasons against it: though another would think it reasonable the proof should lie on him who holds the affirmative. And, after all, this very point which you are now resolved to maintain, without any reason, is in effect what you have more than once during this discourse seen good reason to give up. But, to pass over all this; if I understand you rightly, you say our ideas do not exist without the mind; but that they are copies, images, or representations, of certain originals that do?

Hylas. You take me right.

Philonous. They are then like external things?

Hylas. They are.

Philonous. Have those things a stable and permanent nature, independent of our senses; or are they in a perpetual change, upon our producing any motions in our bodies, suspending, exerting, or altering, our faculties or organs of sense?

Hylas. Real things, it is plain, have a fixed and real nature, which remains the same notwithstanding any change in our senses, or in the posture and motion of our bodies; which indeed may affect the ideas in our minds, but it were absurd to think they had the same effect on things existing without the mind.

Philonous. How then is it possible that things perpetually fleeting and variable as our ideas should be copies or images of anything fixed and constant? Or, in other words, since all sensible qualities, as size, figure, colour, etc., that is, our ideas, are continually changing upon every alteration in the distance, medium, or instruments of sensation; how can any determinate material objects be properly represented or painted forth by several distinct things, each of which is so different from and unlike the rest? Or, if you say it resembles some one only of our ideas, how shall we be able to distinguish the true copy from all the false ones?

Hylas. I profess, *Philonous,* I am at a loss. I know not what to say to this.

Philonous. But neither is this all. Which are material objects in themselves— perceptible or imperceptible.

Hylas. Properly and immediately nothing can be perceived but ideas. All material things, therefore, are in themselves insensible, and to be perceived only by our ideas.

Philonous. Ideas then are sensible, and their archetypes or originals insensible?

Hylas. Right.

Philonous. But how can that which is sensible be like that which is insensible? Can a real thing, in itself *invisible,* be like a *colour;* or a real thing, which is not *audible,* be like a *sound?* In a word, can anything be like a sensation or idea, but another sensation or idea?

Hylas. I must own, I think not.

Philonous. Is it possible there should be any doubt on the point? Do you not perfectly know your own ideas?

Hylas. I know them perfectly; since what I do not perceive or know can be no part of my idea.

Philonous. Consider, therefore, and examine them, and then tell me if there be anything in them which can exist without the mind? or if you can conceive anything like them existing without the mind?

Hylas. Upon inquiry, I find it is impossible for me to conceive or understand how anything but an idea can be like an idea. And it is most evident that *no idea can exist without the mind.*

Philonous. You are therefore, by our principles, forced to deny the reality of sensible things; since you made it to consist in an absolute existence exterior to the mind. That is to say, you are a downright sceptic. So I have gained my point, which was to show your principles led to Scepticism.

Hylas. For the present I am, if not entirely convinced, at least silenced. . . .

The Second Dialogue

Hylas. I beg your pardon, *Philonous,* for not meeting you sooner. All this morning my head was so filled with our late conversation that I had not leisure to think of the time of the day, or indeed of anything else.

Philonous. I am glad you were so intent upon it, in hopes if there were any mistakes in your concessions, or fallacies in my reasonings from them, you will now discover them to me. . . .

Hylas. I own there is a great deal in what you say. Nor can any one be more entirely satisfied of the truth of those odd consequences, so long as I have in view the reasonings that lead to them. But, when these are out of my thoughts, there seems, on the other hand, something so satisfactory, so natural and intelligible, in the modern way of explaining things that, I profess, I know not how to reject it.

Philonous. I know not what way you mean.

Hylas. I mean the way of accounting for our sensations or ideas.

Philonous. How is that?

Hylas. It is supposed the soul makes her residence in some part of the brain, from which the nerves take their rise, and are thence extended to all parts of the body; and that outward objects, by the different impressions they make on the organs of sense, communicate certain vibrative motions to the nerves; and these being filled with spirits propagate them to the brain or seat of the soul, which, according to the various impressions or traces thereby made in the brain, is variously affected with ideas.

Philonous. And call you this an explication of the manner whereby we are effected with ideas?

Hylas. Why not, *Philonous;* have you anything to object against it?

Philonous. I would first know whether I rightly understand your hypothesis. You make certain traces in the brain to be the causes or occasions of our ideas. Pray tell me whether by the *brain* you mean any sensible thing.

Hylas. What else think you I could mean?

Philonous. Sensible things are all immediately perceivable; and those things which are immediately perceivable are ideas; and these exist only in the mind. This much you have, if I mistake not, long since agreed to.

Hylas. I do not deny it.

Philonous. The brain therefore you speak of, being a sensible thing, exists only in the mind. Now, I would fain know whether you think it reasonable to suppose that one idea or thing existing in the mind occasions all other ideas. And, if you think so, pray how do you account for the origin of that primary idea or brain itself?

Hylas. I do not explain the origin of our ideas by that brain which is perceivable to sense, this being itself only a combination of sensible ideas, but by another which I imagine.

Philonous. But are not things imagined as truly *in the mind* as things perceived?

Hylas. I must confess they are.

Philonous. It comes, therefore, to the same thing; and you have been all this while accounting for ideas by certain motions or impressions of the brain, that is, by some alterations in an idea, whether sensible or imaginable it matters not.

Hylas. I begin to suspect my hypothesis.

Philonous. Besides spirits, all that we know or conceive are our own ideas. When, therefore, you say all ideas are occasioned by impressions in the brain, do you conceive this brain or no? If you do, then you talk of ideas imprinted in an idea causing that same idea, which is absurd. If you do not conceive it, you talk unintelligibly, instead of forming a reasonable hypothesis.

Hylas. I now clearly see it was a mere dream. There is nothing in it.

Philonous. You need not be much concerned at it; for after all, this way of explaining things, as you called it, could never have satisfied any reasonable man. What connection is there between a motion in the nerves, and the sensations of sound or colour in the mind? Or how is it possible these should be the effect of that?

Hylas. But I could never think it had so little in it as now it seems to have.

Philonous. Well then, are you at length satisfied that no sensible things have a real existence; and that you are in truth an arrant *sceptic?*

Hylas. It is too plain to be denied.

Philonous. Look! are not the fields covered with a delightful verdure? Is there not something in the woods and groves, in the rivers and clear springs, that soothes, that delights, that transports the soul? At the prospect of the wide and deep ocean, or some huge mountain whose top is lost in the clouds, or of an old gloomy forest, are not our minds filled with a pleasing horror? Even in rocks and deserts is there not an agreeable wildness? How sincere a pleasure is it to behold the natural beauties of the earth! To preserve and renew our relish for them, is not the veil of night alternately drawn over her face, and doth she not change her dress with the seasons? How aptly are the elements disposed! What variety and use in the meanest productions of nature! What delicacy, what beauty, what contrivance, in animal and vegetable bodies! How exquisitely are all things suited, as well to their particular ends, as to constitute opposite parts of the whole! And, while they mutually aid and support, do they not also set off and illustrate each other? Raise now your thoughts from this ball of earth to all those glorious luminaries that adorn the high arch of heaven. The motion and situation of the planets, are they not admirable for use and order? Were those (miscalled *erratic*) globes ever known to stray, in their repeated journeys through the pathless void? Do they not measure areas round the sun ever proportioned to the times? So fixed, so immutable are the laws by which the unseen Author of nature actuates the universe. How vivid and radiant is the luster of the fixed stars! How magnificent and rich that negligent profusion with which they appear to be scattered throughout the whole azure vault! Yet, if you take the telescope, it brings into your sight a new host of stars that escape the naked eye. Here they seem contiguous and minute, but to a nearer view immense orbs of light at various distances, far sunk in the abyss of space. Now you must call imagination to your aid. The feeble narrow sense cannot descry innumerable worlds revolving round the central fires; and in those worlds the energy of an all-perfect Mind displayed in endless forms. But, neither sense nor imagination are big enough to comprehend the boundless extent, with all its glittering furniture. Though the laboring mind exert and strain each power to its utmost reach, there still stands out ungrasped a surplusage immeasurable. Yet all the vast bodies that compose this mighty frame, how distant and remote soever, are by some secret mechanism, some divine art and force, linked in a mutual dependence and intercourse with each other, even with this earth, which was almost slipped from my thoughts and lost in the crowd of worlds. Is not the whole system immense, beautiful, glorious beyond expression and beyond thought! What treatment, then, do those philosophers deserve, who would deprive these noble and delightful scenes of all reality? How should those Principles be entertained that lead us to think all the visible beauty of the creation a false imaginary glare? To be plain, can you expect this Scepticism of yours will not be thought extravagantly absured by all men of sense?

Hylas. Other men may think as they please; but for your part you have nothing to reproach me with. My comfort is, you are as much a sceptic as I am.

Philonous. There, *Hylas,* I must beg leave to differ from you.

Hylas. What! have you all along agreed to the premises, and do you now deny the conclusion, and leave me to maintain those paradoxes by myself which you led me into? This surely is not fair.

Philonous. I deny that I agreed with you in those notions that led to Scepticism. You indeed said the *reality* of sensible things consisted in an *absolute existence* out of the minds of spirits, or distinct from their being perceived. And, pursuant to this notion of reality, you are obliged to deny sensible things any real *existence:* that is, according to your own definition, you profess yourself a sceptic. But I neither said nor thought the reality of sensible things was to be defined after that manner. To me it is evident, for the reasons you allow of, that sensible things cannot exist otherwise than in a mind or spirit. Whence I conclude, not that they have no real existence, but that, seeing they depend not on my thought, and have an existence distinct from being perceived by me, *there must be some other mind wherein they exist.* As sure, therefore, as the sensible world really exists, so sure is there an infinite omnipresent Spirit, who contains and supports it.

Hylas. What! this is no more than I and all Christians hold, nay and all others too who believe there is a God, and that He knows and comprehends all things.

Philonous. Aye, but here lies the difference. Men commonly believe that all things are known or perceived by God, because they believe the being of a God; whereas I, on the other side, immediately and necessarily conclude the being of a God, because all sensible things must be perceived by him. ... It is evident that things I perceive are my own ideas, and that no idea can exist unless it be in a mind. Nor is it less plain that these ideas or things by me perceived, either themselves or their archetypes, exist independently of my mind; since I know myself not to be their author, it being out of my power to determine at pleasure what particular ideas I shall be affected with upon opening my eyes or ears. They must therefore exist in some other mind, whose will it is they should be exhibited to me. The things, I say, immediately perceived are ideas or sensations, call them which you will. But how can any idea or sensation exist in, or be produced by, anything but a mind or spirit? This indeed is inconceivable; and to assert that which is inconceivable is to talk nonsense: is it not?

Hylas. Without doubt.

Philonous. But, on the other hand, it is very conceivable that they should exist in and be produced by a Spirit; since this is no more than I daily experience in myself, inasmuch as I perceive numberless ideas; and, by an act of my will, can form a great variety of them, and raise them up in my imagination: though, it must be confessed, these creatures of the fancy are not altogether so distinct, so strong, vivid, and permanent, as those perceived by my senses, which latter are called *real things*. From all which I conclude, *there is a Mind which affects me every moment with all the sensible impressions I perceive*. And, from the variety, order, and manner of these, I conclude the Author of them to be *wise, powerful, and good, and beyond comprehension.* . . .

[*The* Third Dialogue *is omitted.*]

COMMENT

The speakers in Berkeley's *Dialogues* are Hylas, a "materialist," and Philonous, who represents the point of view of the author. Physical objects, according to Philonous, have no existence independent of thought. The whole universe is made up of minds and the immaterial objects of minds, and nothing more. This doctrine, which is called *idealism (ideaism,* with the *I* inserted for the sake of euphony), may strike beginning students as exceedingly odd; but it is quite possible that the universe is very odd, and the arguments for idealism are strong. Since Berkeley's presentation of these arguments is lucid, they will not be summarized.

Some of Berkeley's arguments are similar to the arguments of Bertrand Russell in discussing the nature and existence of matter (see Chapter 4). Other arguments are unique to Berkeley. Altogether they constitute a powerful case for idealism, certain critical questions are worth reviewing:

1. *Is the Essence of an Object to Be Perceived?* Over and over again, Berkeley insisted that "things" are mere collections of "ideas" and that ideas cannot exist unless they are perceived. The plausibility of his contention depends on his constant use of the word *idea*. We think of "idea" as something in the mind and therefore as incapable of existing apart from the mind. Hence, if we are told that an apple consists entirely of "ideas," it is natural for us to suppose that the apple can exist only in some mind. However, *idea*, as Berkeley used it, really means "immediate object of thought or experience" (including both imaginative and perceptual experience). If we understand idea in this sense, there is a possibility—not lightly to be dismissed—that an object known as a set of ideas may continue to exist when the thought of it ceases.

The point can be illustrated by an amusing passage from Lewis Carroll's *Through the Looking Glass*. Alice is warned by Tweedledum and Tweedledee not to awaken the Red King:

> "He's dreaming now," said Tweedledee: "and what do you think he's dreaming about?"
> Alice said, "Nobody can guess that."
> "What about *you!*" Tweedledee exclaimed, clapping his hands triumphantly. "And if he left off dreaming about you, where do you suppose you'd be?"
> "Where I am now, of course," said Alice.
> "Not you!" Tweedledee retorted contemptuously. "You'd be nowhere. Why, you're only a sort of thing in his dream!"
> "If that there King was to wake," added Tweedledum, "you'd go out—bang!—just like a candle!"

The delicious absurdity of this passage depends upon the supposition of Tweedledum andTweedledee that to *exist* is to be *borne in mind,* and that when Alice is not borne in mind by the Red King, she cannot exist. However, no real person is merely a thought or idea in anybody's mind.

This point would be admitted by Berkeley. His formula for summing up the nature of reality is *"esse est percipi aut percipere"* [essence is to be perceived or to perceive], not just *"esse est percipi."* Though if people can exist independently of someone's idea of them, why cannot a thing exist independently? To argue that an apple must be in our minds because we are thinking of it is like arguing that a person must be in our minds because we are thinking of him or her. If we distiguish clearly between the act of thinking and the object of thought, the act of perceiving and the object perceived, there is no absurdity in supposing that things may exist even when they are unperceived or unthought.

2. *Is the "Egocentric Predicament" a Reason for Believing in Idealism?* Berkeley pointed out that everyone's knowledge is incurably egocentric. Even when you think of the unobserved interior of the earth, you are *thinking* about it, and, in that sense, it is an object before your mind. Every object we ever perceive or think about in any way stands ipso facto in relation to our minds. Does this "egocentric predicament"[1] provide a valid argument for idealism?

Ralph Barton Perry answers in the negative. The fact that we cannot eliminate ourselves as the subject of our own experiences proves nothing at all about the nature of the external world. We may have good reason to suppose that there are unknown stars, unexperienced atoms, unsighted grains of sand in the Sahara Desert, and unobserved physical processes beneath the earth's crust. Our reasons for believing in them should be judged on the basis of logic and evidence and should not be rejected merely because no one can think about these matters without using one's mind.

---

[1] See also Ralph Barton Perry, *Present Philosophical Tendencies* (New York: Longmans, Green, 1929), pp. 129–132.

3. *Does the Relativity of Perception Prove Idealism?* The fact that sense data are relative to the perceiver can scarcely be denied; but does it prove idealism? So long as we can explain *why* things appear differently to different observers, we can still maintain that there are real objective qualities.

Let us consider one of Berkeley's own examples. He pointed out that if one hand has been chilled and the other warmed, and both hands are put simultaneously into the same pan of water, the water will seem warm to one hand and cool to the other. However, this is just what we should expect if the water is *really tepid*. What the person who puts his hands in the water feels is not the temperature of the water but the temperature in his or her hands—and the preheated hand naturally has a different temperature than the prechilled hand. If the two hands remain in the water long enough, the temperature of the water will finally pervade them, and then the water will feel tepid to *both* hands. Similarly, if light and color are truly objective, an object will naturally appear to have a different color in a different light. Or when a microscope enables us to see features of an object that were before invisible, it is not surprising that we see colors and shapes that we did not see before. However variously things may *appear,* we can often distinguish between "appearances" and "realities." Whether we can do so in a sufficient number of cases to invalidate Berkeley's argument is a question worth debating.

4. *Does the Inseparability of Primary and Secondary Qualities Commit Us to Idealism?* Suppose we grant Berkeley's contention that primary and secondary qualities are inseparable. We might therefore conclude that both are objective *(not mind-dependent)* rather than that both are subjective (mind-dependent). Some critics maintain that Berkeley's arguments fail to show that even secondary qualities are "in the mind." They believe that colors, sounds, odors, and textures (though perhaps not tastes) are no less objective than the primary qualities.

Another alternative would be the agnostic position that things-in-themselves are unknowable, and that consequently we can no more assert idealism than we can assert materialism. This is the position favored by Immanuel Kant, David Hume, and the positivists—all of whom admit the inseparability of primary and secondary qualities.

However, it is also possible to reject Berkeley's thesis that primary and secondary qualities are inseparable. Actually, there is a very significant difference between the two sets of qualities. The secondary qualities are *sensory* properties, whereas the primary qualities are *formal* characteristics—the structures, relations, and quantities of things. This difference may justify the supposition that the primary qualities have a different epistemological status than the secondary qualities.

According to modern scientific theories of perception, the secondary qualities seem to depend on physiological and mental factors and thus appear to be qualitative events in the perceiving organisms. Sounds seem to depend on organic reactions to airwaves; colors, on organic reactions to electromagnetic vibrations; and so on. Our *impressions* of primary qualities are similarly dependent on our minds, but there is a significant difference: The laws of physics are framed in terms of abstract orders and quantitative relations—primary qualities—rather than in terms of concrete secondary qualities. We therefore have scientific

warrant for believing that our impressions of primary but not of secondary qualities have objective counterparts—if science is dealing with a real objective world.

Relational properties cannot exist all by themselves; they must attach to the
things related. On this point Berkeley is perfectly right. Yet it is conceivable that
physical science reveals the relational structure of the real world without revealing its content. Atoms may exist and conform to AlbertEinstein's equations even
though their ultimate qualitative nature remains a mystery.

5. *Can We Test the Correspondence between Ideas and Things?* Once we distinguish between objects as we apprehend them and objects as they really are, how
can we ever know that the former agree with the latter? Not only Berkeley, but
Kant and G. W. F. Hegel as well, maintain that the correspondence test of truth is
unworkable.

The impossibility of directly comparing ideas (or sense–data) with things
outside experience must be admitted. However, we can *infer* things that we do
not experience. No one, for example, *directly* observes another person's
toothache, but one can be reasonably certain that the other person is suffering
from a toothache. Such indirect knowledge involves the interpretation of signs,
and we can often infer from signs what we cannot observe.

It is a striking fact that the signs of minds differ very markedly from the signs
of external things. When we hear people talk, see them gesture, or read what they
have written, we are interpreting signs of a very different sort than when we are
looking at a rock. The first set of signs are clearly indicative of thinking people
and their thoughts, whereas the second set of signs, to all appearances, indicates
something nonconscious and nonintelligent. It seems a bit fantastic and gratu-
itous to attribute a *mind* to the rock, or even to the system of nature of which the
rock is a minute part. The sensible aspects of human behavior from which we
infer a human mind have little resemblance to the sensible characteristics of
nature from which Berkeley would have us infer God. Perhaps Kant and the positivists are right—perhaps we can never know the rock as a thing-in-itself—but
such clues as we have for judging the nature of inorganic things are quite different
from the clues whereby we infer the minds of our friends and acquaintances.
Reality *appears* to be dualistic, made up of both mental and physical qualities,
and it involves a sharp break with common sense to suppose that this appearance
is quite illusory.

With respect to our case study involving the twins who share a body, the
issues raised for idealism would seem to be the very reverse of those raised for
materialism, as presented in the previous chapter. How can two distinct minds,
with different ideas, be said to explain a single set of perceptions and sensory
experiences? How would Berkeley account for this seeming breakdown in the
relation between these two minds and their common "physical" experiences?

11

DUALISM

RENÉ DESCARTES (1596–1650)

For a biographical note, see page 55.

MEDITATION I

Of the Things Which May Be Brought Within the Sphere of the Doubtful.

It is now some years since I detected how many were the false beliefs that I had from my earliest youth admitted as true, and how doubtful was everything I had since constructed on this basis; and from that time I was convinced that I must once for all seriously undertake to rid myself of all the opinions which I had formerly accepted, and commence to build anew from the foundation, if I wanted to establish any firm and permanent structure in the sciences. But as this enterprise appeared to be a very great one, I waited until I had attained an age so mature that I could not hope that at any later date I should be better fitted to execute my design. This reason caused me to delay so long that I should feel that I was

doing wrong were I to occupy in deliberation the time that yet remains to me for action. Today, then, since very opportunely for the plan I have in view I have delivered my mind from every care [and am happily agitated by no passions] and since I have procured for myself an assured leisure in a peaceable retirement, I shall at last seriously and freely address myself to the general upheaval of all my former opinions.

Now for this object it is not necessary that I should show that all of these are false—I shall perhaps never arrive at this end. But inasmuch as reason already persuades me that I ought no less carefully to withhold my assent from matters which are not entirely certain and indubitable than from those which appear to me manifestly to be false, if I am able to find in each one some reason to doubt, this will suffice to justify my rejecting the whole. And for that end it will not be requisite that I should examine each in particular, which would be an endless undertaking; for owing to the fact that the destruction of the foundations of necessity brings with it the downfall of the rest of the edifice, I shall only in the first place attack those principles upon which all my former opinions rested.

The following excerpts from the *Meditations* are from *The Philosophical Works of Descartes,* trans. from the Latin by Elizabeth S. Haldane and G. R. T. Ross, and published by Cambridge University Press, 1931. Where it seems desirable, an alternative reading from the French is given in brackets. Reprinted by permission.

All that up to the present time I have accepted as most true and certain I have learned either from the senses or through the senses; but it is sometimes proved to me that these senses are deceptive, and it is wiser not to trust entirely to any thing by which we have once been deceived.

But it may be that although the senses sometimes deceive us concerning things which are hardly perceptible, or very far away, there are yet many others to be met with as to which we cannot reasonably have any doubt, although we recognize them by their means. For example, there is the fact that I am here, seated by the fire, attired in a dressing gown, having this paper in my hands and other similar matters. And how could I deny that these hands and this body are mine, were it not perhaps that I compare myself to certain persons, devoid of sense, whose cerebella are so troubled and clouded by the violent vapors of black bile, that they constantly assure us that they think they are kings when they are really quite poor, or that they are clothed in purple when they are really without covering, or who imagine that they have an earthenware head or are nothing but pumpkins or are made of glass. But they are mad, and I should not be any the less insane were I to follow examples so extravagant.

At the same time I must remember that I am a man, and that consequently I am in the habit of sleeping, and in my dreams representing to myself the same things or sometimes even less probable things, than do those who are insane in their waking moments. How often has it happened to me that in the night I dreamt that I found myself in this particular place, that I was dressed and seated near the fire, whilst in reality I was lying undressed in bed! At this moment it does indeed seem to me that it is with eyes awake that I am looking at this paper; that this head which I move is not asleep, that it is deliberately and of set purpose that I extend my hand and perceive it; what happens in sleep does not appear so clear nor so distinct as does all this. But in thinking over this I remind myself that on many occasions I have in sleep been deceived by similar illusions, and in dwelling carefully on this reflection I see so manifestly that there are no certain indications by which we may clearly distinguish wakefulness from sleep that I am lost in astonishment. And my astonishment is such that it is almost incapable of persuading me that I now dream.

Now let us assume that we are asleep and that all these particulars, e.g., that we open our eyes, shake our head, extend our hands, and so on, are but false delusions; and let us reflect that possibly neither our hands nor our whole body are such as they appear to us to be. At the same time we must at least confess that the things which are represented to us in sleep are like painted representations which can only have been formed as the counterparts of something real and true, and that in this way those general things at least, i.e., eyes, a head, hands, and a whole body, are not imaginary things, but things really existent. For, as a matter of fact, painters, even when they study with the greatest skill to represent sirens and satyrs by forms the most strange and extraordinary, cannot give them natures which are entirely new, but merely make a certain medley of the members of different animals; or if their imagination is extravagant enough to invent something so novel that nothing similar has ever before been seen, and that then their work represents a thing purely fictitious and absolutely false, it is certain all the same that the colors of which this is composed are necessarily real. And for the same reason, although these general things, to wit, a body, eyes, a head, and such like, may be imaginary, we are bound at the same time to confess that there are at least some other objects yet more simple and more universal, which are real and true; and of these just in the same way as with certain real colors, all these images of things which dwell in our thoughts, whether true and real or false and fantastic, are formed.

To such a class of things pertains corporeal nature in general, and its extension, the figure of extended things, their quantity or magnitude and number, as also the place in which they are, the time which measures their duration, and so on.

That is possibly why our reasoning is not unjust when we conclude from this that Physics, Astronomy, Medicine and all other sciences which have as their end the consideration of composite things, are very dubious and uncertain; but that Arithmetic, Geometry and other sciences of that kind which only treat of things that are very simple and very general, without taking great trouble to ascertain whether they are actually existent or not, contain some measure of certainty and an element of the indubitable. For whether I am awake or asleep, two and three together always form five, and the square can never have more than four sides, and it does not seem possible that truths so clear and apparent can be suspected of any falsity [or uncertainty].

Nevertheless I have long had fixed in my mind the belief that an all-powerful God existed by whom I have been created such as I am. But how do I know that He has not brought it to pass that there is no earth, no heaven, no extended body, no magnitude, no place, and that nevertheless [I possess the perceptions of all these things and that] they seem to me to exist just exactly as I now see them? And, besides, as I sometimes imagine that others deceive themselves in the things which they think they know best, how do I know that I am not deceived every time that I add two and three, or count the sides of a square, or judge of things yet simpler, if anything simpler can be imagined? But possibly God has not desired that I should be thus deceived, for He is said to be supremely good. If, however, it is contrary to His goodness to have made me such that I constantly deceive myself, it would also appear to be contrary to His goodness to permit me to be sometimes deceived, and nevertheless I cannot doubt that He does permit this.

There may indeed be those who would prefer to deny the existence of a God so powerful, rather than believe that all other things are uncertain. But let us not oppose them for the present, and grant that all that is said of a God is a fable; nevertheless in whatever way they suppose that I have arrived at the state of being that I have reached—whether they attribute it to fate or to accident, or make out that it is by a continual succession of antecedents, or by some other method—since to err and deceive oneself is a defect, it is clear that the greater will be the probability of my being so imperfect as to deceive myself ever, as is the Author to whom they assign my origin the less powerful. To these reasons I have certainly nothing to reply, but at the end I feel constrained to confess that there is nothing in all that I formerly believed to be true, of which I cannot in some measure doubt, and that not merely through want of thought or through levity, but for reasons which are very powerful and maturely considered; so that henceforth I ought not the less carefully to refrain from giving credence to these opinions than to that which is manifestly false, if I desire to arrive at any certainty [in the sciences].

But it is not sufficient to have made these remarks, we must also be careful to keep them in mind. For these ancient and commonly held opinions still revert frequently to my mind, long and familiar custom having given them the right to occupy my mind against my inclination and rendered them almost masters of my belief; nor will I ever lose the habit of deferring to them or of placing my confidence in them, so long as I consider them as they really are, i.e. opinions in some measure doubtful, as I have just shown, and at the same time highly probable, so that there is much more reason to believe than to deny them. That is why I consider that I shall not be acting amiss, if, taking of set purpose a contrary belief, I allow myself to be deceived, and for a certain time pretend that all these opinions are entirely false and imaginary, until at last, having thus balanced my former prejudices with my later [so that they cannot divert my opinions more to one side than to the other], my judgment will no longer be dominated by bad usage or turned away from the right knowledge of the truth. For I am assured that there can be neither peril nor error in this course, and that I cannot at present yield too much to distrust, since I am not considering the question of action, but only of knowledge.

I shall then suppose, not that God who is supremely good and the fountain of truth, but some evil genius not less powerful than deceitful, has employed his whole energies in deceiving me; I shall consider that the heavens, the earth, colors, figures, sound, and all other external things are nought but the illusions and dreams of which this genius has availed himself in order to lay traps for my credulity; I shall consider myself as having no hands, no eyes, no flesh, no blood, nor any senses, yet falsely believing myself to possess all these things; I shall remain obstinately attached to this idea, and if by this means it is not in my power to arrive at the knowledge of any truth, I may at least do what is in my power [i.e., suspend my judgment], and with firm purpose avoid giving credence to any false thing, or being imposed upon by this arch deceiver, however powerful and deceptive he may be. But this task is a laborious one, and insensibly a certain lassitude leads me into the course of my ordinary life. And just as a captive who in sleep enjoys imaginary liberty, when he begins to suspect that his liberty is but a dream, fears to awaken and conspires with these agreeable illusions that the deception may be prolonged, so insensibly of my own accord I fall back into my former opinions, and I dread awakening from this slumber, lest the laborious wakefulness which would follow the tranquillity of this repose should have to be spent not in daylight, but in the excessive darkness of the difficulties which have just been discussed.

MEDITATION II

Of the Nature of the Human Mind; and That It Is More Easily Known Than the Body

The Meditation of yesterday filled my mind with so many doubts that it is no longer in my power to forget them. And yet I do not see in what manner I can resolve them; and, just as if I had all of a sudden fallen into very deep water, I am so disconcerted that I can neither make certain of setting my feet on the bottom, nor can I swim and so support myself on the surface. I shall nevertheless make an effort and follow anew the same path as that on which I yesterday entered, *i.e.,* I shall proceed by setting aside all that in which the least doubt could be supposed to exist, just as if I had discovered that it was absolutely false; and I shall ever follow in this road until I have met with something which is certain, or at least, if I can do nothing else, until I have learned for certain that there is nothing in the world that is certain.

Archimedes; in order that he might draw the terrestrial globe out of its place, and transport it elsewhere, demanded only that one point should be fixed and immovable; in the same way I shall have the right to conceive high hopes if I am happy enough to discover one thing only which is certain and indubitable.

I suppose, then, that all the things that I see are false; I persuade myself that nothing has ever existed of all that my fallacious memory represents to me. I consider that I possess no senses; I imagine that body, figure, extension, movement and place are but the fictions of my mind. What, then, can be esteemed as true? Perhaps nothing at all, unless that there is nothing in the world that is certain.

But how can I know there is not something different from those things that I have just considered, of which one cannot have the slightest doubt? Is there not some

God, or some other being by whatever name we call it, who puts these reflections into my mind? That is not necessary, for is it not possible that I am capable of producing them myself? I myself, am I not at least something? But I have already denied that I had senses and body. Yet I hesitate, for what follows from that? Am I so dependent on body and senses that I cannot exist without these? But I was persuaded that there was nothing in all the world, that there was no heaven, no earth, that there were no minds, nor any bodies: was I not then likewise persuaded that I did not exist? Not at all; of a surety I myself did exist since I persuaded myself of something [or merely because I thought of something]. But there is some deceiver or other, very powerful and very cunning, who ever employs his ingenuity in deceiving me. Then without doubt I exist also if he deceives me, and let him deceive me as much as he will, he can never cause me to be nothing so long as I think that I am something. So that after having reflected well and carefully examined all things, we must come to the definite conclusion that this proposition: I am, I exist, is necessarily true each time that I pronounce it, or that I mentally conceive it.

But I do not yet know clearly enough what I am, I who am certain that I am; and hence I must be careful to see that I do not imprudently take some other object in place of myself, and thus that I do not go astray in respect of this knowledge that I hold to be the most certain and most evident of all that I have formerly learned. That is why I shall now consider anew what I believed myself to be before I embarked upon these last reflections; and of my former opinions I shall withdraw all that might even in a small degree be invalidated by the reasons which I have just brought forward, in order that there may be nothing at all left beyond what is absolutely certain and indubitable.

What then did I formerly believe myself to be? Undoubtedly I believed myself to be a man. But what is a man? Shall I say a reasonable animal? Certainly not; for then I should have to inquire what an animal is, and what is reasonable; and thus from a single question I should insensibly fall into an infinitude of others more difficult; and I should not wish to waste the little time and leisure remaining to me in trying to unravel subtleties like these. But I shall rather stop here to consider the thoughts which of themselves spring up in my mind, and which were not inspired by anything beyond my own nature alone when I applied myself to the consideration of my being. In the first place, then, I considered myself as having a face, hands, arms, and all that system of members composed of bones and flesh as seen in a corpse which I designated by the name of body. In addition to this I considered that I was nourished, that I walked, that I felt, and that I thought, and I referred all these actions to the soul: but I did not stop to consider what the soul was, or if I did stop, I imagined that it was something extremely rare and subtle like a wind, a flame, or an ether, which was spread throughout my grosser parts. As to body I had no manner of doubt about its nature, but thought I had a very clear knowledge of it; and if I had desired to explain it according to the notions that I had then formed of it, I should have described it thus: By the body I understand all that which can be defined by a certain figure: something which can be confined in a certain place, and which can fill a given space in such a way that every other body will be excluded from it; which can be perceived either by touch, or by sight, or by hearing, or by taste, or by smell: which can be moved in many ways not, in truth, by itself, but by something which is foreign to it, by which it is touched [and from which it receives impressions]: for to have the power of self-movement, as also of feeling or of thinking, I did not consider to appertain to the nature of body: on the contrary, I was rather astonished to find that faculties similar to them existed in some bodies.

But what am I, now that I suppose that there is a certain genius which is extremely powerful, and, if I may say so, malicious, who employs all his powers in deceiving me? Can I affirm that I posssess the least of all those things which I have just said pertain to the nature of body? I pause to consider, I resolve all these things in my mind, and find none of which I can say that it pertains to me. It would be tedious to stop to enumerate them. Let us pass to the attributes of soul and see if there is any one which is in me? What of nutrition or walking [the first mentioned]? But if it is so that I have no body, it is also true that I can neither walk nor take nourishment. Another attribute is sensation. But one cannot feel without body, and besides I have thought I perceived many things during sleep that I recognized in my waking moments as not having been experienced at all. What of thinking? I find here that thought is an attribute that belongs to me; it alone cannot be separated from me. I am, I exist, that is certain. But how often? Just when I think; for it might possibly be the case if I ceased entirely to think, that I should likewise cease altogether to exist. I do not now admit anything which is not necessarily true: to speak accurately I am not more than a thing which thinks, that is to say a mind or a soul, or an understanding, or a reason, which are terms whose significance was formerly unknown to me. I am, however, a real thing and really exist; but what thing? I have answered: a thing which thinks.

And what more? I shall exercise my imagination [in order to see if I am not something more]. I am not a collection of members which we call the human body: I am not a subtle air distributed through these members, I am not a wind, a fire, a vapor, a breath, nor anything at all which I can imagine or conceive; because I have assumed that all these were nothing. Without changing that supposition I find that I only leave myself certain of the fact that I am somewhat. But perhaps it is true that these same things which I supposed were non-existent because they are unknown to me, are really not different from the self

which I know. I am not sure about this, I shall not dispute about it now; I can only give judgement on things that are known to me. I know that I exist, and I inquire what I am, I whom I know to exist. But it is very certain that the knowledge of my existence taken in its precise significance does not depend on things whose existence is not yet known to me; consequently it does not depend on those which I can feign in imagination. And indeed the very term *feign* in imagination proves to me my error, for I really do this if I image myself a something, since to imagine is nothing else than to contemplate the figure or image of a corporeal things. But I already know for certain that I am, and that it may be that all these images, and, speaking generally, all things that relate to the nature of body are nothing but dreams [and chimeras]. For this reason I see clearly that I have as little reason to say, "I shall stimulate my imagination in order to know more distinctly what I am," than if I were to say, "I am now awake," and I perceive somewhat that is real and true: but because I do not yet perceive it distinctly enough, I shall go to sleep of express purpose, so that my dreams may represent the perception with greatest truth and evidence. And, thus, I know for certain that nothing of all that I can understand by means of my imagination belongs to this knowledge which I have of myself, and that it is necessary to recall the mind from this mode of thought with the utmost diligence in order that it may be able to know its own nature with perfect distinctness.

But what then am I? A thing which thinks? What is a thing which thinks? It is a thing which doubts, understands, [conceives], affirms, denies, wills, refuses, which also imagines and feels.

Certainly it is no small matter if all these things pertain to my nature. But why should they not so pertain? Am I not that being who now doubts nearly everything, who nevertheless understands certain things, who affirms that one only is true, who denies all the others, who desires to know more, is averse from being deceived, who imagines many things, sometimes indeed despite his will, and who perceives many likewise, as by the intervention of the bodily organs? Is there nothing in all this which is as true as it is certain that I exist, even though I should always sleep and though he who has given me being employed all his ingenuity in deceiving me? Is there likewise any one of these attributes which can be distinguished from my thought, or which might be said to be separated from myself? For it is so evident of itself that it is I who doubts, who understands, and who desires, that there is no reason here to add anything to explain it. And I have certainly the power of imagining likewise; for although it may happen (as I formerly supposed) that none of the things which I imagine are true, nevertheless this power of imagining does not cease to be really in use, and it forms part of my thought. Finally, I am the same who feels, that is to say, who perceives certain things, as by the organs of sense, since in truth I see light, I hear noise, I feel heat. But it will be said that these phenomena are false and that I am dreaming. Let it be so; still it is at least quite certain that it seems to me that I see light, that I hear noise and that I feel heat. That cannot be false; properly speaking it is what is in me called feeling; and used in this precise sense that is no other thing than thinking.

From this time I begin to know what I am with a little more clearness and distinction than before; but nevertheless it still seems to me, and I cannot prevent myself from thinking, that corporeal things, whose images are framed by thought, which are tested by the senses, are much more distinctly known than that obscure part of me which does not come under the imagination. Although really it is very strange to say that I know and understand more distinctly these things whose existence seems to me dubious, which are unknown to me, and which do not belong to me, than others of the truth of which I am convinced, which are known to me and which pertain to my real nature, in a word, than myself. But I see

clearly how the case stands: my mind loves to wander, and cannot yet suffer itself to be retained within the just limits of truth. Very good, let us once more give it the freest rein, so that, when afterwards we seize the proper occasion for pulling up, it may the more easily be regulated and controlled.

Let us begin by considering the commonest matters, those which we believe to be the most distinctly comprehended, to wit, the bodies which we touch and see; not indeed bodies in general, for these general ideas are usually a little more confused, but let us consider one body in particular. Let us take for example, this piece of wax: it has been taken quite freshly from the hive, and it has not yet lost the sweetness of the honey which it contains; it still retains somewhat of the odor of the flowers from which it has been culled; its color, its figure, its size are apparent; it is hard, cold, easily handled, and if you strike it with the finger, it will emit a sound. Finally all the things which are requisite to cause us distinctly to recognize a body, are met within it. But notice that while I speak and approach the fire what remained of the taste is exhaled, the smell evaporates, the color alters, the figure is destroyed, the size increases, it becomes liquid, it heats, scarcely can one handle it, and when one strikes it, no sound is emitted. Does the same wax remain after this change? We must confess that it remains; none would judge otherwise. What then did I know so distinctly in this piece of wax? It could certainly be nothing of all that the senses brought to my notice, since all these things which fall under taste, smell, sight, touch, and hearing, are found to be changed, and yet the same wax remains.

Perhaps it was what I now think, viz. that this wax was not that sweetness of honey, nor that agreeable scent of flowers, nor that particular whiteness, nor that figure, nor that sound, but simply a body which a little before appeared to me as perceptible under these forms, and which is now perceptible under others. But what, precisely, is that I imagine when I form such conceptions? Let us attentively consider this, and, abstracting from all that does not belong to the wax, let us see what remains. Certainly nothing remains excepting a certain extended thing which is flexible and movable. But what is the meaning of flexible and movable? Is it not that I imagine that this piece of wax being round is capable of becoming square and of passing from a square to a triangular figure? No, certainly it is not that, since I imagine it admits of an infinitude of similar changes, and I nevertheless do not know how to compass the infinitude by imagination, and consequently this conception which I have of the wax is not brought about by the faculty of imagination. What now is this extension? Is it not also unknown? For it becomes greater when the wax is melted, greater when it is boiled, and greater still when the heat increases; and I should not conceive [clearly] according to truth what wax is, if I did not think that even this piece that we are considering is capable of receiving more variations in extension than I have ever imagined. We must then grant that I could not even understand through the imagination what this piece of wax is, and that it is my mind alone which perceives it. I say this piece of wax in particular, for as to wax in general it is yet clearer. But what is this piece of wax which cannot be understood excepting by the [understanding or] mind? It is certainly the same that I see, touch, imagine, and finally it is the same which I have always believed it to be from the beginning.

But what must particularly be observed is that its perception is neither an act of vision, nor of touch, nor of imagination, and has never been such although it may have appeared formerly to be so, but only an intuition of the mind, which may be imperfect and confused as it was formerly, or clear and distinct as it is at present, according as my attention is more or less directed to the elements which are found in it, and of which it is composed.

Yet in the meantime I am greatly astonished when I consider [the great feebleness of mind] and its proneness to fall [insensibly] into error; for although without giving expression to my thoughts I consider all this in my own mind, words often impede me and I am almost deceived by the terms of ordinary language. For we say that we see the same wax, if it is present, and not that we simply judge that it is the same from its having the same color and figure. From this I should conclude that I knew the wax by means of vision and not simply by the intuition of the mind; unless by chance I remember that, when looking from a window and saying I see men who pass in the street, I really do not see them, but infer that what I see is men, just as I say that I see wax. And yet what do I see from the window but hats and coats which may cover automatic machines? Yet I judge these to be men. And similarly solely by the faculty of judgment which rests in my mind, I comprehend that which I believed I saw with my eyes.

A man who makes it his aim to raise his knowledge above the common should be ashamed to derive the occasion for doubting from the forms of speech invented by the vulgar; I prefer to pass on and consider whether I had a more evident and perfect conception of what the wax was when I first perceived it, and when I believed I knew it by means of the external senses or at least by the common as it is called, that is to say by the imaginative faculty, or whether my present conception is clearer now that I have most carefully examined what it is, and in what way it can be known. It would certainly be absurd to doubt as to this. For what was there in this first perception which was distinct? What was there which might not as well have been perceived by any of the animals? But when I distiguish the wax from its external forms, and when, just as if I had taken from it its vestments, I consider it quite naked, it is certain that although some error may still be found in my judgment, I can nevertheless not perceive it thus without a human mind.

But finally what shall I say of this mind, that is, of myself, for up to this point I do not admit in myself anything but mind? What then, I who seem to perceive this piece of wax distinctly, do I not know myself, not only with much more truth and certainty, but also with much more distinctness and clearness? For if I judge that the wax is or exists from the fact that I see it, it certainly follows much more clearly that I am or that I exist myself from the fact that I see it. For it may be that what I see is not really wax, it may also be that I do not possess eyes with which to see anything; but it cannot be that when I see, or (for I no longer take account of the distinction) when I think I see, that I myself who think am nought. So if I judge that the wax exists from the fact that I touch it, the same thing will follow, to wit, that I am; and if I judge that my imagination, or some other cause, whatever it is, persuades me that the wax exists, I shall still conclude the same. And what I have here remarked of wax may be applied to all other things which are external to me [and which are met with outside of me]. And further, if the [notion or] perception of wax has seemed to me clearer and more distinct, not only after the sight or the touch, but also after many other causes

have rendered it quite manifest to me, with how much more [evidence] and distinctness must it be said that I now know myself, since all the reasons which contribute to the knowledge of wax, or any other body whatever, are yet better proofs of the nature of my mind! And there are so many other things in the mind itself which may contribute to the elucidation of its nature, that those which depend on body such as these just mentioned, hardly merit being taken into account.

But finally here I am, having insensibly reverted to the point I desired, for, since it is now manifest to me that even bodies are not properly speaking known by the senses or by the faculty of imagination, but by the understanding only, and since they are not known from the fact that they are seen or touched, but only because they are understood, I see clearly that there is nothing which is easier for me to know than my mind. But because it is difficult to rid oneself so promptly of an opinion to which one was accustomed for so long, it will be well that I should halt a little at this point, so that by the length of my meditation I may more deeply imprint on my memory this new knowledge.

MEDITATION III

Of God: That He Exists

I shall now close my eyes, I shall stop my ears, I shall call away all my senses, I shall efface even from my thoughts all the images of corporeal things, or at least (for that is hardly possible) I shall esteem them as vain and false; and thus holding converse only with myself and considering my own nature, I shall try little by little to reach a better knowledge of and a more familiar acquaintanceship with myself. I am a thing that thinks, that is to say, that doubts, affirms, denies, that knows a few things, that is ignorant of many, [that loves, that hates], that wills, that desires, that also

imagines and perceives; for as I remarked before, although the things which I perceive and imagine are perhaps nothing at all apart from me and in themselves, I am nevertheless assured that these modes of thought that I call perceptions and imaginations, inasmuch only as they are modes of thought, certainly reside [and are met with] in me.

And in the little that I have just said, I think I have summed up all that I really know, or at least all that hitherto I was aware that I knew. In order to try to extend my knowledge further, I shall now look around more carefully and see whether I cannot still discover in myself some other things which I have not hitherto perceived. I am certain that I am a thing which thinks; but do I not then likewise know what is requisite to render me certain of a truth? Certainly in this first knowledge there is nothing that assures me of its truth, excepting the clear and distinct perception of that which I state, which would not indeed suffice to assure me that what I say is true, if it could ever happen that a thing which I conceived so clearly and distinctly could be false; and accordingly it seems to me that already I can establish as a general rule that all things which I perceive very clearly and very distinctly are true.

At the same time I have before received and admitted many things to be very certain and manifest, which yet I afterwards recognized as being dubious. What then were these things? They were the earth, sky, stars and all other objects which I apprehended by means of the senses. But what did I clearly [and distinctly] perceive in them? Nothing more than that the ideas or thoughts of these things were presented to my mind. And not even now do I deny that these ideas are met with in me. But there was yet another thing which I affirmed, and which, owing to the habit which I had formed of believing it, I thought I perceived very clearly, although in truth I did not perceive it at all, to wit, that there were objects outside of me from which these ideas proceeded, and to which they were entirely similar. And it was in this that I erred, or, if perchance my judgment was correct, this was not due to any knowledge arising from my perception.

But when I took anything very simple and easy in the sphere of arithmetic or geometry into consideration, *e.g.* that two and three together made five, and other things of the sort, were not these pres-ent to my mind so clearly as to enable me to affirm that they were true? Certainly if I judged that since such matters could be doubted, this would not have been so for any other reason than that it came into my mind that perhaps a God might have endowed me with such a nature that I may have been deceived even

concerning things which seemed to me most manifest. But every time that this preconceived opinion of the sovereign power of a God presents itself to my thought, I am constrained to confess that it is easy to Him, if He wishes it, to cause me to err, even in matters in which I believe myself to have the best evidence. And, on the other hand, always when I direct my attention to things which I believe myself to perceive very clearly, I am so persuaded of their truth that I let myself break out into words such as these: Let who will deceive me, He can never cause me to be nothing while I think that I am, or some day cause it to be true to say that I have never been, it being true now to say that I am, or that two and three make more or less than five, or any such thing in which I see a manifest contradiction. And certainly, since I have no reason to believe that there is a God who is a deceiver, and as I have not yet satisfied myself that there is a God at all, the reason for doubt which depends on this opinion alone is very slight, and so to speak metaphysical. But in order to be able altogether to remove it, I must inquire whether there is a God as soon as the occasion presents itself; and if I find that there is a God, I must also inquire whether He may be a deceiver; for without a knowledge of these two truths I do not see that I can ever be certain of anything. ...

[To answer this lingering doubt, Descartes "proves" that there is a God who, as perfect, would not deceive him. Since arguments for the existence of God have been considered in detail in Chapter 8, a brief summary of Descartes' arguments will here be sufficient.

His first argument for the existence of God consists of four steps: (1) I have an idea of God. (2) Everything, including my idea, has a cause. (3) Since the greater cannot proceed from the less, nothing less than God is adequate to explain my idea of God. This step involves the notion that the idea of a Perfect Being is, in conception, perfect; that no imperfect being is capable of producing such an idea; and that hence it requires a perfect Cause to produce it. (4) Therefore God exists.

Descartes advances a second argument for God, once again starting with "I think, therefore I am." He argues (still using the first person pronoun) that God is the cause, not only of my idea of God, but of me. This is an argument by elimination. (1) I am not the cause, of myself, for if I were, I would not be the highly imperfect and fallible being that I know myself to be. (2) No other finite being could be the sufficient cause of my existence for if such a being existed, it in turn would have to be explained, as would any prior finite cause as well. I would thus have to trace the causal process back from stage to stage to the ultimate cause, an eternal and necessary being who requires no explanation beyond itself. Only such an infinite cause could be conceived as existing, not merely through my life, but through all the lives involved in the total succession of finite beings—and only such a cause would be adequate to maintain as well as to originate the entire succession. (3) The ultimate cause could not be multiple because I conceive of God as absolutely one, and the cause of this idea must be no less perfect than its effect, not falling short of the idea in its unity or in any other respect. (4) The only possibility that remains is that an infinite and monotheistic God is the cause. of me Therefore God exists.

In Meditation V, which has been omitted from this book, Descartes presents a third argument for God's existence—a restatement of the so-called Ontological Argument of Saint Anselm, an early medieval phioospher. Since this argument is dealt with in Chapter 8, we shall not consider it here.

The importance of God in Descartes' system is that God is used to guarantee not a system of dogma but science and philosophy. Science and philosophy are based upon reason and memory, and God is needed to guarantee their reliability. God, being perfect, would not deceive me—God would not, like a malignant demon, so mislead me as to invalidate my most vivid memory and careful reasoning. Descartes' constructive argument starts with "I think, therefore I am." But, almost surreptitiously, he admits three other "self-evident truths":

1. Whatever is clearly and distinctly perceived is true.
2. Nothing can be without a cause.
3. The cause must be at least as great as the effect.

From these premises he deduces two additional "truths"

4. God exists.
5. God, being perfect, cannot deceive me.

The rest of his argument follows rather quickly. He argues for the existence of other minds and material objects alike on the grounds of God's veracity. This means not that all my ideas are true but simply that the faculties God has given me are reliable when used correctly—without prejudice, hastiness, or naiveté. I can trust only "firm conceptions born in a sound and attentive mind from the light of reason alone" and rigorous deductions from these conceptions.

The remainder of Meditation III and Meditations IV and V are omitted.]

My "idea" of God is a perfect God.

MEDITATION VI

Of the Existence of Material Things, and of the Real Distinction Between the Soul and Body of Man

...First of all I shall recall to my memory those matters which I hitherto held to be true, as having perceived them through the senses, and the foundations on which my belief has rested; in the next place I shall examine the reasons which have since obliged me to place them in doubt; in the last place I shall consider which of them I must now believe.

First of all, then, I perceived that I had a head, hands, feet, and all other members of which this body—which I considered as a part, or possibly even as the whole, of myself—is composed. Further I was sensible that this body was placed amidst manyothers, from which it was capable of being affectedin many different ways, beneficial and hurtful, andI remarked that a certain feeling of pleasure accompanied those that were beneficial, and pain those which were harmful. And in addition to this pleasure and pain, I also experienced hunger, thirst, and other similar appetites, as also certain corporeal inclinations towards joy, sadness, anger, and other similar passions. And outside myself, in addition to extension, figure, and motions of bodies, I remarked in them hardness, heat, and all other tactile qualities, and, further light and color, and scents and sounds, the variety of which gave me the means of distinguishing the sky, the earth, the sea, and generally all the other bodies, one from the other. And certainly, considering the ideas of all these qualities which presented themselves to my mind, and which alone I perceived properly or immediately, it was not without reason that I believed myself to perceive objects quite different from my thought, to wit, bodies from which those ideas proceeded; for I found by experience that these ideas presented themselves to me without my consent being requisite, so that I could not perceive any object, however desirous I might be, unless it were present to the organs of sense; and it was not in my power not to perceive it, when it was present. And because the ideas which I perceived through the senses were much more lively, more clear, and even, in their own way, more distinct than any of those which I could of myself frame in meditation, or than those I found impressed on my memory, it appeared as though they could not have proceeded from my mind, so that they must necessarily have been produced in me by some other things. And having no knowledge of those objects excepting the knowledge which the ideas themselves gave me, nothing was more likely to occur to my mind than that the objects were similar to the ideas which were caused. And because I likewise remembered that I had formerly made use of my senses rather than

my reason, and recognized that the ideas which I formed of myself were not so distinct as those which I perceived through the senses, and that they were most frequently even composed of portions of these last, I persuaded myself easily that I had no idea in my mind which had not formerly come to me through the senses. Nor was it without some reason that I believed that this body (which by a certain special right I call my own) belonged to me more properly and more strictly than any other; for in fact I could never be separated from it as from other bodies; I experienced in it and on account of it all my appetites and affections, and finally I was touched by the feeling of pain and the titillation of pleasure in its parts, and not in the parts of other bodies which were separated from it. But when I inquired, why, from some, I know not what, painful sensation, there follows sadness of mind, and from the pleasurable sensation there arises joy, or why this mysterious emotion of the stomach which I call hunger causes me to desire to eat, and dryness of throat causes a desire to drink, and so on, I could give no reason excepting that nature taught me so; for there is certainly no affinity (that I at least can understand) between the craving of the stomach and the desire to eat, any more than between the perception of whatever causes pain and the thought of sadness which arises from this perception. And in the same way it appeared to me that I had learned from nature all the other judgments which I formed regarding the objects of my senses, since I remarked that these judgments were formed in me before I had the leisure to weigh and consider any reasons which might oblige me to make them.

But afterwards many experiences little by little destroyed all the faith which I had rested in my senses; for I from time to time observed that those towers which from afar appeared to me to be round, more closely observed seemed square, and that colossal statues raised on the summit of these towers, appeared as quite tiny statues when viewed from the bottom; and so in an infinitude of other cases I found error in judgments founded on the external senses. And not only in those founded on the external senses, but even in those founded on the internal as well; for is there anything more intimate or more internal than pain? And yet I have learned from some persons whose arms or legs have been cut off, that they sometimes seemed to feel pain in the part which had been amputated, which made me think that I could not be quite certain that it was a certain member which pained me, even although I felt pain in it. And to those grounds of doubt I have lately added two others, which are very general; the first is that I never have believed myself to feel anything in waking moments which I cannot also sometimes believe myself to feel when I sleep, and as I do not think that these things which I seem to find in sleep, proceed from objects outside of me, I do not see any reason why I should have this belief regarding objects which I seem to perceive while awake. The other was that being still ignorant, or rather supposing myself to be ignorant, of the author of my being, I saw nothing to prevent me from having been so constituted by nature that I might be deceived even in matters which seemed to me to be most certain. And as to the grounds on which I was formerly persuaded of the truth of sensible objects, I had not much trouble in replying to them. For since nature seemed to cause me to lean towards many things from which reason repelled me, I did not believe that I should trust much to the teachings of nature. And although the ideas which I receive by the senses do not depend on my will, I did not think that one should for that reason conclude that they proceeded from things different from myself, since possibly some faculty might be discovered in me—though hitherto unknown to me—which produced them.

But now that I begin to know myself better, and to discover more clearly the author of my being, I do not in truth think that I should rashly admit all the matters which the senses seem to teach us, but, on the other hand, I do not think that I should doubt them all universally.

And first of all, because I know that all things which I apprehend clearly and distinctly can be created by God as I apprehend them, it suffices that I am able to apprehend one thing apart from another clearly and distinctly in order to be certain that the one is different from the other, since they may be made to exist in separation at least by the omnipotence of God; and it does not signify by what power this separation is made in order to compel me to judge them to be different: and, therfore, just because I know certainly that I exist, and that meanwhile I do not remark that any other thing necessarily pertains to my nature or essence excepting that I am a thinking thing, I rightly conclude that my essence consists solely in the fact that I am a thinking thing [or a substance whose whole essence or nature is to think]. And although possibly (or rather certainly, as I shall say in a moment) I possess a body with which I am very intimately conjoined, yet because, on the one side, I have a clear and distinct idea of myself inasmuch as I am only a thinking and unextended thing, and as, on the other, I possess a distinct idea of body, inasmuch as it is only an extended and unthinking thing, it is certain that this I [that is to say, my soul by which I am what I am], is entirely and absolutely distinct from my body, and can exist without it....

There is a great difference between mind and body, inasmuch as body is by nature always divisible, and the mind is entirely indivisible. For, as a matter of fact, when I consider the mind, that is to say, myself inasmuch as I am only a thinking thing, I cannot distinguish in myself any parts, but apprehend myself to be clearly one and entire; and although the whole mind seems to be united to the whole body, yet if a foot, or an arm, or some other part, is separated from my body, I am aware that nothing has been taken away from my mind. And the faculties of willing, feeling, conceiving, etc., cannot be properly speaking said to be its parts, for it is one and the same mind which employs itself in willing and in feeling and understanding. But it is quite otherwise with corporeal or extended objects, for there is not one of these imaginable by me which my mind cannot easily divide into parts, and which consequently I do not recognize as being indivisible; this would be sufficient to teach me that the mind or soul of man is entirely different from the body, if I have not already learned it from other sources. . . .

From this it is quite clear that, notwithstanding the supreme goodness of God, the nature of man, inasmuch as it is composed of mind and body, cannot be otherwise than sometimes a source of deception. For if there is any cause which excites, not in the foot but in some parts of the nerves which are extended between the foot and the brain, or even the brain itself, the same movement which usually is produced when the foot is detrimentally affected, pain will be experienced as though it were in the foot, and the sense will thus naturally be deceived; for since the same movement in the brain is capable of causing but one sensation in the mind, and this sensation is much more frequently excited by a cause which hurts the foot than by another existing in some other quarter, it is reasonable that it should convey to the mind pain in the foot rather than in any other part of the body. And although the parchedness of the throat does not always proceed, as it usually does, from the fact that drinking is essential for the health of the body, but sometimes comes from quite a different cause, as is the case with dropsical patients, it is yet much better that it should mislead on this occasion than if, on the other hand, it were always to deceive us when the body is in good health; and so on in similar cases.

And certainly this consideration is of great service to me, not only in enabling me to recognize all the errors to which my nature is subject, but also in enabling me

to avoid them or to correct them more easily. For knowing that all my senses more frequently indicate to me truth than falsehood respecting the things which concern that which is beneficial to the body, and being able almost always to avail myself of many of them in order to examine one particular thing, and, besides that, being able to make use of my memory in order to connect the present with the past, and of my understanding which already has discovered all the causes of my errors, I ought no longer to fear that falsity may be found in matters every day presented to me by my senses. And I ought to set aside all the doubts of these past days as hyperbolical and ridiculous, particularly that very common uncertainty respecting sleep, which I could not distinguish from the waking state; for at present I find a very notable difference between the two, inasmuch as our memory can never connect our dreams one with the other, or with the whole course of our lives, as it unites events which happen to us while we are awake. And, as a matter of fact, if someone, while I was awake, quite suddenly appeared to me and disappeared as fast as do the images which I see in sleep, so that I could not know from whence the form came nor whither it went, it would not be without reason that I should deem it a specter or a phantom formed by my brain [and similar to those which I form in sleep], rather than a real man. But when I perceive things as to which I know distinctly both the place from which they proceed, and that in which they are, and the time at which they appeared to me; and when, without any interruption, I can connect the perceptions which I have of them with the whole course of my life, I am perfectly assured that these perceptions occur while I am waking and not during sleep. And I ought in no wise to doubt the truth of such matters, if, after having called up all my senses, my memory, and my understanding, to examine them, nothing is brought to evidence by any one of them which is repugnant to what is set forth by the others. For because God is in no wise a deceiver, it follows that I am not deceived in this. But because the exigencies of action often oblige us to make up our minds before having leisure to examine matters carefully, we must confess that the life of man is very frequently subject to error in respect to individual objects, and we must in the end acknowledge the infirmity of our nature.

COMMENT

Dualism Attacked

The distinction between mind and body is closely related to the method of doubt. Descartes notes that he can be certain that he exists as a thinking being even when he is still in doubt whether he has a body; hence, he concludes that the mind and body must be distinct and that his real essence is to think.

Descartes recognized two distinct realms of being. One is the world described by physics, a world that does not depend on our thoughts. It would continue to exist and operate if there were no human beings at all. Its essence is to be extended. The other is the world whose essence is thought—perception, willing, feeling, reasoning, imagining, and the corresponding ideas or mental representations.

A human being, as a compound of mind and body, belongs to both realms. How a person can thus be both two and one poses a difficult problem. Despite the apparent paradox, Descartes believed that mind and body, although radically different, are harmoniously combined in the human organism and that the unextended mind somehow interacts with the extended body.

This dualism is attacked in Gillbert Ryle's famous polemic against "the ghost in the machine." He characterizes the "official theory" of mind and body that stems from Descartes as based on a "category mistake." A mistake of this sort occurs when something is taken to belong to a different type or class than its true one. For example, it would be a category mistake if a spectator at a baseball game wanted to know which player did the pitching, which the catching, and which the exercising of "team spirit." The mistake, in this instance, would be to suppose that exercising team spirit is the same sort of thing as catching and pitching.

The category mistake involved in dualism is to regard both minds and bodies as things of the same logical type, or to use Descartes' terms, as "substances." This leads, declares Ryle, to the false supposition that the mind is an invisible thing somehow having dealings with another thing, the visible body. Each thing is described as having unique and independent properties, bodies being in space and subject to mechanical laws, minds being spaceless and characterized by spiritual capacities. The mental ghost thinks and the bodily machine moves: Somehow each influences the other, although it is strange and mysterious how this interaction takes place.

Ryle objects to the tendency to partition off the mental from the physical. For example, he says,

> When we read novels, biographies, and reminiscences, we do not find the chapters partitioned into section "A," covering the hero's "bodily" doings, and section "B," covering his "mental" doings. We find unpartitioned accounts of what he did and thought and felt, of what he said to others and to himself, of the mountains he tried to climb and the problems he tried to solve.[1]

Reacting against introspectionism, Ryle tries to explain mental life in terms of witnessable activities. "Overt intelligent performances," he declares, "are not clues to the workings of minds; they *are* those workings. Boswell described Johnson's mind when he described how he wrote, talked, ate, fidgeted and fumed."[2]

Whether Ryle succeeds in refuting dualism is debatable. Some critics contend that he is too behavioristic and skips over the more private aspects of mental life. A dream, for example, is directly knowable only by the dreamer. It is different from a table, which you and I and others can inspect. But Ryle does not deny states of consciousness even though he distrusts introspection. He is quite aware that human beings are more than complicated mechanisms. "Man need not be degraded to a machine by being denied to be a ghost in a machine. ..." he writes. "There has yet to be ventured the hazardous leap to the hypothesis that perhaps he is a man."[3]

To return once again to our case study of Abby and Britty, it would seem that Descartes' dualism has at least as much difficulty as do materialism and idealism in explaining how two minds can share one body. Dualism presupposes a one-to-one correlation between minds and bodies, but in this case, there is no such correlation. How are we to understand the reality of the interaction between two minds and one set of perceptual and motor systems? These twins seem to compound the problem of how minds and material bodies can connect up at all, since they have two minds but only one body.

---

[1] *Le Gros Clark, ed., The Physical Basis of Mind (Oxford, England: Basil Blackwell, 1952), p. 77.*

[2] Gilbert Ryle, *The Concept of Mind (New York: Barnes and Noble, 1949), p. 58.*

[3] *Ibid., p. 328.*

12

RELATIONALISM

ALFRED NORTH WHITEHEAD (1861-1947)

The son of a vicar in the Anglican Church, Alfred Whitehead was born at Ramsgate, a village near Canterbury Cathedral. He was educated at Sherborne, one of England's oldest boarding schools, and at Trinity College, Cambridge. He remained in the college for a quarter of a century as a teacher of mathematics and then taught for an additional thirteen years at the University of London.

Meanwhile he had married Evelyn Wade, who bore him a daughter and two sons. "Her vivid life," he wrote in an autobiographical sketch, "has taught me that beauty, moral and esthetic, is the aim of existence; and that kindness, and love, and artistic satisfaction are among its modes of attainment."[1]

In 1924, at the age of sixty-three, he joined the Philosophy Department at Harvard, where he taught until his retirement in 1937. Although he had collaborated with Bertrand Russell in writing the great *Principia Mathematica* (1910–1913), it was not until his later life that he turned to speculative philosophy, writing a brilliant series of books, including *The Concept of Nature* (1920), *Science and the Modern World* (1925), *Process and Reality* (1929), and *Adventures of Ideas* (1933). These works established his reputation as one of the towering figures in modern thought. He died in his eighty-seventh year in his small apartment near Harvard Yard.

OBJECTS AND SUBJECTS

... Τὸ παρὸν ἑχαστω πάθος, ἐξ ὧν αἱ αἰσθήσεις χαὶ αἱ χατὰ ὑαυτας δόξαι γίγνονται, ... *Theaetetus, 179 C.*

(§1) *Prefatory.*—When Descartes, Locke, and Hume undertake the analysis of experience, they utilize those elements in their own experience which lie clear and distinct, fit for the exactitude of intellectual discourse. It is tacitly assumed, except by Plato, that the more fundamental factors will ever lend themselves for discrimination with peculiar clarity. This assumption is here directly challenged.

---

[1] Paul Arthur Schilpp, *The Philosophy of Alfred North Whitehead* (Evanston, IL: Northwestern University, 1941), p. 8.

Reprinted with permission of Macmillam Publishing Company from *Adventures of Ideas* by Alfred North Whitehead. © 1933 by Macmillan Publishing Company; copyright renewed 1961 by Evelyn Whitehead.

(§2) *Structure of Experience.*—No topic has suffered more from this tendency of philosophers than their account of the object-subject structure of experience. In the first place, this structure has been identified with the bare relation of knower to known. The subject is the knower, the object is the known. Thus, with this interpretation, the object-subject relation is the known-knower relation. It then follows that the more clearly any instance of this relation stands out for discrimination, the more safely we can utilize it for the interpretation of the status of experience in the universe of things. Hence Descartes' appeal to clarity and distinctness.

This deduction presupposes that the subject–object relation is the fundamental structural pattern of experience. I agree with this presupposition, but not in the sense in which subject–object is identified with knower–known. I contend that the notion of mere knowledge is a high abstraction, and that conscious discrimination itself is a variable factor only present in the more elaborate examples of occasions of experience. The basis of experience is emotional. Stated more generally, the basic fact is the rise of an affective tone originating from things whose relevance is given.

(§3) *Phraseology.*—Thus the Quaker word 'concern', divested of any suggestion of knowledge, is more fitted to express this fundamental structure. The occasion as subject has a 'concern' for the object. And the 'concern' at once places the object as a component in the experience of the subject, with an affective tone drawn from this object and directed towards it. With this interpretation the subject–object relation is the fundamental structure of experience.

Quaker usages of language are not widely spread. Also each phraseology leads to a crop of misunderstandings. The subject–object relation can be conceived as Recipient and Provoker, where the fact provoked is an affective tone about the status of the provoker in the provoked experience. Also the total provoked occasion is a totality involving many such examples of provocation. Again this phraseology is unfortunate; for the word 'recipient' suggests a passivity which is erroneous.

(§4) *Prehensions.*—A more formal explanation is as follows. An occasion of experience is an activity, analysable into modes of functioning which jointly constitute its process of becoming. Each mode is analysable into the total experience as active subject, and into the thing or object with which the special activity is concerned. This thing is a datum, that is to say, is describable without reference to its entertainment in that occasion. An object is anything performing this function of a datum provoking some special activity of the occasion in question. Thus subject and object are relative terms. An occasion is a subject in respect to its special activity concerning an object; and anything is an object in respect to its provocation of some special activity within a subject. Such a mode of activity is termed a 'prehension'. Thus a prehension involves three factors. There is the occasion of experience within which the prehension is a detail of activity; there is the datum whose relevance provokes the origination of this prehension, this datum is the prehended object, there is the subjective from, which is the affective tone determining the effectiveness of that prehension in that occasion of experience. How the experience constitutes itself depends on its complex of subjective forms.

(§5) *Individuality.*—The individual immediacy of an occasion is the final unity of subjective form, which is the occasion as an absolute reality. This immediacy is its moment of sheer individuality, bounded on either side by essential relativity. The occasion arises from relevant objects, and perishes into the status of an object for other occasions. But it enjoys its decisive moment of absolute self-attainment as emotional unity. As used here the words 'individual' and 'atom' have the same meaning, that they apply to composite things with an absolute reality which their components lack. These words properly apply to an actual entity in its immediacy of self-attainment when it stands out as for itself alone, with its own affective self-enjoyment. The term 'monad' also expresses this essential unity at the decisive moment, which stands between its birth and its perishing. The creativity of the world is the throbbing emotion of the past hurling itself into a new transcendent fact. It is the flying dart, of which Lucretius speaks, hurled beyond the bounds of the world.

(§6) *Knowledge.*—All knowledge is conscious discrimination of objects experienced. But this conscious discrimination, which is knowledge, is nothing more than an additional factor in the subjective form of the interplay of subject with object. This interplay is the stuff constituting those individual things which make up the sole reality of the Universe. These individual things are the individual occasions of experience, the actual entities.

But we do not so easily get rid of knowledge. After all, it is knowledge that philosophers seek. And all knowledge is derived from, and verified by, direct intuitive observation. I accept this axiom of empiricism as stated in this general form. The question then arises how the structure of experience outlined above is directly observed. In answering this challenge I remind myself of the old advice that the doctrines which best repay critical examination are those which for the longest period have remained unquestioned.

(§7) *Sense-perception.*—The particular agelong group of doctrines which I have in mind is: (1) that all perception is by the mediation of our bodily sense-organs, such as eyes, palates, noses, ears, and the diffused bodily organization furnishing touches, aches, and other bodily sensations; (2) that all percepta are bare sensa, in patterned connections, given in the immediate present; (3) that our experience of a social world is an interpretative reaction wholly derivative from this perception; (4) that our emotional and purposive experience is a reflective reaction derived from the original perception, and

intertwined with the interpretative reaction and partly shaping it. Thus the two reactions are different aspects of one process, involving interpretative, emotional, and purpose factors. Of course, we are all aware that there are powerful schools of philosophy which explicitly reject this doctrine. Yet I cannot persuade myself that this rejection has been taken seriously by writers belonging to the schools in question. When the direct question as to things perceived arises, it seems to me that the answer is always returned in terms of sensa perceived.

(§8) *Perceptive Functions.*—In the examination of the sensationalist doctrine, the first question to be asked concerns the general definition of what we mean by those functions of experience which we term 'perceptions'. If we define them as those experiential functions which arise directly from the stimulation of the various bodily sense-organs, then argument ceases. The traditional doctrine then becomes a mere matter of definition of the use of the word 'perception'. Indeed, having regard to long-standing usage, I am inclined to agree that it may be advisable for philosophers to confine the word 'perception' to this limited meaning. But the point on which I am insisting is that this meaning *is* limited, and that there is a wider meaning with which this limited use of the term 'perception' has been tacitly identified.

(§9) *Objects.*—The process of experiencing is constituted by the reception of entities, whose being is antecedent to that process, into the complex fact which is that process itself. These antecedent entities, thus received as factors into the process of experiencing, are termed 'objects' for that experiential occasion. Thus primarily the term 'object' expresses the relation of the entity, thus denoted, to one or more occasions of experiencing. Two conditions must be fulfilled in order that an entity may function as an object in a process of experiencing: (1) the entity must be *antecedent*, and (2) the entity must be experienced in virtue of its antecedence; it must be *given*. Thus an object must be a thing received, and must not be either a *mode* of reception or a thing *generated* in that occasion. Thus the process of experiencing is constituted by the reception of objects into the unity of that complex occasion which is the process itself. The process creates itself, but it does not create the objects which it receives as factors in its own nature.

'Objects' for an occasion can also be termed the 'data' for that occasion. The choice of terms entirely depends on the metaphor which you prefer. One word carries the literal meaning of 'lying in the way of', and the other word carries the literal meaning of 'being given to'. But both words suffer from the defect of suggesting that an occasion of experiencing arises out of a passive situation which is a mere welter of many data.

(§10) *Creativity.*—The exact contrary is the case. The initial situation includes a factor of activity which is the reason for the origin of that occasion of experience. This factor of activity is what I have called 'Creativity'. The initial situation with its creativity can be termed the initial phase of the new occasion. It can equally well be termed the 'actual world' relative to that occasion. It has a certain unity of its own, expressive of its capacity for providing the objects requisite for a new occasion, and also expressive of its conjoint activity whereby it is essentially the primary phase of a new occasion. It can thus be termed a 'real potentiality'. The 'potentiality' refers to the passive capacity, the term 'real' refers to the creative activity, where the Platonic definition of 'real' in the *Sophist* is referred to. This basic situation, this actual world, this primary phase, this real potentiality—however you characterize it—as a whole is active with its inherent creativity, but in its details it provides the passive objects which derive their activity from the creativity of the whole. The creativity is the actualization of potentiality, and the process of actualization is an occasion of experiencing. Thus viewed in abstraction objects are pas-

sive, but viewed in conjunction they carry the creativity which drives the world. The process of creation is the form of unity of the Universe.

(§11) *Perception.*—In the preceding sections, the discovery of objects as factors in experience was explained. The discussion was phrased in terms of an ontology which goes beyond the immediate purpose, although the status of objects cannot be understood in the absence of some such ontology explaining their function in experience, that is to say, explaining why an occasion of experience by reason of its nature requires objects.

The objects are the factors in experience which function so as to express that the occasion originates by including a transcendent universe of other things. Thus it belongs to the essence of each occasion of experience that it is concerned with, an otherness transcending itself. The occasion is one among others, and including the others which it is among. Consciousness is an emphasis upon a selection of these objects. Thus perception is consciousness analysed in respect to those objects selected for this emphasis. Conciousness is the acme of emphasis.

It is evident that this definition of perception is wider than the narrow definition based upon sense-perception, sensa, and the bodily sense-organs.

(§12) *Non-Sensuous Perception.*—This wider definition of perception can be of no importance unless we can detect occasions of experience exhibiting modes of functioning which fall within its wider scope. If we discover such instances of non-sensuous perception, then the tacit identification of perception with sense-perception must be a fatal error barring the advance of systematic metaphysics.

Our first step must involve the clear recognition of the limitations inherent in the scope of sense-perception. This special mode of functioning essentially exhibits percepta as *here, now, immediate,* and *discrete.* Every impression of sensation is a distinct existence, declares Hume; and there can be no reasonable doubt of this doctrine. But even Hume clothes each impression with force and liveliness. It must be distinctly understood that no prehension, even of bare sensa, can be divested of its affective tone, that is to say, of its character of a 'concern' in the Quaker sense. Concernedness is of the essence of perception.

Gaze at a patch of red. In itself as an object, and apart from other factors of concern, this patch of red, as the mere object of that present act of perception, is silent as to the past or the future. How it orginates, how it will vanish, whether indeed there was a past, and whether there will be a future, are not disclosed by its own nature. No material for the interpretation of sensa is provided by the sensa themselves, as they stand starkly, barely, present and immediate. We *do* interpret them; but no thanks for the feat is due to them. The epistemologies of the last two hundred years are employed in the tacit introduction of alien consideration by the uncritical use of current forms of speech. A copious use of simple literary forms can thus provide a philosophy delightful to read, easy to understand, and entirely fallacious. Yet the usages of language do prove that our habitual interpretations of these barren sensa, though in particular instances liable to error. But the evidence on which these interpretations are based is entirely drawn from the vast background and foreground of non-sensuous perception with which sense-perception is fused, and without which it can never be. We can discern no clean-cut sense-perception wholly concerned with present fact.

In human experience, the most compelling example of non-sensuous perception is our knowledge of our own immediate past. I am not referring to our memories of a day past, or of an hour past, or of a minute past. Such memories are blurred and confused by the intervening occasions of our personal existence. But our immediate past is constituted by that occasion, or by that group of fused occasions, which enters into experience devoid of any perceptible medium intervening between it and the present immediate fact. Roughly speaking, it is that portion of our past lying between a tenth of a second and half a second ago. It is gone, and yet it is here. It is our indubitable self, the foundation of our present existence. Yet the present occasion while claiming self-identity, while sharing the very nature of the bye-gone occasion in all its living activities, nevertheless is engaged in modifying it, in adjusting it to *other* influences, in completing it with *other* values, in deflecting it to other purposes. The present moment is constituted by the influx of *the other* into that self-identity which is the continued life of the immediate past within the immediacy of the present.

(§13) *Illustration.*—Consider a reasonably rapid speaker enunciating the proper name 'United States'. There are four syllables here. When the third syllable is reached, probably the first is in the immediate past; and certainly during the word 'States' the first syllable of the phrase lies beyond the immediacy of the present. Consider the speaker's own occasions of existence. Each occasion achieves for him the immediate sense-presentation of sounds, the earlier syllables in the earlier occasions, the word 'States' in the final occasion. As mere sensuous perception, Hume is right in saying that the sound 'United' as a mere sensum has nothing in its nature referent to the sound 'States', and the two conjointly live in the present, by the energizing of the past occasion as it claims its self-identical existence as a living issue in the present. The immediate past as surviving to be again lived through in the present is the palmary instance of nonsensuous perception.

The Humian explanation, involving the 'association of ideas', has its importance for this topic. But it is not the point for this example. The speaker, a citizen of the United States and therefore dominated by an immense familiarity with that phrase, may in fact have been enunciating the phrase 'United Fruit Company'—a corporation which, for all its importance, he may not have heard of till half a minute earlier. In his experience the relation of the later to the earlier parts of this phrase is entirely the same as that described above for the phrase 'United States'. In this latter example it is to be noted that while association would have led him to 'States', the fact of the energizing of the immediate past compelled him to conjoin 'Fruit' in the immediacy of the present. He uttered the word 'United' with the non-sensuous anticipation of an immediate future with the sensum 'Fruit', and he then uttered the word 'Fruit' with the non-sensuous perception of the immediate past with the sensum 'United'. But, unfamiliar as he was with the United Fruit Company, he had no association connecting the various words in the phrase 'United Fruit Company'; while, patriot as he was, the orator had the strongest association connecting the words 'United' and 'States'. Perhaps, indeed, he was the founder of the Company, and also invented the name. He then uttered the mere sounds 'United Fruit Company' for the first time in the history of the English language. There could not have been the vestige of an association to help him along. The final occasion of his experience which drove his body to the utterance of the sound 'Company' is only explicable by his concern with the earlier occasions with their subjective forms of intention to procure the utterance of the complete phrase. Also, in so far as there was consciousness, there was direct observation of the past with its intention finding its completion in the present fact. This is an instance of direct intuitive observation which is incapable of reduction to the sensationalist formula. Such observations have not the clear sharp-cut precision of sense-perception. But surely there can be no doubt about them. For instance, if the speaker had been interrupted after the words 'United Fruit', he might have resumed his speech with the words 'I meant to add the word Company'. Thus during the interruption, the past was energizing in his experience as carrying in itself an unfulfilled intention.

(§14) *Conformation of Feeling.*— Another point emerges in this explanation, namely, the doctrine of the continuity of nature. This doctrine balances and limits the doctrine of the absolute individuality of each occasion of experience. There is a continuity between the subjective form of the immediate past occasion and the subjective from of its primary prehension in the origination of the new occasion. In the process of synthesis of the many basic prehensions modifications enter. But the subjective forms of the immediate past are continuous with those of the present. I will term this doctrine of continuity, the Doctrine of Conformation of Feeling.

Suppose that for some period of time some circumstance of his life has aroused anger in a man. How does he now know that a quarter of a second ago he was angry? Of course, he remembers it; we all know that. But I am enquiring about this very curious fact of memory, and have chosen an overwhelmingly vivid instance. The mere word 'memory' explains nothing. The first phase in the immediacy of the new occasion is that of the conformation of feelings. The feeling as enjoyed by the past occasion is present in the new occasion as datum felt, with a subjective form conformal to that of the datum. Thus if A be the past occasion, D the datum felt by A with subjective form describable as A angry, then this feeling—namely, A feeling D with subjective form of anger—is initially felt by the new occasion B with the same subjective form of anger. The anger is continuous throughout the successive occasions of experience. This continuity of subjective form is the initial sympathy of B for A. It is the primary ground for the continuity of nature.

Let us elaborate the consideration of the angry man. His anger is the subjective form of his feeling some datum D. A quarter of a second later he is, consciously, or unconsciously, embodying his past as a datum in the present, and maintaining in the present the anger which is a datum from the past. In so far as that feeling has fallen within the illumination of conciousness, he enjoys a non-sensuous perception of the past emotion. He enjoys this emotion both objectively, as belonging to the past, and also formally as continued in the present. This continuation is the continuity of nature. I have labored this point, because traditional doctrines involve its denial.

Thus non-sensuous perception is one aspect of the continuity of nature. ...

(§17) *Mind and Nature Compared.*— The doctrine of human experience which I have outlined above, also for its own purposes preserves a doctrine of distinguishable individualities which are the separate occasions of experience, and a doctrine of continuity expressed by the identity of subjective form inherited conformably from one occasion to the other. The physical flux corresponds to the conformal inheritance at the base of each occasions of experience. This inheritance, in spite of its continuity of subjective form, is nevertheless an inheritance from definite individual occasions. Thus, if the analogy is to hold, in the account of the general system of relations binding the past to the present, we should expect a doctrine of quanta, where the individualities of the occasions are relevant, and a doctrine of continuity where the conformal transference of subjective form is the dominating fact.

The notion of physical energy, which is at the base of physics, must then be conceived as an abstraction from the complex energy, emotional and purposeful, inherent in the subjective form of the final synthesis in which each occasion completes itself. It is the total vigor of each activity of experience. The mere phrase that 'physical science is an abstraction', is a confession of philosophic failure. It is the business of rational thought to describe the more concrete fact from which that abstraction is derivable.

(§18) *Personality.*—In our account of human experience we have attenuated human personality into a genetic relation between occasions of human experience. Yet personal unity is an inescapable fact. The Platonic and Christian doctrines of the soul, the Epicurean doctrine of a Concilium of subtle atoms, the Cartesian doctrine of Thinking Substance, the Humanitarian doctrine of the Rights of Man, the general Common Sense of civilized mankind,— these doctrines between them dominate the whole span of Western thought. Evidently there is a fact to be accounted for. Any philosophy must provide some doctrine of personal identity. In some sense there is a unity in the life of each man, from birth to death. The two modern philosophers who most consistently reject the notion of a self-identical Soul-Substance are Hume and William James. But the problem remains for them, as it does for the philosophy of organism, to provide an adequate account of this undoubted personal unity, maintaining itself amidst the welter of circumstance. ...

(§20)*Immanence.*—This is at once the doctrine of the unity of nature, and of the unity of each human life. The conclusion follows that our consciousness of the self-identity pervading our life-thread of occasions, is nothing other than knowledge of a special strand of unity within the general unity of nature. It is a locus within the whole, marked out by its own peculiarities, but otherwise exhibiting the general principle which guides the constitution of the whole. This general principle is the object-to-subject structure of experience. It can be otherwise stated as the vector-structure of nature. Or otherwise, it can be conceived as the doctrine of the immanence of the past energizing in the present.

This doctrine of immanence is practically that doctrine adumbrated by the Hellenistic Christian theologians of Egypt. But they applied the doctrine only to the relation of God to the world, and not to all actualities. ...

COMMENT

Whitehead's Philosophy of Process

Certain philosophers are especially difficult to understand because in addition to dealing with profound issues and engaging in complex analysis, they invent their own vocabulary. Whitehead is one such philosopher. However, in the twentieth century, few thinkers have accomplished as much or become as influential as Whitehead, even though his writings are notoriously complex and idiosyncratic. Generally, his theory of the nature of reality is termed *process philosophy*. Its chief characteristic is its insistence on the *interrelatedness* of all aspects of reality, from the most complex to the simplest. Whitehead saw the world as a vast, organic, weblike reality evolving through time and space by means of continuous connections, disconnections and reconnections.

Whitehead begins by rejecting traditional approaches to metaphysics and epistemology, which assume that the world and our knowledge of it are based on and can be broken down into individual units known as subjects and objects. Adherents of such "atomism" are guilty of what he called "the fallacy of misplaced concreteness." For Whitehead, the fundamental "units" of reality are actually "events," not "things." He termed these free-flowing interchanging happenings *occasions* or *actual entities,* and he saw them as the intersections of the world's continuously evolving energy.

When these events or intersections occur, they are drawn together or coalesce out of what Whitehead calls a mutual "concern"; a relevance arises in which that functioning as the subject and that serving as the object are conjoined. This relationship is always a *relative* one in the sense that the subject can serve as the object for yet another subject, or even for its own object at another time and place, or even simultaneously. The unity formed by this reciprocal interaction is termed by Whitehead a *prehension*. Thus the fundamental nature of reality is relational and processional. Actual entities really are events occurring within the flux of the ongoing process of energy constituting the totality of all that is.

Perhaps a simple, though necessarily limited, illustration will be of help at this juncture. Consider the philosophy class you are presently enrolled in. Rather than thinking of the students in it as the individual units that make it real, try thinking of the interrelatedness of the class itself as that which contributes to the reality of the individual students. This class, as an "actual entity," has come into being and serves to define the students as members of itself. Although each student did exist prior to the class, the class makes a definitive contribution to each individual's identity and character from this point on. Moreover, the whole of reality, consisting of the total sum of all current and previous relationships, not only existed prior to the students but also has functioned as the determining and constitutive factor in their becoming who they are. In short, we are all a function of the relationships in which we find ourselves.

This way of looking at reality is, admittedly, somewhat mind-bending because it asks us to reverse the usual way we think of things. We generally think of relationships as being the result of the individuals that constitute them rather than the other way around. It is a bit like altering our way of locating addresses, according to street names and numbers, to that of the Japanese, who locate places by naming and numbering intersections rather than streets. It takes some getting used to, but Whitehead insists that relational reality is more fundamental than individual reality, that the whole is more than and logically prior to the parts.

The "knowledge" that arises within the prehension that comprises an "occasion" is said by Whitehead to be the result of the creative energy or process that drives the natural order. Both perceptual and non-sensuous knowledge are, for Whitehead, relational realities. In other words, there is no such thing as mere "objective" knowledge; all cognition is based on "concern," or our interactive awareness. This is the point of his example of our knowledge of our immediate past. Knowing is what defines the knower and the known, not vice versa.

Finally, there is, according to Whitehead's view, a basic continuity that runs through all of reality, a kind of networking that ties it all together and provides a sense of "closure" on both the metaphysical and personal levels. There is a dynamic process or energy that animates all reality, from rocks to minds, and that provides a general organic unity to the whole. Individual or personal identity is only "a strand of unity within the general unity of nature." Each occasion is knitted to the next, and together they form what Whitehead calls a nexus. Should a nexus take on increased relevance and prehension, thereby achieving a measurable place in time and space, such as is the case with individual persons, it can be said to exist as a "society."

There are, to be sure, those philosophers who find all this talk of organisms, occasions, and process quite confusing and even misleading. It is one thing, they might say, to invent a fancy vocabulary, quite another to establish its application to reality. There seems to be a stubborn "rightness" about our way of talking about things and qualities as the fundamental building blocks of reality. Moreover, Whitehead's philosophy of relationality does not actually explain how truth can be distinguished from error, even and especially in reference to his own theories. Nonetheless, Whitehead's approach does have the advantage of seeming to be in harmony with Einsteinain relativity and quantum physics of the twentieth century. At the very least it must be admitted that it is a highly creative and influential approach to metaphysics.

It is, indeed, possible to argue that this "relational" understanding of reality does an excellent job of explaining the facts involved in the case of Abby and Britty as twin persons in a single body. For Whitehead, the fundamental realities in this case are the interactions involved and are not some sort of metaphysical "substances" such as "mind" and "matter." Of course, it can still be asked how these interactions can occur prior to there being any entities to interact with each other. How might Whitehead respond to this question with respect to the twins?

13

INTERACTIONISM

PAULO FREIRE (1921–1997)

Paulo Freire was born and raised in Recife, a poverty-stricken area of Brazil. As a young man he struggled with the problems of oppression and exploitation that dominated his country as the result of centuries of Portuguese imperialism. Becoming convinced that the only lasting solution to these difficulties lay in the education of the vast peasant population, Freire earned a Ph.D. in the philosophy of education in 1959 and initiated literacy programs in the villages of rural Brazil. Such activity was extremely threatening to the aristocratic government, and Freire was jailed in 1964. Upon his release, he worked for UNESCO in Chile for several years and taught in the School of Education at Harvard University for several years. His last assignment was as a special consultant to the Office of Education at the World Council of Churches in Geneva, Switzerland.

The following selection, taken from Chapter 3 of his highly influential book *Pedagogy of the Oppressed,* expresses Freire's interactivist understanding of the construction of social reality through political speech and action. In his view, this theory of the world goes hand in hand with a dialogical interpretation of the educative process. The nature of reality is at least partly determined by the nature of cognitivity.

THE POLITICAL CONSTRUCTION OF REALITY

As we attempt to analyze dialogue as a human phenomenon, we discover something which is the essence of dialogue itself: *the word*. But the word is more than just an instrument which makes dialogue possible; accordingly, we must seek its constitutive elements. Within the word we find two dimensions, reflection and action, in such radical interaction that if one is sacrificed—even in part—the other immediately suffers. There is no true word that is not at the same time a praxis.[1] Thus, to speak a true word is to transform the world.[2]

---

[1]
$$\left.\begin{array}{l}\text{Action}\\\text{Reflection}\end{array}\right\} \text{Word} = \text{work} = \text{praxis}$$

Sacrifice of action = verbalism

Sacrifice of reflection = activism

[2] Some of these reflections emerged as a result of conversations with Professor Emani Maria Fiori.

From *Pedagogy of the Oppressed* by Paulo Freire. Copyright © 1970 by Paulo Freire. Reprinted by permission of The Continuum Publishing Co.

An unauthentic word, one which is unable to transform reality, results when dichotomy is imposed upon its constitutive elements. When a word is deprived of its dimension of action, reflection automatically suffers as well; and the word is changed into idle chatter, into *verbalism*, into an alienated and alienating "blah." It becomes an empty word, one which cannot denounce the world, for denunciation is impossible without a commitment to transform, and there is no transformation without action.

On the other hand, if action is emphasized exclusively, to the detriment of reflection, the word is converted into *activism*. The latter—action for action's sake—negates the true praxis and makes dialogue impossible. Either dichotomy, by creating unauthentic forms of existence, creates also unauthentic forms of thought, which reinforce the original dichotomy.

Human existence cannot be silent, nor can it be nourished by false words, but only by true words, with which men transform the world. To exist, humanly, is to *name* the world, to change it. Once named, the world in its turn reappears to the namers as a problem and requires of them a new *naming*. Men are not built in silence,[3] but in word, in work, in action-reflection.

But while to say the true word—which is work, which is praxis—is to transform the world, saying that word is not the privilege of some few men, but the right of every man. Consequently, no one can say a true word alone—nor can he say it *for* another, in a prescriptive act which robs others of their words.

Dialogue is the encounter between men, mediated by the world, in order to name the world. Hence, dialogue cannot occur between those who want to name the world and those who do not wish this naming—between those who deny other men the right to speak their word and those whose right to speak has been denied them. Those who have been denied their primordial right to speak their word must first reclaim this right and prevent the continuation of this dehumanizing aggression.

If it is in speaking their word that men, by naming the world, transform it, dialogue imposes itself as the way by which men achieve significance as men. Dialogue is thus an existential necessity. And since dialogue is the encounter in which the united reflection and action of the dialoguers are addressed to the world which is to be transformed and humanized, this dialogue cannot be reduced to the act of one person's "depositing" ideas in another, nor can it become a simple exchange of ideas to be "consumed" by the discussants. Nor yet is it a hostile, polemical argument between men who are committed neither to the naming of the world, nor to the search for truth, but rather to the imposition of their own truth. Because dialogue is an encounter among men who name the world, it must not be a situation where some men name on behalf of others. It is an act of creation; it must not serve as a crafty instrument for the domination of one man by another. The domination implicit in dialogue is that of the world by the dialoguers; it is conquest of the world for the liberation of men.

Dialogue cannot exist, however, in the absence of a profound love for the world and for men. The naming of the world, which is an act of creation and recreation, is not possible if it is not infused

---

[3] I obviously do not refer to the silence of profound meditation, in which men only apparently leave the world, withdrawing from it in order to consider it in its totality, and thus remaining with it. But this type of retreat is only authentic when the meditator is "bathed" in reality; not when the retreat signifies contempt for the world and flight from it, in a type of "historical schizophrenia."

with love.[4] Love is at the same time the foundation of dialogue and dialogue itself. It is thus necessarily the task of responsible Subjects and cannot exist in a relation of domination. Domination reveals the pathology of love: sadism in the dominator and masochism in the dominated. Because love is an act of courage, not of fear, love is commitment of other men. No matter where the oppressed are found, the act of love is commitment to their cause—the cause of liberation. And this commitment, because it is loving, is dialogical. As an act of bravery, love cannot be sentimental; as an act of freedom, it must not serve as a pretext for manipulation. It must generate other acts of freedom; otherwise, it is not love. Only by abolishing the situation of oppression is it possible to restore the love which that situation made impossible. If I do not love the world—if I do not love life—if I do not love men—I cannot enter into dialogue.

On the other hand, dialogue cannot exist without humility. The naming of the world, through which men constantly recre-ate that world, cannot be an act of arrogance. Dialogue, as the encounter of men addressed to the common task of learning and acting, is broken if the parties (or one of them) lack humility. How can I dialogue if I always project ignorance onto others and never perceive my own? How can I dialogue if I regard myself as a case apart from other men—mere "its" in whom I cannot recognize other "I"s? How can I dialogue if I consider myself a member of the in-group of "pure" men, the owners of truth and knowledge, for whom all non-members are "these people" or "the great unwashed"? How can I dialogue if I start from the premise that naming the world is the task of an elite and that the presence of the people in history is a sign of deterioration, thus to be avoided? How can I dialogue if I am closed to—and even offended by—the contribution of others? How can I dialogue if I am afraid of being displaced, the mere possibility causing me torment and weakness? Self-sufficiency is incompatible with dialogue. Men who lack humility (or have lost it) cannot come to the people, cannot be their partners in naming the world. Someone who cannot acknowledge himself to be as mortal as everyone else still has a long way to go before he can reach the point of encounter. At the point of encounter there are neither utter ignoramuses nor perfect sages; there are only men who are attempting, together, to learn more than they now know.

Dialogue further requires an intense faith in man, faith in his power to make and remake, to create and recreate, faith in his vocation to be more fully human (which is not the privilege of an elite, but the birthright of all men). Faith in man is an *a priori* requirement for dialogue; the "dialogical man" believes in other men even before he meets them face to face. His faith, however, is not naïve. The "dialogical man" is critical and knows that although it is within the power of men to create and transform, in a concrete situation of alienation men may be impaired in the use of

---

[4] I am more and more convinced that truerevo-lutionaries must perceive the revolution, because of its creative and liberating nature, as an act of love. For me, the revolution, which is not possible without a theory of revolution—and therefore science—is not irreconcilable with love. On the contrary: the revolution is made by men to achieve their humanization. What, indeed, is the deeper motive which moves men to become revolutionaries, but the dehumanization of man? The distortion imposed on the word "love" by the capitalist world cannot prevent the revolution from being essentially loving in character, nor can it prevent the revolutionaries from affirming their love of life. Guevara (while admitting the "risk of seeming ridiculous") was not afraid to affirm it: "Let me say, with the risk of appearing ridiculous, that the true revolutionary is guided by strong feelings of love. It is impossible to think of an authentic revolutionary without this quality." *Venceremos—The Speeches and Writings of Che Guevara*, edited by John Gerassi (New York, 1969), p. 398.

that power. Far from destroying his faith in man, however, this possibility strikes him as a challenge to which he must respond. He is convinced that the power to create and transform, even when thwarted in concrete situations, tends to be reborn. And that rebirth can occur—not gratuitously, but in and through the struggle for liberation—in the supersedence of slave labor by emancipated labor which gives zest to life. Without this faith in man, dialogue is a farce which inevitably degenerates into paternalistic manipulation.

Founding itself upon love, humility, and faith, dialogue becomes a horizontal relationship of which mutual trust between the dialoguers is the logicalconsequence. It would be a contradiction in terms if dialogue—loving, humble, and full of faith—did not produce this climate of mutual trust, which leads the dialoguers into ever closer partnership in the naming of the world. Conversely, such trust is obviously absent in the anti-dialogics of the banking method of education. Whereas faith in man is an *a priori* requirement for dialogue, trust is established by dialogue. Should it founder, it will be seen that the preconditions were lacking. False love, false humility, and feeble faith in man cannot create trust. Trust is contingent on the evidence which one party provides the others of his true, concrete intentions; it cannot exist if that party's words do not coincide with his actions. To say one thing and do another—to take one's own word lightly—cannot inspire trust. To glorify democracy and to silence the people is a farce; to discourse on humanism and to negate man is a lie.

Nor yet can dialogue exist without hope. Hope is rooted in men's incompletion, from which they move out in constant search—a search which can be called out only in communion with other men. Hopelessness is a form of silence, of denying the world and fleeing from it. The dehumanization resulting from an unjust order is not a cause for despair but for hope, leading to the incessant pursuit of the humanity denied by injustice. Hope, however, does not consist in crossing one's arms and waiting. As long as I fight, I am moved by hope; and if I fight with hope, then I can wait. As the encounter of men seeking to be more fully human, dialogue cannot be carried on in a climate of hopelessness. If the dialoguers expect nothing to come of their efforts, their encounter will be empty and sterile, bureaucratic and tedious.

Finally, true dialogue cannot exist unless the dialoguers engage in critical thinking—thinking which discerns an indivisible solidarity between the world and men and admits of no dichotomy between them—thinking which perceives reality as process, as transformation, rather than as a static entity—thinking which does not separate itself from action, but constantly immerses itself in temporality withoutfear of the risks involved. Critical thinking contrasts with naïve thinking, which sees "historical time as a weight, a stratification of the acquisitions and experiences of the past,"[5] from which the present should emerge normalized and "well-behaved." For the naïve thinker, the important thing is accommodation to this normalized "today." For the critic, the important thing is the continuing transformation of realty, in behalf of the continuing humanization of men. In the words of Pierre Furter:

> The goal will no longer be to eliminate the risks of temporality by clutching to guaranteed space, but rather to temporalize space.... The universe is revealed to me not as space, imposing a massive presence to which I can but adapt, but as a scope, a domain which takes shape as I act upon it.[6]

For naïve thinking, the goal is precisely to hold fast to this guaranteed space

---

[5] From the letter of a friend.
[6] Pierre Furter, *Educação e Vida* (Rio, 1966), pp. 26–27.

and adjust to it. By thus denying temporality, it denies itself as well.

Only dialogue, which requires critical thinking, is also capable of generating critical thinking. Without dialogue there is no communication, and without communication there can be no true education. Education which is able to resolve the contradiction between teacher and student takes place in a situation in which both address their act of cognition to the object by which they are mediated. Thus, the dialogical character of education as the practice of freedom does not begin when the teacher-student meets with the students-teachers in a pedagogical situation, but rather when the former first asks himself *what* he will dialogue with the latter *about*. And preoccupation with the content of dialogue is really preoccupation with the program content of education.

For the anti-dialogical banking educator, the question of content simply concerns the program about which he will discourse to his students; and he answers his own question, by organizing his own program. For the dialogical, problem-posing teacher–student, the program content of education is neither a gift nor an imposition—bits of information to be deposited in the students—but rather the organized, systematized, and developed "re-presentation" toindividuals of the things about which they want to know more.[7]

Authentic education is not carried on by "A" *for* "B" or by "A" *about* "B," but rather by "A" *with* "B" mediated by the world—a world which impresses and challenges both parties, giving rise to views or opinions about it. These views, impregnated with anxieties, doubts, hopes, or hopelessness, imply significant themes on the basis of which the program content of education can be built. In its desire to create an ideal model of the "good man," a naïvely conceived humanism often overlooks the concrete, existential, present situation of real men. Authentic humanism, in Pierre Furter's words, "consists in permitting the emergence of the awareness of our full humanity, as a condition and as an obligation, as a situation and as a project."[8] We simply cannot go to the laborers—urban or peasant[9]—in the banking style, to give them "knowledge" or to impose upon them the model of the "good man" contained in a program whose content we have ourselves organized. Many political and educational plans have failed because their author designed them according to their own personal views of reality, never once taking into account (except as mere objects of their action) the *men-in-a-situation* to whom their program was ostensibly directed.

For the truly humanist educator and the authentic revolutionary, the object of action is the reality to be transformed by them together with other men—not other men themselves. The oppressors are the ones who act upon men to indoctrinate them and adjust them to a reality which must remain untouched. Unfortunately, however, in their desire to obtain the support of the people for revolutionary action, revolutionary leaders often fall for the banking line of planning program content from the top down. They approach the peasant

---

[7] In a long conversation with Malraux, Mao Tse-tung declared, "You know I've proclaimed for a long time: we must teach the masses clearly what we have received from them confusedly." André Malraux. *Anti-Memoirs* (New York, 1968), pp. 361–362. This affirmation contains an entire dialogical theory of how to construct the program content of education, which cannot be elaborated according to what the *educator* thinks best for *his* students.

[8] Furter, *op. cit.*, p. 165.

[9] The latter, usually submerged in a colonial context, are almost umbilically linked to the world of nature, in relation to which they feel themselves to be component parts rather than shapers.

or urban masses with projects which may correspond to their own view of the world, but not to that of the people.[10] They forget that their fundamental objective is to fight alongside the people for the recovery of the people's stolen humanity, not to "win the people over" to their side. Such a phrase does not belong in the vocabulary of revolutionary leaders, but in that of the oppressor. The revolutionary's role is to liberate, and be liberated, with the people—not to win them over.

In their political activity, the dominant elites utilize the banking concept to encourage passivity in the oppressed, corresponding with the latter's "submerged" state of consciousness, and take advantage of that passivity to "fill that consciousness with slogans which create even more fear of freedom. This practice is incompatible with a truly liberating course of action, which, by presenting the oppressors' slogans as a problem, helps the oppressed to "eject" those slogans from within themselves. After all, the task of the humanists is surely not that of pitting their slogans against the slogans of the oppressors, with the oppressed as the testing ground, "housing" the slogans of first one group and then the other. On the contrary, the task of the humanists is to see that the oppressed become, aware of the fact that as dual beings, "housing" the oppressors within themselves, they cannot be truly human.

This task implies that revolutionary leaders do not go to the people in order to bring them a message of "salvation," but in order to come to know through dialogue with them both their *objective situation* and their *awareness* of that situation—the various levels of perception of themselves and of the world in which and with which they exist. One cannot expect positive results from an educational or political action program which fails to respect the particular view of the world held by the people. Such a program constitutes cultural invasion, good intentions notwithstanding.

The starting point for organizing the program content of education or political action must be the present, existential, concrete situation, reflecting the aspirations of the people. Utilizing certain basic contradictions, we must post this existential, concrete, present situation to the people as a problem which challenges them and requires a response—not just at the intellectual level, but at the level of action.[11]

We must never merely discourse on the pres-ent situation, must never provide the people with programs which have little or nothing to do with their own preoccupations, doubts, hopes, and fears—programs which at times in fact increase the fears of

---

[10] "Our cultural workers must serve the people with great enthusiasm and devotion, and they must link themselves with the masses, not divorce themselves from the masses. In order to do so, they must act in accordance with the needs and wishes of the masses. All work done for the masses must start from their needs and not from the desire of any individual, however well-intentioned. It often happens that objectively the masses need a certain change, but subjectively they are not yet conscious of the need, not yet willing or determined to make the change. In such cases, we should wait patiently. We should not make the change until, through our work, most of the masses have become conscious of the need and are willing and determined to carry it out. Otherwise we shall isolate ourselves from the masses.... There are two principles here: one is the actual needs of the masses rather than what we fancy they need, and the other is the wishes of the masses, who must make up their own minds instead of our making up their minds for them." From the *Selected Works of Mao Tse-tung*, Vol. III. "The United Front in Cultural Work" (October 30, 1944; Peking, 1967), pp. 186–187.

[11] It is as self-contradictory for true humanists to use the banking method as it would be for rightists to engage in problem-posing education. (The latter are always consistent—they never use a problem-posing pedagogy.)

the oppressed consciousness. It is not our role to speak to the people about our own view of the world, nor to attempt to impose that view on them, but rather to dialogue with the people about their view and ours. We must realize that their view of the world, manifested variously in their action, reflects their *situation* in the world. Educational and political action which is not critically aware of this situation runs the risk either of "banking" or of preaching in the desert.

Often, educators and politicians speak and are not understood because their language is not attuned to the concrete situation of the men they address. Accordingly, their talk is just alienated and alienating rhetoric. The language of the educator or the politician (and it seems more and more clear that the latter must also become an educator, in the broadest sense of the word), like the language of the people, cannot exist without thought; and neither language nor thought can exist without a structure to which they refer. In order to communicate effectively, educator and politician must understand the structural conditions in which the thought and language of the people are dialectically framed.

It is to the reality which mediates men, and to the perception of that reality held by educators and people, that we must go to find the program content of education. The investigation of what I have termed the people's "thematic universe"[12]—the complex of their "generative themes"—inaugurates the dialogue of education as the practice of freedom. The methodology of that investigation must likewise be dialogical, affording the opportunity both to discover generative themes and to stimulate people's awareness in regard to these themes. Consistent with the liberating purpose of dialogical education,

the object of the investigation is not men (as if men were anatomical fragments), but rather the thought-language with which men refer to reality, the levels at which they perceive that reality, and their view of the world, in which their generative themes are found.

Before describing a "generative theme" more precisely, which will also clarify what is meant by a "minimum thematic universe," it seems to me indispensable to present a few preliminary reflections. The concept of a generative theme is neither an arbitrary invention nor a working hypothesis to be proved. If it were a hypothesis to be proved, the initial investigation would seek not to ascertain the nature of the theme, but rather the very existence or non-existence of themes themselves. In that event, before attempting to understand the theme in its richness, its significance, its plurality, its transformations, and its historical composition, we would first have to verify whether or not it is an objective fact; only then could we proceed to apprehend it. Although an attitude of critical doubt is legitimate, it does appear possible to verify the reality of the generative theme—not only through one's own existential experience, but also through critical reflection on the men-world relationship and on the relationships between men implicit in the former.

This point deserves more attention. One may well remember—trite as it seems—that, of the uncompleted beings, man is the only one to treat not only his actions but his very self as the object of his reflection; this capacity distinguishes him from the animals, which are unable to separate themselves from their activity and thus are unable to reflect upon it. In this apparently superficial distinction lie the boundaries which delimit the action of each in his life space. Because the animal's activity is an extension of themselves, the results of that activity are also inseparable from themselves: animals can neither set objectives nor infuse their transformation of nature

---

[12] The expression "meaningful thematics" is used with the same connotation.

with any significance beyond itself. More-over, the "decision" to perform this activity belongs not to them but to their species. Animals are, accordingly, fundamentally "beings in themselves."

Unable to decide for themselves, unable to objectify either themselves or their activity, lacking objectives which they themselves have set, living "submerged" in a world to which they can give no meaning, lacking a "tomorrow" and a "today" because they exist in an overwhelming pre-sent, animals are ahistorical. Their ahistori-cal life does not occur in the "world," taken in its strict meaning; for the animal, the world does not constitute a "not-I" which could set him apart as an "I." The human world, which is historical, serves as a mere prop for the "being in itself." Animals are not challenged by the configuration which confronts them; they are merely stimulated. Their life is not one of risk-taking, for they are not aware of taking risks. Risks are not challenges perceived upon reflection, but merely "noted" by the signs which indicate them; they accordingly do not require deci-sion-making responses.

Consequently, animals cannot com-mit themselves. Their ahistorical condition does not permit them to "take on" life. Because they do not "take it on," they can-not construct it; and if they do not construct it, they cannot transform its configuration. Nor can they know themselves to be destroyed by life, for they cannot expand their "prop" world into a meaningful, sym-bolic world which includes culture and his-tory. As a result, animals do not "animalize" their configuration in order to animalize themselves—nor do they "de-animalize" themselves. Even in the forest, they remain "beings-in-themselves," as animal-like there as in the zoo.

In contrast, men—aware of their activity and the world in which they are sit-uated, acting in function of the objectives which they propose, having the seat of their decisions located in themselves and in their relations with the world and with others, infusing the world with their creative pres-ence by means of the transformation they effect upon it—unlike animals, not only live but exist;[13] and their existence is historical. Animals live out their lives on an atempo-ral, flat, uniform "prop"; men exist in a world which they are constantly re-creating and transforming. For animals, "here" is only a habitat with which they enter into contact; for men, "here" signifies not merely a physical space, but also an historical space.

Strictly speaking, "here," "now," "there," "tomorrow," and "yesterday" do not exist for the animal, whose life, lacking self-consciousness, is totally determined. Ani-mals cannot surmount the limits imposed by the "here," the "now," or the "there."

Men, however, because they are aware of themselves and thus of the world— because they are *conscious beings*—exist in a dialectical relationship between the deter-mination of limits and their own freedom. As they separate themselves from the world, which they objectify, as they separate them-selves from their own activity, as they locate the seat of their decisions in themselves and in their relations with the world and oth-ers, men overcome the situations which limit them: the "limit-situations."[14] Once perceived by men as fetters, as obstacles to their liberation, these situations stand

---

[13] In the English language, the terms "live" and "exist" have assumed implications opposite to their etymological origins. As used here, "live" is the more basic term, implying only survival; "exist" implies a deeper involvement in the process of "becoming."

[14] Professor Alvaro Vieira Pinto analyzes with clarity the problem of "limit-situations," using the concept without the pessimistic aspect origi-nally found in Jaspers. For Vieira Pinto, the "limit-situations" are not "the impassable bound-aries where possibilities end, but the real bound-aries where all possibilities begin"; they are not "the frontier which separates being from noth-ingness, but the frontier which separates being from being more." Alvaro Vieira Pinto,*Consciência e Realidade Nacional* (Rio de Janeiro, 1960), Vol. II, p. 284.

out in relief from the background, revealing their true nature as concrete historical dimensions of a given reality. Men respond to the challenge with actions which Vieira Pinto calls "limit-acts": those directed at negating and overcoming, rather than passively accepting, the "given."

Thus, it is not the limit-situations in and of themselves which create a climate of hopelessness, but rather how they are perceived by men at a given historical moment: whether they appear as fetters or as insurmountable barriers. As critical perception is embodied in action, a climate of hope and confidence develops which leads men to attempt to overcome the limit-situations. This objective can be achieved only through action upon the concrete, historical reality in which limit-situations historically are found. As reality is transformed and these situations are superseded, new ones will appear, which in turn will evoke new limit-acts.

The prop world of animals contains no limit-situations, due to its ahistorical character. Similarly, animals lack the ability to exercise limit-acts, which require a decisive attitude towards the world: separation from and objectification of the world in order to transform it. Organically bound to their prop, animals do not distinguish between themselves and the world. Accordingly, animals are not limited by limit-situations—which are historical—but rather by the entire prop. And the appropriate role for animals is not to relate to their prop (in that event, the prop would be a world), but to adapt to it. Thus, when animals "produce" a nest, a hive, or a burrow, they are not creating products which result from "limit-acts," that is, transforming responses. Their productive activity is subordinated to the satisfaction of a physical necessity which is simply stimulating, rather, than challenging. "An animal's product belongs immediately to its physical body, whilst man freely confronts his product."[15]

Only products which result from the activity of a being but do not belong to its physical body (though these products may bear its seal), can give a dimension of meaning to the context, which thus becomes a world. A being capable of such production (who thereby is necessarily aware of himself, is a "being for himself") could no longer be if he were not *in the process of being* in the world with which he relates; just as the world would no longer exist if this being did not exist.

The difference between animals—who (because their activity does not constitute limit-acts) cannot create products detached from themselves—and men—who through their action upon the world create the realm of culture and history—is that only the latter are beings of the praxis. Only men *are* praxis—the praxis which, as the reflection and action which truly transform reality, is the source of knowledge and creation. Animal activity, which occurs without a praxis, is not creative; man's transforming activity is.

It is as transforming and creative beings that men, in their permanent relations with reality, pro-duce not only material goods—tangible objects—but also social institutions, ideas, and concepts.[16] Through their continuing praxis, men simultaneously create history and become historical-social beings. Because—in contrast to animals—men can tri-dimensionalize time into the past, the present, and the future, their history, in function of their own creations, develops as a constant process of transformation within which epochal units materialize. These epochal units are not closed periods of time, static compartments within which men are confined. Were this the case, a fundamental condition of history—its continuity— would disappear. On the contrary, epochal

---

[15] Karl Marx, *Economic and Philosophical Manuscripts of 1844*, Dirk Struik, ed. (New York, 1964), p. 113.

[16] Regarding this point, see Karel Kosik, *Dialéctica de lo Concreto* (Mexico City, 1967).

units interrelate in the dynamics of historical continuity.[17]

An epoch is characterized by a complex of ideas, concepts, hopes, doubts, values, and challenges in dialetical interaction with their opposites, striving towards plenitude. The concrete representation of many of these ideas, values, concepts, and hopes, as well as the obstacles which impede man's full humanization, constitute the themes of that epoch. These themes imply others which are opposing or even antithetical; they also indicate tasks to be carried out and fulfilled. Thus, historical themes are never isolated, independent, disconnected, or static; they are always interacting dialectically with their opposites. Nor can these themes be found anywhere except in the men-world relationship. The complex of interacting themes of an epoch constitutes its "thematic universe."

Confronted by this "universe of themes" in dialectical contradiction, men take equally contradictory positions: some work to maintain the structures, others to change them. As antagonism deepens between themes which are the expression of reality, there is a tendency for the themes and for reality itself to be mythicized, establishing a climate of irrationality and sectarianism. This climate threatens to drain the themes of their deeper significance and to deprive them of their characteristically dynamic aspect. In such a situation, myth-creating irrationality itself becomes a fundamental theme. Its opposing theme, the critical and dynamic view of the world, strives to unveil reality, unmask its mythicization, and achieve a full realization of the human task: the permanent transformation of reality in favor of the liberation of men.

In the last analysis, the *themes*[18] both contain and are contained in *limit-situations*, the *tasks* they imply require *limit-acts*. When the themes are concealed by the limit-situations and thus are not clearly perceived, the corresponding tasks—men's responses in the form of historical action—can be neither authentically nor critically fulfilled. In this situation, men are unable to transcend the limit-situations to discover that beyond these situations—and in contradiction to them—lies an *untested feasibility*.

In sum, limit-situations imply the existence of persons who are directly or indirectly served by these situations, and of those who are negated and curbed by them. Once the latter come to perceive these situations as the frontier between being, and being more human, rather than the frontier between being and nothingness, they begin to direct their increasingly critical actions towards achieving the untested feasibility implicit in that perception. On the other hand, those who are served by the present limit-situation regard the untested feasibility as a threatening limit-situation which must not be allowed to materialize, and act to maintain the status quo. Consequently, liberating actions upon an historical milieu must correspond not only to the generative themes but to the way in which these themes are perceived. This requirement in turn implies another: the investigation of meaningful thematics.

Generative themes can be located in concentric circles, moving from the general to the particular. The broadest epochal unit, which includes a diversified range of

---

[17] On the question of historical epochs, see Hans Freyer, *Teoría de la época actual* (Mexico City).

[18] I have termed these themes "generative" because (however they are comprehended and whatever action they may evoke) they contain the possibility of unfolding into again as many themes, which in their turn call for new tasks to be fulfilled.

units and sub-units—continental, regional, national, and so forth—contains themes of a universal character. I consider the fundamental theme of our epoch to be that of *domination*—which implies its opposite, the theme of *liberation,* as the objective to be achieved. It is this tormenting theme which gives our epoch the anthropological character mentioned earlier. In order to achieve humanization, which presupposes the elimination of dehumanizing oppression, it is absolutely necessary to surmount the limit-situations in which men are reduced to things.

Within the smaller circles, we find themes and limit-situations characteristic of societies (on the same continent or on different continents) which through these themes and limit-situations share historical similarities. For example, underdevelopment, which cannot be understood apart from the relationship of dependency, represents a limit-situation characteristic of societies of the Third World. The task implied by this limit-situation is to overcome the contradictory relation of these "object"-societies to the metropolitan societies; this task constitutes the untested feasibility for the Third World.

Any given society within the broader epochal unit contains, in addition to the universal, continental, or historically similar themes, its own particular themes, its own limit-situations. Within yet smaller circles, thematic diversifications can be found within the same society, divided into areas and sub-areas, all of which are related to the societal whole. These constitute epochal sub-units. For example, within the same national unit one can find the contradiction of the "coexistence of the noncontemporaneous."

Within these sub-units, national themes may or may not be perceived in their true significance. They may simply be *felt*—sometimes not even that. But the nonexistence of themes within the sub-units is absolutely impossible. The fact that individuals in a certain area do not perceive a generative theme, or perceive it in a distorted way, may only reveal a limit-situation of oppression in which men are still submerged.

In general, a dominated consciousness which has not yet perceived a limit-situation in its totality apprehends only its epiphenomena and transfers to the latter the inhibiting force which is the property of the limit-situation.[19] This fact is of great importance for the investigation of generative themes. When men lack a critical understanding of their reality, apprehending it in fragments which they do not perceive as interacting constituent elements of the whole, they cannot truly know that reality. To truly know it, they would have to reverse their starting point: they would need to have a total vision of the context in order subsequently to separate and isolate its constituent elements and by means of this analysis achieve a clearer perception of the whole.

Equally appropriate for the methodology of thematic investigation and for problem-posing education is this effort to present significant dimensions of an individual's contextual reality, the analysis of which will make it possible for him to recognize the interaction of the various components. Meanwhile, the significant dimensions,

---

[19] Individuals of the middle class often demonstrate this type of behavior, although in a different way from the peasant. Their fear of freedom leads them to erect defense mechanisms and rationalizations which conceal the fundamental, emphasize the fortuitous, and deny concrete reality. In the face of a problem whose analysis would lead to the uncomfortable perception of a limit-situation, their tendency is to remain on the periphery of the discussion and resist any attempt to reach the heart of the question. They are even annoyed when someone points out a fundamental proposition which explains the fortuitous or secondary matters to which they had been assigning primary importance.

which in their turn are constituted of parts in interaction, should be perceived as dimensions of total reality. In this way, a critical analysis of a significant existential dimension makes possible a new, critical attitude towards the limit-situations. The perception and comprehension of reality are rectified and acquire new depth. When carried out with a methodology of *conscientização* the investigation of the generative theme contained in the minimum thematic universe (the generative themes in interaction) thus introduces or begins to introduce men to a critical form of thinking about their world.

In the event, however, that men perceive reality as dense, impenetrable, and enveloping, it is indispensable to proceed with the investigation by means of abstraction. This method does not involve reducing the concrete to the abstract (which would signify the negation of its dialectical nature), but rather maintaining both elements as opposites which interrelate dialectically in the act of reflection. This dialectical movement of thought is exemplified perfectly in the analysis of a concrete, existential, "coded" situation.[20] Its "decoding" requires moving from the abstract to the concrete; this requires moving from the part[s] to [the] whole and then returning to the parts; this, in turn that the Subject recognize himself in the object (the coded concrete existential situation) and recognize the object as a situation in which he finds himself, together with other Subjects. If the decoding is well done, this movement of flux and reflux from the abstract to the concrete which occurs in the analysis of a coded situation leads to supersedence of the abstraction *by* the critical perception of the concrete, which has already ceased to be a dense, impenetrable reality.

---

[20] The coding of an existential situation is the representation of that situation, showing some of its constituent elements in interaction. Decoding is the critical analysis of the coded situation.

When an individual is presented with a coded existential situation (a sketch or photograph which leads by abstraction to the concreteness of existential reality), his tendency is to "split" that coded situation. In the process of decoding, this separation corresponds to the stage we call the "description of the situation," and facilitates the discovery of the interaction among the parts of the disjoined whole. This whole (the coded situation), which previously had been only diffusely apprehended, begins to acquire meaning as thought flows back to it from the various dimensions. Since, however, the coding is the representation of an existential situation, the decoder tends to take the step from the representation to the very concrete situation in which and with which he finds himself. It is thus possible to explain conceptually why individuals begin to behave differently with regard to objective reality, once that reality has ceased to look like a blind alley and has taken on its true aspect: a challenge which men must meet.

In all the stages of decoding, men exteriorize their view of the world. And in the way they think about and face the world—fatalistically, dynamically, or statically—their generative themes may be found. A group which does not concretely express a generative thematics—a fact which might appear to imply the nonexistence of themes—is, on the contrary, suggesting a very dramatic theme: *the theme of silence*. The theme of silence suggests a structure of mutism in [the] face of the overwhelming force of the limit-situations.

I must re-emphasize that the generative theme cannot be found in men, divorced from reality; nor yet in reality, divorced from men; much less in "no man's land." It can only be apprehended in the men-world relationship. To investigate the generative theme is to investigate man's thinking about reality and man's action upon reality, which is his praxis. For precisely this reason, the methodology proposed requires that the investigators and the people (who would normally be considered objects of that investigation) should act as *co-investigators*. The more active an attitude men take in regard to the exploration of their thematics, the more they deepen their critical awareness of reality and, in spelling out those thematics, take possession of that reality.

Some may think it inadvisable to include the people as investigators in the search for their own meaningful thematics: that their intrusive influence (N.B., the "intrusion" of those who are mostinterested—or ought to be—in their own education) will "adulterate" the findings and thereby sacrifice the objectivity of the investigation. This view mistakenly presupposes that themes exist, in their original objective purity, outside men—as if themes were *things*. Actually, themes exist in men in their relations with the world, with reference to concrete facts. The same objective fact could evoke different complexes of generative themes in different epochal sub-units. There is, therefore, a relation between the given objective fact, the perception men have of this fact, and the generative themes.

A meaningful thematics is expressed by men, and a given moment of expression will differ from an earlier moment, if men have changed their perception of the objective facts to which the themes refer. From the investigator's point of view, the important thing is to detect the starting point at which men visualize the "given" and to verify whether or not during the process of investigation any transformation has occurred in their way of perceiving reality. (Objective reality, of course, remains unchanged. If the perception of that reality changes in the course of the investigation, that fact does not impair the validity of the investigation.)

We must realize that the aspirations, the motives, and the objectives implicit in the meaningful thematics are *human* aspirations, motives, and objectives. They do not exist "out there" somewhere, as static entities; *they are occurring*. They are as historical as men themselves; consequently, they cannot be apprehended apart from men. To apprehend these themes and to understand them is to understand both the men who embody them and the reality to which they refer. But—precisely because it is not possible to understand these themes apart from men—it is necessary that the men concerned understand them as well. Thematic investigation thus becomes a common striving towards awareness of reality and towards self-awareness, which makes this investigation a starting point for the educational process or for cultural action of a liberating character.

The real danger of the investigation is not that the supposed objects of the investigation, discovering themselves to be co-investigators, might "adulterate" the analytical results. On the contrary, the danger lies in the risk of shifting the focus of the investigation from the meaningful themes to the people themselves, thereby treating the people as objects of the investigation. Since this investigation is to serve as a basis for developing an educational program in which teacher-student and students-teachers combine their cognitions of the same object, the investigation itself must likewise be based on reciprocity of action.

Thematic investigation, which occurs in the realm of the human, cannot be reduced to a mechanical act. As a process of search, of knowledge, and thus of creation, it requires the investigators to discover the interpenetration of problems, in the linking of meaningful themes. The investigation will be most educational when it is most critical, and most critical when it avoids the narrow outlines of partial or "focalized" views of reality, and sticks to the comprehension of *total* reality. Thus, the process of searching for the meaningful thematics should include a concern for the links between themes, a concern to pose these themes as problems, and a concern for their historical-cultural context.

Just as the educator may not elaborate a program to present *to* the people, neither may the investigator elaborate "itineraries" for researching the thematic universe, starting from points which *he* has predetermined. Both education and the investigation designed to support it must be "sympathetic" activities, in the etymological sense of the word. That is, they must consist of communication and of the common experience of a reality perceived in the complexity of its constant "becoming."

The investigator who, in the name of scientific objectivity, transforms the organic into something inorganic, what is becoming into what is, life into death, is a man who fears change. He sees in change (which he does not deny, but neither does he desire) not a sign of life, but a sign of death and decay. He does want to study change—but in order to stop it, not in order to stimulate or deepen it. However, in seeing change as a sign of death and in making people the passive objects of investigation in order to arrive at rigid models, he betrays his own character as a killer of life.

I repeat: the investigation of thematics involves the investigation of the people's thinking—thinking which occurs only in and among men together seeking out reality. I cannot think *for others* or *without others,* nor can others think *for me.* Even if the people's thinking is superstitious, or naïve, it is only as they rethink their assumptions in action that they can change. Producing and acting upon their own ideas—not consuming those of others—must constitute that process.

Men, as beings "in a situation," find themselves rooted in temporal-spatial conditions which mark them and which they also mark. They will tend to reflect on their own "situationality" to the extent that they are challenged by it to act upon it. Men *are* because they *are* in a situation. And they *will be more* the more they not only critically reflect upon their existence but critically act upon it.

Reflection upon situationality is reflection about the very condition of existence: critical thinking by means of which men discover each other to be "in a situation." Only as this situation ceases to present itself as a dense, enveloping reality or a tormenting blind alley, and men can come to perceive it as an objective-problematic situation—only then can commitment exist. Men *emerge* from their *submersion* and acquire the ability to *intervene* in reality as it is unveiled. *Intervention* in reality—historical awareness itself—thus represents a step forward from *emergence,* and results from the *conscientização* of the situation. *Conscientização* is the deepening of the attitude of awareness characteristic of all emergence.

Every thematic investigation which deepens historical awareness is thus really educational, while all authentic education investigates thinking. The more educators and the people investigate the people's thinking, and are thus jointly educated, the more they continue to investigate. Education and thematic investigation, in the problem-posing concept of education, are simply different moments of the same process.

In contrast with the antidialogical and non-communicative "deposits" of the banking method of education, the program content of the problem-posing method—dialogical par excellence—isconstituted and organized by the students' view of the world, where their own generative themes are found. The content thus constantly expands and renews itself. The task of the dialogical teacher in an interdisciplinary team working on the thematic universe revealed by their investigation is to "re-present" that universe to the people from whom he first received it—and "represent" it not as a lecture, but as a problem. . . .

COMMENT

When doing metaphysics and talking about "reality," philosophers traditionally limit their discussions to the consideration of physical and/or mental reality. In the latter half of the twentieth century and into the twenty-first century, however, many important thinkers have become increasingly interested in the powerful significance of social reality as constituting a crucial dimension of the world within which we live. Indeed, the sociopolitical "construction" of reality, rather than merely its discovery and description, may now be a dominant theme of Western intellectual activity. The term "post-modernism" is frequently used to designate the central thrust of this effort to go beyond the limitations of the science and philosophy developed by the modernist thinkers who arose during the Enlightenment.

Paulo Freire may be considered a part of this overall movement in the sense that he viewed human reality as a function of sociopolitical interaction. As he repeatedly emphasized, the reality that we experience is not a static and closed system, but a constantly shifting and evolving world created by the values, desires, thoughts, and actions of human beings. Such interaction not only affects the world in which we live, but as Sandra Harding made clear, it very much affects our understanding and knowledge of reality. Common sense, science, and philosophy itself are all the result of human cultural dialogue and decisions. Thus, Freire's concern was to redefine the educational process so as to bring it into harmony with the dialectical character of the construction processes.

In addition to this concern for a more interactionist view of reality, Freire also agreed with Karl Marx that the dialectical nature of social reality makes it imperative that we not only *understand* the world, but that we seek to *change* it, as well. In this way, Freire spoke as a voice representing "marginalized" peoples of the Third World, who struggle to free themselves from the oppression of colonialism and imperialism. In his book *Pedagogy of the Oppressed,* from which this selection is taken, he explored ways of bringing this radical, social-interactionist approach to our understanding of reality to bear on the education of illiterate peasant folk, so as to empower them to participate in the political dynamics that continuously structure their world.

The philosophical focus of Freire's thought is on the dynamic relationship between language and reality. He saw speech as a powerful form of action, not simply in the process of persuasion and/or propaganda, but in its everyday *naming* functions. Those who initially name the various aspects of our world, be they parents, teachers, or politicians, literally create and shape our common reality. To call someone a "slow learner," a "chick" or a "stud," a "communist" or an "infidel" is at least partially to create such things, for ourselves and the person involved, as well as for others. "Workers" and "owners," "teachers" and "students," "husbands" and "wives," and "citizens" and "aliens" are more generally accepted names that nonetheless carry powerful realities with them.

Freire believed that through *dialogue,* based in love, trust, humility, faith, and critical thinking, human beings can come to understand and alter the problems and barriers that others, as well as we ourselves, have constructed in our world. Honest confrontation and interaction with the results of how we speak and think of the various aspects of life and reality can both dissolve and recreate the world. Central to Freire's view is the belief that education alone will enable people to free themselves from the limits imposed, on both the oppressed and the oppressors, by hierarchical dominance and economic exploitation. For him, true revolution must be based in education, in honest understanding and fresh creation.

The educational process advocated by Freire, and lived out in practice in many activities of his life, involved redefining our understanding of the roles of teacher and student in terms of mutual interaction. Teachers and students must conceive of themselves and each other as "co-learners." In addition, all learning must begin with the perceived needs of those involved and must be problem-centered rather than information-centered. Only in this way will those who learn be engaged by the material in such a way as to be drawn into full participation in the cognitive process. In short, Freire advocated "learning to learn" as the axis around which all educational activity should revolve.

While this understanding of reality as fluid and continuously created is at odds with most traditional approaches to the question of reality, it clearly has much in common with the approach advocated by Whitehead. In a sense, Freire's interactionism might be thought of as providing the sociopolitical dimension or application of Whitehead's relationalism. One marked difference between them would seem to be that whereas Whitehead saw all of reality, including the physical, as characterized by relational processes, Freire seems to have limited his view to the interactions involved within sociopolitical reality. However, this may be more a matter of emphasis than a genuine difference in their thought.

Such radical approaches to the question of the nature of reality are not, to be sure, without their critics. Some would wonder, for instance, if this sort of view does not lead necessarily to relativism and skepticism, since everyone would seem to be free to construct whatever reality struck their fancy. Others would argue that the realities already embodied in our conceptual and political systems reflect the combined labors and insights of hundreds, if not thousands, of years and thus need only be refined, not redefined. Still others might worry about the political and educational ramifications of Freire's recommendations. Would they not lead to instability and confusion on the part of those participating in these respective institutions and fields? By the time the student has read this far in this book, he or she should be able to wrestle with such questions in a meaningful and productive manner on his or her own.

It is perhaps difficult to know how to approach our case study of two persons, Abby and Britty, in one body in relation to Freire's interactionism. In a general way, his view would seem to apply much in the same way as Whitehead's, but at the concrete level, things are not so clear. Just how do we explain the emergence of two distinct persons having different ideas and values from a single set of perceptual and social inputs? Are Abby and Britty any different from other sets of twins raised in a common environment? Can Freire's insights and emphases account for the dialogue that takes place between these two persons in one body?

PART III

THE BASIS OF MORALITY

There are few words more common in the English language than *good, better, worse, right, wrong,* and *ought.* We use these words, or their synonyms every day: "What a good piece of pie!"; "You had better see that movie"; "You ought to obey that traffic signal"; "That is the wrong way to study for exams"; and so on. Each of these utterances expresses a judgment, favorable or unfavorable. Although there are factual implications in each instance, the primary intention is to *evaluate* something rather than merely to state a fact. Purely descriptive sentences, such as "That man is six feet tall," stand in obvious contrast.

Corresponding to these two types of sentences, the evaluative and the descriptive, are two distinct fields of philosophy: *axiology,* or the theory of values, and *metaphysics,* or the theory of reality. In Part II, we have been concerned with metaphysics; in Part III, we shall turn to axiology. In its total scope, axiology is the theory of all types of value—not only the moral good or right, but the holy, the beautiful, the useful, or anything else that is prizeworthy. However, we shall confine ourselves to moral values, which are the subject matter of ethics.

The function of ethics is not to tell you what human beings do but to tell you what they *ought* (in a moral sense) to do. Its fundamental concepts are *good* and *bad* and *right* and *wrong.* How can we tell a good life from a bad one? How can we distinguish between right and wrong acts? These are the questions that ethics seeks to answer. Although such words as *good* and *right* can be used in a nonmoral sense, we shall be concerned with their moral usage.

The readers of this book have already been introduced to ethics in Part I. Socrates, in the *Apology,* was criticizing the ethics of custom and expediency and defending the ideal of wisdom. In Part IV, we shall again meet Socrates, this time as a character in Plato's *Republic.* In this dialogue, Socrates maintains that goodness is the harmonious development of all parts of the personality under the control of reason. Similarly, he defines the good of the state as the harmonious development of all classes under the control of wise men. Some readers of this book will prefer to consider the selections from the *Republic* in connection with the ethical problems of Part III rather than the social problems of Part IV.

In an introductory book, it is impossible to survey the many types of ethics. We have confined our discussion to the following:

1. *Aristotle's theory of rational development.* The good is the active exercise of those faculties distinctive of human beings, especially reason.

2. *The Stoic theory of natural law.* The good is a life lived according to the principles of nature—both the nature of humans and the nature of the environment.

3. *Kant's theory of duty for duty's sake.* The only unqualified good is good will, which is based on respect for duty. Our duty is to obey universal moral laws, regardless of the particular consequences.

4. *Mill's theory of happiness.* The good life excels in both quantity and quality of pleasure. Right acts are the most useful in achieving this goal.

5. *Sartre's theory of absolute freedom.* Moral responsibility can only become a reality when it is affirmed for its own sake, entirely apart from any metaphysical or theological rationalization.

6. *Dewey's theory of moral experiment.* The good life is experimental and has no final end or goal except growth.

7. *Annette Baier's concern for a theory of mortality based on trust.* The "right" and the "good" can only be properly understood as functions of the human need and ability for trust and cooperation.

Once again, we shall set the discussion up by introducing "A Case in Point" that is contemporary.

A CASE IN POINT:

E U T H A N A S I A   O R   A S S I S T E D
S U I C I D E ?

A few years ago, Noel David Earley made the headlines of a number of newspapers across the country by announcing that he was planning to commit suicide. Earley was suffering from what is known as Lou Gehrig's disease; the nerve cells in his brain and spinal cord were being destroyed by the incurable and progressively degenerating illness. The resulting paralysis, pain, and eventual inability to swallow and breathe led Earley to conclude that it would be better for everyone concerned, including himself, if he took his own life.

As a spokesperson for the "right-do-die" movement, Earley took this opportunity not only to announce his imminent self-chosen demise but to do so with a certain degree of flourish; he planned to party with his friends, have sex with his girlfriend, and enjoy some of his favorite foods before injecting himself with a deadly mixture of drugs. Earley was quoted as saying: "I'll do the things I love most in the world—food and sex—then I'll inject myself with a compound ... and I'll go to sleep. Then the fun begins. It's the greatest adventure I'll ever have."

A Vietnam war veteran, Earley was diagnosed with this disease two years before his public announcement of his impending suicide. In that short amount of time, he became bedridden and was being fed through intravenous tubes. For years prior to being diagnosed, Earley had worked for a program to help people with Alzheimer's disease. He remarked ironically that his illness is "the exact opposite of Alzheimer's, since it attacks the body rather than the mind."

Earley received professional advice as to how to go about committing suicide, but he refused to disclose his source so that the person involved would not be prosecuted. Initially, Earley had contacted Dr. Jack Kevorkian, who offered to assist him, but he declined this offer when he found a local source of help. The state of Rhode Island, where Earley resided, has a law against assisted suicide that carries penalties of up to ten years in prison and $10,000 in fines.

Those close to Earley had very mixed feelings about his plans to commit suicide. One of his friends said that while he would honor his friend's right to make such a decision, he really wished he would not go through with it. "It seems awfully young for someone to be dying, particularly since he's taking his own life," his friend was quoted as saying. Earley was forty-seven at the time. The friend went on to say that he felt "kind of cheated because I thought we would be together for a long time." Thus Earley's decision did not affect only himself. Incidentally, Earley actually died before he was able to commit suicide.

The question of the right to kill oneself has always been a difficult one, both legally and morally. Some would argue that no one has the right to end life, whether the person's own or someone else's, because life is a gift of God. Others maintain that each individual has the right to decide for him- or herself whether to go on living or not. These same folks might point out the contradictory character of a law that punishes people for trying to kill themselves, as if living were not difficult enough for such a person without also being burdened with a criminal charge. Earley's case would be an excellent example of the offensiveness of such a law, since it would be hard to imagine how he would be punished.

The question of assisted suicide, where people get help, whether professional or otherwise, in accomplishing their own death, has received a great deal of attention in recent decades. Within the past fifty years there has been a great deal of discussion about the validity of the concept of euthanasia, which in the original Greek means "good death." Generally, this discussion has focused on a medical decision of whether or not doctors, and perhaps nurses, have the right to end a patient's life when there seems to be little hope of recovery and/or an unbearable amount of pain. Perhaps this is more a decision for the nearest of kin, the courts, or the clergy.

More recently this discussion has focused on the legal and moral ramifications of *anyone* assisting people, who have made a choice, in ending their lives. This was the case with Noel David Earley. At the center of the controversy surrounding this issue stands Dr. Jack Kevorkian, who has literally made a profession of assisting people who wish to commit suicide. Moreover, "Doctor Death," as he is referred to in the media, has been an outspoken advocate for the legal and moral right of all persons to put an end to their own lives when they and they alone decide to.

Dr. Kevorkian has assisted dozens of people in their suicides and not only has received but has sought a great deal of publicity for so doing. His avowed aim is to call into question the laws regarding the right to suicide and thereby to force us to rethink the issues involved so that a person's right to decide about his or her own life and death can be honored. In addition, Kevorkian claims that he only minimizes the suffering of people who will die soon anyway. There is, of course, serious debate over whether the sick person is in any condition to make such far-reaching judgments.

In all of his statements and writings about his position on this issue, Kevorkian has repeatedly claimed to follow very strict guidelines and procedures governing whom he chooses to assist in their suicides and how it is to be done. Many critics have argued that he has not always followed his own rules and that even these rules are open to a good deal of debate. Indeed, there seems to have been a case in which the patient was past a point of being able to rationally make that kind of a decision. Kevorkian, who was seventy years old at the time, was brought up on charges and convicted of second-degree murder in Michigan in March 1999. His attorney vowed to appeal the case to the Supreme Court.

While there continues to be a great deal of media debate over the positive and negative aspects of Kevorkian's ideas and practices, there is also a growing concern among moral philosophers about the ethical implications of the entire question of euthanasia in whatever form. Aside from religious issues, there are difficult problems confronting anyone who seeks to clarify exactly how the concepts of "life," "death," "choice," and "killing" are to be understood or defined.

The technological revolution in medicine has rendered these problems more pressing, if not more complex, than ever before.

It should prove profitable to keep these issues, and the specific case of Noel David Earley, in mind while exploring the following selections from the major formulators of the Western philosophical tradition. Each thinker approaches moral problems from a different theoretical perspective, and at times, their views can seem extremely abstract. Thus, it is helpful for the reader to work with a concrete case in point through which to view the key questions and as a means of comparing and contrasting the theories of various philosophers.

14

THE WAY OF REASON

ARISTOTLE (384 B.C.–322 B.C.)

Aristotle was born in Stagira, a town in Macedonia colonized by Greeks. At the time of his birth, Socrates had been dead for fifteen years and Plato was thirty-three. Aristotle's father, Nichomachus, having achieved some renown, became court physician to King Amyntas II of Macedonia. Refusing to follow his father's profession, Aristotle at the age of eighteen migrated to Athens, where he lived for twenty years as a member of Plato's school, the Academy. When the master died, Aristotle left Athens to spend four years on the coast of Asia Minor, engaged mainly in biological research. During this period, he married, and his wife eventually bore him a daughter. Subsequently, he married a second time and had two sons, one of them adopted.

Meanwhile Philip, the son of Amyntas, having become king of Macedonia, invited Aristotle to take charge of the education of his son Alexander, then thirteen years old. In consequence of accepting this invitation, Aristotle must have acquired intimate knowledge of court affairs, but he makes no mention of the great Macedonian empire built up by Philip and Alexander the Great. Perhaps he was too close to kings to be greatly impressed by courtly glitter.

He stayed with Philip for seven years, until the monarch's death, and lingered at the court for about a year after Alexander's accession to the throne. Then he returned to Athens to resume his philosophical career. At this time, the Academy was being reorganized, and Xenocrates, a second-rate philosopher, was made head. Evidently disappointed at the choice, Aristotle withdrew and founded a school of his own, the Lyceum, which he directed for twelve years. It was during this period that he was his most productive.

Aristotle's reputation and the prosperity of his school suffered from the anti-Macedonian reaction that occurred after Alexander's death in 323 B.C. Accused of impiety, Aristotle, unlike Socrates, fled to the island of Euboea, vowing that he would not "give the Athenians a second chance of sinning against philosophy." A year later, in 322 B.C., he died of a stomach disease, at the age of sixty-three.

His writings, as they have come down to us, lack the beauty of Plato's dialogues and are without wit, personal charm, or poetry. He also wrote popular works, including dialogues, which were praised by Cicero for "the incredible flow and sweetness of their diction"; but like many other ancient compositions, these dialogues have been lost. The works that remain touch on almost every phase of human knowledge, and they establish Aristotle's reputation not only as an extremely versatile philosopher but also as an accomplished biologist.

A final word of warning: Although nearly every translator of Aristotle's writings uses the word "happiness" with which to translate the Greek word "eudamonia," it is also true that nearly all scholars agree that this is a very misleading thing to do. Literally speaking, the Greek word means "good spirit," but perhaps "well-being" or "self-fulfillment" would better serve our purposes. The student should not confuse Aristotle's rich concept with our modern, lightweight notion of happiness.

HAPPINESS AND VIRTUE

1. [The Nature of Happiness]

[Aristotle begins, in a way characteristic of his method, with a generalization which, if accepted, will lead to a more exact account of his subject. It is a generalization which is fundamental to his philosophy and in his own mind there is no doubt about the truth of it. Yet he is not at this point asserting its truth. He is content to state a position which he has found reason to hold. It may be defined in some such words as these: The good is that at which all things aim. If we are to understand this, we must form to ourselves a clear notion of what is meant by an aim or, in more technical language, an "end." The first chapter of the Ethics is concerned with making the notion clear.]

It is thought that every activity, artistic or scientific, in fact every deliberate action or pursuit, has for its object the attainment of some good. We may therefore assent to the view which has been expressed that "the good" is "that at which all things aim." ... Since modes of action involving the practiced hand and the instructed brain are numerous, the number of their ends is proportionately large. For instance, the end of medical science is health; of military science, victory; of economic science, wealth. All skills of that kind which come under a single "faculty"—a skill in making bridles or any other part of a horse's gear comes under the faculty or art of horsemanship, while horsemanship itself and every branch of military practice comes under the art of war, and in like manner other arts and techniques are subordinate to yet others—in all these the ends of the master arts are to be preferred to those of the subordinate skills, for it is the former that provide the motive for pursuing the latter. ...

Now if there is an end which as moral agents we seek for its own sake, and which is the cause of our seeking all the other ends—if we are not to go on choosing one act for the sake of another, thus landing ourselves in an infinite progression with the result that desire will be frustrated and ineffectual—it is clear that this must be the good, that is the absolutely good. May we not then argue from this that a knowledge of the good is a great advantage to us in the conduct of our lives? Are we not more likely to hit the mark if we have a target? If this be true, we must do our best to get at least a rough idea of what the good really is, and which of the sciences, pure or applied, is concerned with the business of achieving it.

[Ethics is a branch of politics. That is to say, it is the duty of the statesman to create for the citizen the best possible opportunity of living the good life. It will be seen that the effect of this injunction is not

---

The Ethics of Aristotle, trans. J. A. K. Thomson, George Allen and Unwin, London, and Barnes and Noble, New York, 1953. The sentences in italics are explanatory comments by the translator except where initialed *M.R.*

to degrade morality but to moralize politics. The modern view that "you cannot make men better by act of parliament" would have been repudiated by Aristotle as certainly as by Plato and indeed by ancient philosophers in general.]

Now most people would regard the good as the end pursued by that study which has most authority and control over the rest. Need I say that this is the science of politics? It is political science that prescribes what subjects are to be taught in states, which of these the different sections of the population are to learn, and up to what point. We see also that the faculties which obtain most regard come under this science: for example, the art of war, the management of property, the ability to state a case. Since, therefore, politics makes use of the other practical sciences, and lays it down besides what we must do and what we must not do, its end must include theirs. And that end, in politics as well as in ethics, can only be the good for man. For even if the good of the community coincides with that of the individual, the good of the community is clearly a greater and more perfect good both to get and to keep. This is not to deny that the good of the individual is worth while. But what is good for a nation or a city has a higher, a diviner, quality.

Such being the matters we seek to investigate, the investigation may fairly be represented as the study of politics. . . .

[...Let us consider what is the end of political science. For want of a better word we call it "Happiness." People are agreed on the word but not on its meaning.]

. . . Since every activity involving some acquired skill or some moral decision aims at some good, what do we take to be the end of politics—what is the supreme good attainable in our actions? Well, so far as the name goes there is pretty general agreement. "It is happiness," say both intellectuals and the unsophisticated, meaning by "happiness" living well or faring well. But when it comes to saying in what happiness consists, opinions differ and the account given by the generality of mankind is not at all like that given by the philosophers. The masses take it to be something plain and tangible, like pleasure or money or social standing. Some maintain that it is one of these, some that it is another, and the same man will change his opinion about it more than once. When he has caught an illness he will say that it is health, and when he is hard up he will say that it is money. Conscious that they are out of their depths in such discussions, most people are impressed by anyone who pontificates and says something that is over their heads. Now it would no doubt be a waste of time to examine all these opinions; enough if we consider those which are most in evidence or have something to be said for them. Among these we shall have to discuss the view held by some that, over and above particular goods like those I have just mentioned, there is another which is good in itself and the cause of whatever goodness there is in all these others. . . .

[A man's way of life may afford a clue to his genuine views upon the nature of happiness. It is therefore worth our while to glance at the different types of life.]

. . . There is a general assumption that the manner of a man's life is a clue to what he on reflection regards as the good—in other words happiness. Persons of low tastes (always in the majority) hold that it is pleasure. Accordingly they ask for nothing better than the sort of life which consists in having a good time. (I have in mind the three well-known types of life—that just mentioned, that of the man of affairs, that of the philosophic student.) The utter vulgarity of the herd of men comes out in their preference for the sort of existence a cow leads. Their view would hardly get a respectful hearing, were it not that those who occupy great positions sympathize with a monster of sensuality like Sardanapalus. The gentleman, however, and the man of affairs identify the good with honor, which may fairly be described as the end which men pursue in political or public life. Yet honor is surely too superficial a thing to be the good we are seeking. Honor depends more on those who confer than on him who receives it, and we cannot but feel that the good is something personal and almost inseparable from its possessor. Again, why do men seek honor? Surely in order to confirm the favorable opinion they have formed of themselves. It is at all events by intelligent men who know them personally that they seek to be honored. And for what? For their moral qualities. The inference is clear; public men prefer virtue to honor. It might therefore seem reasonable to suppose that virtue rather than honor is the end pursued in the life of the public servant. But clearly even virtue cannot be quite the end. It is possible, most people think, to possess virtue while you are asleep, to possess it without acting under its influence during any portion of one's life. Besides, the virtuous man may meet with the most atrocious luck or ill-treatment; and nobody, who was not arguing for argument's sake, would maintain that a man with an existence of that sort was "happy." . . . The third type of life is the "contemplative," and this we shall discuss later.

As for the life of the business man, it does not give him much freedom of action. Besides, wealth obviously is not the good we seek, for the sole purpose it serves is to provide the means of getting something else. So far as that goes, the ends we have already mentioned would have a better title to be considered the good, for they are desired on their own account. But in fact even their claim must be disallowed. We may say that they have furnished the ground for many arguments, and leave the matter at that. . . .

[*What then is the good? If it is what all men in the last resort aim at, it must be happiness. And that for two reasons: (1) happiness is everything it needs to be, (2) it has everything it needs to have.*]

. . . [The good] is one thing in medicine and another in strategy, and so in the other branches of human skill. We must inquire, then, what is the good which is the end common to all of them. Shall we say it is that for the sake of which everything else is done? In medicine this is health, in military science victory, in architecture a building, and so on—different ends in different arts; every consciously directed activity has an end for the sake of which everything that it does is done. This end may be described as its good. Consequently, if there be some one thing which is the end of all things consciously done, this will be the double good; or, if there be more than one end, then it will be all of these. . . .

In our actions we aim at more ends than one—that seems to be certain—but, since we choose some (wealth, for example, or flutes and tools or instruments generally) as means to something else, it is clear that not all of them are ends in the full sense of the word, whereas the good, that is the supreme good, is surely such an end. Assuming then that there is some one thing which alone is an end beyond which there are no further ends, we may call *that* the good of which we are in search. If there be more than one such final end, the good will be that end which has the highest degree of finality. An object pursued for its own sake possesses a higher degree of finality than one pursued with an eye to something else. A corollary to that is that a thing which is never chosen as a means to some remoter object has a higher degree of finality than things which are chosen both as ends in themselves and as means to such ends. We may conclude, then, that something which is always chosen for its own sake and never for the sake of something else is without qualification a final end.

Now happiness more than anything else appears to be just such an end, for we always choose it for its own sake and never for the sake of some other thing. It is different with honor, pleasure, intelligence and good qualities generally. We choose them indeed for their own sake in the sense that we should be glad to have them irrespective of any advantage which might accrue from them. But we also choose them for the sake of our happiness in the belief that they will be instrumental in promoting that. On the other hand nobody chooses happiness as a means of achieving them or anything else whatsoever than just happiness.

The same conclusion would seem to follow from another consideration. It is a generally accepted view that the final good is self-sufficient. By "self-sufficient" is meant not what is sufficient for oneself living the life of a solitary but includes parents, wife and children, friends and fellow-citizens in general. For man is a social animal. ... A self-sufficient thing, then, we take to be one which on its own footing tends to make life desirable and lacking in nothing. And we regard happiness as such a thing. . . .

[But we desire a clearer definition of happiness. The way to this may be prepared by a discussion of what is meant by the "function" of a man.]

But no doubt people wilt say, "To call happiness the highest good is a truism. We want a more distinct account of what it is." We might arrive at this if we could grasp what is meant by the "function" of a human being. If we take a flutist or a sculptor or any craftsman—in fact any class of men at all who have some special job or profession—we find that his special talent and excellence comes out in that job, and this is his function. The same thing will be true of man simply as man—that is of course if "man" does have a function. But is it likely that joiners and shoemakers have certain functions or specialized activities, while man as such has none but has been left by Nature a functionless being? Seeing that eye and hand and foot and every one of our members has some obvious function, must we not believe that in like manner a human being has a function over and above these particular functions? Then what exactly is it? The mere act of living is not peculiar to man—we find it even in the vegetable kingdom—and what we are looking for is something peculiar to him. We must therefore exclude from our definition

the life that manifests itself in mere nurture and growth. A step higher should come the life that is confined to experiencing sensations. But that we see is shared by horses, cows and the brute creation as a whole. We are left, then, with a life concerning which we can make two statements. First, it belongs to the rational part of man. Secondly, it finds expression in actions. The rational part may be either active or passive: passive in so far as it follows the dictates of reasoning. A similar distinction can be drawn within the rational life; that is to say, the reasonable element in it may be active or passive. Let us take it that what we are concerned with here is the reasoning power in action, for it will be generally allowed that when we speak of "reasoning" we really mean *exercising* our reasoning faculties. (This seems the more correct use of the word.)

Now let us assume for the moment the truth of the following propositions. (*a*) The function of a man is the exercise of his non-corporeal faculties or "soul" in accordance with, or at least not divorced from, a rational principle. (*b*) The function of an individual and of a *good* individual in the same class—a harp player, for example, and a good harp player, and so through the classes—is generically the same, except that we must add superiority in accomplishment to the function, the function of the harp player being merely to play on the harp, while the function of the good harp player is to play on it well. (*c*) The function of man is a certain form of life, namely an activity of the soul exercised in combination with a rational principle or reasonable ground of action. (*d*) The function of a good man is to exert such activity well. (*e*) A function is performed well when performed in accordance with the excellence proper to it.—If these assumptions are granted, we conclude that the good for man is "an activity of soul in accordance with goodness" or (on the supposition that there may be more than one form of goodness) "in accordance with the best and most complete form of goodness."

[Happiness is more than momentary bliss.]

There is another condition of happiness; it cannot be achieved in less than a complete lifetime. One swallow does not make a summer; neither does one fine day. And one day, or indeed any brief period of felicity, does not make a man entirely and perfectly happy. . . .

[...Our first principle–definition of happiness– should be tested not only by the rules of logic but also by the application to it of current opinions on the subject.]

So we must examine our first principle not only logically, that is as a conclusion from premises, but also in the light of what is currently said about it. For if a thing be true, the evidence will be found in harmony with it; and, if it be false, the evidence is quickly shown to be discordant with it.

But first a note about "goods." They have been classified as (*a*) external, (*b*) of the soul, (*c*) of the body. Of these we may express our belief that goods of the soul are the best and are most properly designated as "good." Now according to our definition happiness is an expression of the soul in considered actions, and that definition seems to be confirmed by this belief, which is not only an old popular notion but is accepted by philosophers. We are justified, too, in saying that the end consists in certain acts or activities, for this enables us to count it among goods of the soul and not among external goods. We may also claim that our description of the happy man as the man who lives or fares well chimes in with our definition. For happiness has pretty much been stated to be a form of such living or faring well. Again, our definition seems to include the elements detected in the various analyses of happiness—virtue, practical wisdom, speculative wisdom, or a combination of these, or one of them in more or less intimate association with pleasure. All these definitions have their supporters, while still others are for

adding material prosperity to the conditions of a happy life. Some of these views are popular convictions of long standing; others are set forth by a distinguished minority. It is reasonable to think that neither the mass of men nor the sages are mistaken altogether, but that on this point or that, or indeed on most points, there is justice in what they say.

Now our definition of happiness as an activity in accordance with virtue is so far in agreement with that of those who say that it is virtue, that such an activity *involves* virtue. But of course it makes a great difference whether we think of the highest good as consisting in the *possession* or in the *exercise* of virtue. It is possible for a disposition to goodness to exist in a man without anything coming of it; he might be asleep or in some other way have ceased to exercise his function of a man. But that is not possible with the activity in our definition. For in "doing well" the happy man will of necessity *do*. Just as at the Olympic Games it is not the best-looking or the strongest men present who are crowned with victory but competitors—the successful competitors, so in the arena of human life the honors and rewards fall to those who show their good qualities in action.

Observe, moreover, that the life of the actively good is inherently pleasant. Pleasure is a psychological experience, and every man finds that pleasant for which he has a liking—"fond of" so and so is the expression people use. For example, a horse is a source of pleasure to a man who is fond of horses, a show to a man who is fond of sight-seeing. In the same way just actions are a source of pleasure to a man who likes to see justice done, and good actions in general to one who likes goodness. Now the mass of men do not follow any consistent plan in the pursuit of their pleasures, because their pleasures are not inherently pleasurable. But men of more elevated tastes and sentiments find pleasure in things which are in their own nature pleasant, for instance virtuous actions, which are pleasant in themselves and not merely to such men. So their life does not need to have pleasure fastened about it like a necklace, but possesses it as a part of itself. We may go further and assert that he is no good man who does not find pleasure in noble deeds. Nobody would admit that a man is just, unless he takes pleasure in just actions; or liberal, unless he takes pleasure in acts of liberality; and so with the other virtues. Grant this, and you must grant that virtuous actions are a source of pleasure in themselves. And surely they are also both good and noble, and that always in the highest degree, if we are to accept, as accept we must, the judgment of the good man about them, he judging in the way I have described. Thus, happiness is the best, the noblest, the most delightful thing in the world, and in it meet all those qualifies which are separately enumerated in the inscription upon the temple at Delos:

> Justice is loveliest, and health is best, And sweetest to obtain is heart's, desire.

All these good qualities inhere in the activities of the virtuous soul, and it is these, or the best of them, which we say constitute happiness.

For all that those are clearly right who, as I remarked, maintain the necessity to a happy life of an addition in the form of material goods. It is difficult, if not impossible, to engage in noble enterprises without money to spend on them; many can only be performed through friends, or wealth, or political influence. There are also certain advantages, such as the possession of honored ancestors or children, or personal beauty, the absence of which takes the bloom from our felicity. For you cannot quite regard a man as happy if he be very ugly to look at, or of humble origin, or alone in the world and childless, or—what is probably worse—with children or friends who have not a single good quality. . . .

[Our definition of happiness compels us to consider the nature of virtue. But before we can do this we must have some conception of how the human soul is constituted. It will serve our purpose to take over

(for what it is worth) the current psychology which divides the soul into "parts."]

Happiness, then, being an activity of the soul in conformity with perfect goodness, it follows that we must examine the nature of goodness. . . . The goodness we have to consider is human goodness. This— I mean human goodness or (if you prefer to put it that way) human happiness—was what we set out to find. By human goodness is meant not fineness of physique but a right condition of the soul, and by happiness a condition of the soul. That being so, it is evident that the statesman ought to have some inkling of psychology, just as the doctor who is to specialize in diseases of the eye must have a general knowledge of physiology. Indeed, such a general background is even more necessary for the statesman in view of the fact that his science is of a higher order than the doctor's. Now the best kind of doctor takes a good deal of trouble to acquire a knowledge of the human body as a whole. Therefore the statesman should also be a psychologist and study the soul with an eye to his profession. Yet he will do so only as far as his own problems make it necessary; to go into greater detail on the subject would hardly be worth the labor spent on it.

Psychology has been studied elsewhere and some of the doctrines stated there may be accepted as adequate for our present purpose and used by us here. The soul is represented as consisting of two parts, a rational and an irrational. . . . As regards the irrational part there is one subdivision of it which appears to be common to all living things, and this we may designate as having a "vegetative" nature, by which I mean that it is the cause of nutrition and growth, since one must assume the existence of some vital force in all things that assimilate food. . . . Now the excellence peculiar to this power is evidently common to the whole of animated nature and not confined to man. This view is supported by the admitted fact that the vegetative part of us is particularly active in sleep, when the good and the bad are hardest to distinguish. . . . Such a phenomenon would be only natural, for sleep is a cessation of that function on the operation of which depends the goodness or badness of the soul. . . . But enough of this, let us say no more about the nutritive part of the soul, since it forms no portion of goodness in the specifically *human* character.

But there would seem to be another constituent of the soul which, while irrational, contains an element of rationality. It may be observed in the types of men we call "continent" and "incontinent." They have a principle—a rational element in their souls—which we commend, because it encourages them to perform the best actions in the right way. But such natures appear at the same time to contain an irrational element in active opposition to the rational. In paralytic cases it often happens that when the patient wills to move his limbs to the right they swing instead to the left. Exactly the same thing may happen to the soul; the impulses of the incontinent man carry him in the opposite direction from that towards which he was aiming. The only difference is that, where the body is concerned, we see the uncontrolled limb, while the erratic impulse we do not see. Yet this should not prevent us from believing that besides the rational an irrational principle exists running opposite and counter to the other. . . . Yet, as I said, it is not altogether irrational; at all events it submits to direction in the continent man, and may be assumed to be still more amenable to reason in the "temperate" and in the brave man, in whose moral make-up there is nothing which is at variance with reason.

We have, then, this clear result. The irrational part of the soul, like the soul itself, consists of two parts. The first of these is the vegetative, which has nothing rational about it at all. The second is that from which spring the appetites and desire in general; and this does in a way participate in reason, seeing that it is submissive and obedient to it. ... That the irrational element in us need not be heedless of the rational is proved by the fact that we find admonition, indeed every form of censure and exhortation, not ineffective. It may be, however, that we ought to speak of the appetitive part of the soul as rational, too. In that event it will rather be the rational part that is divided in two, one division rational in the proper sense of the word and in its nature, the other in the derivative sense in which we speak of a child as "listening to reason" in the person of its father.

These distinctions within the soul supply us with a classification of the virtues. Some are called "intellectual," as wisdom, intelligence, prudence. Others are "moral," as liberality and temperance. When we are speaking of a man's *character* we do not describe him as wise or intelligent but as gentle or temperate. Yet we praise a wise man, too, on the ground of his "disposition" or settled habit of acting wisely. The dispositions so praised are what we mean by "virtues."

2. [Moral Goodness]

[...*We have to ask what moral virtue or goodness is. It is a confirmed disposition to act rightly, the disposition being itself formed by a continuous series of right actions.*]

Virtue, then, is of two kinds, intellectual and moral. Of these the intellectual is in the main indebted to teaching for its production and growth, and this calls for time and experience. Moral goodness, on the other hand, is the child of habit, from which it has got its very name, ethics being derived from *ethos*, "habit." ... This is an indication that none of the moral virtues is implanted in us by nature, since nothing that nature creates can be taught by habit to change the direction of its development. For instance a stone, the natural tendency of which is to fall down, could never, however often you threw it up in the air, be trained to go in that direction. No more can you train fire to burn downwards. Nothing in fact, if the law of its being is to behave in one way, can be habituated to behave in another. The moral virtues, then, are produced in us neither *by* Nature nor *against* Nature. Nature, indeed, prepares in us the ground for their reception, but their complete formation is the product of habit.

Consider again these powers or faculties with which Nature endows us. We acquire the ability to use them before we do use them. The senses provide us with a good illustration of this truth. We have not acquired the sense of sight from repeated acts of seeing, or the sense of hearing from repeated acts of hearing. It is the other way round. We had these senses before we used them, we did not acquire them as a result of using them. But the moral virtues we do acquire by first exercising them. The same is true of the arts and crafts in general. The craftsman has to learn how to make things, but he learns in the process of making them. So men become builders by building, harp players by playing the harp. By a similar process we become just by performing just actions, temperate by performing temperate actions, brave by performing brave actions. Look at what happens in political societies—it confirms our view. We find legislators seeking to make good men of their fellows by making good behavior habitual with them. . . .

We may sum it all up in the generalization, "Like activities produce like dispositions." This makes it our duty to see that our activities have the right character, since the differences of quality in them are repeated in the dispositions that follow in their train. So it is a matter of real importance whether our early education confirms us in one set of habits or another. It would be nearer the truth to say that it makes a very great difference indeed, in fact all the difference in the world. . . .

[There is one way of discovering whether we are in full possession of a virtue or not. We possess it if we feel pleasure in its exercise; indeed, it is just with pleasures and pains that virtue is concerned.]

We may use the pleasure (or pain) that accompanies the exercise of our dis-

positions as an index of how far they have established themselves. A man is temperate who abstaining from bodily pleasures finds this abstinence pleasant; if he finds it irksome, he is intemperate. Again, it is the man who encounters danger gladly, or at least without painful sensations, who is brave; the man who has these sensations is a coward. In a word, moral virtue has to do with pains and pleasures. There are a number of reasons for believing this. (1) Pleasure has a way of making us do what is disgraceful; pain deters us from doing what is right and fine. Hence the importance—I quote Plato—of having been brought up to find pleasure and pain in the right things. True education is just such a training. (2) The virtues operate with actions and emotions, each of which is accompanied by pleasure or pain. This is only another way of saying that virtue has to do with pleasures and pains. (3) Pain is used as an instrument of punishment. For in her remedies Nature works by opposites, and pain can be remedial. (4) When any disposition finds its complete expression it is, as we noted, in dealing with just those things by which it is its nature to be made better or worse, and which constitute the sphere of its operations. Now when men become bad it is under the influence of pleasures and pains when they seek the wrong ones among them, or seek them at the wrong time, or in the wrong manner, or in any of the wrong forms which such offenses may take; and in seeking the wrong pleasures and pains they shun the right. . . .

So far, then, we have got this result. Moral goodness is a quality disposing us to act in the best way when we are dealing with pleasures and pains, while vice is one which leads us to act in the worst way when we deal with them. . . .

[We have now to state the "differentia" of virtue. Virtue is a disposition; but how are we to distinguish it from other dispositions? We may say that it is such a disposition as enables the good man to perform his function well. And he performs

it well when he avoids the extremes and chooses the mean in actions and feelings.]

... Excellence of whatever kind affects that of which it is the excellence in two ways. (1) It produces a good state in it. (2) It enables it to perform its function well. Take eyesight. The goodness of your eye is not only that which makes your eye good, it is also that which makes it function well. Or take the case of a horse. The goodness of a horse makes him a good horse, but it also makes him good at running, carrying a rider and facing the enemy. Our proposition, then, seems to be true, and it enables us to say that virtue in a man will be the disposition which (*a*) makes him a good man, (*b*) enables him to perform his function well. ...
Every form ... of applied knowledge, when it performs its function well, looks to the mean and works to the standard set by that. It is because people feel this that they apply the *cliché,* "You couldn't add anything to it or take anything from it" to an artistic masterpiece, the implication being that too much and too little alike destroy perfection, while the mean preserves it. Now if this be so, and if it be true, as we say, that good craftsmen work to the standard of the mean, then, since goodness like nature is more exact and of a higher character than any art, it follows that goodness is the quality that hits the mean. By "goodness" I mean goodness of moral character, since it is moral goodness that deals with feelings and actions, and it is in them that we find excess, deficiency and a mean. It is possible, for example, to experience fear, boldness, desire, anger, pity, and pleasures and pains generally, too much or too little or to the right amount. If we feel them too much or too little, we are wrong. But to have these feelings at the right times on the right occasions towards the right people for the right motive and in the right way is to have them in the right measure, that is somewhere between the extremes; and this is what characterizes goodness. The same may be said of the mean and extremes in actions. Now it is in the field of

actions and feelings that goodness operates; in them we find excess, deficiency and, between them, the mean, the first two being wrong, the mean right and praised as such. ... Goodness, then, is a mean condition in the sense that it aims at and hits the mean. Consider, too, that it is possible to go wrong in more ways than one. (In Pythagorean terminology evil is a form of the Unlimited, good of the Limited.) But there is only one way of being right. That is why going wrong is easy, and going right difficult; it is easy to miss the bull's eye and difficult to hit it. Here, then, is another explanation of why the too much and the too little are connected with evil and the mean with good. As the poet says.

 Goodness is one, evil is multiform.

[We are now in a position to state our definition of virtue with more precision. Observe that the kind of virtue meant here is moral, not intellectual, and that Aristotle must not be taken as saying that the kind of virtue which he regards as the highest and truest is any sort of mean.]

We may now define virtue as a disposition of the soul in which, when it has to choose among actions and feelings, it observes the mean relative to us, this being determined by such a rule or principle as would take shape in the mind of a man of sense or practical wisdom. We call it a mean condition as lying between two forms of badness, one being excess and the other deficiency; and also for this reason, that, whereas badness either falls short of or exceeds the right measure in feelings and actions, virtue discovers the mean and deliberately chooses it. Thus, looked at from the point of view of its essence as embodied in its definition, virtue no doubt is a mean; judged by the standard of what is right and best, it is an extreme.

[Aristotle enters a caution. Though we have said that virtue observes the mean in actions and passions, we do not say this of all acts and all feelings. Some are essentially evil and, when these

are involved, our rule of applying the mean cannot be brought into operation.]

But choice of a mean is not possible in every action or every feeling. The very names of some have an immediate connotation of evil. Such are malice, shamelessness, envy among feelings, and among actions adultery, theft, murder. All these and more like them have a bad name as being evil in themselves; it is not merely the excess or deficiency of them that we censure. In their case, then, it is impossible to act rightly; whatever we do is wrong. . . .

[Aristotle now suggests some rules for our guidance.]

... We shall find it useful when aiming at the mean to observe these rules. (1) *Keep away from that extreme which is the more opposed to the mean.* It is Calpyso's advice:

Swing round the ship; clear of this surf and surge.

For one of the extremes is always a more dangerous error than the other, and—since it is hard to hit the bull's-eye—we must take the next best course and choose the least of the evils. And it will be easiest for us to do this if we follow the rule I have suggested. (2) *Note the errors into which we personally are most liable to fall.* (Each of us has his natural bias in one direction or another.) We shall find out what ours are by noting what gives us pleasure and pain. After that we must drag ourselves in the opposite direction. For our best way of reaching the middle is by giving a wide berth to our darling sin. It is the method used by a carpenter when he is straightening a warped board. (3) *Always be particularly on your guard against pleasure and pleasant things.* When Pleasure is at the bar the jury is not impartial. So it will be best for us if we feel towards her as the Trojan elders felt towards Helen, and regularly apply their words to her. If we are for packing her off, as they were with Helen, we shall be the less likely to go wrong.

3. [Particular Virtues]

[Aristotle now embarks upon a long analysis of the virtues and vices. These do not include the characteristically Christian virtues of piety, chastity and humility, which are not regarded by him as independent virtues at all. Yet however he may classify and name the moral feelings and habits which form the material for his analysis, that material is substantially the same for him as for us. The picture of the good man which emerges is perfectly recognizable and even familiar to us.]

Let us begin with courage.

We have seen that it is a disposition which aims at the mean in situations inspiring fear and confidence. What we fear are of course things of a nature to inspire fear. Now these are speaking generally, evil things, so that we get the definition of fear as "an anticipation of evil." Well, we do fear all evil things—ill-repute, poverty, sickness, friendlessness, death and so on—but in the opinion of most people courage is to be distinguished from the simple fear of all these. There are some evils which it is proper and honourable to fear and discreditable not to fear—disgrace, for example. The man who fears disgrace has a sense of what is due to himself as a man of character and to other people; the man who does not fear it has a forehead of brass. Such a man indeed is occasionally styled a brave fellow, but only by a transference of epithet made possible by the fact that there is one point of similarity between him and the truly brave man, namely their freedom from timidity. Then one ought not, of course, to fear poverty or illness or, indeed, anything at all that is not a consequence of vice or of one's own misconduct; still we do not call a man who is fearless in facing these things "brave" except once more by analogy. For we find individuals who are cowardly on the field of battle and yet spend money lavishly and meet the loss of it with equanimity. And surely a man is not to be dubbed a coward because he dreads brutality to his wife and children, or the effects of envy towards himself, or anything of that nature. Nor is a man described as brave if he does not turn a hair at the prospect of a whipping.

What, then, are the objects of fear confronting which the brave man comes out in his true colours? Surely one would say the greatest, for it is just in facing fearful issues that the brave man excels. Now the most fearful thing is death; for death is an end, and to the dead man nothing seems good or evil any more for ever. Yet even death may be attended by circumstances which make it seem inappropriate to describe the man confronted by it as "brave." For instance, he might be drowned at sea or pass away in his bed. In what dangers, then, is courage most clearly displayed? Shall we not say, in the noblest? Well, the noblest death is the soldier's, for he meets it in the midst of the greatest and most glorious dangers. This is recognized in the honours conferred on the fallen by republics and monarchs alike. So in the strict meaning of the word the brave man will be one who fearlessly meets an honourable death or some instant threat to life; and it is war which presents most opportunities of that sort. Not but what the brave man will be fearless in plague, or in peril by sea, although it will be a different kind of fearlessness from that of the old salt. For in a shipwreck the brave man does not expect to be rescued, and he hates the thought of the inglorious end which threatens him, whereas the seaman who has weathered many a storm never gives up hope. Courage, too, may be shown on occasions when a man can put up a fight or meet a glorious death. But there is no opportunity for either when you are going down in a ship.

All men have not the same views about what is to be feared, although there are some terrors which are admitted to be more than human nature can face. Terrors of that order are experienced of course by every sane person. But there are great diversities in the extent and degree of the dangers that are humanly tolerable; and there is the same variety in the objects which instil courage. What characterizes the brave man is his unshaken courage wherever courage is humanly possible. No doubt even then he will not always be exempt from fear; but when he fears it will be in the right way, and he will meet the danger according to the rule or principle he has taken to guide his conduct, his object being to achieve moral dignity or beauty in what he does, for that is the end of virtue. Yet it is possible to feel such dangers too much, and possible to fear them too little, and possible also to fear things that are not fearful as much as if they were. One may fear what one ought not to fear, and that is one kind of error; one may fear it in the wrong way, and that is another. A third error is committed when one fears at the wrong time. And so on. We have the same possibilities of error when we deal with things that give us confidence. The brave man is the man who faces or fears the right thing for the right purpose in the right manner at the right moment, or who shows courage in the corresponding ways. . . .

The man who goes to the extreme in fear is a coward—one who fears the wrong things in the wrong way and all the rest of it. He also exhibits a deficiency in boldness. But what one particularly notices is the extremity of his fear in the face of pain. We may therefore describe the coward as a poor-spirited person scared of everything. This is the very opposite of the brave man, for a bold heart indicates a confident temper.

We may say, then, that the coward, the rash man, and the brave man work as it were with the same materials, but their attitudes to them are different. The coward has too much fear and too little courage, the rash man too much courage and too little fear. It is the brave man who has the right attitude, for he has the right disposition, enabling him to observe the mean. We may add that the rash man is foolhardy, ready for anything before the danger arrives; but, when it does, sheering off. On the other hand the brave man is gallant in action but undemonstrative beforehand.

Summing up, let us say that courage is the disposition which aims at the mean in conditions which inspire confidence or fear in the circumstances I have described; it feels confidence and faces danger because it is the fine thing to do so and because it is base to shrink from doing it. Yet to kill oneself as a means of escape from poverty or disappointed love or bodily or mental anguish is the deed of a coward rather than a brave man. To run away from trouble is a form of cowardice and, while it is true that the suicide braves death, he does it not for some noble object but to escape some ill.

[The virtue of which Aristotle now gives an account is Sophrosyne, *a word which cannot be rendered by any modern English equivalent. It is, however, what our moralists until quite recently called "temperance," and this, with its opposite "intemperance," will be used here. What Aristotle means by* Sophrosyne *will gradually appear.]*

Let us next say something about temperance, which like courage is considered to be one of the virtues developed in the irrational parts of the soul.

We have already described it as aiming at the mean in pleasurable experiences. Intemperance is shown in the same field. So we must now say something definite about the quality of the pleasures which are the material on which temperance and its opposite work. Let us begin by drawing a distinction between (*a*) pleasures of the soul and (*b*) pleasures of the body.

(*a*) As an instance of pleasures of the soul consider the love of distinction in public life or in some branch of learning. The devotee in either case takes pleasure in what he loves without any physical sensations. What he feels is a spiritual or intellectual pleasure, and we do not speak of men who seek that kind of pleasure as "temperate" or "intemperate." Nor do we apply these terms to any class of persons whose pleasures are not those of the flesh. For example, the kind of person who likes to

swap stories and anecdotes, and wastes his time discussing trivialities, we call a "gossip" or a "chatterbox," but not "intemperate." Neither should we so describe a man who makes a tragedy out of some loss he has met with of money or of friends.

(*b*) It is then the pleasures of sense that are the concern of temperance, though not all of these. The people who find pleasure in looking at things like colours and forms and pictures are not called temperate or intemperate. At the same time we must suppose that pleasure in these things can be felt too much or too little or in due measure. It is so with the pleasures of listening. A man may take inordinate delight in music or acting. But nobody is prepared to call him intemperate on that account; nor, if he takes neither too much nor too little, do we think of describing him as temperate. It is the same with the pleasures of smell, except when some association comes in. A man is not called intemperate if he happens to like the smell of apples or roses or incense. Yet he may be, if be inhales essences or the emanations of the cuisine, for these are odours which appeal to the voluptuary, because they remind him of the things that arouse his desires. And not only the voluptuary; everybody likes the smell of things to eat when he is hungry. Still the delight in such things is especially characteristic of the voluptuary or intemperate man, because it is on these that his heart is set. And if we extend our observation to the lower animals, we note that they, too, find nothing intrinsically pleasant in these sensations. A hunting-dog gets no pleasure from the scent of a hare. The pleasure is in eating it; all the scent did was to tell him the hare was there. It is not the lowing of an ox that gratifies a lion but the eating it, though the lowing tells him the ox is somewhere about, and that evidently gives him pleasure. Nor does he, as Homer thinks, rejoice when he has caught sight of "stag or goat of the wild," but because he is promising himself a meal.

Such are the pleasures with which temperance and intemperance deal, and they are pleasures in which the lower animals also share. On that account they have the name of being illiberal and brutish, confined as they are to touch and taste. And even taste seems to count for little or nothing in the practice of temperance. It is the function of taste to discriminate between flavours, as connoisseurs do when they sample wines, and chefs when they prepare entrées; although it is not exactly the flavours that please (except, perhaps, with the intemperate), it is the enjoyment of the flavorous article, and that is wholly a tactile experience, whether in eating, drinking or what are called the pleasures of sex. This explains the anecdote of the epicure who prayed that his throat might be made longer than a crane's—the longer the contact, he thought, the more protracted the pleasure. So the sense in respect of which we give an intemperate man that name is the sense that comes nearest to being universal. This may seem to justify its ill-repute, for it belongs to us not as men but as animals. Therefore to delight in such sensations, and to prefer them to any other pleasure, is brutish.

[Aristotle discusses other virtues, such as liberality, the golden mean between stinginess and prodigality; dignified self-respect, between humility and vanity; and friendliness, between quarrelsomeness and obsequiousness. He points out that acts like theft, adultery, and murder, and emotions like shamelessness, envy, and spite, are already excesses or defects and therefore cannot exist in proper moderation. The virtue of justice, as a kind of fairness or impartiality, consists in treating equals equally and unequals unequally in proportion to their deserts. It is a mean, not as the other virtues are, but only in the sense that it produces a state of affairs intermediate between giving too much or too little to one person compared with another.—M.R.]

4. [Self-Love and Friendship]

[How far, and with what justification, may a man love himself?]

Another problem is whether one ought to love oneself or another most. The world blames those whose first thoughts are always for themselves and stigmatizes them as self-centered. It is also generally believed that a bad man does everything from a selfish motive, and does this the more, the worse he is.[1] On the other hand the good man is supposed never to act except on some lofty principle—the loftier the principle, the better the man—and to neglect his own interest in order to promote that of his friend. It is a view which is not borne out by the facts. Nor need this surprise us. It is common ground that a man should love his best friend most. But my best friend is the man who in wishing me well wishes it for my sake, whether this shall come to be known or not. Well, there is no one who fulfills this condition as well as I do in my behaviour towards myself; indeed it may be said of every quality which enters into the definition of a friend—I have it in a higher degree than any of my friends. For, as I have already observed, all the affectionate feelings of a man for others are an extension of his feelings for himself. You will find, too, that all the popular bywords agree on this point. ("Two bodies and one soul," "Amity is parity," "The knee is nearer than the shin.") All the proverbs show how close are the ties of friendship, and they all apply best to oneself. For a man is his own best friend. From this it follows that he ought to love himself best.—Which then of these two opinions ought we to accept in practice? It is a reasonable question, since there is a degree of plausibility in both.

No doubt the proper method of dealing with divergent opinions of this sort is to distinguish between them, and so reach a definite conclusion on the point of how far and in what way each of them is true. So the present difficulty may be cleared up if we can discover what meaning each side attaches to the word "self-love." Those who make it a term of reproach give the epithet of "self-loving" to those who assign to them-

---

[1] A bad man is often accused of "doing nothing until he has to."

selves more than they are entitled to in money, public distinctions and bodily pleasures, these being what most men crave for and earnestly pursue as the greatest blessings, so that they contend fiercely for the possession of them. Well, the man who grasps at more than his fair share of these things is given to the gratification of his desires and his passions generally and the irrational part of his soul. Now most men are like that, and we see from this that the censorious use of the epithet "self-loving" results from the fact that the self-love of most men is a bad thing. Applied to them, the censorious epithet is therefore justified. And unquestionably it is people who arrogate too much of such things to themselves who are called "self-loving" by the ordinary man. For if anybody were to make it his constant business to take the lead himself over everyone else in the performance of just or temperate or any other kind whatever of virtuous actions, generally claiming the honourable role for himself, nobody would stigmatize *him* as a "self-lover." Yet the view might be taken that such a man was exceptionally self-loving. At any rate he arrogates to himself the things of greatest moral beauty and excellence, and what he gratifies and obeys throughout is the magistral part of himself, his higher intelligence. Now just as in a state or any other composite body it is the magistral or dominant part of it that is considered more particularly to *be* the state or body, so with a man; his intelligence, the governing part of him, *is* the man. Therefore he who loves and indulges this part is to the fullest extent a lover of himself. Further, we may note that the terms "continent" and "incontinent" imply that the intellect is or is not in control, which involves the assumption that the intellect is the man. Again, it is our reasoned acts that are held to be more especially those which we have performed ourselves and by our own volition. All which goes to show that a man is, or is chiefly the ruling part of himself, and that a good man loves it beyond any other part of his nature. It follows that such a man will be

self-loving in a different sense from that attached to the word when it is used as a term of reproach. From the vulgar self-lover he differs as far as the life of reason from the life of passion, and as far as a noble purpose differs from mere grasping at whatever presents itself as an expedient. Hence those who are exceptionally devoted to the performance of fine and noble actions receive the approval and commendation of all. And if everyone sought to outdo his neighbour in elevation of character, and laboured strenuously to perform the noblest actions, the common weal would find its complete actualization and the private citizen would realize for himself the greatest of goods, which is virtue.

Therefore it is right for the *good* man to be self-loving, because he will thereby himself be benefited by performing fine actions; and by the same process he will be helpful to others. The bad man on the other hand should not be a self-lover, because he will only be injuring himself and his neighbours by his subservience to base passions. As a result of this subservience what he does is in conflict with what he ought to do, whereas the good man does what he ought to do. For intelligence never fails to choose the course that is best for itself, and the good man obeys his intelligence.

But there is something else which we can truly say about the good man. Many of his actions are performed to serve his friends or his country, even if this should involve dying for them. For he is ready to sacrifice wealth, honours, all the prizes of life in his eagerness to play a noble part. He would prefer one crowded hour of glorious life to a protracted period of quiet existence and mild enjoyment spent as an ordinary man would spend it—one great and dazzling achievement to many small successes. And surely this may be said of those who lay down their lives for others; they choose for themselves a crown of glory. It is also a characteristic trait of the good man that he is prepared to lose money on condition that his friends get more. The friend gets the cash, and he gets the credit, so that he is assigning the greater good to himself. His conduct is not different when it comes to public honours and offices. All these he will freely give up to his friend, because that is the fine and praiseworthy thing for him to do. It is natural then that people should think him virtuous, when he prefers honour to everything else. He may even create opportunities for his friend to do a fine action which he might have done himself, and this may be the nobler course for him to take. Thus in the whole field of admirable conduct we see the good man taking the larger share of moral dignity. In this sense then it is, as I said before, right that he should be self-loving. But in the vulgar sense no one should be so.

[It has been questioned whether the possession of friends is necessary to happiness. Aristotle has no doubt that it is so, and gives his reasons.]

Another debatable point concerning the happy man is this. Will friends be necessary to his happiness or not? It is commonly said that the happy, being sufficient to themselves, have no need of friends. All the blessings of life are theirs already; so, having all resources within themselves, they are not in need of anything else, whereas a friend, being an *alter ego,* is only there to supply what one cannot supply for oneself. Hence that line in the *Orestes* of Euripides:

When Fortune smiles on us, what need of friends?

Yet it seems a strange thing that in the process of attributing every blessing to the happy man we should not assign him friends, who are thought to be the greatest of all external advantages. Besides, if it is more like a friend to confer than to receive benefits, and doing good to others is an activity which especially belongs to virtue and the virtuous man, and if it is better to do a kindness to a friend than to a stranger, the good man will have need of friends as objects of his active benevolence. Hence a second question. Does one need friends more in prosperity than in adversity? There

is a case for either of these alternatives. The unfortunate need people who will be kind to them; the prosperous need people to be kind to.

Surely also there is something strange in representing the man of perfect blessedness as a solitary or a recluse. Nobody would deliberately choose to have all the good things in the world, if there was a condition that he was to have them all by himself. Man is a social animal, and the need for company is in his blood. Therefore the happy man must have company, for he has everything that is naturally good, and it will not be denied that it is better to associate with friends than with strangers, with men of virtue than with the ordinary run of persons. We conclude then that the happy man needs friends. . . .

[A little chapter on the value and influence of Friendship.]

Well then, are we to say that, just as lovers find their chief delight in gazing upon the beloved and prefer sight to all the other senses—for this is the seat and source of love—so friends find the society of one another that which they prefer to all things else? For in the first place friendship is a communion or partnership. Secondly, a man stands in the same relation to his friend as to himself. Now the consciousness which he has of his own existence is something that would be chosen as a good. So the consciousness of his friend's existence must be a good. This consciousness becomes active in the intercourse of the friends, which accordingly they instinctively desire. Thirdly, every man wishes to share with his friends that occupation, whatever it may be, which forms for him the essence and aim of his existence. So we find friends who drink together, and others who dice together, while yet others go in together for physical training, hunting or philosophy. Each set spend their time in one another's company following the pursuit which makes the great pleasure of their lives. As their wish is to be always with their friends, they do what these do and take part with them in these pursuits to the best of their ability. But this means that the friendship of the unworthy is evil, for they associate in unworthy pursuits; and so becoming more and more like each other they turn out badly. But the friendship of the good is good and increases in goodness in consequence of their association. They seem to become positively better men by putting their friendship into operation and correcting each other's faults. For each seeks to transfer to himself the traits he admires in the other. Hence the famous saying:

> From noble men you may learn noble deeds . . .

5. [Intellectual Goodness]

[. . .Aristotle gives reasons for thinking that happiness in its highest and best manifestation is found in cultivating the "contemplative" life.]

. . .If happiness is an activity in accordance with virtue, it is reasonable to assume that it will be in accordance with the highest virtue; and this can only be the virtue of the best part of us. Whether this be the intellect or something else—whatever it is that is held to have a natural right to govern and guide us, and to have an insight into what is noble and divine, either as being itself also divine or more divine than any other part of us—it is the activity of this part in accordance with the virtue proper to it that will be perfect happiness. Now we have seen already that this activity has a speculative or contemplative character. This is a conclusion which may be accepted as in harmony with our earlier arguments and with the truth. For "contemplation" is the highest form of activity, since the intellect is the highest thing in us and the objects which come within its range are the highest that can be known. But it is also the most continuous activity, for we can think about intellectual problems more continuously than we can keep up any sort of physical action. Again, we feel sure that a

modicum of pleasure must be one of the ingredients of happiness. Now it is admitted that activity along the lines of "wisdom" is the pleasantest of all the good activities. At all events it is thought that philosophy ("the pursuit of wisdom") has pleasures marvelous in purity and duration, and it stands to reason that those who have knowledge pass their time more pleasantly than those who are engaged in its pursuit. Again, self-sufficiency will be found to belong in an exceptional degree to the exercise of the speculative intellect. The wise man, as much as the just man and everyone else, must have the necessaries of life. But, given an adequate supply of these, the just man also needs people with and towards whom he can put his justice into operation; and we can use similar language about the temperate man, the brave man, and so on. But the wise man can do more. He can speculate all by himself, and the wiser he is the better he can do it. Doubtless it helps to have fellow workers, but for all that he is the most self-sufficing of men. Finally it may well be thought that the activity of contemplation is the only one that is praised on its own account, because nothing comes of it beyond the act of contemplation, whereas from practical activities we count on gaining something more or less over and above the mere action. Again, it is commonly believed that, to have happiness, one must have leisure; we occupy ourselves in order that we may have leisure, just as we make war for the sake of peace. Now the practical virtues find opportunity for their exercise in politics and in war, but there are occupations which are supposed to leave no room for leisure. Certainly it is true of the trade of war, for no one deliberately chooses to make war for the sake of making it or tries to bring about a war. A man would be regarded as a bloodthirsty monster if he were to make war on a friendly state just to produce battles and slaughter. The business of the politician also makes leisure impossible. Besides the activity itself, politics aims at securing positions of power and honor or the happiness of the politician himself or his fellow citizens—a happiness obviously distinct from that which we are seeking.

We are now in a position to suggest the truth of the following statements. (*a*) Political and military activities, while preeminent among good activities in beauty and grandeur, are incompatible with leisure, and are not chosen for their own sake but with a view to some remoter end, whereas the activity of the intellect is felt to excel in the serious use of leisure, taking as it does the form of contemplation, and not to aim at any end beyond itself, and to own a pleasure peculiar to itself, thereby enhancing its activity. (*b*) In this activity we easily recognize self-sufficiency, the possibility of leisure and such freedom from fatigue as is humanly possible, together with all the other blessings of pure happiness. Now if these statements are received as true, it will follow that it is this intellectual activity which forms perfect happiness for a man—provided of course that it ensures a complete span of life, for nothing incomplete can be an element in happiness.

Yes, but such a life will be too high for *human* attainment. It will not be lived by us in our merely human capacity but in

virtue of something divine within us, and so far as this divine particle is superior to man's composite nature, to that extent will its activity be superior to that of the other forms of excellence. If the intellect is divine compared with man, the life of the intellect must be divine compared with the life of a human creature. And we ought not to listen to those who counsel us *O man, think as man should* and *O mortal, remember your mortality*. Rather ought we, so far as in us lies, to put on immortality and to leave nothing unattempted in the effort to live in conformity with the highest thing within us. Small in bulk it may be, yet in power and preciousness it transcends all the rest. We may in fact believe that this is the true self of the individual, being the sovereign and better part of him. It would be strange, then, if a man should choose to live not his own life but another's. Moreover the rule, as I stated it a little before, will apply here—the rule that what is best and pleasantest for each creature is that which intimately belongs to it. Applying it, we shall conclude that the life of the intellect is the best and pleasantest for man, because the intellect more than anything else is the man. Thus it will be the happiest life as well.

COMMENT

In considering the merits of Aristotle's theory, we should keep certain key questions in mind:

1. *Can we deduce good from the nature of things?* The presupposition of Aristotle's ethics is that each kind of thing has certain characteristic tendencies and that the good is the fulfillment of these tendencies. Man's good, accordingly, can be deduced from human nature. It may be objected that this implies an optimistic and undemonstrated premise (that developed reality is fully good) and allows the tendencies of the actual world to dictate our standards of value. Some philosophers, such as Immanuel Kant, deny that the *ought* (good and right) can be derived from the *is* (matters of fact), and thus take fundamental issue with the basis of Aristotle's ethics.

2. *Is the wider definition of good correct?* We can distinguish, in Aristotle's theory, between a "wide" and a "narrow" definition of ultimate good. In its wide mean-

ing, good is the actualization of potentialities. In its narrow meaning, it is the actualization of *human* potentialities, which are taken to be essentially rational.

Let us first consider the wider definition. It is very wide indeed, for it applies to animals, plants, and even inanimate things. Whether Aristotle would interpret it so broadly is not altogether clear. In his teleological metaphysics, he speaks of "end" or "final cause" in this very inclusive way, but he does not state explicitly that every end is good. If, however, the actualization of potentialities is taken to be the essence of good, there is no logical reason to stop short with conscious or even unconscious organisms.

This very wide definition, a critic might say, confuses an "end" in a temporal sense (the *finis* of a process) with an "end" in an ethical sense (good as an end rather than as a means). Another type of confusion may also be involved. We often say that something is a *good* example of its kind, and good in this sense, a biologist might claim, applies only to a fully developed animal, which clearly exhibits powers and abilities of its species.

However, "good" in this sense does not imply positive value; a cancer specialist might speak of a perfectly good case of cancer, meaning a case so far developed that it clearly exhibits the generic characteristics of the malignancy. Has Aristotle confused good in this sense with good in its value import?

The attempt to extend the meaning of intrinsic goodness to include nonconscious things has often been challenged. If there were no feelings, no desires, no thoughts whatsoever—if all things in the universe were as unconscious as sticks and stones—would there be any value? Some philosophers maintain that a world without consciousness would be without value; if this were so, we should have to reject Aristotle's wider interpretation of good.

3. *Is the narrower definition of good correct?* Aristotle's interpretation of human goodness rests upon two premises: (a) The good is to be found in the life and work peculiar to people; and (b) rationality is the distinctive mark of the human creature. Both premises can be challenged.

(a) Why should we suppose that the human good is to be found in what is distinctive to people? That a certain factor is peculiar to a species does not necessarily imply any ethical superiority in that factor. If all human beings were just like other animals except that they alone had bowlegs, this would not prove that human good is bowleggedness. Perhaps Aristotle is taking it for granted that people *are* superior to other animals and that this superiority must lie in that which people alone possess. However, some philosophers would question this view. Hedonists, for example, would say that good is pleasure, and the fact that a dog can feel pleasure does not detract from human good. We may or may not believe that this view is mistaken and Aristotle's theory correct—but is there any way of supporting our conviction?

(b) Is reason the differentia of humankind? Certain psychologists, such as Wolfgang Köhler, have demonstrated that chimpanzees also have the capacity to reason. These clever animals, for example, can figure out ways of piling up and mounting boxes to reach a bunch of bananas hanging high from the top of their cage. Aristotle would no doubt reply that this is only *practical,* not *theoretical,* reason, but it may be that chimpanzees also have curiosity and enjoy satisfying it. At least it is not at all obvious that reason is *the* distinctive mark of human beings or that any faculty is exclusively human. What fundamentally distinguishes people, it can be argued, is the whole development of their culture, including art and religion and social institutions in addition to philosophy and science. Does Aristotle's rather exclusive emphasis on reason betray the natural bias of a philosopher?

4. *Does Aristotle, in stressing the generic nature of humans, neglect the importance of individuality?* His emphasis is on the reason that all humans share, and only in rare passages does he speak of self-realization in individualistic terms. He would probably have admitted, for example, that a person with very great musical talent should develop that special gift. However, an existentialist such as Søren Kierkegaard would charge that Aristotle shows too little respect for the matchless individuality that is the core of every human life. Who is right?

5. *Is moral virtue to be found in adherence to a mean between the extremes of excess and deficiency?* How adequate is Aristotle's theory of the golden mean? "Be cautious; avoid extremes; follow the mean," it can be argued, is a counsel of prudence and not necessarily of morality—even the wicked and crafty can find it useful. From the standpoint of attaining happiness, does it need to be counterbalanced by a relish for adventure and the careless rapture of intense moments of experience?

Still other questions can be posed. Is pleasure merely contributory to the happy life, as Aristotle supposed, or is it the very essence of happiness, as the hedonists contend? Is the ideal of intellectual contemplation unrealizable by all but the aristocratic few, and if so, should we favor the development of an intellectual elite rather than the cultivation of the masses? Are ethics and politics inseparable in the way in which Aristotle supposed? Do you agree with his characterization of the nature and value of self-love? Of friendship? Other questions will probably occur to the reader.

With respect to the case of Noel David Earley's plan to end his life because it had become unbearable, how would Aristotle respond? It is highly likely that he would argue against Earley's decision because it is "irrational" and fails to allow Earley to fulfill his unique function as a human being. On the other hand, is it not true that Earley had reached his decision through a rational consideration of the alternatives? Does Aristotle's ethical approach apply to cases in which sickness and circumstances beyond one's control arise? What is the difference between Earley's definition of "happiness" and Aristotle's?

15

THE WAY OF
ACCEPTANCE

MARCUS AURELIUS (A.D. 121–180)

Marcus Aurelius was the adopted son of his uncle, the Emperor Antoninus Pius. In early boyhood, he was introduced to the doctrines of Stoicism, and he assumed the simple dress and practiced the austere way of life of the Stoics. After his marriage to the emperor's daughter Faustina, who bore him thirteen children, he was occupied with family affairs and with learning the arts of government. At the death of Antoninus in 161, he became the ruler of the vast Roman Empire.

The remaining nineteen years of his life called for all the Stoic fortitude he could muster, for his reign was beset with calamities—floods, fires, earthquakes, pestilences, insurrections, wars, and barbarian invasions. He instituted many reforms and founded charitable institutions, but he violently persecuted the Christians, whom he regarded as subversive. His *Meditations,* which apparently were private soliloquies intended for no eyes but his own, were written during military campaigns, the hardships of which eventually caused his death at his headquarters near present-day Vienna.

HARMONY WITH NATURE

Book II

Begin the morning by saying to thyself, I shall meet with the busybody, the ungrateful, arrogant, deceitful, envious, unsocial. All these things happen to them by reason of their ignorance of what is good and evil. But I who have seen the nature of the good

---

From *The Meditations of Marcus Aurelius Antoninus,* translated by George Long (1862).

that it is beautiful, and of the bad that it is ugly, and the nature of him who does wrong, that it is akin to me, not only of the same blood or seed, but that it participates in the same intelligence and the same portion of the divinity, I can neither be injured by any of them, for no one can fix on me what is ugly, nor can I be angry with my kinsman, nor hate him. For we are made for co-operation, like feet, like hands, like eyelids like the rows of the upper and lower teeth. To act against one another then is contrary to nature; and it is acting against one another to be vexed and to turn away.

(9) This thou must always bear in mind, what is the nature of the whole, and what is my nature, and how this is related to that, and what kind of a part it is of what kind of a whole; and that there is no one who hinders thee from always doing and saying the things which are according to the nature of which thou are a part.

(16) The soul of man does violence to itself, first of all, when it becomes an abscess and, as it were, a tumour on the universe, so far as it can. For to be vexed at anything which happens is a separation of ourselves from nature, in some part of which the natures of all other things are contained. In the next place, the soul does violence to itself when it turns away from any man, or even moves towards him with the intention of injuring, such as are the souls of those who are angry. In the third place, the soul does violence to itself when it is overpowered by pleasure or by pain. Fourthly, when it plays a part, and does or says anything insincerely and untruly. Fifthly, when it allows any act of its own and any movement to be without an aim, and does anything thoughtlessly and without considering what it is, it being right that even the smallest things be done with reference to an end; and the end of rational animals is to follow the reason and the law of the most ancient city and polity.

(17) Of human life the time is a point, and the substance is in a flux, and the perception dull, and the composition of the whole body subject to putrefaction, and the soul a whirl, and fortune hard to divine, and fame a thing devoid of judgement. And, to say all in a word, everything which belongs to the body is a stream, and what belongs to the soul is a dream and vapour, and life is a warfare and a stranger's sojourn, and after-fame is oblivion. What then is that which is able to conduct a man? One thing and only one, philosophy. But this consists in keeping the daemon within a man free from violence and unharmed, superior to pains and pleasures, doing nothing without a purpose, nor yet falsely and with hypocrisy, not feeling the need of another man's doing or not doing anything; and besides, accepting all that happens, and all that it allotted, as coming from thence, wherever it is, from whence he himself came; and, finally, waiting for death with a cheerful mind, as being nothing else than a dissolution of the elements of which every living being is compounded. But if there is no harm to the elements themselves in each continually changing into another, why should a man have any apprehension about the change and dissolution of all the elements? For it is according to nature, and nothing is evil which is according to nature.

Book III

(2) We ought to observe also that even things which follow after the things which are produced according to nature contain something pleasing and attractive. For instance, when bread is baked some parts are split at the surface, and these parts which thus open, and have a certain fashion contrary to the purpose of the baker's art, are beautiful in a manner, and in a peculiar way excite a desire for eating. And again, figs, when they are quite ripe, gape open; and in the ripe olives the very circumstance of their being near to rottenness adds a peculiar beauty to the fruit. And the ears of corn bending down, and the lion's eyebrows, and the foam which flows from the mouth of wild boars, and many other things—though they are far from being beautiful, if a man should examine them severally—still, because they are consequent upon the things which are formed by nature, help to adorn them, and they please the mind; so that if a man should have a feeling and deeper insight with respect to the things which are produced in the universe, there is hardly one of those which follow by way of consequence which will not seem to him to be in a manner disposed so

as to give pleasure. And so he will see even the real gaping jaws of wild beasts with no less pleasure than those which painters and sculptors show by imitation; and in an old woman and an old man he will be able to see a certain maturity and comeliness; and the attractive loveliness of young persons he will be able to look on with chaste eyes; and many such things will present themselves, not pleasing to every man, but to him only who has become truly familiar with nature and her works.

(11) To the aids which have been mentioned let this one still be added:— Make for thyself a definition or description of the thing which is presented to thee, so as to see distinctly what kind of a thing it is in its substance, in its nudity, in its complete entirety, and tell thyself its proper name, and the names of the things of which it has been compounded, and into which it will be resolved. For nothing is so productive of elevation of mind as to be able to examine methodically and truly every object which is presented to thee in life, and always to look at things so as to see at the same time what kind of universe this is, and what kind of use everything performs in it, and what value everything has with reference to the whole, and what with reference to man, who is a citizen of the highest city, of which all other cities are like families; what each thing is, and of what it is composed, and how long it is the nature of this thing to endure which now makes an impression on me, and what virtue I have need of with respect to it, such as gentleness, manliness, truth, fidelity, simplicity, contentment, and the rest. Wherefore, on every occasion a man should say: this comes from God; and this is according to the apportionment and spinning of the thread of destiny, and such-like coincidence and chance; and this is from one of the same stock, and a kinsman and partner, one who knows not however what is according to his nature. But I know; for this reason I behave towards him according to the natural law of fellowship with benevo-lence and justice. At the same time however in things indifferent I attempt to ascertain the value of each.

Book IV

(4) If our intellectual part is common, the reason also, in respect of which we are rational beings, is common: if this is so, common also is the reason which commands us what to do, and what not to do; if this is so, there is a common law also; if this is so, we are fellow-citizens; if this is so, we are members of some political community; if this is so, the world is in a manner a state. For of what other common political community will any one say that the whole human race are members? And from thence, from this common political community comes also our very intellectual faculty and reasoning faculty and our capacity for law; or whence do they come? For as my earthly part is a portion given to me from certain earth, and that which is watery from another element, and that which is hot and fiery from some peculiar source (for nothing comes out of that which is nothing, as nothing also returns to non-existence), so also the intellectual part comes from some source.

(23) Everything harmonizes with me, which is harmonious to thee, O Universe. Nothing for me is too early nor too late, which is in due time for thee. Everything is fruit to me which thy seasons bring, O Nature: from thee are all things; in thee are all things, to thee all things return. The poet says, Dear city of Cecrops; and wilt not thou say, Dear city of Zeus?

(48) Think continually how many physicians are dead after often contracting their eyebrows over the sick; and how many astrologers after predicting with great pretensions the deaths of others; and how many philosophers after endless discourses on death or immortality; how many heroes after killing thousands; and how many tyrants who have used their power over men's lives with terrible insolence as if they were immortal; and how many cities are entirely

dead, so to speak, Helice and Pompeii and Herculaneum, and others innumerable. Add to the reckoning all whom thou hast known, one after another. One man after burying another has been laid out dead, and another buries him: and all this in a short time. To conclude, always observe how ephemeral and worthless human things are, and what was yesterday a little mucus tomorrow will be a mummy or ashes. Pass then through this little space of time conformably to nature, and end thy journey in content, just as an olive falls off when it is ripe, blessing nature who produced it, and thanking the tree on which it grew.

(49) Be like the promontory against which the waves continually break, but it stands firm and tames the fury of the water around it.

Unhappy am I, because this has happened to me.—Not so, but happy am I, though this has happened to me, because I continue free from pain, neither crushed by the present nor fearing the future. For such a thing as this might have happened to every man; but every man would not have continued free from pain on such an occasion. Why then is that rather a misfortune than this a good fortune? And dost thou in all cases call that a man's misfortune, which is not a deviation from man's nature? And does a thing seem to thee to be a deviation from man's nature, when it is not contrary to the will of man's nature? Well, thou knowest the will of nature. Will then this which has happened prevent thee from being just, magnanimous, temperate, prudent, secure against inconsiderate opinions and falsehood; will it prevent thee from having modesty, freedom, and everything else, by the presence of which man's nature obtains all that is its own? Remember too on every occasion which leads thee to vexation to apply this principle: not that this is a misfortune, but that to bear it nobly is good fortune.

Book V

In the morning when thou risest unwillingly, let this thought be present—I am rising to the work of a human being. Why then am I dissatisfied if I am going to do the things for which I exist and for which I was brought into the world? Or have I been made for this, to lie in the bed-clothes and keep myself warm?—But this is more pleasant.—Dost thou exist then to take thy pleasure, and not at all for action or exertion? Dost thou not see the little plants, the little birds, the ants, the spiders, the bees working together to put in order their several parts of the universe? And art thou willing to do the work of a human being, and dost thou not make haste to do that which is according to thy nature?—But it is necessary to take rest also.—It is necessary: however nature has fixed bounds to this too: she has fixed bounds both to eating and drinking, and yet thou goest beyond these bounds, beyond what is sufficient; yet in thy acts it is not so, but thou stoppest short of what thou canst do. So thou lovest not thyself, for if thou didst, thou wouldst love thy nature and her will. But those who love their several arts exhaust themselves in working at them unwashed and without food; but thou valuest thy own nature less than the turner values the turning art, or the dancer the dancing art, or the lover of money values his money, or the vainglorious man his little glory. And such men, when they have a violent affection to a thing, choose neither to eat nor to sleep rather than to perfect the things which they care for. But are the acts which concern society more vile in thy eyes and less worthy of thy labour?

(2) How easy it is to repel and to wipe away every impression which is troublesome or unsuitable, and immediately to be in all tranquillity.

(3) Judge every word and deed which are according to nature to be fit for thee; and be not diverted by the blame which follows from any people nor by their words, but if a thing is good to be done or said, do not consider it unworthy of thee. For those persons have their peculiar leading principle and follow their peculiar movement; which things do not thou regard, but go straight on, following thy

own nature and the common nature; and the way of both is one.

(16) Such as are thy habitual thoughts, such also will be the character of thy mind; for the soul is dyed by the thoughts. Dye it then with a continuous series of such thoughts as these: for instance, that where a man can live there he can also live well. But he must live in a place;—well then, he can also live well in a palace. And again, consider that for whatever purpose each thing has been constituted, for this it has been constituted, and towards this it is carried; and its end is in that towards which it is carried; and where the end is, there also is the advantage and the good of each thing. Now the good for the reasonable animal is society; for that we are made for society has been shown above. Is it not plain that the inferior exist for the sake of the superior? But the things which have life are superior to those which have not life, and of those which have life the superior are those which have reason.

Book VI

(15) Some things are hurrying into existence, and others are hurrying out of it; and of that which is coming into existence part is already extinguished. Motions and changes are continually renewing the world, just as the uninterrupted course of time is always renewing the infinite duration of ages. In this flowing stream then, on which there is no abiding, what is there of the things which hurry by on which a man would set a high price? It would be just as if a man should fall in love with one of the sparrows which fly by, but it has already passed out of sight. Something of this kind is the very life of every man, like the exhalation of the blood and the respiration of the air. For such as it is to have once drawn in the air and to have given it back, which we do every moment, just the same is it with the whole respiratory power, which thou didst receive at thy birth yesterday and the day before, to give it back to the element from which thou didst first draw it.

(16) Neither is transpiration, as in plants, a thing to be valued, nor respiration, as in domesticated animals and wild beasts, nor the receiving of impressions by the appearances of things, nor being moved by desires as puppets by strings, nor assembling in herds, nor being nourished by food; for this is just like the act of separating and parting with the useless part of our food. What then is worth being valued? To be received with clapping of hands? No. Neither must we value the clapping of tongues, for the praise which comes from the many is a clapping of tongues. Suppose then that thou hast given up this worthless thing called fame, what remains that is worth valuing? This is my opinion, to move thyself and to restrain thyself in conformity to thy proper constitution, to which end both all employments and arts lead. For every art aims at this, that the thing which has been made should be adapted to the work for which it has been made; and both the vine-planter who looks after the vine, and the horse-breaker, and he who trains the dog, seek this end. But the education and the teaching of youth aim at something. In this then is the value of the education and the teaching. And if this is well, thou wilt not seek anything else. Wilt thou not cease to value many other things too? Then thou wilt be neither free, nor sufficient for thy own happiness, nor without passion. For of necessity thou must be envious, jealous, and suspicious of those who can take away those things, and plot against those who have that which is valued by thee. Of necessity a man must be altogether in a state of perturbation who wants any of these things; and besides, he must often find fault with the gods. But to reverence and honour thy own mind will make thee content with thyself, and in harmony with society, and in agreement with the gods, that is, praising all that they give and have ordered.

Book VII

(9) All things are implicated with one another, and the bond is holy; and there is

hardly anything unconnected with any other thing. For things have been co-ordinated, and they combine to form the same universe (order). For there is one universe made up of all things, and one God who pervades all things, and one substance, and one law, one common reason in all intelligent animals, and one truth; if indeed there is also one perfection for all animals which are of the same stock and participate in the same reason.

(55) Do not look around thee to discover other men's ruling principles, but look straight to this, to what nature leads thee, both the universal nature through the things which happen to thee, and thy own nature through the acts which must be done by thee. But every being ought to do that which is according to its constitution; and all other things have been constituted for the sake of rational beings, just as among irrational things the inferior for the sake of the superior, but the rational for the sake of one another.

The prime principle then in man's constitution is the social. And the second is not to yield to the persuasions of the body, for it is the peculiar office of the rational and intelligent motion to circumscribe itself, and never to be overpowered either by the motion of the senses or of the appetites, for both are animal; but the intelligent motion claims superiority and does not permit itself to be overpowered by the others. And with good reason, for it is formed by nature to use all of them. The third thing in the rational constitution is freedom from error and from deception. Let then the ruling principle holding fast to these things go straight on, and it has what is its own.

Book VIII

(7) Every nature is contented with itself when it goes on its way well; and a rational nature goes on its way well, when in its thoughts it assents to nothing false or uncertain, and when it directs its movements to social acts only, and when it confines its desires and aversions to the things which are in its power, and when it is satisfied with everything that is assigned to it by the common nature. For of this common nature every particular nature is a part, as the nature of the leaf is a part of the nature of the plant; except that in the plant the nature of the leaf is part of a nature which has not perception or reason, and is subject to be impeded; but the nature of man is part of a nature which is not subject to impediments, and is intelligent and just, since it gives to everything in equal portions and according to its worth, times, substance, cause (form), activity, and incident. But examine, not to discover that any one thing compared with any other single thing is equal in all respects, but by taking all the parts together of one thing comparing them with all the parts together of another.

(34) If thou didst ever see a hand cut off, or a foot, or a head, lying anywhere apart from the rest of the body, such does a man make himself, as far as he can, who is not content with what happens, and separates himself from others, or does anything unsocial. Suppose that thou hast detached thyself from the natural unity—for thou wast made by nature a part, but now thou hast cut thyself off—yet here there is this beautiful provision, that it is in thy power again to unite thyself. God has allowed this to no other part, after it has been separated and cut asunder, to come together again. But consider the kindness by which he has distinguished man, for he has put it in his power not to be separated at all from the universal; and when he has been separated, he has allowed him to return and to be united and to resume his place as a part.

(47) If thou art pained by any external thing, it is not this thing that disturbs thee, but thy own judgement about it. And it is in thy power to wipe out this judgement now. But if anything in thy own disposition gives thee pain, who hinders thee from correcting thy opinion? And even if thou are pained because thou art not doing some particular thing which seems to thee to be right, why dost thou not rather act than

complain?—But some insuperable obstacle is in the way?—Do not be grieved then, for the cause of its not being done depends not on thee.—But it is not worthwhile to live, if this cannot be done.—Take thy departure then from life contentedly, just as he dies who is in full activity, and well pleased too with things which are obstacles.

Book IX

(3) Do not despise death, but be well content with it, since this too is one of those things which nature wills. For such as it is to be young and to grow old, and to increase and to reach maturity, and to have teeth and beard and grey hairs, and to beget, and to be pregnant and to bring forth, and all the other natural operations which the seasons of thy life bring, such also is dissolution. This, then, is consistent with the character of a reflecting man, to be neither careless nor impatient nor contemptuous with respect to death, but to wait for it as one of the operations of nature. As thou now waitest for the time when the child shall come out of thy wife's womb, so be ready for the time when thy soul shall fall out of this envelope. But if thou requirest also a vulgar kind of comfort which shall reach thy heart, thou wilt be made best reconciled to death by observing the objects from which thou art going to be removed, and the morals of those with whom thy soul will no longer be mingled. For it is no way right to be offended with men, but it is thy duty to care for them and to bear with them gently; and yet to remember that thy departure will be not from men who have the same principles as thyself. For this is the only thing, if there be any, which could draw us the contrary way and attach us to life, to be permitted to live with those who have the same principles as ourselves. But now thou seest how great is the trouble arising from the discordance of those who live together, so that thou mayest say, Come quick, O death, lest perchance I, too, should forget myself.

(9) All things which participate in anything which is common to them all move towards that which is of the same kind with themselves. Everything which is earthy turns towards the earth, everything which is liquid flows together, and everything which is of an aërial kind does the same, so that they require something to keep them asunder, and the application of force. Fire indeed moves upwards on account of the elemental fire, but it is so ready to be kindled together with all the fire which is here, that even every substance which is somewhat dry, is easily ignited, because there is less mingled with it of that which is a hindrance to ignition. Accordingly then everything also which participates in the common intelligent nature moves in like manner towards that which is of the same kind with itself, or moves even more. For so much as it is superior in comparison with all other things, in the same degree also is it more ready to mingle with and to be fused with that which is akin to it. Accordingly among animals devoid of reason we find swarms of bees, and herds of cattle, and the nurture of young birds, and in a manner, loves; for even in animals there are souls, and that power which brings them together is seen to exert itself in the superior degree, and in such a way as never has been observed in plants nor in stones nor in trees. But in rational animals there are political communities and friendships, and families and meetings of people; and in wars, treaties and armistices. But in the things which are still superior, even though they are separated from one another, unity in a manner exists, as in the stars. Thus the ascent to the higher degree is able to produce a sympathy even in things which are separated. See, then, what now takes place. For only intelligent animals have now forgotten this mutual desire and inclination, and in them alone the property of flowing together is not seen. But still though men strive to avoid this union, they are caught and held by it, for their nature is too strong for them; and thou wilt see what I say, if thou only observest. Sooner, then, will one find anything earthy which comes in contact with no earthy

thing than a man altogether separated from other men.

(42) When thou art offended with any man's shameless conduct, immediately ask thyself, is it possible, then, that shameless men should not be in the world? It is not possible. Do not, then, require what is impossible. For this man also is one of those shameless men who must of necessity be in the world. Let the same considerations be present to thy mind in the case of the knave, and the faithless man, and of every man who does wrong in any way. For at the same time that thou dost remind thyself that it is impossible that such kind of men should not exist, thou wilt become more kindly disposed towards every one individually. It is useful to perceive this, too, immediately when the occasion arises, what virtue nature has given to man to oppose to every wrongful act. For she has given to man, as an antidote against the stupid man, mildness, and against another kind of man some other power. And in all cases it is possible for thee to correct by teaching the man who is gone astray; for every man who errs misses his object and is gone astray. Besides wherein hast thou been injured? For thou wilt find that no one among those against whom thou art irritated has done anything by which thy mind could be made worse; but that which is evil to thee and harmful has its foundation only in the mind. And what harm is done or what is there strange, if the man who has not been instructed does the acts of an uninstructed man? Consider whether thou shouldst not rather blame thyself because thou didst not expect such a man to err in such a way. For thou hadst means given thee by the reason to suppose that it was likely that he would commit this error, and yet thou hast forgotten and art amazed that he has erred. But most of all when thou blamest a man as faithless or ungrateful, turn to thyself. For the fault is manifestly thy own, whether thou didst trust that a man who had such a disposition would keep his promise, or when conferring thy kindness thou didst not confer it absolutely, nor yet

in such way as to have received from thy very act all the profit. For what more dost thou want when thou hast done a man a service? Are thou not content that thou hast done something conformable to thy nature, and dost thou seek to be paid for it? Just as if the eye demanded a recompense for seeing, or the feet for walking. For as these members are formed for a particular purpose, and by working according to their several constitutions obtain what is their own; so also as man is formed by nature to acts of benevolence, when he has done anything benevolent or in any other way conducive to the common interest, he has acted conformably to his constitution, and he gets what is his own.

Book X

(2) Observe what thy nature requires, so far as thou art governed by nature only: then do it and accept it, if thy nature, so far as thou art a living being, shall not be made worse by it. And next thou must observe what thy nature requires so far as thou art a living being. And all this thou mayest allow thyself, if thy nature, so far as thou art a rational animal, shall not be made worse by it. But the rational animal is consequently also a political (social) animal. Use these rules, then, and trouble thyself about nothing else.

(6) Whether the universe is a concourse of atoms, or nature is a system, let this first be established, that I am a part of the whole which is governed by nature; next, I am in a manner intimately related to the parts which are of the same kind with myself. For remembering this, inasmuch as I am a part, I shall be discontented with none of the things which are assigned to me out of the whole; for nothing is injurious to the part, if it is for the advantage of the whole. For the whole contains nothing which is not for its advantage; and all natures indeed have this common principle, but the nature of the universe has this principle besides, that it cannot be compelled even by any external cause to gener-

ate anything harmful to itself. By remembering, then, that I am a part of such a whole, I shall be content with everything that happens. And inasmuch as I am in a manner intimately related to the parts which are of the same kind with myself, I shall do nothing unsocial, but I shall rather direct myself to the things which are of the same kind with myself, and I shall turn all my efforts to the common interest, and divert them from the contrary. Now, if these things are done so, life must flow on happily, just as thou mayest observe that the life of a citizen is happy, who continues a course of action which is advantageous to his fellow-citizens, and is content with whatever the state may assign to him.

Book XI

(19) There are four principal aberrations of the superior faculty against which thou shouldst be constantly on thy guard, and when thou hast detected them, thou shouldst wipe them out and say on each occasion thus: this thought is not necessary: this tends to destroy social union: this which thou art going to say comes not from the real thoughts; for thou shouldst consider it among the most absurd of things for a man not to speak from his real thoughts. But the fourth is when thou shalt reproach thyself for anything, for this is an evidence of the diviner part within thee being overpowered and yielding to the less honourable and to the perishable part, the body, and to its gross pleasures.

(20) Thy aërial part and all the fiery parts which are mingled in thee, though by nature they have an upward tendency, still in obedience to the disposition of the universe they are overpowered here in the compound mass (the body). And also the whole of the earthy part in thee and the watery, though their tendency is downward, still are raised up and occupy a position which is not their natural one. In this manner then the elemental parts obey the universal, for when they have been fixed in any place perforce they remain there until

again the universal shall sound the signal for dissolution. Is it not then strange that thy intelligent part only should be disobedient and discontented with its own place? And yet no force is imposed on it, but only those things which are conformable to its nature: still it does not submit, but is carried in the opposite direction. For the movement towards injustice and intemperance and to anger and grief and fear is nothing else than the act of one who deviates from nature. And also when the ruling faculty is discontented with anything that happens, then too it deserts its post: for it is constituted for piety and reverence towards the gods no less than for justice. For these qualities also are comprehended under the generic term of contentment with the constitution of things, and indeed they are prior to acts of justice.

Book XII

(26) When thou art troubled about anything, thou hast forgotten this, that all things happen according to the universal nature; and forgotten this, that a man's wrongful act is nothing to thee; and further thou hast forgotten this, that everything which happens, always happened so and will happen so, and now happens so everywhere; forgotten this too, how close is the kinship between a man and the whole human race, for it is a community, not of a little blood or seed, but of intelligence. And thou hast forgotten this too, that every man's intelligence is a god, and is an efflux of the deity; and forgotten this, that nothing is a man's own, but that his child and his body and his very soul came from the deity; forgotten this, that everything is opinion; and lastly thou hast forgotten that every man lives the present time only, and loses only this.

(36) Man, thou has been a citizen in this great state (the world): what difference does it make to thee whether for five years (or three)? For that which is conformable to the laws is just for all. Where is the hardship then, if no tyrant nor yet an unjust judge sends thee away from the state, but nature

who brought thee into it? The same as if a praetor who has employed an actor dismisses him from the stage.—But I have not finished the five acts, but only three of them.—Thou sayest well, but in life the three acts are the whole drama; for what shall be a complete drama is determined by him who was once the cause of its composition, and now of its dissolution: but thou art the cause of neither. Depart then satisfied, for he also who releases thee is satisfied.

COMMENT

Human Harmony with the Natural Environment

In the writings of Marcus Aurelius, there is a strong overtone of pantheism in the doctrine that people should live in harmony with nature. Just as a soul or life force animates the human body, he maintained, so a spiritual force rolls through all things. This soul or life force can be called God, Nature, Reason—synonyms for the inner essence and animating principle of the universe. It is the productive, formative power, the force that makes for movement and growth. It is divine reason, all-pervasive and all-powerful. Hence, Marcus Aurelius maintained that there is no sheer evil in the world, and nothing is left to chance. From this standpoint, the force is also fate—not a blind mechanical necessity but a purposive, providential force, the living activity of the whole expressing itself through every natural event.

The divine essence is in every person: Reason is our governing principle, the core and center of our being. What corresponds to this reason and expresses our nature also corresponds to the world soul and expresses the universal nature. To "live according to nature" is to express our rational nature and to be in harmony with the rational order of the world. The essence of morality is to make the "things in our power"—our inner attitudes—harmonize with the "things not in our power"—the rational outward course of events.

The need to live in harmony with nature is not just an ancient doctrine. It has been echoed and reechoed during our modern ecological crisis. We may choose to express this need more in scientific than in religious terms, but we too must recognize the necessity to live in symbiotic harmony with nature. Willy-nilly, we have to dwell on this earth if we are to live at all. If the future is to be tolerable, we must bring human breeding under sensible control, we must conserve our dwindling natural resources, and we must bring to a halt the air and water pollution and the bulldozed devastation of the landscape.

Some Major Questions

The great question that is posed by the readings in this chapter is the relation between "facts" and "ideals", between "what is" and "what ought to be." This is a question to which the philosophers represented here in Part III will return again and again, and it is one of the most important and difficult questions in ethics. The serious student of philosophy will need to ponder its meaning and implications and to decide as best as possible what is a reasonable answer.

It seems clear that *good,* in the sense of *what ought to be,* and *right,* in the sense of *what ought to be done,* are not natural characteristics, as are rectangularity or absent-mindedness. Many philosophers have concluded that these concepts have a distinctly *ethical* meaning—a meaning that must be grasped by intuition or *a priori* reason or a peculiar moral sense rather than by empirical science or a descriptive metaphysics. If so, does this invalidate the doctrine discussed in this chapter that morality is based on nature? Here is a question that the reader might ponder.

Another very fundamental question is whether the antirelativistic implications of the theory of natural law are valid. Can we define our legitimate aim as the unfolding of our basic powers according to the laws of our nature and in harmony with our natural environment? Or should we conclude that people are so variously molded by patterns of culture that "human nature" is largely an empty phrase? Or that the natural environment counts less and less in comparison with the artificialities of urban civilization? If so, is this a disaster?

Other questions concern the relation between natural rights and democratic theory. The concept of natural rights has often been linked with the "social contract." This is the idea of an original covenant by which individuals, who possessed natural rights in an original, nonpolitical "state of nature," joined together and through mutual consent formed a state and placed a fiduciary trust in the supreme power of government. The purpose of the covenant is to make these rights more secure, and if the government fails to do so, it forfeits the right to rule. Thus phrased, the theories of the state of nature, natural rights, and the social contract formed the basis of democratic, sometimes revolutionary, tendencies. In Jean Jacques Rousseau's formulation and even more clearly in Immanuel Kant's, the state of nature and the social contract were treated as useful fictions, meant to serve as a criterion for judging the legitimacy of acts of the state. This constellation of ideas has been elaborated by John Rawls' much discussed book, *The Theory of Justice* (Harvard University Press, 1971). The reader may wish to consider whether the tradition of natural law and natural rights is a satisfactory basis for a theory of democratic sovereignty and social justice. Is it an effective way to delineate the meaning of human rights? Or is it too abstract and nonhistorical? Must we seek some other basis for democratic theory, for example, the instrumentalist approach of John Dewey or the socialist approach of Karl Marx? Or should we reject democracy altogether, as Plato and Friedrich Nietzsche would have us do?

There is also the question of whether Marcus Aurelius' interpretation of nature is coherent. Is he being inconsistent in clinging to the doctrines of both fate and free will, cosmopolitanism and self-sufficiency, tacit admission that certain things are preferable and yet explicit, teaching that all happens for the best? If he is inconsistent, can we somehow reconcile these clashing doctrines, or must we choose some and abandon others? If so, how much can we salvage? Can we still admire the main tenets of his Stoicism: the courage, the tranquility, the cosmopolitanism, the sense of universal fellowship, the attempt to see the rational connections and necessity of things, the poise and magnanimity of outlook that result from identifying oneself with the whole frame of nature?

Finally, there is the question of ecological adjustment. As already intimated, this is a crucial issue for the whole of humanity. Our present technology is suicidal—so much of it is devoted to the instruments of death rather than to the means of life, and so much is based on the extraction of exhaustible ores and fossil fuels. These diminishing resources are combined with mounting overpopulation. Control is an unsolved problem even in the developed countries, and starvation is the only surefire method of controlling population in the undeveloped countries. The present rate of population growth cannot continue indefinitely, for it would rapidly exhaust the physical resources and limits of our world. Can we cope with these threats without a fairly radical interference with cherished freedoms and traditional institutions? Can we limit growth without precipitating a new depression? What far-reaching changes in human values will be required?

To return once more to the case of Noel David Earley's plan to commit suicide, one wonders how Marcus Aurelius would respond. Is there any way suicide can be understood as a harmonious adaptation to nature? As an "acceptance" of the divine cosmic plan? It might seem that Marcus Aurelius would fault Earley for failing to exhibit internal strength in the face of adversity, but on the other hand, he might agree that in such circumstances the moral thing to do is to embrace the inevitable and seek to make the most of it. Would Marcus Aurelius think Earley's approach was too individualistic?

16

THE WAY OF DUTY

IMMANUEL KANT (1724–1804)

For a biographical note, see pages 84–85.

THE CATEGORICAL IMPERATIVE

Section I

Transition from Ordinary Moral Conceptions to the Philosophical Conception of Morality

Nothing in the whole world, or even outside of the world, can possibly be regarded as good without limitation except a *good will.* No doubt it is a good and desirable thing to have intelligence, sagacity, judgment, and other intellectual gifts, by whatever name they may be called; it is also good and desirable in many respects to possess by nature such qualities as courage, resolution, and perseverance; but all these gifts of nature may be in the highest degree pernicious and hurtful, if the will which directs them, or what is called the *character,* is not itself good. The same thing applies to *gifts of fortune.* Power, wealth, honor, even good health, and that general

The Philosophy of Kant as Contained in Extracts from His Own Writings, selected and translated by John Watson. Glasgow: Jackson, Wylie and Company, 1888; second edition, 1891. In this version, the original in *The Foundations of the Metaphysic of Morals* is somewhat condensed.

well-being and contentment with one's lot which we call *happiness,* give rise to pride and not infrequently to insolence, if a man's will is not good; nor can a reflective and impartial spectator ever look with satisfaction upon the unbroken prosperity of a man who is destitute of the ornament of a pure and good will. A good will would therefore seem to be the indispensable condition without which no one is even worthy to be happy.

A man's will is good, not because the consequences which flow from it are good, nor because it is capable of attaining the end which it seeks, but it is good in itself, or because it wills the good. By a good will is not meant mere well-wishing; it consists in a resolute employment of all the means within one's reach, and its intrinsic value is in no way increased by success or lessened by failure.

This idea of the absolute value of mere will seems so extraordinary that, although it is endorsed even by the popular judgment, we must subject it to careful scrutiny.

If nature had meant to provide simply for the maintenance, the well-being, in a word the happiness, of beings which have reason and will, it must be confessed that, in making use of their reason, it has hit upon a very poor way of attaining its end. As a matter of fact the very worst way a man of refinement and culture can take to secure enjoyment and happiness is to make use of his reason for that purpose. Hence there is apt to arise in his mind a certain degree of *misology*, or hatred of reason. Finding that the arts which minister to luxury, and even the sciences, instead of bringing him happiness, only lay a heavier yoke on his neck, he at length comes to envy, rather than to despise, men of less refinement, who follow more closely the promptings of their natural impulses, and pay little heed to what reason tells them to do or to leave undone. It must at least be admitted, that one may deny reason to have much or indeed any value in the production of happiness and contentment, without taking a morose or ungrateful view of the goodness with which the world is governed. Such a judgment really means that life has another and a much nobler end than happiness, and that the true vocation of reason is to secure that end.

The true object of reason then, in so far as it is practical, or capable of influencing the will, must be to produce a will which is *good in itself,* and not merely good *as a means* to something else. This will is not the only or the whole good, but it is the highest good, and the condition of all other good, even of the desire for happiness itself. It is therefore not inconsistent with the wisdom of nature that the cultivation of reason which is essential to the furtherance of its first and unconditioned object, the production of a good will, should, in this life at least, in many ways limit, or even make impossible, the attainment of happiness, which is its second and conditioned object.

To bring to clear consciousness the conception of a will which is good in itself, a conception already familiar to the popular mind, let us examine the conception of *duty,* which involves the idea of a good will as manifested under certain subjective limitations and hindrances.

I pass over actions which are admittedly violations of duty, for these, however useful they may be in the attainment of this or that end, manifestly do not proceed *from* duty. I set aside also those actions which are not actually inconsistent with duty, but which yet are done under the impulse of some natural inclination, although *not a direct inclination* to do these particular actions; for in these it is easy to determine whether the action that is consistent with duty, is done *from duty* or with some selfish object in view. It is more difficult to make a clear distinction of motives when there is a *direct* inclination to do a certain action, which is itself in conformity with duty. The preservation of one's own life, for instance, is a duty; but, as everyone has a natural inclination to preserve his life, the anxious care which most men usually devote to this object, has no intrinsic value, nor the maxim from which they act any moral import. They preserve their life in *accordance with* duty, but not *because* of duty. But, suppose adversity and hopeless sorrow to have taken away all desire for life; suppose that the wretched man would welcome death as a release, and yet takes means to prolong his life simply from a sense of duty: then his maxim has a genuine moral import.

But, secondly, an action that is done from duty gets its moral value, *not from the object* which it is intended to secure, but from the maxim by which it is determined. Accordingly, the action has the same moral value whether the object is attained or not, if only the *principle* by which the will is determined to act is independent of every object of sensuous desire. What was said above makes it clear, that it is not the object aimed at, or, in other words, the consequences which flow from an action when these are made the end and motive of the will, that can give to the action an unconditioned and moral value. In what, then, can the moral value of an action consist, if it does not lie in the will itself, as directed to the attainment of a certain object? It can lie only in the principle of the will, no matter whether the object sought can be attained by the action or not. For the will stands as it were at the parting of the ways, between its *a priori* principle, which is formal, and its *posteriori* material motive. As so standing it must be determined by something, and, as no action which is done from duty can be determined by a material principle, it can be determined only by the formal principle of all volition.

From the two propositions just set forth a third directly follows, which may be thus stated, *Duty is the obligation to act from reverence for law*. Now, I may have a natural inclination for the object that I expect to follow from my action, but I can never have reverence for that which is not a spontaneous activity of my will, but merely an effect of it; neither can I have *reverence* for any natural inclination, whether it is my own or another's. If it is my own, I can at most only approve of it; if it is manifested by another, I may regard it as conducive to my own interest, and hence I may in certain cases even be said to have a love for it. But the only thing which I can reverence or which can lay me under an obligation to act, is the law which is connected with my will, not as a consequence, but as a principle; a principle which is not dependent upon natural inclination, but overmasters it, or at least allows it to have no influence whatever in determining my course of action. Now if an action which is done out of regard for duty sets entirely aside the influence of natural inclination and along with it every object of the will, nothing else is left by which the will can be determined but objectively the *law* itself, and subjectively *pure reverence* for the law as a principle of action. Thus there arises the maxim, to obey the moral law even at the sacrifice of all my natural inclinations.

The supreme good which we call moral can therefore be nothing but the *idea of the law* in itself, in so far as it is this idea which determines the will, and not any consequences that are expected to follow. Only a *rational* being can have such an idea, and hence a man who acts from the idea of the law is already morally good, no matter whether the consequences which he expects from his action follow or not.

Now what must be the nature of a law, the idea of which is to determine the will, even apart from the effects expected to follow, and which is therefore itself entitled to be called good absolutely and without qualification? As the will must not be moved to act from any desire for the results expected to follow from obedience to a certain law, the only principle of the will which remains is that of the conformity of actions to universal law. In all cases I must act in such a way that I can at the same time will that my maxim should become a universal law. This is what is meant by conformity to law pure and simple; and this is the principle which serves, and must serve, to determine the will, if the idea of duty is not to be regarded as empty and chimerical. As a matter of fact the judgments which we are wont to pass upon conduct perfectly agree with this principle, and in making them we always have it before our eyes.

May I, for instance, under the pressure of circumstances, make a promise which I have no intention of keeping? The question is not, whether it is prudent to make a false promise, but whether it is morally right. To enable me to answer this question shortly and conclusively, the best way is for me to ask myself whether it would satisfy me that the maxim to extricate myself from embarrassment by giving a false promise should have the force of a universal law, applying to others as well as to myself. And I see at once, that, while I can certainly will the lie, I cannot will that lying should be a universal law. If lying were universal, there would, properly speaking, be no promises whatever. I might say that I intended to do a certain thing at some future time, but nobody would believe me, or if he did at the moment trust to my promise, he would afterwards pay me back in my own coin. My maxim thus proves itself to be self-destructive, so soon as it is taken as a universal law.

Duty, then, consists in the obligation to act from *pure* reverence for the moral law. To this motive all others must give way, for it is the condition of a will which is good *in itself,* and which has a value with which nothing else is comparable.

There is, however, in man a strong feeling of antagonism to the commands of duty, although his reason tells him that those commands are worthy of the highest reverence. For man not only possesses reason, but he has certain natural wants and inclinations, the complete satisfaction of which he calls happiness. These natural inclinations clamorously demand to have their seemingly reasonable claims respected; but reason issues its commands inflexibly, refusing to promise anything to the natural desires, and treating their claims with a sort of neglect and contempt. From this there arises a *natural dialectic,* that is, a disposition to explain away the strict laws of duty, to cast doubt upon their validity, or at least, upon their purity and stringency, and in this way to make them yield to the demands of the natural inclinations.

Thus men are forced to go beyond the narrow circle of ideas within which their reason ordinarily moves, and to take a step into the field of *moral philosophy,* not indeed from any perception of speculative difficulties, but simply on practical grounds. The practical reason of men cannot be long exercised any more than the theoretical, without falling insensibly into a dialectic, which compels it to call in the aid of philosophy; and in the one case as in the other, rest can be found only in a thorough criticism of human reason.

Section II

Transition from Popular Moral Philosophy to the Metaphysic of Morality

So far, we have drawn our conception of duty from the manner in which men employ it in the ordinary exercise of their practical reason. The conception of duty, however, we must not suppose to be therefore derived from experience. On the contrary, we hear frequent complaints, the justice of which we cannot but admit, that no one can point to a single instance in which an action has undoubtedly been done purely from a regard for duty; that there are certainly many actions which are not *opposed* to duty, but none which are indisputably done *from* duty and therefore have a moral value. Nothing indeed can secure us against the complete loss of our ideas of duty, and maintain in the soul a well-grounded respect for the moral law, but the clear conviction, that reason issues its commands on its own authority, without caring in the least whether the actions of men have, as a matter of fact, been done purely from ideas of duty. For reason commands inflexibly that certain actions should be done, which perhaps never have been done; actions, the very possibility of which may seem doubtful to one who bases everything upon experience. Perfect disinterestedness in friendship, for instance, is demanded of every man, although there may never have been a sincere friend; for pure friendship is bound up with the idea of duty as duty, and belongs to the very idea of a reason which determines the will on *a priori* grounds, prior to all experience.

It is, moreover, beyond dispute, that unless we are to deny to morality all truth and all reference to a possible object, the moral law has so wide an application that it is binding, not merely upon man, but upon all *rational beings,* and not merely under certain contingent conditions, and with certain limitations, but absolutely and necessarily.

Only a rational being has the faculty of acting in conformity with the *idea* of law, or from principles; only a rational being, in other words, has a will. And as without reason actions cannot proceed from laws, will is simply practical reason. If the will is infallibly determined by reason, the actions of a rational being are subjectively as well as objectively necessary; that is, will must be regarded as a faculty of choosing *that only* which reason, independently of natural inclination, declares to be practically necessary or good. On the other hand, if the will is not invariably determined by reason alone, but is subject to certain subjective conditions or motives, which are not always in harmony with the objective conditions; if the will, as actually is the case with man, is not in perfect conformity with reason; actions which are recognized to be objectively necessary, are subjectively contingent. The determination of such a will according to objective laws is therefore called *obligation*. That is to say, if the will of a rational being is not absolutely good, we conceive of it as capable of being determined by objective laws of reason, but not as by its very nature necessarily obeying them.

The idea that a certain principle is objective, and binding upon the will, is a command of reason, and the statement of the command in a formula is an *imperative*.

All imperatives are expressed by the word *ought*, to indicate that the will upon which they are binding is not by its subjective constitution necessarily determined in conformity with the objective law of reason. An imperative says, that the doing, or leaving undone of a certain thing would be good, but it addresses a will which does not always do a thing simply because it is good. Now, that is practically *good* which determines the will by ideas of reason, in other words, that which determines it, not by subjective influences, but by principles which are objective, or apply to all rational beings as such. *Good* and *pleasure* are quite distinct. Pleasure results from the influence of purely subjective causes upon the will of the subject, and these vary with the susceptibility of this or that individual, while a principle of reason is valid for all.

A perfectly good will would, like the will of man, stand under objective laws, laws of the good, but it could not be said to be under an *obligation* to act in conformity with those laws. Such a will by its subjective constitution could be determined only by the idea of the good. In reference to the Divine will, or any other holy will, imperatives have no meaning; for here the will is by its very nature necessarily in harmony

with the law, and therefore *ought* has no application to it. Imperatives are formulae, which express merely the relation of objective laws of volition in general to the imperfect will of this or that rational being, as for instance, the will of man.

Now, all imperatives command either *hypothetically* or *categorically*. A hypothetical imperative states that a certain thing must be done, if something else which is willed, or at least might be willed, is to be attained. The categorical imperative declares that an act is in itself or objectively necessary, without any reference to another end.

Every practical law represents a possible action as good, and therefore as obligatory for a subject that is capable of being determined to act by reason. Hence all imperatives are formulae for the determination of an action which is obligatory according to the principle of a will that is in some sense good. If the action is good only because it is a means to *something else*, the imperative is *hypothetical*; if the action is conceived to be good *in itself*, the imperative, as the necessary principle of a will that in itself conforms to reason, is *categorical*.

An imperative, then, states what possible action of mine would be good. It supplies the practical rule for a will which does not at once do an act simply because it is good, either because the subject does not know it to be good, or because, knowing it to be good, he is influenced by maxims which are opposed to the objective principles of a practical reason.

The hypothetical imperative says only that an action is good relatively to a certain *possible* end or to a certain *actual* end. In the former case it is *problematic*, in the latter case *assertoric*. The categorical imperative, which affirms that an action is in itself or objectively necessary without regard to an end, that is, without regard to any other end than itself, is an *apodictic* practical principle.

Whatever is within the power of a rational being may be conceived to be capable of being willed by some rational being, and hence the principles which determine what actions are necessary in the attainment of certain possible ends, are infinite in number.

Yet there is one thing which we may assume that all finite rational beings actually make their end, and there is therefore one object which may safely be regarded, not simply as something that they *may* seek, but as something that by a necessity of their nature they actually *do* seek: This object is *happiness*. The hypothetical imperative, which affirms the practical necessity of an action as the means of attaining happiness, is *assertoric*. We must not think of happiness as simply a possible and problematic end, but as an end that we may with confidence presuppose *a priori* to be sought by everyone, belonging as it does to the very nature of man. Now skill in the choice of means to his own greatest well-being may be called *prudence*, taking the word in its more restricted sense. An imperative, therefore, which relates merely to the choice of means to one's own happiness, that is, a maxim of prudence, must be hypothetical; it commands an action, not absolutely, but only as a means to another end.

Lastly, there is an imperative which directly commands an action, without presupposing as its condition that some other end is to be attained by means of that action. This imperative is *categorical*. It has to do, not with the matter of an action and the result expected to follow from it, but simply with the form and principle from which the action itself proceeds. The action is essentially good if the motive of the agent is good, let the consequences be what they may. This imperative may be called the imperative of *morality*.

How are all these imperatives possible? The question is not, How is an action which an imperative commands actually realized? but, How can we think of the will as placed under obligation by each of those imperatives? Very little need be said to show how an imperative of skill is possible. He who wills the end, wills also the means in his power which are indispensable to the

attainment of the end. Looking simply at the act of will, we must say that this proposition is analytic. If a certain object is to follow as an effect from my volition, my causality must be conceived as active in the production of the effect, or as employing the means by which the effect will take place. The imperative, therefore, simply states that in the conception of the willing of this end there is directly implied the conception of actions necessary to this end. No doubt certain synthetic propositions are required to determine the particular means by which a given end may be attained, but these have nothing to do with the principle or act of the will, but merely state how the object may actually be realized.

Were it as easy to give a definite conception of happiness as of a particular end, the imperatives of prudence would be of exactly the same nature as the imperatives of skill, and would therefore be analytic. For, we should be able to say, that he who wills the end wills also the only means in his power for the attainment of the end. But, unfortunately, the conception of happiness is so indefinite, that, although every man desires to obtain it, he is unable to give a definite and self-consistent statement of what he actually desires and wills. The truth is, that, strictly speaking, the imperatives of prudence are not commands at all. They do not say that actions are objective or *necessary*, and hence they must be regarded as counsels, not as commands of reason. Still, the imperative of prudence would be an analytic proposition, if the means to happiness could only be known with certainty. For the only difference in the two cases is that in the imperative of skill the end is merely possible, in the imperative of prudence it is actually given; and as in both all that is commanded is the means to an end which is assumed to be willed, the imperative which commands that he who wills the end should also will the means, is in both cases analytic. There is therefore no real difficulty in seeing how an imperative of prudence is possible.

The only question which is difficult of solution, is, is, how the imperative of morality is possible. Here the imperative is not hypothetical, and hence we cannot derive its objective necessity from any presupposition. Nor must it for a moment be forgotten, that an imperative of this sort cannot be established by instances taken from experience. We must therefore find out by careful investigation, whether imperatives which seem to be categorical may not be simply hypothetical imperatives in disguise.

One thing is plain at the very outset, namely, that only a categorical imperative can have the dignity of a practical *law,* and that the other imperatives, while they may no doubt be called *principles* of the will, cannot be called laws. An action which is necessary merely as a means to an arbitrary end, may be regarded as itself contingent, and if the end is abandoned, the maxim which prescribes the action has no longer any force. An unconditioned command, on the other hand, does not permit the will to choose the opposite, and therefore it carries with it the necessity which is essential to a law.

It is, however, very hard to see how there can be a categorical imperative or law of morality at all. Such a law is an *a priori* synthetic proposition, and we cannot expect that there will be less difficulty in showing how a proposition of that sort is possible in the sphere of morality than we have found it to be in the sphere of knowledge.

In attempting to solve this problem, we shall first of all inquire, whether the mere conception of a categorical imperative may not perhaps supply us with a formula, which contains the only proposition that can possibly be a categorical imperative....

If I take the mere conception of a hypothetical imperative, I cannot tell what it may contain until the condition under which it applies is presented to me. But I can tell at once from the very conception of a categorical imperative what it must contain. Viewed apart from the law, the imperative simply affirms that the maxim, or subjective principle of action, must con-

form to the objective principle or law. Now the law contains no condition to which it is restricted, and hence nothing remains but the statement, that the maxim ought to conform to the universality of the law as such. It is only this conformity to law that the imperative can be said to represent as necessary.

There is therefore but one categorical imperative, which may be thus stated: *Act in conformity with that maxim, and that maxim only, which you can at the same time will to be a universal....*

The universality of the law which governs the succession of events, is what we mean by *nature,* in the most general sense, that is, the existence of things, in so far as their existence is determined in conformity with universal laws. The universal imperative of duty might therefore be put in this way: *Act as if the maxim from which you act were to become through your will a universal law of nature.*

If we attend to what goes on in ourselves in every transgression of a duty, we find, that we do not will that our maxim should become a universal law. We find it in fact impossible to do so, and we really will that the opposite of our maxim should remain a universal law, at the same time that we assume the liberty of making an exception in favor of natural inclination in our own case, or perhaps only for this particular occasion. Hence, if we looked at all cases from the same point of view, that is, from the point of view of reason, we should see that there was here a contradiction in our will. The contradiction is, that a certain principle is admitted to be necessary objectively or as a universal law, and yet is held not to be universal subjectively, but to admit of exceptions. What we do is, to consider our action at one time from the point of view of a will that is in perfect conformity with reason, and at another time from the point of view of a will that is under the influence of natural inclination. There is, therefore, here no real contradiction, but merely an antagonism of inclination to the command of reason. The universality of the principle is changed into a mere generality, in order that the practical principle of reason may meet the maxim half way. Not only is this limitation condemned by our own impartial judgment, but it proves that we actually recognize the validity of the categorical imperative, and merely allow ourselves to make a few exceptions in our own favor which we try to consider as of no importance, or as a necessary concession to circumstances.

This much at least we have learned, that if the idea of duty is to have any meaning and to lay down the laws of our actions, it must be expressed in categorical and not in hypothetical imperatives. We have also obtained a clear and distinct conception (a very important thing), of what is implied in a categorical imperative which contains the principle of duty for all cases, granting such an imperative to be possible at all. But we have not yet been able to prove *a priori*, that there actually is such an imperative; that there is a practical law which commands absolutely on its own authority, and is independent of all sensuous impulses; and that duty consists in obedience to this law.

In seeking to reach this point, it is of the greatest importance to observe, that the reality of this principle cannot possibly be derived from the *peculiar constitution of human nature*. For by duty is meant the practically unconditioned necessity of an act, and hence we can show that duty is a law for the will of all human beings, only by showing that it is applicable to all rational beings, or rather to all rational beings to whom an imperative applies at all. . . .

Practical principles that abstract from all subjective ends are *formal;* those that presuppose subjective ends, and therefore natural inclinations, are *material*. The ends which a rational being arbitrarily sets before himself as material ends to be produced by his actions, are all merely relative; for that which gives to them their value is simply their relation to the peculiar susceptibility of the subject. They can therefore yield no universal and necessary principles, or practical laws, applicable to all rational beings, and binding upon every will. Upon such relative ends, therefore, only hypothetical imperatives can be based.

Suppose, however, that there is something the existence of which has in itself an absolute value, something which, *as an end in itself,* can be a ground of definite laws; then, there would lie in that, and only in that, the ground of a possible categorical imperative or practical law.

Now, I say, that man, and indeed every rational being as such, *exists* as an end in himself, *not merely as a means* to be made use of by this or that will, and therefore man in all his actions, whether these are directed towards himself or towards other rational beings, must always be regarded as an end. No object of natural desire has more than a conditioned value; for if the natural desires, and the wants to which they give rise, did not exist, the object to which they are directed would have no value at all. So far are the natural desires and wants from having an absolute value, so far are they from being sought simply for themselves, that every rational being must wish to be entirely free from their influence. The value of every object which human action is the means of obtaining, is, therefore, always conditioned. And even beings whose existence depends upon nature, not upon our will, if they are without reason, have only the relative value of means, and are therefore called *things*. Rational beings, on the other hand, are called *persons*, because their very nature shows them to be ends in themselves, that is, something which cannot be made use of simply as a means. A person being thus an object of respect, a certain limit is placed upon arbitrary will. Persons are not purely subjective ends, whose existence has a value *for us* as the effect of our actions, but they are *objective ends*, or beings whose existence is an end in itself, for which no other end can be substituted. If all value were conditioned, and therefore contingent, it would be impossible to show that there is any supreme practical principle whatever.

If, then, there is a supreme practical principle, a principle which in relation to the human will is a categorical imperative, it must be an *objective* principle of the will, and must be able to serve as a universal practical law. For, such a principle must be derived from the idea of that which is necessarily an end for every one because it is an end in itself. Its foundation is this, that *rational nature exists as an end in itself.* Man necessarily conceives of his own existence in this way, and so far this is *a subjective* principle of human action. But in this way also every other rational being conceives of his own existence, and for the very same reason; hence the principle is also *objective,* and from it, as the highest practical ground, all laws of the will must be capable of being derived. The practical imperative will therefore be this: *Act so as to use humanity, whether in your own person or in the person of another, always as an end, never as merely a means.*

The principle, that humanity and every rational nature is an end in itself, is not borrowed from experience. For, in the first place, because of its universality it applies to all rational beings, and no experience can apply so widely. In the second place, it does not regard humanity subjectively, as an end of man, that is, as an object which the subject of himself actually makes his end, but as an objective end, which ought to be regarded as a law that constitutes the supreme limiting condition of all subjective ends, and which must therefore have its source in pure reason. The objective ground of all practical laws consists in the *rule* and the form of universality, which makes them capable of serving as laws, but their *subjective* ground consists in the *end* to which they are directed. Now, by the second principle, every rational being, as an end in himself, is the subject of all ends. From this follows the third practical principle of the will, which is the supreme condition of its harmony with universal practical reason, namely, the idea of *the will of every rational being as a will which lays down universal laws of action.* . . .

At the point we have now reached, it does not seem surprising that all previous attempts to find out the principle of morality should have ended in failure. It was seen that man is bound under law by duty, but it did not strike anyone, that the *universal* system of laws to which he is subject are laws which he *imposes upon himself,* and that he is only under obligation to act in conformity with his own will, a will which by the purpose of nature prescribes universal laws. Now so long as man is thought to be merely subject to law, no matter what the law may be, he must be regarded as stimulated or constrained to obey the law from interest of some kind; for as the law does not proceed from *his own* will, there must be *something external* to his will which compels him to act in conformity with it. This perfectly necessary conclusion frustrated every attempt to find a supreme principle of duty. Duty was never established, but merely the necessity of acting from some form of interest, private or public. The imperative was therefore necessarily always conditioned, and could not possibly have the force of a moral command. The supreme principle of morality I shall therefore call the principle of the *autonomy* of the will, to distinguish it from all other principles, which I call principles of *heteronomy.*

The conception that every rational being in all the maxims of his will must regard himself as prescribing universal laws, by reference to which himself and all his actions are to be judged, leads to a cognate and very fruitful conception, that of a *kingdom of ends.*

By *kingdom,* I mean the systematic combination of different rational beings through the medium of common laws. Now, laws determine certain ends as universal, and hence, if abstraction is made from the individual differences of rational beings, and from all that is peculiar to their private ends, we get the idea of a complete totality of ends combined in a system; in other words, we are able to conceive of a kingdom of ends, which conforms to the principles formulated above.

All rational beings stand under the law, that each should treat himself and others, *never simply as means,* but always as *at the same time ends in themselves.* Thus there arises a systematic combination of rational beings through the medium of common objective laws. This may well be called a kingdom of ends, because the object of those laws is just to relate all rational beings to one another as ends and means. Of course this kingdom of ends is merely an ideal.

Morality, then, consists in the relation of all action to the system of laws which alone makes possible a kingdom of ends. These laws must belong to the nature of every rational being, and must proceed from his own will. The principle of the will, therefore, is, that no action should be done from any other maxim than one which is consistent with a universal law. This may be expressed in the formula: *Act so that the will may regard itself as in its maxims laying down universal laws.* Now, if the maxims of rational beings are not by their very nature in harmony with this objective principle, the principle of a universal system of laws, the necessity of acting in conformity with that principle is called practical obligation or *duty.... Autonomy* is thus the foundation of the moral value of man and of every other rational being.

The three ways in which the principle of morality has been formulated are at bottom simply different statements of the same law, and each implies the other two.

COMMENT

Some Main Issues Presented by Kant's Ethics

The ethics of Kant is the most famous example of a "deontological" type of ethics. The adjective *deontological* is derived from the Greek words *deon* ("duty") and *logos* ("science," or "theory"). A deontological type of ethics is one based on the theory of duty. As the term is commonly used, it means an ethics of duty for duty's sake, expressed in its most uncompromising form in the motto "Let me do right though the heavens fall." The opposite, or utilitarian, point of view is that an act would be wrong because it is disastrous *if* the heavens fell. As indicated by the next chapter, utilitarians such as Jeremy Bentham and John Stuart Mill judge the morality of actions in terms of their consequences for weal or woe. Quite different is Kant's view that the moral quality of acts depends on conformity to laws, rules, or principles of action rather than on goals or results.

Whatever our opinion of Kant's ethics—and there is much to admire as well as to criticize—we cannot deny that he presents issues of great importance. Some of these are as follows:

1. *Are ethical principles empirical or* a priori? The motive of Kant's philosophy is the discovery and justification of *a priori* forms, concepts, and principles. In ethics, he draws a sharp distinction between *is* and *ought* and contends that the moral *ought* must be formulated in *a priori* principles. Is he correct? If empirical science is a knowledge of *existence,* and if an "ideal" or "norm" is what ought to be but *is not,* the conception of a "normative empirical science" is contradictory. And if so, ethics is either merely subjective—as the advocates of the emotive theory contend—or it is *a priori.* Modern philosophers have been deeply disturbed by the problem thus posed.

The proponents of natural law, such as Cicero, try to solve the problem by denying the sharp antithesis between *what is* and *what ought to be*—and on this point they receive support from utilitarians such as Mill and pragmatists such as John Dewey. What ought to be, it can be argued, is what satisfies genuine needs. A need arises when there is an uncompleted tendency in human nature—a frustrated, or at least unconsummated, impulse or desire. These needs can be determined scientifically, and plans to satisfy them can be elaborated with due regard to facts. The objective of securing the greatest possible fulfillment should determine which needs are to receive preferential treatment, and here, too, there are facts to guide us.

Kant would reply that such an empirical procedure is a mere begging of the question. It *assumes* that morality consists in the fulfillment of our needs—but this assumption he would sharply challenge. If *need* is interpreted in a nonmoral sense, it is not a moral concept and hence is irrelevant; but if it is interpreted in a moral sense, it must be connected with obligation—and obligation is not the sort of thing that empirical science can discover and justify. *Moral* objectivity is quite different from *scientific* objectivity, and an objective moral *ought* can never be determined scientifically. Rejecting the emotive view that morality is subjective, Kant concludes that moral objectivity must rest on *a priori* foundations.

2. *Is good will, and good will alone, unconditionally good?* Let us consider Kant's contention that pleasure is good if combined with a good will but evil if combined with a bad will. A hedonist would agree that pleasure gained from wanton torture is bad but would say that it is bad not *in* and *of itself* but in its evil consequences. Its bad effects greatly outweigh its intrinsic goodness—but *as pleasure,* it is intrinsically good. The hedonist would add that what makes good will "intrinsically good" is simply the pleasure that it involves, rather than the accompanying sense of duty. A nonhedonist might admit that good will is intrinsically good but maintain that there are other intrinsic goods, such as truth and beauty, that are no less ultimate and unconditional.

We can ask the question whether there is *any* unconditional good—pleasure or love or respect for duty or anything else. Pleasure can be sadistic, respect for duty can be chill and puritanical, and anything else can be degraded by its context.

3. *Is Kant's distinction between a hypothetical and a categorical imperative sound?* If the criterion of right volition is neither inclination nor consequences, what is it? Kant answers that the rightness of the volition depends on two factors: *right incentive* and *right maxim.*

The right incentive is respect and reverence for moral law. A moral act must be done for duty's sake (although other motivations may be involved). This requirement has already been discussed under the name "good will."

The right maxim is the principle of "the categorical imperative." An imperative is an injunction or command; it says that a person ought to do so and so. A hypothetical imperative always takes a conditional form: "*If* you want to achieve x, then you ought to do y." Rules of skill and counsels of prudence are hypothetical imperatives: They tell us what we ought to do—"ought" in the sense of what we would be well advised to do—*if* we desire certain ends. They may be legitimate, but they are not moral. A categorical imperative, on the other hand, asserts unconditionally, "You ought to act so and so." There is no *if* in front of the *ought.* Obligation is not determined by inclination or expediency but by objective moral necessity, which can be stated in a universal rule.

The question is whether this distinction between a categorical and a hypothetical imperative is sound. Has Kant drawn the distinction too sharply? Is he, in pressing this distinction, too much the absolutist, not enough the relativist? Or is Kant right? Don't we believe that moral imperatives are, somehow or other, distinctive? And has he not correctly formulated the distinction? These are questions for the reader to ponder.

4. *Does Kant's ethics provide a sound test of right?* An opponent might concede that there are categorical imperatives and still find Kant's formulas for determining them unsatisfactory.

His first formula is "Act only on that maxim which you can will as a universal law." One may object that this does not take account of individual differences, which may be ethically decisive. Consider Kant's dispute with the French philosopher Benjamin Constant. The moral duty to tell the truth, Constant argued, is not unconditional. It would be ethically right to lie to a would-be murderer in order to save the intended victim, for a person bent on murder has forfeited all right to a truth that would abet a plot. To this contention Kant replied, "The duty of truthfulness makes no distinction between persons to whom one has this duty and to whom one can exempt himself from this duty; rather, it is an unconditional duty which holds in all circumstances." Hence, we are duty-bound to tell even a truth that would result in murder. This is an extreme position that very few thinkers, whether philosophers or laypeople, would endorse. In the case cited by Constant, there is a conflict between two duties: the duty to tell the truth and the duty to save a life. In such instances, how can we decide which duty is paramount without a consideration of consequences?

Kant would reply that there are "perfect duties," and that the duty to tell the truth is such a duty. We recognize a perfect obligation when we see that it is possible to universalize it and impossible to universalize its violation. For example, it is impossible to universalize lying (the violation of truth-telling) because if everybody lied, no one would believe you—lying is parasitic on truth-telling. Hence, telling the truth, which can be universalized with perfect consistency, is an absolute duty, and lying is an absolute violation of this duty. The duty to protect a life that is threatened is only an "imperfect duty"—derived from the fact that no one could consistently will that one's own life be unprotected under such circumstances. The duties of perfect obligation, forbidding us to lie, break promises, steal, murder, and so forth, admit of no exceptions whatever in favor of duties of imperfect obligation.

Some writers have argued, in Kant's defense, that his universalization formula can be interpreted flexibly enough to meet commonsense objections. For example, we could universalize the principle that people should steal rather than starve to death. Or (to revert to the question that Constant raised) we could universalize the principle that one should lie in order to save an innocent person from the threat of murder. However, can we reason in this way without a more empirical approach to ethics than Kant was prepared to admit? Can we do so without setting aside his concept of "perfect duties"?

A utilitarian could agree with Kant up to a certain point: Granted that an act is right for one person, it must be right *under the same conditions* for everybody. Though, when the conditions (physical or psychological or cultural) vary, philanthropic exception to the general rule may be warranted. If this is so, can morality be *a priori* and universal, as Kant supposed?

His second formula of the categorical imperative is "Act so as to treat humanity, whether in your own person or in that of another, always as an end and never as a means only." This formula expresses our sense of the intrinsic value of the human spirit, and it has a profound moral appeal. However, is it possible to carry out the formula without a view to the effects of our actions? Must we not have some positive idea of the ends of humanity and how to achieve them? If so, is the second formula consistent with the first formula? The first formula, it could be argued, is a "right for right's sake" principle, and the second is a "right for good's sake" principle.

The third formula is "Act as a member of a kingdom of ends." Spelled out, this means that every person, as a rational agent, is ideally a member of a moral community, in which one is both sovereign (free) and subject (responsible), willing the universal laws of morality for oneself and others. The moral law, according to this formula, must be the person's own free voice and is not a whit less a universal law for being freely chosen. However, is genuine freedom consistent with Kant's interpretation of universality? Freedom, it might be objected, does not consist merely in willing the dictates of universal abstract reason; it is warmer, more personal, and creative. In maintaining that morality is obedience to universal law, without regard to the individual and his or her peculiar circumstances. Kant dissolves the individual personality in an ocean of ethical abstraction, like an individual grain of sand dissolved in a vast sea. In so doing, he undermines his very demand for a moral community of free and responsible human beings. So at least existentialists, with their strong emphasis on human individuality, might argue.

In Kant's defense, it can he pointed out that *The Foundations of the Metaphysic of Morals,* from which our selection is taken, is the most abstract and formalistic of his ethical works. In *The Critique of Practical Reason,* Kant corrects the one-sidedness of the *Foundations* by discoursing at length on the concept of "good" as well as "duty," and in his *Lectures on Ethics* and *Metaphysics of Morals* (not to be confused with the *Foundations*), Kant discusses particular duties in a concrete way. The more teleological and less absolutistic elements in his theory emerge in these works.

How, then, would Kant view Noel David Earley's decision to end his life in the face of great pain and impending death as presented in "A Case in Point" at the beginning of this part? Is suicide always an infraction against the categorical imperative to preserve life? Can Earley's choice be universalized such that everyone in similar circumstances *must* do the same? How might Earley himself respond to Kant's ideas of "good will" and of "moral duty"? Is it possible that Earley thought it was his duty to end his own life in such debilitating circumstances? And what about Earley's friends, especially the one who instructed him, and thus assisted him, in how to end his life? Were they behaving "rationally" according to Kant's moral theory?

17

THE WAY OF UTILITY

JEREMY BENTHAM (1748–1832)

The son of a well-to-do London barrister, Jeremy Bentham studied law but never practiced it. He set himself to work out a new system of jurisprudence and to reform both penal and civil law. In pursuit of this aim, he wrote thousands of pages but was curiously indifferent about publishing them. Although his works were collected in eleven large volumes, the only major theoretical work that he published himself was *An Introduction to the Principles of Morals and Legislation* (1789), which contains an exposition of his hedonistic and utilitarian ethics.

Painfully shy, he could hardly endure the company of strangers, and yet he became a powerful political force. As a leader of the "Philosophical Radicals," he attracted such distinguished followers as James Mill and John Stuart Mill. He established the *Westminster Review*, at his own expense, as an organ of his movement, and he and his associates succeeded in founding University College, London. There, his embalmed body, dressed in his customary clothes and topped with a wax model of his head, is still to be seen.

THE HEDONISTIC CALCULUS

Chapter I

Of the Principle of Utility

(I) Nature has placed mankind under the governance of two sovereign masters, *pain* and *pleasure*. It is for them alone to point out what we ought to do, as well as to determine what we shall do. On the one hand the standard of right and wrong, on the other the chain of causes and effects, are fastened to their throne. They govern us in all we do, in all we say, in all we think: every effort we can make to throw off our subjection, will serve but to demonstrate and confirm it. In words a man may pretend to abjure their empire: but in reality he will remain subject to it all the while. *The*

From *An Introduction to the Principles of Morals and Legislation*, new edition, Oxford, 1823. Some of Bentham's footnotes have been omitted. First published in 1789.

principle of utility[1] recognizes this subjection, and assumes it for the foundation of that system, the object of which is to rear the fabric of felicity by the hands of reason and of law. Systems which attempt to question it, deal in sounds instead of sense, in caprice instead of reason, in darkness instead of light.

But enough of metaphor and declamation: it is not by such means that moral science is to be improved.

(II) The principle of utility is the foundation of the present work: it will be proper therefore at the outset to give an explicit and determinate account of what is meant by it. By the principle of utility is meant that principle which approves or disapproves of every action whatsoever, according to the tendency which it appears to have to augment or diminish the happiness of the party whose interest is in question: or, what is the same thing in other words, to promote or to oppose that happiness. I say of every action whatsoever; and therefore not only of every action of a private individual, but of every measure of government.

(III) By utility is meant that property in any object, whereby it tends to produce benefit, advantage, pleasure, good, or happiness, (all this in the present case comes to the same thing) to prevent the happening of mischief, pain, evil, or unhappiness to the party whose interest is considered: if that party be the community in general, then the happiness of the community: if a particular individual, then the happiness of that individual.

(IV) The interest of the community is one of the most general expressions that can occur in the phraseology of morals: no wonder that the meaning of it is often lost. When it has a meaning, it is this. The community is a fictitious *body*, composed of the individual persons who are considered as constituting as it were its *members*. The interest of the community then is, what?— the sum of the interests of the several members who compose it.

(V) It is in vain to talk of the interest of the community, without understanding what is the interest of the individual. A thing is said to promote the interest, or to be *for* the interest, of an individual, when it tends to add to the sum total of his pleasures: or, what comes to the same thing, to diminish the sum total of his pains.

(VI) An action then may be said to be conformable to the principle of utility, or, for shortness sake, to utility, (meaning with respect to the community at large) when the tendency it has to augment the happiness of the community is greater than any it has to diminish it.

(VII) A measure of government (which is but a particular kind of action, performed by a particular person or persons) may be said to be conformable to or dictated by the principle of utility, when in like manner the tendency which it has to

---

[1] Note by the Author, July 1822: To this denomination has of late been added, or substituted, the *greatest happiness or greatest felicity* principle: this for shortness, instead of saying at length *that principle* which states the greatest happiness of all those whose interest is in question, as being the right and proper, and only right and proper and universally desirable, end of human action: of human action in every situation, and in particular in that of a functionary or set of functionaries exercising the powers of Government. The word *utility* does not so clearly point to the ideas of *pleasure* and *pain* as the words *happiness* and *felicity* do: nor does it lead us to the consideration of the *number*, of the interests affected; to the number, as being the circumstance, which contributes, in the largest proportion, to the formation of the standard here in question; the *standard of right and wrong*, by which alone the propriety of human conduct, in every situation can with propriety be tried. This want of a sufficiently manifest connexion between the ideas of *happiness* and *pleasure* on the one hand, and the idea of *utility* on the other, I have every now and then found operating, and with but too much efficiency, as a bar to the acceptance, that might otherwise have been given, to this principle.

augment the happiness of the community is greater than any which it has to diminish it.

(VIII) When an action, or in particular a measure of government, is supposed by a man to be conformable to the principle of utility, it may be convenient, for the purposes of discourse, to imagine a kind of law or dictate, called a law or dictate of utility: and to speak of the action in question, as being conformable to such law or dictate.

(IX) A man may be said to be a partizan of the principle of utility, when the approbation or disapprobation he annexes to any action, or to any measure, is determined by and proportioned to the tendency which he conceives it to have to augment or to diminish the happiness of the community: or in other words, to its conformity or unconformity to the laws or dictates of utility.

(X) Of an action that is conformable to the principle of utility one may always say either that it is one that ought to be done, or at least that it is not one that ought not to be done. One may say also, that it is right it should be done; at least that it is not wrong it should be done: that it is a right action; at least that it is not a wrong action. When thus interpreted, the words *ought,* and *right* and *wrong,* and others of that stamp, have a meaning: when otherwise, they have none.

(XI) Has the rectitude of this principle been ever formally contested? It should seem that it had, by those who have not known what they have been meaning. Is it susceptible of any direct proof? It should seem not: for that which is used to prove every thing else, cannot itself be proved: a chain of proofs must have their commencement somewhere. To give such proof is as impossible as it is needless.

(XII) Not that there is or ever has been that human creature breathing, however stupid or perverse, who has not on many, perhaps on most occasions of his life, deferred to it. By the natural constitution of the human frame, on most occasions of their lives men in general embrace

this principle, without thinking of it: if not for the ordering of their own actions, yet for the trying of their own actions, as well as those of other men. There have been, at the same time, not many, perhaps, even of the most intelligent, who have been disposed to embrace it purely and without reserve. There are even few who have not taken some occasion or other to quarrel with it, either on account of their not understanding always how to apply it, or on account of some prejudice or other which they were afraid to examine into, or could not bear to part with. For such is the stuff that man is made of: in principle and in practice, in a right track and in a wrong one, the rarest of all human qualities is consistency.

(XIII) When a man attempts to combat the principle of utility, it is with reasons drawn, without his being aware of it, from that very principle itself. His arguments, if they prove anything, prove not that the principle is *wrong,* but that, according to the applications he supposes to be made of it, it is *misapplied.* Is it possible for a man to move the earth? Yes; but he must first find out another earth to stand upon.

(XIV) To disprove the propriety of it by arguments is impossible; but, from the causes that have been mentioned, or from some confused or partial view of it, a man may happen to be disposed not to relish it. Where this is the case, if he thinks the settling of his opinions on such a subject worth the trouble, let him take the following steps, and at length, perhaps, he may come to reconcile himself to it.

(1) Let him settle with himself, whether he would wish to discard this principle altogether; if so, let him consider what it is that all his reasonings (in matters of politics especially) can amount to?

(2) If he would, let him settle with himself, whether he would judge and act without any principle, or whether there is any other he would judge and act by?

(3) If there be, let him examine and satisfy himself whether the principle he thinks he has found is really any separate

intelligible principle; or whether it be not a mere principle in words, a kind or phrase, which at bottom expresses neither more nor less than the mere averment of his own unfounded sentiments; that is, what in another person he might be apt to call caprice?

(4) If he is inclined to think that his own approbation or disapprobation, annexed to the idea of an act, without any regard to its consequences, is a sufficient foundation for him to judge and act upon, let him ask himself whether his sentiment is to be a standard of right and wrong, with respect to every other man, or whether every man's sentiment has the same privilege of being a standard to itself?

(5) In the first case, let him ask himself whether his principle is not despotical, and hostile to all the rest of the human race?

(6) In the second case, whether it is not anarchical, and whether at this rate there are not as many different standards of right and wrong as there are men? and whether even to the same man, the same thing, which is right today, may not (without the least change in its nature) be wrong tomorrow? and whether the same thing is not right and wrong in the same place at the same time? and in either case, whether all argument is not at an end? and whether, when two men have said, 'I like this,' and 'I don't like it,' they can (upon such a principle) have any thing more to say?

(7) If he should have said to himself, No: for that sentiment which he proposes as a standard must be grounded on reflection, let him say on what particulars the reflection is to turn? If on particulars having relation to the utility of the act, then let him say whether this is not deserting his own principle, and borrowing assistance from that very one in opposition to which he sets it up: or if not on those particulars, on what other particulars?

(8) If he should be for compounding the matter, and adopting his own principle in part, and the principle of utility in part, let him say how far he will adopt it?

(9) When he has settled with himself where he will stop, then let him ask himself how he justifies to himself the adopting it so far? and why he will not adopt it any farther?

(10) Admitting any other principle than the principle of utility to be a right principle, a principle that it is right for a man to pursue; admitting (what is not true) that the word *right* can have a meaning without reference to utility, let him say whether there is any such thing as a *motive* that a man can have to pursue the dictates of it: if there is, let him say what the motive is, and how it is to be distinguished from those which enforce the dictates of utility: if not, then lastly let him say what it is this other principle can be good for? ...

Value of a Lot of Pleasure or Pain, How To Be Measured

(I) Pleasures then, and the avoidance of pains, are the *ends* which the legislator has in view: it behoves him therefore to understand their *value*. Pleasures and pains are the *instruments* he has to work with: it behoves him therefore to understand their force, which is again, in other words, their value.

(II) To a person considered *by himself,* the value of a pleasure or pain considered *by itself,* will be greater or less, according to the four following circumstances:[2]

1. Its *intensity*.
2. Its *duration*.
3. Its *certainty* or *uncertainty*.
4. Its *propinquity* or *remoteness*.

---

[2] These circumstances have since been denominated *elements* or *dimensions of value* in a pleasure or a pain.

Not long after the publication of the first edition, the following memoriter verses were framed, in the view of lodging more effectually, in the memory, these points, on which the whole fabric of morals and legislation may be seen to rest.

Intense, long, certain, speedy, fruitful, pure—Such marks in *pleasures* and in *pains* endure. Such pleasures seek, if *private* be thy end:

If it be *public,* wide let them *extend*.

Such *pains* avoid, whichever be thy view:

If pains *must* come, let them *extend* to few.

(III) These are the circumstances which are to be considered in estimating a pleasure or a pain considered each of them by itself. But when the value of any pleasure or pain is considered for the purpose of estimating the tendency of any *act* by which it is produced, there are two other circumstances to be taken into the account; these are,

    5. Its *fecundity,* or the chance it has of being followed by sensations of the *same* kind: that is, pleasures, if it be a pleasure: pains, if it be a pain.
    6. Its *purity,* or the chance it has of not being followed by sensations of the opposite kind: that is, pains, if it be a pleasure: pleasures, if it be a pain.

These two last, however, are in strictness scarcely to be deemed properties of the pleasure or the pain itself; they are not, therefore, in strictness to be taken into the account of the value of that pleasure or that pain. They are in strictness to be deemed properties only of the act, or other event, by which such pleasure or pain has been produced; and accordingly are only to be taken into the account of the tendency of such act or such event.

(IV) To a *number* of persons, with reference to each of whom the value of a pleasure or a pain is considered, it will be greater or less, according to seven circumstances: to wit, the six preceding ones; viz.

    1. Its *intensity*.
    2. Its *duration*.
    3. Its *certainty* or *uncertainty*.
    4. Its *propinquity* or *remoteness*.
    5. Its *fecundity*.
    6. Its *purity*.

And one other; to wit:

    7. Its *extent;* that is, the number of persons to whom it extends; or (in other words) who are affected by it.

(V) To take an exact account then of the general tendency of any act, by which the interests of a community are affected, proceed as follows. Begin with any one person of those whose interests seem most immediately to be affected by it: and take an account,

    1. Of the value of each distinguishable *pleasure* which appears to be produced by it in the *first* instance.
    2. Of the value of each *pain* which appears to be produced by it in the *first* instance.
    3. Of the value of each pleasure which appears to be produced by it *after* the first. This constitutes the *fecundity* of the first *pleasure* and the *impurity* of the first *pain*.
    4. Of the value of each *pain* which appears to be produced by it after the first. This constitutes the *fecundity* of the first *pain*, and the *impurity* of the first *pleasure*.
    5. Sum up all the values of all the *pleasures* on the one side, and those of all the pains on the other. The balance, if it be on the side of pleasure, will give the *good* tendency of the act upon the whole, with respect to the interests of that *individual* person; if on the side of pain, the *bad* tendency of it upon the whole.
    6. Take an account of the *number* of persons whose interests appear to be concerned; and repeat the above process with respect to each. *Sum up* the numbers expressive of the degrees of *good* tendency which the act has, with respect to each individual, in regard to whom the tendency of it is good upon the whole: ... do this again with respect to each individual, in regard to whom the tendency of it is *bad* upon the whole. Take the *balance;* which, if on the side of *pleasure*, will give the general *good tendency* of the act, with respect to the total number or community of individuals concerned; if on the side of pain, the general *evil tendency*, with respect to the same community.

(VI) It is not to be expected that this process should be strictly pursued previously to every moral judgement, or to every legislative or judicial operation. It may, however, be always kept in view: and as near as the process actually pursued on these occasions approaches to it, so near will such process approach to the character of an exact one.

(VII) The same process is alike applicable to pleasure and pain, in whatever shape they appear: and by whatever denomination they are distinguished: to pleasure, whether it be called *good* (which is properly the cause or instrument of pleasure) or *profit* (which is distant pleasure, or the cause or instrument of distant pleasure,) or *convenience*, or *advantage, benefit, emolument, happiness*, and so forth: to pain, whether it be called *evil*, (which corresponds to *good*) or *mischief*, or *inconvenience*, or *disadvantage*, or *loss*, or *unhappiness*, and so forth.

(VIII) Nor is this a novel and unwarranted, any more than it is a useless theory. In all this there is nothing but what the practice of mankind, wheresoever they have a clear view of their own interest, is perfectly conformable to. An article of property, an estate in land, for instance, is valuable on what account? On account of the pleasures of all kinds which it enables a man to produce, and what comes to the same thing the pains of all kinds which it enables him to avert. But the value of such an article of property is universally understood to rise or fall according to the length or shortness of the time which a man has in it: the certainty or uncertainty of its coming into possession: and the nearness or remoteness of the time at which, if at all, it is to come into possession. As to the *intensity* of the pleasures which a man may derive from it, this is never thought of, because it depends upon the use which each particular person may come to make of it; which cannot be estimated till the particular pleasures he may come to derive from it, or the particular pains he may come to exclude by means of it, are brought to view. For the same reason, neither does he think of the *fecundity* or *purity* of those pleasures.

JOHN STUART MILL (1806–1873)
19 century.

John Stuart Mill was reared in London and was educated privately by his father, James Mill, a famous political philosopher. No child ever received a more prodigious education. Mill was reading Plato and Thucydides in the original Greek at an age when most children are reading nursery stories in their native language. His father set him to learn Greek at the age of three; Latin, algebra, and geometry at the age of eight; logic at twelve; and political economy at thirteen. Jeremy Bentham was an intimate friend of the family, and young John was thoroughly indoctrinated in his philosophy.

When Mill reached the age of seventeen, he was appointed a clerk in the East India Company, in whose service he remained for thirty-five years, rising steadily to the highest post in his department, that of examiner of correspondence and dispatches to India. This position afforded him considerable leisure for his intense intellectual pursuits.

In his twenty-first year, he fell into a deep mental depression, evidently the result of his unnatural childhood and years of intellectual cramming. He gradually emerged from this illness but with a new sense of the insufficiency of his father's doctrinaire philosophy and a keener appreciation of the value of poetry, especially that of William Wordsworth's. Thereafter he sought to broaden his outlook and succeeded in becoming a much better-rounded (though less consistent) philosopher than either Bentham or his father. An important influence on Mill was Harriet Taylor, the beautiful and talented wife of a London merchant, who finally married him (in 1851) after her husband died. They lived happily together for seven years, until they were separated by her untimely death. It was through her, Mill said, that he came to be more of a democrat and socialist, and *On Liberty* was their joint work.

After his long service in the East India office, he retired on a pension at the age of fifty-two. The remaining fifteen years of his life, although marred by ill health, were packed with intellectual and political activity. In 1865 he consented to run for Parliament as a representative of the working people for the constituency of Westminster; and during his single term of office (1866–1868), he made a considerable impression by his vigorous championing of reform. In 1869 he retired with his stepdaughter, Helen Taylor, to a small white stone cottage near Avignon, in France, where he continued to write. In May 1873 he died, the victim of a local fever.

Among his important books are *Logic* (1843), *The Principles of Political Economy* (1848), *On Liberty* (1859), *Utilitarianism* (1863), *Examination of Sir William Hamilton's Philosophy* (1865), and *Autobiography* (published after his death, in 1873).

UTILITARIANISM

What Utilitarianism Is

A passing remark is all that needs be given to the ignorant blunder of supposing that those who stand up for utility as the test of right and wrong use the term in that restricted and merely colloquial sense in which utility is opposed to pleasure. An apology is due to the philosophical opponents of utilitarianism, for even the momentary appearance of confounding them with anyone capable of so absurd a misconception; which is the more extraordinary, inasmuch as the contrary accusation, of referring everything to pleasure, and that, too, in its grossest form, is another of the common charges against utilitarianism: and, as has been pointedly remarked by an able writer, the same sort of persons, and often the very same persons, denounce the theory "as impracticably dry when the word 'utility' precedes the word 'pleasure,' and as too practicably voluptuous when the word 'pleasure' precedes the word 'utility.'" Those who know anything about the matter are aware that every writer, from Epicurus to Bentham, who maintained the theory of utility, meant by it, not something to be contradistinguished from pleasure, but pleasure itself, together with exemption from pain; and instead of opposing the useful to the agreeable or the ornamental, have always declared that the useful means these, among other things. Yet the common herd, including the herd of writers, not only in newspapers and periodicals, but in books of weight and pretension, are perpetually falling into this shallow mistake. Having caught up the word "utilitarian," while knowing nothing whatever about it but its sound, they habitually express by it the rejection or the neglect of pleasure in some

From *Utilitarianism*, published serially in *Fraser's Magazine* in 1861 and in book form, London, 1863.

of its forms: of beauty, of ornament, or of amusement. Nor is the term thus ignorantly misapplied solely in disparagement, but occasionally in compliment, as though it implied superiority to frivolity and the mere pleasures of the moment. And this perverted use is the only one in which the word is popularly known, and the one from which the new generation are acquiring their sole notion of its meaning. Those who introduced the word, but who had for many years discontinued it as a distinctive appellation, may well feel themselves called upon to resume it if by doing so they can hope to contribute anything towards rescuing it from this utter degradation.

The creed which accepts as the foundation of morals "utility" or the "greatest happiness principle" holds that actions are right in proportion as they tend to promote happiness, wrong as they tend to produce the reverse of happiness. By happiness is intended pleasure, and the absence of pain; by unhappiness, pain, and the privation of pleasure. To give a clear view of the moral standard set up by the theory, much more requires to be said; in particular, what things it includes in the ideas of pain and pleasure; and to what extent this is left an open question. But these supplementary explanations do not affect the theory of life on which this theory of morality is grounded—namely, that pleasure and freedom from pain are the only things desirable as ends; and that all desirable things (which are as numerous in the utilitarian as in any other scheme) are desirable either for the pleasure inherent in themselves, or as means to the promotion of pleasure and the prevention of pain.

Now such a theory of life excites in many minds, and among them in some of the most estimable in feeling and purpose, inveterate dislike. To suppose that life has (as they express it) no higher end than pleasure—no better and nobler object of desire and pursuit—they designate as utterly mean and groveling; as a doctrine worthy only of swine, to whom the followers of Epicurus were, at a very early period, contemp-

tuously likened; and modern holders of the doctrine are occasionally made the subject of equally polite comparisons by its German, French, and English assailants.

When thus attacked, the Epicureans have always answered that it is not they, but their accusers, who represent human nature in a degrading light, since the accusation supposes human beings to be capable of no pleasures except those of which swine are capable. If this supposition were true, the charge could not be gainsaid, but would then be no longer an imputation; for if the sources of pleasure were precisely the same to human beings and to swine, the rule of life which is good enough for the one would be good enough for the other. The comparison of the Epicurean life to that of beasts is felt as degrading, precisely because a beast's pleasures do not satisfy a human being's conceptions of happiness. Human beings have faculties more elevated than the animal appetites and, when once made conscious of them, do not regard anything as happiness which does not include their gratification. I do not, indeed, consider the Epicureans to have been by any means faultless in drawing out their scheme of consequences from the utilitarian principle. To do this in any sufficient manner, many Stoic, as well as Christian, elements require to be included. But there is no known Epicurean theory of life which does not assign to the pleasures of the intellect, of the feelings and imagination, and of the moral sentiments, a much higher value as pleasures than to those of mere sensation. It must be admitted, however, that utilitarian writers in general have placed the superiority of mental over bodily pleasures chiefly in the greater permanency, safety, uncostliness, etc., of the former—that is, in their circumstantial advantages rather than in their intrinsic nature. And on all these points utilitarians have fully proved their case; but they might have taken the other and, as it may be called, higher ground with entire consistency. It is quite compatible with the principle of utility to recognize the fact that some kinds of pleasure are more desirable and more valuable than others. It would be absurd that, while, in estimating all other things, quality is considered as well as quantity, the estimation of pleasures should be supposed to depend on quantity alone.

If I am asked what I mean by difference of quality in pleasures, or what makes one pleasure more valuable than another, merely as a pleasure, except its being greater in amount, there is but one possible answer. Of two pleasures, if there be one to which all or almost all who have experience of both give a decided preference, irrespective of any feeling of moral obligation to prefer it, that is the more desirable pleasure. If one of the two is, by those who are competently acquainted with both, placed so far above the other that they prefer it, even though knowing it to be attended with a greater amount of discontent, and would not resign it for any quantity of the other pleasure which their nature is capable of, we are justified in ascribing to the preferred enjoyment a superiority in quality so far outweighing quantity as to render it, in comparison, of small account.

Now it is an unquestionable fact that those who are equally acquainted with and equally capable of appreciating and enjoying both, do give a most marked preference to the manner of existence which employs their higher faculties. Few human creatures would consent to be changed into any of the lower animals for a promise of the fullest allowance of a beast's pleasures; no intelligent human being would consent to be a fool, no instructed person would be an ignoramus, no person of feeling and conscience would be selfish and base, even though they should be persuaded that the fool, the dunce, or the rascal is better satisfied with his lot than they are with theirs. They would not resign what they possess more than he for the most complete satisfaction of all the desires which they have in common with him. If they ever fancy they would, it is only in cases of unhappiness so extreme that to escape from it they would exchange their lot for almost any other, however undesirable in their own eyes. A being of higher faculties requires more to make him happy, is capable probably of more acute suffering, and certainly accessible to it at more points, than one of an inferior type; but in spite of these liabilities, he can never really wish to sink into what he feels to be a lower grade of existence. We may give what explanation we please of this unwillingness; we may attribute it to pride, a name which is given indiscriminately to some of the most and to some of the least estimable feelings of which mankind are capable: we may refer it to the love of liberty and personal independence, an appeal to which was with the Stoics one of the most effective means for the inculcation of it; to the love of power or to the love of excitement, both of which do really enter into and contribute to it; but its most appropriate appellation is a sense of dignity, which all human beings possess in one form or other, and in some, though by no means in exact, proportion to their higher faculties, and which is so essential a part of the happiness of those in whom it is strong that nothing which conflicts with it could be otherwise than momentarily an object of desire to them. Whoever supposes that this preference takes place at a sacrifice of happiness—that the superior being, in anything like equal circumstances, is not happier than the inferior—confounds the two very different ideas of happiness and content. It is undisputable that the being whose capacities of enjoyment are low has the greatest chance of having them fully satisfied; and a highly endowed being will always feel that any happiness which he can look for, as the world is constituted, is imperfect. But he can learn to bear its imperfections, if they are at all bearable; and they will not make him envy the being who is indeed unconscious of the imperfections, but only because he feels not at all the good which those imperfections qualify. It is better to be a human being dissatisfied than a pig satisfied; better to be Socrates dissatisfied than a fool satisfied. And if the fool, or the pig, are of a different opinion, it is because they only know their own side of the question. The other party to the comparison knows both sides.

It may be objected that many who are capable of the higher pleasures occasionally, under the influence of temptation, postpone them to the lower. But that is quite compatible with a full appreciation of the intrinsic superiority of the higher. Men often, from infirmity of character, make their election for the nearer good, though they know it to be the less valuable; and this no less when the choice is between two bodily pleasures than when it is between bodily and mental. They pursue sensual indulgences to the injury of health, though perfectly aware that health is the greater good. It may be further objected that many who begin with youthful enthusiasm for everything noble, as they advance in years, sink into indolence and selfishness. But I do not believe that those who undergo this very common change voluntarily choose the lower description of pleasures in preference to the higher. I believe that, before they devote themselves exclusively to the one, they have already become incapable of the other. Capacity for the nobler feelings is in most natures a very tender plant, easily killed, not only by hostile influences, but by mere want of sustenance; and in the majority of young persons it speedily dies away if the occupations to which their position in life has devoted them, and the society into which it has thrown them, are not favorable to keeping that higher capacity in exercise. Men lose their high aspirations as they lose their intellectual tastes, because they have not time or opportunity for indulging them; and they addict themselves to inferior pleasures, not because they deliberately prefer them, but because they are either the only ones to which they have access, or the only ones which they are any longer capable of enjoying. It may be questioned whether any one who has remained equally susceptible to both classes of pleasures, every knowingly and calmly preferred the lower, though many, in all ages, have broken down in an ineffectual attempt to combine both.

From this verdict of the only competent judges, I apprehend there can be no appeal. On a question which is the best worth having of two pleasures, or which of two modes of existence is the most grateful to the feelings, apart from its moral attributes and from its consequences, the judgment of those who are qualified by knowledge of both, or, if they differ, that of the majority of them, must be admitted as final. And there needs be the less hesitation to accept this judgment respecting the quality of pleasures, since there is no other tribunal to be referred to even on the question of quantity. What means are there of determining which is the acutest of two pains, or the intensest of two pleasurable sensations, except the general suffrage of those who are familiar with both? Neither pains nor pleasures are homogeneous, and pain is always heterogeneous with pleasure. What is there to decide whether a particular pleasure is worth purchasing at the cost of a particular pain, except the feelings and judgment of the experienced? When, therefore, those feelings and judgment declare the pleasures derived from the higher faculties to be preferable in kind, apart from the question of intensity, to those of which the animal nature, disjointed from the higher faculties, is susceptible, they are entitled on this subject to the same regard.

I have dwelt on this point, as being a necessary part of a perfectly just conception of utility or happiness considered as the directive rule of human conduct. But it is by no means an indispensable condition to the acceptance of the utilitarian standard; for that standard is not the agent's own greatest happiness, but the greatest amount of happiness altogether; and if it may possibly be doubted whether a noble character is always the happier for its nobleness, there can be no doubt that it makes other people happier, and that the world in general is immensely a gainer by it. Utilitarianism, therefore, could only attain its end by the general cultivation of nobleness of character, even if each individual were only benefited by the nobleness of others, and his own, so far as happiness is concerned, were a sheer deduction from the benefit. But the bare enunciation of such an absurdity as this last renders refutation superfluous.

According to the greatest happiness principle, as above explained, the ultimate end, with reference to and for the sake of which all other things are desirable—whether we are considering our own good or that of other people—is an existence exempt as far as possible from pain, and as rich as possible in enjoyments, both in point of quantity and quality; the test of quality and the rule for measuring it against quantity being the preference felt by those who, in their opportunities of experience, to which must be added their habits of self-consciousness and self-observation, are best furnished with the means of comparison. This, being, according to the utilitarian opinion, the end of human action, is necessarily also the standard of morality, which may accordingly be defined "the rules and precepts for human conduct," by the observance of which an existence such as has been described might be, to the greatest extent possible, secured to all mankind; and not to them only, but, so far as the nature of things admits, to the whole sentient creation. . . .

[The remainder of the chapter is devoted to Mill's answer to objections. Some of these objections, for example, that happiness is unobtainable, that utilitarianism is a "godless doctrine," that the doctrine is "worthy only of swine," would no longer be advanced by reputable philosophers, and can here be omitted. But a few of the objections and Mill's answers to them are worthy of attention. We shall begin with his reply to the objection that we should learn to do without happiness, since self-sacrifice is a duty.]

...The utilitarian morality does recognize in human beings the power of sacrificing their own greatest good for the good of others. It only refuses to admit that the sacrifice is itself a good. A sacrifice which does not increase or tend to increase the sum total of happiness, it considers as wasted. The only self-renunciation which it applauds is devotion to the happiness, or to some of the means of happiness, of others, either of mankind collectively or of individuals within the limits imposed by the collective interests of mankind.

I must again repeat what the assailants of utilitarianism seldom have the justice to acknowledge, that the happiness which forms the utilitarian standard of what is right in conduct is not the agent's own happiness but that of all concerned. As between his own happiness and that of others, utilitarianism requires him to be as strictly impartial as a disinterested and benevolent spectator. In the golden rule of Jesus of Nazareth, we read the complete spirit of the ethics of utility. "To do as you would be done by," and "to love your neighbor as yourself," constitute the ideal perfection of utilitarian morality. As the means of making the nearest approach to this ideal, utility would enjoin, first, that laws and social arrangements should place the happiness or (as, speaking practically, it may be called) the interest of every individual as nearly as possible in harmony with the interest of the whole; and, secondly, that education and opinion, which have so vast a power over human character, should so use that power as to establish in the mind of every individual an indissoluble association between his own happiness and the good of the whole, especially between his own happiness and the practice of such modes of conduct, negative and positive, as regard for the universal happiness prescribes; so that not only he may be unable to conceive the possibility of happiness to himself, consistently with conduct opposed to the general good, but also that a direct impulse to promote the general good may be in every individual one of the habitual motives of action, and the sentiments connected therewith may fill a large and prominent place in every human being's sentient existence. If the impugners of the utilitarian morality represented it to their own minds in this its true character, I know not what recommendation possessed by any other morality they could possibly affirm to be wanting to it; what more beautiful or more exalted developments of human nature any other ethical system can be supposed to foster, or what springs of action, not accessible to the utilitarian, such systems rely on for giving effect to their mandates.

The objectors to utilitarianism cannot always be charged with representing it in a discreditable light. On the contrary, those among them who entertain anything like a just idea of its disinterested character sometimes find fault with its standard as being too high for humanity. They say it is exacting too much to require that people shall always act from the inducement of promoting the general interests of society. But this is to mistake the very meaning of a standard of morals, and confound the rule of action with the motive of it. It is the business of ethics to tell us what are our duties, or by what test we may know them; but no system of ethics requires that the sole motive of all we do shall be a feeling of duty; on the contrary, ninety-nine hundredths of all our actions are done from other motives, and rightly so done if the rule of duty does not condemn them. It is the more unjust to utilitarianism that this particular misapprehension should be made a ground of objection to it, inasmuch as utilitarian moralists have gone beyond almost all others in affirming that the motive has nothing to do with the morality of the action, though much with the worth of the agent. He who saves a fellow creature from drowning does what is morally right, whether his motive be duty or the hope of being paid for his trouble; he who betrays the friend that trusts him is guilty of a crime, even if his object be to serve another friend to whom he is under greater obligations. But to speak only of actions done from the motive of duty, and in direct obedience to principle: it is a misapprehension to the utilitarian mode of thought to conceive it as implying that people should fix their minds upon so wide a generality as the world, or society at large.

The great majority of good actions are intended not for the benefit of the world, but for that of individuals, of which the good of the world is made up; and the thoughts of the most virtuous man need not on these occasions travel beyond the particular persons concerned, except so far as is necessary to assure himself that in benefiting them he is not violating the rights, that is, the legitimate and authorized expectations, of any one else. The multiplication of happiness is, according to the utilitarian ethics, the object of virtue: the occasions on which any person (except one in a thousand) has it in his power to do this on an extended scale, in other words, to be a public benefactor, are but exceptional; and on these occasions alone is he called on to consider public utility; in every other case, private utility, the interest or happiness of some few persons, is all he has to attend to. Those alone the influence of whose actions extends to society in general need concern themselves habitually about so large an object. In the case of abstinences indeed—of things which people forbear to do from moral considerations, though the consequences in the particular case might be beneficial—it would be unworthy of an intelligent agent not to be consciously aware that the action is of a class which, if practiced generally, would be generally injurious, and that this is the ground of the obligation to abstain from it. The amount of regard for the public interest implied in this recognition is no greater than is demanded by every system of morals, for they all enjoin to abstain from whatever is manifestly pernicious to society.

The same considerations dispose of another reproach against the doctrine of utility, founded on a still grosser misconception of the purpose of a standard of morality, and of the very meaning of the words "right" and "wrong." It is often affirmed that utilitarianism renders men cold and unsympathizing; that it chills their moral feelings towards individuals; that it makes them regard only the dry and hard consideration of the consequences of actions, not taking into their moral estimate the qualities from which those actions emanate. If the assertion means that they do not allow their judgment respecting the rightness or wrongness of an action to be influenced by their opinion of the qualities of the person who does it, this is a complaint not against utilitarianism, but against any standard of morality at all; for certainly no known ethical standard decides an action to be good or bad because it is done by a good or a bad man, still less because done by an amiable, a brave, or a benevolent man, or the contrary. These considerations are relevant, not to the estimation of actions, but of persons; and there is nothing in the utilitarian theory inconsistent with the fact that there are other things which interest us in persons besides the rightness and wrongness of their actions. The Stoics, indeed, with the paradoxical misuse of language which was part of their system, and by which they strove to raise themselves above all concern about anything but virtue, were fond of saying that he who has that has everything; that he, and only he, is rich, is beautiful, is a king. But no claim of this description is made for the virtuous man by the utilitarian doctrine. Utilitarians are quite aware that there are other desirable possessions and qualities besides virtue, and are perfectly willing to allow to all of them their full worth. They are also aware that a right action does not necessarily indicate a virtuous character, and that actions which are blamable often proceed from qualities entitled to praise. When this is apparent in any particular case, it modifies their estimation, not certainly of the act, but of the agent. . . .

Again, utility is often summarily stigmatized as an immoral doctrine by giving it the name of "expediency," and taking advantage of the popular use of that term to contrast it with principle. But the expedient, in the sense in which it is opposed to the right, generally means that which is expedient for the particular interest of the agent himself; as when a minister sacrifices the interests of his country to keep himself in place. When it means anything better than this, it means that which is expedient for some immediate object, some temporary purpose, but which violates a rule whose observance is expedient in a much higher degree. The expedient, in this sense, instead of being the same thing with the useful, is a branch of the hurtful. Thus it would often be expedient, for the purpose of getting over some momentary embarrassment, or attaining some object immediately useful to ourselves or others, to tell a lie. But inasmuch as the cultivation in ourselves of a sensitive feeling on the subject of veracity is one of the most useful, and the enfeeblement of that feeling one of the most hurtful, things to which our conduct can be instrumental; and inasmuch as any, even unintentional, deviation from truth does that much towards weakening the trustworthiness of human assertion, which is not only the principal support of all present social well-being, but the insufficiency of which does more than any one thing that can be named to keep back civilization, virtue, everything on which human happiness on the largest scale depends— we feel that the violation, for a present advantage, of a rule of such transcendent expediency is not expedient, and that he who, for the sake of convenience to himself or to some other individual, does what depends on him to deprive mankind of the good, and inflict upon them the evil, involved in the greater or less reliance which they can place in each other's word, acts the part of one of their worst enemies. Yet that even this rule, sacred as it is, admits of possible exceptions is acknowledged by all moralists; the chief of which is when the withholding of some fact (as of information from a malefactor, or of bad news from a person dangerously ill) would save an individual (especially an individual other than oneself) from great and unmerited evil, and when the withholding can only be effected by denial. But in order that the exception may not extend itself beyond the need, and may have the least possible effect in weakening reliance on veracity, it ought to be recognized and, if possible, its limits defined; and, if the principle of utility is good for anything, it must be good for weighing these conflicting utilities against one another, and marking out the region within which one or the other preponderates.

Again, defenders of utility often find themselves called upon to reply to such objections as this—that there is not time, previous to action, for calculating and weighing the effects of any line of conduct on the general happiness. This is exactly as if any one were to say that it is impossible to guide our conduct by Christianity because there is no time, on every occasion on which anything has to be done, to read through the Old and New Testaments. The answer to the objection is that there has been ample time, namely, the whole past duration of the human species. During all that time, mankind have been learning by experience the tendencies of actions; on which experience all the prudence, as well as all the morality, of life are dependent. People talk as if the commencement of this course of experience had hitherto been put off, and as if, at the moment when some man feels tempted to meddle with the property or life of another, he had to begin considering for the first time whether murder and theft are injurious to human happiness. Even then I do not think that he would find the question very puzzling; but, at all events, the matter is now done to his hand. It is truly a whimsical supposition that, if mankind were agreed in considering utility to be the test of morality, they would remain without any agreement as to what is useful, and would take no measures for having their notions on the subject taught to the young, and enforced by law and opinion. There is no difficulty in proving any ethical standard whatever to work ill if we suppose universal idiocy to be conjoined with it; but on any hypothesis short of that, mankind must by this time have acquired positive beliefs as to the effects of some actions on their happiness; and the beliefs which have thus come down are the rules of morality for the multi-

tude, and for the philosopher until he has succeeded in finding better. That philosophers might easily do this, even now, on many subjects; that the received code of ethics is by no means of divine right; and that mankind have still much to learn as to the effects of actions on the general happiness, I admit or rather earnestly maintain. The corollaries from the principal of utility, like the precepts of every practical art, admit of indefinite improvement, and, in a progressive state of the human mind, their improvement is perpetually going on. But to consider the rules of morality as improvable is one thing; to pass over the intermediate generalization entirely and endeavor to test each individual action directly by the first principle is another. It is a strange notion that the acknowledgment of a first principle is inconsistent with the admission of secondary ones. To inform a traveler respecting the place of his ultimate destination is not to forbid the use of landmarks and direction-posts on the way. The proposition that happiness is the end and aim of morality does not mean that no road ought to be laid down to that goal, or that persons going thither should not be advised to take one direction rather than another. Men really ought to leave off talking a kind of nonsense on this subject, which they would neither talk nor listen to on other matters of practical concernment. Nobody argues that the art of navigation is not founded on astronomy because sailors cannot wait to calculate the nautical almanac. Being rational creatures, they go to sea with it ready calculated; and all rational creatures go out upon the sea of life with their minds made up on the common questions of right and wrong, as well as on many of the far more difficult questions of wise and foolish. And this, as long as foresight is a human quality, it is to be presumed they will continue to do. Whatever we adopt as the fundamental principle of morality, we require subordinate principles to apply it by; the impossibility of doing without them, being common to all systems, can afford no argument against any one in particular; but gravely to argue as if no such secondary principles could be had, and as if mankind had remained till now, and always must remain, without drawing any general conclusions from the experience of human life, is as high a pitch, I think, as absurdity has ever reached in philosophical controversy....

We are told that a utilitarian will be apt to make his own particular case an exception to moral rules, and, when under temptation, will see a utility in the breach of a rule, greater than he will see in its observance. But is utility the only creed which is able to furnish us with excuses for evil doing, and means of cheating our own conscience? They are afforded in abundance by all doctrines which recognize as a fact in morals the existence of conflicting considerations, which all doctrines do that have been believed by sane persons. It is not the fault of any creed, but of the complicated nature of human affairs, that rules of conduct cannot be so framed as to require no exceptions, and that hardly any kind of action can safely be laid down as either always obligatory or always condemnable. There is no ethical creed which does not temper the rigidity of its laws by giving a certain latitude, under the moral responsibility of the agent, for accommodation to peculiarities of circumstance; and under every creed, at the opening thus made, self-deception and dishonest casuistry get in. There exists no moral system under which there do not arise unequivocal cases of conflicting obligation. These are the real difficulties, the knotty points both in the theory of ethics and in the conscientious guidance of personal conduct. They are overcome practically, with greater or with less success, according to the intellect and virtue of the individual; but it can hardly be pretended that anyone will be the less qualified for dealing with them, from possessing an ultimate standard to which conflicting rights and duties can be referred. If utility is the ultimate source of moral obligations, utility may be invoked to decide between them when their demands are incompatible. Though the application of the standard may be difficult, it is better than none at all; while in other systems, the moral laws all claiming independent authority, there is no common umpire entitled to interfere between them; their claims to precedence one over another rest on little better than sophistry, and, unless determined, as they generally are, by the unacknowledged influence of considerations of utility, afford a free scope for the action of personal desires and partialities. We must remember that only in these cases of conflict between secondary principles is it requisite that first principles should be appealed to.

There is no case of moral obligation in which some secondary principle is not involved; and if only one, there can seldom be any real doubt which one it is, in the mind of any person by whom the principle itself is recognized.

Of What Sort of Proof the Principle of Utility Is Susceptible

It has already been remarked that questions of ultimate ends do not admit of proof, in the ordinary acceptation of the term. To be incapable of proof by reasoning is common to all first principles, to the first premises of our knowledge, as well as to those of our conduct. But the former, being matters of fact, may be the subject of a direct appeal to the faculties which judge of fact—namely, our senses and our internal consciousness. Can an appeal be made to the same faculties on questions of practical ends? Or by what other faculty is cognizance taken of them?

Questions about ends are, in other words, questions what things are desirable. The utilitarian doctrine is that happiness is desirable, and the only thing desirable, as an end; all other things being only desirable as means to that end. What ought to be required of this doctrine, what conditions is it requisite that the doctrine should fulfill—to make good its claim to be believed?

The only proof capable of being given that an object is visible is that people actually see it. The only proof that a sound is audible is that people hear it; and so of the other sources of our experience. In like manner, I apprehend, the sole evidence it is possible to produce that anything is desirable is that people do actually desire it. If the end which the utilitarian doctrine proposes to itself were not, in theory and in practice, acknowledged to be an end, nothing could ever convince any person that it was so. No reason can be given why the general happiness is desirable, except that each person, so far as he believes it to be attainable, desires his own happiness. This, however, being a fact, we have not only all the proof which the case admits of, but all which it is possible to require, that happiness is a good; that each person's happiness is a good to that person, and the general happiness, therefore, a good to the aggregate of all persons. Happiness has made out its title as *one* of the ends of conduct, and consequently one of the criteria of morality.

But it has not, by this alone, proved itself to be the sole criterion. To do that, it would seem, by the same rule, necessary to show, not only that people desire happiness, but that they never desire anything else. Now it is palpable that they do desire things which, in common language, are decidedly distinguished from happiness. They desire, for example, virtue and the absence of vice, no less really than pleasure and the absence of pain. The desire of virtue is not as universal, but it is as authentic a fact as the desire of happiness. And hence the opponents of the utilitarian standard deem that they have a right to infer that there are other ends of human action besides happiness, and that happiness is not the standard of approbation and disapprobation.

But does the utilitarian doctrine deny that people desire virtue, or maintain that virtue is not a thing to be desired? The very reverse. It maintains not only that virtue is to be desired, but that it is to be desired disinterestedly, for itself. Whatever may be the opinion of utilitarian moralists as to the original conditions by which virtue is made

virtue, however they may believe (as they do) that actions and dispositions are only virtuous because they promote another end than virtue, yet this being granted, and it having been decided, from considerations of this description, what is virtuous, they not only place virtue at the very head of the things which are good as means to the ultimate end, but they also recognize as a psychological fact the possibility of its being, to the individual, a good in itself, without looking to any end beyond it; and hold that the mind is not in a right state, nor in a state conformable to utility, not in the state most conducive to the general happiness, unless it does love virtue in this manner—as a thing desirable in itself, even although, in the individual instance, it should not produce those other desirable consequences which it tends to produce, and on account of which it is held to be virtue. This opinion is not, in the smallest degree, a departure from the happiness principle. The ingredients of happiness are very various, and each of them is desirable in itself, and not merely when considered as swelling an aggregate. The principle of utility does not mean that any given pleasure, as music, for instance, or any given exemption from pain, as for example health, is to be looked upon as means to a collective something termed happiness, and to be desired on that account. They are desired and desirable in and for themselves; besides being means, they are a part of the end. Virtue, according to the utilitarian doctrine, is not naturally and originally part of the end, but it is capable of becoming so; and in those who love it disinterestedly it has become so, and is desired and cherished, not as a means to happiness, but as a part of their happiness.

To illustrate this further, we may remember that virtue is not the only thing originally a means, and which if it were not a means to anything else would be and remain indifferent, but which by association with what it is a means to comes to be desired for itself, and that too with the utmost intensity. What, for example, shall we say of the love of money? There is nothing originally more desirable about money than about any heap of glittering pebbles. Its worth is solely that of the things which it will buy; the desires for other things than itself, which it is a means of gratifying. Yet the love of money is not only one of the strongest moving forces of human life, but money is, in many cases, desired in and for itself; the desire to possess it is often stronger than the desire to use it, and goes on increasing when all the desires which point to ends beyond it, to be compassed by it, are falling off. It may, then, be said truly that money is desired not for the sake of an end, but as part of the end. From being a means to happiness, it has come to be itself a principal ingredient of the individual's conception of happiness. The same may be said of the majority of the great objects of human life: power, for example, or fame, except that to each of these there is a certain amount of immediate pleasure annexed, which has at least the semblance of being naturally inherent in them—a thing which cannot be said of money. Still, however, the strongest natural attraction, both of power and of fame, is the immense aid they give to the attainment of our other wishes; and it is the strong association thus generated between them and all our objects of desire which gives to the direct desire of them the intensity it often assumes, so as in some characters to surpass in strength all other desires. In these cases the means have become a part of the end, and a more important part of it than any of the things which they are means to. What was once desired as an instrument for the attainment of happiness has come to be desired for its own sake. In being desired for its own sake it is, however, desired as *part* of happiness. The person is made, or thinks he would be made, happy by its mere possession; and is made unhappy by failure to obtain it. The desire of it is not a different thing from the desire of happiness any more than the love of music or the desire of health. They are included in happiness. They are some of the elements of which the desire of happiness is

made up. Happiness is not an abstract idea but a concrete whole; and these are some of its parts. And the utilitarian standard sanctions and approves their being so. Life would be a poor thing, very ill provided with sources of happiness, if there were not this provision of nature by which things originally indifferent, but conducive to, or otherwise associated with, the satisfaction of our primitive desires, become in themselves sources of pleasure more valuable than the primitive pleasures, both in permanency, in the space of human existence that they are capable of covering, and even in intensity.

Virtue, according to the utilitarian conception, is a good of this description. There was no original desire of it, or motive to it, save its conduciveness to pleasure, and especially to protection from pain. But through the association thus formed it may be felt a good in itself, and desired as such with as great intensity as any other good; and with this difference between it and the love of money, of power, or of fame, that all of these may, and often do, render the individual noxious to the other members of the society to which he belongs, whereas there is nothing which makes him so much a blessing to them as the cultivation of the disinterested love of virtue. And consequently, the utilitarian standard, while it tolerates and approves those other acquired desires, up to the point beyond which they would be more injurious to the general happiness than promotive of it, enjoins and requires the cultivation of the love of virtue up to the greatest strength possible, as being above all things important to the general happiness.

It results from the preceding considerations that there is in reality nothing desired except happiness. Whatever is desired otherwise than as a means to some end beyond itself, and ultimately to happiness, is desired as itself a part of happiness, and is not desired for itself until it has become so. Those who desire virtue for its own sake desire it either because the consciousness of it is a pleasure, or because the consciousness of being without it is a pain, or for both reasons united; as in truth the pleasure and pain seldom exist separately, but almost always together—the same person feeling pleasure in the degree of virtue attained, and pain in not having attained more. If one of these gave him no pleasure, and the other no pain, he would not love or desire virtue, or would desire it only for the other benefits which it might produce to himself or to persons whom he cared for.

We have now, then, an answer to the question, of what sort of proof the principle of utility is susceptible. If the opinion which I have now stated is psychologically true—if human nature is so constituted as to desire nothing which is not either a part of happiness or a means of happiness, we can have no other proof, and we require no other, that these are the only things desirable. If so, happiness is the sole end of human action, and the promotion of it the test by which to judge of all human conduct; from whence it necessarily follows that it must be the criterion of morality, since a part is included in the whole.

And now to decide whether this is really so, whether mankind do desire nothing for itself but that which is a pleasure to them, or of which the absence is a pain, we have evidently arrived at a question of fact and experience, dependent like all similar questions, upon evidence. It can only be determined by practised self-consciousness and self-observation, assisted by observation of others. I believe that these sources of evidence, impartially consulted, will declare that desiring a thing and finding it pleasant, aversion to it and thinking of it as painful, are phenomena entirely inseparable or rather two parts of the same phenomenon; in strictness of language, two different modes of naming the same psychological fact; that to think of an object as desirable (unless for the sake of its consequences) and to think of it as pleasant are one and the same thing; and that to desire anything except in proportion as the idea of it is pleasant, is a physical and metaphysical impossibility.

So obvious does this appear to me that I expect it will hardly be disputed; and the objection made will be, not that desire can possibly be directed to anything ultimately except pleasure and exemption from pain, but that the will is a different thing from desire; that a person of confirmed virtue or any other person whose purposes are fixed carries out his purposes without any thought of the pleasure he has in contemplating them or expects to derive from their fulfilment, and persists in acting on them, even though these pleasures are much diminished by changes in his character or decay of his passive sensibilities, or are outweighed by the pains which the pursuit of the purposes may bring upon him. All this I fully admit and have stated it elsewhere as positively and emphatically as anyone. Will, the active phenomenon, is a different thing from desire, the state of passive sensibility, and, though originally an offshoot from it, may in time take root and detach itself from the parent stock, so much so that in the case of an habitual purpose, instead of willing the thing because we desire it, we often desire it only because we will it. This, however, is but an instance of that familiar fact, the power of habit, and is nowise confined to the case of virtuous actions. Many indifferent things which men originally did from a motive of some sort, they continue to do from habit. Sometimes this is done unconsciously; the consciousness coming only after the action; at other times with conscious volition, but volition which has become habitual and is put in operation by the force of habit, in opposition perhaps to the deliberate preference, as often happens with those who have contracted habits of vicious or hurtful indulgence. Third and last comes the case in which the habitual act of will in the individual instance is not in contradiction to the general intention prevailing at other times, but in fulfilment of it; as in the case of the person of confirmed virtue and of all who pursue deliberately and consistently any determinate end. The distinction between will and desire thus understood is an authentic and highly important psychological fact; but the fact consists solely in this—that will, like all other parts of our constitution, is amenable to habit, and that we may will from habit what we no longer desire for itself, or desire only because we will it. It is not the less true that will, in the beginning, is entirely produced by desire; including in that term the repelling influence of pain as well as the attractive one of pleasure. Let us take into consideration no longer the person who has a confirmed will to do right, but him in whom that virtuous will is still feeble, conquerable by temptation, and not to be fully relied on; by what means can it be strengthened? How can the will to be virtuous, where it does not exist in sufficient force, be implanted or awakened? Only by making the person *desire* virtue— by making him think of it in a pleasurable light, or of its absence in a painful one. It is by associating the doing right with pleasure, or the doing wrong with pain, or by eliciting and impressing and bringing home to the person's experience the pleasure naturally involved in the one or the pain in the other, that it is possible to call forth that will to be virtuous which, when confirmed, acts without any thought of either pleasure or pain. Will is the child of desire, and passes out of the dominion of its parent only to come under that of habit. That which is the result of habit affords no presumption of being intrinsically good; and there would be no reason for wishing that the purpose of virtue should become independent of pleasure and pain were it not that the influence of the pleasurable and painful associations which prompt to virtue is not sufficiently to be depended on for unerring constancy of action until it has acquired the support of habit. Both in feeling and in conduct, habit is the only thing which imparts certainty; and it is because of the importance to others of being able to rely absolutely on one's feelings and conduct, and to oneself of being able to rely on one's own, that the will to do right ought to be cultivated into this habitual independence. In other words, this state of the will is a means to good, not intrinsically a good; and does not contradict the doctrine that nothing is a good to human beings but in so far as it is either itself pleasurable or a means of attaining pleasure or averting pain.

But if this doctrine be true, the principle of utility is proved. Whether it is so or not, must now be left to the consideration of the thoughtful reader.

COMMENT

Bentham and Mill

"What good is happiness? It won't buy money." This witticism reverses the true relation between means and ends. Money is a means, and happiness is an end. Money is important because it contributes to happiness, and happiness is good for its own sake. It is illogical—and hence amusing—to speak as if money were the end and happiness only the means.

The ethical theory known as utilitarianism maintains that right action, like money, is valuable essentially as a means. Unlike Immanuel Kant, the utilitarians make *consequences* the test of right and wrong. An action is right if it brings about the best results.

But what are the *best results?* "The greatest happiness of the greatest number," declared Jeremy Bentham. By happiness he meant the surplus of pleasure over pain; and the proper end of moral action, he maintained, is to bring about this surplus in the lives of as many people as possible. Acts should be judged right in proportion as they tend to increase pleasure or decrease pain among the maximum number of people. The intrinsic value of the pleasure or disvalue of the pain is to be judged quantitatively, not qualitatively. What matters is that we get as much pleasure as possible, not that we get a certain kind. "Quantity of pleasure being equal," Bentham taught, "pushpin [a very simple game] is as good as poetry." The quantity has two dimensions—intensity and duration. The *more* intense and durable a pleasure is, and the *less* intense and durable a pain, the better—apart from future consequences. The pain of a toothache, for example, is worse the longer and more intense it is; the pleasure of a happy friendship is better the more intense and prolonged it is.

Bentham did not deny that there are, in a sense, *bad* pleasures and *good* pains. The pleasures of cruelty or intemperance produce, in the long run, an overbalance of pain—they are good in themselves but bad in their consequences, and their instrumental badness outweighs their intrinsic goodness. Similarly, there are pains with pleasant consequences. However, nothing but pleasure is *intrinsically* good, and nothing but pain is *instrinsically* bad. The art of living well is to calculate the worth of actions in terms of all the plus values of pleasure and the minus values of pain, subtracting the latter from the former. Bentham exercised a great deal of ingenuity in working out the details of this "moral arithmetic."

So far he was expressing an *ethical* theory. In addition, he advanced the *psychological* doctrine that every person is naturally selfish and hence almost invariably seeks pleasure or the avoidance of pain for oneself. This egoistic doctrine is inconsistent with the contention that everyone ought to seek "the greatest happiness of the greatest number." What sense is there in saying that people ought to aim at the greatest social good if their nature is inescapably selfish? Bentham tried to avoid contradiction by arguing that governments should establish a system of rewards and punishments that would induce individuals, on the very basis of their egoism, to further the maximum social happiness.

When Mill undertook the composition of *Utilitarianism,* he was trying to defend the ethical philosophy of his father and Bentham from the attacks made on it, but he was too divided in mind to make a good defense. The conflict between his loyalty to Bentham and his deep independent convictions produced many strains and inconsistencies. His book is, nevertheless, worth very careful study because even his confusions and errors are highly instructive.

Although Mill begins his discussion of utilitarianism with remarks that appear to be in perfect agreement with Bentham's theory, he soon exhibits his independence. This divergence gives rise to some of the most fundamental issues in the whole field of ethics. Let us now consider some of these issues.

The Question of Qualities of Pleasure

In estimating the intrinsic value of pleasures, Mill subordinates Bentham's quantitative standards—intensity and duration— to a standard of quality. The pleasures of the cultivated life, he maintains, are superior in *kind* to the pleasures of the uncultivated. Hence, the pleasures of a human being are qualitatively superior to the pleasures of a pig, and the pleasures of a Socrates are qualitatively superior to the pleasures of an uncultivated fool. This is a radical break with Bentham's quantitative hedonism, which maintains that the pleasure of a dolt is no better or worse intrinsically than the quantitatively equal pleasure of a highly developed person.

Is Mill correct in supposing that there are different kinds of pleasure? At first glance, the facts seem to bear out his view. The pleasure of reading a good philosophical book, for example, apparently differs qualitatively from the pleasure of playing a brisk game of handball. However, is the qualitative difference in the *pleasures,* or is it in the differing *accompaniments* of the pleasures? If we consider pleasant *experiences,* and not bare pleasures, there *are* genuine qualitative differences; but these differences may be not in the pleasures but in the very different *contents* of experience that have the common property of pleasing. In the case of reading, the experience is quiet, meditative, and relaxed; in the case of playing handball, it is exciting, kinesthetic, and strenuous. Some psychologists, such as Edward Titchener in his *Textbook on Psychology,* have maintained that the pleasures in such diverse experiences differ only in intensity and duration and that the only qualitative differences are in such accompaniments as we have just pointed out. Mill inadvertently lends support to this interpretation since he speaks of the "nobility," "dignity," "intellectuality," and so on, of the "pleasures" that he prefers. It would seem that he is talking not about bare pleasures, abstracted from any content, but rather about *experiences,* which contain not only pleasure but also various intellectual, moral, and esthetic qualities.

It is theoretically possible to maintain that there are qualitative differences in pure pleasures and that these differences are ethically important. Just as there are different kinds of colors—red, blue, green, and so on—so there might be different kinds of pleasures. Also, just as one might hold that warm colors, let us say, are qualitatively superior to cool colors, so one might contend that certain kinds of pleasures are qualitatively superior to others. One difficulty with this view is that we do not find such indisputable qualitative differences in pleasures. Even if we did, we might still be unable to tell whether some kinds of pleasure are really better than others.

This sort of qualitative hedonism, in any event, is not Mill's view. He *appears* to be advocating hedonism, but he is really maintaining, albeit unclearly and inconsistently, that the good is the pleasant *development* of the personality. This is a kind of synthesis of hedonism and self-realizationism rather than hedonism pure and simple.

The Question of Moral Arithmetic

Bentham maintained that the business of the legislator or moralist is to calculate the probable effects of alternative acts with a view to maximizing pleasure and minimizing pain. This entails the quantitative assessment of pleasures and pains. That there are great difficulties in comparing intensities with durations, adding up pleasures and pains, and subtracting pains from pleasures has often been pointed out. Bentham might reply that such calculation, although difficult, should be carried out as best we can and that at least a rough estimation of the hedonic consequences of acts is indispensable to any rational direction of our lives.

By introducing questions of quality, Mill greatly restricts the applicability of Bentham's moral arithmetic. His qualitative test is *preference*—not the preference of the average man but that of the moral connoisseur. He tells us that wise persons, such as Socrates, are more competent than the unwise to compare pleasures, to judge which are qualitatively superior, and to decide whether, in a particular instance, considerations of quantity should be sacrificed to considerations of quality. "From this verdict of the only competent judges," he declares, "I apprehend there can be no appeal."

The difference between the approaches of Bentham and of Mill gives rise to a number of questions: To what extent does utilitarianism entail the measurement of pleasures and pains? Are intensities commensurable with durations, and pains with pleasures? Is the preference of the wise a better guide than quantitative assessment? Is the concept of a moral connoisseur sound?

The Question of the Social Distribution of Good

Bentham proposes that the morality of acts be determined by their contribution to "the greatest happiness of the greatest number"—and Mill, at times, employs the same phrase. However, does this formula mean the greatest amount of happiness among men, or the greatest number of men who are happy? And supposing that there is a conflict between greatest happiness and greatest number, should we sacrifice the greatest number to the greatest happiness, or the greatest happiness to the greatest number? Mill's ambiguous formula provides no answer.

There are indications, however, that Bentham is more democratic and equalitarian in his approach to the problem of distribution than Mill. Each person, he declared, should count for one, and no one for more than one. This tenet could be interpreted as meaning that the pleasure of any person is as intrinsically good as the quantitatively equal pleasure of any other person. However, it could also be interpreted to mean that a smaller amount of pleasure *equally* distributed is morally preferable (at least on occasion) to a greater amount *unequally* distributed. If this was Bentham's real conviction, he was not a strict utilitarian and hedonist—for the principle of equality so interpreted is based on a sense of distributive justice rather than on the utilitarian principle of maximizing pleasure and minimizing pain.

Mill's position, in any event, is comparatively aristocratic. Although he verbally subscribes to Bentham's phrases, his emphasis on quality, wisdom, and self-cultivation implies a very different standard than the greatest possible pleasure of the greatest possible number. The word *greatest* indicates a quantitative criterion—whether it be number of people or amount of pleasure. Mill's criterion, on the other hand, is qualitative. In effect, he favors an intellectual aristocracy—though it is worth noting that he does not identify the intellectually superior with the rich and powerful of the earth.

The differences between Bentham and Mill again serve to emphasize an important set of problems. What is a fair and just distribution of good? Can it be reconciled with a quantitative hedonism? Should the controlling consideration be the number of people receiving the good, or the amount of the good? Or should both amount and number be subordinated, as in Mill, to considerations of quality?

The Question of Ultimate Principles

The ethical philosophy of Mill, like that of Bentham, falls into two main parts. The first part is a theory about the nature of right—the doctrine that the proper standard for judging right is best results. This theory is logically independent of hedonism, or of any other particular interpretation of goodness. It simply states that the right must be determined in the light of good consequences—whatever the good may be. The good might be pleasure or satisfaction of desire or actualization of potentialities—or almost anything else. Bentham and Mill speak as if the test of consequences is necessarily linked to one and only one end—namely, "happiness" as each conceives it. However, this is manifestly not the case.

The question of the validity of utilitarianism—in the wide sense of the term—turns largely on whether it can satisfactorily explain our many and varied duties. The nonutilitarian will argue that there are kinds of moral rectitude that cannot be interpreted as utilitarian rightness. He would say, for example, that having made a solemn promise, we have a duty to keep it *even if no more good is thereby to be achieved*. The utilitarian, in contrast, would maintain that there is no valid test of right and wrong except best results. Our duty is to help people and not to hurt them—and the more we help them and the less we hurt them, the better. If it becomes clear that in the long run, keeping a promise will have bad rather than good results, or results less good than some other alternative, our moral obligation is not to keep the promise but to choose whatever alternative yields the best results. This clash between the utilitarians and the nonutilitarians is one of the crucial issues in ethics—and the reader of this book should consider very carefully where the truth lies.

The second part of the ethical philosophy of Bentham and of both Mills is a theory about the nature of ultimate good and evil. Here again, as we have seen, there is disagreement between John Stuart Mill, who embraced a kind of hedonic self-realizationism, and Bentham, who clung to pure quantitative hedonism. The issue is extremely important, but it is not one that can be decided by any conclusive proof. Mill (not realizing the extent of his divergence from Bentham) undertook to "prove" that pleasure alone is ultimately good, but his so-called proof (he admits that *strict or conclusive* proof is impossible) contains some of the most widely advertised fallacies in the history of philosophy. We shall refrain from pointing out these fallacies, leaving to the reader the exercise of discovering them. Whether the fallacies are apparent only, being due to carelessness in the use of language, or whether they are *real* fallacies resulting from mental confusion is a question of interpretation.

To decide the question of what is ultimately good, we must summon up whatever insight we can muster. If we imagine a world of human beings and a world of lower animals, *equal in the amount of pleasure they contain,* it would not follow that the two worlds are equal in ultimate goodness—because the humans, in addition to experiencing pleasure, have insight into truth, love, imagination, excellence of character, enjoyment of beauty, and so forth. The reply of the hedonist, that these things are good as means because they *give* pleasure, would not seem to the antihedonist an adequate answer. The latter would say that it is important not merely to feel pleasure but to feel pleasure in certain ways, with certain accompaniments rather than others. *Real* happiness embraces the great goods of beauty and truth and nobility of character as having intrinsic and not merely instrumental value. To decide who is right, the hedonist or the antihedonist, is a very important question for the reader to answer.

With regard to the utilitarian's approach to the case of Noel David Earley's planned suicide, things begin to get rather complex. On the one hand, it would seem an easy case in which to apply the "hedonistic calculus" in a straightforward manner. This would seem to be what Earley himself did. On the other hand, it seems that Earley failed to include the effects of his decision on those persons with whom he had a relationship. How would Mill react to Earley's focus on the "eat, drink, and be merry" tone of his decision? Are there no higher values than pleasure, even in the face of impending death and severe pain?

18

THE WAY OF FREEDOM

JEAN–PAUL SARTRE (1905–1980)

Jean-Paul Sartre participated in the resistance movement during World War II in Nazi-occupied France. After the war, he emerged as a leading French intellectual, primarily on the basis of his monumental book, *Being and Nothingness* (1943). He became a major figure in the philosophical movement known as Existentialism, mostly due to the influence of his various plays, short stories, and important novel, *Nausea* (1964). The following selection is from his popular lecture, given in 1945, entitled "Existentialism Is a Humanism."

In addition to his philosophical activity, Sartre continued to be politically active throughout his life. He was taken with the Marxist concern for oppressed peoples and sided with the revolutionary cause in Algeria's struggle for independence from France. Although he had worked side by side with the novelist Albert Camus in the resistance against Nazism, the two friends disagreed strongly over Sartre's commitment to communism. Also, Sartre later modified his concept of absolute freedom in light of the sociohistorical criticisms raised by the third "giant" of twentieth-century French philosophy, Maurice Merleau-Ponty.

Sartre maintained a deep and long-term relationship with Simone de Beauvoir, another important French philosopher and one of the most influential feminist thinkers. Beauvoir's book, *The Second Sex*, presents a feminist version of the existentialist approach to ethics.

EXISTENTIALISM IS A HUMANISM

... For in truth this is of all teachings the least scandalous and the most austere: it is intended strictly for technicians and philosophers. All the same, it can easily be defined.

From *Existentialism Is a Humanism* by Jean-Paul Sartre, trans. P. Mairet. Copyright © 1949 by The Philosophical Library, Inc. Reprinted by permission of The Philosophical Library, Inc.

The question is only complicated because there are two kinds of existentialists. There are, on the one hand the Christians, amongst whom I shall name Jaspers and Gabriel Marcel, both professed Catholics; and on the other the existential atheists, amongst whom we must place Heidegger as well as the French existentialists and myself. What they have in common is simply the fact that they believe that *exis-*

tence comes before *essence*—or, if you will, that we must begin from the subjective. What exactly do we mean by that?

If one considers an article of manufacture—as, for example, a book or a paper-knife—one sees that it has been made by an artisan who had a conception of it; and he has paid attention, equally, to the conception of a paper-knife and to the pre-existent technique of production which is a part of that conception and is, at bottom, a formula. Thus the paper-knife is at the same time an article producible in a certain manner and one which, on the other hand, serves a definite purpose, for one cannot suppose that a man would produce a paper-knife without knowing what it was for. Let us say, then, of the paper-knife that its essence—that is to say the sum of the formulae and the qualities which made its production and its definition possible—precedes its existence. The presence of such-and-such a paper-knife or book is thus determined before my eyes. Here, then, we are viewing the world from a technical standpoint, and we can say that production precedes existence.

When we think of God as the creator, we are thinking of him, most of the time, as a supernal artisan. Whatever doctrine we may be considering, whether it be a doctrine like that of Descartes, or of Leibnitz himself, we always imply that the will follows, more or less, from the understanding or at least accompanies it, so that when God creates he knows precisely what he is creating. Thus, the conception of man in the mind of God is comparable to that of the paper-knife in the mind of the artisan: God makes man according to a procedure and a conception, exactly as the artisan manufactures a paper-knife, following a definition and a formula. Thus each individual man is the realisation of a certain conception which dwells in the divine understanding. In the philosophic atheism of the eighteenth century, the notion of God is suppressed, but not, for all that, the idea that essence is prior to existence; something of the idea we still find everywhere, in

Diderot, in Voltaire and even in Kant. Man possesses a human nature; that "human nature," which is the conception of human being, is found in every man; which means that each man is a particular example of an universal con-ception, the conception of Man. In Kant, this universality goes so far that the wild man of the woods, man in the state of nature and the bourgeois are all contained in the same definition and have the same fundamental qualities. Here again, the essence of man precedes that historic existence which we confront in experience.

Atheistic existentialism, of which I am a representative, declares with greater consistency that if God does not exist there is at least one being whose existence comes before its essence, a being which exists before it can be defined by any conception of it. That being is man or, as Heidegger has it, the human reality. What do we mean by saying that existence precedes essence? We mean that man first of all exists, encounters himself, surges up in the world—and defines himself afterwards. If man as the existentialist sees him is not definable, it is because to begin with he is nothing. He will not be anything until later, and then he will be what he makes of himself. Thus, there is no human nature, because there is no God to have a conception of it. Man simply is. Not that he is simply what he conceives himself to be, but he is what he wills, and as he conceives himself after already existing—as he wills to be after that leap towards existence. Man is nothing else but that which he makes of himself. That is the first principle of existentialism. And this is what people call its "subjectivity," using the word as a reproach against us. But what do we mean to say by this, but that man is of a greater dignity than a stone or a table? For we mean to say than man primarily exists—that man is, before all else, something which propels itself towards a future and is aware that it is doing so. Man is, indeed, a project which possesses a subjective life, instead of being a kind of moss, or a fungus or a cauliflower.

Before that projection of the self nothing exists; not even in the heaven of intelligence: man will only attain existence when he is what he purposes to be. Not, however, what he may wish to be. For what we usually understand by wishing or willing is a conscious decision taken—much more often than not—after we have made ourselves what we are. I may wish to join a party, to write a book or to marry—but in such a case what is usually called my will is probably a manifestation of a prior and more spontaneous decision. If, however, it is true that existence is prior to essence, man is responsible for what he is. Thus, the first effect of existentialism is that it puts every man in possession of himself as he is, and places the entire responsibility for his existence squarely upon his own shoulders. And, when we say that man is responsible for himself, we do not mean that he is responsible only for his own individuality, but that he is responsible for all men. The word "subjectivism" is to be understood in two senses, and our adversaries play upon only one of them. Subjectivism means, on the one hand, the freedom of the individual subject and, on the other, that man cannot pass beyond human subjectivity. It is the latter which is the deeper meaning of existentialism. When we say that man chooses himself, we do mean that every one of us must choose himself, but by that we also mean that in choosing for himself he chooses for all men. For in effect, of all the actions a man may take in order to create himself as he wills to be, there is not one which is not creative, at the same time, of an image of man such as he believes he ought to be. To choose between this or that is at the same time to affirm the value of that which is chosen; for we are unable ever to choose the worse. What we choose is always the better; and nothing can be better for us unless it is better for all. If, moreover, existence precedes essence and we will to exist at the same time as we fashion our image, that image is valid for all and for the entire epoch in which we find ourselves. Our responsibility is thus much

greater than we had supposed, for it concerns mankind as a whole. If I am a worker, for instance, I may choose to join a Christian rather than a Communist trade union. And if, by that membership, I choose to signify that resignation is, after all, the attitude that best becomes a man, that man's kingdom is not upon this earth, I do not commit myself alone to that view. Resignation is my will for everyone, and my action is, in consequence, a commitment on behalf of all mankind. Or if, to take a more personal case, I decide to marry and to have children, even though this decision proceeds simply from my situation, from my passion or my desire, I am thereby committing not only myself, but humanity as a whole, to the practice of monogamy. I am thus responsible for myself and for all men, and I am creating a certain image of man as I would have him to be. In fashioning myself I fashion man.

This may enable us to understand what is meant by such terms—perhaps a little grandiloquent—as anguish, abandonment and despair. As you will soon see, it is very simple. First, what do we mean by anguish? The existentialist frankly states that man is in anguish. His meaning is as follows—When a man commits himself to anything, fully realising that he is not only choosing what he will be, but is thereby at the same time a legislator deciding for the whole of mankind—in such a moment a man cannot escape from the sense of complete and profound responsibility. There are many, indeed, who show no such anxiety. But we affirm that they are merely disguising their anguish or are in flight from it. Certainly, many people think that in what they are doing they commit no one but themselves to anything: and if you ask them, "What would happen if everyone did so?" they shrug their shoulders and reply, "Everyone does not do so." But in truth, one ought always to ask oneself what would happen if everyone did as one is doing; nor can one escape from that disturbing thought except by a kind of self-deception. The man who lies in self-excuse, by saying

"Everyone will not do it," must be ill at ease in his conscience, for the act of lying implies the universal value which it denies. By this very disguise his anguish reveals itself. This is the anguish that Kierkegaard called "the anguish of Abraham." You know the story; An angel commanded Abraham to sacrifice his son; and obedience was obligatory, if it really was an angel who had appeared and said, "Thou, Abraham, shalt sacrifice thy son." But anyone in such a case would wonder, first, whether I am really Abraham. Where are the proofs? A certain mad woman who suffered from hallucinations said that people were telephoning to her, and giving her orders. The doctor asked, "But who is it that speaks to you?" She replied: "He says it is God." And what, indeed, could prove to her that it was God? If an angel appears to me, what is the proof that it is an angel; or, if I hear voices, who can prove that they proceed from heaven and not from hell, or from my own subconsciousness or some pathological condition? Who can prove that they are really addressed to me?

Who, then, can prove that I am the proper person to impose, by my own choice, my conception of man upon mankind? I shall never find any proof whatever; there will be no sign to convince me of it. If a voice speaks to me, it is still I myself who must decide whether the voice is or is not that of an angel. If I regard a certain course of action as good, it is only I who choose to say that it is good and not bad. There is nothing to show that I am Abraham: nevertheless I also am obliged at every instant to perform actions which are examples. Everything happens to every man as though the whole human race had its eyes fixed upon what he is doing and regulated its conduct accordingly. So every man ought to say, "Am I really a man who has the right to act in such a manner that humanity regulates itself by what I do?" If a man does not say that, he is dissembling his anguish. Clearly, the anguish with which we are concerned here is not one that could lead to quietism or inaction. It is anguish

pure and simple, of the kind well known to all those who have borne responsibilities. When, for instance, a military leader takes upon himself the responsibility for an attack and sends a number of men to their death, he chooses to do it and at bottom he alone chooses. No doubt he acts under a higher command, but its orders, which are more general, require interpertation by him and upon that interpretation depends the life of ten, fourteen or twenty men. In making the decision, he cannot but feel a certain anguish. All leaders know that anguish. It does not prevent their acting, on the contrary it is the very condition of their action, for the action presupposes that there is a plurality of possibilities, and in choosing one of these, they realise that it has value only because it is chosen. Now it is anguish of that kind which existentialism describes, and moreover, as well shall see, makes explicit through direct responsibility towards other men who are concerned. Far from being a screen which could separate us from action, it is a condition of action itself.

And when we speak of "abandonment"—a favourite word of Heidegger—we only mean to say that God does not exist, and that it is necessary to draw the consequences of his absence right to the end. The existentialist is strongly opposed to a certain type of secular moralism which seeks to suppress God at the least possible expense. Towards 1880, when the French professors endeavoured to formulate a secular morality, they said something like this:—God is a useless and costly hypothesis, so we will do without it. However, it we are to have morality, a society and a law-abiding world, it is essential that certain values should be taken seriously; they must have an *a priori* existence ascribed to them. It must be considered obligatory *a priori* to be honest, not to lie, not to beat one's wife, to bring up children and so forth; so we are going to do a little work on this subject, which will enable us to show that these values exist all the same, inscribed in an intelligible heaven although, of course, there is no God. In other words—and this is, I believe, the purport of all that we in France call radicalism—nothing will be changed if God does not exist; we shall re-discover the same norms of honesty, progress and humanity, and we shall have disposed of God as an out-of-date hypothesis which will die away quietly of itself. The existentialist, on the contrary, finds it extremely embarrassing that God does not exist, for there disappears with Him all possibility of finding values in an intelligible heaven. There can no longer be any good *a priori,* since there is no infinite and perfect consciousness to think it. It is nowhere written that "the good" exists, that one must be honest or must not lie, since we are now upon the plane where there are only men. Dostoievsky once wrote "If God did not exist, everything would be permitted"; and that, for existentialism, is the starting point. Everything is indeed permitted if God does not exist, and man is in consequence forlorn, for he cannot find anything to depend upon either within or outside himself. He discovers forthwith, that he is without excuse. For if indeed existence precedes essence, one will never be able to explain one's action by reference to a given and specific human nature; in other words, there is no determinism—man is free, man is freedom. Nor, on the other hand, if God does not exist, are we provided with any values or commands that could legitimize our behaviour. Thus we have neither behind us, nor before us in a luminous realm of values, any means of justification or excuse. We are left alone, without excuse. That is what I mean when I say that man is condemned to be free. Condemned, because he did not create himself, yet is nevertheless at liberty, and from the moment that he is thrown into this world he is responsible for everything he does. The existentialist does not believe in the power of passion. He will never regard a grand passion as a destructive torrent upon which a man is swept into certain actions as by fate, and which, therefore, is an excuse for them. He thinks that man is responsible for his passion. Neither will an existentialist think that a man can find help through some sign being vouchsafed upon earth for his orientation: for he thinks that the man himself interprets the sign as he chooses. He thinks that every man, without any support or help whatever, is condemned at every instant to invent man. As Ponge has written in a very fine article, "Man is the future of man." That is exactly true. Only, if one took this to mean that the future is laid up in Heaven, that God knows what it is, it would be false, for then it would no longer even be a future. If, however, it means that whatever man may now appear to be, there is a future to be fashioned, a virgin future that awaits him—then it is a true saying. But in the present one is forsaken.

As an example by which you may the better understand this state of abandonment, I will refer to the case of a pupil of mine, who sought me out in the following circumstances. His father was quarrelling with his mother and was also inclined to be a "collaborator"; his elder brother had been killed in the German offensive of 1940 and this young man, with a sentiment somewhat primitive but generous, burned to avenge him. His mother was living alone with him, deeply afflicted by the semi-treason of his father and by the death of her eldest son, and her one consolation was in this young man. But he, at this moment, had the choice between going to England to join the Free French Forces or of staying near his mother and helping her to live. He fully realised that this woman lived only for him and that his disappearance—or perhaps his death—would plunge her into despair. He also realised that, concretely and in fact, every action he performed on his mother's behalf would be sure of effect in the sense of aiding her to live, whereas anything he did in order to go and fight would be an ambiguous action which might vanish like water into sand and serve no purpose. For instance, to set out for England he would have to wait indefinitely in a Spanish camp on the way through Spain; or, on arriving in England or in Algiers he might be put into an office to fill up forms. Consequently, he found himself confronted by two very different modes of action: the one concrete, immediate but directed towards only one individual; and the other an action addressed to an end infinitely greater, a national collectivity, but for that very reason ambiguous—and it might be frustrated on the way. At the same time, he was hesitating between two kinds of morality; on the one side the morality of sympathy, of personal devotion and, on the other side, a morality of wider scope but of more debatable validity. He had to choose between these two. What could help him to choose? Could the Christian doctrine? No. Christian doctrine says: Act with charity, love your neighbour, deny yourself for others, choose the way which is hardest, and so forth. But which is the harder road? To Whom does one owe the more brotherly love, the patriot or the mother? Which is the more useful aim, the general one of fighting in and for the whole community, or the precise aim of helping one particular person to live? Who can give an answer to that *a priori*? No one. Nor is it given in any ethical scripture. The Kantian ethic says, Never regard another as a means, but always as an end. Very well; if I remain with my mother, I shall be regarding her as the end and not as a means: but by the same token I am in danger of treating as means those who are fighting on my behalf; and the converse is also true, that if I go to the aid of the combatants I shall be treating them as the end at the risk of treating my mother as a means.

If values are uncertain, if they are still too abstract to determine the particular, concrete case under consideration, nothing remains but to trust in our instincts. That is what this young man tried to do; and when I saw him he said, "In the end, it is feeling that counts; the direction in which it is really pushing me is the one I ought to choose. If I feel that I love my mother enough to sacrifice everything else for her—my will to be avenged, all my longings for action and adventure—then I stay with her. If, on the contrary, I feel that my love

for her is not enough, I go." But how does one estimate the strength of a feeling? The value of his feeling for his mother was determined precisely by the fact that he was standing by her. I may say that I love a certain friend enough to sacrifice such or such a sum of money for him, but I cannot prove that unless I have done it. I may say, "I love my mother enough to remain with her," if actually I have remained with her. I can only estimate the strength of this affection if I have performed an action by which it is defined and ratified. But if I then appeal to this affection to justify my action, I find myself drawn into a vicious circle....

What is at the very heart and centre of existentialism is the absolute character of the free commitment, by which every man realises himself in realising a type of humanity—a commitment always understandable, to no matter whom in no matter what epoch—and its bearing upon the relativity of the cultural pattern which may result from such absolute commitment. One must observe equally the relativity of Cartesianism and the absolute character of the Cartesian commitment. In this sense you may say, if you like, that every one of us makes the absolute by breathing, by eating, by sleeping or by behaving in any fashion whatsoever. There is no difference between free being—being as self-committal, as existence choosing its essence—and absolute being. And there is no difference whatever between being as an absolute, temporarily localised—that is, localised in history—and universally intelligible being....

Existentialism is nothing else but an attempt to draw the full conclusions from a consistently atheistic position. ... Not that we believe God does exist, but we think that the real problem is not that of His existence; what man needs is to find himself again and to understand that nothing can save him from himself, not even a valid proof of the existence of God. In this sense existentialism is optimistic, it is a doctrine of action, and it is only by self-deception, by confusing their own despair with ours that Christians can describe us as without hope.

COMMENT

Sartre begins by distinguishing himself, as a representative of "atheistic existentialism," from such religious existentialists as Karl Jaspers and Gabriel Marcel. He most surely would include Søren Kierkegaard in this latter group, as well. The defining characteristic that separates these two versions of this highly influential approach to philosophy pertains to the relationship between *essence* and *existence*. Those who believe that there is an overall meaning and purpose to human life, generally associated with a divine being, would maintain that our essence, our fundamental humanity, is logically prior to our particular existence or character. What we can do and can become is thus determined by our inherent nature. Sartre, on the other hand, and those who side with him would argue that we *choose* our nature and character as we live from day to day. This is especially true if God is not in the picture, since then there exists no preexistent plan or nature to which we must conform.

While many, if not most, people find the idea of our being merely "thrown" into existence, or "condemned to freedom," a fearful one, Sartre thinks it is just the opposite. Although it may be difficult to face up to having full responsibility for one's own choices and destiny, since now there is no one else to blame for the results, this radical freedom also liberates us from such debilitating notions as fate and/or predestination. In Sartre's view, which is quite similar to that of Friedrich Nietzsche, this challenge can only be met in a positive manner by those who accept the possibility of moral maturity. Since we no longer *can* hide behind metaphysical or theological "excuses," we no longer *need* to. To become a mature, responsible moral agent is at once both stark and invigorating, honest and empowering.

Sartre provides us with a helpful example of how this existentialist rationale works in the case of his student who comes to him for advice. After cataloguing all the different factors and moves the young man could make, Sartre concludes, in a paragraph not included in the reading, that all anyone can do in such cases is *choose* and then continue to work with the ongoing results, that is to say, continue to choose. In the final analysis, no matter which ethical posture we adopt, whether Christian, Kantian, or even Sartrean, *we ourselves* are making the choice of whom to listen to and follow. Even in rejecting the existentialist approach, we *choose* to do so, so in the end we alone are responsible for our actions.

Although this approach to moral questions is often taken to be the height of subjectivity, Sartre refuses this implication. He argues, on the contrary, that in choosing for ourselves we implicitly choose for all humankind, since we claim to be choosing *responsibly*. Thus absolute freedom does not give one the right to do simply as he or she pleases; rather, it demands that each person act in a manner which reflects the goals and values he or she has chosen. Sartre seems to think that if each person would behave in this way, the important needs and aspirations of human existence would be fulfilled.

Many thinkers have raised questions and criticisms of this radical approach to morality. Perhaps the most important pertain to the difficulty of moving from the abstract notion of absolute freedom to the practical issues of daily social life. In addition to there being few, if any, ethical guidelines, there also seem to be no criteria for connecting these decisions with those of other moral agents. In other words, it is difficult to know how the concepts of "good" and "right" are to function in an ethical sense, whether on the individual or social level, once responsibility is interpreted in such an individualist fashion. It would seem that Sartre's concept of "freedom" leaves the moral agent trapped within an existentialist vacuum.

In Sartre's defense, it may prove instructive to work through possible dialogues that might take place between him and the other moral theorists we have considered in this section. Such comparisons and contrasts may well reveal, at the very least, how easy it is to hide behind the intricacies of a complex moral theory, or at best become mired down in them. The tensions and even contradictions within and between the theories of Kant and the Utilitarians, for instance, may make Sartre's radical freedom seem rather appealing. Nevertheless, it does remain true that it is difficult to tell the difference between two equally responsible actions which lead to quite opposite results, given Sartre's exclusive focus on the act of choosing itself. How are lying, murder, and exploitation, for example, to be understood if an individual or group decides that they are willing to deal with the consequences thereof?

Although he may not have provided "the answer" to the fundamental issues of morality, Sartre certainly focuses some of the most important questions pertaining to them. It is our responsibility to engage these questions seriously.

The case of Noel David Earley provides an excellent "case in point" for such engagement, especially with regard to Sartre's existentialist posture. At first glance, it might appear that Sartre would applaud Earley's decision to take his own life because it arose from his own moral, individual agency. However, one might ask whether Earley can so choose and at the same time choose for everyone else, as Sartre seems to suggest he must. Is it possible that from an existentialist point of view Earley must be viewed as taking the easy, self-indulgent way out? Did he exhibit the sort of moral courage that goes with the "authentic" way of life?

19

THE WAY OF EXPERIMENT

JOHN DEWEY (1859-1952)

For a biographical note, see pages 149–150.

RECONSTRUCTION IN MORAL CONCEPTIONS

The impact of the alteration in methods of scientific thinking upon moral ideas is, in general, obvious. Goods, ends are multiplied. Rules are softened into principles, and principles are modified into methods of understanding. Ethical theory began among the Greeks as an attempt to find a regulation for the conduct of life which should have a rational basis and purpose instead of being derived from custom. But reason as a substitute for custom was under the obli-gation of supplying objects and laws as fixed as those of custom had been. Ethical theory ever since has been singularly hypnotized by the notion that its business is to discover some final end or good or some ultimate and supreme law. This is the common element among the diversity of theories. Some have held that the end is loyalty or obedience to a higher power or authority; and they have variously found this higher principle in Divine Will, the will of the secular ruler, the maintenance of institutions in which the purpose of superiors is embodied, and the rational consciousness of duty. But they have differed from one another because there was one point in which they were agreed: a single and final source of law. Others have asserted that it is impossible to locate morality in conformity to law-giving power, and that it must be sought in ends that are good. And some have sought the good in self-realization, some in holiness, some in happiness, some in the greatest possible aggregate of pleasures. And yet these schools have agreed in the assumption that there is a single, fixed and final good. They have been able to dispute with one another only because of their common premise.

The question arises whether the way out of the confusion and conflict is not to go to the root of the matter by questioning this common element. Is not the belief in

From *Reconstruction in Philosophy* (originally given as lectures in Japan), New York: Henry Holt and Company, 1920; enlarged edition, Boston: Beacon Press, 1948.

the single, final and ultimate (whether conceived as good or as authoritative law) an intellectual product of that feudal organization which is disappearing historically and of that belief in a bounded, ordered cosmos, wherein rest is higher than motion, which has disappeared from natural science? It has been repeatedly suggested that the present limit of intellectual reconstruction lies in the fact that it has not as yet been seriously applied in the moral and social disciplines. Would not this further application demand precisely that we advance to a belief in a plurality of changing, moving, individualized goods and ends, and to a belief that principles, criteria, laws are intellectual instruments for analyzing individual or unique situations?

The blunt assertion that every moral situation is a unique situation having its own irreplaceable good may seem not merely blunt but preposterous. For the established tradition teaches that it is precisely the irregularity of special cases which makes necessary the guidance of conduct universals, and that the essence of the virtuous disposition is willingness to subordinate every particular case to adjudication by a fixed principle. It would then follow that submission of a generic end and law to determination by the concrete situation entails complete confusion and unrestrained licentiousness. Let us, however, follow the pragmatic rule, and in order to discover the meaning of the idea ask for its consequences. Then it surprisingly turns out that the primary significance of the unique and morally ultimate character of the concrete situation is to transfer the weight and burden of morality to intelligence. It does not destroy responsibility; it only locates it. A moral situation is one in which judgment and choice are required antecedently to overt action. The practical meaning of the situation—that is to say the action needed to satisfy it—is not self-evident. It has to be searched for. There are conflicting desires and alternative apparent goods. What is needed is to find the right course of action, the right good. Hence,

inquiry is exacted: observation of the detailed makeup of the situation; analysis into its diverse factors; clarification of what is obscure; discounting the more insistent and vivid traits; tracing the consequences of the various modes of action that suggest themselves; regarding the decision reached as hypothetical and tentative until the anticipated or supposed consequences which led to its adoption have been squared with actual consequences. This inquiry is intelligence. Our moral failures go back to some weakness of disposition, some absence of sympathy, some one-sided bias that makes us perform the judgment of the concrete case carelessly or perversely. Wide sympathy, keen sensitiveness, persistence in the face of the disagreeable, balance of interests enabling us to undertake the work of analysis and decision intelligently are the distinctively moral traits—the virtues or moral excellences.

It is worth noting once more that the underlying issue is, after all, only the same as that which has been already threshed out in physical inquiry. There too it long seemed as if rational assurance and demonstration could be attained only if we began with universal conceptions and subsumed particular cases under them. The men who initiated the methods of inquiry that are now everywhere adopted were denounced in their day (and sincerely) as subverters of truth and foes of science. If they have won in the end, it is because, as has already been pointed out, the method of universals confirmed prejudices and sanctioned ideas that had gained currency irrespective of evidence for them; while placing the initial and final weight upon the individual case, stimulate painstaking inquiry into facts and examination of principles. In the end, loss of eternal truths was more than compensated for in the accession of quotidian facts. The loss of the system of superior and fixed definitions and kinds was more than made up for by the growing system of hypotheses and laws used in classifying facts. After all, then, we are only pleading for the adoption in moral reflection of the logic that has been proved to make for security, stringency and fertility in passing judgment upon physical phenomena. And the reason is the same. The old method in spite of its nominal and esthetic worship of reason discouraged reason, because it hindered the operation of scrupulous and unremitting inquiry.

More definitely, the transfer of the burden of the moral life from following rules or pursuing fixed ends over to the detection of the ills that need remedy in a special case and the formation of plans and methods for dealing with them, eliminates the causes which have kept moral theory controversial, and which have also kept it remote from helpful contact with the exigencies of practice. The theory of fixed ends inevitably leads thought into the bog of disputes that cannot be settled. If there is one *summum bonum,* one supreme end, what is it? To consider this problem is to place ourselves in the midst of controversies that are as acute now as they were two thousand years ago. Suppose we take a seemingly more empirical view, and say that while there is not a single end, there also are not as many as there are specific situations that require amelioration; but there are a number of such natural goods as health, wealth, honor or good name, friendship, esthetic appreciation, learning and such moral goods as justice, temperance, benevolence, etc. What or who is to decide the right of way when these ends conflict with one another, as they are sure to do? Shall we resort to the method that once brought such disrepute upon the whole business of ethics: Casuistry? Or shall we have recourse to what Bentham well called the *ipse dixit* method: the arbitrary preference of this or that person for this or that end? Or shall we be forced to arrange them all in an order of degrees from the highest good down to the least precious? Again we find ourselves in the middle of unreconciled disputes with no indication of the way out.

Meantime, the special moral perplexities where the aid of intelligence is required

go unenlightened. We cannot seek or attain health, wealth, learning, justice or kindness in general. Action is always specific, concrete, individualized, unique. And consequently judgments as to acts to be performed must be similarly specific. To say that a man seeks health or justice is only to say that he seeks to live healthily or justly. These things, like truth, are adverbial. They are modifiers of action in special cases. How to live healthily or justly is a matter which differs with every person. It varies with his past experience, his opportunities, his temperamental and acquired weaknesses and abilities. Not man in general but a particular man suffering from some particular disability aims to live healthily, and consequently health cannot mean for him exactly what it means for any other mortal. Healthy living is not something to be attained by itself apart from other ways of living. A man needs to be healthy *in* his life, not apart from it, and what does life mean except the aggregate of his pursuits and activities? A man who aims at health as a distinct end becomes a valetudinarian, or a fanatic, or a mechanical performer of exercises, or an athlete so one-sided that his pursuit of bodily development injures his heart. When the endeavor to realize a so-called end does not temper and color all other activities, life is portioned out into strips and fractions. Certain acts and times are devoted to getting healthy, others to cultivating religion, others to seeking learning, to being a good citizen, a devotee of fine art and so on. This is the only logical alternative to subordinating all aims to the accomplishment of one alone—fanaticism. This is out of fashion at present, but who can say how much of distraction and dissipation in life, and how much of its hard and narrow rigidity is the outcome of men's failure to realize that each situation has its own unique end and that the whole personality should be concerned with it? Surely, once more, what a man needs is to live healthily, and this result so affects all the activities of his life that it cannot be set up as a separate and independent good.

Nevertheless the general notions of health, disease, justice, artistic culture are of great importance: Not, however, because this or that case may be brought exhaustively under a single head and its specific traits shut out, but because generalized science provides a man as physician and artist and citizen, with questions to ask, investigations to make, and enables him to understand the meaning of what he sees. Just in the degree in which a physician is an artist in his work he uses his science, no matter how extensive and accurate, to furnish him with tools of inquiry into the individual case, and with methods of forecasting a method of dealing with it. Just in the degree in which, no matter how great his learning, he subordinates the individual case to some classification of diseases and some generic rule of treatment, he sinks to the level of the routine mechanic. His intelligence and his action become rigid, dogmatic, instead of free and flexible.

Moral goods and ends exist only when something has to be done. The fact that something has to be done proves that there are deficiencies, evils in the existent situation. This ill is just the specific ill that it is. It never is an exact duplicate of anything else. Consequently the good of the situation has to be discovered, projected and attained on the basis of the exact defect and trouble to be rectified. It cannot intelligently be injected into the situation from without. Yet it is the part of wisdom to compare different cases, to gather together the ills from which humanity suffers, and to generalize the corresponding goods into classes. Health, wealth, industry, temperance, amiability, courtesy, learning, esthetic capacity, initiative, courage, patience, enterprise, thoroughness and a multitude of other generalized ends are acknowledged as goods. But the *value* of this systematization is intellectual or analytic. Classifications *suggest* possible traits to be on the lookout for in studying a particular case; they suggest methods of action to be tried in removing the inferred causes of ill. They are tools of insight; their value is in promoting an individualized response in the individual situation.

Morals is not a catalogue of acts nor a set of rules to be applied like drugstore prescriptions or cookbook recipes. The need in morals is for specific methods of inquiry and of contrivance: Methods of inquiry to locate difficulties and evils; methods of contrivance to form plans to be used as working hypotheses in dealing with them. And the pragmatic import of the logic of individualized situations, each having its own irreplaceable good and principle, is to transfer the attention of theory from preoccupation with general conceptions to the problem of developing effective methods of inquiry.

Two ethical consequences of great moment should be remarked. The belief in fixed values has bred a division of ends into intrinsic and instrumental, of those that are really worth while in themselves and those that are of importance only as means to intrinsic goods. Indeed, it is often thought to be the very beginning of wisdom, of moral discrimination, to make this distinction. Dialectically, the distinction is interesting and seems harmless. But carried into practice it has an import that is tragic. Historically, it has been the source and justification of a hard and fast difference between ideal goods on one side and material goods on the other. At present those who would be liberal conceive intrinsic goods as esthetic in nature rather than as exclusively religious or as intellectually contemplative. But the effect is the same. So-called intrinsic goods, whether religious or esthetic, are divorced from those interests of daily life which because of their constancy and urgency form the preoccupation of the great mass. Aristotle used this distinction to declare that slaves and the working class though they are necessary *for* the state—the commonweal—are not constituents of it. That which is regarded as *merely* instrumental must approach drudgery; it cannot command either intellectual, artistic or moral attention and respect. Anything becomes *unworthy* whenever it is thought of as intrinsically lacking worth. So men of "ideal" interests have chosen for the most part the way of neglect and escape. The urgency and pressure of "lower" ends have been covered up by polite conventions. Or, they have been relegated to a baser class of mortals in order that the few might be free to attend to the goods that are really or intrinsically worth while. This withdrawal, in the name of higher ends, has left, for mankind at large and especially for energetic "practical" people, the lower activities in complete command.

No one can possibly estimate how much of the obnoxious materialism and brutality of our economic life is due to the fact that economic ends have been regarded as *merely* instrumental. Often they are recognized to be as intrinsic and final in their place as any others, then it will be seen that they are capable of idealization, and that if life is to be worth while, they must acquire ideal and intrinsic value. Esthetic, religious and other "ideal" ends are now thin and meager or else idle and luxurious because of the separation from "instrumental" or economic ends. Only in connection with the latter can they be woven into the texture of daily life and made substantial and pervasive. The vanity and irresponsibility of values that are merely final and not also in turn means to the enrichment of other occupations of life ought to be obvious. But now the doctrine of "higher" ends gives aid, comfort and support to every socially isolated and socially irresponsible scholar, specialist, esthete and religionist. It protects the vanity and irresponsibility of his calling from observation by others and by himself. The moral deficiency of the calling is transformed into a cause of admiration and gratulation.

The other generic change lies in doing away once for all with the traditional distinction between moral goods, like the virtues, and natural goods like health, economic security, art, science and the like. The point of view under discussion is not the only one which has deplored this rigid distinction and endeavored to abolish it. Some schools have even gone so far as to regard moral excellencies, qualities of character as of value only because they promote natural goods. But the experimental logic when carried into morals makes every quality that is judged to be good according as it contributes to amelioration of existing ills. And in so doing, it enforces the moral meaning of natural science. When all is said and done in criticism of present social deficiencies, one may well wonder whether the root difficulty does not lie in the separation of natural and moral science. When physics, chemistry, biology, medicine, contribute to the detection of concrete human woes and to the development of plans for remedying them and relieving the human estate, they become moral; they become part of the apparatus of moral inquiry or science. The latter then loses its peculiar flavor of the didactic and pedantic; its ultra-moralistic and hortatory tone. It loses its thinness and shrillness as well as its vagueness. It gains agencies that are efficacious. But the gain is not confined to the side of moral science. Natural science loses its divorce from humanity; it becomes itself humanistic in quality. It is something to be pursued not in a technical and specialized way for what is called truth for its own sake, but with the sense of its social bearing, its intellectual indispensableness. It is technical only in the sense that it provides the technique of social and moral engineering.

When the consciousness of science is fully impregnated with the consciousness of human value, the greatest dualism which now weighs humanity down, the split between the material, the mechanical, the scientific and the moral and ideal will be destroyed. Human forces that now waver because of this division will be unified and reinforced. As long as ends are not thought of as individualized according to specific needs and opportunities, the mind will be content with abstractions, and the adequate stimulus to the moral or social use of natural science and historical data will be lacking. But when attention is concentrated upon the diversified concretes, recourse to all intellectual materials needed to clear up the special cases will be imperative. At the same time that morals are made to focus in intelligence, things intellectual are moralized. The vexatious and wasteful conflict between naturalism and humanism is terminated.

These general considerations may be amplified. First: Inquiry, discovery take the same place in morals that they have come to occupy in sciences of nature. Validation, demonstration become experimental, a matter of consequences. Reason, always an honorific term in ethics, becomes actualized in the methods by which the needs and conditions, the obstacles and resources, of situations are scrutinized in detail, and intelligent plans of improvement are worked out. Remote and abstract generalities promote jumping at conclusions, "anticipations of nature." Bad consequences are then deplored as due to natural perversity and untoward fate. But shifting the issue to analysis of a specific situation makes inquiry obligatory and alert observation of consequences imperative. No past decision nor old principle can ever be wholly relied upon to justify a course of action. No amount of pains taken in forming a purpose in a definite case is final; the consequences of its adoption must be carefully noted, and a purpose held only as a working hypothesis until results confirm its rightness. Mistakes are no longer either mere unavoidable accidents to be mourned or moral sins to be expiated and forgiven. They are lessons in wrong methods of using intelligence and instructions as to a better course in the future. They are indications of the need of revision, development, readjustment. Ends grow, standards of judgment are improved. Man is under just as much obligation to develop his most advanced standards and ideals as to use conscientiously those which he already possesses. Moral life is protected from falling into formalism and rigid repetition. It is rendered flexible, vital, growing.

In the second place, every case where moral action is required becomes of equal moral importance and urgency with every other. If the need and deficiencies of a specific situation indicate improvement of health as the end and good, then for the situation health is the ultimate and supreme good. It is no means to something else. It is a final and intrinsic value. The same thing is true of improvement of economic status, of making a living, of attending to business and family demands—all of the things which under the sanction of fixed ends have been rendered of secondary and merely instrumental value, and so relatively base and unimportant. Anything that in a given situation is an end and good at all is of equal worth, rank and dignity with every other good of any other situation, and deserves the same intelligent attention.

We note thirdly the effect in destroying the roots of Phariseeism. We are so accustomed to thinking of this as deliberate hypocrisy that we overlook its intellectual premises. The conception which looks for the end of action within the circumstances of the actual situation will not have the same measure of judgment for all cases. When one factor of the situation is a person of trained mind and large resources, more will be expected than with a person of backward mind and uncultured experience. The absurdity of applying the same standard of moral judgment to savage peoples that is used with civilized will be apparent. No individual or group will be judged by whether they come up to or fall short of some fixed result, but by the direction in which they are moving. The bad man is the man who no matter how good he *has* been is beginning to deteriorate, to grow less good. The good man is the man who no matter how morally unworthy he *has* been is moving to become better. Such a conception makes one severe in judging himself and humane in judging others. It excludes that arrogance which always accompanies judgment based on degree of approximation to fixed ends.

In the fourth place, the process of growth, of improvement and progress, rather than the static outcome and result, becomes the significant thing. Not health as an end fixed once and for all, but the needed improvement in health—a continual process—is the end and good. The end is no longer a terminus or limit to be reached. It is the active process of transforming the existent situation. Not perfection as a final goal, but the ever-enduring process of perfecting, maturing, refining is the aim in living. Honesty, industry, temperance, justice, like health, wealth and learning, are not goods to be possessed as they would be if they expressed fixed ends to be attained. They are directions of change in the quality of experience. Growth itself is the only moral "end."

Although the bearing of this idea upon the problem of evil and the controversy between optimism and pessimism is too vast to be here discussed, it may be worth while to touch upon it superficially. The problem of evil ceases to be a theological and metaphysical one, and is perceived to be the practical problem of reducing, alleviating, as far as may be removing, the evils of life. Philosophy is no longer under obligation to find ingenious methods of proving that evils are only apparent, not real, or to elaborate schemes for explaining them away or, worse yet, for justifying them. It assumes another obligation:—That of contributing in however humble a way to methods that will assist us in discovering the causes of humanity's ills. Pessimism is a paralyzing doctrine. In declaring that the world is evil wholesale, it makes futile all efforts to discover the remedial causes of specific evils and thereby destroys at the root every attempt to make the world better and happier. Wholesale optimism, which has been the consequence of the attempt to explain evil away, is, however, equally an incubus.

After all, the optimism that says that the world is already the best possible of all worlds might be regarded as the most cynical of pessimisms. If this is the best possible, what would a world which was fundamentally bad be like? Meliorism is the belief that the specific conditions which exist at one moment, be they comparatively bad or comparatively good, in any event may be bettered. It encourages intelligence to study the positive means of good and the obstructions to their realization, and to put forth endeavor for the improvement of conditions. It arouses confidence and a reasonable hopefulness as optimism does not. For the latter in declaring that good is already realized in ultimate reality tends to make us gloss over the evils that concretely exist. It becomes too readily the creed of those who live at ease, in comfort, of those who have been successful in obtaining this world's rewards. Too readily optimism makes the men who hold it callous and blind to the sufferings of the less fortunate, or ready to find the cause of troubles of others in their personal viciousness. It thus cooperates with pessimism, in spite of the extreme nominal differences between the two, in benumbing sympathetic insight and intelligent effort in reform. It beckons men away from the world of relativity and change into the calm of the absolute and eternal.

The import of many of these changes in moral attitudes focuses in the idea of happiness. Happiness has often been made the object of the moralists' contempt. Yet the most ascetic moralist has usually restored the idea of happiness under some other name, such as bliss. Goodness without happiness, valor and virtue without satisfaction, ends without conscious enjoyment—these things are as intolerable practically as they are self-contradictory in conception. Happiness is not, however, a bare possession; it is not a fixed attainment. Such a happiness is either the unworthy selfishness which moralists have so bitterly condemned, or it is, even if labeled bliss, an insipid tedium, a millennium of ease in relief from all struggle and labor. It could satisfy only the most delicate of mollycoddles. Happiness is found only in success; but success means succeeding, getting forward, moving in advance. It is an active process, not a passive outcome. Accordingly it includes the overcoming of obstacles, the elimination of sources of defect and ill. Esthetic sensitiveness and enjoyment are a large constituent in any worthy happiness. But the esthetic appreciation which is totally separated from renewal of spirit, from recreation of mind and purification of emotion is a weak and sickly thing, destined to speedy death from starvation. That the renewal and re-creation come unconsciously, not by set intention, but makes them the more genuine.

Upon the whole, utilitarianism has marked the best in the transition from the classic theory of ends and goods to that which is now possible. It had definite merits. It insisted upon getting away from vague generalities, and down to the specific and concrete. It subordinated law to human achievement instead of subordinating humanity to external law. It taught that institutions are made for man and not man for institutions; it actively promoted all issues of reform. It made moral good natural, humane, in touch with the natural goods of life. It opposed unearthly and otherworldly morality. Above all, it acclimatized in human imagination the idea of social welfare as a supreme test. But it was still profoundly affected in fundamental points by old ways of thinking. It never questioned the idea of a fixed, final and supreme end. It only questioned the current notions as to the nature of this end; and then inserted pleasure and the greatest possible aggregate of pleasures in the position of the fixed end.

Such a point of view treats concrete activities and specific interests not as worth while in themselves, or as constituents of happiness, but as mere external means to getting pleasures. The upholders of the old tradition could therefore easily accuse utilitarianism of making not only virtue but art, poetry, religion and the state into mere servile means of attaining sensuous enjoyment. Since pleasure was an outcome, a result valuable on its own account independently of the active processes that achieve it, happiness was a thing to be possessed and held onto. The acquisitive instincts of man were exaggerated at the expense of

the creative. Production was of importance not because of the intrinsic worth of invention and reshaping the world, but because its external results feed pleasure. Like every theory that sets up fixed and final aims, in making the end passive and possessive, it made all active operations *mere* tools. Labor was an unavoidable evil to be minimized. Security in possession was the chief thing practically. Material comfort and ease was magnified in contrast with the pains and risk of experimental creation. . . . The idea of a fixed and single end lying beyond the diversity of human needs and acts rendered utilitarianism incapable of being an adequate representative of the modern spirit. It has to be reconstructed through emancipation from its inherited elements.

If a few words are added upon the topic of education, it is only for the sake of suggesting that the educative process is all one with the moral process, since the latter is a continuous passage of experience from worse to better. Education has been traditionally thought of as preparation: as learning, acquiring certain things because they will later be useful. The end is remote, and education is getting ready, is a preliminary to something more important to happen later on. Childhood is only a preparation for adult life, and adult life for another life. Always the future, not the present, has been the significant thing in education: acquisition of knowledge and skill for future use and enjoyment; formation of habits required later in life in business, good citizenship and pursuit of science. Education is thought of also as something needed by some human beings merely because of their dependence upon others. We are born ignorant, unversed, unskilled, immature, and consequently in a state of social dependence. Instruction, training, moral discipline are processes by which the mature, the adult, gradually raise the helpless to the point where they can look out for themselves. The business of childhood is to grow into the independence of adulthood by means of the guidance of those who have already attained it. Thus the process of education as the main business of life ends when the young have arrived at emancipation from social dependence.

These two ideas, generally assumed but rarely explicitly reasoned out, contravene the conception that growing, or the continuous reconstruction of experience, is the only end. If at whatever period we choose to take a person, he is still in process of growth, then education is not, save as a by-product, a preparation for something coming later. Getting from the present the degree and kind of growth there is in it is education. This is a constant function, independent of age. The best thing that can be said about any special process of education, like that of the formal school period, is that it renders its subject capable of further education: more sensitive to conditions of growth and more able to take advantage of them. Acquisition of skill, possession of knowledge, attainment of culture are not ends: they are marks of growth and means to its continuing.

The contrast usually assumed between the period of education as one of social dependence and of maturity as one of social independence does harm. We repeat over and over that man is a social animal, and then confine the significance of this statement to the sphere in which sociality usually seems least evident, politics. The heart of the sociality of man is in education. The idea of education as preparation and of adulthood as a fixed limit of growth are two sides of the same obnoxious untruth. If the moral business of the adult as well as the young is a growing and developing experience, then the instruction that comes from social dependencies and interdependencies is as important for the adult as for the child. Moral independence for the adult means arrest of growth, isolation means induration. We exaggerate the intellectual dependence of childhood so that children are too much kept in leading strings, and then we exaggerate the independence of adult life from intimacy of contact and communication with others. When the identity of the moral process with the processes of specific growth is realized, the more conscious and formal education of childhood will be seen to be the most economical and efficient means of social advance and reorganization, and it will also be evident that the test of all the institutions of adult life is their effect in furthering continued education. Government, business, art, religion, all social institutions have a meaning, a purpose. That purpose is to set free and to develop the capacities of human individuals without respect to race, sex, class or economic status. And this is all one with saying that the test of their value is the extent to which they educate every individual into the full stature of his possibility. Democracy has many meanings, but if it has a moral meaning, it is found in resolving that the supreme test of all political institutions and industrial arrangements shall be the contribution they make to the all-around growth of every member of society.

COMMENT

Main Emphases in Dewey's Ethics

John Dewey shifts the emphasis in ethical theory from *value* to *valuation,* being more concerned with the process of appraisal than with the qualities appraised. Valuation, he maintains, should be in accordance with the methods of experimental logic. No one has insisted more strenuously than Dewey on scientific study of the actual needs of human beings and the concrete, experimental means of satisfying these needs. "Not all who say Ideals, Ideals," he remarks, "shall enter into the kingdom of the ideal, but those who know and respect the roads that conduct to the kingdom."[1] His main contribution to ethical theory has been to explore the roads rather than to describe the destination. Indeed, he does not believe in a fixed destination but rather in a never-ending and exploratory journey. Since conditions are constantly changing, rules cannot be made nor goals ascertained in advance. Living well is an experiment, and there should be flexible reappraisal and reorientation as the experiment progresses.

Valuation is stimulated by tension, conflict, and unsatisfactoriness; and successful valuation points to ways of resolving the tensions and releasing the pent-up energies. In regard to ethics, as in pragmatist theory in general, inquiry is conceived to be instrumentalist—a tool for controlling experience. Values are not passively "given," without intelligent effort, but are actively constructed. There is a fundamental difference between what is merely "liked" and what is genuinely "likable," merely "desired" and really "desirable," merely "admired" and truly "admirable," merely "satisfying" and dependably "satisfactory." Only the latter are *values* in the sense that they have been *validated*. They can be achieved only if we know the conditions and consequences of our desires, affections, and enjoyments and if we learn intelligently to coordinate and control them. The idea of a *good* should be treated as a hypothesis, to be tested like any other.

In the testing, we must see ends and means as "continuous"—the ends as means to future satisfactions, and the means as not merely instrumentally but also intrinsically valuable or disvaluable. Immanuel Kant, for example, was fundamentally mistaken in exalting virtue as an end apart from being a means, for the very qualities that make it good as end make it good as means also. Dewey believed that experience is most satisfactory when the instrumental and the consummatory are closely linked—when action and contemplation fructify each other. We should neither subordinate growth and spontaneity to static contemplation nor concentrate merely on activity to the neglect of rational goals. Life should combine both repose and stimulation—the sense of achievement and the sense of adventure. In thus insisting on "the continuity of means and ends," Dewey is exhibiting the antidualistic tendency that pervades his entire philosophy. He protests strongly against the inveterate tendency to think in terms of hard-and-fast distinctions between, for example, facts and values, experience and nature, freedom and organization, learning and doing; and he seeks to resolve all such sharp dualisms by insisting on the continuity and interpenetration of "opposites." Values are to be studied as natural facts, and facts are to be evaluated; experience is to be regarded as inseparable from nature, and nature is to be interpreted in terms of experience; freedom is to be secured by organization, and organization is to be liberalized by freedom; learning is to be achieved by doing, and doing is to be directed by learning. His whole philosophy can thus be regarded as a "revolt against dualism." In this respect he has much in common with Alfred Whitehead.

---

[1] "The Pragmatic Acquiescence," New Republic, Vol. 49 (Jan. 5, 1927), p. 189.

There is no sense, according to Dewey, in talking about *the* end of life—as if there were a single end or final consummation. Life is simply an ongoing process, with a plurality of ends that function also as means. His stress is on the dynamic rather than the static, the specific rather than the general, the concrete and plural rather than the abstract and monistic. "Faith in the varied possibilities of diversified experience," he declares, "is attended with the joy of constant discovery and constant growing."[2] Growth provides its own sufficient criterion, and it is a mistake to seek anything more fixed and constant.

On the Distinction between Science, Technology, and Morals

According to some critics, Dewey's ethical philosophy is strong in method but weak in vision; strong in delineating the variety of experience but weak in revealing the unity of life; strong in its awareness of novelty but weak in its blindness to universal and enduring values; strong in opposing static absolutism but weak in yielding to mercurial relativism; strong in realizing the need for growth but weak in criticizing the direction of growth; strong in relating science, technology, and morals, but weak in failing to distinguish them. Whether this estimate is justified we shall leave to the readers of this book to decide. The last point of criticism, however, calls for more detailed comment.

The heart of Dewey's ethical philosophy is the attempt to link science, technology, and morals, and it is therefore important to consider their interrelations. We can begin by noting three realms of discourse, as illustrated by the following sentences:

> "That is a strong poison."
> "You ought to use a strong poison" (said to a would-be murderer)
> "You ought not to murder."

The first sentence is *descriptive,* it simply indicates a matter of fact, with no commendation or disparagement. The second sentence is *evaluative,* but in what Kant would call a *hypothetical* rather than a categorical sense. The "ought" here simply means that *if* you want to murder this man, you ought to use a poison strong enough to accomplish your purpose. It does not express a *duty* to use a strong poison. The third sentence is also *evaluative,* but in what Kant would call a *categorical* rather than a hypothetical sense. It expresses a duty to refrain from murdering. Sentences of the first type are characteristic of pure science; sentences of the second type are characteristic of technology; and sentences of the third type are characteristic of morals. (To accept these distinctions, we would not have to agree with Kant's formulas for determining categorical imperatives. If we were utilitarians, for example, our formula might read, "So act that in every case there shall be no better results." If our duty is to achieve the best results possible, it is still our *duty*.)

---

[2] "What I Believe," Forum (March 1930), p. 179.

The charge that can be made against Dewey is that he has failed to distinguish clearly between science, technology, and morals. In his laudable effort to relate them, he has obscured their differences. We shall not discuss the adequacy of his distinction between pure science and technology—this question is relevant to the issues presented in Chapter 5 and might well be debated in that connection. At present, we are concerned only with the relation between morals and science and between morals and technology.

1. *Morals and science.* "Experience," Dewey notes, "actually presents esthetic and moral traits."[3] These stand on "the same level" as the redness of a rose or the absent-mindedness of a professor—they are matters of fact, which can be studied like any other. There is a valid point here that should not be denied. Human beings do exhibit esthetic and moral traits and experience satisfactions and enjoyments. These can be described like any other natural facts. Moral theories that try to exclude consideration of human nature and its environment are hopelessly unrealistic. If this is all that Dewey means, we need not disagree with him. However, it is still the case that a psychologist bent on *describing* human nature has a different task than the moralist bent on *evaluating* moral alternatives. Such words as *good, right, ought,* as used by the moralist, are nouns and adjectives of commendation, not of description. How can we make the leap from description to evaluation? How can we get, for example, from *desired* to *ethically desirable?* The latter does not mean *psychologically* desirable, in the sense that someone *can* desire it. It means *worth* desiring—desiring in the sense that it *ought* to be desired. A naturalistic theory of ethics, such as that of Dewey, seems to overlook the nondescriptive, purely ethical character of the moral *ought.*

Dewey could reply that *desirable* means that which one desires *after* one has seen all its conditions and consequences. However, this does not solve the problem because it is perfectly possible for a malevolent person to desire something that is morally evil after that person has thoroughly understood its connections with other things. Dewey could also reply that the ethically desirable is that which is desired by a fair and impartial judge. This definition is circular, however; it amounts to saying that something *is* ethically desirable (good or right) when it is approved by somebody who approves only what *is* ethically desirable. The only solution, Dewey's critics would say, is to admit a clear-cut distinction between facts and norms, morals and science—and this he fails to do. So runs the criticism that could be directed against Dewey. The reader should weigh this criticism carefully and decide whether it is valid.

2. *Morals and technology.* Dewey often appears to be identifying morality with technology, or to be thinking of it as a kind of supertechnology. There would seem to be much to support this point of view. The language of technological discourse, as we have already noted, is distinguished by normative terms, such as *ought* or *ought not,* or by imperatives, such as *do this* or *do not do that.* Such lan-

---

[3] *Experience and Nature* (Chicago: Open Court, 1929), p. 2.

guage is intended to direct choice among alternative possibilities. There are different kinds of norms and normative statements belonging to different levels of technological discourse. Many technological imperatives are mere counsels of skill, as when a carpenter says to his helper, "You ought to sharpen the teeth of that saw." He means, "*If* you want to use your saw effectively for the purpose at hand, you ought to sharpen its teeth." At a somewhat higher and more general level, the norms have a quasi-ethical or esthetic character, as in the case of the artistic norm of "beauty," the legal norm of "justice," the medical norm of "health," and the economic norm of "prosperity." Finally, there are highest-level norms that pertain to a total economy of values. They are invoked when there is a conflict between low-level *oughts,* and may be thought of as decidedly ethical. Morality will then be conceived as a technology of technologies, the function of which is to coordinate all the various techniques that a society has at its disposal.

This view of morality is by no means new. Aristotle had a similar conception of the art of arts, the technology of technologies. In the opening paragraphs of his *Ethics,* as we have seen, he pointed out that the arts are to be distinguished by the ends that they serve. Health is the aim of medicine, vessels of shipbuilding, victory of military strategy, and wealth of economics. The ends and the corresponding arts form a hierarchy, some being subservient to others. Bridle-making is subservient to horsemanship, horsemanship to strategy, and so on. Finally we arrive at some ultimate end and the art corresponding to it. This is the art of arts— the art whose function it is to harmonize and control all the other arts and whose end, therefore, is not this or that particular good but the good for humanity. Aristotle calls this highest art the art of politics, of which ethics, since it defines the ultimate good, is an integral part. Here the word *art* is being used in the same sense as that which we intend by *technology,* and Aristotle's conception of politics as an "art of arts" is analogous to the conception of morality as a "technology of technologies."

Up to a point, this way of looking at morality seems sound, but it is important to recognize that morality, as a kind of supreme technology, is fundamentally different from ordinary technology—so different, indeed, that we should perhaps not call it a technology at all. An ordinary technological norm is an *instrument* of a decision maker, not a *control;* and therefore, to interpret moral norms as ordinary technological norms would imply that technology needs no control or is somehow self-regulating. Such a view is exceedingly mischievous, especially in this age of nuclear fission. Consequently, there must be norms controlling the decision maker rather than norms that are merely his or her instruments. The right use of instrumental norms presupposes some noninstrumental criteria.

In the case of ordinary technology, in other words, it is not the right motivation of the agent that is in question but the skill to be used in carrying out a motivation that is taken for granted. In the case of morality, on the other hand, it is precisely the motivation that is most in question, and the problem of finding the right means is secondary. The norms of ordinary technology usually prescribe how to perform some action. The moral question, on the other hand, is not simply *how* to do something but *what* to do.

Here, then, is a possible ground for criticism. Pragmatists such as Dewey, the critics might say, are prone to exaggerate the similarity between ordinary technology and morality. They are so intent on the fluidity and instrumentality of norms that they neglect or even deny the question of *ultimate* motivation. They are inclined to take "the problematic situation" as it arises and to interpret right action as "problem solving" within the context of this situation. The problem, as they see it, is "solved" when the diverse competing interests in the situation are brought into some kind of moving equilibrium, which leads to new "problematic situations" and thus to new and revised norms. So understood, morality is closely akin to ordinary technology. However, morality cannot afford merely to implement and reconcile interests that are taken for granted. Its task is more radical. It criticizes interests in light of ultimate norms; and in exercising this sort of stubborn and very radical criticism, it differentiates itself from technology.

The question that we have posed is whether Dewey has sufficiently realized this fact, and whether he has also realized the clear-cut difference between morality (or ethics, as its theoretical basis) and natural science.

This question even arises when we return to the case of Noel David Earley's decision to end his life, since whatever means he chose to use in some way would involve technology in the more common, scientific sense of the word. Dewey would, of course, stress that Earley may have been employing "scientific reasoning" in coming to his decision, although he may well have left certain important factors out of his analysis. Was Earley's approach to his situation a good example of the pragmatist "reconstruction" of values perspective? Are there any final goals or axioms at work here, in the sense that Aristotle and Kant would advocate?

20

THE WAY OF FEMINISM

ANNETTE C. BAIER (1929–   )

Annette Baier is professor of philosophy at the University of Pittsburgh. In the following essay, she is reflecting on the implications of Carol Gilligan's book, *In a Different Voice,* for the development of moral theory. In this book, Gilligan provides empirical evidence and psychological analysis that strongly suggest that the respective ways young girls and boys are enculturated to think about moral issues differ markedly. Boys tend to emphasize *reciprocity,* focusing on such concepts as equality, justice, rights, impartiality, logical objectivity, and so on. Girls, on the other hand, tend to stress *responsiveness,* focused in such notions as care, love, trust, compassion, mercy, and so on. These factors seem to indicate quite different modes of moral reasoning.

Baier takes as her point of departure the simple fact that most, if not all, significant moral theorists have been men. So, as a philosopher herself, she begins to develop an ethical theory rooted in the "different voice" expressed in the responsiveness emphasis embodied in the female approach to ethical questions and dilemmas. Here, then, is the seedplot for a feminist moral theory.

WHAT DO WOMEN WANT IN A MORAL THEORY?

When I finished reading Carol Gilligan's *In a Different Voice,*[1] I asked myself the obvious question for a philosopher reader, namely what differences one should expect in the moral philosophy done by women, supposing Gilligan's sample of women representative, and supposing her analysis of their moral attitudes and moral development to be correct. Should one expect them to want to produce moral theories, and if so, what sort of moral theories? How will any moral theories they produce differ from those produced by men?

Obviously one does not have to make this an entirely *a priori* and hypothetical question. One can look and see what sort of contributions women have made to

Annette C. Baier, "What Do Women Want in a Moral Theory?" *Noûs.* vol. 19 (March, 1985), 53–63. Copyright © 1985 by *Noûs* Publications, Indiana University. Reprinted by permission of the author and Blackwell Publishers.

[1] Cambridge, Mass.: Harvard University Press, 1982.

419

moral philosophy. Such a look confirms, I think, Gilligan's findings. What one finds is a bit different in tone and approach from the standard sort of moral philosophy as done by men following in the footsteps of the great moral philosophers (all men). Generalizations are extremely rash, but when I think of Philippa Foot's work on the moral virtues, of Elizabeth Anscombe's work on intention and on modern moral philosophy, of Iris Murdoch's philosophical writings, of Ruth Barcan Marcus' work on moral dilemmas, of the work of the radical feminist moral philosophers who are not content with orthodox Marxist lines of thought, of Jenny Teichman's book on illegitimacy, of Susan Wolf's recent articles, of Claudia Card's essay on mercy, Sabina Lovilbond's recent book, Gabriele Taylor's work on pride, love and on integrity, Cora Diamond's and Mary Midgeley's work on our attitude to animals, Sissela Bok's work on lying and on secrecy, Virginia Held's work, the work of Alison Jaggar, Marilyn Frye, and many others, I seem to hear a different voice from the standard moral philosophers' voice. I hear the voice Gilligan heard, made reflective and philosophical. What women want in moral philosophy is what they are providing. And what they are providing seems to me to confirm Gilligan's theses about women. One has to be careful here, of course, for not all important contributions to moral philosophy by women fall easily into the Gilligan stereotype, nor its philosophical extension. Nor has it been only women who recently have

been proclaiming discontent with the standard approach in moral philosophy, and trying new approaches. Michael Stocker, Alasdair MacIntyre, Ian Hacking when he assesses the game theoretic approach to morality,[2] all should be given the status of honorary women, if we accept the hypothesis that there are some moral insights which for whatever reason women seem to attain more easily or more reliably than men do. Still, exceptions confirm the rule, so I shall proceed undaunted by these important exceptions to my generalizations.

If Hacking is right, preoccupation with prisoner's and prisoners' dilemma is a big boys' game, and a pretty silly one too. It is, I think, significant that women have not rushed into the field of game-theoretic moral philosophy, and that those who have dared enter that male locker room have said distinctive things there. Edna Ullman Margalit's book *The Emergence of Norms*[3] put prisoners' dilemma in its limited moral place. Supposing that at least part of the explanation for the relatively few women in this field is disinclination rather than disability, one might ask if this disinclination also extends to a disinclination for the construction of moral theories. For although we find out what sort of moral philosophy women want by looking to see what they have provided, if we do that for moral theory, the answer we get seems to be "none." For none of the contributions to moral philosophy by women really count as moral theories, nor are seen as such by their authors.

---

[2] Ian Hacking "Winner Takes Less," a review of *The Evolution of Cooperation* by Robert Axelrod, *New York Review of Books*, June 28, 1984.

The "game theoretic" approach to morality compares situations requiring moral decisions to games in which individuals try to maximize their self-interest. The most-discussed example is the "prisoners' dilemma," which is mentioned in the following paragraph. In this imaginary dilemma, two prisoners guilty of a crime are interrogated separately. Both prisoners know (1) that if *neither*

confesses, they will both get rather light sentences; (2) that if one confesses and the other does not, the one who confesses will fare best (by turning state's evidence) and the one who does not will fare worst (by receiving a vindictive sentence); and (3) that if they *both* confess, they will both avoid the worst but neither will attain the best. Each prisoner faces the dilemma of whether to confess or not.

[3] Oxford, England: Clarendon Press, 1977.

Is it that reflective women, when they become philosophers, want to do without moral theory, want no part in the construction of such theories? To conclude this at this early stage, when we have only a few generations of women moral philosophers to judge from, would be rash indeed. The term "theory" can be used in wider and narrower ways, and in its widest sense a moral theory is simply an internally consistent fairly comprehensive account of what morality is and when and why it merits our acceptance and support. In that wide sense, a moral theory is something it would take a sceptic, or one who believes that our intellectual vision is necessarily blurred or distorted when we let it try to take in too much, to be an anti-theorist. Even if there were some truth in the latter claim, one might compatibly with it still hope to build up a coherent total account by a mosaic method, assembling a lot of smaller scale works until one had built up a complete account—say taking the virtues or purported virtues one by one until one had a more or less complete account. But would that sort of comprehensiveness in one's moral philosophy entitle one to call the finished work a moral theory? If it does, then many women moral philosophers today can be seen as engaged in moral theory construction. In the weakest sense of "theory," namely coherent near-comprehensive account, then there are plenty incomplete theories to be found in the works of women moral philosophers. And in *that* sense of theory, most of what are recognized as the current moral theories are also incomplete, since they do not purport to be yet really comprehensive. Wrongs to animals and wrongful destruction of our physical environment are put to one side by Rawls,[4] and in most "liberal" theories there are only hand waves concerning our proper attitude to our children,

to the ill, to our relatives, friends and lovers.

Is comprehensiveness too much to ask of a moral theory? The paradigm examples of moral theories—those that are called by their authors "moral theories," are distinguished not by the comprehensiveness of their internally coherent account, but by the *sort* of coherence which is aimed at over a fairly broad area. Their method is not the mosaic method, but the broad brush-stroke method. Moral theories, as we know them, are, to change the art form, vaults rather than walls—they are not built by assembling painstakingly made brick after brick. In this sense of theory, namely fairly tightly systematic account of a fairly large area of morality, with a key stone supporting all the rest, women moral philosophers have not yet, to my knowledge, produced moral theories, nor claimed that they have.

Leaving to one side the question of what good purpose (other than good clean intellectual fun) is served by such moral theories, and supposing for the sake of argument that women can, if they wish, systematize as well as the next man, and if need be systematize in a mathematical fashion as well as the next mathematically minded moral philosopher, then what key concept, or guiding *motif*, might hold together the structure of a moral theory hypothetically produced by a reflective woman, Gilligan-style, who has taken up moral theorizing as a calling? What would be a suitable central question, principle, or concept, to structure a moral theory which might accommodate those moral insights women tend to have more readily than men, and to answer those moral questions which, it seems, worry women more than men? I hypothesized that the women's theory, expressive mainly of women's insights and concerns, would be an ethics of love, and this hypothesis seems to be Gilligan's too, since she has gone on from *In a Different Voice* to write about the limitations of Freud's under-

---

[4] John Rawls, *A Theory of Justice* (Cambridge, Mass.: Harvard University Press, 1971).

standing of love as women know it.[5] But presumably women theorists will be like enough to men to want their moral theory to be acceptable to all, so acceptable both to reflective women and to reflective men. Like any good theory, it will need not to ignore the partial truth of previous theories. So it must accommodate both the insights men have more easily than women, and those women have more easily than men. It should swallow up its predecessor theories. Women moral theorists, if any, will have this very great advantage over the men whose theories theirs supplant, that they can stand on the shoulders of men moral theorists, as no man has yet been able to stand on the shoulders of any woman moral theorist. There can be advantages, as well as handicaps, in being latecomers. So women theorists will need to connect their ethics of love with what has been the men theorists' preoccupation, namely obligation.

The great and influential moral theorists have in the modern era taken *obligation* as the key and the problematic concept, and have asked what justifies treating a person as morally bound or obliged to do a particular thing. Since to be bound is to be unfree, by making obligation central one at the same time makes central the question of the justification of coercion, of forcing or trying to force someone to act in a particular way. The concept of obligation as justified limitation of freedom does just what one wants a good theoretical concept to do—to divide up the field (as one looks at different ways one's freedom may be limited, freedom in different spheres, different sorts and versions and levels of justification) and at the same time hold the subfields together. There must in a theory be some generalization and some speciation or diversification, and a good rich key concept guides one

both in recognizing the diversity and in recognizing the unity in it. The concept of obligation has served this function very well for the area of morality it covers, and so we have some fine theories about that area. But as Aristotelians and Christians, as well as women, know, there is a lot of morality *not* covered by that concept, a lot of very great importance even for the area where there are obligations.

This[6] is fairly easy to see if we look at what lies behind the perceived obligation to keep promises. Unless there is some good moral reason why someone should assume the responsibility of rearing a child to be *capable* of taking promises seriously, once she understands what a promise is, the obligation to obey promises will not effectively tie her, and any force applied to punish her when she breaks promises or makes fraudulent ones will be of questionable justice. Is there an *obligation* on someone to make the child into a morally competent promisor? If so, on whom? Who have failed in their obligations when, say, war orphans who grew up without parental love or any other love arrive at legal adulthood very willing to be untrue to their word? Who failed in what obligation in all those less extreme cases of attempted but unsuccessful moral education? The parents who didn't produce promise-keeping offspring? Those who failed to educate the parents in how to educate their children (whoever it might be who might plausibly be thought to have the responsibility for training parents to fulfill their obligations)? The liberal version of our basic moral obligations tends to be fairly

---

[5] "The Conquistador and the Dark Continent: Reflections on the Psychology of Love," *Daedalus*, Summer 1994.

[6] This paragraph and the following one were not included in the version of the article published in *Noûs* (vol. 19, March 1985, pp. 53–63). They were supplied by Professor Baier for use in this anthology and are reprinted with her kind permission. These two paragraphs form part of a longer section omitted from the *Noûs* version. The complete version of the article will appear in Professor Baier's forthcoming collection, *Moral Prejudices*.

silent on who has what obligations to new members of the moral community, and it would throw most theories of the justification of obligations into some confusion if the obligation to lovingly rear one's children were added to the list of obligations. Such evidence as we have about the conditions in which children do successfully "learn" the morality of the community of which they are members suggests that we cannot substitute "conscientiously" for "lovingly" in this hypothetical extra needed obligation. But an obli-gation to love, in the strong sense needed, would be an embarrassment to the theorist, given most accepted versions of "ought implies can."

It is hard to make fair generalizations here, so I shall content myself with indicating how this charge I am making against the current men's moral theories, that their version of the justified list of obligations does not ensure the proper care of the young, so does nothing to ensure the stability of the morality in question over several generations, can be made against what I regard as the best of the men's recent theories, namely John Rawls' theory of justice. One of the great strengths of Rawls' theory is the careful attention given to the question of how just institutions produce the conditions for their continued support, across generations, and in particular of how the sense of justice will arise in children, once there are minimally just institutions structuring the social world into which they are born. Rawls, more than most moral theorists, has attended to the question of the stability of his just society, given what we know about child development. But Rawls' sensitive account of the conditions for the development of that sense of justice needed for the maintenance of his version of a just society takes it for granted that there will be loving parents rearing the children in whom the sense of justice is to develop. "The parents, we may suppose, love the child, and in time the child comes to love and trust the parents." Why may we suppose this? Not because compliance with Rawls' version of our obligations and duties

will ensure it. Rawls' theory, like so many other theories of obligation, in the end must take out a loan not only on the natural duty of parents to care for children (which he will have no trouble including), but on the natural *virtue* of parental love (or even a loan on the maternal instinct?). The virtue of being a *loving* parent must supplement the natural duties and the obligations of justice, if the just society is to last beyond the first generation....

Granted that the men's theories of obligation need supplementation, to have much chance of integrity and coherence, and that the women's hypothetical theories will want to cover obligation as well as love, then what concept brings them together? My tentative answer is—the concept of appropriate trust, oddly neglected in moral theory. This concept also nicely mediates between reason and feeling, those tired old candidates for moral authority, since to trust is neither quite to believe something about the trusted, nor necessarily to feel any emotion towards them—but to have a belief-informed and action-influencing attitude. To make it plausible that the neglected concept of appropriate trust is a good one for the enlightened moral theorist to make central, I need to show, or begin to show, how it could include obligation, indeed shed light on obligations and their justification, as well as include love and the other moral concerns of Gilligan's women, and many of the topics women moral philosophers have chosen to address, mosaic fashion. I would also need to show that it could connect all of these in a way which holds out promise both of synthesis and of comprehensive moral coverage. A moral theory which looked at the conditions for proper trust of all the various sorts we show, and at what sorts of reasons justify inviting such trust, giving it, and meeting it, would, I believe, not have to avoid turning its gaze on the conditions for the survival of the practices it endorses, so it could avoid that unpleasant choice many current liberal theories seem to have—

between incoherence and bad faith. I do not pretend that we will easily agree once we raise the questions I think we should raise, but at least we may have a language adequate to the expression of both men's and women's moral viewpoints.

My trust in the concept of trust is based in part on my own attempts to restate and consider what was right and what wrong with men's theories, especially Hume's,[7] which I consider the best of the lot. There I found myself reconstructing his account of the artifices of justice as an account of the progressive enlargement of a climate of trust, and found that a helpful way to see it. It has some textual basis, but is nevertheless a reconstruction, and one I found, immodestly, an improvement. So it is because I have tried the concept, and explored its dimensions a bit—the variety of goods we may trust others not to take from us, the variety of sort of security or insurance we have when we do, the sorts of defenses or potential defenses we lay down when we trust, the various conditions for reasonable trust of various types—that I am hopeful about its power as a theoretical not just an exegetical tool. I also found myself needing to use it, when I made a brief rash attempt at that women's topic, caring (invited in by a man philosopher,[8] I should say). That it does generalize some central moral features both of the recognition of binding obligations and moral virtues, and of loving, as well as of other important relations between persons, such as teacher-pupil, confider-confidante, worker to co-worker in the same cause, professional to client, I am reasonably sure.

Indeed it is fairly obvious that love, the main moral phenomenon women want attended to, involves trust, so I anticipate little quarrel when I claim that, if we had a moral theory spelling out the conditions for appropriate trust and distrust, that would include a morality of love in all its variants—parental love, love of children for their parents, love of family members, love of friends, of lovers in the strict sense, of co-workers, of one's country, and its figureheads, of exemplary heroines and heros, of goddesses and gods.

Love and loyalty demand maximal trust of one sort, and maximal trustworthiness, and in investigating the conditions for maximal trust and maximal risk we must think about the ethics of love. More controversial may be my claim that the ethics of obligation will also be covered. I see it as covered since to recognize a set of obligations is to trust some group of persons to install them, to demand that they be met, possibly to levy sanctions if they are not, and this is to trust persons with very significant coercive power over others. Less coercive but still significant power is possessed by those shaping our conception of the virtues, and expecting us to display them, approving when we do, disapproving and perhaps shunning us when we do not. Such coercive and manipulative power over others requires justification, and is justified only if we have reason to trust those who have it to use it properly and to use the discretion which is always given when trust is given in a way which serves the purpose of the whole system of moral control, and not merely self-serving or morally improper purposes. Since the question of the justification of coercion becomes, at least in part, the question of the wisdom of trusting the coercers to do their job properly, the morality of obligation, in as far as it reduces to the morality of coercion, is covered by the morality of proper trust. Other forms of trust may also be involved, but trusting enforcers with the use of force is the most problematic form of trust involved.

---

[7] David Hume (1711–1776) was a Scottish philosopher and historian.

[8] "Caring About Caring," a response to Harry Frankfurt's "What We Care About," both in *Matters of the Mind, Synthese* 52 (November 1982): 257–290.

Baier's article is reprinted in her collection *Postures of the Mind* (Minneapolis: University of Minnesota Press, 1985).

The coercers and manipulators are, to some extent, all of us, so to ask what our obligations are and what virtues we should exhibit is to ask what it is reasonable to trust us to demand, expect, and contrive to get, from one another. It becomes, in part, a question of what powers we can in reason trust ourselves to exercise properly. But self-trust is a dubious or limit case of trust, so I prefer to postpone the examination of the concept of proper self-trust at least until proper trust of others is more clearly understood. Nor do we distort matters too much if we concentrate on those cases where moral sanctions and moral pressure and moral manipulation is not self applied but applied to others, particularly by older persons to younger persons. Most moral pressuring that has any effects goes on in childhood and early youth. Moral sanctions may continue to be applied, formally and informally, to adults, but unless the criminal courts apply them it is easy enough for adults to ignore them, to brush them aside. It is not difficult to become a sensible knave, and to harden one's heart so that one is insensible to the moral condemnation of one's victims and those who sympathize with them. Only if the pressures applied in the morally formative stage have given one a heart that rebels against the thought of such ruthless independence of what others think will one see any reason *not* to ignore moral condemnation, not to treat it as mere powerless words and breath. Condemning sensible knaves is as much a waste of breath as arguing with them—all we can sensibly do is to try to protect children against their influence, and ourselves against their knavery. Adding to the criminal law will not be the way to do the latter, since such moves will merely challenge sensible knaves to find new knavish exceptions and loopholes, not protect us from sensible knavery. Sensible knaves are precisely those who exploit us without breaking the law. So the whole question of when moral pressure of various sorts, formative, reformative, and punitive, ought to be brought to bear by whom is subsumed under the question of whom to trust when and with what, and for what good reasons.

In concentrating on obligations, rather than virtues, modern moral theorists have chosen to look at the cases where more trust is placed in enforcers of obligations than is placed in ordinary moral agents, the bearers of the obligations. In taking, as contractarians do, contractual obligations as the model of obligations, they concentrate on a case where the very minimal trust is put in the obligated person, and considerable punitive power entrusted to the one to whom the obligation is owed (I assume here that Hume is right in saying that when we promise or contract, we formally subject ourselves to the penalty, in case of failure, of never being trusted as a promisor again). This is an interesting case of the allocation of trust of various sorts, but it surely distorts our moral vision to suppose that *all* obligations, let alone all morally pressured expectations we impose on others, conform to that abnormally coercive model. It takes very special conditions for it to be safe to trust persons to inflict penalties on other persons, conditions in which either we can trust the penalizers to have the virtues necessary to penalize wisely and fairly, or else we can rely on effective threats to keep unvirtuous penalizers from abusing their power—that is to say, rely on others to coerce the first coercers into proper behaviour. But that reliance too will either be trust, or will have to rely on threats from coercers of the coercers of coercers, and so on. Morality on this model becomes a nasty, if intellectually intriguing, game of mutual mutually corrective threats. The central question of who should deprive whom of what freedom soon becomes the question of whose anger should be dreaded by whom (the theory of obligation) supplemented perhaps by an afterthought on whose favor should be courted by whom (the theory of the virtues).

Undoubtedly some important part of morality does depend in part on a system of threats and bribes, at least for its survival in difficult conditions when normal goodwill and normally virtuous dispositions may be insufficient to motivate the conduct required for the preservation and justice of the moral network of relationships. But equally undoubtedly life will be nasty, emotionally poor, and worse than brutish (even if longer), if that is all morality is, or even if that coercive structure of morality is regarded as the backbone, rather than as an available crutch, should the main support fail. For the main support has to come from those we entrust with the job of rearing and training persons so that they can be trusted in various ways, some trusted with extraordinary coercive powers, some with public decision-making powers, all trusted as parties to promise, most trusted by some who love them and by one or more willing to become co-parents with them, most trusted by dependent children, dependent elderly relatives, sick friends, and so on. A very complex network of a great variety of sorts of trust structures our moral relationships with our fellows, and if there is a *main* support to this network it is the trust we place in those who respond to the trust of new members of the moral community, namely to children, and prepare them for new forms of trust.

A theory which took as its central question "Who should trust whom with what, and why?" would not have to forego the intellectual fun and games previous theorists have had with the various paradoxes of morality—curbing freedom to increase freedom, curbing self interest the better to satisfy self interest, not aiming at happiness in order to become happier. For it is easy enough to get a paradox of trust, to accompany or, if I am right, to generalize the paradoxes of freedom, self interest and hedonism. To trust is to make oneself or let oneself be more vulnerable than one might have been to harm from others—to give them an opportunity to harm one, in the confidence that they will not take it, because they have no good reason to. Why would one take such a risk? For risk it

always is, given the partial opaqueness to us of the reasoning and motivation of those we trust and with whom we cooperate. Our confidence may be, and quite often is, misplaced. That is what we risk when we trust. If the best reason to take such a risk is the expected gain in security which comes from a climate of trust, then in trusting we are always giving up security to get greater security, exposing our throats so that others become accustomed to not biting. A moral theory which made proper trust its central concern could have its own categorical imperative,[9] could replace obedience to self-made laws and freely chosen restraint on freedom with security-increasing sacrifice of security, distrust in the promoters of a climate of distrust, and so on.

Such reflexive use of one's central concept, negative or affirmative, is an intellectually satisfying activity which is bound to have appeal to those system-lovers who want to construct moral theories, and it may help them design their theory in an intellectually pleasing manner. But we should beware of becoming hypnotized by our slogans, or of sacrificing truth to intellectual elegance. Any theory of proper trust should not *prejudge* the question of when distrust is proper. We might find more objects of proper distrust than just the contributors to a climate of reasonable distrust, just as freedom should be restricted not just to increase human freedom but to protect human life from poisoners and other killers. I suspect, however, that all the objects of reasonable distrust are more reasonably seen as falling into the category of ones who contribute to a decrease in the scope of proper trust, than can all who are reasonably coerced be seen as themselves guilty of wrongful coercion. Still, even if all proper trust turns out to be for such persons

---

[9] *categorical imperative:* an unconditionally binding moral command. The term comes from the German philosopher Immanuel Kant (1724–1804).

and on such matters as will increase the scope or stability of a climate of reasonable trust, and all proper distrust for such persons and on such matters as increase the scope of reasonable distrust, overreliance on such nice reflexive formulae can distract us from asking all the questions about trust which need to be asked, if an adequate moral theory is to be constructed around that concept. These questions should include when to *respond* to trust with *un*trustworthiness, when and when not to invite trust, as well as when to give and refuse trust. We should not assume that promiscuous trustworthiness is any more a virtue than is undiscriminating distrust. It is appropriate trustworthiness, appropriate trustingness, appropriate encouragement to trust, which will be virtues, as will be judicious untrustworthiness, selective refusal to trust, discriminating discouragement of trust.

Women are particularly well placed to appreciate these last virtues, since they have sometimes needed them to get into a position to even consider becoming moral theorizers. The long exploitation and domination of women by men depended on men's trust in women and women's trustworthiness to play their allotted role and so to perpetuate their own and their daughters' servitude. However keen women now are to end the lovelessness of modern moral philosophy, they are unlikely to lose sight of the cautious virtue of appropriate distrust, or of the tough virtue of principled betrayal of the exploiters' trust.

Gilligan's girls and women saw morality as a matter of preserving valued ties to others, of preserving the conditions for that care and mutual care without which human life becomes bleak, lonely, and after a while, as the mature men in her study found, not self affirming, however successful in achieving the egoistic goals which had been set. The boys and men saw morality as a matter of finding workable traffic rules for self assertors, so that they not needlessly frustrate one another, and so

that they could, should they so choose, cooperate in more positive ways to mutual advantage. Both for the women's sometimes unchosen and valued ties with others, and for the men's mutual respect as sovereigns and subjects of the same minimal moral traffic rules (and for their more voluntary and more selective associations of profiteers) trust is important. Both men and women are concerned with cooperation, and the dimensions of trust-distrust structure the different cooperative relations each emphasize. The various considerations which arise when we try to defend an answer to any question about the appropriateness of a particular form of cooperation with its distinctive form of trust or distrust, that is when we look into the terms of all sorts of cooperation, at the terms of trust in different cases of trust, at what are fair terms and what are trust-enhancing and trust-preserving terms, are suitably many and richly interconnected. A moral theory (or family of theories) that made trust its central problem could do better justice to men's and women's moral intuitions than do the going men's theories. Even if we don't easily agree on the answer to the question of who should trust whom with what, who should accept and who should meet various sorts of trust, and why, these questions might enable us better to morally reason together than we can when the central moral questions are reduced to those of whose favor one must court and whose anger one must dread. But such programmatic claims as I am making will be tested only when women standing on the shoulders of men, or men on the shoulders of women, or some theorizing Tiresias,[10] actually work out such a theory. I am no Tiresias, and have not foresuffered all the labor pains of such a theory. I aim here only to fertilize.

---

[10] Tiresias was a legendary blind seer of the ancient Greek city of Thebes.

COMMENT

The core of Baier's approach to moral thinking is the distinction between the male way of doing ethical theory and the female way. She claims that the women who engage in philosophical reasoning in general, and in moral theorizing in particular, do so in a manner quite different from their male counterparts. Baier does not want to exempt a "feminist ethic" from the usual criteria of clarity, comprehensiveness, and coherence. On the contrary, she maintains that women *can* and *should* meet these standards as well as men. The crucial difference, according to Baier, lies more in the contrast between the key concepts of *obligation* and *trust*.

The fundamental difference between these two concepts is that the former tends to be defined and worked out according to a *hierarchical* structure, while the latter is more *bilateral* in character. Rights and obligations can be said to move up and down, whereas caring and trust are seen as moving outward, establishing connections. Another way to put this difference is by saying that in a hierarchial pattern what is aimed at are answers and solutions, while in a bilateral format what is sought are possibilities and resolutions. Baier stresses Gilligan's conclusion that the female approach sees "morality as a matter of preserving valued ties to others, of preserving the conditions for that mutual care without which human life becomes bleak, lonely, and … not self-affirming."

Thus, by placing the dynamics of trust and distrust at the axis of moral theorizing, Baier suggests that cooperation and life-sustaining emphases, rather than deontological and teleological goals, become the main themes of moral theory. It should be clear that she is not advocating "blind-trust" or naive caring as the chief characteristic of the ethical life. There is a need to explore and establish useful and stable criteria for trustworthiness and distrustfulness alike. Nevertheless, the feminist claim is that when moral theory is approached in this way, many of the traditional approaches, together with their attendant difficulties and dilemmas, may well be transcended.

It is interesting and helpful to compare Baier's approach to that of Simone de Beauvoir on the one hand and Alasdair MacIntyre on the other. Although Beauvoir clearly presents a feminist perspective, in her book *The Second Sex*, it is also clear that since she draws heavily on the philosophy of Jean-Paul Sartre her approach is, in Baier's terms, essentially male-oriented. Beauvoir begins by accepting the existentialist definition of what it means to be fully human, namely to *act* in the world, to accomplish things, and then proceeds to argue that in Western culture women have been systematically excluded from fulfilling themselves as persons in this way. Baier's approach would seem to begin with different assumptions about the nature of human personhood. She tends to define persons in terms of their capacity for entering into and sustaining relationships, which perhaps includes acting in the world, but does not place it in a paramount position. Individual actions are more susceptible to evaluation in terms of contracts, obligations, and justice than are ongoing relational interactions.

On the other hand, Alasdair MacIntyre, whom Baier mentions, has recently become the leading exponent of what has been termed "character ethics," which advocates basing moral considerations more on such qualities as human *virtue* than on the rightness of individual actions. Following Aristotle, MacIntyre suggests that morality is a function of a person's character yielding certain forms of behavior, rather than the other way around. Thus one can see that MacIntyre's approach, even though offered by a man, is more in line with that of Baier than is that of Beauvoir, a woman. Trust, care, and love are qualities of character rather than attributes of individual actions.

As Baier herself admits, her suggestions are largely programmatic, leaving a great deal of work to be done in developing a full-blown feminist moral theory. Some thinkers would argue, for instance, that the ethics of trust are well-suited to the interactions amongst the members of a family or a relatively small group of people associating out of selective choice, but are hardly sufficient for an entire society composed of diverse ethnic backgrounds and varying aspirations. It remains to be shown how a moral theory based on trust can be developed so as to deal with the needs of a large, pluralistic culture. Nevertheless, Baier's perspective is surely one that deserves and will receive a good deal of attention in current discussions of the basis of morality.

Finally, it is instructive to ask how Baier would analyze the case of Noel David Earley's suicide plans. Over and against the traditional concern to establish certain fundamental "principles" upon which to base moral judgments, she would clearly stress the importance of dialogue and trust in coming to such decisions. Is there any indication that Earley engaged in dialogue with others about his situation, and did trust play a role as well? Might she ask what his girlfriend thought about his plans, and would this reflect quite a different "voice" from that of Earley and/or the other moral philosophers we have considered? What would Baier's overall approach to the question of suicide be?

PART IV

SOCIAL IDEALS

Social philosophy is not a sharply distinct and separate field. The fundamental issues that divide social philosophers are ultimately metaphysical, epistemological or ethical. Among the questions debated are the following: What is the basis of political obligation? What is the nature of good social order? What is right social action? Is the state an organism? Are the actions of government to be justified by reference to the ends of the individual or of society? Does history have a pattern that can be known and predicted? All these questions involve metaphysical, epistemological or ethical issues.

An example may help to make clear the nature of social philosophy. In his *Discourse on Political Economy,* Jean Jacques Rousseau declares,

> The body politic … is also a moral being possessed of a will; and this general will, which tends always to the preservation and welfare of the whole and of every part, and is the source of the laws, constitutes for all the members of the State, in their relations to one another and to it, the rule of what is just or unjust.[1]

This sentence is replete with philosophical notions: that the body politic is a moral being, that it possesses a "general will" distinct from the individual wills of its members; that the general will is a good will; and that it defines, through the medium of law, what is just and what is unjust in the relations of citizens to one another and to the state. Philosophers, and not social scientists, are best fitted to clarify and criticize ideas.

The philosophers represented in the following chapters discuss questions of great interest to all students of human affairs. Other important social philosophers, such as Aristotle, Rousseau, and G. W. F. Hegel, are omitted for lack of space. Each of the philosophers chosen represents a social ideal.

It may be helpful to indicate in advance some of the issues that will arise in studying these thinkers:

---

[1] *The Social Contract,* Everyman's Edition (New York: Dutton, 1913), p. 253.

1. Plato maintains that values are absolute, not relative; that genuine knowledge—especially the knowledge of absolute values—is restricted to the few; that these few, when thoroughly educated, should rule the state; that the choice goods are to be preferred to the common goods; and that the foremost virtue, in the state or in the individual, is wisdom.

2. Thomas Hobbes contends that values are relative, not absolute; that people, being naturally egoistic, tend to prey upon one another; that the state is brought into existence to eliminate this anarchy and to attain peace and security; and that it is rational for citizens to obey their sovereign so long as they are protected.

3. John Locke affirms the necessity of a social contract between those governed and the state that is based in constitutional law and guarantees individual rights to life, property, and liberty, through democracy.

4. John Stuart Mill believes that the ultimate good is the happiness and self-realization of individuals; that actions are right to the extent that they promote individual welfare; that virtually all opinions are liable to error; that it is wrong to suppress dissident opinions; and that the progress of society depends upon the cultivation of a rich variety among individuals.

5. Karl Marx argues that it is possible to know and to predict accurately the course of history; that the most fundamental factor in determining the history of any society is economic development; that human rights and values are relative to the stages of historical evolution; that conflict, especially class struggle, is the basic mode of revolutionary change; that humankind after passing through various stages of class society—slavery, feudalism, capitalism—will finally attain a free, just, and classless social order; and that it is right and rational to assist the historical process by whatever means—even violent and dictatorial—that may be found necessary.

6. Frantz Fanon explores the social problems that are the legacy of colonial occupation and exploitation in Third World countries. He warns that as such newly independent nations seek to redefine and restructure themselves they must avoid allowing an oligarchy of a privileged, capitalist class to establish itself. True nationalism must be "of, for, and by the people" who constitute the majority of the population.

To some extent these theories involve questions of fact, which social scientists are best prepared to answer, but to a great extent they involve questions of ethics, epistemology, or metaphysics, which philosophers are best qualified to discuss. Such questions are too momentous, however, to be left to experts, whether philosophers or social scientists. All of us should ponder them.

A CASE IN POINT:

CIVIL DISOBEDIENCE OR CRIMINAL ACTIVITY?

In the late 1970s and early 1980s, the countries in Central America were undergoing violent upheaval. The Sandinista Revolution in Nicaragua had replaced the former dictatorship with a socialist form of government, and the United States was providing support for those who were trying to overthrow the new leadership. The dictatorial government of Guatemala was engaging in a repressive war against those of its own people, mostly native peasants, who were seeking political representation and social justice. In El Salvador, a similar conflict was underway, and in both cases, the United States was supportive of the oppressive governments then in power.

Tens of thousands of refugees from these countries came north across Mexico into the United States seeking political asylum. They had suffered great persecution in their homeland, and many had been tortured and had witnessed the murder of their family members. Our own government, however, refused to grant political asylum to these folks because they were not refugees from countries whose governments the United States opposed. Thus, these refugees were considered illegal entrants and were sent back to their home countries, where their lives were in real danger.

A group of church people in and around Tucson, Arizona—Catholics, Quakers, and Presbyterians—began to rally in support of these refugees. Eventually, this church group invoked the ancient concept of "sanctuary," granting these Central Americans immunity from the law under the auspices of the church. They actively engaged in illegally bringing thousands of these refugees over the Mexico–U.S. border and in finding shelter for them all over North America. This movement became known as the Sanctuary Movement.

The principal public figures in this illegal enterprise were the Reverend John Fife of the Southside Presbyterian Church in Tucson and Jim Corbett, a retired librarian and part-time rancher of the Quaker persuasion. Many other supporters, both clergy and lay folk, participated in the Sanctuary Movement in the Tucson area, and eventually it spread to many churches throughout the country. Although the concrete task of actually transporting Central Americans across the border was carried out in strict secrecy, the group made no effort to conceal the fact that it was thus engaged.

Every individual being considered as an illegal entrant was screened carefully to make sure he or she was actually a political refugee in need of sanctuary. It was a difficult yet challenging time for everyone involved, and many folks were putting their lives, their families, and their jobs on the line in order to see justice done for these oppressed and displaced persons. They all saw their task as one of obeying a law higher than that of the U.S. government, the moral law of providing protection for persecuted people, much in the same way some Europeans tried to protect Jewish folk from the Nazi concentration camps in World War II.

Eventually, the Immigration and Naturalization Service (INS) infiltrated the Sanctuary Movement and collected information that led to a federal indictment in 1985 of thirteen of those participating in bringing refugees into the United States illegally. The trial was held in Tucson and lasted about six months. Jim Corbett was found not guilty because there was no direct evidence that he had transported illegal refugees. John Fife and the others were deemed guilty and each sentenced to five years' probation.

The main reason for the minimal sentencing seems to have been the fact that by the time the trial was over the mood of the country toward U.S. policy in Central America had shifted dramatically. Five hundred and thirty church congregations, seventeen cities, and the State of New Mexico, along with many colleges and universities, had declared themselves as sanctuaries. Indeed, in 2000, President Clinton made a trip to Guatemala in order to offer a public apology for the way our government contributed to the violence there. Also, the policy of the CIA supporting dictators throughout Latin America had come under severe criticism, both in the media and in congressional discussion.

From both a legal and a moral point of view, one of the more interesting aspects of the Sanctuary trial was the fact that at the outset the judge stipulated that no evidence would be permitted that pertained to the reasons why these refugees had sought asylum or why those indicted had tried to help them. No references to international law or higher moral laws were to be allowed. The only issue was whether or not those providing sanctuary had in fact broken laws governing immigration. This is standard judicial practice.

The people involved in the Sanctuary Movement saw themselves as engaged in a form of civil disobedience, much like that engaged in by the civil rights workers during the 1960s. They knew they were breaking the immigration laws, but they felt these laws were being applied to Central Americans in a wrongful if not illegal manner. Their conviction was that civil disobedience is always called for when one's own government violates its own constitutional principles. The fact that these refugees were not fleeing from a communist country but from our "official" allies should not matter.

Civil disobedience can take the form of either passive resistance or active resistance, and clearly those working in the Sanctuary Movement had chosen the latter course. They were not just failing to comply with the current laws, they actively sought to disobey them on behalf of those who were being punished or abused by these laws. Clearly, there are forms of government, both in theory and in practice, in which such disobedience is never tolerated. However, in a constitutional democracy, provision is made for the right to resist a given law in order to test whether or not it does in fact reflect the will of the people and/or the constitution.

In the 1950s and 1960s, Martin Luther King, Jr., and his followers repeatedly broke local and state laws that they deemed to be unconstitutional and immoral. King fully expected to be found guilty for his acts of civil disobedience and to serve time in prison as well, which he often did. Eventually, he was able to get legislation passed that made segregation of the races illegal in the United States.

In like manner, in the 1940s, Mahatma Gandhi challenged the British government's imperial rule over India according to which the people of India had been subjected to prolonged exploitation and oppression. He, too, was successful in overturning this racist situation by continually organizing large-scale acts of civil disobedience and forced the British to acknowledge the immorality of their own rule. After World War II, the British removed their own government and military from India.

Throughout modern times, there have been a number of such cases wherein civil disobedience has at first been judged illegal and morally wrong but later been declared to be just. It is very difficult at best to determine the criteria for the making of such judgments. Moreover, it is important to see the difference between legal issues and moral ones. Although these two domains often overlap in interesting and confusing ways, it should be clear that it is possible for something that is illegal to be moral, and vice versa. It is, in fact, one of the crucial tasks of any society to determine just what the roles of law and morality are with respect to its own culture and government. The ongoing debate over abortion is but one example of this difficult task.

The different visions of the good society offered by the philosophers presented in this part entail varying answers to the questions of civil disobedience. Just when, if ever, a person or group is justified in actively disobeying the law depends on a complex set of issues and principles. If one accepts the idea that laws are subject to continuous and thorough review, then this process can be understood a bit more easily, to be sure. However, such an admission carries with it the implication that what is morally correct may in fact change with time, thus suggesting moral relativism.

It will be interesting and instructive to explore what each of the thinkers in this part would have to say about the morality or lack thereof of the Sanctuary Movement in Tucson in the 1980s. Plato and Hobbes might be seen as lining up on one side, though for quite different reasons, while Locke and Mill would come down in roughly the same place at the other end of the continuum. Both Karl Marx and Frantz Fanon would seem to be more amenable to the importance of active disobedience on the part of those who are being exploited and oppressed by the ruling class.

21

ARISTOCRACY

PLATO (428/7–348/7 B.C.)

For a biographical note, see page 47.

THE IDEAL REPUBLIC

The Ring of Gyges

Good, said Glaucon. Listen then, and I will begin with my first point: the nature and origin of justice.

What people say is that to do wrong is, in itself, a desirable thing; on the other hand, it is not at all desirable to suffer wrong, and the harm to the sufferer outweighs the advantage to the doer. Consequently, when men have had a taste of both, those who have not the power to seize the advantage and escape the harm decide that they would be better off if they made a compact neither to do wrong nor to suffer it. Hence they began to make laws and covenants with one another; and whatever the law prescribed they called lawful and right. That is what right or justice is and how it came into existence; it stands halfway between the best thing of all—to do wrong with impunity—and the worst,

Translated with introduction and notes by Francis MacDonald Cornford, Oxford University Press, London, 1941; some of Cornford's footnotes have been omitted. The italicized glosses are his except for those supplied by the editor and marked by the word "Editors."

which is to suffer wrong without the power to retaliate. So justice is accepted as a compromise, and valued, not as good in itself, but for lack of power to do wrong; no man worthy of the name, who had that power, would ever enter into such a compact with anyone; he would be mad if he did. That, Socrates, is the nature of justice according to this account, and such the circumstances in which it arose.

The next point is that men practise it against the grain, for lack of power to do wrong. How true that is, we shall best see if we imagine two men, one just, the other unjust, given full licence to do whatever they like, and then follow them to observe where each will be led by his desires. We shall catch the just man taking the same road as the unjust; he will be moved by self-interest, the end which it is natural to every creature to pursue as good, until forcibly turned aside by law and custom to respect the principle of equality.

Now, the easiest way to give them that complete liberty of action would be to imagine them possessed of the talisman found by Gyges, the ancestor of the famous Lydian. The story tells how he was a shepherd in the King's service. One day there was a great storm, and the ground where his flock was feeding was rent by an earthquake. Astonished at the sight, he went down into the chasm and saw, among other wonders of which the story tells, a brazen horse, hollow, with windows in its sides. Peering in, he saw a dead body, which seemed to be of more than human size. It was naked save for a gold ring, which he took from the finger and made his way out. When the shepherds met, as they did every month, to send an account to the King of the state of his flocks, Gyges came wearing the ring. As he was sitting with the others, he happened to turn the bezel of the ring inside his hand. At once he became invisible, and his companions, to his surprise, began to speak of him as if he had left them. Then, as he was fingering the ring, he turned the bezel outwards and became visible again. With that, he set about testing the ring to see if it really had this power, and always with the same result: according as he turned the bezel inside or out he vanished and reappeared. After this discovery he contrived to be one of the messengers sent to the court. There he seduced the Queen, and with her help murdered the King and seized the throne.

Now suppose there were two such magic rings, and one were given to the just man, the other to the unjust. No one, it is commonly believed, would have such iron strength of mind as to stand fast in doing right or keep his hands off other men's goods, when he could go to the market-place and fearlessly help himself to anything he wanted, enter houses and sleep with any woman he chose, set prisoners free and kill men at his pleasure, and in a word go about among men with the powers of a god. He would behave no better than the other; both would take the same course. Surely this would be strong proof that men do right only under compulsion; no individual thinks of it as good for him personally, since he does wrong whenever he finds he has the power. Every man believes that wrongdoing pays him personally much better, and, according to this the-

ory, that is the truth. Granted full licence to do as he liked, people would think him a miserable fool if they found him refusing to wrong his neighbours or to touch their belongings, though in public they would keep up a pretence of praising his conduct, for fear of being wronged themselves. So much for that.

Finally, if we are really to judge between the two lives, the only way is to contrast the extremes of justice and injustice. We can best do that by imagining our two men to be perfect types, and crediting both to the full with the qualities they need for their respective ways of life. To begin with the unjust man: he must be like any consummate master of a craft, a physician or a captain, who, knowing just what his art can do, never tries to do more, and can always retrieve a false step. The unjust man, if he is to reach perfection, must be equally discreet in his criminal attempts, and he must not be found out, or we shall think him a bungler; for the highest pitch of injustice is to seem just when you are not. So we must endow our man with the full complement of injustice; we must allow him to have secured a spotless reputation for virtue while committing the blackest crimes; he must be able to retrieve any mistake, to defend himself with convincing eloquence if his misdeeds are denounced, and, when force is required, to bear down all opposition by his courage and strength and by his command of friends and money.

Now set beside this paragon the just man in his simplicity and nobleness, one who, in Aeschylus' words, "would be, not seem, the best." There must, indeed, be no such seeming; for if his character were apparent, his reputation would bring him honours and rewards, and then we should not know whether it was for their sake that he was just or for justice's sake alone. He must be stripped of everything but justice, and denied every advantage the other enjoyed. Doing no wrong, he must have the worst reputation for wrong-doing, to test whether his virtue is proof against all that comes of having a bad name; and under this lifelong imputation of wickedness, let him hold on his course of justice unwavering to the point of death. And so, when the two men have carried their justice and injustice to the last extreme, we may judge which is the happier.

My dear Glaucon, I exclaimed, how vigorously you scour these two characters clean for inspection, as if you were burnishing a couple of statues![1]

I am doing my best, he answered. Well, given two such characters, it is not hard, I fancy, to describe the sort of life that each of them may expect; and if the description sounds rather coarse, take it as coming from those who cry up the merits of injustice rather than from me. They will tell you that our just man will be thrown into prison, scourged and racked, will have his eyes burnt out, and after every kind of torment, be impaled. That will teach him how much better it is to seem virtuous than to be so. In fact those lines of Aeschylus I quoted are more fitly applied to the unjust man, who, they say, is a realist and does not live for appearances: "he would be, not seem" unjust,

> … reaping the harvest sown
> In those deep furrows of the thoughtful heart
> Whence wisdom springs.

With his reputation for virtue, he will hold offices of state, ally himself by marriage to any family he may choose, become a partner in any business, and, having no scruples about being dishonest, turn all these advantages to profit. If he is involved in a lawsuit, public or private, he will get the better of his opponents, grow rich on the proceeds, and be able to help his friends and harm his enemies. Finally, he can

make sacrifices to the gods and dedicate offerings with due magnificence, and, being in a much better position than the just man to serve the gods as well as his chosen friends, he may reasonably hope to stand higher in the favour of heaven. So much better, they say, Socrates, is the life prepared for the unjust by gods and men.

[Socrates sees no way of immediately refuting the theory advanced by Glaucon and suggests that an answer can best be found if the argument is projected from the level of the individual to that of the community. He proposes to study the origin and nature of the state, in the hope of thereby discovering the nature of justice and other virtues. Editors.]

The Virtues in the State

[Plato's original aim in constructing an ideal state was to find in it justice exemplified on a larger scale than in the individual. Assuming that four cardinal qualities make up the whole of virtue, he now asks wherein consist the wisdom, courage, temperance, and justice of the state, or, in other words, of the individuals composing the state in their public capacity as citizens.

Wisdom in the conduct of state affairs will be the practical prudence or good counsel of the deliberative body. Only the philosophic Rulers will possess the necessary insight into what is good for the community as a whole. They will have "right belief" grounded on immediate knowledge of the meaning of goodness in all its forms. The Auxiliaries will have only a right belief accepted on the authority of the Rulers. Their functions will be executive, not deliberative.

The Courage of the state will obviously be manifested in the fighting force. Socrates had defined courage as knowledge of what really is, or is not, to be feared, and he had regarded it as an inseparable part of all virtue, which consists in knowing what things are really good or evil. If the only real evil is moral evil, then poverty, suffering, and all the so-called evils that others can inflict on us, including death itself, are not to be feared, since, if they are met in the right spirit, they cannot make us worse men. This knowledge only the philosophic Rulers will possess to the full. The courage of the

---

[1] At Elis and Athens officials called *phaidryntai*, 'burnishers,' had the duty of cleaning cult statues (A. B. Cook, *Zeus*, iii. 967). Later, where this passage is recalled, it is admitted to be an extravagant supposition, that the just and unjust should exchange reputations.

Auxiliaries will consist in the power of holding fast to the conviction implanted by their education.

Temperance is not, as we might expect, the peculiar virtue of the lowest order in the state. As self-mastery, it means the subordination of the lower elements to the higher; but government must be with the willing consent of the governed, and temperance will include the unanimous agreement of all classes as to who should rule and who obey.[2] It is consequently like a harmony pervading and uniting all parts of the whole, a principle of solidarity. In the Laws, which stresses the harmonious union of different and complementary elements, this virtue overshadows even justice.

Justice is the complementary principle of differentiation, keeping the parts distinct. It has been before us all through the construction of the state since it first appeared on the economic level as the division of labor based on natural aptitudes. "Doing one's own work" now has the larger sense of a concentration on one's peculiar duty or function in the community. This conception of "doing and possessing what properly belongs to one" is wide enough to cover the justice of the lawcourts, assuring to each man his due rights. Injustice will mean invasion and encroachment upon the rights and duties of others.

The virtue described in this chapter is what Plato calls "civic" or "popular" virtue. Except in the Rulers, it is not directly based on that ultimate knowledge of good and evil which is wisdom, to be attained only at the end of the higher education of the philosopher.]

So now at last, son of Ariston, said I, your commonwealth is established. The next thing is to bring to bear upon it all the light you can get from any quarter, with the help of your brother and Polemarchus and all the rest, in the hope that we may see where justice is to be found in it and where injustice, how they differ, and which of the two will bring happiness to its possessor, no matter whether gods and men see that he has it or not.

Nonsense, said Glaucon; you promised to conduct the search yourself, because it would be a sin not to uphold justice by every means in your power.

That is true; I must do as you say, but you must all help.

We will.

I suspect, then, we may find what we are looking for in this way. I take it that our state, having been founded and built up on the right lines, is good in the complete sense of the word.

It must be.

Obviously, then, it is wise, brave, temperate, and just.

Obviously.

Then if we find some of these qualities in it, the remainder will be the one we have not found. It is as if we were looking somewhere for one of any four things: if we detected that one immediately, we should be satisfied; whereas if we recognized the other three first, that would be enough to indicate the thing we wanted; it could only be the remaining one. So here we have four qualities. Had we not better follow that method in looking for the one we want?

Surely.

To begin then: the first quality to come into view in our state seems to be its wisdom; and there appears to be something odd about this quality.[3]

What is there odd about it?

I think the state we have described really has wisdom; for it will be prudent in counsel, won't it?

Yes.

And prudence in counsel is clearly a form of knowledge; good counsel cannot be due to ignorance and stupidity.

Clearly.

But there are many and various kinds of knowledge in our commonwealth. There is the knowledge possessed by the carpen-

---

[2] At *Statesman* 276 E the true king is distinguished from the despot by the voluntary submission of his subjects to his rule.

[3] Because the wisdom of the whole resides in the smallest part, as explained below.

ters or the smiths, and the knowledge how to raise crops. Are we to call the state wise and prudent on the strength of these forms of skill?

No, they would only make it good at furniture-making or working in copper or agriculture.

Well then, is there any form of knowledge, possessed by some among the citizens of our new-founded commonwealth, which will enable it to take thought, not for some particular interest, but for the best possible conduct of the state as a whole in its internal and external relations?

Yes, there is.

What is it, and where does it reside?

It is precisely that art of guardianship which resides in those Rulers whom we just now called Guardians in the full sense.

And what would you call the state on the strength of that knowledge?

Prudent and truly wise.

And do you think there will be more or fewer of these genuine Guardians in our state than there will be smiths?

Far fewer.

Fewer, in fact, than any of those other groups who are called after the kind of skill they possess?

Much fewer.

So, if a state is constituted on natural principles, the wisdom it possesses as a whole will be due to the knowledge residing in the smallest part, the one which takes the lead and governs the rest. Such knowledge is the only kind that deserves the name of wisdom, and it appears to be ordained by nature that the class privileged to possess it should be the smallest of all.

Quite true.

Here then we have more or less made out one of our four qualities and its seat in the structure of the commonwealth.

To my satisfaction, at any rate.

Next there is courage. It is not hard to discern that quality or the part of the community in which it resides so as to entitle the whole to be called brave.

Why do you say so?

Because anyone who speaks of a state as either brave or cowardly can only be thinking of that part of it which takes the field and fights in its defence; the reason being, I imagine, that the character of the state is not determined by the bravery or cowardice of the other parts.

No.

Courage, then, is another quality which a community owes to a certain part of itself. And its being brave will mean that, in this part, it possesses the power of preserving, in all circumstances, a conviction about the sort of things that it is right to be afraid of—the conviction implanted by the education which the law-giver has established. Is not that what you mean by courage?

I do not quite understand. Will you say it again?

I am saying that courage means preserving something.

Yes, but what?

The conviction, inculcated by lawfully established education, about the sort of things which may rightly be feared. When I added "in all circumstances," I meant preserving it always and never abandoning it, whether under the influence of pain or of pleasure, or desire or of fear. If you like, I will give an illustration.

Please do.

You know how dyers who want wool to take a purple dye, first select the white wool from among all the other colors, next treat it very carefully to make it take the dye in its full brilliance, and only then dip it in the vat. Dyed in that way, wool gets a fast color, which no washing, even with soap, will rob of its brilliance; whereas if they choose wool of any color but white, or if they neglect to prepare it, you know what happens.

Yes, it looks washed-out and ridiculous.

That illustrates the result we were doing our best to achieve when we were choosing our fighting men and training their minds and bodies. Our only purpose was to contrive influences whereby they might take the color of our institutions like a dye, so that, in virtue of having both the right temperament and the right education, their convictions about what ought to be feared and on all other subjects might be indelibly fixed, never to be washed out by pleasure and pain, desire and fear, solvents more terribly effective than all the soap and fuller's earth in the world. Such a power of constantly preserving, in accordance with our institutions, the right conviction about the things which ought, or ought not, to be feared, is what I call courage. That is my position, unless you have some objection to make.

None at all, he replied; if the belief were such as might be found in a slave or an animal—correct, but not produced by education—you would hardly describe it as in accordance with our institutions, and you would give it some other name than courage.

Quite true.

Then I accept your account of courage.

You will do well to accept it, at any rate as applying to the courage of the ordinary citizen;[4] if you like we will go into it more fully some other time. At present we are in search of justice, rather than of courage; and for that purpose we have said enough.

I quite agree.

Two qualities, I went on, still remain to be made out in our state, temperance and the object of our whole inquiry, justice. Can we discover justice without troubling ourselves further about temperance?

I do not know, and I would rather not have justice come to light first, if that means that we should not go on to consider temperance. So if you want to please me, take temperance first.

Of course I have every wish to please you.

Do go on then.

I will. At first sight, temperance seems more like some sort of concord or harmony than the other qualities did.

How so?

Temperance surely means a kind of orderliness, a control of certain pleasures and appetites. People use the expression, "master of oneself," whatever that means, and various other phrases that point the same way.

Quite true.

Is not "master of oneself" an absurd expression? A man who was master of himself would presumably be also subject to himself, and the subject would be master; for all these terms apply to the same person.

No doubt.

I think, however, the phrase means that within the man himself, in his soul, there is a better part and a worse; and that he is his own master when the part which is better by nature has the worse under its control. It is certainly a term of praise; whereas it is considered as disgrace, when, through bad breeding or bad company, the better part is overwhelmed by the worse, like a small force outnumbered by a multitude. A man in that condition is called a slave to himself and intemperate.

Probably that is what is meant.

Then now look at our newly founded state and you will find one of these two conditions realized there. You will agree that it deserves to be called master of itself, if temperance and self-mastery exist where the better part rules the worse.

Yes, I can see that is true.

It is also true that the great mass of multifarious appetites and pleasures and pains will be found to occur chiefly in children and women and slaves, and, among free men so called, in the inferior multitude; whereas the simple and moderate desires which, with the aid of reason and right belief, are guided by reflection, you will find only in a few, and those with the best inborn dispositions and the best educated.

Yes, certainly.

---

[4] As distinct from the perfect courage of the philosophic Ruler, based on immediate knowledge of values.

Do you see that this state of things will exist in your commonwealth, where the desires of the inferior multitude will be controlled by the desires and wisdom of the superior few? Hence, if any society can be called master of itself and in control of pleasures and desires, it will be ours.

Quite so.

On all these grounds, then, we may describe it as temperate. Furthermore, in our state, if anywhere, the governors and the governed will share the same conviction on the question who ought to rule.[5] Don't you think so?

I am quite sure of it.

Then, if that is their state of mind, in which of the two classes of citizens will temperance reside—in the governors or in the governed?

In both, I suppose.

So we were not wrong in divining a resemblance between temperance and some kind of harmony. Temperance is not like courage and wisdom, which made the state wise and brave by residing each in one particular part. Temperance works in a different way; it extends throughout the whole gamut of the state, producing a consonance of all its elements from the weakest to the strongest as measured by any standard you like to take—wisdom, bodily strength, numbers, or wealth. So we are entirely justified in identifying with temperance this unanimity or harmonious agreement between the naturally superior and inferior elements on the question which of the two should govern, whether in the state or in the individual.

I fully agree.

Good, said I. We have discovered in our commonwealth three out of our four qualities, to the best of our present judgment. What is the remaining one, required to make up its full complement of goodness? For clearly this will be justice.

Clearly.

Now is the moment, then, Glaucon, for us to keep the closest watch, like huntsmen standing round a covert, to make sure that justice does not slip through and vanish undetected. It must certainly be somewhere hereabouts; so keep your eyes open for a view of the quarry, and if you see it first, give me the alert.

I wish I could, he answered; but you will do better to give me a lead and not count on me for more than eyes to see what you show me.

Pray for luck, then, and follow me.

The thicket looks rather impenetrable, said I; too dark for it to be easy to start up the game. However, we must push on.

Of course we must.

Here I gave the view "halloo." Glaucon, I exclaimed, I believe we are on the track and the quarry is not going to escape us altogether.

That is good news.

Really, I said, we have been extremely stupid. All this time the thing has been under our very noses from the start, and we never saw it. We have been as absurd as a person who hunts for something he has all the time got in his hand. Instead of looking at the thing, we have been staring into the distance. No doubt that is why it escaped us.

What do you mean?

I believe we have been talking about the thing all this while without ever understanding that we were giving some sort of account of it.

Do come to the point. I am all ears.

Listen, then, and judge whether I am right. You remember how, when we first began to establish our commonwealth and several times since, we have laid down, as a universal principle, that everyone ought to perform the one function in the community for which his nature best suited him. Well, I believe that that principle, or some form of it, is justice.

We certainly laid that down.

---

[5] This principle of freedom—government with consent of the governed—is thus recognized. The "democratic" freedom to "do whatever you like" is condemned in later chapters.

Yes, and surely we have often heard people say that justice means minding one's own business and not meddling with other men's concerns; and we have often said so ourselves.

We have.

Well, my friend, it may be that this minding of one's own business, when it takes a certain form, is actually the same thing as justice. Do you know what makes me think so?

No, tell me.

I think that this quality which makes it possible for the three we have already considered, wisdom, courage, and temperance, to take their place in the commonwealth, and so long as it remains present secures their continuance, must be the remaining one. And we said that, when three of the four were found, the one left over would be justice.

It must be so.

Well now, if we had to decide which of these qualities will contribute most to the excellence of our commonwealth, it would be hard to say whether it was the unanimity of rules and subjects, or the soldier's fidelity to the established conviction about what is, or is not, to be feared, or the watchful intelligence of the Rulers; or whether its excellence were not above all due to the observance by everyone, child or woman, slave or freeman or artisan, ruler or ruled, of this principle that one should do his own proper work without interfering with others.

It would be hard to decide, no doubt.

It seems, then, that this principle can at any rate claim to rival wisdom, temperance, and courage as conducing to the excellence of a state. And would you not say that the only possible competitor of these qualities must be justice?

Yes, undoubtedly.

Here is another thing which points to the same conclusion. The judging of lawsuits is a duty that you will lay upon your Rulers, isn't it?

Of course.

And the chief aim of their decisions will be that neither party shall have what

belongs to another or be deprived of what is his own.

Yes.

Because that is just?

Yes.

So here again justice admittedly means that a man should possess and concern himself with what properly belongs to him.[6]

True.

Again, do you agree with me that no great harm would be done to the community by a general interchange of most forms of work, the carpenter and the cobbler exchanging their positions and their tools and taking on each other's jobs, or even the same man undertaking both?

Yes, there would not be much harm in that.

But I think you will also agree that another kind of interchange would be disastrous. Suppose, for instance, someone whom nature designed to be an artisan or tradesman should be emboldened by some advantage, such as wealth or command of votes or bodily strength, to try to enter the order of fighting men; or some member of that order should aspire, beyond his merits, to a seat in the council-chamber of the Guardians. Such interference and exchange of social positions and tools, or the attempt to combine all these forms of work in the same person, would be fatal to the commonwealth.

Most certainly.

Where there are three orders, then, any plurality of functions or shifting from one order to another is not merely utterly harmful to the community, but one might fairly call it the extreme of wrongdoing. And you will agree that to do the greatest of wrongs to one's own community is injustice.

Surely.

This, then, is injustice. And, conversely, let us repeat that when each order—trades-

---

[6] Here the legal conception of justice is connected with its moral significance.

man, Auxiliary, Guardian—keeps to its own proper business in the commonwealth and does its own work, that is justice and what makes a just society.

I entirely agree.

The Three Parts of the Soul

[It has been shown that justice in the state means that the three chief social functions—deliberative and governing, executive, and productive—are kept distinct and rightly performed. Since the qualities of a community are those of the component individuals we may expect to find three corresponding elements in the individual soul. All three will be present in every soul; but the structure of society is based on the fact that they are developed to different degrees in different types of character.

The existence of three elements or "parts" of the soul is established by an analysis of the conflict of motives. A simple case is the thirsty man's appetite for drink, held in check by the rational reflection that to drink will be bad for him. That two distinct elements must be at work here follows from the general principle that the same thing cannot act or be affected in two opposite ways at the same time. By "thirst" is meant simply the bare craving for drink; it must not be confused with a desire for some good (e.g., health or pleasure) expected as a consequence of drinking. This simple craving says, "Drink"; Reason says, "Do not drink": the contradiction shows that two elements are at work.

A third factor is the "spirited" element, akin to our "sense of honor," manifested in indignation, which takes the side of reason against appetite, but cannot be identified with reason, since it is found in children and animals and it may be rebuked by reason.

This analysis is not intended as a complete outline of psychology; that could be reached only by following "a longer road." It is concerned with the factors involved in moral behavior. . . .]

The Virtues in the Individual

[The virtues in the state were the qualities of the citizen, as such, considered as playing the special part in society for which he was qualified by the pre-

dominance in his nature of the philosophic, the pugnacious, or the commercial spirit. But all three elements exist in every individual, who is thus a replica of society in miniature. In the perfect man reason will rule, with the spirited element as its auxiliary, over the bodily appetites. Self-control or temperance will be a condition of internal harmony, all the parts being content with their legitimate satisfactions. Justice finally appears, no longer only as a matter of external behavior toward others, but as an internal order of the soul, from which right behavior will necessarily follow. Injustice is the opposite state of internal discord and faction. To ask whether justice or injustice pays the better is now seen to be as absurd as to ask whether health is preferable to disease.]

And so, after a stormy passage, we have reached the land. We are fairly agreed that the same three elements exist alike in the state and in the individual soul.

That is so.

Does it not follow at once that state and individual will be wise or brave by virtue of the same element in each and in the same way? Both will possess in the same manner any quality that makes for excellence.

That must be true.

Then it applies to justice: We shall conclude that a man is just in the same way that a state was just. And we have surely not forgotten that justice in the state meant that each of the three orders in it was doing its own proper work. So we may henceforth bear in mind that each one of us likewise will be a just person, fulfilling his proper function, only if the several parts of our nature fulfill theirs.

Certainly.

And it will be the business of reason to rule with wisdom and forethought on behalf of the entire soul; while the spirited element ought to act as its subordinate and ally. The two will be brought into accord, as we said earlier, by that combination of mental and bodily training which will tune up one string of the instrument and relax the other, nourishing the reasoning part on the study of noble literature and allaying the other's wildness by harmony and rhythm. When both have been thus nurtured and trained to know their own true functions, they must be set in command over the appetites, which form the greater part of each man's soul and are by nature insatiably covetous. They must keep watch lest this part, by battening on the pleasures that are called bodily, should grow so great and powerful that it will no longer keep to its own work, but will try to enslave the others and usurp a dominion to which it has no right, thus turning the whole of life upside down. At the same time, those two together will be the best of guardians for the entire soul and for the body against all enemies from without: the one will take counsel, while the other will do battle, following its ruler's commands and by its own bravery giving effect to the ruler's designs.

Yes, that is all true.

And so we call an individual brave in virtue of this spirited part of his nature, when, in spite of pain or pleasure, it holds fast to the injunctions of reason about what he ought or ought not to be afraid of.

True.

And wise in virtue of that small part which rules and issues these injunctions, possessing as it does the knowledge of what is good for each of the three elements and for all of them in common.

Certainly.

And, again, temperate by reason of the unanimity and concord of all three, when there is no internal conflict between the ruling element and its two subjects, but all are agreed that reason should be ruler.

Yes, that is an exact account of temperance, whether in the state or in the individual.

Finally, a man will be just by observing the principle we have so often stated.

Necessarily.

Now is there any indistinctness in our vision of justice, that might make it seem somehow different from what found it to be in the state?

I don't think so.

Because, if we have any lingering doubt, we might make sure by comparing it with some commonplace notions. Suppose, for instance, that a sum of money were entrusted to our state or to an individual of corresponding character and training, would anyone imagine that such a person would be specially likely to embezzle it?

No.

And would he not be incapable of sacrilege and theft, or of treachery to friend or country; never false to an oath or any other compact; the last to be guilty of adultery or of neglecting parents or the due service of the gods?

Yes.

And the reason for all this is that each part of his nature is exercising its proper function, of ruling or of being ruled.

Yes, exactly.

Are you satisfied, then, that justice is the power which produces states or individuals of whom that is true, or must we look further?

There is no need; I am quite satisfied.

And so our dream has come true—I mean the inkling we had that, by some happy chance, we had lighted upon a rudimentary form of justice from the very moment when we set about founding our commonwealth. Our principle that the born shoemaker or carpenter had better stick to his trade turns out to have been an adumbration of justice; and that is why it has helped us. But in reality justice, though evidently analogous to this principle, is not a matter of external behavior, but of the inward self and of attending to all that is, in the fullest sense, a man's proper concern. The just man does not allow the several elements in his soul to usurp one another's functions; he is indeed one who sets his house in order, by self-mastery and discipline coming to be at peace with himself, and bringing into tune those three parts, like the terms in the proportion of a musical scale, the highest and lowest notes and the mean between them, with all the intermediate intervals. Only when he has linked these parts together in well-tempered harmony and has made himself one man instead of many, will he be ready to go about whatever he may have to do whether it be making money and satisfying bodily wants, or business transactions, or the affairs of state. In all these fields when he speaks of just and honorable conduct, he will mean the behavior that helps to produce and to preserve this habit of mind; and by wisdom he will mean the knowledge which presides over such conduct. Any action which tends to break down this habit will be for him unjust; and the notions governing it he will call ignorance and folly.

That is perfectly true, Socrates.

Good, said I. I believe we should not be thought altogether mistaken, if we claimed to have discovered the just man and the just state, and wherein their justice consists.

Indeed we should not.

Shall we make that claim, then?

Yes, we will.

So be it, said I. Next, I suppose, we have to consider injustice.

Evidently.

This must surely be a sort of civil strife among the three elements, whereby they usurp and encroach upon one another's functions and some one part of the soul rises up in rebellion against the whole, claiming a supremacy to which it has no right because its nature fits it only to be the servant of the ruling principle. Such turmoil and aberration we shall, I think, identify with injustice, intemperance, cowardice, ignorance, and in a word with all wickedness.

Exactly.

And now that we know the nature of justice and injustice, we can be equally clear about what is meant by acting justly and again by unjust action and wrongdoing.

How do you mean?

Plainly, they are exactly analogous to those wholesome and unwholesome activities which respectively produce a healthy or unhealthy condition in the body; in the same way just and unjust conduct produce a just or unjust character. Justice is produced in the soul, like health in the body, by establishing the elements concerned in their natural relations of control and subordination, whereas injustice is like disease and means that this natural order is inverted.

Quite so.

It appears, then, that virtue is as it were the health and comeliness and well-being of the soul, as wickedness is disease, deformity, and weakness.

True.

And also that virtue and wickedness are brought about by one's way of life, honorable or disgraceful.

That follows.

So now it only remains to consider which is the more profitable course: to do right and live honorably and be just, whether or not anyone knows what manner of man you are, or to do wrong and be unjust, provided that you can escape the chastisement which might make you a better man.

But really, Socrates, it seems to me ridiculous to ask that question now that the nature of justice and injustice has been brought to light. People think that all the luxury and wealth and power in the world cannot make life worth living when the bodily constitution is going to rack and ruin; and are we to believe that, when the very principle whereby we live is deranged and corrupted, life will be worth living so long as a man can do as he will, and wills to do anything rather than to free himself from vice and wrongdoing and to win justice and virtue?

Yes, I replied, it is a ridiculous question. . . .

The Paradox: Philosophers Must Be Kings

[Challenged to show that the ideal state can exist, Socrates first claims that an idea is none the worse for not being realizable on earth. The assertion that theory comes closer than practice to truth or reality is characteristically Platonic. The ideal state or man is the true state or man; for if men, who are in fact

always imperfect, could reach perfection, they would only be realizing all that their nature aims at being and might conceivably be. Further, the realm of ideals is the real world, unchanging and eternal, which can be known by thought. The visible and tangible things commonly called real are only a realm of fleeting appearance, where the ideal is imperfectly manifested in various degrees of approximation. ...

An ideal has an indispensable value for practice, in that thought thereby gives to action its right aim. So, instead of proving that the ideal state or man can exist here, it is enough to discover the least change, within the bounds of possibility, that would bring the actual state nearest to the ideal. This change would be the union, in the same persons, of political power and the love of wisdom, so as to close the gulf, which had been growing wider since the age of Pericles, between the men of thought and the men of action. The corresponding change in the individual is the supremacy of the reason, the divine element in man, over the rest of our nature.]

But really, Socrates, Glaucon continued, if you are allowed to go on like this, I am afraid you will forget all about the question you thrust aside some time ago: whether a society so constituted can ever come into existence, and if so, how. No doubt, if it did exist, all manner of good things would come about. I can even add some that you have passed over. Men who acknowledged one another as fathers, sons, or brothers and always used those names among themselves would never desert one another; so they would fight with unequaled bravery. And if their womenfolk went out with them to war, either in the ranks or drawn up in the rear to intimidate the enemy and act as a reserve in case of need, I am sure all this would make them invincible. At home, too, I can see many advantages you have not mentioned. But, since I admit that our commonwealth would have all these merits and any number more, if once it came into existence, you need not describe it in further detail. All we have now to do is to convince ourselves that it can be brought into being and how.

This is a very sudden onslaught, said I; you have no mercy on my shillyshallying. Perhaps you do not realize that, after I have barely escaped the first two waves,[7] the third, which you are now bringing down upon me, is the most formidable of all. When you have seen what it is like and heard my reply, you will be ready to excuse the very natural fears which made me shrink from putting forward such a paradox for discussion.

The more you talk like that, he said, the less we shall be willing to let you off from telling us how this constitution can come into existence; so you had better waste no more time.

Well, said I, let me begin by reminding you that what brought us to this point was our inquiry into the nature of justice and injustice.

True; but what of that?

Merely this: suppose we do find out what justice is,[8] are we going to demand that a man who is just shall have a character which exactly corresponds in every respect to the ideal of justice? Or shall we be satisfied if he comes as near to the ideal as possible and has in him a larger measure of that quality than the rest of the world?

That will satisfy me.

If so, when we set out to discover the essential nature of justice and injustice and what a perfectly just and a perfectly unjust man would be like, supposing them to exist, our purpose was to use them as ideal patterns: we were to observe the degree of happiness or unhappiness that each exhibited, and to draw the necessary inference that our own destiny would be like that of the one we most resembled. We did not set out to show that these ideals could exist in fact.

---

[7] The equality of women and the abolition of the family. [These concepts have been spoken of as waves, and the wave metaphor is now continued. Editors.]

[8] Justice, as a "civic" virtue, has been defined . . . but the wise man's virtue, based on knowledge, has still to be described.

That is true.

Then suppose a painter had drawn an ideally beautiful figure complete to the last touch, would you think any the worse of him, if he could not show that a person as beautiful as that could exist?

No, I should not.

Well, we have been constructing in discourse the pattern of an ideal state. Is our theory any the worse, if we cannot prove it possible that a state so organized should be actually founded?

Surely not.

That, then, is the truth of the matter. But if, for your satisfaction, I am to do my best to show under what conditions our ideal would have the best chance of being realized, I must ask you once more to admit that the same principle applies here. Can theory ever be fully realized in practice? Is it not in the nature of things that action should come less close to truth than thought? People may not think so; but do you agree or not?

I do.

Then you must not insist upon my showing that this construction we have traced in thought could be reproduced in fact down to the last detail. You must admit that we shall have found a way to meet your demand for realization, if we can discover how a state might be constituted in the closest accordance with our description. Will not that content you? It would be enough for me.

And for me too.

Then our next attempt, it seems, must be to point out what defect in the working of existing states prevents them from being so organized, and what is the least change that would effect a transformation into this type of government—a single change if possible, or perhaps two; at any rate let us make the changes as few and insignificant as may be.

By all means.

Well, there is one change which, as I believe we can show, would bring about this revolution—not a small change, certainly, nor an easy one, but possible.

What is it?

I have now to confront what we called the third and greatest wave. But I must state my paradox, even though the wave should break in laughter over my head and drown me in ignominy. Now mark what I am going to say.

Go on.

Unless either philosophers become kings in their countries or those who are now called kings and rulers come to be sufficiently inspired with a genuine desire for wisdom; unless, that is to say, political power and philosophy meet together, while the many natures who now go their several ways in the one or the other direction are forcibly debarred from doing so, there can be no rest from troubles, my dear Glaucon, for states, nor yet, as I believe, for all mankind; nor can this commonwealth which we have imagined ever till then see the light of day and grow to its full stature. This it was that I have so long hung back from saying; I knew what a paradox it would be, because it is hard to see that there is no other way of happiness either for the state or for the individual. ...

Definition of the Philosopher: The Two Worlds

[The word "philosophy" originally meant curiosity, the desire for fresh experience, such as led Solon to travel and see the world (Herod. i. 30). or the pursuit of intellectual culture, as in Pericles' speech: "We cultivate the mind (φιλοσοφοῦμεν) without loss of manliness" (Thuc, ii. 40). This sense has to be excluded: the Rulers are not to be dilettanti or mere amateurs of the arts. They are to desire knowledge of the whole of truth and reality, and hence of the world of essential Forms, in contrast with the world of appearances.

The doctrine of Forms is here more explicitly invoked. Corresponding to the two worlds, the mind has two faculties: Knowledge of the real and Belief in appearances (doxa). Faculties can be distinguished only by (1) the states of mind they produce, and (2) their fields of objects. By both tests Knowledge and Belief differ. (1) Knowledge is infallible (there is no false knowledge); Belief may be true or false. (2) Knowledge, by definition, is of unique, unchanging objects. Just in this respect the Forms resemble the laws of nature sought by modern natural science: a law is an unseen intelligible principle, a unity underlying an unlimited multiplicity of similar phenomena, and supposed to be unalterable. The Forms, however, are not laws of the sequence or coexistence of phenomena, but ideals or patterns, which have a real existence independent of our minds[9] and of which the many individual things called by their names in the world of appearances are like images or reflections. If we are disposed, with Aristotle, to deny that Platonic Forms or ideals exist apart from individual things in the visible world, we should remember that the essence of the doctrine is the conviction that the differences between good and evil, right and wrong, true and false, beautiful and ugly, are absolute, not 'relative' to the customs or tastes or desires of individual men or social groups. We can know them or (as is commonly the case) not know them; they cannot change or vary from place to place or from time to time. This conviction has been, and is, held by many who cannot accept, at its face value, Plato's mode of expressing it.

A Form, such as Beauty itself, excludes its opposite, Ugliness: it can never be or become ugly. But any particular beautiful thing may be also ugly in some aspects or situations: it may cease to be beautiful and become ugly, it may seem beautiful to me, ugly to you; and it must begin and cease to exist in time. Such things cannot be objects of knowledge. Our apprehension of these many changing things is here called doxa and compared to dream experience, which is neither wholly real nor utterly nonexistent. Doxa is usually rendered by "Opinion." Here 'Belief' is preferred as having a corresponding verb which, unlike 'opine,' is in common use. But both terms are inadequate. Doxa and its cognates denote our apprehension of anything that 'seems': (1) what seems to exist, sensible appearances, phenomena; (2) what seems true, opinions, beliefs, whether really true or false; (3) what seems right, legal and deliberative decisions, and the "many conventional notions" of current morality (479 D), which vary from place to place and from time to time. The amateur of the arts and the politician live in the twilight realm of these fluctuating beliefs.]

Now, I continued, if we are to elude those assailants you have described, we must, I think, define for them whom we mean by these lovers of wisdom who, we have dared to assert, ought to be our rulers. Once we have a clear view of their character, we shall be able to defend our position by pointing to some who are naturally fitted to combine philosophic study with political leadership, while the rest of the world should accept their guidance and let philosophy alone.

Yes, this is the moment for a definition.

Here, then, is a line of thought which may lead to a satisfactory explanation. Need I remind you that a man will deserve to be called a lover of this or that, only if it is clear that he loves that things as a whole, not merely in parts?

You must remind me, it seems; for I do not see what you mean.

That answer would have come better from someone less susceptible to love than yourself, Glaucon. You ought not to have forgotten that any boy in the bloom of youth will arouse some sting of passion in a man of your amorous temperament and seem worthy of his attentions. Is not this your way with your favourites? You will praise a snub nose as piquant and a hooked one as giving a regal air, while you call a straight nose perfectly proportioned; the swarthy, you say, have a manly look, the fair are children of the gods; and what do you think is that word 'honey-pale,' if not the euphemism of some lover who had no fault to find with sallowness on the cheek of youth? In a word, you will carry pretence and extravagance to any length sooner than reject a single one that is in the flower of his prime.

If you insist on taking me as an example of how lovers behave, I will agree for the sake of argument.

---

[9] Hence most modern critics avoid the term 'idea,' though this is Plato's word, because it now suggests a thought existing only in our minds.

Again, do you not see the same behaviour in people with a passion for wine? They are glad of any excuse to drink wine of any sort. And there are the men who covet honour, who, if they cannot lead an army, will command a company, and if they cannot win the respect of important people, are glad to be looked up to by nobodies, because they must have someone to esteem them.

Quite true.

Do you agree, then, that when we speak of a man as having a passion for a certain kind of thing, we mean that he has an appetite for everything of that kind without discrimination?

Yes.

So the philosopher, with his passion for wisdom, will be one who desires all wisdom, not only some part of it. If a student is particular about his studies, especially while he is too young to know which are useful and which are not, we shall say he is no lover of learning or of wisdom; just as, if he were dainty about his food, we should say he was not hungry or fond of eating, but had a poor appetite. Only the man who has a taste for every sort of knowledge and throws himself into acquiring it with an insatiable curiosity will deserve to be called a philosopher. Am I not right?

That description, Glaucon replied, would include a large and ill-assorted company. It is curiosity, I suppose, and a delight in fresh experience that gives some people a passion for all that is to be seen and heard at theatrical and muscial performances. But they are a queer set to reckon among philosophers, considering that they would never go near anything like a philosophical discussion, though they run round at all the Dionysiac festivals in town or country as if they were under contract to listen to every company of performers without fail. Will curiosity entitle all these enthusiasts, not to mention amateurs of the minor arts, to be called philosophers?

Certainly not; though they have a certain counterfeit resemblance?

And whom do you mean by the genuine philosophers?

Those whose passion it is to see the truth.

That must be so; but will you explain?

It would not be easy to explain to everyone; but you, I believe, will grant my premiss.

Which is—?

That since beauty and ugliness are opposite, they are two things; and consequently each of them is one. The same holds of justice and injustice, good and bad, and all the essential Forms: each in itself is one; but they manifest themselves in a great variety of combinations, with actions, with material things, and with one another, and so each seems to be many.[10]

That is true.

On the strength of this premiss, then, I can distinguish your amateurs of the arts and men of action from the philosophers we are concerned with, who are alone worthy of the name.

What is your distinction?

Your lovers of sights and sounds delight in beautiful tones and colours and shapes and in all the works of art into which these enter; but they have not the power of thought to behold and to take delight in the nature of Beauty itself. That power to approach Beauty and behold it as it is in itself, is rare indeed.

Quite true.

Now if a man believes in the existence of beautiful things, but not of Beauty itself, and cannot follow a guide who would lead him to a knowledge of it, is he not living in a dream? Consider: does not dreaming, whether one is awake or asleep, consist in mistaking a semblance for the reality it resembles?

I should certainly call that dreaming.

Contrast with him the man who holds that there is such a thing as Beauty itself

---

[10] At *523 A* ff., it is explained how confused impressions of opposite qualities in sense-perception provoke reflection to isolate and define the corresponding universals or Forms.

and can discern that essence as well as the things that partake of its character, without ever confusing the one with the other—is he a dreamer or living in a waking state?

He is very much awake.

So may we say that he knows, while the other has only a belief in appearances; and might we call their states of mind knowledge and belief?

Certainly.

But this person who, we say, has only belief without knowledge may be aggrieved and challenge our statement. Is there any means of soothing his resentment and converting him gently, without telling him plainly that he is not in his right mind?

We surely ought to try.

Come then, consider what we are to say to him. Or shall we ask him a question, assuring him that, far from grudging him any knowledge he may have, we shall be only too glad to find that there is something he knows? But, we shall say, tell us this: When a man knows, must there not be something that he knows? Will you answer for him, Glaucon?

My answer will be, that there must.

Something real or unreal?

Something real; how could a thing that is unreal ever be known?

Are we satisfied, then, on this point, from however many points of view we might examine it: that the perfectly real is perfectly knowable, and the utterly unreal is entirely unknowable?

Quite satisfied.

Good. Now if there is something so constituted that it both *is* and *is not,* will it not lie between the purely real and the utterly unreal?

It will.

Well then, as knowledge corresponds to the real, and absence of knowledge necessarily to the unreal, so, to correspond to this intermediate thing, we must look for something between ignorance and knowledge, if such a thing there be.

Certainly.

Is there not a thing we call belief?

Surely.

A different power from knowledge, or the same?

Different.

Knowledge and belief, then, must have different objects, answering to their respective powers.

Yes.

And knowledge has for its natural object the real—to know the truth about reality. However, before going further, I think we need a definition. Shall we distinguish under the general name of "faculties"[11] those powers which enable us—or anything else—to do what we can do? Sight and hearing, for instance, are what I call faculties, if that will help you to see the class of things I have in mind.

Yes, I understand.

Then let me tell you what view I take of them. In a faculty I cannot find any of those qualities, such as colour or shape, which, in the case of many other things, enable me to distinguish one thing from another. I can only look to its field of objects and the state of mind it produces, and regard these as sufficient to identify it and to distinguish it from faculties which have different fields and produce different states. Is that how you would go to work?

Yes.

Let us go back, then, to knowledge. Would you class that as a faculty?

Yes; and I should call it the most powerful of all.

And is belief also a faculty?

It can be nothing else, since it is what gives us the power of believing.

But a little while ago you agreed that knowledge and belief are not the same thing.

Yes; there could be no sense in identifying the infallible with the fallible.[12] Good.

---

[11] The Greek here uses only the common word for "power" (*dynamis*), but Plato is defining the special sense we express by "faculty."

[12] This marks one distinction between the two states of mind. Further, even if true, belief, unlike knowledge, (1) is produced by persuasion, not by instruction; (2) cannot "give an account" of itself; and (3) can be shaken by persuasion (*Timaeus* 51 E).

So we are quite clear that knowledge and belief are different things?

They are.

If so, each of them, having a different power, must have a different field of objects.

Necessarily.

The field of knowledge being the real; and its power, the power of knowing the real as it is.

Yes.

Whereas belief, we say, is the power of believing. Is its object the same as that which knowledge knows? Can the same things be possible objects of knowledge and of belief?[13]

Not if we hold to the principles we agreed upon. If it is of the nature of a different faculty to have a different field, and if both knowledge and belief are faculties and, as we assert, different ones, it follows that the same things cannot be possible objects of both.

So if the real is the object of knowledge, the object of belief must be something other than the real.

Yes.

Can it be the unreal? Or is that an impossible object even for belief? Consider: if a man has a belief, there must be something before his mind; he cannot be believing nothing, can he?

No.

He is believing something, then; whereas the unreal could only be called nothing at all.

Certainly.

Now we said that ignorance must correspond to the unreal, knowledge to the real. So what he is believing cannot be real nor yet unreal.

True.

Belief, then, cannot be either ignorance or knowledge.

---

[13] If "belief" bore its common meaning, we might answer, yes. But in this context it is essentially belief in *appearances*. It includes perception by the senses, and these can never perceive objects of thought, such as Beauty itself.

It appears not.

Then does it lie outside and beyond these two? Is it either more clear and certain than knowledge or less clear and certain than ignorance?

No, it is neither.

It rather seems to you to be something more obscure than knowledge, but not so dark as ignorance, and so to lie between the two extremes?

Quite so.

Well, we said earlier that if some object could be found such that it both *is* and at the same time *is not,* that object would lie between the perfectly real and the utterly unreal; and that the corresponding faculty would be neither knowledge nor ignorance, but a faculty to be found situated between the two.

Yes.

And now what we have found between the two is the faculty we call belief.

True.

It seems, then, that what remains to be discovered is that object which can be said both to be and not to be and cannot properly be called either purely real or purely unreal. If that can be found, we may justly call the object of belief, and so give the intermediate faculty the intermediate object, while the two extreme objects will fall to the extreme faculties.

Yes.

On these assumptions, then, I shall call for an answer from our friend who denies the existence of Beauty itself or of anything that can be called an essential Form of Beauty remaining unchangeably in the same state for ever, though he does recognize the existence of beautiful things as a plurality—that lover of things seen who will not listen to anyone who says that Beauty is one, justice is one, and so on. I shall say to him, Be so good as to tell us: of all these many beautiful things is there one which will not appear ugly? Or of these many just or righteous actions, is there one that will not appear unjust or unrighteous?

No, replied Glaucon, they must inevitably appear to be in some way both beautiful and ugly; and so with all the other terms your question refers to.

And again the many things which are doubles are just as much halves as they are doubles. And the things we call large or heavy have just as much right to be called small or light.

Yes; any such thing will always have a claim to both opposite designations.

Then, whatever any one of these many things may be said to be, can you say that it absolutely is that, any more than that it *is not* that?

They remind me of those punning riddles people ask at dinner parties, or the child's puzzle about what the eunuch threw at the bat and what the bat was perched on.[14] These things have the same ambiguous character, and one cannot form any stable conception of them either as being or as not being, or as both being and not being, or as neither.

Can you think of any better way of disposing of them than by placing them between reality and unreality? For I suppose they will not appear more obscure and so less real than unreality, or clearer and so more real than reality.

Quite true.

It seems, then, we have discovered that the many conventional notions of the mass of mankind about what is beautiful or honourable or just and so on are adrift in a sort of twilight between pure reality and pure unreality.

We have.

And we agreed earlier that, if any such object were discovered, it should be called the object of belief and not of knowledge. Fluctuating in that halfway region, it would be seized upon by the intermediate faculty.

Yes.

So when people have an eye for the multitude of beautiful things or of just actions or whatever it may be, but can neither behold Beauty or justice itself nor follow a guide who would lead them to it, we shall say that all they have is beliefs, without any real knowledge of the objects of their belief.

That follows.

But what of those who contemplate the realities themselves as they are for ever in the same unchangeable state? Shall we not say that they have, not mere belief, but knowledge?

That too follows.

And, further, that their affection goes out to the objects of knowledge, whereas the others set their affections on the objects of belief; for it was they, you remember, who had a passion for the spectacle of beautiful colours and sounds, but would not hear of Beauty itself being a real thing.

I remember.

So we may fairly call them lovers of belief rather than of wisdom—not philosophical, in fact, but philosophical. Will they be seriously annoyed by that description?

Not if they will listen to my advice. No one ought to take offence at the truth.

The name of philosopher, then, will be reserved for those whose affections are set, in every case, on the reality.

By all means.

The Philosopher's Fitness to Rule

[The above definition of the philosopher might suggest an unpractical head-in-air, unfit to control life in the state. But the qualities most valuable in a ruler will follow naturally from the master passion for truth in a nature of the type described earlier, when it is perfected by time and education.]

So at last, Glaucon, after this long and weary way, we have come to see who are the philosophers and who are not.

I doubt if the way could have been shortened.

---

[14] A man who was not a man (eunuch), seeing and not seeing (seeing imperfectly) a bird that was not a bird (bat) perched on a bough that was not a bough (a reed), pelted and did not pelt it (aimed at it and missed) with a stone that was not a stone (pumice-stone).

Apparently not. I think, however, that we might have gained a still clearer view if this had been the only topic to be discussed; but there are so many others awaiting us, if we mean to discover in what ways the just life is better than the unjust.

Which are we to take up now?

Surely the one that follows next in order. Since the philosophers are those who can apprehend the eternal and unchanging, while those who cannot do so, but are lost in the mazes of multiplicity and change, are not philosophers, which of the two ought to be in control of a state?

I wonder what would be a reasonable solution.

To establish as Guardians whichever of the two appear competent to guard the laws and ways of life in society.

True.

Well, there can be no question whether a guardian who is to keep watch over anything needs to be keen-sighted or blind. And is not blindness precisely the condition of men who are entirely cut off from knowledge of any reality, and have in their soul no clear pattern of perfect truth, which they might study in every detail and constantly refer to, as a painter looks at his model, before they proceed to embody notions of justice, honour, and goodness in earthly institutions or, in their character of Guardians, to preserve such institutions as already exist?

Certainly such a condition is very like blindness.

Shall we, then, make such as these our Guardians in preference to men who, besides their knowledge of realities, are in no way inferior to them in experience and in every excellence of character?

It would be absurd not to choose the philosophers, whose knowledge is perhaps their greatest point of superiority, provided they do not lack those other qualifications.

What we have to explain, then, is how those qualifications can be combined in the same persons with philosophy.

Certainly.

The first thing, as we said at the outset, is to get a clear view of their inborn disposition.[15] When we are satisfied on that head, I think we shall agree that such a combination of qualities is possible and that we need look no further for men fit to be in control of a commonwealth. One trait of the philosophic nature we may take as already granted: a constant passion for any knowledge that will reveal to them something of that reality which endures for ever and is not always passing into and out of existence. And, we may add, their desire is to know the whole of that reality; they will not willingly renounce any part of it as relatively small and insignificant, as we said before when we compared them to the lover and to the man who covets honour.

True.

Is there not another trait which the nature we are seeking cannot fail to possess—truthfulness, a love of truth and a hatred of falsehood that will not tolerate untruth in any form?

Yes, it is natural to expect that.

It is not merely natural, but entirely necessary that an instinctive passion for any object should extend to all that is closely akin to it; and there is nothing more closely akin to wisdom than truth. So the same nature cannot love wisdom and falsehood; the genuine lover of knowledge cannot fail, from his youth up, to strive after the whole of truth.

I perfectly agree.

Now we surely know that when a man's desires set strongly in one direction, in every other channel they flow more feebly, like a stream diverted into another bed. So when the current has set towards knowledge and all that goes with it, desire will abandon those pleasures of which the body is the instrument and be concerned only with the pleasure which the soul enjoys independently—if, that is to say, the love of

---

[15] The subject of the present chapter. The next will explain why the other qualifications, of experience and character, are too often lacking.

wisdom is more than a mere pretence. Accordingly, such a one will be temperate and no lover of money; for he will be the last person to care about the things for the sake of which money is eagerly sought and lavishly spent.

That is true.

Again, in seeking to distinguish the philosophic nature, you must not overlook the least touch of meanness. Nothing could be more contrary than pettiness to a mind constantly bent on grasping the whole of things, both divine and human.

Quite true.

And do you suppose that one who is so high-minded and whose thought can contemplate all time and all existence will count this life of man a matter of such concern?

No, he could not.

So for such a man death will have no terrors.

None.

A mean and cowardly nature, then, can have no part in the genuine pursuit of wisdom.

I think not.

And if a man is temperate and free from the love of money, meanness, pretentiousness, and cowardice, he will not be hard to deal with or dishonest. So, as another indication of the philosophic temper, you will observe whether, from youth up, he is fair-minded, gentle, and sociable.

Certainly.

Also you will not fail to notice whether he is quick or slow to learn. No one can be expected to take a reasonable delight in a task in which much painful effort makes little headway. And if he cannot retain what he learns, his forgetfulness will leave no room in his head for knowledge; and so, having all his toil for nothing, he can only end by hating himself as well as his fruitless occupation. We must not, then, count a forgetful mind as competent to pursue wisdom; we must require a good memory.

By all means.

Further, there is in some natures a crudity and awkwardness that can only

tend to a lack of measure and proportion; and there is a close affinity between proportion and truth. Hence, besides our other requirements, we shall look for a mind endowed with measure and grace, which will be instinctively drawn to see every reality in its true light.

Yes.

Well then, now that we have enumerated the qualities of a mind destined to take its full part in the apprehension of reality, have you any doubt about their being indispensable and all necessarily going together?

None whatever.

Then have you any fault to find with a pursuit which none can worthily follow who is not by nature quick to learn and to remember, magnanimous and gracious, the friend and kinsman of truth, justice, courage, temperance?

No; Momus[16] himself could find no flaw in it.

Well then, when time and education have brought such characters as these to maturity, would you entrust the care of your commonwealth to anyone else? . . .

The Allegory of the Cave

[The progress of the mind from the lowest state of unenlightenment to knowledge of the Good is now illustrated by the famous parable comparing the world of appearance to an underground Cave. In Empedocles' religious poem the powers which conduct the soul to its incarnation say, "We have come under this cavern's roof." The image was probably taken from mysteries held in caves or dark chambers representing the underworld, through which the candidates for initiation were led to the revelation of sacred objects in a blaze of light. The idea that the body is a prison-house, to which the soul is condemned for past misdeeds, is attributed by Plato to the Orphics.

One moral of the allegory is drawn from the distress caused by a too sudden passage from darkness to light. The earlier warning against plunging untrained minds into the discussion of

---

[16] The spirit of faultfinding, one of the children of Night in Hesoid's *Theogony.*

moral problems (498 A), as the Sophists and Socrates himself had done, is reinforced by the picture of the dazed prisoner dragged out into the sunlight. Plato's ten years' course of pure mathematics is to habituate the intellect to abstract reasoning before moral ideas are called in question (537 E, ff.).]

Next, said I, here is a parable to illustrate the degrees in which our nature may be enlightened or unenlightened. Imagine the condition of men living in a sort of cavernous chamber underground, with an entrance open to the light and a long passage all down the cave.[17] Here they have been from childhood, chained by the leg and also by the neck, so that they cannot move and can see only what is in front of them, because the chains will not let them turn their heads. At some distance higher up is the light of a fire burning behind them; and between the prisoners and the fire is a track[18] with a parapet built along it, like the screen at a puppet-show, which hides the performers while they show their puppets over the top.

I see, said he.

Now behind this parapet imagine persons carrying along various artificial objects, including figures of men and animals in wood or stone or other materials, which project above the parapet. Naturally, some of these persons will be talking, others silent.[19]

It is a strange picture, he said, and a strange sort of prisoners.

Like ourselves, I replied; for in the first place prisoners so confined would have seen nothing of themselves or of one another, except the shadows thrown by the fire-light on the wall of the Cave facing them, would they?

Not if all their lives they had been prevented from moving their heads.

And they would have seen as little of the objects carried past.

Of course.

Now, if they could talk to one another, would they not suppose that their words referred only to those passing shadows which they saw?[20]

Necessarily.

And suppose their prison had an echo from the wall facing them? When one of the people crossing behind them spoke, they could only suppose that the sound came from the shadow passing before their eyes.

No doubt.

In every way, then, such prisoners would recognize as reality nothing but the shadows of those artificial objects.[21]

Inevitably.

Now consider what would happen if their release from the chains and the healing of their unwisdom should come about in this way. Suppose one of them set free and forced suddenly to stand up, turn his head, and walk with eyes lifted to the light; all these movements would be painful, and he would be too dazzled to make out the objects whose shadows he had been used to see. What do you think he would say, if someone told him that what he had formerly seen was meaningless illusion, but now, being somewhat nearer to reality and

---

[17] The length of the "way in" (eisodos) to the chamber where the prisoners sit is an essential feature, explaining why no daylight reaches them.

[18] The track crosses the passage into the cave at right angles, and is above the parapet built along it.

[19] A modern Plato would compare his Cave to an underground cinema, where the audience watches the play of shadows thrown by the film passing before a light at their backs. The film itself is only an image of "real" things and events in the world outside the cinema. For the film Plato has to substitute the clumsier apparatus of a procession of artificial objects carried on their heads by persons who are merely part of the machinery, providing for the movement of the objects and the sounds whose echo the prisoners hear. The parapet prevents these persons' shadows from being cast on the wall of the Cave.

[20] The prisoners, having seen nothing but shadows, cannot think their words refer to the objects carried past behind their backs. For them shadows (images) are the only realities.

[21] The state of mind called *eikasia* in the previous chapter.

turned towards more real objects, he was getting a truer view? Suppose further that he were shown the various objects being carried by and were made to say, in reply to questions, what each of them was. Would he not be perplexed and believe the objects now shown him to be not so real as what he formerly saw?[22]

Yes, not nearly so real.

And if he were forced to look at the fire-light itself, would not his eyes ache, so that he would try to escape and turn back to the things which he could see distinctly, convinced that they really were clearer than these other objects now being shown to him?

Yes.

And suppose someone were to drag him away forcibly up the steep and rugged ascent and not let him go until he had hauled him out into the sunlight, would he not suffer pain and vexation at such treatment, and, when he had come out into the light, find his eyes so full of its radiance that he could not see a single one of the things that he was now told were real?

Certainly he would not see them all at once.

He would need, then, to grow accustomed before he could see things in that upper world.[23] At first it would be easiest to make out shadows, and then the images of men and things reflected in water, and later on the things themselves. After that, it would be easier to watch the heavenly bodies and the sky itself by night, looking at the light of the moon and stars rather than the Sun and the Sun's light in the day-time.

Yes, surely.

Last of all, he would be able to look at the Sun and contemplate its nature, not as it appears when reflected in water or any

alien medium, but as it is in itself in its own domain.

No doubt.

And now he would begin to draw the conclusion that it is the Sun that produces the seasons and the course of the year and controls everything in the visible world, and moreover is in a way the cause of all that he and his companions used to see.

Clearly he would come at last to that conclusion.

Then if he called to mind his fellow prisoners and what passed for wisdom in his former dwelling-place, he would surely think himself happy in the change and be sorry for them. They may have had a practice of honouring and commending one another, with prizes for the man who had the keenest eye for the passing shadows and the best memory for the order in which they followed or accompanied one another, so that he could make a good guess as to which was going to come next.[24] Would our released prisoner be likely to covet those prizes or to envy the men exalted to honour and power in the Cave? Would he not feel like Homer's Achilles, that he would far sooner "be on earth as a hired servant in the house of a landless man"[25] or endure anything rather than go back to his old beliefs and live in the old way?

Yes, he would prefer any fate to such a life.

Now imagine what would happen if he went down again to take his former seat in the Cave. Coming suddenly out of the sunlight, his eyes would be filled with darkness. He might be required once more to deliver his opinion on those shadows, in competition with the prisoners who had never been released, while his eyesight was

---

[22] The first effect of Socratic questioning is perplexity.

[23] Here is the moral—the need of habituation by mathematical study before discussing moral ideas and ascending through them to the Form of the Good.

[24] The empirical politician, with no philosophic insight, but only a "knack of remembering what usually happens" (*Gorg. 501 A*). He has *eikasia* = conjecture as to what is likely (*eikos*).

[25] This verse (already quoted at 386 c), being spoken by the ghost of Achilles, suggests that the Cave is comparable with Hades.

still dim and unsteady; and it might take some time to become used to the darkness. They would laught at him and say that he had gone up only to come back with his sight ruined; it was worth no one's while even to attempt the ascent. If they could lay hands on the man who was trying to set them free and lead them up, they would kill him.[26]

Yes, they would.

Every feature in this parable, my dear Glaucon, is meant to fit our earlier analysis. The prison dwelling corresponds to the region revealed to us through the sense of sight, and the fire-light within it to the power of the Sun. The ascent to see the things in the upper world you may take as standing for the upward journey of the soul into the region of the intelligible; then you will be in possession of what I surmise, since that is what you wish to be told. Heaven knows whether it is true; but this, at any rate, is how it appears to me. In the world of knowledge, the last thing to be perceived and only with great difficulty is the essential Form of Goodness. Once it is perceived, the conclusion must follow that, for all things, this is the cause of whatever is right and good; in the visible world it gives birth to light and to the lord of light, while it is itself sovereign in the intelligible world and the parent of intelligence and truth. Without having had a vision of this Form no one can act with wisdom, either in his own life or in matters of state.

So far as I can understand, I share your belief.

Then you may also agree that it is no wonder if those who have reached this height are reluctant to manage the affairs of men. Their souls long to spend all their time in that upper world—naturally enough, if here once more our parable holds true. Nor, again, is it at all strange that one who comes from the contemplation of divine things to the miseries of human life should appear awkward and ridiculous when, with eyes still dazed and not yet accustomed to the darkness, he is compelled, in a lawcourt or elsewhere, to dispute about the shadows of justice or the images that cast those shadows, and to wrangle over the notions of what is right in the minds of men who have never beheld justice itself.[27]

It is not at all strange.

No; a sensible man will remember that the eyes may be confused in two ways—by a change from light to darkness or from darkness to light; and he will recognize that the same thing happens to the soul. When he sees it troubled and unable to discern anything clearly, instead of laughing thoughtlessly, he will ask whether, coming from a brighter existence, its unaccustomed vision is obscured by the darkness, in which case he will think its condition enviable and its life a happy one; or whether, emerging from the depths of ignorance, it is dazzled by excess of light. If so, he will rather feel sorry for it; or, if he were inclined to laugh, that would be less ridiculous than to laugh at the soul which has come down from the light.

That is a fair statement.

If this is true, then, we must conclude that education is not what it is said to be by some, who profess to put knowledge into a soul which does not possess it, as if they could put sight into blind eyes. On the contrary, our own account signifies that the soul of every man does possess the power of learning the truth and the organ to see it with; and that, just as one might have to turn the whole body round in order that the eye should see light instead of darkness, so the entire soul must be turned away from this changing world, until its eye can bear to contemplate reality and that supreme splendour which we have called the Good. Hence there may well be an art whose aim would be to effect this very thing, the conversion of the soul, in the readiest way; not

---

[26] An allusion to the fate of Socrates.

[27] In the *Gorgias* 486 A, Callicles, forecasting the trial of Socrates, taunts him with the philosopher's inability to defend himself in a court.

to put the power of sight into the soul's eye, which already has it, but to ensure that, instead of looking in the wrong direction, it is turned the way it ought to be.

Yes, it may well be so.

It looks, then, as though wisdom were different from those ordinary virtues, as they are called, which are not far removed from bodily qualities, in that they can be produced by habituation and exercise in a soul which has not possessed them from the first. Wisdom, it seems, is certainly the virtue of some diviner faculty, which never loses its power, though its use for good or harm depends on the direction towards which it is turned. You must have noticed in dishonest men with a reputation for sagacity the shrewd glance of a narrow intelligence piercing the objects to which it is directed. There is nothing wrong with their power of vision, but it has been forced into the service of evil, so that the keener its sight, the more harm it works.

Quite true.

And yet if the growth of a nature like this had been pruned from earliest childhood, cleared of those clinging overgrowths which come of gluttony and all luxurious pleasure and, like leaden weights charged with affinity to this mortal world, hang upon the soul, bending its vision downwards; if, freed from these, the soul were turned round towards true reality, then this same power in these very men would see the truth as keenly as the objects it is turned to now.

Yes, very likely.

Is it not also likely, or indeed certain after what has been said, that a state can never be properly governed either by the uneducated who know nothing of truth or by men who are allowed to spend all their days in the pursuit of culture? The ignorant have no single mark before their eyes at which they must aim in all the conduct of their own lives and of affairs of state; and the others will not engage in action if they can help it, dreaming that, while still alive, they have been translated to the Islands of the Blest.

Quite true.

It is for us, then, as founders of a commonwealth, to bring compulsion to bear on the noblest natures. They must be made to climb the ascent to the vision of Goodness, which we called the highest object of knowledge; and, when they have looked upon it long enough, they must not be allowed, as they now are, to remain on the heights, refusing to come down again to the prisoners or to take any part in their labours and rewards, however much or little these may be worth.

Shall we not be doing them an injustice, if we force on them a worse life than they might have?

You have forgotten again, my friend, that the law is not concerned to make any one class specially happy, but to ensure the welfare of the commonwealth as a whole. By persuasion or constraint it will unite the citizens in harmony, making them share whatever benefits each class can contribute to the common good; and its purpose in forming men of that spirit was not that each should be left to go his own way, but that they should be instrumental in binding the community into one.

You will see, then, Glaucon, that there will be no real injustice in compelling our philosophers to watch over and care for the other citizens. We can fairly tell them that their compeers in other states may quite reasonably refuse to collaborate: there they have sprung up, like a self-sown plant, in despite of their country's institutions; no one has fostered their growth, and they cannot be expected to show gratitude for a care they have never received. "But," we shall say, "it is not so with you. We have brought you into existence for your country's sake as well as for your own, to be like leaders and king-bees in a hive; you have been better and more thoroughly educated than those others and hence you are more capable of playing your part both as men of thought and as men of action. You must go down, then, each in his turn, to live with the rest and let your eyes grow accustomed to the darkness. You will then see a thousand times better than those who live there always; you will recognize every image for what it is and know what it represents, because you have seen justice, beauty, and goodness in their reality; and so you and we shall find life in our commonwealth no mere dream, as it is in most existing states, where men live fighting one another about shadows and quarrelling for power, as if that were a great prize; whereas in truth government can be at its best and free from dissension only where the destined rulers are least desirous of holding office."

Quite true.

Then will our pupils refuse to listen and to take their turns at sharing in the work of the community, though they may live together for most of their time in a purer air?

No; it is a fair demand, and they are fair-minded men. No doubt, unlike any ruler of the present day, they will think of holding power as an unavoidable necessity.

Yes, my friend; for the truth is that you can have a well-governed society only if you can discover for your future rulers a better way of life than being in office; then only will power be in the hands of men who are rich, not in gold, but in the wealth that brings happiness, a good and wise life. All goes wrong when, starved for lack of anything good in their lives, men turn to public affairs hoping to snatch from thence the happiness they hunger for. They set about fighting for power, and this internecine conflict ruins them and their country. The life of true philosophy is the only one that looks down upon offices of state; and access to power must be confined to men who are not in love with it; otherwise rivals will start fighting. So whom else can you compel to undertake the guardianship of the commonwealth, if not those who, besides understanding best the principles of government, enjoy a nobler life than the politician's and look for rewards of a different kind?

There is indeed no other choice.

COMMENT

The Means of Achieving the Ideal

Since the foregoing excerpts from the *Republic* state Plato's ideal as well as his philosophical premises, only a few remarks need to be added to complete the exposition and show how Plato believed his idea could be implemented.

If the Guardians are to be wise, they must be very carefully bred, selected, reared, and educated. The biological fitness of the ruling class should be guaranteed by a comprehensive program of eugenics; the most select parents should be induced to have the greatest number of children. Even more important is education, which Plato regards as the main foundation of the state.

He conceives education as a journey of the mind from the concrete practicalities of sensory experience to the external and abstract realities of the intellect. It begins with the arts and gymnastics and mounts upward through mathematics, astronomy, and harmonics (the mathematical theory of musical form) to philosophy. The preliminary education continues until about the age of eighteen; then follows two years of military training, for males and females alike. The Guardians are then provisionally selected by "ordeals of toil and pain," and only those who manifest the proper character and intelligence will receive the highest training. The program of mathematical and scientific training will occupy the prospective Guardians from the age of twenty to thirty, and they will then have intensive training in philosophy ("dialectics") for five additional years, or until they have "grasped by pure intelligence the very nature of Goodness itself." The students who have distinguished themselves throughout this long and arduous training will serve a political apprenticeship for about fifteen years, discharging the subordinate functions "suitable to the young." Finally, those who have fully proved their mettle, both men and women, will be selected at the age of fifty to fulfill the high function of philosopher-kings. Others, fit to be soldiers but incapable of the highest intellectual flights, remain Auxiliaries; and the great mass of the people, as members of the producing class, receive the lesser education appropriate to their station.

Every precaution should be taken to ward off temptations and keep the Guardians and Auxiliaries faithful to the state. The chief temptations arise from private interests. The competitive struggle for property, Plato believes, is incompatible with full devotion to the social good. Hence he proposes that the Guardians and Auxiliaries should have no private possessions or acquisitive occupations and that they should receive their maintenance from the state. This proposal is not the same as modern communism since it applies only to the Auxiliaries and Guardians and not to the producers, who constitute the bulk of the population.

Plato also believes that normal marriage and family life are incompatible with wholehearted devotion to the state since there is always a temptation to prefer family interests to community welfare. Hence he proposes to abolish private homes and monogamous marriage among the Guardians and Auxiliaries. They should live and share their meals together, realizing the principle that "friends have all things in common." Sexual intercourse should be strictly controlled in the interests of the eugenics program.

Such is the pattern of the aristocratic state. However, even the "best" of states may decay, and Plato imaginatively sketches, in a section here omitted, the decline of the state through successive stages of timocracy—the rule of the military class; oligarchy—the rule of the wealthy; democracy—the rule of the many; and tyranny—the rule of the irresponsible dictator. Finally, he discusses art and rewards and punishments after death, but these topics do not now concern us.

Some Main Issues

No one will agree with all of the details of Plato's arguments, but even when we least agree we can find his ideas challenging. Among the principal issues that he presents are the following:

1. *Force versus morality.* In Books I and II of the *Republic,* Plato raises one of the basic issues in political philosophy—the question of whether force or morality is the foundation of the state. Against Thrasymachus, Socrates (as a character in the dialogue) argues that the authority of the ruler is morally based on right rather than might. In reply to Glaucon and Adeimantus, he maintains that social obligation is based on duty rather than selfish expediency. The policies of the state, he insists, should conform to the pattern of the Good, which wise persons, long disciplined by education, can alone discern. He distinguishes between *opinion* and

knowledge about goodness and maintains that genuine knowledge requires an intellectual grasp of *forms.* The form is the universal essence that is somehow exemplified in particular instances. All beautiful things, for example, exemplify the form of beauty, and all just acts and institutions exemplify the form of justice.

According to Plato, these forms or universals are real, but they exist in their full and essential reality apart from particular things. The perfection, unity, and eternality of the forms separate them from the imperfection, multiplicity, and impermanence of particular things. The sensible nature of the thing declares itself as relative and contingent and points to the imperishable essence that is connected with it and yet independent of it—a form free from limitation, change, defilement. The nature of this superreality is hard to define—Plato appears to have struggled with the problem throughout his whole philosophical career. In the *Phaedo,* the particulars are said to "participate" in the forms, or the forms are said to be "present" in the particulars. Elsewhere in Plato's dialogues the individual things are said to "imitate" the forms or to be related as an imperfect "copy" to a pattern or archetype. However, all such language is metaphorical, and the essential truth is that the universal somehow transcends the particulars. In the *Republic,* this is taken to mean that the pattern of the ideal state is eternal and hence exempt from the relativities of power politics and shifting expediency.

Whether Plato's theory—or any doctrine of eternal and objective universals—is sound has been one of the principal questions of philosophy from his day until the present. It is possible to agree with him that universals are real and yet to differ from him in holding that they are immanent in particulars rather than separate and transcendent. "Justice" really exists, but in particular instances—not in "a heaven above the heavens" or as a separate, eternal essence. The "form," in this sense, is simply the characteristic common to all members of the class of things (in this case, the class of just things). The human mind has the power to notice resemblances and to abstract (that is, mentally to extricate) the common characteristics. Thus, universals can be said to consist, on the one hand, of common properties in things, and on the other hand, of concepts that represent these properties. This theory of real but immanent universals is the doctrine of Aristotle, and it serves as well as Plato's theory as an alternative to moral relativism. What is required is that moral concepts must conform to real, objective distinctions, and on this point Plato and Aristotle agree.

2. *The "closed" versus the "open" society.* With his vision fixed on eternal forms, Plato wishes, after a fundamental revolution in human affairs, to arrest history and preserve the ideal state in its static perfection. As means to this end, he proposes rigorous censorship of the arts and religion; the use of myths and "noble lies" to reconcile the lower classes to their subordinate status; and the regulation of all details of social life, including marriage and the ownership of property, among the Guardians and Auxiliaries. In effect, he insists on a tight, "closed" unity of the body politic.

This emphasis on a static unity is related to his organic theory of the state. Plato maintains that the state is the human soul writ large, just as the soul is the state writ small. There is some question of how literally we should understand this doctrine, but it seems to imply that the state, like the individual personality, is an organism—that is, a living being with a life and worth of its own. Individuals appear mainly to derive their character and value from their relation to this organic whole. This sort of ethical organism receives its most express and elaborate expression in the social philosophy of G. W. F. Hegel, but it is foreshadowed in the *Republic*.

The contrasting ideal of an "open" society—in which the freedom and intrinsic value of the individual are primarily emphasized—was eloquently formulated by John Stuart Mill in *On Liberty* (see Chapter 24). Both Mill and Plato, in a sense, maintain an ethics of self-realization, but Plato contends that the private interest of the individual is at one with the interest of the state, whereas Mill is distrustful of the state and believes that self-realization lies in the cultivation of individuality.

We can roughly divide political philosophers into two schools of thought corresponding to their positions on this issue. In one camp are the organic theorists—Plato, Rousseau, Hegel, and Marx—who stress the importance of the general will and the value and significance of collective processes. In the other group are the individualistic theorists—Hume, Bentham, Mill, and Jefferson—who disbelieve in the organic nature of society and regard social institutions as means to the happiness of individuals. The dispute between these two schools of thought is perhaps the most important conflict in the whole of political philosophy.

3. *Aristocracy versus democracy.* The basic tenet of Plato's social philosophy, as we have seen, is that philosopher-kings should rule. This conviction is consistent with his general attitude toward life: He habitually prefers the choice goods to the common goods. Hence he ranks democracy, whose slogan is "equality," as fourth in his classification of five types of government, superior only to tyranny and inferior to aristocracy, timocracy, and oligarchy. The typical democrat seems to him an ill-educated and superficial fellow who wishes to drag all excellent things down to the mediocre level of the average.

The democrat might reply that philosopher-kings are difficult to find or to produce and that a government *of* the few is almost certain to be a government *for* the few. No one can be trusted with irresponsible power, not even the so-called wise. It is the wearer of the shoe who knows where it pinches, and consequently we cannot allow the few aristocrats to choose our shoes for us. If the state exacts duties of its citizens, moreover, it should grant them rights—for responsibility implies freedom. It is only by living as free people—by participating in government and exercising self-rule—that we cease to be mere imitators and become fully developed human beings. With such arguments, the democrat might answer Plato.

If we democrats and liberals are sensible, however, we will not indiscriminately reject the whole of Plato's social philosophy. We need experts in our government and wisdom in our lives. We should adapt to our own ends Plato's great ideal of a state based on education, and we should seek to reconcile the aristocratic ideal of excellence with the democratic ideal of sharing. Our goals should be a culture both high in attainment and broad in terms of democratic participation.

The case in point with which we began this part, dealing with the issue of civil disobedience in the Sanctuary Movement, provides a useful device for focusing Plato's social philosophy. He might well be skeptical about the knowledge and wisdom at work among those who chose to break the law by bringing illegal immigrants across the border. Would he not maintain that the laws established by the rulers should be adhered to for the overall good of the society? Might he even question the wisdom of the sort of "rulers" we have in our modern democratic societies? In Plato's ideal republic, is there ever any place for civil disobedience? What would he say to those who claim that there are "higher," more "noble" laws than those of the state? Does not this claim sound a bit like Plato's own philosophy?

22

PEACE AND SECURITY

THOMAS HOBBES (1588–1679)

Thomas Hobbes was the son of a poor and ignorant country parson who could scarcely read the church prayers. A precocious lad, he attracted the attention of his schoolmaster by translating the Greek text of Euripides' *Medea* into Latin verse. At fifteen he entered Oxford, the cost of his education being paid by his uncle, a prosperous tradesman. He found the university instruction still dominated by medieval logic and Aristotelian philosophy, and most of the students "debauched to drunkenness, wantonness, gaming, and other vices." After taking his degree, he became tutor and then secretary to William Cavendish, later the second Earl of Devonshire. This connection with the influential Cavendish family was to last, with some interruptions, for the remainder of his life. It opened the door to cultivated society, and Hobbes became acquainted with Francis Bacon, William Harvey, and other distinguished men. His secretarial duties were light, and he found ample leisure for scholarly pursuits, which included a translation of Thucydides, published in 1628. He also accompanied his master on trips to the Continent, where he met Galileo in Florence and Mersenne, Gassendi, and other French philosophers in Paris.

In 1637 he returned to England, resolved to write philosophy and study politics. At the ripe age of fifty-two, he published his first original book, a volume entitled *The Elements of Law Natural and Politic*. Meanwhile, the civil wars were brewing, and Hobbes, finding his ideas sharply attacked, took alarm and fled to France. He spent the next eleven years in Paris, while insurrection and civil war raged in England. During this period, he engaged in controversy with René Descartes; wrote a second political treatise, *De Cive;* and served briefly as tutor to the Prince of Wales, later Charles II. In 1651 he published his greatest work, *Leviathan*, a plea for materialism and political absolutism. This book offended the Republicans for its defense of absolutism, the Royalists for its scorn of the divine right of kings, and the clergy for its championship of the state over the Church. Finding himself unpopular among the exiles in Paris, Hobbes returned to England and submitted to Oliver Cromwell.

Hobbes now devoted himself to philosophy, expounding his materialistic metaphysics in *De Corpore* (1655). He also engaged in furious controversy with his critics, not always creditably. In 1660 the Stuarts were restored, with Hobbes' former student and friend, now Charles II, on the throne. Despite his friendship with the king, however, his public reputation was that of an atheist and blasphemer, and the House of Commons considered the advisability of ordering a public burning of his books. Since he could not obtain leave in England to publish works on controversial subjects, his *Behemoth: The History of the Causes of the Civil Wars of England* (1688) had to be published abroad. By this time he was old in years but indefatigable in spirit, singing by night and playing tennis by day, as intellectually keen as he was physically vigorous. At eighty-four he wrote an autobiography in Latin verse, and in the next few years translated the whole of Homer's *Iliad* and *Odyssey*. He died in his boots at the age of ninety-one, stricken by apoplexy.

LEVIATHAN

Chapter XIII

Of the Natural Condition of Mankind as Concerning Their Felicity, and Misery

Nature hath made men so equal, in the faculties of the body and mind; as that, though there be found one man sometimes manifestly stronger in body or of quicker mind than another, yet when all is reckoned together, the difference between man and man is not so considerable, as that one man can thereupon claim to himself any benefit, to which another may not pretend as well as he. For as to the strength of body, the weakest has strength enough to kill the strongest, either by secret machination, or by confederacy with others that are in the same danger with himself.

And as to the faculties of the mind—setting aside the arts grounded upon words, and especially that skill of proceeding upon general and infallible rules, called science; which very few have, and but in few things; as being not a native faculty, born with us; nor attained, as prudence, while we look after somewhat else—I find yet a greater equality amongst men, than that of strength. For prudence is but experience, which equal time equally bestows on all men, in those things they equally apply themselves unto. That which may perhaps make such equality incredible, is but a vain conceit of one's own wisdom, which almost all men think they have in a greater degree than the vulgar; that is, than all men but themselves, and a few others, whom by fame, or for concurring with themselves, they approve. For such is the nature of men, that howsoever they may acknowledge many others to be more witty, or more eloquent, or more learned, yet they will hardly believe there be many so wise as themselves; for they see their own wit at hand, and other men's at a distance. But this proveth rather than men are in that point equal, than unequal. For there is not ordinarily a greater sign of the equal distribution of anything, than that every man is contented with his share.

From this equality of ability, ariseth equality of hope in the attaining of our ends. And therefore if any two men desire the same thing, which nevertheless they cannot both enjoy, they become enemies; and in the way to their end, which is principally their own conservation, and sometimes their delectation only, endeavor to destroy, or subdue one another. And from hence it comes to pass that where an invader hath no more to fear than another man's single power; if one plant, sow, build, or possess a convenient seat, others may probably be expected to come prepared with forces united, to dispossess and

---

Reprinted from *Leviathan* by Thomas Hobbes.

deprive him, not only of the fruit of his labor, but also of his life or liberty. And the invader again is in the like danger of another.

And from this diffidence of one another, there is no way for any man to secure himself so reasonable as anticipation; that is, by force or wiles to master the persons of all men he can, so long, till he see no other power great enough to endanger him: and this is no more than his own conservation requireth, and is generally allowed. Also because there be some, that taking pleasure in contemplating their own power in the acts of conquest, which they pursue farther than their security requires; if others, that otherwise would be glad to be at ease within modest bounds, should not by invasion increase their power, they would not be able long time, by standing only on their defence, to subsist. And by consequence, such augmentation of dominion over men being necessary to a man's conservation, it ought to be allowed him.

Again, men have no pleasure, but on the contrary a great deal of grief, in keeping company, where there is no power able to overawe them all. For every man looketh that his companion should value him at the same rate he sets upon himself; and upon all signs of contempt, or undervaluing, naturally endeavors, as far as he dares (which amongst them that have no common power to keep them in quiet, is far enough to make them destroy each other), to extort a greater value from his contemners by damage, and from others by the example.

So that in the nature of man, we find three principal causes of quarrel. First, competition; second, diffidence; thirdly, glory.

The first maketh men invade for gain; the second, for safety; and the third, for reputation. The first use violence to make themselves masters of other men's persons, wives, children, and cattle; the second, to defend them; the third, for trifles, as a work, a smile, a different opinion, and any other sign of undervalue, either direct in their persons, or by reflection in their kindred, their friends, their nation, their profession, or their name.

Hereby it is manifest that during the time men live without a common power to keep them all in awe, they are in that condition which is called war; and such a war as is of every man against every man. For *war* consisteth not in battle only, or the act of fighting, but in a tract of time wherein the will to contend by battle is sufficiently known, and therefore the notion of *time* is to be considered in the nature of war, as it is in the nature of weather. For as the nature of foul weather lieth not in a shower or two of rain, but in an inclination thereto of many days together; so the nature of war consisteth not in actual fighting, but in the known disposition thereto, during all the time there is no assurance to the contrary. All other time is *peace*.

Whatsoever therefore is consequent to a time of war, where every man is enemy to every man; the same is consequent to the time, wherein men livewithout other security than what their own strength and their own invention shall furnish them withal. In such condition there is no place for industry, because the fruit thereof is uncertain: and consequently no culture of the earth; no navigation, nor use of the commodities that may be imported by sea; no commodious building; no instruments of moving, and removing, such things as require more force; no knowledge of the face of the earth; no account of time; no arts; no letters; no society; and which is worst of all,continual fear, and danger of violent death; and the life of man, solitary, poor, nasty, brutish, and short.

It may seem strange to some man that has not well weighed these things, that nature should thus dissociate, and render men apt to invade and destroy one another; and he may therefore, not trusting to this inference, made from the passions, desire perhaps to have the same confirmed by experience. Let him therefore consider with himself, when taking a journey, he arms himself and seeks to go well accompanied; when going to sleep, he locks his doors; when even in his house he locks his chests; and this when he knows there be laws, and public officers, armed, to revenge all injuries shall be done him: what opinion he has of his fellow-subjects, when he rides armed; of his fellow citizens, when he locks his doors; and of his children, and servants, when he locks his chests. Does he not there as much accuse mankind by his actions, as I do by my words? But neither of us accuse man's nature in it. The desires, and other passions of man, are in themselves no sin. No more are the actions that proceed from those passions, till they know a law that forbids them: which till laws be made they cannot know; nor can any law be made, till they have agreed upon the person that shall make it.

It may peradventure be thought, there was never such a time nor condition of war as this; and I believe it was never generally so, over all the world: but there are many places where they live so now. For the savage people in many places of America, except the government of small families, the concord whereof dependeth on natural lust, have no government at all; and live at this day in that brutish manner, as I said before. Howsoever, it may be perceived what manner of life there would be, where there were no common power to fear; by the manner of life which men that have formerly lived under a peaceful government, use to degenerate into in a civil war.

But though there had never been any time wherein particular men were in a condition of war one against another; yet in all times kings and persons of sovereign authority, because of their independency, are in continual jealousies, and in the state and posture of gladiators; having their weapons pointing, and their eyes fixed on one another; that is, their forts, garrisons, and guns upon the frontiers of their kingdoms; and continual spies upon their neighbors; which is a posture of war. But because they uphold thereby the industry of their subjects, there does not follow from it that misery which accompanies the liberty of particular men.

To this war of every man against every man, this also is consequent: *that nothing can be unjust.* The notions of right and wrong, justice and injustice, have there no place. Where there is no common power, there is no law; where no law, no injustice. Force and fraud are in war the two cardinal virtues, justice and injustice are none of the faculties neither of the body nor mind. If they were, they might be in a man that were alone in the world, as well as his senses and passions. They are qualities that relate to men in society, not in solitude. It is consequent also to the same condition, that there be no propriety, no domination, no *mine* and *thine* distinct; but only that to be every man's, that he can get; and for so long as he can keep it. And thus much for the ill condition which man by mere nature is actually placed in; though with a possibility to come out of it, consisting partly in the passions, partly in his reason.

The passions that incline man to peace are fear of death, desire of such things as are necessary to commodious living, and a hope by their industry to obtain them. And reason suggesteth convenient articles of peace, upon which men may be drawn to agreement. These articles are they which otherwise are called the Laws of Nature; whereof I shall speak more particularly in the two following chapters.

Chapter XIV

Of the First and Second Natural Laws, and of Contracts

The right of nature, which writers commonly call *jus naturale,* is the liberty each man hath to use his own power, as he will himself, for the preservation of his own nature; that is to say, of his own life; and consequently, of doing anything, which in his own judgment and reason, he shall conceive to be the aptest means thereunto.

By *liberty,* is understood, according to the proper signification of the word, the absence of external impediments: which impediments, may oft take away part of man's power to do what he would; but cannot hinder him from using the power left him, according as his judgment, and reason shall dictate to him.

A *law of nature, lex naturalis,* is a precept or general rule, found out by reasons, by which a man is forbidden to do that which is destructive of his life, or taketh away the means of preserving the same; and to omit that by which he thinketh it may be best preserved. For though they that speak of this subject, use to confound *jus* and *lex, right* and *law;* yet they ought to be distinguished: because *right* consisteth in liberty to do or to forbear, whereas *law* determineth and bindeth to one of them; so that law, and right differ as much as obligation and liberty; which in one and the same matter are inconsistent.

And because the condition of man, as hath been declared in the precedent chapter, is a condition of war of everyone against everyone; in which case everyone is governed by his own reason, and there is nothing he can make use of that may not be a help unto him in preserving his life against his enemies: it followeth, that in such a condition every man has a right to everything; even to one another's body. And therefore, as long as this natural right of every man to everything endureth, there can be no security to any man, how strong or wise soever he be, of living out the time which nature ordinarily alloweth men to live. And consequently it is a precept, or general rule of reason, *that every man ought to endeavor peace, as far as he has hope of obtaining it; and when he cannot obtain it, that he may seek and use all helps and advantages of war.* The first branch of which rule containeth the first and fundamental law of nature; which is, *to seek peace and follow it.* The second, the sum of the right of nature; which is, *by all means we can, to defend ourselves.*

From this fundamental law of nature, by which men are commanded to endeavor peace, is derived this second law: *that a man be willing, when others are so too, as far forth as for peace and defence of himself he shall think it necessary, to lay down this right to all things; and be contented with so much liberty against other men, as he would allow other men against himself.* For as long as every man holdeth this right, of doing anything he liketh, so long are all men in the condition of war. But if other men will not lay down their right, as well as he, then there is no reason for anyone to divest himself of his: for that were to expose himself to prey, which no man is bound to, rather than to dispose himself to peace. . . .

Whensoever a man transferreth his right, or renounceth it; it is either in consideration of some right reciprocally transferred to himself, or for some other good he hopeth for thereby. For it is a voluntary act; and of the voluntary acts of every man, the object is some *good to himself.* And therefore there be some rights which no man can be understood by any words, or other signs, to have abandoned or transferred. As first a man cannot lay down the right of resisting them that assault him by force, to take away his life; because he cannot be understood to aim thereby, at any good to himself. The same may be said of wounds, and chains, and imprisonment: both because there is no benefit consequent to such patience, as there is to the patience of suffering another to be wounded or imprisoned; as also because a man cannot tell, when he seeth men proceed against him by violence, whether they intend his death or not. And lastly the motive, an end for which this renouncing and transferring of right is introduced, is nothing else but the security of a man's person, in his life, and in the means of so preserving life as not to be weary of it. And therefore if a man by words, or other signs, seem to despoil himself of the end for which those signs were intended, he is not to be understood as if he meant it, or that it was his will, but that he was ignorant of how such words and actions were to be interpreted.

The mutual transferring of right, is that which men call *contract*.

Chapter XV

Of Other Laws of Nature

From that law of nature by which we are obliged to transfer to another such rights as, being retained, hinder the peace of mankind, there followeth a third; which is this, *that men perform their covenants made*: without which, covenants are in vain, and but empty words; and the right of all men to all things remaining, we are still in the condition of war.

And in this law of nature, consisteth the fountain and original of *justice*. For where no covenant hath preceded, there hath no right been transferred, and every man has right to everything; and consequently, no action can be unjust. But when a covenant is made, then to break it is *unjust;* and the definition of *injustice* is no other than *the not performance of covenant.* And whatsoever is not unjust, is *just*.

But because covenants of mutual trust, where there is a fear of not performance on either part, as hath been said in the former chapter, are invalid; though the original of justice be the making of covenants; yet injustice actually there can be none, till the cause of such fear be taken away; which while men are in the natural condition of war, cannot be done. Therefore before the names of just and unjust can have place, there must be some coercive power, to compel men equally to the performance of their covenants, by the terror of some punishment greater than the benefit they expect by the breach of their covenant; and to make good that propriety which by mutual contract men acquire, in recompense of the universal right they abandon: and such power there is none before the erection of a commonwealth. And this is also to be gathered out of the ordinary definition of justice in the Schools; for they say, that *justice is the constant will of giving to every man his own.* And therefore where there is no *own* that is no propriety, there is no injustice; and where is no coercive power erected, that is, where there is no commonwealth, there is no propriety; all men having right to all things: therefore where there is no commonwealth, there nothing is unjust. So that the nature of justice consisteth in keeping of valid covenants; but the validity of covenants begins not but with the constitution of a civil power sufficient to compel men to keep them, and then it is also that propriety begins. . . .

Chapter XVII

Of the Causes, Generation, and Definition of a Commonwealth

The final cause, end, or design of men who naturally love liberty and dominion over others, in the introduction of that restraint upon themselves in which we see them live in commonwealths, is the foresight of their own preservation, and of a more contented life thereby; that is to say, of getting themselves out from that miserable condition of war, which is necessarily consequent, as hath been shown in Chapter XIII, to the natural passions of men, when there is no visible power to keep them in awe, and tie them by fear of punishment to the performance of their covenants and observation of those laws of nature set down in the fourteenth and fifteenth chapters.

For the laws of nature, as justice, equity, modesty, mercy, and, in sum, *doing to others as we would be done to,* of themselves, without the terror of some power to cause them to be observed, are contrary to our natural passions, that carry us to partiality, pride, revenge, and the like. And covenants, without the sword, are but words, and of no strength to secure a man at all. Therefore notwithstanding the laws of nature, which everyone hath then kept, when he has the will to keep them when he can do it safely; if there be no power erected, or not great enough for our security, every man will, and may, lawfully rely on his own strength and art, for caution against all other men. And in all places where men have lived by small families, to rob and spoil one another has been a trade, and so far from being reputed against the law of nature, that the greater spoils they gained, the greater was their honor; and men observed no other laws therein but the laws of honor; that is, to abstain from cruelty, leaving to men their lives, and instruments of husbandry. And as small families did then; so now do cities and kingdoms, which are but greater families, for their own security enlarge their dominions, upon all pretences of danger and fear of invasion, or assistance that may be given to invaders, and endeavor as much as they can to subdue or weaken their neighbors, by open force and secret arts, for want of other caution, justly; and are remembered for it in after ages with honor.

Nor is it the joining together of a small number of men, that gives them this security; because in small numbers, small additions on the one side or the other make the advantage of strength so great, as is sufficient to carry the victory, and therefore gives encouragement to an invasion. The multitude sufficient to confide in for our security, is not determined by any certain number, but by comparison with the enemy we fear; and is then sufficient, when the odds of the enemy is not of so visible and conspicuous moment, to determine the event of war, as to move him to attempt.

And be there never so great a multitude, yet if their actions be directed according to their particular judgments and particular appetites, they can expect thereby no defence nor protection, neither against a common enemy nor against the injuries of one another. For being distracted in opinions concerning the best use and application of their strength, they do not help but hinder one another; and reduce their strength by mutual opposition to nothing: whereby they are easily, not only subdued by a very few that agree together; but also when there is no common enemy, they make war upon each other, for their particular interests. For if we could suppose a great multitude of men to consent in the observation of justice, and other laws of nature, without a common power to keep them all in awe, we might as well suppose all mankind to do the same; and then there neither would be, nor need to be any civil government or commonwealth at all, because there would be peace without subjection.

Nor is it enough for the security, which men desire should last all the time of their life, that they be governed and directed by one judgment for a limited time, as in one battle or one war. For though they obtain a victory by their unanimous endeavor against a foreign enemy; yet afterwards, when either they have no common enemy, or he that by one part is held for an enemy, is by another part held for a friend, they must needs by the difference of their interests dissolve, and fall again into a war amongst themselves.

It is true that certain living creatures, as bees and ants, live sociably one with another, which are therefore by Aristotle numbered amongst political creatures; and yet have no other direction than their particular judgments and appetites; nor speech, whereby one of them can signify to another what he thinks expedient for the common benefit: and therefore some man may perhaps desire to know why mankind cannot do the same. To which I answer:

First, that men are continually in competition for honor and dignity, which these creatures are not; and consequently amongst men there ariseth on that ground, envy and hatred, and finally war; but amongst these not so.

Secondly, that amongst these creatures, the common good differeth not from the private; and being by nature inclined to their private, they procure thereby the common benefit. But man, whose joy consisteth in comparing himself with other men, can relish nothing but what is eminent.

Thirdly, that these creatures, having not, as man, the use of reason, do not see, nor think they see, any fault in the administration of their common business; whereas amongst men, there are very many that think themselves wiser, and able to govern the public better, than the rest; and these strive to reform and innovate, one this way, another that way; and thereby bring it into distraction and civil war.

Fourthly, that these creatures, though they have some use of voice in making known to one another their desires and other affections; yet they want that art of words by which some men can represent to others, that which is good in the likeness of evil, and evil in the likeness of good, and augment or diminish the apparent greatness of good and evil; discontenting men and troubling their peace at their pleasure.

Fifthly, irrational creatures cannot distinguish between *injury* and *damage;* and therefore as long as they be at ease, they are not offended with their fellows: whereas man is then most troublesome when he is most at ease; for then it is that he loves to show his wisdom, and control the actions of them that govern the commonwealth.

Lastly, the agreement of these creatures is natural; that of men is by covenant only, which is artificial: and therefore it is no wonder if there be somewhat else required, besides covenant, to make their agreement constant and lasting; which is a common power, to keep them in awe, and to direct their actions to the common benefit.

The only way to erect such a common power, as may be able to defend them from the invasion of foreigners and the injuries of one another, and thereby to secure them in such sort as that, by their own industry, and by the fruits of the earth, they may nourish themselves and live contentedly; is, to confer all their power and strength upon one man, or upon one assembly of men, that may reduce all their wills, by plurality of voices, unto one will: which is as much as to say, to appoint one man, or assembly of men, to bear their person; and everyone to own and acknowledge himself to be author of whatsoever he that so beareth their person, shall act or cause to be acted in those things which concern the common peace and safety; and therein to submit their wills, everyone to his will, and their judgments, to his judgment. This is more than consent, or concord; it is a real unity of them all, in one and the same person, made by covenant of every man with every man, in such manner as if every man should say to every man, *"I authorize and give up my right of governing myself to this man, or to this assembly of men, on this condition, that thou give up thy right to him, and authorize all his actions in like manner."* This done, the multitude so united in one person, is called a *commonwealth,* in Latin *civitas.* This is the generation of that great *LEVIATHAN,* or rather, to speak more reverently, of that *mortal god,* to which we owe under the *immortal God,* our peace and defence. For by this authority, given him by every particular man in the commonwealth, he hath the use of so much power and strength conferred on him, that by terror thereof he is enabled to perform the wills of them all, to peace at home and mutual aid against their enemies abroad. And in him consisteth the essence of the commonwealth; which, to define it, *is one person, of whose acts a great multitude, by mutual covenants one with another, have made themselves every one the author, to the end he may use the strength and means of them all, as he shall think expedient, for their peace and common defence.*

And he that carrieth this person, is called *sovereign,* and said to have sovereign power; and everyone besides; his *subject. ...*

C O M M E N T

The Premises of Hobbes' Argument

Hobbes was born prematurely, as the story goes, because his mother took fright at the near approach of the Spanish Armada. In commenting on the circumstances of his birth, he said, "Fear and I were twins." This remark, made in his old age, expresses his realization that fear had been a dominant motive in his life. His social philosophy is concerned primarily with the need for security.

He lived during the most unstable period of English history. Among the shifts and disturbances that occurred during his lifetime were the First Civil War between King and Parliament (1642–1645), the Second Civil War (1648), the rule of the "Rump Parliament" (1649–1653), Cromwell's dictatorship (1654–1658), and the Restoration of the Stuarts (1660). Hobbes' emphasis on security was a natural reaction to a period so unsettled.

This emphasis rested on several premises: (1) an interpretation of human nature, (2) an analysis of moral experience, and (3) a conception of the precivil condition of human life.

1. *An interpretation of human nature.* Hobbes believed that a person is a kind of elaborate machine, whose "vital motions" are determined by outward stimuli. If a stimulus is favorable to the machine's operations, it evokes *desire* or motion toward; if unfavorable, it evokes *aversion* or motion away from. More complex motives and emotions are all derived from these elementary reactions of advance or retreat. The emotions springing from desire, such as love and hope, are generally pleasant; the emotions springing from aversion, such as hate and fear, are unpleasant. If the effect is pleasant, the organism seeks to continue or renew the stimulus; if unpleasant, to avoid it. "The object of man's desire is not to enjoy once only, and for one instant of time; but to assure for ever the way of his future desire."[1] There is no lasting repose, no final breathing space, but only ceaseless pursuit of power. Power is defined as the "present means to obtain future, apparent good." Since the means are precarious, there is no limit to the power that men seek. "I put for a general inclination of all mankind," declares Hobbes, "a perpetual and restless desire of power after power, which ceases only in death."[2]

Motivated by egoistic concern for one's own power, each person tends to conflict with others. "If any two men desire the same thing, which they nevertheless cannot both enjoy, they become enemies and ... endeavor to destroy or subdue one another."[3] The result would be a constant and intolerable war of each against all if it were not for the faculty of reason. By means of this faculty, we "acquire the knowledge of consequences, and dependence of one fact upon another."[4] Reason does not select the ends of action—these are determined by

---

[1] *Leviathan,* XI.

[2] Ibid.

[3] Ibid., XIII.

[4] Ibid., V.

desire and aversion—but it reflects on the consequences of acts and judges how the ends can be most fully achieved. By its means, we escape from the suicidal anarchy that our predatory natures would force on us.

2. *An analysis of moral experience*. At the most primitive and presocial level of human life, *good* simply means "whatsoever is the object of any man's appetite or desire," and *evil* means "the object of his hate and aversion."[5] Values are derived from human drives, and since the drives are invariably egoistic, good and evil are always relative to the individual.

> These words of good, evil, and contemptible are ever used with relation to the person that useth them: there being nothing simply and absolutely so; nor any common rule of good and evil to be taken from the nature of the objects themselves; but from the person of the man, where there is no commonwealth; or, in a commonwealth, from the person that representeth it; or from an arbitrator or judge, whom men disagreeing shall by consent set up, and make his sentence rule thereof.[6]

This quotation points to two levels of moral experience: the level *before* and the level *after* the creation of the commonwealth. *Before* there is no moral authority except the desires and aversions of the individual, whoever he or she may be. However, *after* the creation of the state, the ultimate moral authority is the sovereign or judicial arbitrator. The social concepts of law and justice arise only within the state.

In speaking of a precivil level of morality, Hobbes did not mean that he actually *finds* individuals at this level. He was pointing out the kind of morality they would have if they lacked civil institutions, and he was saying that the second or higher level of morality requires an organized political state.

3. *The precivil condition of humankind*. That "the state of nature" is a nasty condition of anarchy follows from Hobbes' analysis of human nature. Since everyone naturally preys upon one's fellows, the consequence is "such a war as is of every man against every man." It is easy to misunderstand Hobbes' meaning. "The state of nature" may never have existed; and whether it did or not does not really affect his argument. This is the state that *would* exist if people were wholly dominated by passions, without the restraint of reason and civil society. It is an analytical, not a historical, concept. Hobbes, in effect, was saying that we must permanently be on guard because the brutish state of nature would be our lot if we should abandon reason and destroy political sovereignty. It is an emphatic way of saying that the civil state is extremely necessary.

Natural Law and the Social Contract

The state of nature is haunted by "continual fear and danger of violent death," and reason therefore impels human beings to set up the coercive power of a central government, which alone can establish peace and security. The contrast

---

[5] Ibid., VI.
[6] Ibid.

between the condition of humankind *outside* and in a duly constituted state is sharply drawn.

> Out of it, any man may rightly spoil or kill another; in it, none but one. Out of it, we are protected by our own forces; in it, by the power of all. Out of it, no man is sure of the fruit of his labors; in it, all men are. Lastly, out of it, there is a dominion of passions, war, fear, poverty, slovenliness, solitude, barbarism, ignorance, cruelty; in it, the dominion of reason, peace, security, riches, decency, society, elegancy, sciences and benevolence.[7]

What is required to pass from the natural to the civil state is determined by "the laws of nature." These laws are the dictates of reason defining what needs to be done to safeguard life. They are "natural" in the sense that they are based on the instinct of self-preservation aided by reason. In substance these laws state that peace, cooperation, and the keeping of covenants are essential to survival, but that if these be lacking, it is rational to defend oneself with the most effective means available.

In conformity to natural law, reason impels individuals to escape from the lethal anarchy of the state of nature, and to set up, by mutual agreement, the civil state. Every individual must agree to live in peace in consideration of the like agreement of others. However, human nature being what it is, mere agreement to live peaceably together is insufficient. For this reason, people must form a contract with one another to set up a common power "to keep them in awe, and to direct their actions to the Common Benefit."[8]

The idea of a "social contract" was not original with Hobbes. Its roots are to be found in ancient Greek philosophy, and it had become a commonplace in political theory by the time Hobbes wrote *Leviathan*. His account is distinguished by its sharp insistence that the conferring of absolute power on a sovereign is the only refuge from chronic war, which would break out again if ever the civil power should crumble. The power of the sovereign is absolute since no limiting conditions were stipulated when he or she received power. Indeed, no effective condition could have been stipulated since covenants are only words without the power of enforcement until the sovereign is established. According to this interpretation, the contract is not between citizen and ruler but between citizen and citizen—every citizen covenanting with every other to form a civil society *and to obey the government*.

The government is not necessarily a monarchy. Hobbes personally thought monarchy the safest and best type of government, but he recognized that the sovereign *might* be an assembly. There is nothing in his theory that presupposes a king or single ruler, provided that the sovereign group is sufficiently united to maintain authority.

It is sometimes said that the power conferred on the sovereign is irrevocable. This is a misinterpretation of Hobbes' theory. He insisted that the sovereign

---

[7] De Cive, ed. Sterling P. Lamprecht (New York: Appleton-Century-Crofts, 1949), p. 114.

[8] Op. cit. XVII.

power must be undisputed as long as it is effective in keeping the peace; but if the government does not in fact govern, if anarchy breaks out afresh, there is no longer reason for submission. The citizens are then thrown back on their natural resources for self-preservation and may rightly set up a new sovereign who can protect them.

The social contract, like the state of nature, should not be interpreted historically. Only in special circumstances do states originate by deliberate contract. The "social contract" is the *logical* basis of the state, which, as far as people are governed by reason, remains operative as a continuing tacit agreement. The function of this type of theory is to emphasize the activity of reason in devising, and the activity of will in instituting, the political community. Among democratic theorists, such as John Locke, it is a way of insisting that legitimate government rests on the consent of the governed.

Application to International Politics

The clearest example of "the state of nature" is the relation of sovereign states to one another:

> … In all times, kings, and persons of sovereign authority, because of their independency, are in continual jealousies, and in the state and posture of gladiators; having their weapons pointing, and their eyes fixed on one another; that is, their forts, garrisons, and guns upon the frontiers of their kingdoms; and continual spies upon their neighbors; which is a posture of war.[9]

Hobbes remarked that this international anarchy does not occasion as much misery as anarchy among individuals.

Living in the seventeenth century, Hobbes could not foresee how powerfully his social philosophy would apply to international affairs in recent times. We now know that a hydrogen bomb can obliterate a city like Moscow or New York in an instant, and that the fallout from such a bomb can destroy life over a vastly wider area. Competent authorities have declared that an atomic world war might so poison the earth's atmosphere as to cause universal death. Here is danger on a scale that Hobbes never even dreamed of.

The remedy for anarchy, as he clearly perceived, is the creation of government with power to enforce its decisions. It is not sufficient for nations to promise not to go to war with one another, for "covenants, without the sword, are but words."[10] A binding covenant must be a surrender of sovereignty, whether of individuals or of nations, to some effective central authority.

The establishment of the United Nations was a step toward world government. The supreme question is whether this beginning can be transformed into an international authority with power to enforce peace. The human race has now reached the point at which it must either abandon war and the dogma of unlim-

---

[9] Ibid., XIII.

[10] Ibid., XVII.

ited national sovereignty or accept the possibility of universal annihilation. Hobbes' argument that we should obey the dictates of self-preservation applies today with terrific force.

Some Critical Remarks

The main defect of Hobbes' social philosophy is fairly obvious. His insistence on the necessity of coercive government is excessive because his account of human nature is too grim. Having described human beings as essentially selfish and predatory, he concluded that only fear and coercion could hold them in cheek. There is a vein of realism in this argument that should not be overlooked, but it does scant justice to the fraternal aspects of human life. The impulse to cooperate is as real as the impulse to compete; sympathy is as real as selfishness. Hobbes speaks as if rational self-interest alone impels individuals to unite in a political order, but it is at least as true to say, with Aristotle, that a human being is naturally a political animal.

Hobbes' one-sided characterization of human nature leads to a paradoxical theory of the state. At the same time that he demands unlimited power for his sovereign, he virtually limits the sovereign's functions to the safeguarding of life and limb. Thus his state is maximal in powers but minimal in functions. It may be instructive to compare Hobbes' view with that of Abraham Lincoln, who also lived during a period of civil strife. "The legitimate object of government," declared Lincoln, "is 'to do for the people what needs to be done, but which they cannot, by individual effort, do at all, or do so well, for themselves.'"[11] The emphasis is positive rather than negative—on the promotion of welfare rather than the suppression of antisocial impulses. Lincoln would limit the powers of the state but not its functions; Hobbes would limit its functions but not its powers.

Hobbes was so insistent on the unfettered power of the sovereign that he had no sympathy for a bill of rights or a system of constitutional checks. He did not recognize, as did Locke and Thomas Jefferson, that irresponsible absolute power corrupts absolutely or that the social contract should be a democratic instrument, based on the will and participation of the governed. He conceived of law as the mere command of the rulers rather than as a body of principles limiting their arbitrary power and applying to sovereign and subjects alike.

The social-contract theory, as he developed it, is inadequate to explain the inner cohesion of society. Purely selfish interests, even though enlightened by reason, cannot provide social unity or generate a binding social contract. In opposition to Hobbes, Jean Jacques Rousseau pointed out that there is a great difference between a real community of interests and a mere sum of selfish interests. He maintained that society must be "a moral, collective body," which essentially binds people together, their wills merged and transformed in a corporate will. His theory has defects of its own, but it lacks the particular defects of Hobbes' egoistic theory.

---

[11] Michael D. Oakeshott, The Social and Political Doctrines of Contemporary Europe (Cambridge, England: Cambridge University Press, 1939), p. 19.

The strength of Hobbes' argument is most evident when we consider its application to international affairs. In the atomic age, the simple dictates of self-preservation demand an international authority with power to maintain peace. However, even here the argument can easily be oversimplified—there are many causes of war besides political anarchy among nations. Poverty, imperialism, racial antagonism, and the conflict of ideologies—to mention only a few factors—are also productive of international strife. There is no single cause of war and no single remedy. We must act in many fields at once—political, economic, moral, religious, and philosophical—creating a real world community to give force and substance to international peace.

It would seem that Hobbes' response to the case study regarding the civil disobedience of the Sanctuary Movement would be rather straightforward. Does he not say that in entering into a contract with their sovereign leadership such people have forfeited the right to disobey the law? But would not those engaging in civil disobedience in the name of a higher law claim that such behavior is justified when the leadership fails to keep its contractual responsibilities? Just what is the place of law in Hobbes' view? Is it strictly "dos" and "don'ts," or does it have a broader, more constructive role? Does it make a difference if those involved in civil disobedience accept their punishment in order to call into question a particular law as a matter of principle?

23

SOCIAL CONTRACT

JOHN LOCKE (1632–1704)

John Locke was born in England and raised according to strict Puritan discipline. In 1656 he completed his degree in Oxford and became a teacher of Latin and Greek. After his father's death in 1661, he took up the study of medicine as a result of his growing interest in the sciences. In 1667 Locke began an impressive career in politics, though for some years he was forced to live in exile in Holland. In addition to his very influential *Essay Concerning Human Understanding,* which is often regarded as the first work in psychology, Locke wrote a number of political essays and *Treatise on Civil Government,* from which the following pages have been selected. Locke's work in epistemology lay the foundations for the empiricism of David Hume, even as his political writings provided much of the inspiration for the beliefs of Thomas Jefferson.

THE BASIS OF CIVIL SOCIETY

Of the State of Nature

To understand political power aright, and derive it from its original, we must consider what state all men are naturally in, and that is a state of perfect freedom to order their actions and dispose of their possessions and persons as they think fit, within the bounds of the law of nature, without asking leave, or depending upon the will of any other man.

A state also of equality, wherein all the power and jurisdiction is reciprocal, no one having more than another; there being nothing more evident than that creatures of the same species and rank, promiscuously born to all the same advantages of nature, and the use of the same faculties, should also be equal one amongst another without subordination or subjection, unless the Lord and Master of them all should by any manifest declaration of Hits will set one above another, and confer on him by an evident and clear appointment an undoubted right to dominion and sovereignty.

This quality of men by nature the judicious Hooker looks upon as so evident in itself and beyond all question, that he makes it the foundation of that obligation to mutual love amongst men on which he builds the duties they owe one another,

From *Treatise on Civil Government,* ed. C. K. Sherman, New York: Appleton-Century-Crofts, 1937. Reprinted by permission of Irvington Publishers.

and from whence he derives the great maxims of justice and charity. His words are:—

"The like natural inducement hath brought men to know that it is no less their duty to love others than themselves; for seeing those things which are equal must needs all have one measure, if I cannot but wish to receive good, even as much at every man's hands as any man can wish unto his own soul, how should I look to have any part of my desire herein satisfied, unless myself be careful to satisfy the like desire, which is undoubtedly in other men weak, being of one and the same nature? To have anything offered them repugnant to this desire, must needs in all respects grieve them as much as me, so that, if I do harm, I must look to suffer, there being no reason that others should show greater measures of love to me than they have by me showed unto them. My desire, therefore, to be loved of my equals in nature as much as possible may be, imposeth upon me a natural duty of bearing to themward fully the like affection; from which relation of equality between ourselves and them that are as ourselves, what several rules and canons natural reason hath drawn for direction of life no man is ignorant."—"Eccl. Pol.," lib. I.

But though this be a state of liberty, yet it is not a state of licence; though man in that state have an uncontrollable liberty to dispose of his person or possessions, yet he has not liberty to destroy himself, or so much as any creature in his possession, but where some nobler use than its bare preservation calls for it. The state of nature has a law of nature to govern it, which obligates every one; and reason, which is that law, teaches all mankind who will but consult it, that being all equal and independent, no one ought to harm another in his life, health, liberty, or possessions. For men being all the workmanship of one omnipotent and infinitely wise Maker—all the servants of one sovereign Master, sent into the world by His order, and about His business—they are His property, whose workmanship they are, made to last during His,

not one another's pleasure; and being furnished with like faculties, sharing all in one community of nature, there cannot be supposed any such subordination among us, that may authorise us to destroy one another, as if we were made for one another's uses, as the inferior ranks of creatures are for ours. Every one, as he is bound to preserve himself, and not to quit his station wilfully, so, by the like reason, when his own preservation comes not in competition, ought he, as much as he can, to preserve the rest of mankind, and not, unless it be to do justice on an offender, take away or impair the life, or what tends to the preservation of the life, the liberty, health, limb, or goods of another.

And that all men may be restrained from invading others' rights, and from doing hurt to one another, and the law of nature be observed, which willeth the peace and preservation of all mankind, the execution of the law of nature is in that state put into every man's hand, whereby every one has a right to punish the transgressors of that law to such a degree as may hinder its violation. For the law of nature would, as all other laws that concern men in this world, be in vain if there were nobody that, in the state of nature, had a power to execute that law, and thereby preserve the innocent and restrain offenders. And if any one in the state of nature may punish another for any evil he has done, every one may do so. For in that state of perfect equality, where naturally there is no superiority or jurisdiction of one over another, what any may do in prosecution of that law, every one must needs have a right to do.

And thus in the state of nature one man comes by a power over another; but yet no absolute or arbitrary power, to use a criminal, when he has got him in his hands, according to the passionate heats or boundless extravagance of his own will; but only to retribute to him so far as calm reason and conscience dictate what is proportionate to his transgression, which is so much as may serve for reparation and restraint. For these two are the only reasons why one man may lawfully do harm to another, which is that we call punishment. In transgressing the law of nature, the offender declares himself to live by another rule than that of common reason and equity, which is that measure God has set to the actions of men, for their mutual security; and so he becomes dangerous to mankind, the tie which is to secure them from injury and violence being slighted and broken by him. Which, being a trespass against the whole species, and the peace and safety of it, provided for by the law of nature, every man upon this score, by the right he hath to preserve mankind in general, may restrain, or, where it is necessary, destroy things noxious to them, and so may bring such evil on any one who hath transgressed that law, as may make him repent the doing of it, and thereby deter him, and by his example others, from doing the like mischief. And in this case, and upon this ground, every man hath a right to punish the offender, and be executioner of the law of nature.

I doubt not but this will seem a very strange doctrine to some men; but before they condemn it, I desire them to resolve me by what right any prince or State can put to death or punish an alien, for any crime he commits in their country. 'Tis certain their laws, by virtue of any sanction they receive from the promulgated will of the legislature, reach not a stranger: they speak not to him, nor, if they did, is he bound to hearken to them. The Legislative authority, by which they are in force over the subjects of that commonwealth, hath no power over him. Those who have the supreme power of making laws in England, France, or Holland, are to an Indian but like the rest of the world—men without authority. And, therefore, if by the law of nature every man hath not a power to punish offences against it, as he soberly judges the case to require, I see not how the magistrates of any community can punish an alien of another country; since in reference to him they can have no more power than

what every man naturally may have over another.

Besides the crime which consists in violating the law, and varying from the right rule of reason, whereby a man so far becomes degenerate, and declares himself to quit the principles of human nature, and to be a noxious creature, there is commonly injury done, and some person or other, some other man receives damage by his transgression, in which case he who hath received any damage, has, besides the right of punishment common on him with other men, a particular right to seek reparation from him that has done it. And any other person who finds it just, may also join with him that is injured, and assist him in recovering from the offender so much as may make satisfaction for the harm he has suffered.

From those two distinct rights—the one of punishing the crime, for restraint and preventing the like offence, which right of punishing is in everybody; the other of taking reparation, which belongs only to the injured party—comes it to pass that the magistrate, who by being magistrate hath the common right of punishing put into his hands, can often, where the public good demands not the execution of the law, remit the punishment of criminal offences by his own authority, but yet cannot remit the satisfaction due to any private man for the damage he has received. That he who has suffered the damage has a right to demand in his own name, and he alone can remit. The damnified person has this power of approaching to himself the goods or service of the offender, by right of self-preservation, as every man has a power to punish the crime, to prevent its being committed again, by the right he has of preserving all mankind, and doing all reasonable things he can in order to that end. And thus it is that every man in the state of nature has a power to kill a murderer, both to deter others from doing the like injury, which no reparation can compensate, by the example of the punishment that attends it from everybody, and also to secure men from the attempts of a criminal who having renounced reason, the common rule and measure God hath given to mankind, hath by the unjust violence and slaughter he hath committed upon one, declared war against all mankind, and therefore may be destroyed as a lion or a tiger, one of those wild savage beasts with whom men can have no society nor security. And upon this is grounded that great law of nature. "Whoso sheddeth man's blood, by man shall his blood be shed." And Cain was so fully convinced that every one had a right to destroy such a criminal, that after the murder of his brother he cries out, "Every one that findeth me shall slay me;" so plain was it writ in the hearts of mankind.

By the same reason may a man in the state of nature punish the lesser breaches of that law. It will perhaps be demanded, With death? I answer, each transgression may be punished to that degree, and with so much severity, as will suffice to make it an ill bargain to the offender, give him cause to repent, and terrify others from doing the like. Every offence that can be committed in the state of nature, may in the state of nature be also punished equally, and as far forth as it may, in a commonwealth. For though it would be beside my present purpose to enter here into the particulars of the law of nature, or its measures of punishment, yet it is certain there is such a law, and that, too, as intelligible and plain to a rational creature and a studier of that law as the positive laws of commonwealths; nay, possibly plainer, as much as reason is easier to be understood than the fancies and intricate contrivances of men, following contrary and hidden interests put into words; for truly so are a great part of the municipal laws of countries, which are only so far right as they are founded on the law of nature, by which they are to be regulated and interpreted.

To this strange doctrine—viz, That in the state of nature—every one has the executive power of the law of nature I doubt not but it will be objected that it is unreasonable for men to be judges in their own cases, that self-love will make men partial to themselves and their friends. And on the other side, that ill-nature, passion, and revenge will carry them too far in punishing others; and hence nothing but confusion and disorder will follow; and that therefore God hath certainly appointed government to restrain the partiality and violence of men. I easily grant that civil government is the proper remedy for the inconveniences of the state of nature, which must certainly be great where men may be judges in their own case, since 'tis easy to be imagined that he who was so unjust as to do his brother an injury, will scarce be so just as to condemn himself for it. But I shall desire those who make this objection, to remember that absolute monarchs are but men, and if government is to be the remedy of those evils which necessarily follow from men's being judges in their own cases, and the state of nature is therefore not to be endured, I desire to know what kind of government that is, and how much better it is than the state of nature, where one man commanding a multitude, has the liberty to be judge in his own case, and may do to all his subjects whatever he pleases, without the least question or control of those who execute his pleasure; and in whatsoever he doth, whether led by reason, mistake, or passion, must be submitted to, which men in the state of nature are not bound to do one to another? And if he that judges, judges amiss in his own or any other case, he is answerable for it to the rest of mankind.

'Tis often asked as a mighty objection, Where are, or ever were there, any men in such a state of nature? To which it may suffice as an answer at present: That since all princes and rulers of independent governments all through the world are in a state of nature, 'tis plain the world never was, nor ever will be, without numbers of men in that state. I have named all governors of independent communities, whether they are or are not in league with others. For 'tis not every compact that puts an end to the state of nature between men, but only this one of agreeing together mutually to enter into one community, and make one body politic; other promises and compacts men may make one with another, and yet still be in the state of nature. The promises and bargains for truck, etc., between the two men in Soldania, in or between a Swiss and an Indian, in the woods of America, are binding to them, though they are perfectly in a state of nature in reference to one another. For truth and keeping of faith belong to men as men, and not as members of society.

To those that say there were never any men in the state of nature, I will not only oppose the authority of the judicious Hooker—"Eccl. Pol.," lib. i, sec. 10, where he says, "The laws which have been hitherto mentioned," *i.e.,* the laws of nature, "do bind men absolutely, even as they are men, although they have never any settled fellowship, and never any solemn agreement amongst themselves what to do or not to do; but forasmuch as we are not by ourselves sufficient to furnish ourselves with competent store of things needful for such a life as our nature doth desire—a life fit for the dignity of man—therefore to supply those defects and imperfections which are in us, as living single and solely by overselves, we are naturally induced to seek communion and fellowship with others; this was the cause of men's uniting themselves at first in politic societies"—but I moreover affirm that all men are naturally in that state, and remain so, till by their own consents they make themselves members of some politic society; and I doubt not, in the sequel of this discourse, to make it very clear. . . .

Of Property . . .

God, who hath given the world to men in common, hath also given them reason to make use of it to the best advantage of life and convenience. The earth and all that is therein is given to men for the support and comfort of their being. And though all the fruits it naturally produces, and beasts it feeds, belong to mankind in common, as they are produced by the spontaneous hand of nature; and nobody has originally a private dominion exclusive of the rest of mankind in any of them as they are thus in their natural state; yet being given for the use of men, there must of necessity be a means to appropriate them some way or other before they can be of any use or at all beneficial to any particular man. The fruit or venison which nourishes the wild Indian, who knows no enclosure, and is still a tenant in common, must be his, and so his, *i.e.,* a part of him, that another can no longer have any right to it, before it can do any good for the support of his life.

Though the earth and all inferior creatures be common to all men, yet every man has a property in his own person; this nobody has any right to but himself. The labour of his body and the work of his hands we may say are properly his. Whatsoever, then, he removes out of the state that nature hath provided and left it in, he hath mixed his labour with, and joined to it something that is his own, and thereby makes it his property. It being by him removed from the common state nature placed it in, it hath by this labour something annexed to it that excludes the common right of other men. For this labour being the unquestionable property of the labourer, no man but he can have a right to what that is once joined to, at least where there is enough, and as good left in common for others. . . .

Of Political or Civil Society . . .

Man being born, as has been proved, with a title to perfect freedom, and an uncontrolled enjoyment of all the rights and privileges of the law of nature equally with any other man or number of men in the world, hath by nature a power not only to preserve his property—that is, his life, liberty, and estate—against the injuries and attempts of other men, but to judge of and punish the breaches of that law in others as he is persuaded the offence deserves, even with death itself, in crimes where the heinousness of the fact in his opinion requires it. But because no political society can be nor subsist without having in itself the power to preserve the property, and, in order thereunto, punish the offences of all those of that society, there, and there only, is political society, where every one of the members hath quitted this natural power, resigned it up into the hands of the community in all cases that exclude him not from appealing for protection to the law established by it; and thus all private judgment of every particular member being excluded, the community comes to be umpire, and by understanding indifferent rules and men authorized by the community for their execution, decides all the differences that may happen between any members of that society concerning any matter of right and punishes those offences which any member hath committed against the society with such penalties as the law has established; whereby it is easy to discern who are and who are not in political society together. Those who are united into one body, and have a common established law and judicature to appeal to, with authority to decide controversies between them and punish offenders, are in civil society one with another; but those who have no such common appeal—I mean on earth—are still in the state of nature, each being, where there is no other, judge for himself and executioner, which is, as I have before shown it, the perfect state of nature.

And thus the commonwealth comes by a power to set down what punishment shall belong to the several transgressions which they think worthy of it committed amongst the members of that society, which is the power of making laws, as well as it has the power to punish any injury done unto any of its members by any one that is not of it, which is the power of war and peace; and all this for the preservation of the property of all the members of that society as far as is possible. But though every man entered into civil society, has acquitted his power to punish offences against the law of nature in prosecution of his own private judgment, yet with the judgment of offences, which he has given up to the legislature in all cases where he can appeal to the magistrate, he has given a right to the commonwealth to employ his force for the execution of the judgments of the commonwealth whenever he shall be called to it; which, indeed, are his own judgments, they being made by himself or his representative. And herein we have the original of the legislative and executive power of civil society, which is to judge by standing laws how far offences are to be punished when committed within the commonwealth, and also by occasional judgments founded on the present circumstances of the fact, how far injuries from without are to be vindicated; and in both these to employ all the force of all the members when there shall be need.

Wherever, therefore, any number of men so unite into one society, as to quit every one his executive power of the law of nature, and to resign it to the public, there, and there only, is a political, or civil society. And this is done wherever any number of men, in the state of nature, enter into society to make one people, one body politic, under one supreme government, or else when any one joins himself to, and incorporates with, any government already made. For thereby he authorises the society, or, which is all one, the legislative thereof, to make laws for him, as the public good of the society shall require, to the execution whereof his own assistance (as to his own decrees) is due. And this puts men out of a state of nature into that of a commonwealth, by setting up a judge on earth with authority to determine all the controversies and redress the injuries that may happen to any member of the commonwealth; which judge is the legislative, or magistrates appointed by it. And wherever there are any number of men, however associated, that have no such decisive power to appeal to, there they are still in the state of nature.

Hence it is evident that absolute monarchy, which by some men is counted the only government in the world, is indeed inconsistent with civil society, and so can be no form of civil government at all. For the end of civil society being to avoid and remedy those inconveniences of the state of nature which necessarily follow from every man's being judge in his own case, by setting up a known authority to which every one of that society may appeal upon any injury received or controversy that may arise, and which every one of the society ought to obey; wherever any persons are who have not such an authority to appeal to and decide any difference between them there, those persons are still in the state of nature. And so is every absolute prince, in respect of those who are under his dominion.

For he being supposed to have all, both legislative and executive power in himself alone, there is no judge to be found; no appeal lies open to any one who may fairly and indifferently and with authority decide, and from whence relief and redress may be expected of any injury or inconvenience that may be suffered from or by his order; so that such a man, however entitled—Czar, or Grand Seignior, or how you please—is as much in the state of nature, with all under his dominion, as he is with the rest of mankind. For wherever any two men are, who have no standing rule and common judge to appeal to on earth for the determination of controversies of right betwixt them, there they are still in the state of nature, and under all the inconveniences of it, with only this woeful difference to the subject, or rather slave, of an absolute prince: that, whereas in the ordinary state of nature he has a liberty to judge of his right, and according to the best of his power to maintain it, now, whenever his property is invaded by the will and order of his monarch, he has not only no appeal, as those in the society ought to have, but, as if he were degraded from the common state of rational creatures, is denied a liberty to judge of or to defend his right; and so is

exposed to all the misery and inconveniences that a man can fear from one who, being in the unrestrained state of nature, is yet corrupted with flattery, and armed with power. . . .

Of the Ends of Political Society and Government ...

The great and chief end, therefore, of men's uniting into commonwealths, and putting themselves under government, is the preservation of their property; to which in the state of nature there are many things wanting.

First, There wants an established settled, known law, received and allowed by common consent to be the standard of right and wrong, and the common measure to decide all controversies between them. For though the law of nature be plain and intelligible to all rational creatures; yet men, being biased by their interest, as well as ignorant for want of study of it, are not apt to allow of it as a law binding to them in the application of it to their particular cases.

Secondly, In the state of nature there wants a known and indifferent judge, with authority to determine all differences according to the established law. For every one in that state, being both judge and executioner of the law of nature, men being partial to themselves, passion and revenge is very apt to carry them too far, and with too much heat in their own cases, as well as negligence and unconcernedness, to make them too remiss in other men's.

Thirdly, In the state of nature there often wants power to back and support the sentence when right, and to give it due execution. They who by any injustice offend, will seldom fail, where they are able by force to make good their injustice; such resistance many times makes the punishment dangerous, and frequently destructive to those who attempt it.

Thus mankind, notwithstanding all the privileges of the state of nature, being but in an ill condition, while they remain in it, are quickly driven into society. Hence it comes to pass that we seldom find any number of men live any time together in this state. . . .

Of the Extent of the Legislative Power

The great end of men's entering into society being the enjoyment of their properties in peace and safety, and the great instrument and means of that being the laws established in that society: the first and fundamental positive law of all commonwealths, is the establishing of the legislative power; as the first and fundamental natural law, which is to govern even the legislative itself, is the preservation of the society, and (as far as will consist with the public good) of every person in it. This legislative is not only the supreme power of the commonwealth, but sacred and unalterable in the hands where the community have once placed it; nor can any edict of anybody else, in what form soever conceived, or by what power soever backed, have the force and obligation of a law, which has not its sanction from that legislative which the public has chosen and appointed. For without this the law could not have that, which is absolutely necessary to its being a law, the consent of the society over whom nobody can have a power to make laws; but by their own consent, and by authority received from them; and therefore all the obedience, which by the most solemn ties any one can be obliged to pay, ultimately terminates in this supreme power, and is directed by those laws which it enacts; nor can any oaths to any foreign power whatsoever, or any domestic subordinate power discharge any member of the society from his obedience to the legislative, acting pursuant to their trust; nor oblige him to any obedience contrary to the laws so enacted, or farther than they do allow; it being ridiculous to imagine one can be tied ultimately to obey any power in the society which is not the supreme.

Though the legislative, whether placed in one or more, whether it be always in being, or only by intervals, though it be the supreme power in every commonwealth, yet,

First, It is not nor can possibly be absolutely arbitrary over the lives and fortunes of the people. For it being but the joint power of every member of the society given up to that person, or assembly, which is legislator; it can be no more than those persons had in a state of nature before they entered into society, and gave it up to the community. For nobody can transfer to another more power than he has in himself; and nobody has an absolute arbitrary power over himself, or over any other to destroy his own life, or take away the life or property of another. A man as has been proved cannot subject himself to the arbitrary power of another; and having in the state of nature no arbitrary power over the life, liberty, or possession of another, but only so much as the law of nature gave him for the preservation of himself, and the rest of mankind; this is all he doth, or can give up to the commonwealth, and by it to the legislative power, so that the legislative can have no more than this. Their power in the utmost bounds of it, is limited to the public good of society. It is power that hath no other end but preservation, and therefore can never have a right to destroy, enslave, or designedly to impoverish the subjects. The obligations of the law of nature cease not in society, but only in many cases are drawn closer, and have by human laws known penalties annexed to them to enforce their observation. Thus the law of nature stands as an eternal rule to all men, legislators as well as others. The rules that they make for other men's actions must, as well as their own, and other men's actions be conformable to the law of nature, *i.e.* to the will of God, of which that is declaration, and the fundamental law of nature being the preservation of mankind, no human sanction can be good or valid against it.

Secondly, The legislative, or supreme authority, cannot assume to itself a power to rule by extemporary arbitrary decrees, but is bound to dispense justice, and decide the rights of the subject by promulgated standing laws, and known authorised judges. For the law of nature being unwritten, and so nowhere to be found but in the minds of men, they who through passion or interest shall miscite or misapply it, cannot so easily be convinced of their mistake where there is no established judge. And so it serves not, as it ought, to determine the rights, and fence the properties of those that live under it, especially where every one is judge, interpreter, executioner of it too, and in his own case; and he that has right on his side, having ordinarily but his own single strength hath not force enough to defend himself from injuries, or punish delinquents. To avoid these inconveniences, which disorder men's properties in the state of nature, men unite into societies that they may have the united strength of the whole society to secure and defend their properties, and may have standing rules to bound it, by which every one may know what is his. To this end it is that men give up all their natural power to the society which they enter into, and the community put the legislative power into such hands as they think fit, with this trust, that they shall be governed by declared laws, or else their peace, quiet, and property, will still be at the same uncertainty as it was in the state of nature.

Absolute arbitrary power, or governing without settled standing laws, can neither of them consist with the ends of society and government, which men would not quit the freedom of the state of nature for, and tie themselves up under, were it not to preserve their lives, liberties, and fortunes; and by stated rules of right and property to secure their peace and quiet. It cannot be supposed that they should intend, had they a power so to do, to give to any one, or more, an absolute arbitrary power over their persons and estates, and put a force into the magistrate's hand to execute his unlimited will arbitrarily upon them. This were to put themselves into a worse condition than the state of nature, wherein they had a liberty to defend their right against the injuries of others, and were upon equal terms of force to maintain it, whether

invaded by a single man or many in combination. Whereas, by supposing they have given up themselves to the absolute arbitrary power and will of a legislator, they have disarmed themselves, and armed him, to make prey of them when he pleases. He being in a much worse condition that is exposed to the arbitrary power of one man who has the command of 100,000 than he that is exposed to the arbitrary power of 100,000 single men; nobody being secure that his will, who hath such a command, is better than that of other men, though his force be 100,000 times stronger. And, therefore, whatever form the commonwealth is under, the ruling power ought to govern by declared and received laws, and not by extemporary dictates and undetermined resolutions. For then mankind will be in a far worse condition than in the state of nature, if they shall have armed one, or a few men, with the joint power of a multitude to force them to obey at pleasure the exorbitant and unlimited decrees of their sudden thoughts, or unrestrained, and, till that moment, unknown wills, without having any measures set down which may guide and justify their actions. For all the power the government has, being only for the good of the society, as it ought not to be arbitrary and at pleasure, so it ought to be exercised by established and promulgated laws; that both the people may know their duty and be safe and secure within the limits of the law; and the rules too kept within their due bounds, and not be tempted by the power they have in their hands to employ it to such purposes, and by such measures as they would not have known, and own not willingly.

Thirdly, The supreme power cannot take from any man any part of his property without his own consent. For the preservation of property being the end of government, and that for which men enter into society, it necessarily supposes and requires that the people should have property, without which they must be supposed to lose that by entering into society, which was the end for which they entered into it, too gross an absurdity for any man to own. Men, therefore, in society having property, they have such a right to the goods which by the law of the community are theirs, that nobody hath a right to take them or any part of them from them, without their own consent; without this they have no property at all. For I have truly no property in that which another can by right take from me when he pleases, against my consent. Hence it is a mistake to think that the supreme or legislative power of any commonwealth can do what it will, and dispose of the estates of the subjects arbitrarily, or take any part of them at pleasure. This is not much to be feared in government where the legislative consists wholly, or in part, in assemblies which are variable, whose members, upon the dissolution of the assembly, are subjects under the common laws of their country, equally with the rest. But in governments where the legislative is in one lasting assembly, always in being, or in one man, as in absolute monarchies, there is danger still, that they will think themselves to have a distinct interest from the rest of the community, and so will be apt to increase their own riches and power by taking what they think fit from the people. For a man's property is not at all secure, though there be good and equitable laws to see the bounds of it between him and his fellow subjects, if he who commands those subjects have power to take from any private man what part he pleases of his property, and use and dispose of it as he thinks good.

But government, into whosesoever hands it is put, being, as I have before shown, entrusted with this condition, and for this end, that men might have and secure their properties, the prince, or senate, however it may have power to make laws for the regulating of property between the subjects one amongst another, yet can never have a power to take to themselves the whole or any part of the subject's property without their own consent. For this would be in effect to leave them no property at all. And to let us see that even absolute power, where

it is necessary, is not arbitrary by being absolute, but is still limited by that reason, and confined to those ends which required it in some cases to be absolute, we need look no farther than the common practice of martial discipline. For the preservation of the army, and in it the whole commonwealth, requires an absolute obedience to the command of every superior officer, and it is justly death to disobey or dispute the most dangerous or unreasonable of them; but yet we see that neither the sergeant, that could command a soldier to march up to the mouth of a cannon, or stand in a breach, where he is almost sure to perish, can command that soldier to give him one penny of his money; nor the general that can condemn him to death for deserting his post, or not obeying the most desperate orders, cannot yet, with all his absolute power of life and death, dispose of one farthing of that soldier's estate, or seize one jot of his goods, whom yet he can command anything, and hang for the least disobedience. Because such a blind obedience is necessary to that end for which the commander has his power, *viz.*, the preservation of the rest; but the disposing of his goods has nothing to do with it.

'Tis true governments cannot be supported without great charge, and it is fit every one who enjoys a share of the protection should pay out of his estate his proportion for the maintenance of it. But still it must be with his own consent, *i.e.*, the consent of the majority giving it either by themselves or their representatives chosen by them. For if any one shall claim a power to lay and levy taxes on the people, by his own authority, and without such consent of the people, he thereby invades the fundamental law of property, and subverts the end of government. For what property have I in that which another may by right take when he pleases to himself?

Fourthly, The legislative cannot transfer the power of making laws to any other hands; for it being but a delegated power from the people, they who have it cannot pass it over to others. The people alone can appoint the form of the commonwealth, which is by constituting the legislative, and appointing in whose hands that shall be. And when the people have said we will submit to rules, and be governed by laws made by such men, and in such forms, nobody else can say other men shall make laws for them; nor can the people be bound by any laws but such as are enacted by those whom they have chosen and authorised to make laws for them.

These are the bounds which the trust that is put in them by society, and the law of God and Nature, have set to the legislative power of every commonwealth, in all forms of government.

First, They are to govern by promulgated established laws, not to be varied in particular cases, but to have one rule for rich and poor, for the favourite at court and the countryman at plough.

Secondly, These laws also ought to be designed for no other end ultimately but the good of the people.

Thirdly, They must not raise taxes on the property of the people without the consent of the people, given by themselves or their deputies. And this properly concerns only such governments where the legislative is always in being, or at least where the people have not reserved any part of the legislative to deputies, to be from time to time chosen by themselves.

Fourthly, The legislative neither must nor can transfer the power of making laws to anybody else, or place it anywhere but where the people have.

COMMENT

Like Thomas Hobbes, Locke believed that apart from civil society, human beings would live in a "state of nature," enjoying an existence little better than that of animals, or what they termed "savages." Unlike Hobbes, however, Locke believed that the "social contract" on which civil society is based is itself grounded not in fear and power, but in a mutual desire to sustain and improve human life. Whereas Hobbes thought that the chief goal of political organization and authority is to provide peace and security, Locke thought that these provisions are the necessary means to the greater end of the free and productive life. Thus for Locke, civil society has a positive function, whereas for Hobbes its function is primarily negative.

Another crucial difference between Locke and Hobbes is that the former maintained that since the state exists to facilitate the "rights and privileges" of its citizens, its power can never be used to deprive its citizens of these basic rights and privileges. The social contract, for Locke, is subject to adjudication, as it were, by a higher authority; either side, including the state, can be guilty of breaking the contract and thus be found deserving of punishment and recompense. For Hobbes, on the other hand, the only way to ensure peace and security is to give the state absolute power over the needs and wishes of its individual citizens. The law, in Locke's view, stands above both the state and the individual, and either can call the other to task for breaking the social contract between them.

To put these points in a slightly different manner, for Hobbes once the original contract is made, the state holds and executes sole authority. For Locke, the authority of the state is subject to systematic review by means of the democratic process under constitutional law. Exactly how Locke viewed the democratic process and how it was to be connected to the concept of private property is too complex to go into at this juncture. It is sufficient to say that Locke's notions of social contract and private property have had a profound influence upon the planning and development of Western political and economic life, as well as upon democracy and capitalism as the pillars of "the American way." Chapter 25, on the philosophy of Marxism, will return to these issues.

Another way of understanding Locke's idea of the social contract is to compare it to that of Jean Jacques Rousseau. Locke saw government as providing the foundation for civil society by means of a conscious agreement between the state and its citizens to abide by law. Rousseau, on the other hand, saw society itself, in all of its natural and unspoken interrelationships, as the foundation for civil government and the state. For Rousseau, the real social contract exists at the society or cultural level, and the state is at best a necessary evil. In other words, where Hobbes and Locke saw the human "state of nature" negatively, and civil government positively, Rousseau saw things just the other way around.

In addition to the potential criticisms of Locke's position implied by the foregoing comparisons with those of Hobbes and Rousseau, there remain several other issues that bear mentioning. There is, of course, serious question as to whether human beings ever have existed in a "state of nature." Perhaps social and political life are actually coextensive with the very definition of human nature. Also, there are those thinkers who, from a Marxist perspective, suggest that far from being a natural right, private property is actually a form of robbery. Surely many primal peoples know nothing of this way of life. For most, the world is considered a "home" in which people dwell and share its resources. Socialists would suggest that only when resources and capital are held in common can democracy actually work. The Scandinavian countries, which practice democratic socialism, have the world's highest standard of living.

Finally, questions can be raised as to whether Locke's perspective does not presuppose some form of "Divine" or "Natural" law upon which civil law is to be based. Apart from some such grounding, one is hard pressed to see how the notion of social contract can work since for Locke it is not based on an earthly sovereign. Many modern philosophers have objected to the idea that there is something inherent within nature itself that grounds human-made laws; even more have doubted the rationality of a belief in a heavenly sovereign. The big question would appear to be: Is it possible to provide an adequate basis for the state without appealing either to God, Natural Law, or to the power of a dictator?

As the primary philosophical source for the constitutional law under which the United States functions, it would be valuable to explore Locke's possible response to the case in point with which this part began. Locke surely would agree with the right of those engaged in civil disobedience, but what would he think of this specific instance? Those indicted by the immigration office tried to appeal to a "higher law," either that of mortality or that of international law, but the judge refused to acknowledge such notions in this case. How would Locke adjudicate between these claims? Does Rousseau's idea of a community or cultural social contract that forms the basis for any political social contract factor into this controversy? Was such an idea operative in the claims of the Sanctuary Movement?

24

LIBERAL DEMOCRACY

JOHN STUART MILL (1806–1873)

For a biographical note, see pages 378–379.

ON LIBERTY

Chapter I

Introductory

… The object of this Essay is to assert one very simple principle, as entitled to govern absolutely the dealings of society with the individual in the way of compulsion and control, whether the means used be physical force in the form of legal penalties, or the moral coercion of public opinion. That principle is, that the (sole) end for which mankind are warranted, individually or collectively, in interfering with the liberty of action of any of their number, is self-protection. That the only purpose for which power can be rightfully exercised over any member of a civilized community, against his will, is to prevent harm to others. His own good, either physical or moral, is not a sufficient warrant. He cannot rightfully be compelled to do or forbear because it will be better for him to do so, because it will make him happier, because, in the opinions of others, to do so would be wise, or even right. These are good reasons for remonstrating with him, or reasoning with

him, or persuading him, or entreating him, but not for compelling him, or visiting him with any evil in case he do otherwise. To justify that, the conduct from which it is desired to deter him must be calculated to produce evil to some one else. The only part of the conduct of anyone, for which he is amenable to society, is that which concerns others. In the part which merely concerns himself, his independence is, of right, absolute. Over himself, over his own body and mind, the individual is sovereign.

It is perhaps hardly necessary to say that this doctrine is meant to apply only to human beings in the maturity of their faculties. We are not speaking of children, or of young persons below the age which the law may fix as that of manhood or womanhood. Those who are still in a state to require being taken care of by others, must be protected against their own actions as well as against external injury. For the same reason, we may leave out of consideration those backward states of society in which the race itself may be considered as in its nonage. The early difficulties in the way of spontaneous progress are so great, and there is seldom any choice of means for overcoming them; and a ruler full of the

On Liberty was first published in London in 1859.

spirit of improvement is warranted in the use of any expedients that will attain an end, perhaps otherwise unattainable. Despotism is a legitimate mode of government in dealing with barbarians, provided the end be their improvement, and the means justified by actually effecting that end. Liberty, as a principle, has no application to any state of things anterior to the time when mankind have become capable of being improved by free and equal discussion. Until then, there is nothing for them but implicit obedience to an Akbar or a Charlemagne, if they are so fortunate as to find one. But as soon as mankind have attained the capacity of being guided to their own improvement by conviction or persuasion (a period long since reached in all nations with whom we need here concern ourselves), compulsion, either in the direct form or in that of pains and penalties for noncompliance, is no longer admissible as a means to their own good, and justifiable only for the security of others.

It is proper to state that I forego any advantage which could be derived to my argument from the idea of abstract right, as a thing independent of utility. I regard utility as the ultimate appeal on all ethical questions; but it must be utility in the largest sense, grounded on the permanent interests of a man as a progressive being. Those interests, I contend, authorized the subjection of individual spontaneity to external control, only in respect to those actions of each which concern the interest of other people. If anyone does an act hurtful to others, there is a *prima facie* case for punishing him, by law, or, where legal penalties are not safely applicable, by general disapprobation. There are also many positive acts for the benefit of others, which he may rightfully be compelled to perform: such as to give evidence in a court of justice; to bear his fair share in the common defense, or in any other joint work necessary to the interest of the society of which he enjoys the protection; and to perform certain acts of individual beneficence, such as saving a fellow-creature's life, or interpos-

ing to protect the defenseless against ill-usage, things which wherever it is obviously a man's duty to do, he may rightfully be made responsible to society for not doing. A person may cause evil to others not only by his actions but by his inaction, and in either case he is justly accountable to them for the injury. The latter case, it is true, requires a much more cautious exercise of compulsion than the former. To make anyone answerable for doing evil to others is the rule; to make him answerable for not preventing evil is, comparatively speaking, the exception. Yet there are many cases clear enough and grave enough to justify that exception. In all things which regard the external relations of the individual, he is *de jure* amenable to those whose interests are concerned, and, if need be, to society as their protector. There are often good reasons for not holding him to the responsibility; but these reasons must arise from the special expediencies of the case: either because it is a kind of case in which he is on the whole likely to act better, when left to his own discretion, than when controlled in any way in which society have it in their power to control him; or because the attempt to exercise control would produce other evils, greater than those which it would prevent. When such reasons as these preclude the enforcement of responsibility, the conscience of the agent himself should step into the vacant judgment seat, and protect those interests of others which have no external protection; judging himself all the more rigidly, because the case does not admit of his being made accountable to the judgment of his fellow-creatures.

But there is a sphere of action in which society, as distinguished from the individual, has, if any, only an indirect interest; comprehending all that portion of a person's life and conduct which affects only himself, or if it also affects others, only with their free, voluntary, and undeceived consent and participation. When I say only himself, I mean directly, and in the first instance; for whatever affects himself, may affect others through himself; and the objection which may be grounded on this contingency, will receive consideration in the sequel. This, then, is the appropriate region of human liberty. It comprises, *first*, the inward domain of consciousness; demanding liberty of conscience in the most comprehensive sense; liberty of thought and feeling; absolute freedom of opinion and sentiment on all subjects, practical or speculative, scientific, moral or theological. The liberty of expressing and publishing opinions may seem to fall under a different principle, since it belongs to that part of the conduct of an individual which concerns other people; but, being almost of as much importance as the liberty of thought itself, and resting in great part on the same reasons, is practically inseparable from it. *Secondly*, the principle requires liberty of tastes and pursuits; of framing the plan of our life to suit our own character; of doing as we like, subject to such consequences as may follow: without impediment from our fellow-creatures, so long as what we do does not harm them, even though they should think our conduct foolish, perverse, or wrong. *Thirdly*, from this liberty of each individual, follows the liberty, within the same limits, of combination among individuals; freedom to unite, for any purpose not involving harm to others: the persons combining being supposed to be of full age, and not forced or deceived.

No society in which these liberties are not, on the whole, respected, is free, whatever may be its form of government; and none is completely free in which they do not exist absolute and unqualified. The only freedom which deserves the name, is that of pursuing our own good in our own way, so long as we do not attempt to deprive others of theirs, or impede their efforts to obtain it. Each is the proper guardian of his own health, whether bodily, or mental and spiritual. Mankind are greater gainers by suffering each other to live as seems good to themselves, than by compelling each to live as seems good to the rest.

Though this doctrine is anything but new, and, to some persons, may have the air of a truism, there is no doctrine which stands more directly opposed to the general tendency of existing opinion and practice.... There is ... an inclination to stretch unduly the powers of society over the individual, both by the force of opinion and even by that of legislation; and as the tendency of all the changes taking place in the world is to strengthen society, and diminish the power of the individual, this encroachment is not one of the evils which tend spontaneously to disappear, but, on the contrary, to grow more and more formidable. The disposition of mankind, whether as rulers or as fellow-citizens, to impose their own opinions and inclinations as a rule of conduct on others, is so energetically supported by some of the best and by some of the worst feelings incident to human nature, that it is hardly ever kept under restraint by anything but want of power; and as the power is not declining, but growing, unless a strong barrier of moral conviction can be raised against the mischief, we must expect, in the present circumstances of the world, to see it increase....

Chapter II

Of the Liberty of Thought and Discussion

The time, it is to be hoped, is gone by, when any defence would be necessary of the "liberty of the press" as one of the securities against corrupt or tyrannical government.... Speaking generally, it is not, in constitutional countries, to be apprehended that the government, whether completely responsible to the people or not, will often attempt to control the expression of opinion, except when in doing so it makes itself the organ of the general intolerance of the public. Let us suppose, therefore, that the government is entirely at one with the people, and never thinks of exerting any power of coercion unless in agreement with what it conceives to be their voice. But I deny the right of the people to exercise such coercion, either by themselves or by their government. The power itself is illegitimate. The best government has no more title to it than the worst. It is as noxious, or more noxious, when exerted in accordance with public opinion, than when in opposition to it. If all mankind minus one were of one opinion, and only one person were of the contrary opinion, mankind would be no more justified in silencing that one person, than he, if he had the power, would be justified in silencing mankind. Were an opinion a personal possession of no value except to the owner; if to be obstructed in the enjoyment of it were simply a private injury, it would make some difference whether the injury was inflicted only on a few persons or on many. But the peculiar evil of silencing the expression of an opinion is, that it is robbing the human race: posterity as well as the existing generation; those who dissent from the opinion, still more than those who hold it. If the opinion is right, they are deprived of the opportunity of exchanging error for truth; if wrong, they lose, what is almost as great a benefit, the clearer perception and livelier impression of truth, produced by its collision with error.

It is necessary to consider separately these two hypotheses, each of which has a distinct branch of the argument corresponding to it. We can never be sure that the opinion we are endeavoring to stifle is a false opinion; and if we were sure, stifling it would be an evil still.

First: the opinion which it is attempted to suppress by authority may possibly be true. Those who desire to suppress it, of course deny its truth; but they are not infallible. They have no authority to decide the question for all mankind, and exclude every other person from the means of judging. To refuse a hearing to an opinion, because they are sure that it is false, is to assume that *their* certainty is the same thing as *absolute* certainty. All silencing of discussion is an assumption of infallibility. Its condemnation may be allowed to rest on this common argument, not the worse for being common.

Unfortunately for the good sense of mankind, the fact of their fallibility is far from carrying the weight in their practical judgment which is always allowed to it in theory; for while everyone well knows himself to be fallible, few think it necessary to take any precautions against their own fallibility, or admit the supposition that any opinion of which they feel very certain, may be one of the examples of the error to which they acknowledge themselves to be liable. Absolute princes, or others who are accustomed to unlimited deference, usually feel this complete confidence in their own opinions on nearly all subjects. People more happily situated, who sometimes hear their opinions disputed, and are not wholly unused to be set right when they are wrong, place the same unbounded reliance only on such of their opinions as are shared by all who surround them, or to whom they habitually defer; for in proportion to a man's want of confidence in his own solitary judgment, does he usually repose, with implicit trust, on the infallibility of "the world" in general. And the world, to each individual, means the part of it with which he comes in contact—his party, his sect, his church, his class of society; the man may be called, by comparison, almost liberal and large-minded to whom it means anything so comprehensive as his own country or his own age. Nor is his faith in this collective authority at all shaken by his being aware that other ages, countries, sects, churches, classes, and parties have thought, and even now think, the exact reverse. He devolves upon his own world the responsibility of being in the right against the dissentient worlds of other people; and it never troubles him that mere accident has decided which of these numerous worlds is the object of his reliance, and that the same causes which make him a Churchman in London, would have made him a Buddhist or a Confucian in Peking. Yet it is as evident in itself as any amount of argument can make it, that ages are no more infallible than individuals; every age having held many opinions which subsequent ages have deemed not only false but absurd; and it is as certain that many opinions now general will be rejected by future ages, as it is that many, once general, are rejected by the present.

The objection likely to be made to this argument would probably take some such form as the following. There is no greater assumption of infallibility in forbidding the propagation of error, than in any other thing which is done by public authority on its own judgment and responsibility. Judgment is given to men that they may use it. Because it may be used erroneously, are men to be told that they ought not to use it at all? To prohibit what they think pernicious, is not claiming exemption from error, but fulfilling the duty incumbent on them, although fallible, of acting on their conscientious conviction. If we were never to act on our opinions, because those opinions may be wrong, we should leave all our interests uncared for, and all our duties unperformed. An objection which applies to all conduct can be no valid objection to any conduct in particular. It is the duty of governments, and of individuals, to form the truest opinions they can; to form them carefully, and never impose them upon others unless they are quite sure of being right. But when they are sure (such reasoners may say), it is not conscientiousness but cowardice to shrink from acting on their opinions, and allow doctrines which they honestly think dangerous to the welfare of mankind, either in this life or in another, to be scattered abroad without restraint, because other people, in less enlightened times, have persecuted opinions now believed to be true. Let us take care, it may be said, not to make the same mistake; but governments and nations have made mistakes in other things, which are not denied to be fit subjects for the exercise of authority: they have laid on bad taxes, made unjust wars. Ought we therefore to lay on no taxes, and, under whatever provocation, make no wars? Men, and governments, must act to the best of their ability. There is no such thing as absolute certainty, but there is assurance sufficient for the purposes of human life. We may, and must, assume our opinion to be true for the guidance of our own conduct: and it is assuming no more when we forbid bad men to pervert society by the propagation of opinions which we regard as false and pernicious.

I answer that it is assuming very much more. There is the greatest difference between presuming an opinion to be true because, with every opportunity for contesting it, it has not been refuted, and assuming its truth for the purpose of not permitting its refutation. Complete liberty of contradicting and disproving our opinion is the very condition which justifies us in assuming its truth for purposes of action; and on no other terms can a being with human faculties have any rational assurance of being right.

When we consider either the history of opinion, or the ordinary conduct of human life, to what is it to be ascribed that the one and the other are no worse than they are? Not certainly to the inherent force of the human understanding; for, on any matter not self-evident, there are ninety-nine persons totally incapable of judging of it for one who is capable; and the capacity of the hundredth person is only comparative: for the majority of the eminent men of every past generation held many opinions now known to be erroneous, and did or approved numerous things which no one will now justify. Why is it, then, that there is on the whole a preponderance among mankind of rational opinions and rational conduct? If there really is this preponderance—which there must be unless human affairs are, and have always been, in an almost desperate state—it is owing to a quality of the human mind, the source of everything respectable in man either as an intellectual or as a moral being, namely, that his errors are corrigible. He is capable of rectifying his mistakes, by discussion and experience. Not by experience alone. There must be discussion, to show how experience is to be interpreted. Wrong opinions and practices gradually yield to fact and argument; but facts and arguments, to produce any effect on the mind, must be brought before it. Very few facts are able to tell their own story, without comments to bring out their meaning. The whole strength and value, then, of human judgment, depending on the one property, that it can be set right when it is wrong, reliance can be placed on it only when the means of setting it right are kept constantly at hand. In the case of any person whose judgment is really deserving of confidence, how has it become so? Because he has kept his mind open to criticism of his opinions and conduct. Because it has been his practice to listen to all that could be said against him; to profit by as much of it as was just, and expound to himself, and upon occasion to others, the fallacy of what was fallacious. Because he has felt that the only way in which a human being can make some approach to knowing the whole of a subject, is by hearing what can be said about it by persons of every variety of opinion, and studying all modes in which it can be looked at by every character of mind. No wise man ever acquired his wisdom in any mode but this; nor is it in the nature of human intellect to become wise in any other manner. The steady habit of correcting and completing his own opinion by collating it with those of others, so far from causing doubt and hesitation in carrying it into practice, is the only stable foundation for a just reliance on it: for, being cognizant of all that can, at least obviously, be said against him, and having taken up his position against all gainsayers—knowing that he has sought for objections and difficulties, instead of avoiding them, and has shut out no light which can be thrown upon the subject from any quarter—he has a right to think his judgment better than that of any person, or any multitude, who have not gone through a similar process.

It is not too much to require that what the wisest of mankind, those who are best entitled to trust their own judgment, find necessary to warrant their relying on it, should be submitted to by that miscellaneous collection of a few wise and many foolish individuals, called the public. The most intolerant of churches, the Roman Catholic Church, even at the canonization of a saint, admits, and listens patiently to, a "devil's advocate." The holiest of men, it appears, cannot be admitted to posthumous honors, until all that the devil could say against him is known and weighed. If even the Newtonian philosophy were not permitted to be questioned, mankind could not feel as complete assurance of its truth as they now do. The beliefs which we have most warrant for, have no safeguard to rest on but a standing invitation to the whole world to prove them unfounded. If the challenge is not accepted, or is accepted and the attempt fails, we are far enough from certainty still; but we have done the best that the existing state of human reason admits of; we have neglected nothing that could give the truth a chance of reaching us: if the lists are kept open, we may hope that if there be a better truth, it will be found when the human mind is capable of receiving it; and in the meantime we may rely on having attained such approach to truth as is possible in our own day. This is the amount of certainty attainable by a fallible being, and this the sole way of attaining it.

Strange it is that men should admit the validity of the arguments for free discussion, but object to their being "pushed to an extreme"; not seeing that unless the reasons are good for an extreme case they are not good for any case. Strange that they should imagine that they are not assuming infallibility, when they acknowledge that there should be free discussion on all subjects which can possibly be *doubtful,* but think that some particular principle or doctrine should be forbidden to be questioned because it is so *certain,* that is, because *they are certain* that it is certain. To call any proposition certain while there is anyone who would deny its certainty if permitted, but who is not permitted, is to assume that we ourselves, and those who agree with us, are the judges of certainty, and judges without hearing the other side.

In the present age—which has been described as "destitute of faith, but terrified at scepticism"—in which people feel sure, not so much that their opinions are true, as that they should not know what to do without them—the claims of an opinion to be protected from public attack are rested not so much on its truth, as on its importance to society. There are, it is alleged, certain beliefs so useful, not to say indispensable, to well-being that it is as much the duty of governments to uphold those beliefs, as to protect any other of the interests of society. In a case of such necessity, and so directly in the line of their duty, something less than infallibility may, it is maintained, warrant, and even bind, governments to act on their own opinion, confirmed by the general opinion of mankind. It is also often argued, and still oftener thought, that none but bad men would desire to weaken these salutary beliefs; and there can be nothing wrong, it is thought, in restraining bad men, and prohibiting what only such men would wish to practice. This mode of thinking makes the justification of restraints on discussion not a question of the truth of doctrines, but of their usefulness; and flatters itself by that means to escape the responsibility of claiming to be an infallible judge of opinions. But those who thus satisfy themselves, do not perceive that the assumption of infallibility is merely shifted from one point to another. The usefulness of an opinion is itself matter of opinion: as disputable, as open to discussion, and requiring discussion as much as the opinion itself. There is the same need of an infallible judge of opinions to decide an opinion to be noxious, as to decide it to be false, unless the opinion condemned has full opportunity of defending itself. And it will not do to say that the heretic may be allowed to maintain the utility or harmlessness of his opinion, though forbidden to maintain its truth. The truth of an opinion is part of its utility. If we would know whether or not it is desirable that a proposition should be believed, is it possible to exclude the consideration of whether or not it is true? In the opinion, not of bad men, but of the best men, no belief which is contrary to truth can be really useful; and can you prevent such men from urging that plea, when they are charged with culpability for denying some doctrine which they are told is useful, but which they believe to be false? Those who are on the side of received opinions never fail to take all possible advantages of this plea: you do not find *them* handling the question of utility as if it could be completely abstracted from that of truth; on the contrary, it is, above all, because their doctrine is "the truth," that the knowledge or the belief of it is held to be so indispensable. There can be no fair discussion of the question of usefulness when an argument so vital may be employed on one side, but not on the other. And in point of fact, when law or public feeling do not permit the truth of an opinion to be disputed, they are just as little tolerant of a denial of its usefulness. The utmost they allow is an extenuation of its absolute necessity, or of the positive guilt of rejecting it.

In order more fully to illustrate the mischief of denying a hearing to opinions because we, in our own judgment, have condemned them, it will be desirable to fix down the discussion to a concrete case; and I choose, by preference, the cases which are least favorable to me—in which the argument against freedom of opinion, both on the score of truth and on that of utility, is considered the strongest. Let the opinions impugned be the belief in a God and in a future state, or any of the commonly received doctrines of morality. To fight the battle on such ground gives a great advantage to an unfair antagonist; since he will be sure to say (and many who have no desire to be unfair will say it internally), "Are these the doctrines which you do not deem sufficiently certain to be taken under the protection of laws? Is the belief in a God one of the opinions to feel sure of which you hold to be assuming infallibility?" But I must be permitted to observe that it is not the feeling sure of a doctrine (be it what it may) which I call an assumption of infallibility. It is the undertaking to decide that question *for others,* without allowing them to hear what can be said on the contrary side. And I denounce and reprobate this pretension not the less if put forth on the side of my most solemn convictions. However positive anyone's persuasion may be, not only of the falsity but of the pernicious consequences—not only of the pernicious consequences, but (to adopt expressions which I altogether condemn) the immorality and impiety of an opinion; yet if, in pursuance of that private judgment, though backed by the public judgment of his country or his contemporaries, he prevents the opinion from being heard in its defense, he assumes infallibility. And so far from the assumption being less objectionable or less dangerous because the opinion is called immoral or impious, this is the case of all others in which it is most fatal. These are exactly the occasions on which the men of one generation commit those dreadful mistakes which excite the astonishment and horror of posterity. It is among such that we find the instances memorable in history, when the arm of the law has been employed to root out the best men and the noblest doctrines; with deplorable success as to the men, though some of the doctrines have survived to be (as if in mockery) invoked in defense of similar conduct toward those who dissent from *them,* or from their received interpretation.

Mankind can hardly be too often reminded, that there was once a man named Socrates, between whom and the legal authorities and public opinion of his time there took place a memorable collision. Born in an age and country abounding in individual greatness, this man has been handed down to us by those who best knew both him and the age, as the most virtuous man in it; while we know him as the head and prototype of all subsequent teachers of virtue, the source equally of the lofty inspiration of Plato and the judicious utilitarianism of Aristotle . . . the two headsprings of ethical as of all other philosophy. This acknowledged master of all the eminent thinkers who have since lived—whose

fame, still growing after more than two thousand years, all but outweighs the whole remainder of the names which make his native city illustrious—was put to death by his countrymen, after a judicial conviction, for impiety and immorality. Impiety, in denying the gods recognized by the State; indeed his accuser asserted (see the *Apologia*) that he believed in no gods at all. Immorality, in being, by his doctrines and instructions, a "corruptor of youth." Of these charges the tribunal, there is every ground for believing, honestly found him guilty, and condemned the man who probably of all then born had deserved best of mankind to be put to death as a criminal.

To pass from this to the only other instance of judicial iniquity, the mention of which, after the condemnation of Socrates, would not be an anticlimax: the event which took place on Calvary rather more than eighteen hundred years ago. The man who left on the memory of those who witnessed his life and conversation such an impression of his moral grandeur that eighteen subsequent centuries have done homage to him as the Almighty in person, was ignominiously put to death, as what? As a blasphemer. Men did not merely mistake their benefactor; they mistook him for the exact contrary of what he was, and treated him as that prodigy of impiety which they themselves are now held to be for their treatment of him. The feelings with which mankind now regard these lamentable transactions, especially the later of the two, render them extremely unjust in their judgment of the unhappy actors. These were, to all appearance, not bad men—not worse than men commonly are, but rather the contrary; men who possessed in a full, or somewhat more than a full measure, the religious, moral, and patriotic feelings of their time and people: the very kind of men who, in all times, our own included, have every chance of passing through life blameless and respected. The high-priest who rent his garments when the words were pronounced which, according to all the ideas of his country, constituted the blackest guilt, was in all probability quite as sincere in his horror and indignation as the generality of respectable and pious men now are in the religious and moral sentiments they profess; and most of those who now shudder at his conduct, if they had lived in his time, and been born Jews, would have acted precisely as he did. Orthodox Christians who are tempted to think that those who stoned to death the first martyrs must have been worse men than they themselves are, ought to remember that one of those persecutors was Saint Paul.

Let us add one more example, the most striking of all, if the impressiveness of an error is measured by the wisdom and virtue of him who falls into it. If ever anyone possessed of power had grounds for thinking himself the best and most enlightened among his contemporaries, it was the Emperor Marcus Aurelius. Absolute monarch of the whole civilized world, he preserved through life not only the most unblemished justice, but what was less to be expected from his Stoical breeding, the tenderest heart. The few failings which are attributed to him were all on the side of indulgence; while his writings, the highest ethical product of the ancient mind, differ scarcely perceptibly, if they differ at all, from the most characteristic teachings of Christ. This man, a better Christian in all but the dogmatic sense of the word than almost any of the ostensibly Christian sovereigns who have since reigned, persecuted Christianity. Placed at the summit of all the previous attainments of humanity, with an open, unfettered intellect, and a character which led him of himself to embody in his moral writings the Christian ideal, he yet failed to see that Christianity was to be a good and not an evil to the world, with his duties to which be was so deeply penetrated. Existing society he knew to be in a deplorable state. But such as it was, he saw, or thought he saw, that it was held together, and prevented from being worse, by belief and reverence of the received divinities. As a ruler of mankind, he deemed it his duty not to suffer society to fall in pieces; and saw not

how, if its existing ties were removed, any others could be formed which could again knit it together. The new religion openly aimed at dissolving these ties: unless, therefore, it was his duty to adopt that religion, it seemed to be his duty to put it down. Inasmuch then as the theology of Christianity did not appear to him true or of divine origin; inasmuch as this strange history of a crucified God was not credible to him, and a system which purported to rest entirely upon a foundation to him so wholly unbelievable, could not be foreseen by him to be that renovating agency which, after all abatements, it has in fact proved to be; the gentlest and most amiable of philosophers and rulers, under a solemn sense of duty, authorized the persecution of Christianity. To my mind this is one of the most tragical facts in all history. It is a bitter thought, how different a thing the Christianity of the world might have been, if the Christian faith had been adopted as the religion of the empire under the auspices of Marcus Aurelius instead of those of Constantine. But it would be equally unjust to him and false to truth to deny that no one plea which can be urged for punishing anti-Christian teaching was wanting to Marcus Aurelius for punishing as he did the propagation of Christianity. No Christian more firmly believes that atheism is false, and tends to the dissolution of society, than Marcus Aurelius believed the same things of Christianity; he who, of all men then living, might have been thought the most capable of appreciating it. Unless anyone who approves of punishment for the promulgation of opinions, flatters himself that he is a wiser and better man than Marcus Aurelius—more deeply versed in the wisdom of his time, more elevated in his intellect above it— more earnest in his search for truth, or more single-minded in his devotion to it when found; let him abstain from that assumption of the joint infallibility of himself and the multitude, which the great Antoninus made with so unfortunate a result. . . .

Let us now pass to the second division of the argument, and dismissing the supposition that any of the received opinions may be false, let us assume them to be true, and examine into the worth of the manner in which they are likely to be held, when their truth is not freely and openly canvassed. However unwilling a person who has a strong opinion may admit the possibility that his opinion may be false, he ought to be moved by the consideration that, however true it may be, if it is not fully, frequently, and fearlessly discussed, it will be held as a dead dogma, not a living truth.

There is a class of persons (happily not quite so numerous as formerly) who think it enough if a person assents undoubtingly to what they think true, though he has no knowledge whatever of the grounds of the opinion, and could not make a tenable defense of it against the most superficial objections. Such persons, if they can once get their creed taught from authority, naturally think that no good, and some harm, comes of its being allowed to be questioned. Where their influence prevails, they make it nearly impossible for the received opinion to be rejected wisely and considerately, though it may still be rejected rashly and ignorantly; for to shut out discussion entirely is seldom possible, and when it once gets in, beliefs not grounded on conviction are apt to give way before the slightest semblance of an argument. Waiving, however, this possibility—assuming that the true opinion abides in the mind, but abides as a prejudice, a belief independent of, and proof against, argument—this is not the way in which truth ought to be held by a rational being. This is not knowing the truth. Truth, thus held, is but one superstition the more, accidentally clinging to the words which enunciate a truth.

If the intellect and judgment of mankind ought to be cultivated, a thing which Protestants at least do not deny, on what can these faculties be more appropriately exercised by anyone, than on the things which concern him so much that it is considered necessary for him to hold opinions on them? If the cultivation of the understanding consists in one thing more

than in another, it is surely in learning the grounds of one's own opinions. Whatever people believe, on subjects on which it is of the first importance to believe rightly, they ought to be able to defend against at least the common objections. But, some one may say, "Let them be *taught* the grounds of their opinions. It does not follow that opinions must be merely parroted because they are never heard controverted. Persons who learn geometry do not simply commit the theorems to memory, but understand and learn likewise the demonstrations; and it would be absurd to say that they remain ignorant of the grounds of geometrical truths, because they never hear any one deny, and attempt to disprove them." Undoubtedly: and such teaching suffices on a subject like mathematics, where there is nothing at all to be said on the wrong side of the question. The peculiarity of the evidence of mathematical truths is that all the argument is on one side. There are no objections, and no answers to objections. But on every subject on which difference of opinion is possible, the truth depends on a balance to be struck between two sets of conflicting reasons. Even in natural philosophy, there is always some other explanation possible of the same facts—some geocentric theory instead of heliocentric, some phlogiston instead of oxygen—and it has to be shown why that other theory cannot be the true one; and until this is shown, and until we know how it is shown, we do not understand the grounds of our opinion. But when we turn to subjects infinitely more complicated, to morals, religion, politics, social relations, and the business of life, three-fourths of the arguments for every disputed opinion consist in dispelling appearances which favor some opinion different from it. The greatest orator, save one, of antiquity, has left it on record that he always studied his adversary's case with as great, if not still greater, intensity than even his own. What Cicero practiced as the means of forensic success requires to be imitated by all who study any subject in order to arrive at the truth. He who knows only his own side of the case, knows little of that. His reasons may be good, and no one may have been able to refute them. But if he is equally unable to refute the reasons on the opposite side; if he does not so much as know what they are, he has no ground for preferring either opinion. The rational position for him would be suspension of judgment, and unless he contents himself with that, he is either led by authority, or adopts, like the generality of the world, the side to which he feels most inclination, Nor is it enough that he should hear the arguments of adversaries from his own teachers, presented as they state them, and accompanied by what they offer as refutations. That is not the way to do justice to the arguments, or bring them into real contact with his own mind. He must be able to hear them from persons who actually believe them; who defend them in earnest, and do their very utmost for them. He must know them in their most plausible and persuasive form; he most feel the whole force of the difficulty which the true view of the subject has to encounter and dispose of; else he will never really possess himself of the portion of truth which meets and removes that difficulty. Ninety-nine in a hundred of what are called educated men are in this condition; even of those who can argue fluently for their opinions. Their conclusion may be true, but it might be false for anything they know: they have never thrown themselves into the mental position of those who think differently from them, and considered what such persons may have to say; and consequently they do not, in any proper sense of the word, know the doctrine which they themselves profess. They do not know those parts of it which explain and justify the remainder; the considerations which show that a fact which seemingly conflicts with another is reconcilable with it, or that, of two apparently strong reasons, one and not the other ought to be preferred. All that part of the truth which turns the scale, and decides the judgment of a completely informed mind, they are strangers to; nor is it ever really known but to those who have

attended equally and impartially to both sides, and endeavored to see the reasons of both in the strongest light. So essential is this discipline to a real understanding of moral and human subjects, that if opponents of all important truths do not exist, it is indispensable to imagine them, and supply them with the strongest arguments which the most skilful devil's advocate can conjure up. . . .

If, however, the mischievous operation of the absence of free discussion, when the received opinions are true, were confined to leaving men ignorant of the grounds of those opinions, it might be thought that this, if an intellectual, is no moral evil, and does not affect the worth of the opinions, regarded in their influence on the character. The fact, however, is that not only the grounds of the opinion are forgotten in the absence of discussion, but too often the meaning of the opinion itself. The words which convey it cease to suggest ideas, or suggest only a small portion of those they were originally employed to communicate. Instead of a vivid conception and a living belief, there remain only a few phrases retained by rote; or, if any part, the shell and husk only of the meaning is retained, the finer essence being lost. The great chapter in human history which this fact occupies and fills, cannot be too earnestly studied and meditated on. . . .

It is the fashion of the present time to disparage negative logic—that which points out weaknesses in theory or errors in practice, without establishing positive truths. Such negative criticism would indeed be poor enough as an ultimate result; but as a means to attaining any positive knowledge or conviction worthy the name, it cannot be valued too highly; and until people are again systematically trained to it, there will be few great thinkers, and a low general average of intellect, in any but the mathematical and physical departments of speculation. On any other subject no one's opinions deserve the name of knowledge, except so far as he has either had forced upon him by others, or gone through of himself, the same mental process which would have been required of him in carrying on an active controversy with opponents. That, therefore, which when absent, it is so indispensable, but so difficult, to create, how worse than absurd it is to forego, when spontaneously offering itself! If there are any persons who contest a received opinion, or who will do so if law or opinion will let them, let us thank them for it, open our minds to listen to them, and rejoice that there is some one to do for us what we otherwise ought, if we have any regard for either the certainty or the vitality of our convictions, to do with much greater labor for ourselves.

It still remains to speak of one of the principal causes which make diversity of opinion advantageous, and will continue to do so until mankind shall have entered a stage of intellectual advancement which at present sees at an incalculable distance. We have hitherto considered only two possibilities: that the received opinion may be false, and some other opinion consequently true; or that, the received opinion being true, a conflict with the opposite error is essential to a clear apprehension and deep feeling of its truth. But there is a commoner case than either of these: when the conflicting doctrines, instead of being one true and the other false, share the truth between them; and the nonconforming opinion is needed to supply the remainder of the truth, of which the received doctrine embodies only a part. Popular opinions, on subjects not palpable to sense, are often true, but seldom or never the whole truth. They are a part of the truth; sometimes a greater, sometimes a smaller part, but exaggerated, distorted, and disjointed from the truths by which they ought to be accompanied and limited. Heretical opinions, on the other hand, are generally some of these suppressed and neglected truths, bursting the bonds which kept them down, and neither seeking reconciliation with the truth contained in the common opinion, or fronting it as enemies, and setting themselves up, with similar exclusiveness, as the whole truth. The latter case is hitherto the most frequent, as, in the human mind, one-sidedness has always been the rule and many-sidedness the exception. Hence, even in revolutions of opinion, one part of the truth usually sets while another rises. Even progress, which ought to superadd, for the most part only substitutes, one partial and incomplete truth for another; improvement consisting chiefly in this, that the new fragment of truth is more wanted, more adapted to the needs of the time, than that which it displaces. Such being the partial character of prevailing opinions, even when resting on a true foundation, every opinion which embodies somewhat of the portion of truth which the common opinion omits, ought to be considered precious, with whatever amount of error and confusion that truth may be blended. No sober judge of human affairs will feel bound to be indignant because those who force on our notice truths which we should otherwise have overlooked, overlook some of those which we see. Rather, he will think that so long as popular truth is one-sided, it is more desirable than otherwise that unpopular truth should have one-sided assertors too; such being usually the most energetic, and the most likely to compel reluctant attention to the fragment of wisdom which they proclaim as if it were the whole.

Thus, in the eighteenth century, when nearly all the instructed, and all those of the uninstructed who were led by them, were lost in admiration of what is called civilization, and of the marvels of modern science, literature, and philosophy, and while greatly overrating the amount of unlikeness between the men of modern and those of ancient times, indulged the belief that the whole of the difference was in their own favor; with what a salutary shock did the paradoxes of Rousseau explode like bombshells in the midst, dislocating the compact mass of one-sided opinion, and forcing its elements to recombine in a better form and with additional ingredients. Not that the current opinions were on the whole farther from the truth than

Rousseau's were: on the contrary, they were nearer to it: they contained more of positive truth, and very much less of error. Nevertheless there lay in Rousseau's doctrine, and has floated down the stream of opinion along with it, a considerable amount of exactly those truths which the popular opinion wanted; and these are the deposit which was left behind when the flood subsided. The superior worth of simplicity of life, the enervating and demoralizing effect of the trammels and hypocrisies of artificial society, are ideas which have never been entirely absent from cultivated minds since Rousseau wrote; and they will in time produce their due effect, though at present needing to be asserted as much as ever, and to be asserted by deeds, for words, on this subject, have nearly exhausted their power.

In politics, again, it is almost a commonplace, that a party of order or stability, and a party of progress or reform, are both necessary elements of a healthy state of political life; until the one or the other shall have so enlarged its mental grasp as to be a party equally of order and of progress, knowing and distinguishing what is fit to be preserved from what ought to be swept away. Each of these modes of thinking derives its utility from the deficiencies of the other; but it is in a great measure the opposition of the other that keeps each within the limits of reason and sanity. Unless opinions favorable to democracy and to aristocracy, to property and to equality, to coöperation and to competition, to luxury and to abstinence, to sociality and individuality, to liberty and discipline, and all the other standing antagonisms of practical life, are expressed with equal freedom, and enforced and defended with equal talent and energy, there is no chance of both elements obtaining their due: one scale is sure to go up, and the other down. Truth, in the great practical concerns of life, is so much a question of the reconciling and combining of opposites, that very few have minds sufficiently capacious and impartial to make the adjustment with an approach

to correctness, and it has to be made by the rough process of a struggle between combatants fighting under hostile banners. On any of the great open questions just enumerated, if either of the two opinions has a better claim than the other, not merely to be tolerated, but to be encouraged and countenanced, it is the one which happens at the particular time and place to be in a minority. That is the opinion which, for the time being, represents the neglected interests, the side of human well-being which is in danger of obtaining less than its share. I am aware that there is not, in this country, any intolerance of differences of opinion on most of these topics. They are adduced to show, by admitted and multiplied examples, the universality of the fact that only through diversity of opinion is there, in the existing state of human intellect, a chance of fair play to all sides of the truth. When there are persons to be found who form an exception to the apparent unanimity of the world on any subject, even if the world is in the right, it is always probable that dissentients have something worth hearing to say for themselves, and that truth would lose something by their silence. . . .

We have now recognized the necessity to the mental well-being of mankind (on which all their other well-being depends) of freedom of opinion, and freedom of the expression of opinion, on four distinct grounds; which we will now briefly recapitulate.

✷ First, if any opinion is compelled to silence, that opinion may, for aught we can certainly know, be true. To deny this is to assume our own infallibility.

✷ Secondly, though the silenced opinion be an error, it may, and very commonly does, contain a portion of truth; and since the general or prevailing opinion on any subject is rarely or never the whole truth, it is only by the collision of adverse opinions that the remainder of the truth has any chance of being supplied.

✷ Thirdly, even if the received opinion be not only true, but the whole truth; unless it is suffered to be, and actually is, vigorously and earnestly contested, it will, by most of those who receive it, be held in the manner of a prejudice, with little comprehension or feeling of its rational grounds. And not only this, but, fourthly, the meaning of the doctrine itself will be in danger of being lost, or enfeebled, and deprived of its vital effect on the character and conduct: the dogma becoming a mere formal procession, inefficacious for good, but cumbering the ground, and preventing the growth of any real and heartfelt conviction, from reason or personal experience. . . .

Chapter III

Of Individuality, As One of the Elements of Well-being

Such being the reasons which make it imperative that human beings should be free to form opinions, and to express their opinions without reserve; and such the baneful consequences to the intellectual, and through that to the moral nature of man, unless this liberty is either conceded, or asserted in spite of prohibition; let us next examine whether the same reasons do not require that men should be free to act upon their opinions—to carry these out in their lives, without hindrance, either physical or moral, from their fellowmen, so long as it is at their own risk and peril. This last proviso is of course indispensable. No one pretends that actions should be as free as opinions. On the contrary, even opinions lose their immunity when the circumstances in which they are expressed are such as to constitute their expression a positive instigation to some mischievous act. An opinion that corn-dealers are starvers of the poor, or that private property is robbery, ought to be unmolested when simply circulated through the press, but may justly incur punishment when delivered orally to an excited mob assembled before the house of a corn-dealer, or when handed about among the same mob in the form of a placard. Acts, of whatever kind, which without justifiable cause do harm to others may be,

and in the more important cases absolutely require to be, controlled by the unfavorable sentiments, and, when needful, by the active interference of mankind. The liberty of the individual must be thus far limited; he must not make himself a nuisance to other people. But if he refrains from molesting others in what concerns them, and merely acts according to his own inclination and judgment in things which concern himself, the same reasons which show that opinion should be free, prove also that he should be allowed, without molestation, to carry his opinions into practice at his own cost. That mankind are not infallible; that their truths, for the most part, are only half-truths; that unity of opinion, unless resulting from the fullest and freest comparison of opposite opinions, is not desirable, and diversity not an evil, but a good, until mankind are much more capable than at present of recognizing all sides of the truth, are principles applicable to men's modes of action, not less than to their opinions. As it is useful that while mankind are imperfect there should be different opinions, so it is that there should be different experiments of living; that free scope should be given to varieties of character, short of injury to others; and that the worth of different modes of life should be proved practically, when any one thinks fit to try them. It is desirable, in short, that in things which do not primarily concern others, individuality should assert itself. Where not the person's own character, but the traditions or customs of other people are the role of conduct, there is wanting one of the principal ingredients of human happiness, and quite the chief ingredient of individual and social progress.

In maintaining this principle, the greatest difficulty to be encountered does not lie in the appreciation of means toward an acknowledged end, but in the indifference of persons in general to the end in itself. If it were felt that the free development of individuality is one of the leading essentials of well-being; that it is not only a coördinate element with all that is designated by the terms civilization, instruction, education, culture, but is itself a necessary part and condition of all those things; there would be no danger that liberty should be under-valued, and the adjustment of the boundaries between it and social control would present no extraordinary difficulty. But the evil is, that individual spontaneity is hardly recognized by the common modes of thinking as having any intrinsic worth, or deserving any regard on its own account. The majority, being satisfied with the ways of mankind as they now are (for it is they who make them what they are), cannot comprehend why those ways should not be good enough for everybody; and what is more, spontaneity forms no part of the ideal of the majority of moral and social reformers, but is rather looked on with jealousy, as a troublesome and perhaps rebellious obstruction to the general acceptance of what these reformers, in their own judgment, think would be best for mankind. Few persons, out of Germany, even comprehend the meaning of the doctrine which Wilhelm von Humboldt, so eminent both as a *savant* and as a politician, made the text of a treatise—that "the end of man, or that which is prescribed by the eternal or immutable dictates of reason, and not suggested by vague and transient desires, is the highest and most harmonious development of his powers to a complete and consistent whole"; that, therefore, the object "towards which every human being must ceaselessly direct his efforts, and on which especially those who design to influence their fellow-men must ever keep their eyes, is the individuality of power and development"; that for this there are two requisites, "freedom, and variety of situations"; and that from the union of these arise "individual vigor and manifold diversity," which combine themselves in "originality."[1]

Little, however, as people are accustomed to a doctrine like that of von Humboldt, and surprising as it may be to them to

[1] *The Sphere and Duties of Government,* from the German of Baron Wilhelm von Humboldt, pp. 1–13.

find so high a value attached to individuality, the question, one must nevertheless think, can only be one of degree. No one's idea of excellence in conduct is that people should do absolutely nothing but copy one another. No one would assert that people ought not to put into their mode of life, and into the conduct of their concerns, any impress whatever of their own judgment, or of their own individual character. On the other hand, it would be absurd to pretend that people ought to live as if nothing whatever had been known in the world before they came into it; as if experience had as yet done nothing toward showing that one mode of existence, or of conduct, is preferable to another. Nobody denies that people should be so taught and trained in youth as to know and benefit by the ascertained results of human experience. But it is the privilege and proper condition of a human being, arrived at the maturity of his faculties, to use and interpret experience in his own way. It is for him to find out what part of recorded experience is properly applicable to his own circumstances and character. The traditions and customs of other people are to a certain extent, evidence of what their experience has taught *them*: presumptive evidence and as such, have a claim to his deference. But in the first place, their experience may be too narrow, or they may not have interpreted it rightly. Secondly, their interpretation of experience may be correct, but unsuitable to him. Customs are made for customary circumstances and customary characters, and his circumstances or his character may be uncustomary. Thirdly, though the customs be both good as customs, and suitable to him, yet to conform to custom, merely as custom, does not educate or develop in him any of the qualities which are the distinctive endowment of a human being. The human faculties of perception, judgment, discriminative feeling, mental activity, and even moral preference, are exercised only in making a choice. He who does anything because it is the custom makes no choice. He gains no practice either in discerning or

crowd is the nature

in desiring what is best. The mental and moral, like the muscular powers, are improved only by being used. The faculties are called into no exercise by doing a thing merely because others do it, no more than by believing a thing only because others believe it. If the grounds of an opinion are not conclusive to the person's own reason, his reason cannot be strengthened, but is likely to be weakened, by his adopting it; and if the inducements to an act are not such as are consentaneous to his own feelings and character (where affection, or the rights of others, are not concerned) it is so much done toward rendering his feelings and character inert and torpid, instead of active and energetic.

He who lets the world, or his own portion of it, choose his plan of life for him, has no need of any other faculty than the ape-like one of imitation. He who chooses his plan for himself, employs all his faculties. He must use observation to see, reasoning and judgment to foresee, activity to gather materials for decision, discrimination to decide, and when he has decided, firmness and self-control to hold to his deliberate decision. And these qualities he requires and exercises exactly in proportion as the part of his conduct which he determines according to his own judgment and feelings is a large one. It is possible that he might be guided in some good path, and kept out of harm's way, without any of these things. But what will be his comparative worth as a human being? It really is of importance, not only what men do, but also what manner of men they are that do it. Among the works of man which human life is rightly employed in perfecting and beautifying, the first in importance surely is man himself. Supposing it were possible to get houses built, corn grown, battles fought, causes tried, and even churches erected and prayers said, by machinery—by automatons in human form—it would be a considerable loss to exchange for these automatons even the men and women who at present inhabit the more civilized parts of the world, and who assuredly are but

starved specimens of what nature can and will produce. Human nature is not a machine to be built after a model, and set to do exactly the work prescribed for it, but a tree, which requires to grow and develop itself on all sides, according to the tendency of the inward forces which make it a living thing.

It will probably be conceded that it is desirable people shall exercise their understandings, and that an intelligent following of custom, or even occasionally an intelligent deviation from custom, is better than a blind and simple mechanical adhesion to it. To a certain extent it is admitted that our understanding should be our own: but there is not the same willingness to admit that our desires and impulses should be our own likewise; or that to possess impulses of our own, and of any strength, is anything but a peril and a snare. Yet desires and impulses are as much a part of a perfect human being as beliefs and restraints; and strong impulses are only perilous when not properly balanced—when one set of aims and inclinations is developed into strength, white others, which ought to coexist with them, remain weak and inactive. It is not because men's desires are strong that they act ill; it is because their consciences are weak. There is no natural connection between strong impulses and a weak conscience. The natural connection is the other way. To say that one person's desires and feelings are stronger and more various than those of another, is merely to say that he has more of the raw material of human nature, and is therefore capable, perhaps of more evil, but certainly of more good. Strong impulses are but another name for energy. Energy may be turned to bad uses; but more good may always be made of an energetic nature than of an indolent and impassive one. Those who have most natural feeling are always those whose cultivated feelings may be made the strongest. The same strong susceptibilities which make the personal impulses vivid and powerful, are also the source from whence are generated the most passionate love of virtue, and the sternest selfcontrol. It is through the cultivation of these that society both does its duty and protects its interests; not by rejecting the stuff of which heroes are made because it knows not how to make them. A person whose desires and impulses are his own—are the expression of his own nature, as it has been developed and modified by his own culture—is said to have a character. One whose desires and impulses are not his own, has no character, no more than a steam-engine has a character. If, in addition to being his own, his impulses are strong, and are under the government of a strong will, he has an energetic character. Whoever thinks that individuality of desires and impulses should not be encouraged to unfold itself, must maintain that society has no need of strong natures—is not the better for containing many persons who have much character— and that a high general average of energy is not desirable. . . .

It is not by wearing down into uniformity all that is individual in themselves, but by cultivating it, and calling it forth, within the limits imposed by the rights and interests of others, that human beings become a noble and beautiful object of contemplation; and as the works partake the character of those who do them, by the same process human life also becomes rich, diversified, and animating, furnishing more abundant aliment to high thoughts and elevating feelings, and strengthening the tie which binds every individual to the race, by making the race infinitely better worth belonging to. In proportion to the development of his individuality, each person becomes more valuable to himself, and is therefore capable of being more valuable to others. There is a greater fullness of life about his own existence, and when there is more life in the units there is more in the mass which is composed of them. As much compression as is necessary to prevent the stronger specimens of human nature from encroaching on the rights of others cannot be dispensed with; but for this there is ample compensation even in the point of view of human development. The means of development which the individual loses by being prevented from gratifying his inclinations to the injury of others, are chiefly obtained at the expenses of the development of other people. And even to himself there is a full equivalent in the better development of the social part of his nature, rendered possible by the restraint put upon the selfish part. To be held to rigid rules of justice for the sake of others, develops the feelings and capacities which have the good of others for their object. But to be restrained in things not affecting their good, by their mere displeasure, develops nothing valuable, except such force of character as may unfold itself in resisting the restraint. If acquiesced in, it dulls and blunts the whole nature. To give any fair play to the nature of each, it is essential that different persons should be allowed to lead different lives. In proportion as this latitude has been exercised in any age, has that age been noteworthy to posterity. Even despotism does not produce its worst effects, so long as individuality exists under it; and whatever crushes individuality is despotism, by whatever name it may be called, and whether it professes to be enforcing the will of God or the injunctions of men.

Having said that the individuality is the same thing with development, and that it is only the cultivation of individuality which produces, or can produce, well-developed human beings, I might here close the argument: for what more or better can be said of any condition of human affairs than that it brings human beings themselves nearer to the best thing they can be? or what worse can be said of any obstruction to good than that it prevents this? Doubtless, however, these considerations will not suffice to convince those who most need convincing; and it is necessary further to show that these developed human beings are of some use to the undeveloped—to point out to those who do not desire liberty, and would not avail themselves of it, that they may be in some intelligible manner rewarded for allowing other people to make use of it without hindrance.

In the first place, then, I would suggest that they might possibly learn something from them. It will not be denied by anybody that originality is a valuable element in human affairs. There is always need of persons not only to discover new truths, and point out when what were once truths are true no longer, but also to commence new practices, and set the example of more enlightened conduct, and better taste and sense in human life. This cannot well be gainsaid by anybody who does not believe that the world has already attained perfection in all its ways and practices. It is true that this benefit is not capable of being rendered by everybody alike: there are but few persons, in comparison with the whole of mankind, whose experiments, if adopted by others, would be likely to be any improvement on established practice. But these few are the salt of the earth; without them, human life would become a stagnant pool. Not only is it they who'd introduce good things which did not before exist; it is they who keep the life in those which already exist. If there were nothing new to be done, would human intellect cease to be necessary? Would it be a reason why those who do the old things should forget why they are done, and do them like cattle, nor like human beings? There is only too great a tendency in the best beliefs and practices to degenerate into the mechanical; and unless there were a succession of persons whose over-recurring originality prevents the grounds of those beliefs and practices from becoming merely traditional, such dead matter would not resist the smallest shock from anything really alive, and there would be no reason why civilization should not die out, as in the Byzantine Empire. Persons of genius, it is true, are, and are always likely to be, a small minority; but in order to have them, it is necessary to preserve the soil in which they grow. Genius can only breathe freely in an *atmosphere* of freedom. Persons of genius are, *ex vi termini* [by the force of the phraseology], more individual than any other people—less capable, consequently, of fitting themselves, without hurtful compression, into any of the small number of molds which society provides in order to save its members the trouble of forming their own character. If from timidity they consent to be forced into one of these molds, and to let all that part of themselves which cannot expand under the pressure remain unexpanded, society will be little the better for their genius. If they are of a strong character, and break their fetters, they become a mark for the society which has not succeeded in reducing them to commonplace, to point out with solemn warning as "wild," "erratic," and the like; much as if one should complain of the Niagara river for not flowing smoothly between its banks like a Dutch canal. . . .

The despotism of custom is everywhere the standing hindrance to human advancement, being in unceasing antagonism to that disposition to aim at something better than customary, which is called, according to circumstances, the spirit of liberty, or that of progress or improvement. The spirit of improvement is not always a spirit of liberty, for it may aim at forcing improvements on an unwilling people; and the spirit of liberty, in so far as it resists such attempts, may ally itself locally and temporarily with the opponents of improvement; but the only unfailing and permanent source of improvement is liberty, since by it there are as many possible independent centers of improvement as there are individuals. The progressive principle, however, in either shape, whether as the love of liberty or of improvement, is antagonistic to the sway of custom, involving at least emancipation from that yoke; and the contest between the two constitutes the chief interest of the history of mankind. . . .

What has made the European family of nations an improving, instead of a stationary portion of mankind? Not any superior excellence in them, which, when it exists, exists as the effect not as the cause; but their remarkable diversity of character and culture. Individuals, classes, nations, have been extremely unlike one another:

they have struck out a great variety of paths, each leading to something valuable; and although at every period those who travelled in different paths have been intolerant of one another, and each would have thought it an excellent thing if all the rest could have been compelled to travel his road, their attempts to thwart each other's development have rarely had any permanent success, and each has in time endured to receive the good which the others have offered. Europe is, in my judgment, wholly indebted to this plurality of paths for its progressive and many-sided development. But it already begins to possess this benefit in a considerably less degree. M. de Tocqueville, in his last important work, remarks how much more the Frenchmen of the present day resemble one another than did those even of the last generation. The same remark might be made of Englishmen in a far greater degree. In a passage already quoted from Wilhelm von Humboldt, he points out two things as necessary conditions of human development, because necessary to render people unlike one another: namely, freedom, and variety of situations. The second of these two conditions is in this country every day diminishing. The circumstances which surround different classes and individuals, and shape their characters, are daily becoming more assimilated. Formerly, different ranks, different neighborhoods, different trades and professions, lived in what might be called different worlds; at present to a great degree in the same. Comparatively speaking, they now read the same things, listen to the same things, see the same things, go to the same places, have their hopes and fears directed to the same objects, have the same rights and liberties and the same means of asserting them. Great as are the differences of position which remain, they are nothing to those which have ceased. And the assimilation is still proceeding. All the political changes of the age promote it, since they all tend to raise the low and to lower the high. Every extension of education promotes it, because education brings people under common influences and gives them access to the general stock of facts and sentiments. Improvement in the means of communication promotes it, by bringing the inhabitants of distant places into personal contact, and keeping up a rapid flow of changes of residence between one place and another The increase of commerce and manufactures promotes it, by diffusing more widely the advantages of easy circumstances, and opening all objects of ambition, even the highest, to general competition, whereby the desire of rising becomes no longer the character of a particular class, but of all classes. A more powerful agency than even all these, in bringing about a general similarity among mankind, is the complete establishment, in this and other free countries, of the ascendancy of public opinion in the State. As the various social eminences which enabled persons entrenched on them to disregard the opinion of the multitude gradually become leveled; as the very idea of resisting the will of the public; when it is positively known that they have a will, disappears more and more from the minds of practical politicians: there ceases to be any social support for nonconformity—any substantive power in society which, itself opposed to the ascendancy of numbers, is interested in taking under its protection opinions and tendencies at variance with those of the public.

The combination of all these causes forms so great a mass of influences hostile to individuality, that it is not easy to see how it can stand its ground. It will do so with increasing difficulty, unless the intelligent part of the public can be made to feel its value—to see that it is good there should be differences, even though not for the better, even though, as it may appear to them, some should be for the worse. If the claims of individuality are ever to be asserted, the time is now, while much is still wanting to complete the enforced assimilation. It is only in the earlier stages that any stand can be successfully made against the encroachment. The demand that all other people shall resemble ourselves grows by what if feeds on. If resistance waits till life is reduced *nearly* to one uniform type, all deviations from that type will come to be considered impious, immoral, even monstrous and contrary to nature. Mankind speedily become unable to conceive diversity, when they have been for some time unaccustomed to see it.

COMMENT

The Basis of Mill's Argument

The older liberals, especially John Locke and Thomas Jefferson, espoused liberty as an inalienable natural right. Mill, in contrast, avowedly based his argument on "utility, in the largest sense." Progress, he maintained, is desirable for human welfare, and free thought and action are necessary for that end. The ultimate standard for judging social institutions is their contribution to happiness. Mill thus began by running up the banner of utilitarianism.

The real premise of his argument, however, is not the calculation of pleasure and pain but the inner value of character and unhampered individuality. In Chapter III of *On Liberty,* he mentions with approval the doctrine of "self-realization" advocated by Wilhelm von Humboldt. "The end of man," according to this German writer, "is the highest and most harmonious development of his powers to a complete and consistent whole," and for this there are two requisites, "freedom and variety of situations." This theory of self-realization is the focus of Mill's teaching. It underlies his decided preference for highly developed individuals rather than "ape-like imitators." Liberty enables a person to be a person—to attain the full use and development of one's powers. To live freely is to unfold one's individual human capacities; to live servilely—by custom, imitation, social pressure, or repressive political rule—is to be less than a human being. Liberty is the acknowledgment of the peculiar dignity of a person as a person—and of *each* person's matchless individuality. There is slight trace in this essay of the earlier teaching of the utilitarians that it does not matter what people are like provided that they have as much pleasure and as little pain as possible.

Mill had become convinced that the modern enemy of liberty is the tyranny of the majority. No longer is the problem that of overthrowing a trannical king or the oligarchy of a few. It is the much more difficult problem of freeing dissident individuals and minorities from the pressure of a mass society. Mill had been shocked by Alexis de Tocqueville's classic study, *Democracy in America* (1835–1840), which maintained that the ultimate triumph of democracy is inevitable and that its tendency is to reduce all people to a level of equal mediocrity. Sharing Tocqueville's alarm, Mill believed that a truly liberal society must be created as a safeguard against mass illiberalism. Such a society would be deeply respectful of human freedom. His argument, therefore, is primarily a defense of individuality against the conventionalities of society, the despostism of social custom, and the overweening powers of government.

Individual and Social Standards of Human Fulfillment

The traditional theory of democracy is the doctrine of natural rights. The language of the American Declaration of Independence and the French Declaration of the Rights of Man, for example, is largely derived from this tradition. Mill believed that his doctrine of the supreme importance of individuality contradicts the natural rights tradition, but his standard of self-realization is not so far removed from that of natural rights as might be supposed at first glance. What distinguishes his doctrine from most theories of natural rights is the strong emphasis on the diversity of human nature. To live freely is to unfold one's *individual* human capacities. His theory in this sense is complementary rather than contradictory to the natural rights theory. It calls attention to the individual, and not merely the generic, elements in human nature.

More than the older natural rights theorists, such as Locke and Jean Jacques Rousseau, Mill was aware that society must adapt itself to changing historical circumstances. Similarly, John Dewey, in his version of democratic liberalism, was keenly aware of the tides of historical change and their relevance to democratic ideals. This is also the characteristic approach of Marxists who insist that "democracy," "socialism," and "communism" are historical concepts with changing meaning and content. Typical is Karl Marx's remark in *The Critique of the Gotha Program* that "right can never be higher than the economic structure of the society and the cultural development conditioned by it." However, Mill, more than Marx, insisted on the autonomy and self-fulfillment of the individual.

The contrast between the more individualistic emphasis of Mill and the more social emphasis of Marx should incite lively discussion. While thinking about these differences, however, we should not overlook the similarities. Mill became increasingly convinced as he grew older that real freedom requires the resources and opportunities that enable people to fulfill their potentialities and effectuate their choices. In his essay on Samuel Taylor Coleridge, he contended that "a State ought to be considered a great benefit society, or mutual insurance company, for helping (under the necessary regulations for preventing abuse) that large proportion of its members who cannot help themselves." He was inclined to favor cooperative ownership and management of industry by the workers instead of either capitalistic or state-socialistic operation. "There can be little doubt," he said in *Principles of Political Economy,* "that the relation of masters and workpeople will be gradually superseded by partnership in one of two forms: in some cases, association of the labourers with the capitalist; in others, and perhaps finally in all, association of labourers among themselves." In his *Autobiography,* he declared that "the social problem of the future" is "how to unite the greatest individual liberty of action with a common ownership of the raw materials of the globe, and an equal participation of all in the benefits of combined labour." He was nevertheless opposed to state intervention "to chain up the free agency of individuals."

Conclusion

So far we have examined the ideas of four major figures in social philosophy—Plato, Hobbes, Locke, and Mill. They differ in many respects, and not least in their attitudes toward democracy. Plato believed in the cultivation of excellence by the rule of the wise—he rejected democracy because its leaders are neither wise nor devoted to excellence. Hobbes felt that democracy will dissolve into anarchy and chaos. Only a strong sovereign can bring peace. Locke saw democracy, along with constitutional law, as the foundation of social peace and productivity. Mill regarded representative democracy as the best form of government for a modern civilized society, but he warned against the tyranny of the majority and defended the liberties of the dissident individual. If we add to these characterizations other relevant ideas, such as the concept of natural rights, we have a wide and rich gamut of theories.

One of the major questions from Mill's perspective on liberty arising out of a consideration of the Sanctuary case study introduced at the outset of this part is whether and to what extent his insistence on freedom applies across national borders. Do all people have the absolute right to "life, liberty, and the pursuit of happiness"? And what should our response be when those who do not have these rights come to us for help? Would Mill argue that the judge in the Sanctuary trial should have listened to the reasons given for breaking the law?

25

COMMUNISM

KARL MARX (1818–1883)

Born in Treves in the German Rhineland, Karl Marx was the son of well-to-do Jewish parents who had been converted to Christianity. He studied law, history, and philosophy at the universities of Bonn, Berlin, and Jena, imbibing the doctrines of G. W. F. Hegel, then at the height of his fame. His doctoral thesis was on the materialism of Democritus and Epicurus. In 1842 through 1843, he edited a newspaper at Cologne that was suppressed by the Prussian government because of its advanced ideas. After marrying Jennie von Westphalen, a beautiful young woman of aristocratic lineage, he went to Paris, where he studied the socialist movement. There he met Friedrich Engels, a young German who worked first as clerk, eventually as manager and part owner in the family business of Ermen and Engels, cotton spinners in Manchester. On the basis of the socialist convictions that they shared, the two young men formed a friendship that endured throughout their lives.

In 1845 the Prussian government, incensed by Marx's continued attacks, persuaded the French authorities to deport him. He then went with Engels to live in Brussels, where he continued his political and journalistic activities. During this period, he wrote, singly or in collaboration with Engels, a number of socialist works, the most famous of which is the *Communist Manifesto,* published on the eve of the revolutionary disturbances of 1848. Expelled in turn from Belgium, Marx returned to Cologne, where he founded a radical newspaper and participated in the revolutionary uprisings of 1848–1849. The ensuing political reaction compelled him to seek refuge in England.

With his family, he spent the remainder of his life in London. There he worked for years in the British Museum, accumulating the research materials for his indictment of capitalist society. Having only a small income as a correspondent for the New York *Daily Tribune,* he lived with his wife and children in a squalid attic, often without sufficient food, decent clothing, or other basic necessities. His later years were saddened by ill health and the death of three of his children, but nothing could divert him from unremitting service to his ideals. In 1864 he helped to organize the First International, a radical political organization, which continued under his direction until 1872. His major work is *Capital,* a detailed historical and economic analysis of capitalist society, which he referred to as "the task to which I have sacrificed my health, my happiness in life, and my family." Volume One was published in 1867 and the two remaining volumes after his death.

COMMUNISM AND HISTORY

I. The Materialist Conception of History

I was led by my studies to the conclusion that legal relations as well as forms of state could neither be understood by themselves, nor explained by the so-called general progress of the human mind, but that they are rooted in the material conditions of life, which are summed up by Hegel after the fashion of the English and French writers of the eighteenth century under the name civil society, and the anatomy of *civil society* is to be sought in political economy. The study of the latter which I had begun in Paris, I continued in Brussels where I had emigrated on account of an expulsion order issued by M. Guizot. The general conclusion at which I arrived and which, once reached, continued to serve as the guiding thread in my studies, may be formulated briefly as follows: In the social production which men carry on they enter into definite relations that are indispensable and independent of their will; these relations of production correspond to a definite stage of development of their material powers of production. The totality of these relations of production constitutes the economic structure of society—the real foundation, on which legal and political

All passages except the speech at the Anniversary of the *People's Paper* are taken from *Karl Marx: Selected Writings in Sociology and Social Philosophy,* ed. T. B. Bottomore and M. Rubel (London: C. A. Watts & Co. Ltd., 1956), or *Karl Marx: Early Writings,* ed. T B. Bottomore (London: C. A. Watts & Co. Ltd., 1963). Translations are by Bottomore. Reprinted by permission of the publisher. Each passage is followed by a reference to its original source.

superstructures arise and to which definite forms of social consciousness correspond. The mode of production of material life determines the general character of the social, political and spiritual processes of life. It is not the consciousness of men that determines their being, but, on the contrary, their social being determines their consciousness. At a certain stage of their development, the material forces of production in society come in conflict with the existing relations of production, or—what is but a legal expression for the same thing—with the property relations within which they had been at work before. From forms of development of the forces of production these relations turn into their fetters. Then occurs a period of social revolution. With the change of the economic foundation the entire immense superstructure is more or less rapidly transformed. In considering such transformations the distinction should always be made between the material transformation of the economic conditions of production which can be determined with the precision of natural science, and the legal, political, religious, aesthetic or philosophical—in short ideological, forms in which men become conscious of this conflict and fight it out. Just as our opinion of an individual is not based on what he thinks of himself, so can we not judge of such a period of transformation by its own consciousness; on the contrary, this consciousness must rather be explained from the contradictions of material life, from the existing conflict between the social forces of production and the relations of production. No social order ever disappears before all the productive forces for which there is room in it have been developed; and new, higher relations of production never appear before the material conditions of their existence have matured in the womb of the old society. Therefore, mankind always sets itself only such problems as it can solve; since, on closer examination, it will always be found that the problem itself arises only when the material conditions necessary for its solution already exist or are at least in the process of formation. In broad outline we can designate the Asiatic, the ancient, the feudal, and the modern bourgeois modes of production as progressive epochs in the economic formation of society. The bourgeois relations of production are the last antagonistic form of the social process of production; not in the sense of individual antagonisms, but of conflict arising from conditions surrounding the life of individuals in society. At the same time the productive forces developing in the womb of bourgeois society create the material conditions for the solution of that antagonism. With this social formation, therefore, the prehistory of human society comes to an end.

Preface to A Contribution to the Critique of Political Economy *(1859)*

The premises from which we begin are not arbitrary ones, not dogmas, but real premises from which abstraction can be made only in the imagination. They are the real individuals, their activity and their material conditions of life, including those which they find already in existence and those produced by their activity. These premises can thus be established in a purely empirical way.

The first premise of all human history is, of course, the existence of living human individuals. The first fact to be established, therefore, is the physical constitution of these individuals and their consequent relation to the rest of Nature. Of course we cannot here investigate the actual physical nature of man or the natural conditions in which man finds himself—geological, orohydrographical, climatic and so on. All historiography must begin from these natural bases and their modification in the course of history by men's activity.

Men can be distinguished from animals by consciousness, by religion, or by anything one likes. They themselves begin to distinguish themselves from animals as soon as they begin to *produce* their means of subsistence, a step which is determined by their physical constitution. In producing their means of subsistence men indirectly produce their actual material life.

The way in which men produce their means of subsistence depends in the first place on the nature of the existing means which they have to reproduce. This mode of production should not be regarded simply as the reproduction of the physical existence of individuals. It is already a definite form of activity of these individuals, a definite way of expressing their life, a definite *mode of life*. As individuals express their life, so they are. What they are, therefore, coincides with their production, with *what* they produce and with *how* they produce it. What individuals are, therefore, depends on the material conditions of their production. . . .

This conception of history, therefore, rests on the exposition of the real process of production, starting out from the simple material production of life, and on the comprehension of the form of intercourse connected with and created by this mode of production, i.e. of civil society in its various stages as the basis of all history, and also in its action as the State. From this starting point, it explains all the different theoretical productions and forms of consciousness, religion, philosophy, ethics, etc., and traces their origins and growth, by which means the matter can of course be displayed as a whole (and consequently, also the reciprocal action of these various sides on one another). Unlike the idealist view of history, it … remains constantly on the real ground of history; it does not explain practice from the idea but explains the formation of ideas from material practice, and accordingly comes to the conclusion that all the forms of and products of consciousness can be dissolved, not by intellectual criticism . . . but only by the practical overthrow of the actual relations . . . that not criticism but revolution is the driving force of history, as well as of religion, philosophy, and all other types of theory. It shows that history does not end by being resolved into "self-consciousness," as "spirit of the spirit," but that at each stage of history there is found a material result, a sum of productive forces, a historically created relation on individuals to Nature and to one another, which is handed down to each generation from its predecessors, a mass of productive forces, capital, and circumstances, which is indeed modified by the new generation but which also prescribes for it its conditions of life and gives it a definite devel-opment, a special character. It shows that circumstances made men just as much as men make circumstances. . . .

The fact is, therefore, that determinate individuals, who are productively active in a definite way, enter into these determinate social and political relations. Empirical observation must, in each particular case, show empirically, and without any mystification or speculation, the connection of the social and political structure with production. The social structure and the State are continually evolving out of the life-process of determinate individuals, of individuals not as they may appear in their own or other people's imagination, but as they really are: i.e. as they act, produce their material life, and are occupied within determinate material limits, presuppositions and conditions, which are independent of their will.

The production of ideas, conceptions and consciousness is at first directly interwoven with the material activity and the material intercourse of men, the language of real life. Representation and thought, the mental intercourse of men, still appear at this stage as the direct emanation of their material behaviour. The same applies to mental production as it is expressed in the political, legal, moral, religious and metaphysical language of a people. Men are the producers of their conceptions, ideas, etc.,—real, active men, as they are conditioned by a determinate development of their productive forces, and of the intercourse which corresponds to these, up to its most extensive forms. Consciousness can never be anything else than conscious existence, and the existence of men is their actual life process. If in all ideology men and their circumstances appear upside down as in a *camera obscura*, this phenomenon arises from their historical life process just as the inversion of objects on the retina does from their physical life–process.

In direct contrast to German philosophy, which descends from heaven to earth, here we ascend from earth to heaven. That is to say, we do not set out from what men say, imagine, or conceive, nor from what has been said, thought, imagined, or conceived of men, in order to arrive at men in the flesh. We begin with real, active men, and from their real life-process show the development of the ideological reflexes and echoes of this life-process. The phantoms of the human brain also are necessary sublimates of men's material life-process, which can be empirically established and which is bound to material preconditions. Morality, religion, metaphysics, and other ideologies, and their corresponding forms of consciousness, no longer retain therefore their appearance of autonomous existence. They have no history, no development; it is men, who, in developing their material production and their material intercourse, change, along with this their real existence, their thinking and the products of their thinking. Life is not determined by consciousness, but consciousness by life. Those who adopt the first method of approach begin with consciousness, regarded as the living individual; those who adopt the second, which corresponds with real life, begin with the real living individuals themselves, and consider consciousness only as *their* consciousness. . . .

The ideas of the ruling class are, in every age, the ruling ideas: i.e. the class which is the dominant *material* force in society is at the same time is dominant *intellectual* force. The class which has the means of material production at its disposal, has control at the same time over the means of mental production, so that in consequence the ideas of those who lack the means of mental production are, in general, subject to it. The dominant ideas are nothing more than the ideal expression of the dominant material relationships, the dominant material relationships grasped as ideas, and thus of the relationships which make one class the ruling one; they are consequently the ideas of its dominance. The individuals composing the ruling class possess among other things consciousness, and therefore think. In so far, therefore, as they rule as a class and determine the whole extent of an epoch, it is self-evident that they do this in their whole range and thus, among other things, rule also as thinkers, as producers of ideas, and regulate the production and distribution of the ideas of their age. Consequently their ideas are the ruling ideas of the age. For instance, in an age and in a country where royal power, aristocracy and the bourgeoisie are contending for domination and where, therefore, domination is shared, the doctrine of the separation of powers appears as the dominant idea and is enunciated as an "eternal law." The division of labour, which we saw earlier as one of the principal forces of history up to the present time, manifests itself also in the ruling class, as the division of mental and material labour, so that within this class one part appears as the thinkers of the class (its active conceptualizing ideologists, who make it their chief source of livelihood to develop and perfect the illusions of the class about itself), while the others have a more passive and receptive attitude to these ideas and illusions, because they are in reality the active members of this class and have less time to make up ideas and illusions about themselves. This cleavage within the ruling class may even develop into a certain opposition and hostility between the two parts, but in the event of a practical collision in which the class itself is endangered, it disappears of its own accord and with it also the illusion that the ruling ideas were not the ideas of the ruling class and had a power distinct from the power of this class. The existence of revolutionary ideas in a particular age presupposes the existence of a revolutionary class. . . .

If, in considering the course of history, we detach the ideas of the ruling class from the ruling class itself and attribute to them an independent existence, if we confine ourselves to saying that in a particular age these or those ideas were dominant, without paying attention to the conditions of production and the world conditions which are the source of the ideas, it is possible to say, for instance, that during the time that the aristocracy was dominant the concepts honour, loyalty, etc., were dominant; during the dominance of the bourgeoisie the concepts freedom, equality, etc. The ruling class itself in general imagines this to be the case. This conception of history which is common to all historians, particularly since the eighteenth century, will necessarily come up against the phenomenon that increasingly abstract ideas hold sway, i.e. ideas which increasingly take on the form of universality. For each new class which puts itself in the place of the one ruling before it, is compelled, simply in order to achieve its aims, to represent its interest as the common interest of all members of society, i.e. employing an ideal formula, to give its ideas the form of universality and to represent them as the only rational and universally valid ones. The class which makes a revolution appears from the beginning not as a class but as the representative of the whole of society, simply because it is opposed to a *class*. It appears as the whole mass of society confronting the single ruling class. It can do this because at the beginning its interest really is more closely connected with the common interest of all other non-ruling classes and has been unable under the constraint of the previously existing conditions to develop as the particular interest of a particular class. Its victory, therefore, also benefits many individuals of the other classes which are not achieving a dominant position, but only in so far as it now puts these individuals in a position to raise themselves into the ruling class. When the French bourgeoisie overthrew the rule of the aristocracy it thereby made it possible for many proletarians to raise themselves above the proletariat, but only in so far as they became bourgeois. Every new class, therefore, achieves its domination only on a broader basis than that of the previous ruling class. On the other hand, the opposition of the non-ruling class to the new ruling class later develops all the more sharply and profoundly. These two characteristics entail that the struggle to be waged against this new ruling class has as its object a more decisive and radical negation of the previous conditions of society than could have been accomplished by all previous classes which aspired to rule.

The German Ideology (with Engels, 1845–1846)

II. Alienation

We shall begin from a *contemporary* economic fact. The worker becomes poorer the more wealth he produces and the more his production increases in power and extent. The worker becomes an ever cheaper commodity the more goods he creates. The *devaluation* of the human world increases in direct relation with the *increase in value* of the world of things. Labor does not only create goods; it also produces itself and the worker as a *commodity,* and indeed in the same proportion as it produces goods.

This fact simply implies that the object produced by labor, its product, now stands opposed to it as an *alien being,* as a *power independent* of the producer. The product of labor is labor which has been embodied in an object and turned into a physical thing; this product is an *objectification* of labor. The performance of work is at the same time its objectification. The performance of work appears in the sphere of political economy as a *vitiation* of the worker, objectification as a *loss* and as *servitude* to *the object,* and appropriation as *alienation*.

So much does the performance of work appear as vitiation that the worker is vitiated to the point of starvation. So much does objectification appear as loss of the object that the worker is deprived of the most essential things not only of life but also of work. Labor itself becomes an object which he can acquire only by the greatest effort and with unpredictable interruptions. So much does the appropriation of the object appear as alienation that the more objects the worker produces the fewer he can possess and the more he falls under the domination of his product, of capital.

All these consequences follow from the fact that the worker is related to the *product of his labor* as to an *alien* object. For it is clear on this presupposition that the more the worker expends himself in work the more powerful becomes the world of objects which he creates in face of himself, the poorer he becomes in his inner life, and the less he belongs to himself. It is just the same as in religion. The more of himself man attributes to God the less he has left in himself. The worker puts his life into the object, and his life then belongs no longer to himself but to the object. The greater his activity, therefore, the less he possesses. What is embodied in the product of his labor is no longer his own. The greater this product is, therefore, the more he is diminished. The *alienation* of the worker in his product means not only that his labor becomes an object, assumes an external existence, but that it exists independently, *outside himself,* and alien to him, and that it stands opposed to him as an autonomous power. The life which he has given to the object sets itself against him as an alien and hostile force.

Let us now examine more closely the phenomenon of *objectification,* the worker's production and the *alienation* and *loss* of the object it produces, which is involved in it. The worker can create nothing without *nature,* without the *sensuous external world.* The latter is the material in which his labor is realized, in which it is active, out of which and through which it produces things.

But just as nature affords the *means of existence* of labor in the sense that labor cannot *live* without objects upon which it can be exercised, so also it provides the *means of existence* in a narrower sense; namely the means of physical existence for the *worker* himself. Thus, the more the worker *appropriates* the external world of sensuous nature by his labor the more he deprives himself of *means of existence* in two respects: first, that the sensuous external world becomes progressively less an object belonging to his labor or a means of existence of his labor, and secondly, that it becomes progressively less a means of existence in the direct sense, a means for the physical subsistence of the worker.

In both respects, therefore, the worker becomes a slave of the object; first, in that he receives an *object of work,* i.e., receives work, and secondly that he receives *means of subsistence.* Thus the object enables him to exist, first as a *worker* and secondly, as a *physical subject.* The culmination of this enslavement is that he can only maintain himself as a *physical subject* so far as he is worker, and that it is only as a *physical subject* that he is a worker.

(The alienation of the worker in his object is expressed as follows in the laws of political economy: the more the worker produces the less he has to consume; the more value he creates the more worthless he becomes; the more refined his product the more crude and misshapen the worker; the more civilized the product the more barbarous the worker; the more powerful the work the more feeble the worker; the more the work manifests intelligence the more the worker declines in intelligence and becomes a slave of nature.)

Political economy conceals the alienation in the nature of labor insofar as it does not examine the direct relationship between the worker (work) and production. Labor certainly produces marvels for the rich but it produces privation for the worker. It produces palaces, but hovels for the worker. It produces beauty, but deformity for the worker. It replaces labor by machinery, but it casts some of the workers back into a barbarous kind of work and turns the others into machines. It produces intelligence, but also stupidity and cretinism for the workers.

The direct relationship of labor to its products is the relationship of the worker to the objects of his production. The relationship of property owners to the objects of production and to production itself is merely a *consequence* of this first relationship and confirms it. We shall consider this second aspect later.

Thus, when we ask what is the important relationship of labor, we are concerned with the relationship of the *worker* to production.

So far we have considered the alienation of the worker only from one aspect; namely, *his relationship with the products of his labor.* However, alienation appears not only in the result, but also in the *process,* of *production, within productive activity* itself. How could the worker stand in an alien relationship to the product of his activity if he did not alienate himself in the act of production itself? The product is indeed only the *résumé* of activity, of production. Consequently, if the product of labor is alienation, production itself must be active alienation—the alienation of activity and the activity of alienation. The alienation of the object of labor merely summarizes the alienation in the work activity itself.

What constitutes the alienation of labor? First, that the work is *external* to the worker, that it is not part of his nature; and that, consequently, he does not fulfill himself in his work but denies himself, has a feeling of misery rather than well being, does not develop freely his mental and physical energies but is physically exhausted and mentally debased. The worker therefore feels himself at home only during his leisure time, whereas at work he feels homeless. His work is not voluntary but imposed, *forced labor*. It is not the satisfaction of a need, but only a *means* for satisfying other needs. Its alien character is clearly shown by the fact that as soon as there is no physical or other compulsion it is avoided like the plague. External labor, labor in which man alienates himself, is a labor of self-sacrifice, of mortification. Finally, the external character of work for the worker is shown by the fact that it is not his own work but work for someone else, that in work he does not belong to himself but to another person. Just as in religion the spontaneous activity of human fantasy, of the human brain and heart, reacts independently as an alien activity of gods or devils upon the individual, so the activity of the worker is not his own spontaneous activity. It is another's activity and a loss of his own spontaneity.

We arrive at the result that man (the worker) feels himself to be freely active only in his animal functions—eating, drinking and procreating, or at most also in his dwelling and in personal adornment—while in his human functions he is reduced to an animal. The animal becomes human and the human becomes animal.

Eating, drinking and procreating are of course also genuine human functions. But abstractly considered, apart from the environment of other human activities, and turned into final and sole ends, they are animal functions.

We have now considered the act of alienation of practical human activity, labor, from two aspects: (1) the relationship of the worker to the *product of labor* as an alien object which dominates him. This relationship is at the same time the relationship to the sensuous external world, to natural objects, as an alien and hostile world; (2) the relationship of labor to the *act of production* within *labor*. This is the relationship of the worker to his own activity as something alien and not belonging to him, activity as suffering (passivity), strength as powerlessness, creation as emasculation,

the *personal* physical and mental energy of the worker, his personal life (for what is life but activity?) as an activity which is directed against himself, independent of him and not belonging to him. This is *self-alienation* as against the above-mentioned alienation of the thing.

We have now to infer a third characteristic of *alienated labor* from the two we have considered.

Man is a species-being[1] not only in the sense that he makes the community (his own as well as those of other things) his objects both practically and theoretically, but also (and this is simply another expression for the same thing) in the sense that he treats himself as the present, living species, as a *universal* and consequently free being.

Species-life, for man as for animals, has its physical basis in the fact that man (like animals) lives from inorganic nature, and since man is more universal than an animal so the range of inorganic nature from which he lives is more universal. Plants, animals, minerals, air, light, etc. constitute, from the theoretical aspect, a part of human consciousness as objects of natural science and art; they are man's spiritual inorganic nature, his intellectual means of life, which he must first prepare for enjoyment and perpetuation. So also, from the practical aspect they form a part of human life and activity. In practice man lives only from these natural products, whether in the form of food, heating, clothing, housing, etc. The universality of man appears in practice in the universality which makes the whole of nature into his inorganic body: (1) as a direct means, of life; and equally

---

[1] The term 'species-being' is taken from Feuerbach's *Das Wasen des Christentums* (The Essence of Christianity). Feuerbach used the notion in making a distinction between consciousness in man and in animals. Man is conscious not merely of himself as an individual but of the human species or 'human essence.'—*Tr. Note.*

(2) as the material object and instrument of his life activity. Nature is the *inorganic body* of man; that is to say, nature excluding the human body itself. To say that man *lives* from nature means that nature is his *body* with which he must remain in a continuous interchange in order not to die. The statement that the physical and mental life of man, and nature, are interdependent means simply that nature is interdependent with itself, for man is a part of nature.

Since alienated labor: (1) alienates nature from man; and (2) alienates man from himself, from his own active function, his life activity; so it alienates him from the species. It makes *species-life* into a means of individual life. In the first place it alienates species-life and individual life, and secondly, it turns the latter, as an abstraction, into the purpose of the former, also in its abstract and alienated form.

For labor, *life activity, productive life,* now appear to man only as *means* for the satisfaction of a need, the need to maintain his physical existence. Productive life is, however, species-life. It is life creating life. In the type of life activity resides the whole character of a species, its species-character; and free, conscious activity is the species-character of human beings. Life itself appears only as *means of life.*

The animal is one with its life activity. It does not distinguish the activity from itself. It is its *activity.* But man makes his life activity itself an object of his will and consciousness. He has a conscious life activity. It is not a determination with which he is completely identified. Conscious life activity distinguishes man from the life activity of animals. Only for this reason is he a species-being. Or rather, he is only a self-conscious being, i.e. his own life is an object for him, because he is a species-being. Only for this reason is his activity free activity. Alienated labor reverses the relationship, in that man because he is a self-conscious being makes his life activity, his *being,* only a means for his *existence.*

The practical construction of an *objective world,* the *manipulation* of inor-

ganic nature, is the confirmation of man as a conscious species-being, i.e. a being who treats the species as his own being or himself as a species-being. Of course, animals also produce. They construct nests, dwellings, as in the case of bees, beavers, ants, etc. But they only produce what is strictly necessary for themselves or their young. They produce only in a single direction, while man produces universally. They produce only under the compulsion of direct physical need, while man produces when he is free from physical need and only truly produces in freedom from such need. Animals produce only themselves, while man reproduces the whole of nature. The products of animal production belong directly to their physical bodies, while man is free in face of his product. Animals construct only in accordance with the standards and needs of the species to which they belong, while man knows how to produce in accordance with the standards of every species and knows how to apply the appropriate standard to the object. Thus man constructs also in accordance with the laws of beauty.

It is just in his work upon the objective world that man really proves himself as a *species-being.* This production is his active species life. By means of it nature appears as his work and his reality. The object of labor is, therefore, the *objectification of man's species life;* for he no longer reproduces himself merely intellectually, as in consciousness, but actively and in a real sense, and he sees his own reflection in a world which he has constructed. While, therefore, alienated labor takes away the object of production from man, it also takes away his *species life,* his real objectivity as a species-being, and changes his advantage over animals into a disadvantage in so far as his inorganic body, nature, is taken from him.

Just as alienated labor transforms free and self-directed activity into a means, so it transforms the species-life of man into a means of physical existence.

Consciousness, which man has from his species, is transformed through alienation so that species life becomes only a means for him.

(3) Thus alienated labor turns the *species life of man,* and also nature as his mental species-property, into an *alien* being and into a *means* for his *individual existence.* It alienates from man his own body, external nature, his mental life and his human life.

(4) A direct consequence of the alienation of man from the product of his activity and from his species life is that *man is alienated* from other men. When man confronts himself he also confronts *other* men. What is true of man's relationship to his work, to the product of his work and to himself, is also true of his relationship to other men, to their labor and to the objects of their labor.

In general, the statement that man is alienated from his species life means that each man is alienated from others, and that each of the others is likewise alienated from human life.

Human alienation, and above all the relation of man to himself, is first realized and expressed in the relationship between each man and other men. Thus in the relationship of alienated labor every man regards other men according to the standards and relationships in which he finds himself placed as a worker.

We began with an economic fact, the alienation of the worker and his production. We have expressed this fact in conceptual terms as *alienated labor,* and in analyzing the concept we have merely analyzed an economic fact.

Let us now examine further how this concept of alienated labor must express and reveal itself in reality. If the product of labor is alien to me and confronts me as an alien power, to whom does it belong? If my own activity does not belong to me but is an alien, forced activity, to whom does it belong? To a being *other* than myself. And who is this being? The *gods?* It is apparent in the earliest stages of advanced production, e.g., temple building, etc. in Egypt, India, Mexico, and in the service rendered

to gods, that the product belonged to the gods. But the gods alone were never the lords of labor. And no more was *nature.* What a contradiction it would be if the more man subjugates nature by his labor, and the more the marvels of the gods are rendered superfluous by the marvels of industry, he should abstain from his joy in producing and his enjoyment of the product for love of these powers.

The *alien* being to whom labor and the product of labor belong, to whose service labor is devoted, and to whose enjoyment the product of labor goes, can only be *man* himself. If the product of labor does not belong to the worker, but confronts him as an alien power, this can only be because it belongs to *a man other than the worker.* If his activity is a torment to him it must be a source of enjoyment and pleasure to another. Not the gods, nor nature, but only man himself can be this alien power over men.

Economic and Philosophical
Manuscripts (1844)

The so-called Revolutions of 1848 were but poor incidents—small fractures and fissures in the dry crust of European society. However, they denounced the abyss. Beneath the apparently solid surface, they betrayed oceans of liquid matter, only needing expansion to rend into fragments continents of hard rock. Noisely and confusedly they proclaimed the emancipation of the proletarian, *i.e.,* the secret of the nineteenth century, and of the revolution of that century. That social revolution, it is true, was no novelty invented in 1848. Steam, electricity, and the self-acting mule were revolutionists of a rather more dangerous character than even citizens Barbès, Raspail and Blanqui. But, although the atmosphere in which we live weighs upon everyone with a 20,000 pound force, do you feel it? No more than European society before 1848 felt the revolutionary atmosphere enveloping and pressing it from all sides.

There is one great fact, characteristic of this, our nineteenth century, a fact which no party dares deny. On the one hand, there have started into life industrial and scientific forces, which no epoch of the former human history had ever suspected. On the other hand, there exist symptoms of decay, far surpassing the horrors recorded of the latter times of the Roman empire. In our days everything seems pregnant with its contrary; machinery gifted with the wonderful power of shortening and fructifying human labor, we behold starving and overworking it. The newfangled sources of wealth, by some strange weird spell, are turned into sources of want. The victories of art seem bought by the loss of character. At the same pace that mankind masters nature, man seems to become enslaved to other men or to his own infamy. Even the pure light of science seems unable to shine but on the dark background of ignorance. All our inventions and progress seem to result in endowing material forces with intellectual life, and in stultifying human life into a material force. This antagonism between modern industry and science on the one hand, modern misery and dissolution on the other hand; this antagonism between the productive powers and the social relations of our epoch, is a fact, palpable, overwhelming, and not to be controverted. Some parties may wail over it; others may wish to get rid of modern arts in order to get rid of modern conflicts. Or they may imagine that so signal a progress in industry wants to be completed by as signal a regress in politics.

On our part, we do not mistake the shape of the shrewd spirit that continues to mark all these contradictions. We know that to work well the newfangled forces of society, they only want to be mastered by newfangled men—and such are the working men. They are as much the invention of modern times as machinery itself. In the signs that bewilder the middle class, the aristocracy and the poor prophets of regression, we do recognize our brave friend, Robin Goodfellow, the old mole that can work in the earth so fast, that worthy pioneer—the revolution. The English working men are the first born sons of modern industry. They will then, certainly, not be the last in aiding the social revolution produced by that industry, a revolution, which means the emancipation of their own class all over the world, which is as universal as capital-rule and wages-slavery. I know the heroic struggles the English working class have gone through since the middle of the last century—struggles less glorious because they are shrouded in obscurity and burked by the middle class historians to revenge the misdeeds of the ruling class.

There existed in the middle ages in Germany a secret tribunal, called the "Vehmgericht." If a red cross was seen marked on a house people knew that its owner was doomed by the "Vehm." All the houses of Europe are now marked with the mysterious red cross. History is the judge—its executioner, the proletarian.

Speech by Marx at the anniversary celebration of the *People's Paper*, a Chartist publication, in April 1856.

III. Communist Revolution and Future Society

(1) In the development of the productive forces a stage is reached where productive forces and means of intercourse are called into being which, under the existing relations, can only work mischief, and which are, therefore, no longer productive, but destructive, forces (machinery and money). Associated with this is the emergence of a class which has to bear all the burdens of society without enjoying its advantages, which is excluded from society and is forced into the most resolute opposition to all other classes; a class which comprises the majority of the members of society and in which there develops a consciousness of the need for a fundamental revolution, the communist consciousness. This consciousness can, of course, also arise in other classes from the observation of the situation of this class.

(2) The conditions under which determinate productive forces can be used

are also the conditions for the dominance of a determinate social class, whose social power, derived from its property ownership, invariably finds its *practical* and ideal expression in a particular form of the State. Consequently, every revolutionary struggle is directed against the class which has so far been dominant.

(3) In all former revolutions the form of activity was always left unaltered and it was only a question of redistributing this activity among different people, of introducing a new division of labour. The communist revolution, however, is directed against the former *mode* of activity, does away with *labour,* and abolishes all class rule along with the classes themselves, because it is effected by the class which no longer counts as a class in society, which is not recognized as a class, and which is the expression of the dissolution of all classes, nationalities, etc., within contemporary society.

(4) For the creation on a mass scale of this communist consciousness, as well as for the success of the cause itself, it is necessary for men themselves to be changed on a large scale, and this change can only occur in a practical movement, in a *revolution.* Revolution is necessary not only because the ruling class cannot be overthrown in any other way, but also because only in a revolution can *the class which overthrows it* rid itself of the accumulated rubbish of the past and become capable of reconstructing society. ...

The transformation of personal powers (relationships) into material powers through the division of labour cannot be undone again merely by dismissing the idea of it from one's mind, but only by the action of individuals who reestablish their control over these material powers and abolish the division of labour. This is not possible without a community. Only in association with others has each individual the means of cultivating his talents in all directions. Only in a community therefore is personal freedom possible. In the previous substitutes for community, in the State,

etc., personal freedom existed only for those individuals who grew up in the ruling class and only in so far as they were members of this class. The illusory community in which, up to the present, individuals have combined, always acquired an independent existence apart from them, and since it was a union of one class against another it represented for the dominated class not only a completely illusory community but also a new shackle. In a genuine community individuals gain their freedom in and through their association.

The German Ideology (1845–1846)

The possessing class and the proletarian class express the same human alienation. But the former is satisfied with its situation, feels itself well established in it, recognizes this self-alienation as *its own* power, and thus has the appearance of a human existence. The latter feels itself crushed by this self-alienation, sees in it its own impotence and the reality of all inhuman situation. It is, to use an expression of Hegel's, "in the midst of degradation the *revolt* against degradation," a revolt to which it is forced by the contradiction between its *humanity* and its situation, which is an open, clear and absolute negation of its humanity.

Within the framework of alienation, therefore, the property owners are the *conservative* and the proletarians the *destructive* party.

It is true that, in its economic development, private property advances towards its own dissolution; but it only does this through a development which is independent of itself, unconscious and achieved against its will—solely because it produces the proletariat *as* proletariat, poverty conscious of its moral and physical poverty, degradation conscious of its degradation, and for this reason trying to abolish itself. The proletariat carries out the sentence which private property, by creating the proletariat, passes upon itself, just as it carries out the sentence which wage-labour, by creating wealth for others and poverty for itself, passes upon itself. If the proletariat triumphs this does not mean that it becomes the absolute form of society, for it is only victorious by abolishing itself as well as its opposite. Thus the proletariat disappears along with the opposite which conditions it, private property.

If socialist writers attribute this world-historical role to the proletariat this is not at all ... because they regard the proletarians as *gods*. On the contrary, in the fully developed proletariat, everything human is taken away, even the *appearance* of humanity. In the conditions of existence of the proletariat are condensed, in their most inhuman form, all the conditions of existence of present-day society. Man has lost himself but he has not only acquired, at the same time, a theoretical consciousness of his loss, he has been forced, by an ineluctable and imperious *distress*—by practical *necessity*—to revolt against this inhumanity. It is for these reasons that the proletariat can and must emancipate itself. But it can only emancipate itself by destroying its own conditions of existence. It can only destroy its own conditions of existence by destroying *all* the inhuman conditions of existence of present-day society, conditions which are epitomized in its situation. It is not in vain that it passes through the rough but stimulating school of *labour*. It is not a matter of knowing what this or that proletarian, or even the proletariat as a whole, *conceives* as its aims at any particular moment. It is a question of knowing *what* the proletariat *is*, and what it must historically accomplish in accordance with its *nature*. Its aim and its historical activity are ordained for it, in a tangible and irrevocable way, by its own situation as well as by the whole organization of present-day civil society. It is unnecessary to show here that a large part of the English and French proletariat has already become *aware* of its historic mission, and works incessantly to clarify this awareness.

The Holy Family (1985)

The realm of freedom only begins, in fact, where that labour which is determined by need and external purposes, ceases; it is therefore, by its very nature, outside the sphere of material production proper. Just as the savage must wrestle with Nature in order to satisfy his wants, to maintain and reproduce his life, so also must civilized man, and he must do it in all forms of society and under any possible mode of production. With his development the realm of natural necessity expands, because his wants increase, but at the same time the forces of production, by which these wants are satisfied, also increase. Freedom in this field cannot consist of anything else but the fact that socialized mankind, the associated producers, regulate their interchange with Nature rationally, bring it under their common control, instead of being ruled by it as by some blind power, and accomplish their task with the least expenditure of energy and under such conditions as are proper and worthy for human beings. Nevertheless, this always remains a realm of necessity. Beyond it begins that development of human potentiality for its own sake, the true realm of freedom, which however can only flourish upon that realm of necessity as its basis. The shortening of the working day is its fundamental prerequisite.

Capital, Vol. III (published posthumously)

What we have to deal with here is a communist society, not as it has *developed* on its own foundation, but, on the contrary, just as it *emerges* from capitalist society; and which is thus in every respect, economically, morally and intellectually, still stamped with the birthmarks of the old society from whose womb it emerges. Accordingly, the individual producer receives back from society—after the deductions have been made—exactly what he contributes to it. What he has contributed to it is his individual quantum of labour. For example, the social working day consists of the sum of the individual hours of work; the individual labour-time of the individual producer is the part of the social working day contributed by him, his share in it. He receives a certificate from society that he has furnished such and such an amount of labour (after deducting his labour for the common funds), and with this certificate he draws from the social stock of means of consumption as much as costs the same amount of labour. The same amount of labour which he has given to society in one form he receives back in another.

Here obviously the same principle prevails as that which regulates the exchange of commodities, as far as this is exchange of equal values. Content and form are changed, because under the altered conditions no one can give anything except his labour, and because, on the other hand, nothing can pass into the ownership of individuals except individual means of consumption. But, as far as the distribution of the latter among the individual producers is concerned, the same principle prevails as in the exchange of commodity–equivalents: a given amount of labour in another form.

Hence, *equal right* here is still in principle—*bourgeois right,* although principle and practice are no longer at loggerheads, whereas the exchange of equivalents in commodity exchange only exists *on the average* and not in the individual case.

In spite of this advance, *equal right* is still burdened with bourgeois limitations. The right of the producers is *proportional* to the labour they supply; the equality consists in the fact that measurement is made with an *equal standard, labour.*

But one man is superior to another physically or mentally and so supplies more labour in the same time, or can labour for a longer time; and labour, to serve as a measure, must be defined by its duration or intensity, otherwise it ceases to be a standard of measurement. The *equal right* is an unequal right for unequal labour. It recognizes no class differences, because everyone is only a worker like everyone else; but it tacitly recognizes unequal individual endowment, and thus

natural privileges in respect of productive capacity. *It is, therefore, in its content, a right of inequality, like every right.* Right by its very nature can consist only in the application of an equal standard; but unequal individuals (and they would not be different individuals if they were not unequal) can only be assessed by an equal standard in so far as they are regarded from a single aspect, from one particular side only, as for instance, in the present case, they are regarded *only as workers,* and nothing more is seen in them, everything else being ignored. Further, one worker is married, another not; one has more children than another, and so on. Thus, with an equal performance of labour, and hence an equal share in the social consumption fund, one individual will in fact receive more than another, one will be richer than another, and so on. To avoid all these defects, right instead of being equal would have to be unequal.

But these defects are inevitable in the first phase of communist society as it is when it has just emerged after prolonged birth-pangs from capitalist society. Right can never be higher than the economic structure of society and the cultural development conditioned by it.

In a higher phase of communist society, when the enslaving subordination of the individual to the division of labour, and with it the antithesis between mental and physical labour, has vanished; when labour is no longer merely a means of life but has become life's principal need; when the productive forces have also increased with the all-round development of the individual, and all the springs of co-operative wealth flow more abundantly— only then will it be possible completely to transcend the narrow outlook of bourgeois right and only then will society be able to inscribe on its banners: From each according to his ability, to each according to his needs!

Critique of the Gotha Program
(1875)

COMMENT

In this chapter, we are dealing with an extremely complex thinker whose ideas were not only ambiguous but subject to change and development. Marx once even remarked, "One thing I know and that is that I am not a Marxist."[1] He was aware of the common tendency among "Marxists" to reduce and distort his ideas, being perhaps as misinterpreted by friends as by foes.

Despite some unguarded statements, his theory was neither a simpleminded economic determinism nor a rigid scheme of historical development. He maintained that the economic system primarily determines the history of a social order, but he believed that all sorts of other forces enter into the very complex interaction of causal factors. Contrary to the usual interpretation of his doctrine, he did not suppose that all history can be arranged in a definite series of stages, beginning with primitive communism and going on to slavery, feudalism, capitalism, socialism, and finally advanced communism. He pointed out that the historical development in India and China, and to a considerable extent in Russia, deviated greatly from the pattern in western Europe, and he recognized that the future is somewhat uncertain. In 1844, in his *Economic and Philosophical Manuscripts,* he said that communism may appear in a democratic or an autocratic form, and in his famous speech at The Hague in 1872, he declared that the "emancipation of the workers" may be achieved peacefully in the more democratic countries. Thus he advocated—not always consistently—a complex, multilinear theory of history rather than the very simple unilinear theory that is usually attributed to him.[2]

He also foresaw that communism may take the form of a raw and repressive system. "This entirely crude and unreflective communism," he declared, "would negate the personality of man in every sphere.... It would be a system in which universal envy sets itself up as a power, and ... in this form of envy, it would reduce everything to a common level.... Crude communism," he went on to say, "is only the culmination of such envy and levelling down to a preconceived minimum." He spoke of it as "the negation of the whole world of culture and civilization."[3]

These remarks were made in 1844, but in his later works, Marx occasionally recognized the dangers of collectivism and bureaucracy. In the 1850s, he wrote articles for the New York *Daily Tribune* in which he characterized "Oriental despotism," the state managerialism of the old Asiatic societies, as dooming the masses to a kind of "general [state] slavery."[4] In his comments of 1871 on the Paris Commune, he emphasized the need for popular control of the revolutionary government, warning against bureaucracy and militarism. His ultimate ideal was to abolish the coercive state and to organize society on a decentralized basis. His

---

[1] Karl Marx and Friedrich Engels, Selected Correspondence (New York: International Publishers, 1936), p. 472.

[2] See Melvin Rader, Ethics and the Human Community (New York: Holt, Rinehart and Winston, 1964), Ch. 12, for a fuller discussion.

[3] Economic and Philosophical Manuscripts, in T. B. Bottomore, Karl Marx: Early Writings (London: C. A. Watts, 1963), pp. 153–154.

[4] See Karl Wittfogel, Oriental Despotism (New Haven, CT: Yale University Press, 1959).

works contain an impassioned protest against the dehumanizing process of mass industry, with its tendency toward the depersonalization of life. Although expressed most fully in the early *Economic and Philosophical Manuscripts,* his theory of "alienation" remains basic in the later works, but more often implicit than explicit. For example, Marx's speech at the anniversary celebration of the *People's Paper* (1856) mentions two basic sides of the process of alienation: first, material forces taking on "life" and dominating human beings ("objectification"), and second, human life being stultified into a material force ("self-alienation"). Although Marx seldom used the *word* "alienation" in these later works, he still thought of human beings as estranged from themselves, from other people, from their work, from their products, from their society, from nature. He also clung to the ideal of dealienation, demanding that human beings be treated as human beings, and things as things. A nonalienated person would be *really* a person, a free, creative, well-rounded being, no longer the victim of impersonal forces.

No well-informed liberal would deny that there are totalitarian trends in the writings of Marx. In his criticism of the Gotha Program of the German Social-Democrats, he insisted on the dictatorship of the proletariat as a necessary step in the transition from capitalism to socialism. In the *Communist Manifesto,* he proposed "to centralize all instruments of production in the hands of the state." The more orthodox Marxists have selected and elaborated such features of the original Marxist creed, whereas the revisionists have seized on the more liberal elements. Both sides can point to authentic Marxist texts.

In various respects we can question and debate the validity of Marx's ideas, but we shall leave this task to the readers of this book. We need to be sensitive, as Marx was sensitive, to the enormous burden of human suffering. His humanitarian concern does honor to him as a man. If we were as sincerely concerned, it would be very much to our credit. However, Marx, even though his ideas are far from the caricature that is so often presented, was too sure about the way history would go, too one-sided in his emphasis on economic forces, and too ready to accept dictatorship in his eagerness for revolutionary change. With our different tradition of civil liberties and human rights, we need to cherish the free, humane values of our civilization—and so we have to revise Marx. However, insofar as his moral passion is concerned, we have to heed him.

It is interesting and instructive to note that the so-called "Liberation Theology," which inspired many of the Central American refugees involved in the Sanctuary Movement, has often been accused of relying too heavily on Marxist thought. Thus, those who were put on trial for helping these refugees were frequently thought of as "Marxists" and "communists." Just what would Marx have to say about such acts of civil disobedience on behalf of those fleeing social and political persecution? Would his view of the foundational character of economic life put him in sympathy with refugees from totalitarian governments? Would he feel that the fact that these refugees came from totalitarian governments justifies a group to engage in civil disobedience against its own government in order to help such people? Do capitalism and democracy necessarily go together, or could one have the latter without the former? Are acts of civil disobedience the result of purely economic factors, or are there other principles that contribute to them?

26

COLONIALISM AND NATIONALISM

FRANTZ FANON (1925–1961)

Frantz Fanon was born and raised on the island of Martinique. After studying medicine and psychiatry in France, he worked as a psychiatrist in the Antilles. On the basis of this experience, he wrote his first book, *Black Skin, White Masks*. During the French-Algerian War, he was assigned by the French government to a hospital in Algeria, where he found himself identifying strongly with the revolutionary cause. Out of this experience came his most influential book, *The Wretched of the Earth* (1961), from which the following selection is taken. Fanon died of cancer in 1961 without ever knowing that his written work would come to serve as a virtual handbook for Third World freedom fighters around the world. In his preface for *The Wretched of the Earth,* Jean-Paul Sartre challenged the white, Western world to "have the courage to read this book."

THE PITFALLS OF NATIONAL CONSCIOUSNESS

History teaches us clearly that the battle against colonialism does not run straight away along the lines of nationalism. For a very long time the native devotes his energies to ending certain definite abuses: forced labor, corporal punishment, inequality of salaries, limitation of political rights, etc. This fight for democracy against the oppression of mankind will slowly leave the confusion of neo-liberal universalism to emerge, sometimes laboriously, as a claim to nationhood. It so happens that the unpreparedness of the educated classes, the lack of practical links between them and the mass of the people, their laziness, and, let it be said, their cowardice at the decisive moment of the struggle will give rise to tragic mishaps.

National consciousness, instead of being the all-embracing crystallization of the innermost hopes of the whole people, instead of being the immediate and most

From *The Wretched of the Earth* by Frantz Fanon. Copyright © 1963 by Presence Africaine, copyright renewed 1991 by Presence Africaine. Used with the permission of Grove/Atlantic Monthly Press.

obvious result of the mobilization of the people, will be in any case only an empty shell, a crude and fragile travesty of what it might have been. The faults that we find in it are quite sufficient explanation of the facility with which, when dealing with young and independent nations, the nation is passed over for the race, and the tribe is preferred to the state. These are the cracks in the edifice which show the process of retrogression, that is so harmful and prejudicial to national effort and national unity. We shall see that such retrograde steps with all the weaknesses and serious dangers that they entail are the historical result of the incapacity of the national middle class to rationalize popular action, that is to say their incapacity to see into the reasons for that action.

This traditional weakness, which is almost congenital to the national consciousness of underdeveloped countries, is not solely the result of the mutilation of the colonized people by the colonial regime. It is also the result of the intellectual laziness of the national middle class, of its spiritual penury, and of the profoundly cosmopolitan mold that its mind is set in.

The national middle class which takes over power at the end of the colonial regime is an underdeveloped middle class. It has practically no economic power, and in any case it is in no way commensurate with the bourgeoisie of the mother country which it hopes to replace. In its narcissism, the national middle class is easily convinced that it can advantageously replace the middle class of the mother country. But that same independence which literally drives it into a corner will give rise within its ranks to catastrophic reactions, and will oblige it to send out frenzied appeals for help to the former mother country. The university and merchant classes which make up the most enlightened section of the new state are in fact characterized by the smallness of their number and their being concentrated in the capital, and the type of activities in which they are engaged: business, agriculture, and the liberal profes-

sions. Neither financiers nor industrial magnates are to be found within this national middle class. The national bourgeoisie of underdeveloped countries is not engaged in production, nor in invention, nor building, nor labor; it is completely canalized into activities of the intermediary type. Its innermost vocation seems to be to keep in the running and to be part of the racket. The psychology of the national bourgeoisie is that of the businessman, not that of a captain of industry; and it is only too true that the greed of the settlers and the system of embargoes set up by colonialism have hardly left them any other choice.

Under the colonial system, a middle class which accumulates capital is an impossible phenomenon. Now, precisely, it would seem that the historical vocation of an authentic national middle class in an underdeveloped country is to repudiate its own nature in so far as it is bourgeois, that is to say in so far as it is the tool of capitalism, and to make itself the willing slave of that revolutionary capital which is the people.

In an underdeveloped country an authentic national middle class ought to consider as its bounden duty to betray the calling fate has marked out for it, and to put itself to school with the people: in other words to put at the people's disposal the intellectual and technical capital that it has snatched when going through the colonial universities. But unhappily we shall see that very often the national middle class does not follow this heroic, positive, fruitful, and just path; rather, it disappears with its soul set at peace into the shocking ways—shocking because anti-national—of a traditional bourgeoisie, of a bourgeoisie which is stupidly, contemptibly, cynically bourgeois.

The objective of nationalist parties as from a certain given period is, we have seen, strictly national. They mobilize the people with slogans of independence, and for the rest leave it to future events. When such parties are questioned on the economic program of the state that they are clamoring for, or on the nature of the regime which they propose to install, they are incapable of replying, because, precisely, they are completely ignorant of the economy of their own country.

This economy has always developed outside the limits of their knowledge. They have nothing more than an approximate, bookish acquaintance with the actual and potential resources of their country's soil and mineral deposits; and therefore they can only speak of these resources on a general and abstract plane. After independence this underdeveloped middle class, reduced in numbers and without capital, which refuses to follow the path of revolution, will fall into deplorable stagnation. It is unable to give free rein to its genius, which formerly it was wont to lament, though rather too glibly, was held in check by colonial domination. The precariousness of its resources and the paucity of its managerial class force it back for years into an artisan economy. From its point of view, which is inevitably a very limited one, a national economy is an economy based on what may be called local products. Long speeches will be made about the artisan class. Since the middle classes find it impossible to set up factories that would be more profit-earning both for themselves and for the country as a whole, they will surround the artisan class with a chauvinistic tenderness in keeping with the new awareness of national dignity, and which moreover will bring them in quite a lot of money. This cult of local products and this incapability to seek out new systems of management will be equally manifested by the bogging down of the national middle class in the methods of agricultural production which were characteristic of the colonial period.

The national economy of the period of independence is not set on a new footing. It is still concerned with the groundnut harvest, with the cocoa crop and the olive yield. In the same way there is no change in the marketing of basic products, and not a single industry is set up in the country. We go on sending out raw materials; we go on being Europe's small farmers, who specialize in unfinished products.

Yet the national middle class constantly demands the nationalization of the economy and of the trading sectors. This is because, from their point of view, nationalization does not mean placing the whole economy at the service of the nation and deciding to satisfy the needs of the nation. For them, nationalization does not mean governing the state with regard to the new social relations whose growth it has been decided to encourage. To them, nationalization quite simply means the transfer into native hands of those unfair advantages which are a legacy of the colonial period.

Since the middle class has neither sufficient material nor intellectual resources (by intellectual resources we mean engineers and technicians), it limits its claims to the taking over of business offices and commercial houses formerly occupied by the settlers. The national bourgeoisie steps into the shoes of the former European settlement: doctors, barristers, traders, commercial travelers, general agents, and transport agents. It considers that the dignity of the country and its own welfare require that it should occupy all these posts. From now on it will insist that all the big foreign companies should pass through its bands, whether these companies wish to keep on their connections with the country, or to open it up. The national middle class discovers its historic mission: that of intermediary.

Seen through its eyes, its mission has nothing to do with transforming the nation; it consists, prosaically, of being the transmission line between the nation and a capitalism, rampant though camouflaged, which today puts on the mask of neo-colonialism. The national bourgeoisie will be quite content with the role of the Western bourgeoisie's business agent, and it will play its part without any complexes in a most dignified manner. But this same lucrative role, this cheap-Jack's function, this meanness of outlook and this absence of all ambition symbolize the incapability of the national middle class to fulfill its historic role of bourgeoisie. Here, the dynamic, pioneer aspect, the characteristics of the inventor and of the discoverer of new worlds which are found in all national bourgeoisies are lamentably absent. In the colonial countries, the spirit of indulgence is dominant at the core of the bourgeoisie; and this is because the national bourgeoisie identifies itself with the Western bourgeoisie, from whom it has learnt its lessons. It follows the Western bourgeoisie along its path of negation and decadence without ever having emulated it in its first stages of exploration and invention, stages which are an acquisition of that Western bourgeoisie whatever the circumstances. In its beginnings, the national bourgeoisie of the colonial countries identifies itself with the decadence of the bourgeoisie of the West. We need not think that it is jumping ahead; it is in fact beginning at the end. It is already senile before it has come to know the petulance, the fearlessness, or the will to succeed of youth.

The national bourgeoisie will be greatly helped on its way toward decadence by the Western bourgeoisies, who come to it as tourists avid for the exotic, for big game hunting, and for casinos. The national bourgeoisie organizes centers of rest and relaxation and pleasure resorts to meet the wishes of the Western bourgeoisie. Such activity is given the name of tourism, and for the occasion will be built up as a national industry. If proof is needed of the eventual transformation of certain elements of the ex-native bourgeoisie into the organizers of parties for their Western opposite numbers, it is worth while having a look at what has happened in Latin America. The casinos of Havana and of Mexico, the beaches of Rio, the little Brazilian and Mexican girls, the half-breed thirteen-year-olds, the ports of Acapulco and Copacabana—all these are the stigma of this depravation of the national middle class. Because it is bereft of ideas, because it lives to itself and cuts itself off from the people,

undermined by its hereditary incapacity to think in terms of all the problems of the nation as seen from the point of view of the whole of that nation, the national middle class will have nothing better to do than to take on the role of manager for Western enterprise, and it will in practice set up its country as the brothel of Europe.

Once again we must keep before us the unfortunate example of certain Latin American republics. The banking magnates, the technocrats, and the big businessmen of the United States have only to step onto a plane and they are wafted into subtropical climes, there for a space of a week or ten days to luxuriate in the delicious depravities which their "reserves" hold for them.

The behavior of the national landed proprietors is practically identical with that of the middle classes of the towns. The big farmers have, as soon as independence is proclaimed, demanded the nationalization of agricultural production. Through manifold scheming practices they manage to make a clean sweep of the farms formerly owned by settlers, thus reinforcing their hold on the district. But they do not try to introduce new agricultural methods, nor to farm more intensively, nor to integrate their farming systems into a genuinely national economy.

In fact, the landed proprietors will insist that the state should give them a hundred times more facilities and privileges than were enjoyed by the foreign settlers in former times. The exploitation of agricultural workers will be intensified and made legitimate. Using two or three slogans, these new colonists will demand an enormous amount of work from the agricultural laborers, in the name of the national effort of course. There will be no modernization of agriculture, no planning for development, and no initiative, for initiative throws these people into a panic since it implies a minimum of risk, and completely upsets the hesitant, prudent, landed bourgeoisie, which gradually slips more and more into the lines laid down by colonialism. In the districts where this is the case, the only efforts made to better things are due to the government; it orders them, encourages them, and finances them. The landed bourgeoisie refuses to take the slightest risk, and remains opposed to any venture and to any hazard. It has no intention of building upon sand; it demands solid investments and quick returns. The enormous profits which it pockets, enormous if we take into account the national revenue, are never reinvested. The money-in-the-stocking mentality is dominant in the psychology of these landed proprietors. Sometimes, especially in the years immediately following independence, the bourgeoisie does not hesitate to invest in foreign banks the profits that it makes out of its native soil. On the other hand large sums are spent on display: on cars, country houses, and on all those things which have been justly described by economists as characterizing an underdeveloped bourgeoisie.

We have said that the native bourgeoisie which comes to power uses its class aggressiveness to corner the positions formerly kept for foreigners. On the morrow of independence, in fact, it violently attacks colonial personalities: barristers, traders, landed proprietors, doctors, and higher civil servants. It will fight to the bitter end against these people "who insult our dignity as a nation." It waves aloft the notion of the nationalization and Africanization of the ruling classes. The fact is that such action will become more and more tinged by racism, until the bourgeoisie bluntly puts the problem to the government by saying "We must have these posts." They will not stop their snarling until they have taken over everyone. . . .

It is from this viewpoint that we must interpret the fact that in young, independent countries, here and there federalism triumphs. We know that colonial domination has marked certain regions out for privilege. The colony's economy is not integrated into that of the nation as a whole. It is still organized in order to complete the economy of the different mother countries. Colonialism hardly ever exploits the whole of a country. It contents itself with bringing to light the natural resources, which it extracts, and exports to meet the needs of the mother country's industries, thereby allowing certain sectors of the colony to become relatively rich. But the rest of the colony follows its path of underdevelopment and poverty, or at all events sinks into it more deeply.

Immediately after independence, the nationals who live in the more prosperous regions realize their good luck, and show a primary and profound reaction in refusing to feed the other nationals. The districts which are rich in groundnuts, in cocoa, and in diamonds come to the forefront, and dominate the empty panorama which the rest of the nation presents. The nationals of these rich regions look upon the others with hatred, and find in them envy and covetousness, and homicidal impulses. Old rivalries which were there before colonialism, old interracial hatreds come to the surface. The Balubas refuse to feed the Luluas; Katanga forms itself into a state, and Albert Kalondji gets himself crowned king of South Kasai.

African unity, that vague formula, yet one to which the men and women of Africa were passionately attached, and whose operative value served to bring immense pressure to bear on colonialism, African unity takes off the mask, and crumbles into regionalism inside the hollow shell of nationality itself. The national bourgeoisie, since it is strung up to defend its immediate interests, and sees no further than the end of its nose, reveals itself incapable of simply bringing national unity into being, or of building up the nation on a stable and productive basis. The national front which has forced colonialism to withdraw cracks up, and wastes the victory it has gained.

This merciless fight engaged upon by races and tribes, and this aggressive anxiety to occupy the posts left vacant by the departure of the foreigner, will equally give rise to religious rivalries. In the country districts and the bush, minor confraternities, local religions, and maraboutic cults will show a new vitality and will once more take up their round of excommunications. In the big towns, on the level of the administrative classes, we will observe the coming to grips of the two great revealed religions, Islam and Catholicism.

Colonialism, which had been shaken to its very foundations by the birth of African unity, recovers its balance and tries now to break that will to unity by using all the movement's weaknesses. Colonialism will set the African peoples moving by revealing to them the existence of "spiritual" rivalries. In Senegal, it is the newspaper *New Africa* which week by week distills hatred of Islam and of the Arabs. The Lebanese, in whose hands is the greater part of the small trading enterprises on the western seaboard, are marked out for national obloquy. The missionaries find it opportune to remind the masses that long before the advent of European colonialism the great African empires were disrupted by the Arab invasion. There is no hesitation in saying that it was the Arab occupation which paved the way for European colonialism; Arab imperialism is commonly spoken of, and the cultural imperialism of Islam is condemned. Moslems are usually kept out of the more important posts. In other regions the reverse is the case, and it is the native Christians who are considered as conscious, objective enemies of national independence. . . .

As we see it, the bankruptcy of bourgeoisie is not apparent in the economic field only. They have come to power in the name of a narrow nationalism and representing a race; they will prove themselves incapable of triumphantly putting into practice a program with even a minimum humanist content, in spite of fine-sounding declarations which are devoid of meaning since the speakers bandy about in irresponsible fashion phrases that come straight out of European treatises on morals and political philosophy. When the bourgeoisie is strong, when it can arrange everything and everybody to serve its power, it does not hesitate

to affirm positively certain democratic ideas which claim to be universally applicable. There must be very exceptional circumstances if such a bourgeoisie, solidly based economically, is forced into denying its own humanist ideology. The Western bourgeoisie, though fundamentally racist, most often manages to mask this racism by a multiplicity of nuances which allow it to preserve intact its proclamation of mankind's outstanding dignity.

The Western bourgeoisie has prepared enough fences and railings to have no real fear of the competition of those whom it exploits and holds in contempt. Western bourgeois racial prejudice as regards the nigger and the Arab is a racism of contempt; it is a racism which minimizes what it hates. Bourgeois ideology, however, which is the proclamation of an essential equality between men, manages to appear logical in its own eyes by inviting the submen to become human, and to take as their prototype Western humanity as incarnated in the Western bourgeoisie.

The racial prejudice of the young national bourgeoisie is a racism of defense, based on fear. Essentially it is no different from vulgar tribalism, or the rivalries between septs or confraternities. We may understand why keen-witted international observers have hardly taken seriously the great flights of oratory about African unity, for it is true that there are so many cracks in that unity visible to the naked eye that it is only reasonable to insist that all these contradictions ought to be resolved before the day of unity can come.

The peoples of Africa have only recently come to know themselves. They have decided, in the name of the whole continent, to weigh in strongly against the colonial regime. Now the nationalist bourgeoisies, who in region after region hasten to make their own fortunes and to set up a national system of exploitation, do their utmost to put obstacles in the path of this "Utopia." The national bourgeoisies, who are quite clear as to what their objectives are, have decided to bar the way to that unity, to that coordinated effort on the part of two hundred and fifty million men to triumph over stupidity, hunger, and inhumanity at one and the same time. This is why we must understand that African unity can only be achieved through the upward thrust of the people, and under the leadership of the people, that is to say, in defiance of the interests of the bourgeoisie.

As regards internal affairs and in the sphere of institutions, the national bourgeoisie will give equal proof of its incapacity. In a certain number of underdeveloped countries the parliamentary game is faked from the beginning. Powerless economically, unable to bring about the existence of coherent social relations, and standing on the principle of its domination as a class, the bourgeoisie chooses the solution that seems to it the easiest, that of the single party. It does not yet have the quiet conscience and the calm that economic power and the control of the state machine alone can give. It does not create a state that reassures the ordinary citizen, but rather one that rouses his anxiety.

The state, which by its strength and discretion ought to inspire confidence and disarm and lull everybody to sleep, on the contrary seeks to impose itself in spectacular fashion. It makes a display, it jostles people and bullies them, thus intimating to the citizen that he is in continual danger. The single party is the modern form of the dictatorship of the bourgeoisie, unmasked, unpainted, unscrupulous, and cynical.

It is true that such a dictatorship does not go very far. It cannot halt the processes of its own contradictions. Since the bourgeoisie has not the economic means to ensure its domination and to throw a few crumbs to the rest of the country; since, moreover, it is preoccupied with filling its pockets as rapidly as possible but also as prosaically as possible, the country sinks all the more deeply into stagnation. And in order to hide this stagnation and to mark this regression, to reassure itself and to give itself something to boast about, the bourgeoisie can find nothing better to do than to erect grandiose buildings in the capital and to lay out money on what are called prestige expenses.

The national bourgeoisie turns its back more and more on the interior and on the real facts of its undeveloped country, and tends to look toward the former mother country and the foreign capitalists who count on its obliging compliance. As it does not share its profits with the people, and in no way allows them to enjoy any of the dues that are paid to it by the big foreign companies, it will discover the need for a popular leader to whom will fall the dual role of stabilizing the regime and of perpetuating the domination of the bourgeoisie. . . .

After independence, the party sinks into an extraordinary lethargy. The militants are only called upon when so-called popular manifestations are afoot or international conferences, or independence celebrations. The local party leaders are given administrative posts, the party becomes an administration, and the militants disappear into the crowd and take the empty title of citizen. Now that they have fulfilled their historical mission of leading the bourgeoisie to power, they are firmly invited to retire so that the bourgeoisie may carry out *its* mission in peace and quiet. But we have seen that the national bourgeoisie of underdeveloped countries is incapable of carrying out any mission whatever. After a few years, the break-up of the party becomes obvious, and any observer, even the most superficial, can notice that the party, today the skeleton of its former self, only serves to immobilize the people. The party, which during the battle had drawn to itself the whole nation, is falling to pieces. The intellectuals who on the eve of independence rallied to the party, now make it clear by their attitude that they gave their support with no other end in view than to secure their slices of the cake of independence. The party is becoming a means of private advancement.

There exists inside the new regime, however, an inequality in the acquisition of wealth and in monopolization. Some have a double source of income and demonstrate that they are specialized in opportunism. Privileges multiply and corruption triumphs, while morality declines. Today the vultures are too numerous and too voracious in proportion to the lean spoils of the national wealth. The party, a true instrument of power in the hands of the bourgeoisie, reinforces the machine, and ensures that the people are hemmed in and immobilized. The party helps the government to hold the people down. It becomes more and more clearly antidemocratic, an implement of coercion. The party is objectively, sometimes subjectively, the accomplice of the merchant bourgeoisie. In the same way that the national bourgeoisie conjures away its phase of construction in order to throw itself into the enjoyment of its wealth, in parallel fashion in the institutional sphere it jumps the parliamentary phase and chooses a dictatorship of the national–socialist type. We know today that this fascism at high interest which has triumphed for half a century in Latin America is the dialectic result of states which were semi-colonial during the period of independence.

In these poor, underdeveloped countries, where the rule is that the greatest wealth is surrounded by the greatest poverty, the army and the police constitute the pillars of the regime; an army and a police force (another rule which must not be forgotten) which are advised by foreign experts. The strength of the police force and the power of the army are proportionate to the stagnation in which the rest of the nation is sunk. By dint of yearly loans, concessions are snatched up by foreigners; scandals are numerous, ministers grow rich, their wives doll themselves up, the members of parliament feather their nests and there is not a soul down to the simple policeman or the customs officer who does not join in the great procession of corruption.

The opposition becomes more aggressive and the people at once catch on to its propaganda. From now on their hostility to the bourgeoisie is plainly visible. This young bourgeoisie which appears to be afflicted with precocious senility takes no heed of the advice showered upon it, and reveals itself incapable of understanding that it would be in its interest to draw a veil, even if only the flimsiest kind, over its exploitation. It is the most Christian newspaper, *The African Weekly*, published in Brazzaville, which addresses the princes of the regime thus:

> You who are in good positions, you and your wives, today you enjoy many comforts; perhaps a good education, a fine house, good contacts, and many missions on which you are delegated which open new horizons to you. But all your wealth forms a hard shell which prevents your seeing the poverty that surrounds you. Take care.

This warning coming from *The African Weekly* and addressed to the henchmen of Monsieur Youlou has, we may imagine, nothing revolutionary about it. What *The African Weekly* wants to point out to the starvers of the Congolese people is that God will punish their conduct. It continues: "If there is no room in your heart for consideration toward those who are beneath you, there will be no room for you in God's house."

It is clear that the national bourgeoisie hardly worries at all about such an indictment. With its wave lengths tuned in to Europe, it continues firmly and resolutely to make the most of the situation. The enormous profits which it derives from the exploitation of the people are exported to foreign countries. The young national bourgeoisie is often more suspicious of the regime that it has set up than are the foreign companies. The national bourgeoisie refuses to invest in its own country and behaves toward the state that protects and nurtures it with, it must be remarked, astonishing ingratitude. It acquires foreign securities in the European markets, and goes off to spend the weekend in Paris or Hamburg.

The behavior of the national bourgeoisie of certain underdeveloped countries is reminiscent of the members of a gang, who after every holdup hide their share in the loot from the other members who are their accomplices and prudently start thinking about their retirement. Such behavior shows that more or less consciously the national bourgeoisie is playing to lose if the game goes on too long. They guess that the present situation will not last indefinitely but they intend to make the most of it. Such exploitation and such contempt for the state, however, inevitably gives rise to discontent among the mass of the people. It is in these conditions that the regime becomes harsher. In the absence of a parliament it is the army that becomes the arbiter: but sooner or later it will realize its power and will hold over the government's head the threat of a manifesto.

As we see it, the national bourgeoisie of certain underdeveloped countries has learned nothing from books. If they had looked closer at the Latin American countries they doubtless would have recognized the dangers which threaten them. We may thus conclude that this bourgeoisie in miniature that thrusts itself into the forefront is condemned to mark time, accomplishing nothing. In underdeveloped countries the bourgeois phase is impossibly arid. Certainly, there is a police dictatorship and a profiteering caste, but the construction of an elaborate bourgeois society seems to be condemned to failure. The ranks of decked-out profiteers whose grasping hands scrape up the bank notes from a poverty-stricken country will sooner or later be men of straw in the hands of the army, cleverly handled by foreign experts. In this way the former mother country practices indirect government, both by the bourgeoisie that it upholds and also by the national army led by its experts, an army that pins the people down, immobilizing and terrorizing them. . . .

What holds up the taking of a decision by the profoundly democratic elements of the young nation and adds to their timidity is the apparent strength of the bourgeoisie. In newly independent underdeveloped countries, the whole of the ruling class swarms into the towns built by colonialism. The absence of any analysis of the total population induces onlookers to think that there exists a powerful and perfectly organized bourgeoisie. In fact, we know today that the bourgeoisie in underdeveloped countries is non-existent. What creates a bourgeoisie is not the bourgeois spirit, nor its taste or manners, nor even its aspirations. The bourgeoisie is above all the direct product of precise economic conditions.

Now, in the colonies, the economic conditions are conditions of a foreign bourgeoisie. Through its agents, it is the bourgeoisie of the mother country that we find present in the colonial towns. The bourgeoisie in the colonies is, before independence, a Western bourgeoisie, a true branch of the bourgeoisie of the mother country, that derives its legitimacy, its force, and its stability from the bourgeoisie of the homeland. During the period of unrest that precedes independence, certain native elements, intellectuals, and traders, who live in the midst of that imported bourgeoisie, try to identify themselves with it. A permanent wish for identification with the bourgeois representatives of the mother country is to be found among the native intellectuals and merchants.

This native bourgeoisie, which has adopted unreservedly and with enthusiasm the ways of thinking characteristic of the mother country, which has become wonderfully detached from its own thought and has based its consciousness upon foundations which are typically foreign, will realize, with its mouth watering, that it lacks something essential to a bourgeoisie: money. The bourgeoisie of an underdeveloped country is a bourgeoisie in spirit only. It is not its economic strength, nor the dynamism of its leaders, nor the breadth of its ideas that ensures its peculiar quality as bourgeoisie. Consequently it remains at the beginning and for a long time afterward a bourgeoisie of the civil service. It is the positions that it holds in the new national administration which will give it strength and serenity. If the government gives it enough time and opportunity, this bourgeoisie will manage to put away enough money to stiffen its domination. But it will always reveal itself as incapable of giving birth to an authentic bourgeois society with all the economic and industrial consequences which this entails.

From the beginning the national bourgeoisie directs its efforts toward activities of the intermediary type. The basis of its strength is found in its aptitude for trade and small business enterprises, and in securing commissions. It is not its money that works, but its business acumen. It does not go in for investments and it cannot achieve that accumulation of capital necessary to the birth and blossoming of an authentic bourgeoisie. At that rate it would take centuries to set on foot an embryonic industrial revolution, and in any case it would find the way barred by the relentless opposition of the former mother country, which will have taken all precautions when setting up neo-colonialist trade conventions. . . .

In an underdeveloped country, the setting up of dynamic district officials stops the process whereby the towns become top-heavy and the incoherent rush toward the cities of the mass of country people. The setting up early in the days of independence of regional organizations and officials who have full authority to do everything in their power to awaken such a region, to bring life to it, and to hasten the growth of consciousness in it is a necessity from which there is no escape for a country that wishes to progress. Otherwise, the government big-wigs and the party officials group themselves around the leader. The government services swell to huge proportions, not because they are developing and specializing, but because new-found cousins and fresh militants are looking for jobs and hope to edge themselves into the government machine. And the dream of every citizen is to get up to the capital, and

to have his share of the cake. The local districts are deserted; the mass of the country people with no one to lead them, uneducated and unsupported, turn their backs on their poorly labored fields and flock toward the outer ring of suburbs, thus swelling out of all proportion the ranks of the *lumpenproletariat.*

The moment for a fresh national crisis is not far off. To avoid it, we think that a quite different policy should be followed: that the interior, the back country, ought to be the most privileged part of the country. Moreover, in the last resort, there is nothing inconvenient in the government choosing its seat elsewhere than in the capital. The capital must be deconsecrated; the outcast masses must be shown that we have decided to work for them. It is with this idea in mind that the government of Brazil tried to found Brasilia. The dead city of Rio de Janeiro was an insult to the Brazilian people. But, unfortunately, Brasilia is just another new capital, as monstrous as the first. The only advantage of this achievement is that today, there exists a road through the bush to it.

No, there is no serious reason which can be opposed to the choice of another capital, or to the moving of the government as a whole toward one of the most underpopulated regions. The capital of underdeveloped countries is a commercial notion inherited from the colonial period. But we who are citizens of the underdeveloped countries, we ought to seek every occasion for contacts with the rural masses. We must create a national policy, in other words a policy for the masses. We ought never to lose contact with the people which has battled for its independence and for the concrete betterment of its existence.

The native civil servants and technicians ought not to bury themselves in diagrams and statistics, but rather in the hearts of the people. They ought not to bristle up every time there is question of a move to be made to the "interior." We should no longer see the young women of the country threaten their husbands with divorce if they do not manage to avoid being appointed to a rural post. For these reasons, the political bureau of the party ought to treat these forgotten districts in a very privileged manner; and the life of the capital, an altogether artificial life which is stuck onto the real national life like a foreign body, ought to take up the least space possible in the life of the nation, which is sacred and fundamental. In an underdeveloped country, the party ought to be organized in such fashion that it is not simply content with having contacts with the masses. The party should be the direct expression of the masses. The party is not an administration responsible for transmitting government orders; it is the energetic spokesman and the incorruptible defender of the masses. In order to arrive at this conception of the party, we must above all rid ourselves of the very Western, very bourgeois and therefore contemptuous attitude that the masses are incapable of governing themselves. In fact, experience proves that the masses understand perfectly the most complicated problems. One of the greatest services that the Algerian revolution will have rendered to the intellectuals of Algeria will be to have placed them in contact with the people, to have allowed them to see the extreme, ineffable poverty of the people, at the same time allowing them to watch the awakening of the people's intelligence and the onward progress of their consciousness. The Algerian people, that mass of starving illiterates, those men and women plunged for centuries in the most appalling obscurity have held out against tanks and airplanes, against napalm and "psychological services," but above all against corruption and brainwashing, against traitors and against the "national" armies of General Bellounis. This people has held out in spite of hesitant or feeble individuals, and in spite of would-be dictators. This people has held out because for seven years its struggle has opened up for it vistas that it never dreamed existed. Today, arms factories are working in the midst of the mountains several yards underground; today, the people's tribunals are functioning at every level, and local planning commissions are organizing the division of large-scale holdings, and working out the Algeria of tomorrow. An isolated individual may obstinately refuse to understand a problem, but the group or the village understands with disconcerting rapidity. It is true that if care is taken to use only a language that is understood by graduates in law and economics, you can easily prove that the masses have to be managed from above. But if you speak the language of everyday, if you are not obsessed by the perverse desire to spread confusion and to rid yourself of the people, then you will realize that the masses are quick to seize every shade of meaning and to learn all the tricks of the trade. If recourse is had to technical language, this signifies that it has been decided to consider the masses as uninitiated. Such a language is hard put to it to hide the lecturers' wish to cheat the people and to leave them out of things. The business of obscuring language is a mask behind which stands out the much greater business of plunder. The people's property and the people's sovereignty are to be stripped from them at one and the same time. Everything can be explained to the people, on the single condition that you really want them to understand. And if you think that you don't need them, and that on the contrary they may hinder the smooth running of the many limited liability companies whose aim it is to make the people even poorer, then the problem is quite clear.

For if you think that you can manage a country without letting the people interfere, if you think that the people upset the game by their mere presence, whether they slow it down or whether by their natural ignorance they sabotage it, then you must have no hesitation: you must keep the people out. Now, it so happens that when the people are invited to partake in the management of the country, they do not slow the movement down but on the contrary they speed it up, We Algerians have had the occasion and the good fortune during the course of this war to handle a fair number of questions. In certain country districts, the politico-military leaders of the revolution found themselves in fact confronted with situations which called for radical solutions. ...

A government which calls itself a national government ought to take responsibility for the totality of the nation; and in an underdeveloped country the young people represent one of the most important sectors. The level of consciousness of young people must be raised; they need enlightenment. If the work of explanation had been carried on among the youth of the nation, and if the Young Peoples National Union had carried out its task of integrating them into the nation, those mistakes would have been avoided which have threatened or already undermined the future of the Latin American republics. The army is not always a school of war, more often, it is a school of civic and political education. The soldier of an adult nation is not a simple mercenary but a citizen who by means of arms defends the nation. That is why it is of fundamental importance that the soldier should know that he is in the service of his country and not in the service of his commanding officer, however great that officer's prestige may be. We must take advantage of the national military and civil service in order to raise the level of the national consciousness; and to detribalize and unite the nation. In an underdeveloped country every effort is made to mobilize men and women as quickly as possible; it must guard against the danger of perpetuating the feudal tradition which holds sacred the superiority of the masculine element over the feminine. Women will have exactly the same place as men, not in the clauses of the constitution but in the life of every day: in the factory, at school, and in the parliament. If in the Western countries men are shut up in barracks, that is not to say that this is always the best procedure. Recruits need not necessarily be militarized. The national service may be civil or military, and in any case it is advisable that every able-bodied citizen can at any

moment take his place in a fighting unit for the defense of national and social liberties.

It should be possible to carry out large-scale undertakings in the public interest by using recruited labor. This is a marvelous way of stirring up inert districts and of making known to a greater number of citizens the needs of their country. Care must be taken to avoid turning the army into an autonomous body which sooner or later, finding itself idle and without any definite mission, will "go into politics" and threaten the government. Drawing-room generals, by dint of haunting the corridors of government departments, come to dream of manifestoes. The only way to avoid this menace is to educate the army politically, in other words to nationalize it. In the same way another urgent task is to increase the militia. In case of war, it is the whole nation which fights and works. It should not include any professional soldiers, and the number of permanent officers should be reduced to a minimum. This is in the first place because officers are very often chosen from the university class, who would be much more useful elsewhere; an engineer is a thousand times more indispensable to his country than an officer; and secondly, because the crystallization of the caste spirit must be avoided. We have seen in the preceding pages that nationalism, that magnificent song that made the people rise against their oppressors, stops short, falters, and dies away on the day that independence is proclaimed. Nationalism is not a political doctrine, nor a program. If you really wish your country to avoid regression, or at best halts and uncertainties, a rapid step must be taken from national consciousness to political and social consciousness. The nation does not exist in a program which has been worked out by revolutionary leaders and taken up with full understanding and enthusiasm by the masses. The nation's effort must constantly be adjusted into the general background of underdeveloped countries. The battle line against hunger, against ignorance, against poverty, and against unawareness ought to be ever present in the muscles and the intelligences of men and women. The work of the masses and their will to overcome the evils which have for centuries excluded them from the mental achievements of the past ought to be grafted onto the work and will of all underdeveloped peoples. On the level of underdeveloped humanity there is a kind of collective effort, a sort of common destiny. The news which interests the Third World does not deal with King Baudouin's marriage nor the scandals of the Italian ruling class. What we want to hear about are the experiments carried out by the Argentinians or the Burmese in their efforts to overcome illiteracy or the dictatorial tendencies of their leaders. It is these things which strengthen us, teach us, and increase our efficiency ten times over. As we see it, a program is necessary for a government which really wants to free the people politically and socially. There must be an economic program; there must also be a doctrine concerning the division of wealth and social relations. In fact, there must be an idea of man and of the future of humanity, that is to say that no demagogic formula and no collusion with the former occupying power can take the place of a program. The new peoples, unawakened at first but soon becoming more and more clearminded, will make strong demands for this program. The African people and indeed all underdeveloped peoples, contrary to common belief, very quickly build up a social and political consciousness. What can be dangerous is when they reach the stage of social consciousness before the stage of nationalism. If this happens, we find in underdeveloped countries fierce demands for social justice which paradoxically are allied with often primitive tribalism. The underdeveloped peoples behave like starving creatures; this means that the

end is very near for those who are having a good time in Africa. Their government will not be able to prolong its own existence indefinitely. A bourgeoisie that provides nationalism alone as food for the masses fails in its mission and gets caught up in a whole series of mishaps. But if nationalism is not made explicit, if it is not enriched and deepened by a very rapid transformation into a consciousness of social and political needs, in other words into humanism, it leads up a blind alley. The bourgeois leaders of underdeveloped countries imprison national consciousness in sterile formalism. It is only when men and women are included on a vast scale in enlightened and fruitful work that form and body are given to that consciousness. Then the flag and the palace where sits the government cease to be the symbols of the nation. The nation deserts these brightly lit, empty shells and takes shelter in the country, where it is given life and dynamic power. The living expression of the nation is the moving consciousness of the whole of the people; it is the coherent, enlightened action of men and women. The collective building up of a destiny is the assumption of responsibility on the historical scale. Otherwise there is anarchy, repression, and the resurgence of tribal parties and federalism. The national government, if it wants to be national, ought to govern by the people and for the people, for the outcasts and by the outcasts. No leader, however valuable he may he, can substitute himself for the popular will; and the national government, before concerning itself about international prestige, ought first to give back their dignity to all citizens, fill their minds and feast their eyes with human things, and create a prospect that is human because conscious and sovereign men dwell therein.

COMMENT

Writing in 1960, Fanon faced a world that was awakening to the cries of rising nationalism and independence. After World War II, the imperial powers of Western Europe began to withdraw their control over the colonies they had established in Africa, India, and Southeast Asia. In many cases, this withdrawal was a forced option due to the revolutionary activity of the various colonized peoples. A focusing of national consciousness and a desire to be free of foreign exploitation fueled a great deal of revolutionary activity, much of which involved extremely violent battles.

On the basis of his experience in the Algerian revolution, Fanon feared that these young new nations would themselves soon become entangled in the snares that all too frequently follow a revolution. In this selection from his major work, he seeks to pinpoint and document just where these potential difficulties lie. In particular, Fanon warns against the nearly overwhelming tendency for the national bourgeoisie to take the place of the colonial power and continue business as usual. The major pitfall to be avoided is the all-too-human propensity of the new, national leadership to mimic the now departed foreign ruling class in order to preserve their own personal or tribal advantage.

Fanon goes into great detail documenting the various dimensions of national political life that can be turned against the desire for independence and democracy. The end result is an oppression that in many ways is more devastating to national consciousness than colonialism itself, because it perpetuates itself as the *answer* to oppression. In addition to continued economic exploitation, a young nation striving for independence is subject to the tendency of its new ruling class to pander to the wishes of various Western powers. This leads to an overemphasis on urban and tourist interests, with a corresponding neglect of rural peoples and agricultural development. Moreover, the influence of Western popular culture, in movies, music, fashion, and food, undermines the people's own sense of identity. This is especially true for young people.

While it is true that nearly all of the political philosophies presented in this section were worked out against the backdrop of real and concrete political upheaval, Fanon actually wrote in the context of our contemporary, post-World War II times. This renders his concerns and analysis especially relevant to our consideration of various social ideals. Even though those of us who live in countries outside the Third World do not face these issues directly, as the world continues to shrink and becomes more and more a "global village," the issues confronting these nations are increasingly relevant to us. Not only are we in the West becoming increasingly intertwined with Third World countries day by day, but our own countries are themselves becoming more and more multicultural. Moreover, in most cases our own "free world" independence also resulted from revolutionary action. Finally, in many places throughout Eastern Europe and the Near East, there are continuing conflicts fueled by nationalism and racisim.

The pressing urgency of such considerations comes even closer to home in connection with the relationship between the United States and the countries of Central and South America. In order to protect our own economic interests in these countries, which supply us with coffee, rubber, sugar, bananas, and the like, we have engaged in various direct and indirect military activities there. Fanon himself mentions the lessons of Latin America in his essay. In fact, there are many ways in which his analysis of the pitfalls facing the efforts to develop a national consciousness and independence is every bit as relevant to Latin America as it is to Africa.

At the heart of Fanon's analysis lies the difference between a commitment to the needs and aspirations of the vast majority of the people of a given nation and a commitment to the ambitions and preferences of those who constitute the privileged class. In his concern to protect and develop the political and social rights of the working class, Fanon clearly sides with Karl Marx over against such theorists as Plato, Thomas Hobbes, and John Stuart Mill, who in one way or another advocate some form of aristocracy. Like John Locke, Fanon believes that all the people must participate in the political processes that control their common destiny. However, whether he would agree with Locke's preference for private property as the basis of the national economy, or be more in favor of the strong socialized economy advocated by Marx, is not altogether clear. What is clear is that Fanon deeply distrusts the corrupting power of political and economic privilege. It does no good to substitute a local version of the ruling class for its colonial counterpart.

Some thinkers would extrapolate from Fanon's critique by applying it to our own situation in Western democracies. Serious questions can be raised about the reality of a political system that purports to be democratic but whose elected officials are beholden to reelection pressures and the financial support of special interest groups. In addition, one may well wonder what degree of democracy remains in a culture dominated by media images, big-time advertising, and materialistic values. Seen in this light, Fanon's fears about the possibility of a true national consciousness avoiding the pitfalls of political corruption loom large indeed. His voice, too, is a "marginalized" one since he speaks on behalf of millions of people who are still without any real say in the shaping of their own future. In this way, he joins with Sandra Harding, Paulo Freire, and Annette Baier in calling for a rethinking of the processes and criteria by means of which we have traditionally responded to "the enduring questions." This challenge is one that we all must struggle to meet.

It seems clear that Fanon would strongly favor the civil disobedience of those taking part in the Sanctuary Movement, as presented in the case study earlier on. The conditions in Central American countries were almost exactly as Fanon describes situations in which revolutionary action is called for. One might ask, however, whether such acts of civil disobedience would ever be justified, in Fanon's view, in the sort of society he would admire and advocate. Is there some way neighboring peoples can actually help rectify the political tyranny and corruption of countries that oppress and exploit their own people? Is there a place for civil disobedience, such as the Sanctuary Movement, as a means of raising the moral consciousness and conscience of one's own nation?

GLOSSARY

Most key terms and concepts are defined as they are introduced in the individual selections in the text.

Absolutism: The view that there is a single set of truths and/or moral standards appropriate to all societies and time periods.

ad hominem: Latin expression for an argument that focuses on the individual rather than on the truth of his or her argument.

Agnosticism: The view that no one can know whether or not God exists.

Altruism: The belief that one should put the interests of others ahead of one's own.

Analytic: A statement whose truth or falsity can be determined merely by logical analysis.

Anthropomorphism: The practice of ascribing human qualities to God.

a posteriori: Knowledge based exclusively on experience.

a priori: Knowledge gained independently of all experience.

Atomism: The view that reality is composed exclusively of individual, undividable units.

Begging the question: To argue in a circle by assuming the truth of one's conclusion at the beginning of the argument.

Behaviorism: The belief that human life consists only of physical behavior and does not involve mental activity.

Capitalism: An economic system of private ownership in which people are free to sell and buy as they choose.

Categorical imperative: Kant's term to indicate that moral duty is always universal, never conditional.

Coherence criterion of truth: The belief that truth is determined on the basis of the agreement of all the evidence available.

Cognitivity: Thought processes yielding truth and knowledge.

Contingent: Not necessary, could have been otherwise.

Correspondence criterion of truth: The belief that truth is determined on the basis of a one-to-one match between a belief and the data of experience.

Cosmology: Theories about the nature of the universe, its origin, patterns, and meaning.

Deduction: The process of deriving a conclusion from a set of premises with certainty.

Deism: The belief that God created the universe but lets it operate according to its own natural principles without intervening.

Determinism: The belief that all events, including all human actions and decisions, are entirely the result of previous causal factors.

Dialectic: The developmental process of moving from one idea—a thesis—to the opposite idea—an antithesis—to a conclusion—a synthesis.

Dualism: The view that reality is composed of only two basic yet separate aspects, mind and matter.

Empirical: Based exclusively on sensory experience.

Functionalism: The theory that all realities are entirely the result of function or the use they serve in the world.

Hedonism: The belief that sensory pleasure is the chief goal in life.

Humanism: The view that humanity is the highest value in the universe.

Idealism: The theory that reality is composed entirely of minds and ideas.

Ideology: Any system of beliefs and values.

Indeterminism: The belief that at least some events are not caused by antecedent conditions.

Innate ideas: Ideas that are already in the knower's mind at birth.

Intuition: A process of discerning the truth of a belief directly, without experience and/or reasoning.

Materialism: The belief that reality is composed exclusively of matter and its patterns of organization.

Mechanism: The view that the universe functions according to strict causal principles, like a machine.

Monism: The view that only one reality—mind or matter—exists.

Natural theology: The attempt to know about God through the use of human reason unaided by revelation.

Naturalism: The belief that all reality, including God and humanity, is a part of the natural universe.

Nihilism: The view that there is no overall purpose to life.

Nominalism: The view that abstract nouns function merely as names for collections of individual items and do not refer to any independent realities.

Omnipotence: The capacity of being all-powerful.

Omniscience: The capacity of being all-knowing.

Ontology: The study of being, of what there is and why.

Perspectivism: The view that truth is a function of one's individual and/or cultural perspective.

Pragmatism: The theory that all truth and values should be determined on the basis of their consequences.

Primary qualities: The sensible qualities of an entity that it essentially possesses, such as weight and size.

reductio ad absurdum: Latin phrase meaning to refute an argument by showing that it leads to an absurd conclusion.

Relationalism: The view that reality is essentially composed of relationships rather than objects.

Relativism: The belief that no values or truth claims are absolute or universal.

Secondary qualities: The sensible qualities of an entity that depend on the experience of the perceiver, such as color, smell, and sound.

Skepticism: The belief that knowledge is humanly impossible.

Socialism: The economic system that values the needs of the community above the freedom of the individual.

Solipsism: The claim that people can only know that they and their ideas exist.

Syllogism: A deductive argument in which the conclusion is claimed to follow from the premises with certainty.

Synthetic: A statement whose truth or falsity can only be determined by empirical investigation.

Teleology: The idea that every aspect of reality has a purpose or is goal-oriented.

Theism: The belief that God created and controls the world.

Theodicy: The justification of the ways God deals with the world, especially in relation to human suffering.

Transcendent: Beyond the limitations of the world and humanity.

Valid: The quality of an argument in which the conclusion follows necessarily from the premises.

Worldview: Any theory of the nature and value structure of the whole of reality and the human place in it.

BIBLIOGRAPHY
for Introductory Students

General Introductory Resources

Coplestone, F. *History of Philosophy.* 7 vols. Garden City, NY: Doubleday, 1961–1965.

Edwards, P., Ed. *The Encyclopedia of Philosophy.* 8 vols. New York: Macmillan and Free Press, 1967.

Feinberg, J. *Doing Philosophy.* Belmont, CA: Wadsworth, 1997.

Stumpf, S. *Socrates to Sartre.* New York: McGraw-Hill, 1966.

Part I: The Ways of Understanding

Barrett, W. M. *Irrational Man.* New York: Doubleday, 1958.

Belenky, M., Clinchy, B., Goldberger, N., and Tarule, J., Eds. *Women's Ways of Knowing.* New York: Basic Books, 1986.

Bernstein, R. *John Dewey.* New York: Washington Square Press, 1966.

Ewing, A. C. *A Short Commentary on Kant's Critique of Pure Reason.* London: Methuen, 1938.

Flew, A. *Hume's Philosophy of Belief.* New York: Humanities Press, 1961.

Goodman, N. *Ways of World Making.* Indianapolis, IN: Hackett, 1978.

Grave, S. A. *The Scottish Philosophy of Common Sense.* Oxford: Oxford University Press, 1960.

Hanna, T. *The Bergsonian Heritage.* New York: Columbia University Press, 1962.

Joachim, H. H. *Descartes' Rules for the Direction of the Mind.* London: Allen and Unwin, 1957.

Kaufmann, W. *Existentialism from Dostoevsky to Sartre.* New York: Harcourt, Brace, and World, 1956.

Kuhn, T. *The Structure of Scientific Revolutions.* Chicago: University of Chicago Press, 1970.

Malcolm, N. *Knowledge and Certainty.* Englewood Cliffs, NJ: Prentice-Hall, 1963.

Reck, A. J. *Introduction to William James.* Bloomington, IN: Indiana University Press, 1967.

Schilpp, P. A., Ed. *The Philosophy of Bertrand Russell.* Evanston, IL: Northwestern University Press, 1944.

Smith, J. *The Spirit of American Philosophy.* Oxford: Oxford University Press, 1963.

Smith, N. K. *The Philosophy of David Hume.* London: Macmillan, 1941.

Strawson, P. F. *The Bounds of Sense.* London: Methuen, 1966.

Part II: The Nature of Reality

Anderson, A., Ed. *Minds and Machines.* Englewood Cliffs, NJ: Prentice-Hall, 1964.

Beck, L. *The Metaphysics of Descartes.* Oxford: Clarendon Press, 1965.

Berger, P. and Luckman, T. *The Social Construction of Reality.* Garden City, NY: Doubleday, 1967.

Ewing, A. C. *Idealism: A Critical Survey.* London: Methuen, 1954.

Gibson, A. B. *The Philosophy of Descartes.* London: Russell and Russell, 1967.

Hartshorne, C. *The Logic of Perfection.* LaSalle, IL: Open Court, 1962.

Hick, J. *Evil and the God of Love.* London: Macmillan, 1966.

Longino, H. *Science as Social Knowledge.* Princeton, NJ: Princeton University Press, 1990.

Lowe, V. *Understanding Whitehead.* Baltimore, MD: Johns Hopkins University Press, 1962.

Schilpp, P. A., Ed. *The Philosophy of Alfred North Whitehead.* Evanston, IL: Northwestern University Press, 1941.

Smart, J. J. C. *Philosophy and Scientific Realism.* London: Routledge and Kegan Paul, 1963.

Smith, J. *Reason and God.* New Haven, CT: Yale University Press, 1961.

Part III: The Basis of Morality

DeBeauvoir, S. *The Ethics of Ambiguity.* New York: Philosophical Library, 1949.

Frankena, W. M. *Ethics.* Englewood Cliffs, NJ: Prentice-Hall, 1963.

Gilligan, C. *In a Different Voice.* Cambridge, MA: Harvard University Press, 1982.

Jeanson, F. *Sartre and the Problem of Morality.* Bloomington, IN: Indiana University Press, 1980.

Narveson, J. *Morality and Utility.* Baltimore, MD: Johns Hopkins University Press, 1966.

Paton, H. *The Categorical Imperative.* London: Hutchinson, 1947.

Pearsall, M. Ed. *Women and Values: Readings in Recent Feminist Philosophy.* Belmont, CA: Wadsworth, 1986.

Rescher, N. *Distributive Justice.* Indianapolis, IN: Bobbs Merrill, 1966.

Rist, J., Ed. *The Stoics.* Berkeley, CA: University of California Press, 1978.

Sandbach, F. *The Stoics.* New York: W. W. Norton, 1975.

Shapiro, H. and Walsh, J., Eds. *Aristotle's Ethics.* Belmont, CA: Wadsworth, 1967.

Toulmin, S. *The Place of Reason in Ethics.* Cambridge, England: Cambridge University Press, 1950.

Part IV: Social Ideals

Arendt, H. *The Origins of Totalitarianism.* New York: Harcourt, Brace, 1966.

Berlin, I. *Two Concepts of Liberty.* Oxford: Oxford University Press, 1958.

————. *Karl Marx: His Life and Environment.* New York: Oxford University Press, 1959.

Britton, K. *John Stuart Mill.* New York: Penguin Books, 1953.

Dupre, L. *The Philosophical Foundations of Marxism.* New York: Harcourt, Brace, 1966.

Gough, J. *John Locke's Political Philosophy.* Oxford: The Clarendon Press, 1950.

Koyre, A. *Discovering Plato.* New York: Columbia University Press, 1945.

Marcuse, H. *Reason and Revolution.* New York: Humanities Press, 1954.

Nickoloff, J., Ed. *Gustavo Gutierrez: Essential Writings.* Maryknoll, NY: Orbis Books, 1996.

O'Conner, J. *John Locke: A Critical Introduction.* New York: Penguin Books, 1952.

Peters, R. *Hobbes.* New York: Penguin Books, 1956.

Popper, K. *The Open Society and Its Enemies.* Princeton, NJ: Princeton University Press, 1950.

Radcliff, P. *Limits of Liberty: Studies on Mill's On Liberty.* Belmont, CA: Wadsworth, 1966.

Sesonske, A. *Plato's Republic.* Belmont, CA: Wadsworth, 1966.

Warrender, H. *The Political Philosophy of Hobbes.* Oxford: The Clarendon Press, 1957.